The AI Act Handbook

Natascha Windholz et al.

The AI Act Handbook

Compliant Usage of Artificial Intelligence
in the Private and Public Sectors

With Contributions from Kristina Altrichter, Gabriele Bolek-Fügl,
Karin Bruckmüller, Alexandra Ciarnau, Veronica Cretu,
Julia Eisner, Julia Fuith, Valerie Hafez, Isabella Hinterleitner,
Manuela Machner, Renate Rechinger, Sabine Singer, Merve
Taner, Theresa Tisch, Natascha Windholz, Carina Zehetmaier,
Klaudia Zoltzmann-Koch

HANSER

Hanser Publishers, Munich

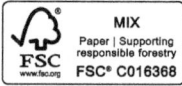

Print-ISBN: 978-1-56990-314-8
E-Book-ISBN: 978-1-56990-324-7
Epub-ISBN: 978-1-56990-483-1

Bibliographic information of the German National Library:
The German National Library lists this publication in the German National Bibliography; detailed bibliographic data are available on the Internet at http://dnb.d-nb.de.

© 2025 Carl Hanser Verlag GmbH & Co. KG, Munich
Vilshofener Straße 10 | 81679 Munich | info@hanser.de
www.hanserpublications.com
www.hanser-fachbuch.de
Editor: Sylvia Hasselbach
Production Management: le-tex publishing services GmbH, Leipzig
Cover concept: Marc Müller-Bremer, www.rebranding.de, München
Cover design: Thomas West
Cover picture: © AdobeStock / Maxim_Kazmin
Production Management: le-tex publishing services GmbH, Leipzig

Typesetting: Eberl & Koesel Studio, Kempten

Table of Contents

10   Governance in the Company   393

Gabriele Bolek-Fügl, Karin Bruckmüller, Veronica Cretu, Valerie Hafez,
Klaudia Zotzmann-Koch

Foreword

Actually, AI is not a new topic; the roots of this supposedly "innovative" technology go back to the 1950s. However, the general public only became aware of AI with the publication of various models of generative AI for creating images, texts, music or programming code.

The EU's AI Act has been a key milestone on the path to human rights-friendly and innovation-promoting compliance when using AI in companies, in administration and also in law enforcement. The EU Commission addressed AI back in 2018 and published a on AI in Europe. In 2021, three years later, the first draft of the AI Act was published. The emergence of "general-purpose AI" and generative AI in the public eye and the possibility of AI being used by the general public have given the negotiations on the AI Act another new twist. This has raised new questions as to whether and how such AI models should be regulated. Following a political agreement in December 2023, the final texts were published in the Official Journal of the EU in July 2024. The aim was to launch the new AI Act before the EU elections in June 2024.

The practical handbook on the AI Act was primarily developed within the *Women in AI Austria* network. The contributions of the members reflect their different professional backgrounds.

Women in AI Austria is an Austrian association whose goal is to increase the participation and representation of women and girls in the field of artificial intelligence. We are also committed to promoting gender diversity in AI based on a digital-humanistic approach. Members of the association are exclusively natural persons, regardless of their gender, education or profession. All members are volunteers. The association was founded in 2020 as part of the global network of *Women in AI* and its members are involved in research, making statements in politics, distributing educational material, organizing events and representing the association at events. Women in AI

Austria strives to provide an interdisciplinary setting where people can exchange ideas about AI.

Specialists, entrepreneurs and lawyers from Women in AI Austria and from a wide range of specialist fields have contributed their knowledge, expertise, time and effort to jointly shape and publish this handbook. The aim was not only to analyze the AI Act, but also to look at areas of law with which there are significant overlaps, to analyze use cases and to work out what it means to use AI in certain industries or sectors. After all, the AI Act was and will never be a "standalone law". Rather, it has an impact on a wide range of product specifications and, above all, data protection issues and the topic of intellectual property. Without the network of Women in AI Austria (*https://www.womeninai.at/*) and the authors' diverse, wide-ranging knowledge of AI, this handbook would not have been possible. You can also follow us on LinkedIn (*https://at.linkedin.com/company/women-in-ai-austria*)

Many thanks to *Women in AI Austria* and the authors for their commitment!

Natascha Windholz   Vienna, August 2024

1

What is AI and How Do Data Science and Data Analytics Differ?

Gabriele Bolek-Fügl

Artificial intelligence is at the center of a revolution that is not only changing the way machines think and learn, but also challenging our understanding of intelligence itself. This revolution is driven by big data and the extraordinary computing power of modern computers, which can perform complex statistical calculations with a speed and precision that has long been unimaginable.

AI has many faces. From simple programs that perform individual tasks with an accuracy that surpasses human ability, to complex systems that learn to adapt and make decisions that are reminiscent of the human mind.

Increasing digitalization can free us from repetitive and tedious tasks and give us the freedom to act more creatively and strategically. If you have little talent or experience in one area, you can compensate for this with virtual assistants. AI offers opportunities to expand our skills and push our boundaries. However, to take full advantage, we need to learn how to work effectively with AI.

But what exactly makes a machine "intelligent"? Is it its ability to recognize and respond to human speech? Its efficiency to make decisions in milliseconds that a human could only make with difficulty and after long deliberation? Or is it the ability to learn from experience and improve over time?

In fact, AI encompasses a spectrum of technologies that are as diverse as the definitions that seek to capture them. So let's begin our journey into the world of AI with a look at the basic components and the various techniques that are summarized under the term "artificial intelligence".

1.1 The Cornerstones of AI

In the field of AI, names and terms are often used without knowing the exact definitions and backgrounds. But in the world of mathematicians, computer scientists and architects of AI, precision is essential. Clear, unambiguous definitions are needed to push the boundaries of what is possible and develop the next generation of intelligent systems.

When developing any AI system, there are components that are necessary regardless of the specific technology or use case. These cornerstones form the foundation on which more complex AI algorithms can be built. Let's therefore take a look at these components of AI-systems and define the associated details:

Table 1.1 Overview of important AI Components

Component	Description	Importance	Complexity	Customizability
Data	Information for learning and decision-making	High	Variable	High
Algorithms	Procedures or methods for processing data	High	High	High
Computing power	For processing large amounts of data and complex calculations	High	Medium	Medium
Storage	Necessary for storing data, models and results	Medium	Low	Medium
Measurement and model optimization	Important for evaluating the effectiveness of AI models and their optimization	High	High	High
Interfaces for interaction	Enable interaction between humans and AI systems	Medium	Medium	High
Security and data protection	Protect data from unauthorized access and misuse, ensure compliance with legal standards	High	High	Medium

Importance: A rating of "High" means that this component is very important in the context of the correct and efficient operation of an AI system. Medium and Low indicate less important criteria.

Complexity: The rating refers to the degree of difficulty with which reliably correct or performant results are generated by the AI.

Adaptability: The rating indicates how flexibly a company can adapt the components of an AI to its own needs and tasks.

Let us now take a closer look at the individual components. The following explanations represent only the most important aspects and do not claim to be exhaustive.

1.1.1 Data

Data is the fuel for AI models. Similar to a vehicle, the AI model would be of no use without data. It provides the information needed to recognize patterns, make decisions and learn from experience.

> Data is the lifeblood of AI. Without data, AI would have no point of reference to analyze, learn or improve. The quality of the data used is therefore of particular importance! If the quality is not sufficiently high, it will not be possible to achieve good results.

From simple Data Sets to today's Big Data Approach

The availability and quality of data has steadily increased in recent years. The development of the internet and digital technologies has led to an exponential increase in the amount and variety of data that AI systems now use for learning and analysis.

Data must always be in context of its use in order to understand its meaning and value. Context provides insight into what data represents, the context in which it was collected and how it should be interpreted. For example, depending on the context, the number 9 could represent a temperature (in degrees Celsius), a length (in centimeters), a duration (in minutes) or a variety of other measurements.

In data analysis and artificial intelligence, the context is crucial for drawing correct conclusions and making accurate predictions. Models require training with data that is not only accurate and cleansed, but also presented in a suitable framework. The context therefore directly influences the outcome of an AI model:

Table 1.2 Goals and Challenges for the Context of AI Result Generation

Range	Goal	Challenge	Example
Data selection	Selection of data that is relevant and representative of the problem.	Insufficient or distorted data can lead to poor model performance.	Selection of patient data for an AI model to predict diabetes.
Feature engineering	Development and transformation of features to improve the presentation of information for the model.	Overfitting to training data and neglecting generalizability.	Creation of time windows for customer buying behavior in an AI model to predict sales.

Table 1.2 Goals and Challenges for the Context of AI Result Generation *(continued)*

Range	Goal	Challenge	Example
Model interpretation	Analyze and explain the results produced by an AI model.	The traceability and verification of the decision-making processes of complex models such as deep neural networks are often difficult to carry out.	Interpretation of the credit rating in a financial model.

Depending on the format in which the data is available, the context can be better or worse recognized and processed.

- **Structured data** are organized in a predefined format, usually in tabular form, which facilitates their analysis and processing. Examples of this are databases and Excel tables.

- **Unstructured data** on the other hand, have no predefined format or structure. It includes texts, books, images, videos and more. Processing this data requires more complex methods, as structuring is necessary first.

Extensive and well-prepared data sets are required for the training of AI models. These data sets are divided into three main categories:

1. **Training data** is the data on which the model is trained. They form the basis for learning patterns and correlations.

2. **Validation data** is used to evaluate the performance of the model during training and to adjust the parameters.

3. **Testing data** are used to evaluate the final performance of the model. They must be independent of the training and validation data in order to ensure an objective evaluation.

The quality of the data is also crucial for the performance of AI models. High-quality data is accurate, complete, consistent and up-to-date. Poor data quality leads to unreliable models that deliver distorted or incorrect results. It is often not until the results after the training phase that you realize that the data quality is not sufficient for the intended purpose and then have to rework the data.

Another major challenge is the legally compliant processing of sensitive and personal data as well as data from minorities. Solutions such as anonymization of data and methods to reduce bias must be discussed and implemented in every project. Options and criteria for this are the subject of the following chapters.

1.1.2 Algorithms

An algorithm is a precisely defined rule or set of instructions for solving a problem or performing a task. Basically, one can think of an algorithm like a recipe in a cookbook: It gives step-by-step instructions on how to get from an initial state (raw potato) to a desired final state (French fries).

In computer science, an algorithm consists of a finite sequence of well-defined, executable steps that solve a task or problem. In AI, algorithms are the processes or methods used to learn from data, solve a task, make predictions and decisions or recognize patterns in data.

A particularly popular area of AI at the moment is machine learning. Unlike a programmer who has to explicitly formulate each instruction in rule-based software, an AI system in machine learning learns from the data provided and independently identifies patterns in order to derive the underlying rules. Here are some key concepts that are frequently used in machine learning:

- **Supervised Learning**

  This is one of the most common categories of AI algorithms in which the model learns from a data set that already contains the correct answers (labels). The aim is to make predictions for new, unknown data (e. g. spam detection or price prediction).

- **Unsupervised Learning**

  Here, the model learns from data without predefined labels in order to recognize patterns or structures independently. Typical applications are the grouping of data points based on similarities (e. g. customer segmentation).

- **Semi-supervised learning**

  A mixed form in which the model is trained with a data set that contains both labeled and unlabeled data. This technique is useful when labeled data is limited or expensive to obtain.

- **Reinforcement learning**

  In this approach, an agent learns how to act in an environment in order to maximize a reward. It is based on the principle of trial and error and is used in areas such as games (e. g. chess) and autonomous vehicles.

- **Deep Learning**

  A subset of machine learning based on deep neural networks. These networks are able to recognize complex patterns in large amounts of data. Applications include image and speech recognition as well as natural language processing (NLP).

■ **Transfer Learning**

This involves transferring knowledge from one area to another, which is particularly useful if not enough training data is available for the target application. This concept has become increasingly important in deep learning, particularly in the processing of images and language.

1.1.3 Computing Power

Modern AI techniques, especially deep learning, require considerable amounts of computing power. This power is necessary to process the large amounts of data and perform the complex calculations of the mathematical methods required to train AI models.

Computing power has increased exponentially over the last few decades, driven by advances in semiconductor technology (known as Moore's Law[1]) and innovations in computer architecture. From the early days of mainframe computers to today's high-performance GPUs (graphics processing units), the increasing availability of computing power has dramatically improved the complexity of the AI models we can train today.

Cloud technology can also be used for training AI models to avoid having to purchase one's own server. In this way, it enables the flexible use of computing power exactly according to current requirements. This is significantly higher during training than during operation.

1.1.4 Storage

Storage is used in all areas of artificial intelligence, from storing large training data sets for machine learning to storing status information in real-time applications such as autonomous vehicles.

To store, access and process data, AI systems need adequate storage capacity for both short-term storage (for current data processing) and long-term storage (for storing models and results). The further development of storage technologies has therefore significantly influenced the possibilities of AI systems. While access times were very slow with magnetic tapes, modern solid-state drives (SSDs) and in-memory databases have increased storage capacity and accelerated access.

---

[1] Moore's Law: Formulated by Gordon Moore, co-founder of Intel, in 1965, it states that the number of transistors on a microchip doubles approximately every two years, which means a corresponding increase in computing power (see "Algorithms for Dummies" by John Paul Mueller, Luca Massaron[1]).

1.1.5 Measurement and Model Optimization

The measurement of the performance and optimization of AI models are crucial steps in the development process of artificial intelligence. They ensure that models not only make accurate predictions, but are also efficient and usable under real-world conditions. It is important to evaluate the performance of AI models to ensure their accuracy, efficiency and fairness. Through evaluation, weaknesses can be identified and improvements can be made. Optimization techniques are necessary to improve the models and adapt their performance to specific requirements.

> Continuous measurement and optimization are also essential for the development of responsible AI models. This is the only way to ensure and prove that AI systems perform their tasks in a fair and comprehensible manner.
>
> Evidence is determined and archived by previously defined control actions.

1.1.6 Interfaces for Interaction

User interfaces (UI) and application programming interfaces (API) are necessary to enable people to interact with AI systems. They facilitate the input of data, the configuration of models and access to the results of data processing or decision-making by the AI.

The interaction interfaces should be adapted for the respective AI application and the individual user group. In the case of a personal assistant or customer service bot for a non-technical customer group, the UI should be kept intuitive, while in the case of complex control systems for robotics and smart devices for technicians, more prior knowledge can be expected. These examples illustrate how different interfaces improve the accessibility and user-friendliness of AI systems and help to avoid errors. The following aspects should also be taken into account:

- **Accessibility:** Ensuring that AI interfaces are accessible to all users, including people with disabilities and special needs.

- **Natural interaction:** development of interfaces that enable natural and intuitive communication.

- **Data protection and security:** Ensuring that interaction with AI systems protects the privacy of users.

Future developments could include immersive technologies such as virtual reality (VR) and augmented reality (AR), which enable new types of interaction. Advances could lead to more personalized and adaptive interfaces that adapt to the preferences and needs of the individual user.

1.1.7 Security and Data Protection

As AI systems often work with sensitive or personal data, robust security and data protection measures are essential. These measures protect the information from unauthorized access and misuse and ensure compliance with legal and ethical standards.

Fundamental risks and legal requirements are:

- **Data protection:** Concepts such as data minimization, purpose limitation and transparency must be implemented to ensure that personal data is protected and treated confidentially.

- **Copyright:** Proof should be provided that the data and works used are not copyrighted by other persons and that the organization owns the rights to use them.

- **Security risks in AI systems:** Measures must be taken to detect and prevent threats and attack scenarios against AI systems. One example of this is adversarial attacks, in which input data is manipulated by users in order to provoke incorrect predictions or decisions. This risk must be minimized by analysing the input data.

- **Encryption and anonymization:** Techniques must be implemented to protect data, both during transmission and storage. Anonymization should be implemented for personal and sensitive data.[2] or pseudonymization[3] of the data are taken into account.

> It is important to document which protective measures have been implemented for which purpose and how protection is ensured throughout the entire life cycle of the AI. To this end, control actions must be defined and compliance with them must be archived in a traceable manner.

Security and data protection are crucial aspects that shape the success and acceptance of AI technologies. By continuously adapting to new threats and complying with strict data protection standards, AI systems can be used confidently and responsibly.

---

[2] This means that the link between a person and their data is irreversibly deleted. No one can be identified from the data.

[3] In pseudonymization, names and other identifying features are replaced by an identifier so that only authorized persons can link a person to their data. Examples of this are a license plate number or a customer number.

1.2 Data Science and Data Analytics

Terms like "Data science" and "Data analytics" are often used interchangeably, although there are differences. While data science is a broader field that deals with the creation of models and algorithms to analyze data, data analytics focuses more on the interpretation of data to answer immediate questions. The following table illustrates the differences based on basic criteria:

Table 1.3 Differentiation between Data Science and Data Analytics

Criterion	Data science	Data analytics
Primary goal	Discovering patterns and predicting future trends and behaviors by analyzing data.	Interpretation of historical data to answer specific questions or solve problems.
Focal points	Data preparation, exploration, modeling, machine learning, predictive analytics.	Data collection, data cleansing, descriptive analysis, reporting.
Methods and techniques	Machine learning, (deep learning) learning algorithms, statistical models, data mining.	Statistical analyses, explorative data analysis, visualization tools, process mining.
Application examples	Development of new product ideas, fraud detection, risk management, personalized recommendation systems.	Sales and market analyses, customer behavior analyses, operational efficiency, quality control.
Required skills	Statistics, machine learning, programming (e. g. Python, R), database knowledge, business understanding.	Statistics, analytical thinking, knowledge of BI tools (e. g. Tableau, Power BI), basic knowledge of programming.

Data science therefore deals with the collection, cleansing and analysis of data in order to recognize patterns, make predictions and make decisions based on large data sets. Data scientists use complex algorithms, machine learning and statistical methods to work with data. They look for answers to questions that have not yet been asked and create new ways of using data.

Data analytics focuses more on the processing and analysis of existing data from an organization's manufacturing processes to answer specific questions related to the business area. Data analysts use statistical tools and techniques to help organizations make operational decisions. In contrast to data science, which is often more exploratory and forward-looking, data analytics is usually more focused and geared towards solving specific problems.

However, there are no "fixed" definitions of these terms, as the field of data science and analytics is rapidly evolving and the boundaries between disciplines are often blurred. Companies should specify the precise areas of responsibility and areas of application in job advertisements and position descriptions to avoid unfulfilling or disappointing expectations.

1.3 Development of AI in SMEs

The use of artificial intelligence offers a number of opportunities for small and medium-sized enterprises (SMEs) and start-ups in particular. With AI technologies, they can automate processes, increase efficiency and develop innovative products or services that can provide a competitive advantage.

For SMEs s, the use of AI opens up the possibility of using resources more efficiently by providing the workforce with an AI assistant that takes over time-consuming tasks and supports decision-making processes with data-driven insights. This can lead to a significant reduction in costs and improved customer service.

Start-ups experimenting with AI can develop customized solutions tailored to specific industry needs and thus open up new markets or disrupt existing markets.

In addition, the use of AI in both types of company promotes a culture of data focus and innovation. This is essential for long-term growth and adaptability to rapidly changing market conditions. In a world where data has become the new most important resource, AI technologies provide SMEs and start-ups with the tools to harness these valuable resources and develop future-proof business models.

The use of AI in SMEs and start-ups therefore holds considerable potential, but also presents them with significant challenges. One of the main problems is the recruitment and retention of qualified personnel who are skilled in the development and implementation of AI technologies. Other challenges include

- **Recruitment of experts**
  - Skills shortage: There is a global shortage of experts in the field of AI and machine learning. This makes it particularly difficult for SMEs and start-ups to attract talented professionals who are familiar with the latest technologies and methods.
  - Competing with large companies: Start-ups and SMEs are competing with large, established companies for AI talent. Large companies can often offer more attractive salaries, benefits and career development opportunities.

- **Financial resources**
    - High costs: The development and implementation of AI solutions can be expensive, especially when it comes to purchasing the necessary hardware or software. For start-ups and SMEs with limited budgets, this can be a significant barrier.
    - ROI uncertainty: Investing in AI brings uncertainties regarding the return on investment (ROI), especially if the company is new to this area. This can lead to hesitation in the allocation of resources.
- **Data and data protection**
    - Data quality and availability: Effective AI systems require large amounts of high-quality data. However, many SMEs and start-ups struggle to gain access to such data or to collect and process it in a meaningful way.
    - Data protection regulations: Compliance with data protection laws such as the GDPR can be a challenge for companies working with personal data. Developing AI systems that meet these requirements requires specific knowledge and resources.
    - IT security: Implementing and continuously ensuring IT security measures in the organization's infrastructure requires experienced specialists, expensive software and time resources. This also applies to the integration of security features in software or AI products.
- **Technological integration**
    - Process integration: Integrating AI solutions into existing business processes and systems can be complex and challenging. Compatibility issues and the need for customized solutions can delay or increase the cost of implementation.
    - Controls: Defining internal control and governance measures for digital services can be a challenge for SMEs or start-ups because many activities are implemented with a small workforce. Often, the knowledge or people to implement the separation of functions or the dual control principle are not available in the company.
- **Knowledge and cultural change**
    - Established small companies: The introduction of AI often requires a cultural change within the organization. In SMEs, this can quickly lead to anxiety and resistance if the workforce is not properly trained.
    - Start-ups: In new, technology-driven companies, there is often an atmosphere of innovation and new beginnings, without paying attention to continuity in the use of tools or to ensuring that they are used securely (in terms of trade secrets, data protection, etc.) and in compliance with laws (in accordance with copyright, rights of use).

▪ Knowledge building: Technological cycles and new AI products are coming at ever shorter intervals, and it is challenging to stay up to date alongside daily work. In smaller companies in particular, it is often difficult to continuously build up the knowledge of specialists and transfer it to the rest of the workforce.

These challenges highlight the need for start-ups and SMEs to consider strategic partnerships, seek external advice and support, and invest in training and upskilling their workforce. Despite these obstacles, however, the integration of AI offers great opportunities to optimize business processes, explore new growth opportunities and remain competitive in the long term.

> The EU Commission will draw up guidelines for the practical implementation of the AI Regulation, paying particular attention to the needs of SMEs, including start-ups (Art. 96 AI Act).

The following checklist for the use of AI in start-ups and SMEs can help to take a structured approach and ensure that all important aspects for planning the use of AI in the organization are taken into account:

▪ **Needs analysis and objectives for AI initiatives**
  ▪ Define clear goals for the use of AI in your company.
  ▪ Identify specific problems or processes that could be improved by AI.
  ▪ Evaluate the company's current technological status and level of maturity with regard to AI.
  ▪ Discuss as a team potential risks and ethical concerns associated with the use of AI, including data protection and the impact on workplaces.

▪ **Market and technology research**
  ▪ What current and future trends in AI technology will have an impact on your industry?
  ▪ Research available AI tools and solutions that are or can be tailored to your needs.
  ▪ Compile a list of available AI technologies and platforms that are relevant to the company's business model.
  ▪ Evaluate the market readiness and reliability of potential AI technologies.
  ▪ Research the reliability and reputation of different AI technology providers.
  ▪ Identify how competitors are using AI technologies and evaluate their successes and failures.
  ▪ Which AI-based products or services are in demand in your market segment and which customer needs can be addressed?

- **Resource planning**
  - Check whether the necessary financial and human resources are available for the implementation and maintenance of AI solutions.
  - Plan training courses for your team to build up the necessary knowledge to successfully use AI technologies.
  - Assess whether the company's current IT infrastructure is suitable to support new AI solutions or whether upgrades are required.

- **Data preparation**
  - Make sure you have access to high-quality data that can be used to train AI models.
  - Check the data for completeness, accuracy, timeliness and relevance in relation to the AI use case.
  - A large amount of training data is often required to train powerful AI models. Make sure that enough data is available to develop robust models and also consider the diversity of the data.
  - Check existing data protection and data security requirements to ensure compliance.
  - Prepare the data using techniques such as normalization, scaling and coding of categorical data to prepare the data for training AI models.
  - Organize data storage efficiently for quick access and easy management.

- **Selection of the AI solution**
  - Decide whether you want to develop a customized AI solution or use AI software available on the market.
  - Compare different providers and products in terms of performance, costs and support.
  - Clarify the legal requirements that must be taken into account when implementing the planned AI technology.
  - Investigate how the potential AI solutions can be integrated into the existing technology landscape.

- **Pilot project and evaluation**
  - Start with a pilot project to test the effectiveness and integration of the AI solution.
  - Measure the results and the impact of the AI solution on the defined objectives.
  - Don't forget to include the legal requirements and specific contractual regulations in the evaluation.
  - Evaluate the risks in terms of data protection and data security for the specific AI solution.

- Document learning effects and best practices from the pilot project and transfer knowledge from the project.

- **Integration and scaling**
  - Integrate the AI solution into existing systems and workflows.
  - Train the workforce so that they can handle the AI and the generated results appropriately.
  - Plan to scale the AI solution to cover other areas of your company.

- **Continuous monitoring and optimization**
  - Set up processes for continuous monitoring of AI performance.
  - Set up control procedures to verify that implementation complies with the law.
  - Use feedback and performance data to continuously improve the AI solution.

- **Data security and ethics**
  - Implement strong security measures to protect AI-powered systems and data.
  - Work with specialists on data management and processing.
  - Develop a robust data architecture that effectively supports the growth and scalability of the data. Also consider archiving requirements.
  - Consider ethical[4] Aspects and effects of the use of AI on employees, customers and society.

- **Feedback and customization**
  - Collect regular feedback on the AI solution from users and stakeholders.
  - Don't start collecting feedback from (potential) customers too late.
  - Be prepared to make adjustments to maximize the effectiveness and acceptance of AI.

> This checklist serves as a framework for start-ups and SMEs planning to integrate AI technologies into their business processes. The key to success lies in careful design, selecting the right technologies and continuously assessing the impact on the business.

Sources

[1] Mueller, J. P., Massaron, L. in *Algorithmen für Dummies*, (2017) WILEY-VCH Verlag, Weinheim

[2] IEEE 7000–2021, *Model Process for Addressing Ethical Concerns during System Design* (2021) IEEE Computer Society, Piscataway, New Jersey

[3] HEG-KI, *Ethics Guidelines for Trustworthy AI* (2018), Europäische Kommission, accessed in March 2024

---

[4] The IEEE 7000-2021 standard [2] or the EU Ethics Guidelines for Trustworthy AI [3], for example, can be used for support.

2 Geopolitics of Artificial Intelligence

Veronica Cretu

> ✓ **Definitions**
> - **Geopolitics according to the Encyclopædia Britannica**: "the study of how geography and economics have an influence on politics and on the relations between nations; the political and geographical parts of something."
> - **Geopolitics according to the Cambridge Dictionary**: "the study of the way a country's size, position, etc. influence its power and its relationships with other countries political activity as influenced by the physical features of a country or areas of the world."
> - **OECD-definition of AI systems** (as of March 2024): "An AI system is a machine-based system that, for explicit or implicit objectives, infers, from the input it receives, how to generate outputs such as predictions, content, recommendations, or decisions that can influence physical or virtual environments. Different AI systems vary in their levels of autonomy and adaptiveness after deployment."

Taking the above definitions into account, the *geopolitics of AI* can be defined as follows:

> ✓ Geopolitics of AI explores how artificial intelligence systems - i. e. machine-based entities capable of generating predictions, content, recommendations or decisions that impact both physical and virtual environments - are changing influence, economic strategies and relationships between nations beyond traditional geographic and economic factors.

The geopolitics of AI therefore examines how the characteristics, capabilities and deployment of AI technologies affect global power dynamics, influence the strategic positioning of countries, international cooperation and competition. It encompasses the role of AI in enhancing or challenging the economic and military status of nations, in shaping political decisions and in redefining the geopolitical landscape in a world where technological dominance increasingly determines national sovereignty and international relations. It reflects a nation's ability to lead or innovate in technology, particularly in areas such as artificial intelligence (AI), cybersecurity and digital infrastructure, highlighting its power, influence and authority, as well as its strategic autonomy [8][1] on the global stage.

2.1 Emerging Landscape of AI Regulations

In recent years, the world has entered a race for AI, driven by a mix of hopes for economic benefits, safety improvements, technological breakthroughs, ethical progress and better societies.

Governments around the world have recognized that leadership in AI can give them a decisive strategic advantage and are investing heavily to secure their position at the forefront of this transformative technological revolution. The AI landscape remains remarkably diverse, however, reflecting the varying degrees of maturity of government approaches and strategies around the world - from governments with robust, forward-looking AI strategies to those that have yet to fully recognize the potential of AI.

Stanford's Artificial Intelligence Report 2023 [3], a study of legislative documents from 127 countries, shows a significant increase in the adoption of legislation mentioning "artificial intelligence", rising from a single bill in 2016 to 37 in 2022. Similarly, a study of parliamentary discussions on AI in 81 countries shows that references to AI in legislation have increased 6.5-fold since 2016.

---

[1] The concept of strategic autonomy, as formulated by Josep Borrell, EU High Representative for Foreign Affairs and Security Policy and Vice-President of the European Commission, highlights its long-standing application in the military sphere, which has historically been limited to issues of European security and defense. Borrell describes strategic autonomy as a critical "process of political survival" for the European Union and argues that its underlying logic should be extended to a broader range of sectors beyond the traditional military domain, such as technological and digital development and data management.

Number of AI-Related Bills Passed Into Law by Country, 2016–22
Source: AI Index, 2022 | Chart: 2023 AI Index Report

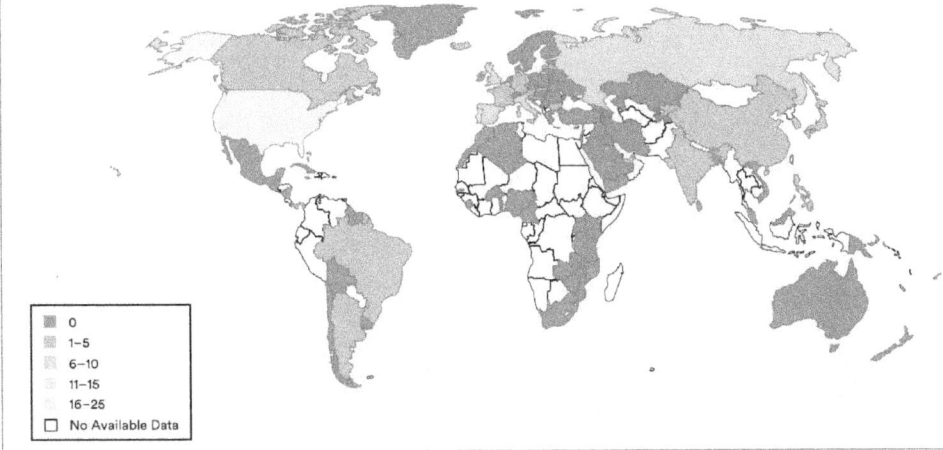

Legend:
- 0
- 1–5
- 6–10
- 11–15
- 16–25
- No Available Data

Figure 2.1 Number of Regulations Related to AI per Country

From the research results of the AI Index show that the legislative trends of 2022 follow the global trend towards the responsible and ethical integration of AI into society. Countries are developing lawsthat not only promote the advancement of artificial intelligence, but also aim to mitigate its risks, ensure safety and promote fairly distributed benefits for society as a whole.

- The importance and impact of AI on various areas of society – from the creative industries to national security – is clearly recognized. Countries are actively seeking to create a regulatory framework that not only promotes the development of AI, but also addresses its potential risks and impacts. Legislation and regulations are being enacted to address the challenges and opportunities of a rapidly evolving AI revolution.

- Countries are making significant efforts to modernize their legal frameworks in response to the rapid development of AI and its impact on society.

- The legislation reflects a wide range of AI applications, from promoting the creative industries and education to ensuring national security and promoting fair and non-discriminatory decision-making in public administration.

- Several countries are in the process of introducing regulations to protect against the misuse of AI, with a focus on safety, ethics and minimizing bias.

- The introduction of training programs addresses the need to prepare and train workers for the AI-driven future.

The Global AI Index [16] is another comprehensive metric that assesses the state of artificial intelligence in 62 countries. It comprises 111 indicators drawn from 28 public and private data sources and information from 62 governments, covering seven sub-pillars: talent or skills, infrastructure, operating environment, research, development, government strategy and commercial sectors.

	Overall	Talent	Infrastructure	Operating Environment	Research	Development	Government Strategy	Commercial	Scale	Intensity
United States	10...	100.0	100.0	82.8	100.0	100.0	60.3	100.0	10...	60.5
China	61.5	30.0	92.1	89.7	54.7	80.8	93.5	43.1	67.8	39.3
Singapore	49.7	56.9	92.3	85.7	48.8	24.4	81.8	26.2	28.1	10...
United Kingdom	41.8	53.8	81.8	79.5	38.1	19.8	89.2	20.0	34.6	62.8
Canada	40.3	46.0	62.1	93.1	34.0	18.9	93.4	18.9	31.9	56.9
South Korea	40.3	35.1	74.4	91.4	24.3	80.3	91.9	5.3	31.3	57.3
Israel	40.0	45.5	80.5	85.1	24.8	22.2	31.8	40.5	23.5	76.1
Germany	39.2	57.0	68.2	90.7	25.3	19.5	93.9	10.3	34.7	46.4
Switzerland	37.7	44.5	68.0	81.9	41.3	24.9	9.0	13.3	23.5	71.6
Finland	34.9	34.5	73.0	97.7	27.4	13.1	82.7	9.5	24.2	62.0
Netherlands	34.5	45.2	65.7	90.3	27.1	15.7	71.8	7.9	25.5	55.5
Japan	33.9	38.0	80.8	92.4	18.6	22.2	80.3	6.9	32.2	36.4
France	32.8	41.5	66.9	84.2	21.4	8.9	87.3	10.8	29.5	39.7
India	31.4	36.2	34.7	81.1	12.0	7.6	56.0	8.9	33.7	20.0
Australia	30.9	34.2	54.3	53.8	34.4	11.7	83.3	7.0	23.6	47.5
Denmark	30.5	30.6	67.5	100.0	19.4	8.8	75.0	8.3	23.3	50.9
Sweden	30.3	33.7	82.3	95.9	22.4	11.4	47.0	8.6	22.5	50.1
Luxembourg	29.2	24.0	74.9	90.4	19.4	7.5	66.8	8.8	19.0	53.1
Ireland	28.8	31.8	60.8	88.0	13.6	19.2	71.7	8.6	20.1	49.6
Spain	27.7	31.5	65.2	50.2	14.5	4.3	93.4	4.7	24.6	34.5
Austria	27.7	27.6	57.0	94.7	21.3	7.4	63.1	5.8	21.7	44.0
Belgium	26.6	27.4	55.3	84.8	21.9	5.1	57.0	8.6	21.6	41.4

Figure 2.2 Countries with the Most Points in the Global AI Index

The data from this index clearly shows the following:

- The United States leads the global AI landscape with optimal scores in skills/talent and development, reflecting its robust AI ecosystem supported by leading universities and technology companies.

- China is performing strongly overall, particularly in the areas of infrastructure and government strategy, due to significant government investment and the strategic prioritization of AI.

- Despite being a small country, Singapore ranks at the top with good results in infrastructure and operating environment, indicating favorable conditions for AI growth.

- European countries have different strengths. Countries such as Finland are characterized by an excellent infrastructure, which indicates a solid foundation for AI technologies, while others such as Germany have a strong government strategy that could drive their national AI agendas.

- India stands out in comparison to its overall ranking with a remarkably high skills and talent score.

- There are notable differences in the trade pillar: some countries, such as the United States, perform extremely well, while others lag behind despite strong government support and capabilities, possibly due to different industrial strategies or market conditions.

- The index distinguishes between "scope" and "intensity" of AI activities, with some countries scoring high on intensity (such as Israel), even if their scope is not as large, suggesting a concentrated and strong AI capability.

- Austria shows a solid performance in the area of "Operational Environment". However, Austria's scores in the areas of capabilities and government strategy are relatively low compared to the operating environment.

The Government AI Readiness Index Government 2023 [1] shows that international collaboration on AI governance and ethics saw significant growth in 2023. The year was also characterized by an increasing number of AI summits and initiatives, demonstrating growing global awareness and concerted action to understand the societal impact of AI.

Notable events included the launch of the Hiroshima AI process at the G7 summit in May [17] and the *UK AI Safety Summit* [4] in November 2023. These and other gatherings underlined the global commitment to shaping future AI governance.

A number of proposals for guidelines and principles for AI have been made, including the G7's *International Guiding Principles for Advanced AI Systems* [11] and the *UK AI Safety Summit's Bletchley Declaration* [15]. These new proposals join a number of established frameworks and recommendations aimed at ethical AI development, such as the *2019 OECD AI Principles* [5], the 2021 UNESCO Recommendation on the Ethics of Artificial Intelligence [14]. UNESCO's role in promoting AI ethics through methodologies such as the *Readiness Assessment Methodology (RAM)* [18] and *ethical impact assessment* [14] has been central. UNESCO has supported an initial group of 50 countries, mainly developing countries, in implementing these methodologies. This initiative, which potentially prioritizes ethics over the development of comprehensive national AI strategies, could revolutionize the way governments around the world approach AI, particularly as it relates to public services.

Regional efforts in the field of artificial intelligence have also intensified. In Latin America and the Caribbean, the *Santiago Declaration* was signed by twenty countries [13] in 2023, while the countries of Southern Africa came together in Namibia in 2022 to agree on the *Windhoek Declaration* [20], which emphasizes regional action on AI in the areas of data, education and governance.

The beginning of 2024 is characterized by two important developments in the field of AI governance:

- On March 13, 2024, the European Parliament [10] approved the Artificial Intelligence Regulation ("AI Act"), the first ever regulatory framework for AI that addresses the risks of AI and enables Europe to take a leading role globally.

- The *Framework Convention on Artificial Intelligence, Human Rights, Democracy and the Rule of Law* [7] was finalized by the Council of Europe Committee on Artificial Intelligence on March 14, 2024. The draft text will be submitted to the Committee of Ministers for adoption and opened for signature at a later date.

Although the EU's position is being challenged by the technological dominance of the USA and China with the AI regulation, it is of central importance due to its regulatory influence.

2.2 The Race for AI Regulation – the Big Three

The EU, the USA and China are currently in a race for regulation of AI, with each country pursuing different goals [Scarre, P and Chilukiri, V [19]].

- The EU's AI regulation pursues a comprehensive, "risk-based" strategy that focuses on minimizing social harms, such as discrimination in AI-driven recruitment processes. This approach aims to mitigate the risks associated with AI technologies through detailed regulation, with a focus on protecting social values and human rights.

- China's approach to regulating AI focuses on strengthening state control over information. The regulations are designed to enforce state authority and ensure that AI development is in line with state interests and security concerns, rather than primarily promoting innovation in the AI sector.

- The US is still in the process of defining its position on AI governance. While the Biden administration's AI executive order is an important first step, comprehensive regulation requires legislative action. The US is seeking a regulatory framework that balances the need for an open and competitive AI ecosystem, safety and control of harmful AI technologies, while maintaining technological leadership and addressing the strategic challenge posed by China.

Table 2.1 Overview of the AI Regulatory Frameworks in EU, USA and China

Global leader in AI governance	Approach to AI governance
European Union (EU)	The EU approach to AI governance is comprehensive, prudent and multi-stakeholder based. It aims to balance technological progress with ethical considerations and public trust. The EU's approach includes consultation and involvement of a broad range of stakeholders, including AI developers, users, public authorities, academics and civil society, to ensure that the AI Act and other AI measures are comprehensive and address the concerns of all stakeholders. This collaborative approach reflects the diverse interests and values of European citizens. The European Union is determined to set a global benchmark with the AI Act, reflecting its potential to lead the creation of international standards. However, in the competition for technological leadership, Europe is faced with strong competition from technology giants from the USA and China. The EU's commitment to technological sovereignty is therefore called into question by the need for greater investment and the lack of a European counterpart to "Silicon Valley", which is home to large technology companies. "The EU's pursuit of indigenous AI innovation underscores the critical importance of AI in strengthening European technological sovereignty and reducing strategic dependencies." (Carnegie Europe, March 2024) Important provisions of the AI Act: The purpose of the AI Regulation is to "improve the functioning of the internal market by establishing a single legal framework, in particular for the development, placing on the market, deployment and use of artificial intelligence systems in the Union, in accordance with Union values, to promote the deployment of human-centric and trustworthy artificial intelligence while ensuring a high level of protection of health, safety and fundamental rights enshrined in the Charter, including democracy and the rule of law, protection of the environment, against harmful effects of artificial intelligence systems in the Union and to promote innovation. This Regulation ensures the free movement of AI-based goods and services across borders and prevents Member States from restricting the development, marketing and use of artificial intelligence (AI) systems, except as expressly authorized by this Regulation.". "Artificial intelligence should be a technology that puts people at the center. It should serve as a tool for people that ultimately aims to increase human well-being."

Table 2.1 Overview of the AI Regulatory Frameworks in EU, USA and China *(continued)*

Global leader in AI governance	Approach to AI governance
	The AI Act proposes a regulatory framework that classifies AI systems according to their level of risk:
	▪ Unacceptable risks are prohibited (e. g. social rating systems and manipulative AI).
	▪ The majority of the text deals with the regulation of high-risk AI systems.
	▪ A smaller section deals with AI systems with limited risk, which are subject to transparency obligations: Developers and deployers must ensure that end users are aware that they are interacting with AI (chatbots and deepfakes).
	▪ The lowest risk is unregulated (including most AI applications currently available in the EU single market, such as spam filters).
	Most obligations apply to providers (i. e. developers in particular) of high-risk AI systems. Users are natural or legal persons who use an AI system professionally, but not affected end users. Providers of AI models for general purposes must adhere to certain documentation and transparency standards, especially if their AI systems are classified as systems with systemic risks.
	Article 5 of the AI Act prohibits certain types of AI systems:
	▪ AI that manipulates behavior through subliminal techniques or exploits vulnerabilities, causing significant damage.
	▪ Systems that classify individuals based on sensitive attributes without appropriate context or law enforcement categorization.
	▪ Social scoring practices that have negative consequences for the individual ("social scoring").
	▪ AI that predicts criminal behavior based solely on profiles, without concrete, factual links to actual criminal activity.
	▪ The non-targeted collection of facial recognition data for databases.
	▪ AI that derives emotions in work or educational environments, with the exception of medical or security applications.
	▪ Real-time remote biometric identification ("RBI") by law enforcement agencies in public spaces, with narrow exceptions for urgent matters such as searching for missing persons or preventing imminent threats, including serious crimes.
	The law prescribes a strict procedure for the assessment and approval of high-risk AI applications, particularly those used in law enforcement and public surveillance. These systems must undergo a fundamental rights impact assessment and receive the necessary approvals prior to deployment to ensure that their use is both lawful and ethical.

Global leader in AI governance	Approach to AI governance
	The regulation places great emphasis on protecting the fundamental rights of individuals and ensuring transparency in the use of AI systems. This includes clear communication with the public about the use of potentially intrusive technologies such as real-time biometric identification and ensuring that AI systems do not perpetuate biases or violate privacy and other fundamental rights and freedoms.
United States of America	The United States is taking a stand by having the highest total private investment in this area in the world. In 2022, the U. S. will provide $47.4 billion in AI investment, about 3.5 times more than China, which is the next highest investor. The United States also has the highest number of AI start-ups, almost double the total number of companies in the EU and the UK and 3.4 times as many in China [9]. In October 2023, President Biden issued an executive order [12] aimed at making the United States a leader in artificial intelligence (AI) while managing its risks. This executive order sets new standards for the safety of AI, emphasizes the protection of privacy, the promotion of equality and civil rights, the protection of consumers and workers, the promotion of innovation and competition, and the strengthening of American leadership on a global level. The main objectives of the Executive Order include: <ul><li>The developers of the most powerful AI systems should be required to share the results of their security tests and other important information with the US government.</li><li>The National Institute of Standards and Technology (NIST) will establish rigorous standards for extensive testing to ensure safety prior to public release.</li><li>Protect against the risks of using AI in the development of hazardous biological materials by developing rigorous new standards for screening biological syntheses.</li><li>Protect Americans from AI-powered fraud and deception by establishing standards and best practices for recognizing AI-generated content and authenticating official content.</li><li>Address the discrimination and bias potential of AI in different sectors and provide clear guidance to mitigate these risks.</li><li>Ensuring that AI benefits consumers without causing harm and promoting positive change in healthcare and education through AI.</li><li>Looking at the impact of AI on the workforce, promoting vocational training and developing best practices to maximize the benefits of AI for workers.</li><li>Aims to maintain America's leadership in AI innovation by supporting research and ensuring a competitive AI ecosystem.</li></ul>

Table 2.1 Overview of the AI Regulatory Frameworks in EU, USA and China *(continued)*

Global leader in AI governance	Approach to AI governance
	▪ Expand international cooperation to promote the safe and responsible use of AI worldwide to ensure that the use of AI is in line with safety standards and ethical considerations. ▪ Provides guidance to federal agencies on the procurement and use of AI to ensure that the government's use of AI is safe, ethical, and effective. This Executive Order represents a comprehensive approach to AI that balances the need for innovation with the need to address the ethical and safety challenges posed by AI technologies (see section 9.2.2 for more details on the Executive Order).
China	China reports investments of 13.4 billion dollars in AI for 2022 [9]. Based on the paper on AI governance in China [2]: China's approach to AI governance is characterized by seeking a balance between supporting AI development and regulatory control to mitigate social and economic threats. The Chinese government has gradually increased its regulatory attention to AI, taking a targeted approach that aims to avoid stifling innovation. This approach includes high cybersecurity and data protection requirements, with most regulatory documents at this stage being non-binding and experimental. It is expected that more specific requirements will be included in future provincial AI laws and regulations over time to clarify the legislation for all sectors. The paper highlights the most important phases of AI regulation in China: ▪ Years 2017–2020: Initially, China focused on industry self-regulation and strategic opportunities for AI by introducing basic policies without imposing strict regulatory barriers. ▪ Years 2020–2022: During this period, national standards for AI technologies and machine learning applications were formulated, reflecting a shift towards direct government involvement in AI governance. ▪ From 2022 to today: Recently, the focus has shifted to enacting specific, binding regulations for individual industries and technologies, led by the Cyberspace Administration of China (CAC). This trend towards more targeted and sector-specific regulations is likely to continue with the creation of a legal framework for AI. Pilot cities such as Shenzhen and Shanghai [6] have taken a pioneering role in enacting regulations to promote AI development and have conducted administrative experiments at the local level to attract AI investment and policy approval from the central government.

Global leader in AI governance	Approach to AI governance
	Main pillar of Chinese AI governance: ■ Content moderation: Management of online content with a focus on traceability, authenticity and restriction of information that violates applicable regulations. ■ Data protection: is briefly addressed in the context of AI governance, drawing on the provisions of existing data protection legislation to cover the processing of personal data in AI services. ■ "Algorithmic governance": Ensuring the security, ethics and clarity of algorithms, with a particular focus on security assessments, ethical standards and transparent service provision. With an evolving framework aimed at supporting AI innovation while managing its potential risks, China's governance model mirrors government oversight and industry growth in the broader context of digital and data governance.
Comparison EU vs. USA vs. China	Scope: ■ The EU AI Act is a comprehensive legal framework that classifies AI systems based on their risk levels and provides a set of requirements for different categories of AI applications. It aims to mitigate risks by imposing strict obligations on high-risk AI systems, with a focus on protecting fundamental rights and ensuring safety. ■ President Biden's Executive Order is an administrative directive that outlines the U.S. government's approach to promoting AI innovation while managing its risks. It emphasizes national security, economic competitiveness, privacy, equality and the ethical use of AI and directs specific actions across federal agencies. ■ China promotes state supervision, focusing on maintaining social order, economic development and improving state control over information. Regulatory approach: ■ The EU emphasizes a preventive, risk-based regulatory approach that seeks to proactively address potential harms associated with AI technologies, focusing in particular on social risks such as discrimination. ■ The US strategy set out in the executive order aims to promote innovation and competitiveness in the AI sector, while also addressing safety and ethical concerns. It proposes a more flexible, adaptable framework that will evolve with AI technologies. ■ China's approach includes both supportive measures for AI development and prudential regulations to mitigate risk, with a focus on content moderation, data protection and algorithmic governance.

Table 2.1 Overview of the AI Regulatory Frameworks in EU, USA and China *(continued)*

Global leader in AI governance	Approach to AI governance
	Implementation and enforcement:
	▪ The EU AI Act is designed to be directly applicable in all EU Member States and establishes uniform rules and obligations for AI systems that are enforced by national supervisory authorities.
	▪ The U. S. Executive Order directs federal agencies to develop and implement standards, policies and measures to ensure the responsible development and deployment of AI. It calls for collaboration with Congress to create a more robust regulatory framework that emphasizes a more decentralized and sector-specific approach.
	▪ China uses a mix of mandatory regulations and non-binding standards, with provincial governments and industry self-regulation playing an important role in the early stages and moving to more specific and targeted regulations over time.
	Leadership qualities:
	▪ While both the EU and the US recognize the global nature of AI challenges and the need for international cooperation, the EU AI Act positions the EU as a standard setter in global AI governance and seeks to influence international norms and practices.
	▪ The U. S. approach, according to the Executive Order, focuses on maintaining U. S. leadership in AI innovation and ensuring the safe and ethical use of AI both domestically and internationally. It emphasizes the U. S. role in shaping global frameworks and standards through bilateral and multilateral commitments.
	▪ China emphasizes domestic control and the strategic use of AI for national development and social management, focusing on setting its own rules for cyberspace while engaging in international cooperation to influence global standards and norms.

Sources

[1] 2023 Government AI Readiness Index

[2] AI Governance in China: Strategies, Initiatives, and Key Considerations. URL *https://www.twobirds. com/en/insights/2024/china/ai-governance-in-china-strategies-initiatives-and-key-considerations* – accessed: 2024/03/31

[3] AI Index Steering Committee, Institute for Human-Centered AI, Stanford University: The AI Index 2023 Annual Report. URL *https://aiindex.stanford.edu/wp-content/uploads/2023/04/HAI_AI-Index-Report_ 2023.pdf* – accessed: 2024/03/31

[4] AI Safety Summit 2023 – GOV.UK. URL *https://www.gov.uk/government/topical-events/ai-safety-sum mit-2023* – accessed: 2024/03/31

[5] AI-Principles Overview. URL *https://oecd.ai/en/principles* – accessed: 2024/03/31

[6] *https://www-ssme-sh-gov-cn.translate.goog/public/news!loadNewsDetail.do?id=2c91c28d83647d7001837 da955a60a55&_x_tr_sl=auto&_x_tr_tl=de&_x_tr_hl=de&_x_tr_pto=wapp* – accessed: 2024/03/31

[7] Artificial Intelligence, Human Rights, Democracy and the Rule of Law Framework Convention – Artificial Intelligence – *www.coe.int*. URL *https://www.coe.int/en/web/artificial-intelligence/-/artificial-intelligence-human-rights-democracy-and-the-rule-of-law-framework-convention* – accessed: 2024/03/31

[8] Csernatoni, Raluca: The EU's Rise as a Defense Technological Power: From Strategic Autonomy to Technological Sovereignty. URL *https://carnegieeurope.eu/2021/08/12/eu-s-rise-as-defense-technological-power-from-strategic-autonomy-to-technological-sovereignty-pub-85134* – accessed: 2024/03/31 – Carnegie Europe

[9] Csernatoni, Raluca: Charting the Geopolitics and European Governance of Artificial Intelligence. URL *https://carnegieeurope.eu/2024/03/06/charting-geopolitics-and-european-governance-of-artificial-intelligence-pub-91876* – accessed: 2024/03/31 – Carnegie Europe

[10] EU Parliament IMCOLIBE: Draft Compromise Amendments on the Draft Report Artificial Intelligence Act.

[11] Hiroshima Process International Guiding Principles for Advanced AI system | Shaping Europe's digital future. URL *https://digital-strategy.ec.europa.eu/en/library/hiroshima-process-international-guiding-principles-advanced-ai-system* – accessed: 2024/03/31

[12] House, The White: FACT SHEET: President Biden Issues Executive Order on Safe, Secure, and Trustworthy Artificial Intelligence. URL *https://www.whitehouse.gov/briefing-room/statements-releases/2023/10/30/fact-sheet-president-biden-issues-executive-order-on-safe-secure-and-trustworthy-artificial-intelligence/* – accessed: 2024/03/31 – The White House

[13] InvestChile: Chile leads regional initiative on ethical Artificial Intelligence. URL *https://blog.investchile.gob.cl/chile-ethical-artificial-intelligence* – accessed: 2024/03/31

[14] Recommendation on the Ethics of Artificial Intelligence – UNESCO Digital Library. URL *https://unesdoc.unesco.org/ark:/48223/pf0000380455.:~:text=Member%20States%20should%20put%20in,or%20social%20inequalities%2C%20prejudice%2C%20the* – accessed: 2024/03/31

[15] The Bletchley Declaration by Countries Attending the AI Safety Summit, 1–2 November 2023. URL *https://www.gov.uk/government/publications/ai-safety-summit-2023-the-bletchley-declaration/the-bletchley-declaration-by-countries-attending-the-ai-safety-summit-1-2-november-2023* – accessed: 2024/03/31 – GOV.UK

[16] The Global AI Index. URL *https://www.tortoisemedia.com/intelligence/global-ai/* – accessed: 2024/03/31 – Tortoise

[17] The Hiroshima AI Process: Leading the Global Challenge to Shape Inclusive Governance for Generative AI. URL *https://www.japan.go.jp/kizuna/2024/02/hiroshima_ai_process.html* – accessed: 2024/03/31 – The Government of Japan – JapanGov

[18] Using the RAM as a tool to ensure trustworthy AI | UNESCO. URL *https://www.unesco.org/en/articles/using-ram-tool-ensure-trustworthy-ai* – accessed: 2024/03/31

[19] What an American Approach to AI Regulation Should Look Like. URL *https://time.com/6848922/ai-regulation/* – accessed: 2024/03/31 – TIME

[20] Windhoek Statement on Artificial Intelligence in Southern Africa, Windhoek (Namibia), 9 September 2022 – UNESCO Digital Library. URL *https://unesdoc.unesco.org/ark:/48223/pf0000383197* – accessed: 2024/03/31

3 AI Act: Rights and Obligations

Gabriele Bolek-Fügl, Veronica Cretu, Julia Fuith,
Merve Taner, Natascha Windholz, Carina Zehetmaier

In the era of the digital revolution, artificial intelligence has taken its place as the driving force behind countless innovations and improvements in various areas of life. From the optimization of industrial processes to the personalization of user experience in digital media and support in medical diagnostics – the capabilities of AI systems seem limitless. However, this rapid development is also accompanied by significant ethical and legal challenges, particularly with regard to the protection of fundamental rights.

The AI Act is fundamentally based on the idea of protecting fundamental rights, ensuring security and protecting democracy, the rule of law and the environment. The law represents the world's first comprehensive AI law (see chapter 2 "Geopolitics") and aims to harness the potential benefits of AI for society while mitigating the risks associated with certain AI systems.

The risk-based approach to classifying AI systems into different categories ensures that regulatory efforts are focused on AI applications that have a significant impact on the safety and fundamental rights of individuals as protected by the EU Charter of Fundamental Rights. The regulation lists high-risk AI systems, detailing the obligations for providers of such systems, including the need for a conformity assessment before these systems can be placed on the market or otherwise put into operation.

In addition, the regulation prohibits certain AI practices that are deemed unacceptable because they contradict EU values by violating fundamental rights. Examples include social rating systems, the exploitation of vulnerabilities through subliminal techniques and certain uses of real-time remote biometric recognition.

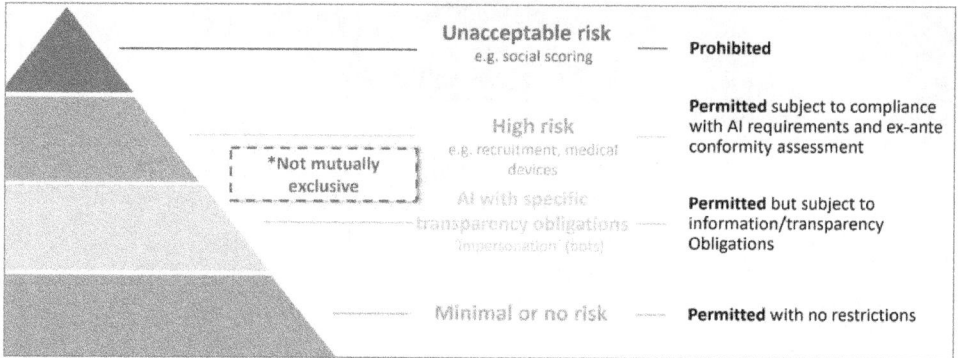

Figure 3.1 A Risk-based Approach to Regulation (Source: © European Commission)

Requirements for cooperation with authorities, the re-establishment of authorities (especially the AI office) and high penalties complete the picture.

3.1 Introduction to the AI Act

Gabriele Bolek-Fügl

Basic information on the AI Act

The EU regulation on the regulation of artificial intelligence, known as the AI Act or AI Regulation, has the full, official title "Regulation (EU) 2024/1689 of the European Parliament and of the Council of 13 June 2024 laying down harmonized rules on artificial intelligence" and was published in the Official Journal of the EU on 12 July 2024. The AI Act applies from August 2, 2024 in accordance with Art. 113 AI Act, but certain provisions will not come into force until later.

The European Parliament adopted the AI Act on March 13, 2024. The approval of the EU Council took place in May 2024. On July 12, 2024, the Regulation was published in the Official Journal of the EU and entered into force 20 days later, on August 2, 2024, to be applied in principle two years later (Art. 113 AI Act and Recital 179 AI Act). However, some areas enter into force at other times, see section 3.1.3 "Start of Application of the AI Act".

As a regulation, the provisions of the AI Act become directly effective in all EU Member States in all its parts without the need for transposition into national law (Art. 113 AI Act).

Start of Application of the AI Act

Recital 179 AI Act further states that "In view of the unacceptable risk associated with the use of AI in certain ways," some provisions should be applied earlier, such as the rules on prohibited systems. In contrast, it is envisaged that the provisions for the high-risk systems listed in Art. 6 para. 1 AI Act will only apply three years after entry into force.

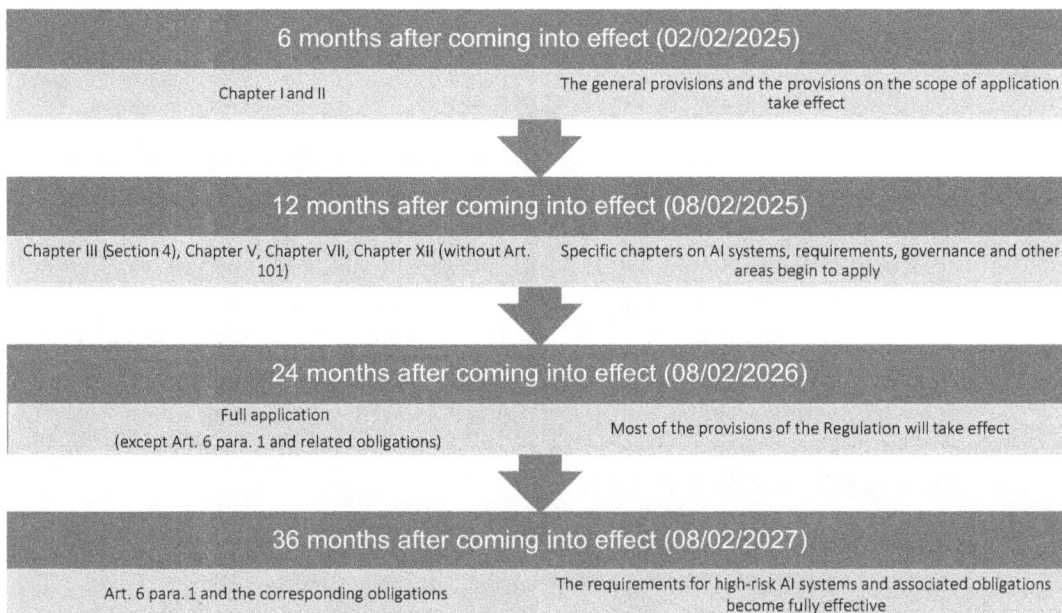

6 months after coming into effect (02/02/2025)	
Chapter I and II	The general provisions and the provisions on the scope of application take effect

12 months after coming into effect (08/02/2025)	
Chapter III (Section 4), Chapter V, Chapter VII, Chapter XII (without Art. 101)	Specific chapters on AI systems, requirements, governance and other areas begin to apply

24 months after coming into effect (08/02/2026)	
Full application (except Art. 6 para. 1 and related obligations)	Most of the provisions of the Regulation will take effect

36 months after coming into effect (08/02/2027)	
Art. 6 para. 1 and the corresponding obligations	The requirements for high-risk AI systems and associated obligations become fully effective

The overview illustrates the staggered timetable for the entry into force of the various sections of the regulation. This phased approach gives all stakeholders, from AI developers and providers to users, the opportunity to prepare for the new requirements and ensure that their systems and processes meet the new requirements. The different timeframes for the entry into force of individual chapters reflect the desire to strike a balance between protecting citizens immediately and providing companies with a reasonable implementation period.

Objectives of the AI Act

The EU Artificial Intelligence Regulation is a comprehensive set of rules aimed at shaping the development and use of AI systems in Europe. It represents a decisive step towards fostering both innovation and trust in the technology by striking a balance between protecting the public interest, security and fundamental rights, and support for technological progress.

Functioning of the EU Market	Human-centric and trustworthy AI	High level of protection against harmful effects	To support innovation
• Uniform legal framework in all Member States • Harmonised EU market • Cross-border free movement of goods	• Protection of personal data • Ensuring safety • Ensuring health • Protection of fundamental rights • Building Competencies	• Protection of democracy • Protection of the rule of law • Civil rights • Environmental protection • Promoting employment	• The development • Placing on the market • Commissioning • The use of AI systems • Support for SMEs and start-ups

Figure 3.2 Objectives of the EU AI Regulation

A key objective of the AI Act is to ensure the smooth functioning of the internal market. This is achieved by introducing uniform rules for the development, placing on the market and use of AI systems within the European Union. Such a harmonized approach prevents fragmentation of the market through different national laws and promotes coherent application and compliance across national borders.

Another key element of the regulation is the promotion of human-centered and trustworthy AI. This means that the development and use of AI technologies must be in line with the fundamental values and rights upheld in the European Union. These include protecting personal data, ensuring the safety and health of citizens and protecting democracy and the rule of law.

Art. 1 para. 1 AI Act

The purpose of this Regulation is to improve the functioning of the internal market and to promote the deployment of human-centric and trustworthy artificial intelligence (AI), while ensuring a high level of protection of health, safety and fundamental rights enshrined in the Charter of Fundamental Rights, including democracy, the rule of law and environmental protection, from the harmful effects of artificial intelligence (AI) systems in the Union and supporting innovation.

Recital 6 AI Act also requires "that AI is a human-centered technology. It should serve as a tool for people and ultimately improve human well-being". The EU's clear call is therefore to use artificial intelligence as a tool to improve people's quality of life, whether by facilitating work processes, improving healthcare, increasing efficiency in various sectors or helping to tackle global challenges such as climate change or resource and energy efficiency (Recital 4 AI Act).

Scope of Application of the AI Act

Article 2 AI Act defines the scope of application of the Regulation and essentially includes all AI systems that are created, distributed and operated in the EU or applied to persons located within the Union (Art. 2 para.1 litg AI Act).

The following overview illustrates the areas of application of the regulation and those areas to which it does not apply:

Table 3.1 Scope of Application of the EU AI Act

Scope of Application of the AI Act	Not in the Area of Application
▪ Providers who place AI models with a general purpose on the market (Art. 2 para. 1 lit a AI Act) ▪ Providers and deployers of AI systems, regardless of whether they are based in the EU or in a third country, provided that the systems are used in the EU or the result is used in the EU (Art. 2 para. 1 lit a to c AI Act) ▪ Product manufacturers who place AI systems on the market or put them into operation together with their product under their own name or trademark (Art. 2 para. 1lit e AI Act) ▪ AI systems that are placed on the market, put into service or used in the EU. This applies to providers, deployers, importers and distributors of AI systems (Art. 2 para. 1 AI Act) ▪ Authorized representatives of providers who are not established in the EU (Art. 2 para. 1 lit f Act)	▪ AI systems that can be used for personal, non-commercial Activities of individuals (Art. 2 para. 10 AI Act) ▪ AI systems used in areas not covered by Union law (e. g. national security) and AI systems used exclusively for military purposes or national security (Art. 2 para. 3 AI Act) ▪ AI systems used for the sole purpose of research and development are developed and operated (Art. 2 para. 6 AI Act) ▪ AI systems for research, testing and development activities before they are placed on the market or put into operation, except for real-world testing (Art. 2 para. 8 AI Act) ▪ Authorities in third countries and international organizations, provided that appropriate safeguards exist with regard to the protection of individuals (Art. 2 para. 4 GDPR)

AI systems that pose certain risks to the health, safety or fundamental rights of citizens are called high-risk AI systems.

Art. 2 para. 2 AI Act specifies the areas of application and exemptions for high-risk AI systemsassociated with products covered by specific Union harmonization legislation as listed in Annex I Section B AI Act. This paragraph clarifies that only Art. 112 AI Act (Assessment and verification) applies to these specific high-risk AI-systems. Art. 57 AI Act (AI sandboxes) applies, but only to the extent that the requirements for high-risk AI systems have been integrated into the aforementioned Union harmonization legislation.

This regulation reflects an effort to avoid overlaps or conflicts between the AI Act and existing, already harmonized EU legislation. It is recognized that certain products incorporating or deemed to incorporate AI technology may already be regulated by other EU directives or EU regulations. The specific reference to Art. 112 AI Act and the conditional application of Art. 57 AI Act are intended to ensure that compliance with the requirements for high-risk AI systems is in line with the already existing harmonized legal framework, without creating redundant or contradictory regulation.

Recital 9 AI Act mentions further harmonized EU regulations that remain unaffected. These are explicitly the "areas of data protection, consumer protection, fundamental rights, employment, employee protection and product safety", "including health and safety at work and relations between employers and employees".

Art. 2 para. 11 AI Act reinforces these concerns by requiring "the maintenance or introduction of laws, regulations or administrative provisions which are more favorable to employees with regard to the protection of their rights when employers use AI systems".

Art. 2 para. 12 AI Act states that AI systems that are made freely available to everyone and whose source code is openly accessible and usable (open source) are not subject to the rules of the AI Act, with the exception of the following cases:

- The open source AI system is classified as high-risk: High-risk AI systems have a potentially serious impact on people's safety, health or fundamental rights. If such a system, even if it is open source, is marketed or used in the EU, it must comply with the strict requirements of the AI Act.

- The AI system falls under Art. 5 AI Act or Art. 50 AI Act: Both articles deal with certain types of AI systems and their use, which are specifically regulated due to their potential impact. Article 5 deals with prohibited practices in the field of AI and Article 50 with transparency obligations for providers and deployers of certain AI systems. If an open source AI system falls into these categories, it is also subject to the provisions of the law.

> In principle, the use of an open source license does not exclude the applicability of the AI Act. The decisive factor is the type of system and the context of its use, in particular if it involves risks for persons or falls under the special provisions of Art. 5 AI Act or Art. 50 AI Act.

3.1.1 Definition of AI systems

The definition of AI system under the AI Act is deliberately broad in order to cover a wide range of technologies and forms of application and to keep pace with the rapid technical development of the regulation. This is to ensure that the regulation remains applicable even if the technology continues to develop.

> According to the AI Act, the term **AI system** includes a machine-based system that is designed to operate with varying degrees of autonomy, that can be adaptive once deployed, and that derives from the inputs received for explicit or implicit goals how to produce results such as predictions, content, recommendations or decisions that can influence physical or virtual environments (Art. 3 no. 1 AI Act).

This definition is conceptually comprehensive and includes both current and future developments in AI technology. It focuses on systems that can process and interpret data in order to perform tasks, make decisions or generate content that simulates or replaces human work.

A **general-purpose AI model** is defined in Art. 3 no. 63 AI Act as an AI model that is designed to perform a variety of tasks rather than being limited to a specific function. These models are particularly flexible and can be used in a wide variety of areas. Some key characteristics are

- **Significant general usability:** The model is not limited to a specific application or task, but can be used for a wide range of tasks. This flexibility distinguishes it from AI systems that are developed for specific purposes.

- **Ability to perform tasks competently:** It can perform a wide variety of tasks effectively. This means that it can be useful and effective in many different areas or contexts.

- **Integration into downstream systems or applications:** It can be embedded in a variety of different systems or applications. This makes it a versatile component that can be used in various products or services.

- **Training with large amounts of data under extensive self-monitoring:** Often these models are developed by training with large amounts of data, where advanced techniques such as self-monitoring can be used. This allows the model to learn from a wide variety of information and improve its ability to perform tasks across different domains.

- **Exception for research and development:** AI models that are used exclusively for research and development purposes or for the creation of prototypes prior to their market launch do not fall under this category. This means that certain models that are still in the development phase and are used for experimental or research purposes are not considered general-purpose AI models.

A **general-purpose AI system** is an AI system that is based on a general-purpose AI model and is capable of serving a variety of purposes both for direct use and for integration into other AI systems (Art. 3 no. 66 AI Act).

3.1.2 Roles of Natural or Legal Persons

The AI Act defines various designations for the roles that can be assumed by a natural or legal person, authority, institution or other body. These are summarized under the term **"operator"**.

The individual roles in the AI Act are described as follows:

Role	Description	Duties
Provider (Art. 3 no. 3 AI Act)	Developer or who has developed an AI system or AI model with a general purpose who places it on the market or puts it into operation under his name or trademark, whether for payment or free of charge.	Responsibility for the conformity of the AI system with the requirements of the AI Regulation, including carrying out a conformity assessment, providing the necessary documentation and registering high-risk AI systems.
Deployer (Art. 3 no. 4 AI Act)	Users of an AI system on their own responsibility, except for personal and non-professional use.	Ensuring compliance with the operating regulations of the AI system, in particular with regard to transparency and information obligations towards data subjects and compliance with data protection regulations.
Authorized representative (Art. 3 no. 5 AI Act)	A person appointed in writing by a provider who is based in the EU and who assumes the obligations of the provider with regard to compliance with the AI Act.	Assume the obligations set out in the Regulation on behalf of the provider, including ensuring compliance and carrying out necessary procedures.
Importer (Art. 3 no. 6 AI Act)	Places an AI system on the market in the EU under the name or trademark of a person established outside the EU.	Ensures that the AI system imported into the EU complies with the requirements of the AI Act before it is placed on the market, including conformity assessment and provision of the necessary documentation.

Role	Description	Duties
Distributors (Art. 3 no. 7 AI Act)	Any person in the supply chain who makes an AI system available on the EU market, with the exception of the supplier or importer.	Must check that the AI system has the correct markings, that the required documents are available and that the AI system provider has met the EU requirements.
Product manufacturer (Art. 2 para. 1 lit e AI Act)	Brings an AI system together with its product onto the market or into operation under its own name or trademark.	Responsible for ensuring that the product, including the integrated AI system, complies with the applicable EU safety and conformity requirements before being placed on the market.

In addition, the term "downstream provider" means a provider of an AI system, including a general-purpose AI system, that integrates an AI model, regardless of whether the model is provided and vertically integrated by itself or provided by another entity on the basis of contractual relationships (Art. 3 no. 68 AI Act).

3.1.3 Market Launch Phases

The various phases in the life cycle of an AI system include not only the development and use of AI systems, but above all their market launch. From a legal perspective, the following phases are the definitions for the deployment phases of an AI from Art. 3 AI Act:

Name of the Phase	Explanation
Placing on the market (Art. 3 no. 9 AI Act)	Refers to the first time an AI system or general-purpose AI model is made available on the Union market. It marks the point in time when a new product is made commercially available for the first time.
Making available on the market (Art. 3 no. 10 AI Act)	Refers to the provision of an AI system or an AI model with a general purpose for distribution or use on the Union market in the context of a business activity, whether in return for payment or free of charge. This phase includes the commercial distribution and availability of the product.

Name of the Phase	Explanation
Putting into service (Art. 3 no. 11 AI Act)	The provision of an AI-system by the provider in the Union for first use directly to the deployer or for own use in accordance with its intended purpose. This is the moment when the AI-system is actually activated and used for its intended purpose.
Recall of an AI system (Art. 3 no. 16 AI Act)	Any measure aimed at returning an AI system already made available to providers to the deployer or decommissioning or shutting it down.
Withdrawal of an AI system (Art. 3 no. 17 AI Act)	Any measure intended to prevent an AI system in the supply chain from being made available on the market.

The legal definitions of the various phases are largely based on the application in the productive use of AI, as the development and test phase is not part of the regulation in the AI Act. The timing of the transitions from one phase to another is important, as this has an impact on responsibility and supervisory duties.

An exception to this is **testing under real-life conditions**, which enables developers to gain valuable insights into the practical application and effectiveness of their AI system and helps to ensure that it complies with legal requirements before it is officially placed on the market or put into operation. This testing process aims to collect data and insights on the functioning of the AI system under real-life conditions (Art. 3 no. 57 AI Act).

3.1.4 Terms for the Use of AI Systems

The key terms that are central to the understanding, use and processes that apply to the development, assessment and monitoring of AI systems under the AI Regulation are listed and explained below. They form the basis for robust safety and quality management:

Designation of Use	Description
Intended purpose (Art. 3 no. 12 AI Act)	This refers to the use(s) or function(s) of an AI system as specified by the provider, as indicated in the accompanying documentation, instructions or promotional materials. The intended purpose specifies the tasks for which or the conditions under which the AI system was designed.

Designation of Use	Description
Reasonably foreseeable misuse (Art. 3 no. 13 AI Act)	A term that describes situations in which an AI system is used in a way that was not intended by the provider, but which may arise due to the behavior of end users or a reasonably foreseeable interaction with other systems. Developers must therefore recognize both the risks they are aware of and those that are reasonably foreseeable. This includes misuse of the AI system based on how humans normally act. This includes misuse or improper use of the system that could lead to risk or harm.
Conformity assessment (Art. 3 no. 20 AI Act)	A procedure that ensures that an AI system meets the requirements set out in the regulation. It includes a review of the technical documentation, a review of the safety and risk management processes and, if necessary, further tests or inspections. The conformity assessment can be carried out internally or externally.
Risk management-system (Art. 9 para. 2 AI Act)	An ongoing process established by the provider of an AI system to continuously identify, assess, mitigate and monitor risks associated with the use of the AI system. This includes measures to prevent and mitigate risks to the health, safety and fundamental rights of individuals. "Risk" is the combination of the likelihood of harm occurring and the severity of that harm (Art. 3 no. 2 AI Act).
Systemic risk (Art. 3 no. 65 AI Act)	Refers to a specific risk associated with the wide-ranging capabilities of general-purpose AI models. It arises from their potential or foreseeable negative impact on public health, safety, fundamental rights or society and can have a significant impact on the EU market by spreading extensively along the value chain.
Performance of an AI system (Art. 3 no. 18 AI Act)	Refers to the ability of an AI system to perform the defined and expected tasks under the intended operating conditions. Performance can be measured using various criteria such as accuracy, reliability, robustness and efficiency. Performance evaluation is critical to ensure that the AI system fulfills its intended purpose and does not pose undesirable risks.

Designation of Use	Description
Significant change (Art. 3 no. 23 AI Act)	A substantial change is any modification to an AI system after it has been placed on the market or put into service that could affect its conformity with the essential requirements inArt. 8 et seq. AI Act, requirements for high-risk AI systems. This includes changes to the functionality, operating environment or components of the system that potentially change its safety, performance or risk profile. Significant changes require a reassessment of the conformity of the AI system.
CE marking (Art. 3 no. 24 AI Act)	The CE marking is a mark indicating that a product, including an AI system, complies with the applicable EU regulations and can be freely marketed in the European Economic Area (EEA). The affixing of the CE marking is the result of a conformity assessment procedure which confirms that the product complies with EU safety, health and environmental protection requirements.
Post-market monitoring system (Art. 3 no. 25 AI Act)	Process or activity established by AI system providers to continuously monitor the performance and safety of the AI system after it has been introduced to the market. This includes collecting and analyzing user feedback, monitoring incidents, identifying potential safety issues and implementing necessary corrective actions. The aim is to minimize risks and ensure that the AI system remains safe and effective throughout its lifecycle.

3.1.5 Data-related Designations

The AI Act emphasizes the importance of transparency and traceability of AI systems. Detailed information about the data used helps to understand and comprehend the decisions and actions of an AI system. This is particularly important for accountability and trust in AI technologies.

It is therefore essential that the naming of the data is precise in order to always speak about the correct information. The following designations are therefore used for the AI training phase in accordance with Art. 3 no. 29-32 AI Act:

Training data
- Data used to train an AI system. The learnable parameters of the system are adjusted during this process.

Validation data
- Data used to evaluate and fine-tune the trained AI system. Helps to avoid underfitting or overfitting by adjusting non-learnable parameters and the learning process.

Validation dataset
- A separate dataset or a portion of the training dataset that is used for validation with a fixed or variable split.

Test data
- Data used for an independent evaluation of the AI system before its market launch or deployment. Helps confirm the expected performance of the system.

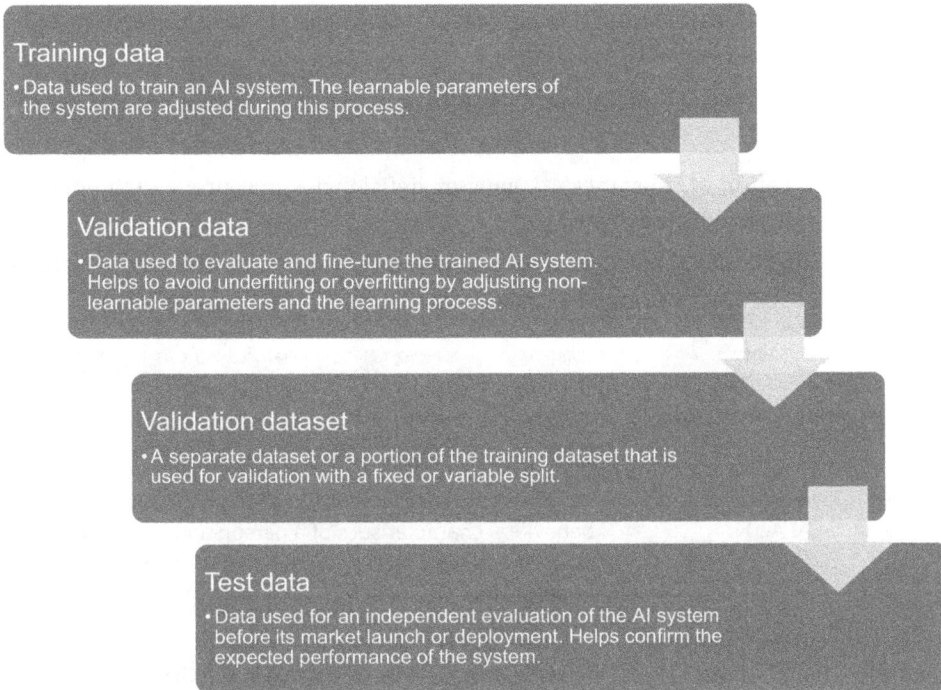

Figure 3.3 Designation of Data for Training and Test Phase

Access to high-quality data is crucial to ensure the functionality and safety of advanced AI systems, especially when models are trained by data. This is necessary to guarantee that high-risk AI systems fulfill their intended purpose, operate safely and do not cause discrimination in violation of EU law. This requires high-quality training-validation- and testing data sets which in turn requires effective data governance and management practices. These data sets must not only be relevant and representative in relation to the objective of the system, but also as accurate and complete as possible, including accurate labeling (Recital 67 AI Act).

Specific data governance and data management procedures that are precisely tailored to the purpose of the system are essential for the training, validation and testing data sets of high-risk AI systems. According to Art. 10 para. 2 AI Act, these include a number of critical steps (selection):

- the selection and justification of the underlying conceptual decisions
- the methods of data collection and origin, including consideration of the original purpose of collection for personal data
- Important data preparation processes such as annotations, labeling, cleansing, updating, expanding and merging

- the definition of assumptions, in particular with regard to the information to be collected and presented by the data

- the implementation of measures to identify, prevent and mitigate recognized distortions

- the identification of relevant data gaps or deficiencies that prevent compliance and strategies to address them

Data is also differentiated in terms of its content and composition. The following table contains definitions in this regard:

Term	Description
Input data (Art. 3 no. 33 AI Act)	Data that is fed into an AI system or collected directly by it and on the basis of which the system generates a result.
Biometric data (Art. 3 no. 34 AI Act)	Personal data that records the physical, physiological or behavioral characteristics of a person and is obtained using special technical procedures, e. g. facial images or fingerprints.
Special categories of personal data (Art. 3 no. 37 AI Act)	Categories of personal data containing particularly sensitive information, as defined in the GDPR.
Personal data (Art. 3 no. 50 AI Act)	According to Art. 4 no. 1 GDPR, this is any information relating to an identified or identifiable natural person ("data subject").
Non-personal data (Art. 3 no. 51 AI Act)	Data that is not personal data in the meaning of the GDPR. This data does not relate to identified or identifiable natural persons or has been anonymized in such a way that the data subject cannot or can no longer be identified. Non-personal data can be freely processed and used as long as this process does not violate other laws or removes the anonymization and makes persons identifiable.
Sensitive operational data (Art. 3 no. 38 AI Act)	Operational data relating to the prevention, detection, investigation or prosecution of criminal offenses, the disclosure of which could jeopardize the integrity of criminal proceedings.

The protection of sensitive and personal data is crucial to safeguard the privacy, security and fundamental rights of data subjects. In a world where data is considered the new oil, the consequences of inadequate data protection can be severe for the individuals concerned. From identity theft and financial fraud to unwanted surveillance and discrimination, the potential detriments that can arise from misuse of this information can range.

In addition, the unauthorized use or loss of personal data can significantly undermine trust in technologies, companies and even government institutions.

Art. 3 no. 60 AI Act

"Deepfake" refers to content – whether in the form of images, sound recordings or videos – that has been created or manipulated using artificial intelligence. This content imitates real people, objects, places or events so convincingly that it could appear authentic and truthful to an unprepared person.

3.1.6 AI Literacy

It is crucial that developers ("providers") and users ("deployers") of AI systems ensure that their teams and all persons interacting with these systems on their behalf have the required competencies and knowledge in the field of artificial intelligence (Art. 4 AI Act). This includes technical understanding, practical experience, formal education and training. The following key aspects should be considered:

- **Technical knowledge and experience:** It is important that staff not only have basic knowledge of AI, but can also gain specific experience with the respective AI systems.

- **Education and training** Employees should be kept up to date with the latest technology through education and ongoing training. This helps to ensure that they can use the AI systems effectively and safely.

- **Context of use:** The specific conditions and framework in which the AI systems are to be used must be taken into account when developing skills. Different areas of application can entail different requirements and challenges.

- **Target groups:** It is also important to consider the people or groups for whom or to whom the AI systems will be used. Understanding the needs and potential risks for these target groups can help to better design and adapt the use of AI systems.

There is a need for competent handling of AI systems by well-trained personnel to ensure their safe and effective use. It also emphasizes that adequate training and experience are essential to fully exploit the potential benefits of AI technologies while minimizing risks.

According to Art. 3 no. 56 AI Act, "AI literacy" comprises the skills, knowledge and understanding that enable providers, deployers and data subjects, taking into account their respective rights and obligations under this Regulation, to use AI systems competently and to be aware of the opportunities and risks of AI and the potential harm it can cause.

3.2 AI Literacy for Providers

Veronica Cretu

This section provides a structured approach to AI literacy and emphasizes the need for continuous learning and adaptation to the evolving AI landscape. By following the suggested framework, providers can ensure that their employees are well equipped to handle AI technologies responsibly and effectively. In addition, they will be able to foster a culture of ethical AI use, promote transparency and accountability, and drive innovation within their organizations. The framework outlines key recommendations for improving the digital readiness of institutions, enhancing the digital skills of staff, promoting data literacy, providing AI-specific training, promoting continuous learning, investing in talent development, implementing change management strategies and establishing communities of practice. These measures will help AI providers meet the requirements of the AI Act, ensure robust AI competencies and responsible AI use, and ultimately contribute to the development of a better informed and ethically minded workforce.

3.2.1 Introduction

The digital transformation transformation, particularly through the use of artificial intelligence (AI), has become a priority for both private and public organizations.

Governments are using technology to better understand and meet the needs of citizens. For this transformation to be successful, a comprehensive and inclusive approach is required. This requires changes in governance models, structures and organizations to address the new challenges and opportunities presented by digital technologies. Governments are faced with complex and unpredictable challenges that put pressure on the public sector to increase.

A report by the Working Group on AI Capacity Building [3] points to significant gaps in the **digital skills** of governments, particularly in the Global South. The failure of digital transformation projects is often due to inadequate IT infrastructure and policy frameworks, as well as insufficient digital skills and the difficulty of applying them effectively. Therefore, governments around the world are focusing on the essential competencies – beyond knowledge, skills and attitudes – that civil servants need to use digital tools, develop and implement digital transformation projects and effectively address complex governance issues. Many public organizations lack in-house expertise in AI and data analytics, so they rely heavily on external consultants and organizations for AI projects. This reliance is partly due to lower salaries in the public sector, making it difficult to attract and retain top talent.

In addition, the public sector must make **complex ethical and legal considerations** when using AI. Issues such as privacy, bias and accountability are of paramount importance, which is a further difficulty compared to the private sector where such constraints are less pronounced. Despite these challenges, there is a growing recognition in the public sector that AI capabilities need to be developed. Governments around the world are increasingly focusing on building the necessary digital skills among civil servants to be able to use AI effectively. This involves not only acquiring technical skills, but also fostering a culture that supports digital transformation.

In contrast, the **private sector** benefits from benefits from higher salaries and better resources, which attracts top AI talent. Private companies have access to advanced infrastructure, including the high-performance computing resources required for AI development. The culture in private companies is often focused on rapid innovation and risk-taking, allowing them to quickly implement and adapt new AI technologies. Employees at these companies typically have extensive skills that enable them to effectively develop, maintain and operate sophisticated AI systems. Nonetheless, the private sector faces the same significant **AI skills gap** as the public sector. Based on data from a survey conducted in 2023 by Access Partnership and Amazon Web Services (AWS) with 3297 employees and 1340 companies in the US, 73% of employers have hiring AI professionals as a priority, 75% are struggling to find the talent they need [11]. The demand is not limited to technical skills; critical and creative thinking is also highly valued. Unfortunately, the majority of employers and employees are unsure which specific AI skills to target and are unaware of available training programs. The same survey shows that by 2028, more than 90% of US companies plan to integrate AI-powered solutions into their operations. Various departments are expected to benefit from this change, with IT departments leading the way, followed by sales, marketing and human resources. Key benefits of AI include automating tasks, improving workflows, enhancing communication and helping employees learn new skills.

The demand for AI skills is also leading to changes in the labor market. Companies are willing to offer significantly higher salaries to employees with AI skills, with IT staff potentially earning 47% more, according to the AWS report. This trend extends to other departments as well, reflecting the broad applicability of AI skills. Nearly 80% of workers are interested in developing AI skills, including a significant proportion of older workers who see value in upskilling. It is predicted that AI will fundamentally improve productivity. 88% of employees expect to be using AI on a daily basis by 2028. Employers believe that AI could increase overall productivity by up to 49% – a remarkable increase compared to recent productivity growth rates.

Research from the year 2023 by Coursera [7], in which 650 managers from the areas of L&D **(Learning & Development)** and HR (Human Resources) executives from eight countries, shows a clear shift towards more investment in talent development. More than 95% of these executives stated that budgets for L&D have increased, with 51% of executives recognizing L&D as a strategic business function.

The key findings of the survey show that L&D is experiencing unprecedented support from senior management. This shift underscores the critical role that L&D and HR leaders now play in achieving organizational goals. The majority of executives indicated that budget increases are driven by the need to improve employee engagement and develop critical skills that are essential to remaining competitive. In particular, 75% of executives indicated that management is prioritizing investment in L&D to ensure the success of their technology ambitions.

The urgency of retraining and upskilling is determined by several factors. Increasing productivity, maintaining competitiveness, fostering employee engagement, adapting to technological change and retaining employees are top priorities. L&D and HR leaders are focusing on business and people skills such as project management, leadership, adaptability and agility as these are critical to the changing workplace. Digital and data skills are also high on the priority list, reflecting the ongoing digital transformation.

Interestingly, AI skills were ranked as a lower priority: Only 19% of executives consider it a primary focus, and only 20% have effective metrics for AI skills. This is likely due to the fact that many organizations are still in the early stages when it comes to how to integrate and leverage AI. Nonetheless, the potential impact of generative AI on different job roles presents an opportunity for HR leaders to drive change by working with business and technology leaders.

One of the biggest challenges for L&D leaders is creating meaningful learning experiences amidst an overwhelming amount of available content, a phenomenon referred to as "content chaos". Nearly half of executives cited this as their biggest challenge, citing that too many learning initiatives to measure leaves too little time for strategic planning. Nevertheless, performance and productivity improvements, along with skills development, are seen as key indicators of program success. Of particular note, 46% of managers reported that their employees are using the skills acquired through L&D programs more in their daily work compared to the previous year. The findings from this report serve as a catalyst for new ideas that will enable organizations to build more engaged and flexible workforces that are ready to tackle future challenges.

All in all, it is important to mention that research on AI literacy is still in its infancy and there is little literature on this topic [8].

Nonetheless, the insights into AI literacy gained from these and other new findings are crucial to align with the AI Act, which aims to regulate the development and deployment of AI across the European Union. The law emphasizes high standards of transparency, accountability and ethical considerations and highlights the need for robust AI competencies. Addressing the significant gaps in digital skills identified in the report is essential for compliance with the AI Act. Both the public and private sectors must invest in **education and training** to ensure their workforces are prepared for these stringent requirements. Furthermore, the law's focus on ethical and legal considerations aligns with the challenges faced by the public sector, highlighting the need for targeted capacity building initiatives. The increasing investment in L&D, driven by the need for organizational agility, reflects a proactive approach to meeting the requirements of the AI Act and ensuring responsible and effective AI deployment.

3.2.2 Definition of AI Literacy

First of all, it is important to define **literacy**. According to UNESCO, the acquisition of reading and writing skills is not a one-off act. Beyond the traditional concept of literacy and numeracy, literacy is now understood as a means of identifying, understanding, interpreting, creating and communicating in an increasingly digital, text-mediated, information-rich and rapidly changing world. Literacy is a continuum of learning and mastery of reading, writing and numeracy throughout life and is part of a broader set of skills that include digital literacy, media literacy, education for sustainable development and global citizenship, and job-specific skills. Literacy skills themselves are expanding and developing as people become more and more exposed to information and learning through digital technologies [9].

Literacy, a fundamental human right, encompasses cognitive, linguistic, social, affective, relational and cultural skills [5]. It goes beyond the mere decoding and understanding of texts and promotes critical thinking and a deeper understanding of information.

AI skills, like general knowledge, are essential to navigate the modern world, especially as AI becomes increasingly integrated into different areas of life.

Just as traditional literacy is a human right, AI literacy can be seen as a crucial right in the digital age. It enables individuals to understand, interact with and critically evaluate AI technologies to ensure they are not left behind in an increasingly AI-driven world. AI literacy empowers people to grasp the far-reaching impact of AI on society and encourages critical thinking about its implications and applications.

AI literacy encompasses the **ability to understand, apply, monitor and critically reflect on AI applications without having to develop AI models**. It has parallels with other forms of technological literacy, such as digital literacy, media literacy and data literacy [8].

The term "AI Literacy" was first used in an online article in 2015 and appeared shortly afterwards in an empirical article [12]. AI literacy is defined as *"a set of competencies that enable individuals to critically evaluate AI technologies, communicate and collaborate effectively with AI, and use AI as a tool online, at home and at work"* [10]. AI literacy is primarily aimed at learners without a computer science background and emphasizes the need for the general population to be AI literate. As AI permeates areas such as education, healthcare, transportation, social services, marketing and others, understanding AI becomes critical to both personal and professional interactions with the technology.

Other sources [2] indicate that AI literacy encompasses a holistic set of competencies that enable individuals not only to use AI tools, but also to **critically evaluate and understand the broader context in which AI operates**. By developing technical skills, critical thinking and contextual understanding, individuals can effectively engage with AI technologies, make informed decisions and contribute to the responsible development and use of AI in society.

In summary, fostering AI literacy helps people to better navigate the increasingly AI-driven world and improve their ability to critically engage with AI technologies and use them effectively in different areas.

3.2.3 AI Literacy and the Provisions of the AI Act

Providing knowledge about artificial intelligence (AI) is a decisive factor for the responsible use and operation of AI systems.

Art. 4 AI Act states: *"Providers and deployers of AI systems shall take measures to ensure, to the best of their ability **that their personnel and other persons involved in the operation and use of AI-systems on their behalf have a sufficient level of AI literacy,** taking into account their technical knowledge, experience, education and training and the context in which the AI-systems are intended to be used and the persons or groups of persons with whom the AI-systems are intended to be used."*

Further provisions on AI literacy in the AI Act:

- **Recital 20 AI Act:** *"In order to maximize the benefits of AI-systems while safeguarding fundamental rights, health and safety and enabling democratic oversight, **AI literacy should equip providers, deployers and data subjects with the necessary concepts to make informed decisions about AI-systems.** These concepts may vary depending on the context and may include understanding the correct application of technical elements in the development phase of the AI system, the measures to be applied in its use and the appropriate interpretation of the outputs of the AI system and, in the case of data subjects, the knowledge necessary to understand how decisions made using AI will affect them. In the context of the application of this Regulation, **AI literacy should provide all relevant operators in the AI value chain with the knowledge necessary to ensure appropriate compliance and proper enforcement of the Regulation.** In addition, the full implementation of AI literacy measures and the introduction of appropriate follow-up measures could help to improve working conditions and ultimately support the consolidation and innovation pathway of trustworthy AI in the Union. A European Panel on Artificial Intelligence ('the AI Panel') **should support the Commission in promoting***

AI literacy tools and public awareness and education on the benefits, risks, safeguards, rights and obligations related to the use of AI systems. In coope-ration with relevant stakeholders, the Commission and the Member States should facilitate the development of voluntary codes of conduct to promote AI liter-acy among persons involved in the development, operation and use of AI."

- **Art. 3 no. 56 AI Act:** *"... the term 'AI literacy' means the skills, knowledge and under-standing that enable providers, deployers and data subjects, taking into account their respective rights and obligations under this Regulation, to use AI systems in an informed manner and to be aware of the opportunities and risks of AI and the poten-tial harm it may cause."*

- **Recital 91 AI Act:** "Given the nature of AI-systems and the risks to safety and fundamental rights that may be associated with their use, it is appropriate to lay down specific responsibilities for deployers, including with regard to the need to ensure adequate monitoring of the performance of an AI-system in real-life condi-tions. In particular, deployers should take appropriate technical and organiza-tional measures to ensure that they use high-risk AI-systems in accordance with the instructions for use and certain other obligations should be laid down in rela-tion to the monitoring of the functioning of the AI systems and, where appropri-ate, record-keeping obligations. In addition, deployers should ensure that the per-sons entrusted with the implementation of the instructions for use and human oversight in accordance with this Regulation have the necessary competence, in particular an appropriate level of AI literacy, training and authority, to properly perform those tasks. Those obligations should be without prejudice to other obli-gations of the deployer in relation to high-risk AI-systems under Union or national law."

- **Recital 165 AI Act:** "The development of AI-systems other than high-risk AI-sys-tems in accordance with the requirements of this Regulation may lead to a greater uptake of ethical and trustworthy AI in the Union. Providers of non-high-risk AI-systems should be encouraged to establish codes of conduct, including associated governance mechanisms, to promote voluntary application of some or all of the requirements applicable to high-risk AI-systems, adapted in light of the intended purpose of the systems and the lower risk, and taking into account available tech-nical solutions and industry best practices such as model and data cards. In addi-tion, providers and, where appropriate, deployers of all AI systems, whether high-risk or not, and of all AI models should also be encouraged to voluntarily apply additional requirements, e. g. in relation to the elements of the Union Ethics Guide-lines for Trustworthy AI, environmental sustainability, measures for AI literacy, inclusive and diverse design and development of AI systems, including with a focus on vulnerable persons and accessibility for persons with disabilities, stake-holder participation, involving, where appropriate, relevant stakeholders such as business associations and civil society organizations, academia, research organisations, trade unions and consumer protection organisations in the design and development of AI systems, and diversity of development teams, including gender balance. (...)"

- **Art. 66 lit. f AI Act:** "... *support the Commission in* **promoting AI literacy**, *raising awareness and educating the public on the benefits, risks, safeguards, rights and obligations related to the use of AI systems*".

3.2.4 Proposal for a Maturity Framework for AI providers

One of the starting points for defining a maturity level-framework for AI literacy is the Recommendation on key competences for lifelong learning of the Council of the European Union, which was adopted in May 2018 [4]. The Recommendation identifies eight key competences that are essential for citizens in terms of personal fulfilment, healthy and sustainable lifestyles, employability, active citizenship and social inclusion.

Digital competence one of the eight competences, encompasses the confident, critical and responsible use of and engagement with digital technologies for learning, work and participation in society. It includes information and data literacy, communication and collaboration, media literacy, digital content creation (including programming), security (including digital wellbeing and cybersecurity skills), intellectual property issues, problem solving and critical thinking.

Essential knowledge, skills and attitudes related to this competence: Individuals should understand how digital technologies can support communication, creativity and innovation and be aware of their possibilities, limitations, impacts and risks. They should understand the general principles, mechanisms and logic underlying evolving digital technologies and know the basic function and use of different devices, software and networks. Individuals should critically consider the validity, reliability and impact of information and data provided by digital means and be aware of the legal and ethical principles associated with the use of digital technologies.

As a starting point for digital capacity building, many governments, international organizations, think tanks and universities have developed competency frameworks, courses and curricula to lay the foundations for training public sector officials on digital transformation [3]. UNESCO's analysis identified the following common competencies in the frameworks studied: *Digital leadership; problem identification; digital literacy; open data; data-driven approaches;* **artificial intelligence** *human-centeredness; iteration-based improvements in product and service development.*

For the purposes of this section, the following maturity framework for AI literacy is proposed. The framework can be easily adapted and extended. By following it, AI providers can ensure that their employees and other relevant individuals have the necessary knowledge, skills and attitudes to develop, deploy and manage AI systems effectively and ethically. This meets the requirements of **Art. 4 AI Act** and helps to promote a culture of responsible use of AI.

Table 3.2 Maturity framework for AI literacy

Maturity level	Knowledge	Skills	Attitudes	Implications for AI providers
Base level	Basic understanding of AI principles, terminology and concepts. Knowledge of the AI Act and its impact on the development and use of AI.	Basic knowledge of digital tools and understanding of simple AI applications. Basic data skills, including basic data collection, storage and security practices.	Openness to learning about AI and its ethical implications. Awareness of the importance of data protection, security and ethical considerations in the field of AI.	Implementation of AI introduction programs for all employees. Promoting a culture of continuous learning and curiosity about AI. Ensure that all employees know and understand the basic principles of the AI Act.
Middle level	In-depth understanding of AI algorithms data processing techniques and ethical guidelines. Familiarity with the specific requirements of the AI Act relevant to their role. Basic understanding of design thinking principles [13][1] and human-centered AI design [6][2].	Knowledge of AI tools and platforms for data analysis and decision-making. Ability to handle and analyze large amounts of data and understand its impact on AI systems. Understanding the role of AI in improving operational processes. Applying design thinking principles to AI projects to improve user experience and usability.	Critical approach to evaluating AI results in terms of accuracy and bias. Commitment to ethical AI practices and compliance with legal and regulatory standards. Emphasizing the central role of humans in the development and use of AI.	Provide targeted training on advanced AI concepts and tools. Promoting critical thinking and ethical decision-making in AI-related tasks. Ensure that employees are able to interpret and apply the AI Act and adopt a human-centered approach in their daily work.

Table 3.2 Maturity framework for AI literacy *(continued)*

Maturity level	Knowledge	Skills	Attitudes	Implications for AI providers
Advanced level	Comprehensive understanding of AI technologies, including machine learning and neural networks. Thorough knowledge of the AI Act, including specific compliance requirements. Advanced understanding of the principles of design thinking and its application in AI development.	Ability to develop and implement sophisticated AI solutions. Advanced data analysis and problem solving skills. Leadership skills in managing AI projects and initiatives that focus on user experience and human-centered design.	Advocating the ethical use of AI and the responsible use of AI systems. Promoting transparency and accountability in AI processes and decisions. Commitment to the development of AI systems that prioritize human needs and ethical considerations.	Development of advanced AI training programs with a focus on leadership and innovation. Promoting a culture of ethical use of AI and transparency. Ensure that employees are able to carry out AI projects in accordance with the AI Act and the principles of design thinking.
Expert level	Mastery of the latest AI technologies and innovations. Expert knowledge of global AI standards, regulations and ethical considerations, including the AI Regulation. Understanding the environment of the various stakeholders, including the perspectives of governments, industry, academia and civil society.	Leading AI research and development initiatives. Development and implementation of AI policies and strategies. Guiding organizations on ethical and compliant AI practices. Facilitate collaboration and dialog between different stakeholders to shape AI policy and standards with a human-centric approach.	Provide leadership in promoting the responsible use of AI and influencing AI policy and standards. Commitment to continuous learning and innovation in the field of AI. Advocating integrative and participatory approaches in AI governance. Advocating for inclusive, participatory and human-centered approaches in AI governance.	Supporting the continuous professional development of senior employees and managers in the field of AI. Promote participation in global AI policy discussions and standard-setting activities. Fostering relationships between different stakeholders to ensure that different perspectives are taken into account in the development and deployment of AI.

Maturity level	Knowledge	Skills	Attitudes	Implications for AI providers
	Expert knowledge of design thinking principles and human-centered AI [1] [3] and their strategic application in AI.		Prioritizing the impact of AI on human well-being and societal well-being.	Ensure that the organization is at the forefront of the development and use of AI from an ethical and humane perspective by engaging with various stakeholders.

1 Design thinking differs from other innovation and idea generation processes in that it is solution-oriented and user-centered rather than problem-oriented. This means that it focuses on the solution to a problem and not on the problem itself.

2 If you really focus on augmenting human capabilities, that's human-centered AI [6]

3 Seven principles for human-centered AI [1]

Key Recommendations for AI Providers to Develop and Promote Continuous AI Literacy within Companies

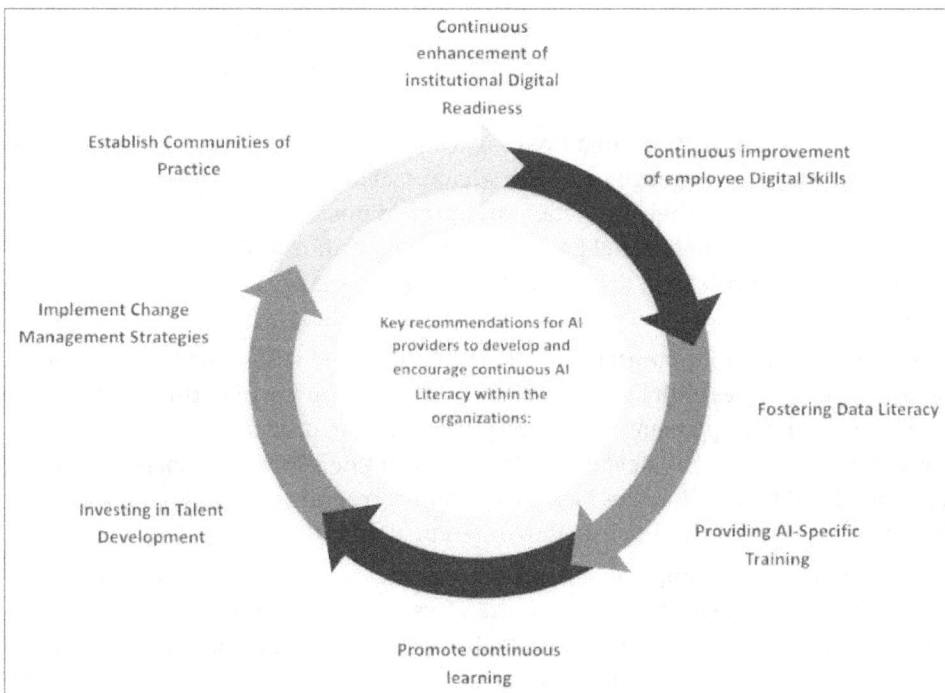

Figure 3.4 Key Recommendations for AI Literacy

Continuously improve institutional digital readiness within the organization: Conduct a comprehensive digital readiness assessment to identify gaps in technology infrastructure, digital policies and governance frameworks. Develop a strategic plan to improve digital readiness, including modernizing IT systems, establishing clear digital policies and fostering a culture that supports digital transformation.

Continuous improvement of employees' digital skills: Establish digital skills training programs for all employees to ensure that they master digital tools and understand digital processes. Develop and implement comprehensive digital skills training covering the most important digital tools and platforms. Offer specialized training modules tailored to employees' tasks and responsibilities. Encourage participation in online courses, webinars and workshops on new digital trends.

Promoting data literacy: Promoting data literacy throughout the organization to ensure that employees can effectively collect, analyze and interpret data and make data-driven decisions. Integrate data literacy training into the onboarding process and ongoing professional development programs. Provide access to data analysis tools and resources. Create data-oriented workshops and seminars to improve employees' analytical skills.

Provide AI-specific training: Develop targeted AI-specific training programs to build expertise in AI technologies, their application and ethical considerations. Partner with universities and online platforms to offer AI certification programs. Conduct internal AI workshops and trainings led by industry experts. Develop internal expertise on AI. Ensure training covers AI ethics, regulatory compliance and the practical application of AI.

Promoting continuous learning: Creating a culture of continuous learning to keep employees at the cutting edge of AI and digital technologies. Provide incentives for employees to continue their education and professional development in AI and related areas. Establish an internal knowledge sharing platform where employees have access to the latest research, articles and training materials. Encourage participation in conferences, seminars and networking events related to AI and digital innovation.

Invest in talent development: Focus on developing talent within the organization by identifying employees with high potential and giving them the opportunity to expand their AI expertise. Implement a mentoring and coaching program to promote professional development in the field of AI. Create a talent development pipeline for roles that are critical to AI initiatives. Provide a rotation program and project-based learning experiences to expose employees to different aspects of AI.

Implementation of change management strategies: development and implementation of effective change management strategies to facilitate the introduction of AI technologies and processes. Involving employees in the change process through feedback sessions and participation in pilot projects. Providing support and resources to overcome resistance and ensure a smooth transition to AI-supported workflows.

Establish communities of practice (CoP): Create communities of practice within the organization to foster collaboration, knowledge sharing and innovation in the field of AI. Establish internal AI interest groups or forums where employees can discuss AI trends, challenges and best practices. Encourage cross-departmental collaboration on AI projects to leverage different perspectives and expertise. Organize regular meetings, hackathons and innovation challenges to encourage active engagement and continuous improvement of AI skills.

3.3 Risk-based Approach

Gabriele Bolek-Fügl

The AI Act divides AI systems into different categories, depending on the level of risk they pose to the health, safety or fundamental rights of natural persons.

The classification of an AI system into the risk categories as defined by the AI Act appears to be the most important step for a potential providerwho wants to place their system on the market or put it into operation in the EU.

3.3.1 Prohibited AI Systems

Chapter II AI Act is dedicated to "Prohibited Practices in the field of artificial intelligence". According to the AI Act, specific uses of AI are prohibited in order to protect the health, safety and fundamental rights of individuals. These prohibited applications of AI include

a) **Practices of manipulation:**

Placing on the marketplacing on the market, putting into service or using an AI system to induce persons to engage in behavior that may cause them or others significant harm by means of subliminal techniques or by exploiting their vulnerabilities is prohibited. This includes AI applications that aim to influence human behavior in a way that undermines people's ability to make independent decisions (Art. 5 para. 1 lit a AI Act).

b) **Exploitation of weaknesses:**

The placing on the market, putting into service or use of an AI system that is specifically designed to exploit the vulnerabilities of a particular group of persons based on their age, physical or mental condition in order to induce them to engage in behavior that is likely to cause, or is reasonably likely to cause, harm to them or others is also prohibited (Art. 5 para. 1 lit b AI Act).

c) **Social rating systems:**

The placing on the market, putting into service or use of AI for the purpose of assessing or classifying the trustworthiness of persons on the basis of their social behavior or known, inferred or predicted personal characteristics over a period of time, with the result that certain persons or groups are disadvantaged or excluded, is prohibited. This applies in particular if such assessments lead to unfair or unfavorable treatment in various areas of life (Art. 5 para. 1 lit c AI Act).

It is prohibited to discriminate against or disadvantage certain natural persons or entire groups of persons

I. in social contexts unrelated to the circumstances in which the data was originally generated or collected (Art. 5 para. 1 lit c sublit. i AI Act),

II. in a way that is unjustified or disproportionate with regard to their social conduct or its scope (Art. 5 para. 1 lit c sublit i AI Act).

d) **Restrictions for risk-based assessments by AI:**

It is not permitted to market, commission or use AI systems that aim to determine the likelihood of a person committing a crime based solely on profiling or the assessment of their personal characteristics. This prohibition does not apply to AI systems that support human assessments, provided that these are based on objective and verifiable facts directly related to a criminal offense (Art. 5 para. 1 lit d AI Act).

e) **Ban on the creation of facial recognition databases:**

It is prohibited to bring AI systems onto the market, put them into operation or use them that create facial recognition databases through the unspecific reading of facial images from the internet or surveillance videos, to create or expand facial recognition databases (Art. 5 para. 1 lit e AI Act).

f) **Limitations in emotion recognition:**

the placing on the market, putting into service or use of AI systems for detecting or inferring the emotions of persons in the workplace or in educational institutions is prohibited, unless these systems are introduced or placed on the market for medical or safety reasons (Art. 5 para. 1 lit f AI Act).

g) **Prohibition of biometric categorization:**

The placing on the market, commissioning or use of AI systems that identify persons on the basis of biometric data to draw conclusions about race, political views, trade union membership, religious or philosophical beliefs, sex life or sexual orientation is prohibited. Exceptions exist for the legally permissible labeling or filtering of biometric data sets, such as the sorting of images according to biometric characteristics, or for use in law enforcement under specific conditions (Art. 5 para. 1 g AI Act).

h) **Real-time remote biometrics in public spaces:**

The placing on the market, commissioning or use of AI systems for real-time re-mote biometrics-identification of natural persons in publicly accessible areas for law enforcement purposes is only permitted under strictly defined conditions and is generally prohibited. Exceptions only apply in precisely defined and narrowly limited situations involving a significant threat to security or serious crimes (Art. 5 para. 1 lit h AI Act), such as

I. Targeted search for specific victims of abduction, human trafficking or sexual exploitation and search for missing persons (Art. 5 para. 1 lit h sublit i AI Act)

II. Averting a specific, substantial and imminent danger to the life or physical integrity of natural persons or an actual and present or actual and foresee-able danger of a terrorist attack (Art. 5 para. 1 lit h sublit ii AI Act)

III. Tracing or identifying a person suspected of having committed a criminal offense for the purpose of conducting a criminal investigation, prosecution or execution of a sentence for the offenses listed in Annex II, which is punish-able under the law of the Member State concerned by a custodial sentence or a detention order for a maximum period of at least four years (Art. 5 para. 1 lit h sublit iii AI Act)

> The use of real-time biometric remote identification systems in publicly accessi-ble areas for law enforcement purposes is generally prohibited in accordance with Art. 5 para. 1 sublit h AI Act, except in specific and urgent situations.

AI has the ability to recognize people based on their appearance and movement. In the case of a child abduction or a missing person from a nursing home, the police could use biometric recognition systems to quickly find these people in public spaces such as train stations or shopping centers. Or if there is a specific threat to public safety, such as the imminent threat of a terrorist attack, such systems could be used to identify a suspect before they can cause harm.

However, strict criteria must be observed when using this technology in accordance with Art. 5 para. 2) AI Act:

a) Assessment of the situation: The use of the technology must be necessary to pre-vent significant damage.

Example: The use of biometric identification could be considered if a known dan-gerous fugitive is suspected at a major event and there is a high risk to public safety.

b) Assessment of the impact: The impact on rights and freedoms of people must be carefully weighed up. It is important to protect the privacy and data of bystanders and to ensure that the technology is not used too extensively or invasively.

Additional protective measures must also be observed:

- The deployment must be strictly limited in terms of time, geography and the persons concerned.

- A prior assessment of the impact on fundamental rights (fundamental rights impact assessment) in accordance with Art. 27 AI Act is required (see section 3.4).

- The technology must be registered in the EU database in accordance with Art. 49 AI Act in order to ensure transparency and monitoring. In urgent cases, this registration can be carried out retrospectively.

These rules are intended to ensure that the use of such invasive technologies only takes place in truly necessary and justified cases in order to ensure both public safety and to protect the privacy and freedoms of citizens. Therefore, Art. 5 para. 3 AI Act requires prior authorization for the use of real-time biometric remote identification:

- Every time a police department plans to use real-time remote biometric identification technology in publicly accessible areas, it must first obtain authorization. This authorization must be granted by a judicial authority or an independent administrative authority in the respective country, based on a thorough review of the application. The authority then makes a binding decision on whether or not to approve the use of the technology.

- In very urgent situations where there is no time to obtain authorization before deployment, the police may use the technology provisionally. However, they must apply for authorization within 24 hours of the start of the operation. If this approval is refused, use must be stopped immediately and all data and results collected must be deleted.

- Authorization will only be granted if there is convincing evidence or clear indications that the use of the technology is necessary for one of the permitted objectives. The authority must also ensure that the use is strictly limited in terms of time, geography and persons affected and does not go beyond what is absolutely necessary.

- It must be taken into account that no decisions that could have negative legal consequences for a person are made solely on the basis of the results of biometric identification. This means that the results of this technology must only be considered as part of the evidence.

The authorization and use of real-time remote biometric identification in public areas for law enforcement is therefore strictly regulated to ensure the protection of privacy and civil rights. Authorities may only use this technology in clearly defined and urgent cases, and even then, strict guidelines must be adhered to.

Regardless of certain exceptions, any use of a real-time remote biometric recognition system in public areas for police purposes must be notified to the competent authorities for market surveillance and national data protection in accordance with the specific national rules. This notification must contain certain required information, but must not include any confidential details of use (Art. 5 para. 4 AI Act).

According to Art. 5 para. 5 AI Act, each EU Member State has the option of allowing the use of real-time biometric remote identification systems within the limits and under the conditions laid down by law. This means that the use of such systems is not automatically permitted in every EU country, but depends on the specific regulations of each country. To this end, the Member States must take the following actions:

1. **Legislation:** Countries must lay down detailed regulations for the entire process in their national legislation, from the application to the approval and use of such systems. This also includes regulations on monitoring and reporting on the use of these technologies.

2. **Authorization purposes:** National laws must clarify for which specific purposes and under which circumstances law enforcement authorities may be authorized to use this technology. These include, for example, the search for missing persons, the prevention of threats to public safety or the prosecution of certain serious crimes.

3. **Notification to the EU Commission:** Member States are obliged to inform the EU Commission of their national regulations no later than 30 days after these regulations have entered into force.

4. **Stricter national regulations:** In addition, countries can also adopt stricter rules than those provided for at EU level, as long as they are in line with Union law. This allows Member States to provide additional safeguards for the privacy and fundamental rights of citizens at national level.

Example

Suppose a country decides that real-time remote biometric identification systems may only be used to search for missing children and prevent terrorist attacks. The national laws would then describe in detail how an authority applies for authorization for such use, which criteria must be met and how the use is monitored and documented. They would also have to notify the EU Commission of these regulations and could decide not to allow the use of this technology to monitor demonstrations under any circumstances, even if this would be permitted at EU level under certain circumstances.

Art. 5 para. 6 AI Act refers to the monitoring and reporting of the use of real-time biometric remote identification systems in publicly accessible spaces for law enforcement purposes by the Member States of the European Union.

- The national market surveillance authorities and the national data protection authorities of the EU Member States are obliged to submit annual reports to the European Commission.

- These reports relate to the use of real-time remote biometric identification systems in public areas for law enforcement purposes.

- The reports contain information on the number of cases in which a judicial authority or an independent administrative authority has decided on applications for authorization to use this technology.

- The reports also record the outcome of these decisions, i. e. whether the applications were approved or rejected.

- To ensure that the reports are uniform and contain all the necessary information, the European Commission provides the Member States and the market surveillance and data protection authorities with a standardized reporting template.

- This annual reporting provides an overview of how often and under what circumstances real-time biometric remote identification systems are used for law enforcement purposes in the EU.

- It serves the purpose of transparency and monitoring to ensure that the use of such technologies complies with legal requirements and the fundamental rights of citizens.

The EU Commission is responsible for publishing annual reports on the use of real-time biometric remote identification systems in publicly accessible areas for law enforcement purposes in accordance with Art. 5 para. 7 AI Act. These reports are based on the summarized (aggregated) data from the annual reports of the individual EU Member States. These national reports contain information on the authorization and use of such systems.

It is important to note that these published annual reports must not contain any sensitive operational information. This means that details that could jeopardize security measures or ongoing investigations are not disclosed.

The purpose of these reports is to create transparency and provide the public, policy makers and other stakeholders with an overview of the use of these technologies in the EU. The aim is to create an understanding of how often and under what conditions biometric identification is used in practice without compromising the work of law enforcement authorities.

Example

Suppose a real-time remote biometric identification system is used in a way that meets the specific requirements of this article but violates the General Data Protection Regulation (GDPR) because it does not follow the principles of data minimization or purpose limitation. In this case, the use of the system, despite compliance with the requirements for use for law enforcement purposes, would violate the GDPR and would therefore be inadmissible.

The purpose of this provision is to clarify that compliance with the specific require-ments of this Article does not exempt from the obligation to comply with all other relevant EU legislation. It underlines the need to take into account a wide range of legal bases and principles when deploying AI systems, especially those with a signifi-cant potential impact on fundamental rights.

3.3.2 High-risk AI Systems

Julia Fuith

The Regulation on Artificial Intelligence (hereinafter: AI Act) divides AI systems into into different categories, depending on the level of risk they pose to the health, safety or fundamental rights of natural persons.

The classification of an AI system into the risk categories as defined by the AI Act ap-pears to be the most important step for a potential providerwho wants to place their system on the market or put it into operation in the EU. Classification as a high-risk AI system means that it must meet certain requirements and that the provider is subject to certain obligations.

3.3.2.1 Classification of AI as a High-risk AI System

So how can a provider of an AI system determine whether it should be classified as high-risk or not? The EU Commission's original proposal [1], apart from distinguish-ing between those AI systems that contain safety components of a product covered by the Union harmonization legislation listed in Annex I AI Act or are themselves such a product, and those stand-alone AI systems that fall under Annex III AI Act, there are no further indications for the classification.

However, this changed in the course of the negotiations to the extent that it was rec-ognized that the originally envisaged provision on the classification of stand-alone AI systems covered by Annex III AI Act does not provide enough guidance for providers, as it appears to be formulated too generally. It was therefore decided to include de-tailed criteria in Art. 6 AI Act [2], which define the cases in which an AI system is not to be classified as high-risk in accordance with Art. 6 para. 2 (see Recital 52 AI Act).

Art. 6 para. 3 AI Act provides that "by way of derogation from paragraph 2, an AI sys-tem listed in Annex III shall not be considered high-risk if it does not present a sig-nificant risk of harm to the health, safety or fundamental rights of natural persons, including by not significantly influencing the outcome of decision-making.

The first subparagraph shall apply if one of the following conditions is met:

a) the AI system is intended to perform a narrowly defined procedural task;

b) the AI system is designed to improve the result of a previously completed human activity;

c) the AI system is intended to recognize decision-making patterns or deviations from previous decision-making patterns and is not intended to replace or influence the previously completed human assessment without appropriate human review; or

d) the AI-system is intended to perform a preparatory task for an assessment relevant for the purposes of the use cases listed in Annex III.

Recital 53 AI Act explains in more detail what is meant by the phrase "not having a significant impact on the outcome of the decision-making process", namely that it "does not have a significant impact on the content and therefore the outcome of the decision-making process, regardless of whether the decisions are human or automated". Furthermore, this recital also outlines examples of the above criteria and explains them in more detail in order to provide providers with further guidance for the classification of their AI system.

According to Recital 53, the AI systems referred to in Art. 6 para. 3 lit a AI Act for performing a narrowly defined procedural task would include, for example, an AI system "that converts unstructured data into structured data, an AI system that classifies incoming documents into categories or an AI system that is used to detect duplicates among a large number of applications".

According to Recital 53, the AI systems referred to in Art. 6 para. 3 lit b AI Act for the improvement of a previously completed human activity would include, for example, an AI system that "is intended to improve the language used in previously written documents, such as the professional tone, the scientific style of language or to adapt the text to a particular style associated with a trademark".

According to Recital 53, the AI systems referred to in Art. 6 para. 3 lit. c AI Act for detecting decision-making patterns or deviations from previous decision-making patterns would include, for example, AI systems "which can be used in relation to a particular marking pattern of a teacher to check retrospectively whether the teacher may have deviated from the marking pattern in order to draw attention to possible inconsistencies or irregularities".

According to Recital 53, the AI systems referred to in Art. 6 para. 3 lit d AI Act for performing preparatory tasks for the purposes of the use cases listed in Annex III would include, for example, "intelligent solutions for processing dossiers, including various functions such as indexing, searching, text and language processing or linking data with other data sources, or AI systems for translating documents".

Since profiling of natural persons is considered a significant interference with their fundamental rights, Art. 6 para. 3 AI Act stipulates that such AI systems must always be classified as high-risk, even if they would meet the criteria listed above.

If providers determine that their AI-system meets one or more of the criteria set out in Art. 6 para. 3, they are obliged under Art. 6 para. 4 AI Act to document this assessment before placing it on the market or putting it into service and to register the AI-system in the EU database for high-risk AI-systems within the meaning of Art. 49 para. 2 AI Act. This documentation must also be submitted at the request of the competent national authority.

The EU Commission has drafted the AI Act as a legal act for which it should be possible to adapt certain provisions to new technological developments as quickly as possible. In most cases, delegated acts are provided for this purpose, which can be processed more quickly in procedural terms than in the ordinary legislative procedure. In the case of the above-mentioned criteria of Art. 6 para. 3, it is therefore possible for the EU Commission to adopt delegated acts in accordance with Art. 6 para. 6 AI Act. which extend, amend or delete the list of these criteria – however, this is subject to strict conditions, which are explained in more detail in this paragraph.

As additional support for providers, Art. 6 para. 5 AI Act stipulates that the EU Commission – after consulting the European Artificial Intelligence Board – must provide guidelines on the practical implementation of this article and a comprehensive list of practical examples of use cases for high-risk and non-high-risk AI systems no later than 18 months after the Regulation enters into force.

Furthermore, the recitals, which explain the individual provisions of the AI Act in more detail, can also provide additional assistance for the interpretation of Art. 6 AI Act in this case in order to "better" classify AI systems as high-risk systems that could fall under Art. 6 para. 1 or 2. Recitals 46-63 explain in more detail what the EU legislator had in mind when formulating the provisions on high-risk AI systems (Art. 6 in conjunction with Annex I and Annex III).

As mentioned above, Art. 6 AI Act distinguishes between two different types of high-risk AI systems:

Art. 6 para. 1 AI Act concerns those AI systems that are considered safety components for a product that is already subject to regulation under one of the EU legal acts listed in Annex I, or which are themselves such a product and are subject to a conformity assessment procedure in accordance with the relevant EU legal acts listed in Annex I by a conformity assessment body acting as a third party (so-called "notified body").

The harmonization provisions listed in Annex I Section A AI Act, which are based on the New Legislative Framework concern products such as machinery, toys, elevators, equipment and protective systems intended for use in potentially explosive atmospheres, radio equipment, pressure equipment, recreational craft equipment, cableways, equipment for the combustion of gaseous fuels, medical devices and in vitro diagnostic medical devices.

The EU legislator's intention with this provision, namely Art. 6 para. 1 AI Act, was to focus on AI applications that have a real impact on safety (and in particular on the safety of products). The intention was to take into account already established and comprehensive legislation that regulates many risky products (examples given in the previous paragraph) and to ensure that the AI Act is fully integrated into the relevant sectoral legislation. This is done by ensuring that relevant definitions (e. g. "safety component") are harmonized, but also the fact that the conformity assessment of the product in the sectoral legislation as a criterion for a high level of risk and by using the enforcement instrument of the sectoral legislation.

What does this mean in concrete terms for providers whose AI system is such a safety component of a product or is the product itself that falls under one of the legal acts listed in Annex I Section A AI Act and for which a conformity assessment procedure must be carried out by a conformity assessment body acting as a third party in accordance with one of the listed EU legal acts? Such an AI system is classified as high-risk within the meaning of Art. 6 para. 1 AI Act. Therefore, in this case too, providers must comply with the obligations listed in Art. 16 et seq. AI Act (see section 3.3.2.3 Requirements for High-risk AI Systems). If the AI system in question also interacts with humans or generates synthetic audio, image, video or text content, the provider must also comply with transparency obligations pursuant to Art. 50 AI Act.

If the safety component of an AI system or the AI system as a product itself is related to those EU legal acts listed in Annex I Section B AI Act, only Art. 112 of the AI Act (review of the AI Act, amendment of the Annexes, reports on the AI Act) applies in accordance with Art. 2 para. 2 AI Act. The non-application of the rest of the AI Regulation in this case is due to the fact that the regulatory logic for AI and these legal acts differ considerably. Examples of areas covered by Annex I Section B AI Act include civil aviation, agricultural and forestry vehicles, motor vehicles and their trailers, marine equipment, etc.

Art. 6 para. 2 AI Act stipulates that all AI systems that fall into one of the areas listed in Annex III AI Act are to be classified as high-risk. In addition to the high risk of harm to the health and safety or fundamental rights of persons, Recital 52 AI Act requires the provider to "take into account both the seriousness of the potential harm and the likelihood of its occurrence." According to Recital 52, the methodology and criteria for determining such systems is the same as that provided for future amendments to the list of high-risk AI systems in Annex III pursuant to Art. 7 AI Act in order to take into account the rapid pace of technological development and possible changes in the use of AI systems. Art. 7 AI Act lays down strict criteria for the adoption of delegated acts by the EU Commission regarding the addition, modification or deletion of use cases in Annex III AI Act.

As explained in the previous paragraph, an AI-system is to be classified as high-risk if, among other things, it poses a significant risk to the fundamental rights of individuals. Recital 48 AI Act emphasizes that the extent of the adverse effects on the fundamental rights protected by the European Charter of Fundamental Rights [4] is particularly important for the classification of an AI system as high-risk. These are then listed in the relevant recital, including human dignity, respect for private and family life, protection of personal data and many more (see section 3.4).

The areas and use cases covered by Annex III AI Act are outlined below. Furthermore, some examples of such use cases are given to illustrate to providers which AI systems could actually fall into one of the areas listed in Annex III in practice in the future. At this point – as already mentioned – reference is once again made to Art. 6 para. 5 AI Act, which provides for an obligation on the part of the EU Commission to provide guidelines for practical implementation in this context, including a list of practical examples of high-risk and non-high-risk use cases, no later than 18 months after the AI Act enters into force.

3.3.2.2 Annex III

1. Biometrics, insofar as their use is permitted under relevant EU law or national law:

a) biometric remote identification systems.
    This shall not include AI systems intended to be used for biometric verification the sole purpose of which is to confirm that a specific natural person is the person he or she claims to be;
b) AI systems intended to be used for biometric categorisation, according to sensitive or protected attributes or characteristics based on the inference of those attributes or characteristics;
c) AI systems intended to be used for emotion recognition.

What is a remote biometric identification system? Art. 3 para. 41 AI Act defines this as an AI system "which serves the purpose of identifying natural persons without their active involvement and, as a rule, remotely by matching the biometric data of a person with the biometric data stored in a reference database".

Recital 54 AI Act explains in more detail why the classification of remote biometric identification systems as high-risk seems so important: "Technical inaccuracies of AI systems intended for the remote biometric identification of natural persons may lead to biased results and have a discriminatory effect. The risk of such biased results and discriminatory effects is of particular importance when it comes to age, ethnicity, race, gender or disability."

The EU Commission's original proposal [1] did not provide for the use cases listed in Annex III/1b) and c), AI systems for biometric categorization and those for emotion recognition were only subject to transparency obligations. In the final text of the Regulation [2], these use cases are included to the effect that AI systems used for biometric categorization according to sensitive attributes or characteristics protected on the basis of biometric data pursuant to Art. 9 para. 1 GDPR [3] and AI systems for emotion recognition are classified as high-risk. At this point, reference is made to section 3.3.1 on prohibited practices, as other applications of biometric categorization and emotion recognition within the meaning of Art. 5 AI Act [2] are prohibited.

2. Critical infrastructure

AI systems intended to be used as safety components in the management and operation of critical digital infrastructure, road traffic or the supply of water, gas, heating or electricity.

Why are these systems classified as high-risk? Recital 55 AI Act states that "security components of critical infrastructure, including critical digital infrastructure, are used to protect the physical integrity of critical infrastructure or the health and safety of persons and property, but are not necessary for the system to function. Failures or malfunctions of such components can lead directly to risks to the physical integrity of critical infrastructure and thus to risks to the health and safety of persons and property." As examples of such systems, the present recital mentions systems for monitoring water pressure or fire alarm control systems in cloud computing centers.

3. Education and vocational training

a) AI systems intended to be used to determine access or admission or to assign natural persons to educational and vocational training institutions at all levels;

b) AI systems intended to be used to evaluate learning outcomes, including when those outcomes are used to steer the learning process of natural persons in educational and vocational training institutions at all levels;

c) AI systems intended to be used for the purpose of assessing the appropriate level of education that an individual will receive or will be able to access, in the context of or within educational and vocational training institutions at all levels;

d) AI systems intended to be used for monitoring and detecting prohibited behaviour of students during tests in the context of or within educational and vocational training institutions at all levels.

Recital 56 AI Act explains in more detail why the use cases listed in the education sector are classified as high-risk, even if the use of AI to promote education and the acquisition of digital skills is in principle to be welcomed. The use cases listed in Annex III/3a-d AI Act would "determine the course of a person's education and professional life and may therefore affect their ability to earn a living. If improperly designed and used, such systems can be very intrusive and violate the right to education and the right to non-discrimination and perpetuate historical patterns of discrimination, for example against women, certain age groups and persons with disabilities or persons with a particular racial or ethnic origin or sexual orientation".

4. Employment, worker's management and access to self-employment

a)   AI systems intended to be used for the recruitment or selection of natural persons, in particular to place targeted job advertisements, to analyse and filter job applications, and to evaluate candidates;

b)   AI systems intended to be used to make decisions affecting terms of work-related relationships, the promotion or termination of work-related contractual relationships, to allocate tasks based on individual behaviour or personal traits or characteristics or to monitor and evaluate the performance and behaviour of persons in such relationships.

Recital 57 AI Act explains the classification of the use cases listed in Annex III/4a and b AI Act as high-risk by stating that "these systems may have a significant impact on the future career prospects and livelihoods of these individuals and on workers' rights". These use cases also pose the risk of perpetuating historical patterns of discrimination, similar to the use cases listed in Annex III/3 AI Act. AI systems that are used to monitor the performance and behavior of these individuals could also affect their fundamental rights to data protection and privacy.

5. Access to and enjoyment of essential private and public services and benefits:

a)   AI systems intended to be used by public authorities or on behalf of public authorities to evaluate the eligibility of natural persons for essential public assistance benefits and services, including healthcare services, as well as to grant, reduce, revoke, or reclaim such benefits and services;

b)   AI systems intended to be used to evaluate the creditworthiness of natural persons or establish their credit score, with the exception of AI systems used for the purpose of detecting financial fraud;

c)   AI systems intended to be used for risk assessment and pricing in relation to natural persons in the case of life and health insurance;

d)   AI systems intended to evaluate and classify emergency calls by natural persons or to be used to dispatch, or to establish priority in the dispatching of, emergency first response services, including by police, firefighters and medical aid, as well as of emergency healthcare patient triage systems.

Recital 58 AI Act explains in detail why the classification of AI systems as high-risk in this area is particularly important and why certain listed use cases can particularly interfere with some fundamental rights of individuals.

AI systems under Annex III/5a AI Act, which assess the eligibility of natural persons for basic state support benefits such as health benefits, social security benefits or social services in cases such as maternity, sickness, accidents at work, dependency or old age and job loss, as well as social and housing support, "may have a significant impact on the livelihood of individuals and violate their fundamental rights, such as the right to social protection, non-discrimination, human dignity or an effective remedy" (Recital 58 AI Act).

AI systems in accordance with Annex III/5b are to be classified as high-risk "as they determine the access of these persons to financial resources or essential services such as housing, electricity and telecommunications services" (Recital 58 AI Act). Furthermore, there is also a risk of discrimination and the perpetuation of historical patterns of discrimination, such as on the basis of racial or ethnic origin, gender, disability, age or sexual orientation, or the risk of new forms of discrimination.

However, AI systems "used under Union law for the detection of fraud in the provision of financial services or for prudential purposes for the calculation of capital requirements of credit institutions and insurance undertakings" are to be exempted here (Recital 58 AI Act).

The use case according to Annex III/5c AI Act was not included in the original proposal [1]. However, it was included in Annex III during the negotiations, as the decision to use such an AI system "can also have a significant impact on people's livelihoods and, if not properly designed, developed and used, can have serious consequences for people's lives and health, including financial exclusion and discrimination" (Recital 58 AI Act).

AI systems in accordance with Annex III/5d AI Act are classified as high-risk "as they make decisions in situations that are highly critical for the life and health of persons and for their property" (Recital 58 AI Act).

6. Law enforcement, insofar as their use is permitted and relevant Union or national law:

    a)   AI systems intended to be used by or on behalf of law enforcement authorities, or by Union institutions, bodies, offices or agencies in support of law enforcement authorities or on their behalf to assess the risk of a natural person becoming the victim of criminal offences;

    b)   AI systems intended to be used by or on behalf of law enforcement authorities or by Union institutions, bodies, offices or agencies in support of law enforcement authorities as polygraphs or similar tools;

    c)   AI systems intended to be used by or on behalf of law enforcement authorities, or by Union institutions, bodies, offices or agencies, in support of law enforcement authorities to evaluate the reliability of evidence in the course of the investigation or prosecution of criminal offences;

    d)   AI systems intended to be used by law enforcement authorities or on their behalf or by Union institutions, bodies, offices or agencies in support of law enforcement authorities for assessing the risk of a natural person offending or re-offending not solely on the basis of the profiling of natural persons as referred to in Article 3(4) of Directive (EU) 2016/680, or to assess personality traits and characteristics or past criminal behaviour of natural persons or groups;

    e)   AI systems intended to be used by or on behalf of law enforcement authorities or by Union institutions, bodies, offices or agencies in support of law enforcement authorities for the profiling of natural persons as referred to in Article 3(4) of Directive (EU) 2016/680 in the course of the detection, investigation or prosecution of criminal offences.

Recital 59 AI Act explains in more detail why certain use cases should be classified as high-risk, particularly in the area of criminal prosecution.

AI systems used by law enforcement authorities are characterized by a significant imbalance of power and could have a massive negative impact on the fundamental rights enshrined in the Charter [4] for the individuals concerned. In this area, it seems particularly critical if AI systems do not meet the requirements of the AI Act regarding the quality of data for the training of AI systems, do not meet the requirements for its performance, accuracy or robustness, or if it is not properly designed and tested, as this could lead to discrimination against data subjects. A lack of transparency, explainability and documentation could hinder the exercise of important fundamental procedural rights, such as the right to an effective remedy and an impartial tribunal, as well as the right of defense and the presumption of innocence.

For these reasons, the use cases listed in Annex III/6a-e AI Act are classified as high-risk.

> **7. Migration, asylum and border control, in so far as their use is permitted under relevant Union or national law:**
> a) AI systems intended to be used by or on behalf of competent public authorities or by Union institutions, bodies, offices or agencies as polygraphs or similar tools;
> b) AI systems intended to be used by or on behalf of competent public authorities or by Union institutions, bodies, offices or agencies to assess a risk, including a security risk, a risk of irregular migration, or a health risk, posed by a natural person who intends to enter or who has entered into the territory of a Member State;
> c) AI systems intended to be used by or on behalf of competent public authorities or by Union institutions, bodies, offices or agencies to assist competent public authorities for the examination of applications for asylum, visa or residence permits and for associated complaints with regard to the eligibility of the natural persons applying for a status, including related assessments of the reliability of evidence;
> d) AI systems intended to be used by or on behalf of competent public authorities, or by Union institutions, bodies, offices or agencies, in the context of migration, asylum or border control management, for the purpose of detecting, recognising or identifying natural persons, with the exception of the verification of travel documents.

Recital 60 AI Act justifies the classification of the use cases listed in Annex III/7a-d AI Act as high-risk in that the AI systems used in this area would affect people in precarious situations who are dependent on the outcome of the measures taken by the competent authorities. Therefore, the accuracy, non-discriminatory nature and transparency of these AI systems are important for safeguarding the fundamental rights of the persons concerned (in particular the rights to freedom of movement, non-discrimination, protection of private life and personal data, international protection and good administration).

AI systems in the area of migration, asylum and border control that fall under one of the use cases listed in Annex III/7a-d AI Act should comply with relevant Union procedural rules and should not be used to circumvent international obligations, such as those arising from the Geneva Convention on Refugees. Furthermore, the principle of non-refoulement and the right to international protection must be observed (Recital 60 AI Act).

8. Administration of justice and democratic processes

a)   AI systems intended to be used by a judicial authority or on their behalf to assist a judicial authority in researching and interpreting facts and the law and in applying the law to a concrete set of facts, or to be used in a similar way in alternative dispute resolution;

b)   AI systems intended to be used for influencing the outcome of an election or referendum or the voting behaviour of natural persons in the exercise of their vote in elections or referenda. This does not include AI systems to the output of which natural persons are not directly exposed, such as tools used to organise, optimise or structure political campaigns from an administrative or logistical point of view.

AI systems in this area are classified as high-risk according to Recital 61 AI Act, as these systems can have a significant impact on democracy, the rule of law, individual freedoms and the right to an effective remedy and an impartial court. In connection with the use case in Annex III/8a AI Act, it is emphasized in Recital 61 AI Act that such an AI system in the judicial area can only ever support the decision-making power of judges or the independence of the judiciary, but never replace it. The final decision-making process must remain a human-controlled activity. AI systems for purely ancillary administrative activities, such as the anonymization or pseudonymization of court judgments, documents or data that do not affect the actual administration of justice in individual cases, should not be classified as high-risk.

The use case listed in Annex III/8b AI Act was not included in the original proposal [1]. However, it was included in Annex III in order to counter the "risks of undue external interference with the right to vote enshrined in Article 39 of the Charter [4] and adverse effects on democracy and the rule of law" (Recital 62 AI Act).

Sources

[1] European Commission, Propsal for a Regulation laying down harmonized rules on Artificial Intelligence (Artificial Intelligence Act) and amending certain union legislative Acts (COM/2021/206 final), 21.04.2021.

[2] Regulation (EU) 2024/1689 of 13 June 2024 laying down harmonised rules on artificial intelligence and amending Regulations (EC) No 300/2008, (EU) No 167/2013, (EU) No 168/2013, (EU) 2018/858, (EU) 2018/1139 und (EU) 2019/2144 and Directives 2014/90/EU, (EU) 2016/797 and (EU) 2020/1828 (Artificial Intelligence Act), OJ L, 2024/1689, 12.07.2024.

[3] Regulation (EU) 2016/679 of 27 April 2016 on the protection of natural persons with regard to the processing of personal data and on the free movement of such data, and reaplealing Directive 95/46/EC (General Data Protection Regulation), OJ L 119, 04.05.2016, p. 1.

[4] Charter of Funamental Rights of the European Union, OJ C 326, 26.10.2012, p. 391.

3.3.2.3 Requirements for High-risk AI Systems

Natascha Windholz

The classification of high-risk AI systems was described in the previous section 3.3.2.1, but once the classification has been determined, the high-risk AI system must meet certain requirements. These are set out in Art. 8 et seq. AI Act.

Art. 8 AI Act itself only refers in para. 1 to the fact that the state of the art must be taken into account and that a risk management system as described inArt. 9 AI Act must be in place. Para. 2 explicitly states that, in accordance with Annex 1 Section A AI Act, the provider must ensure that the product must first meet the requirements of this specific standard and that the requirements of the AI Act regarding high-risk AI are added "on top". For example, a medical device whose safety component is a high-risk AI system would first have to fulfill the requirements of the Medical Devices Regulation and subsequently the requirements of Art. 8 et seq. AI Act. To avoid duplication of work, providers may integrate compliance with the requirements of the AI Act into their product documentation in accordance with the applicable Annex I legal framework. To continue the example given, the provider would therefore not have to keep two sets of documentation, one in accordance with the Medical Devices Regulation and one in accordance with the AI Act, but may integrate the documentation of the AI Act into that of the Medical Devices Regulation.

3.3.2.3.1 Risk Management System

Every high-risk AI system must have a risk management system in accordance with-Art. 9 AI Act, which is planned, implemented, maintained and regularly reviewed over the entire life cycle of the AI system.

Only those risks that can be appropriately mitigated or eliminated by the development or design of the high-risk AI system or by providing sufficient technical information need to be considered. Completely unforeseeable risks (also referred to as "black swans" in risk management) do not need to be considered.

> The AI Act expects the deployer to have the necessary technical expertise to eliminate or reduce the risks associated with the use of high-risk AI.

Checklist: Steps in risk management

1. Identification and analysis of known and foreseeable risks
   - *Assessment question: What risks does the high-risk AI system pose to health, safety or fundamental rights if it is used in accordance with its intended purpose?*

2. Assessment and evaluation of risks
   * *Assessment question: What risks can arise if the high-risk AI system is used in accordance with its intended purpose or in the context of reasonably foreseeable misuse?*
3. Assessment of other risks that may arise
   * *Assessment question: How can risks that arise after the* product *has been placed on the market be* mitigated*by evaluating the data from the monitoring system in accordance with* Art. 72 AI Act *?*
4. Taking appropriate and targeted risk management measures
   * *Assessment question: What measures can be taken to address the risks identified in the first question?*
   * *Assessment question: Are impacts and possible interactions duly taken into account?*
   * *Assessment question: Are measures taken to ensure that the residual risk associated with a specific hazard and the overall residual risk can be classified as acceptable?*
       * *Sub-question: Are the risks eliminated or reduced as far as technically possible through appropriate design and development of the AI system?*
       * *Sub-question: Are appropriate mitigation and control measures taken to manage a risk that cannot be ruled out?*
       * *Sub-question: Is the necessary information provided in accordance with Art. 13 or is the deployer trained?*
   * *Assessment question: Has the AI system been tested to determine the most appropriate measures? (see section 3.8.3 on testing outside of AI sandboxes)*
       * *Sub-question: Was the system tested during the entire development process or at least before it was placed on the market/put into operation?*
   * *Assessment question: Has consideration been given to whether the AI system is likely to have an adverse impact on persons under the age of 18 or other vulnerable groups?*
   * *Assessment question: Were other applicable legal provisions considered in the risk management process?*

3.3.2.3.2 Data and Data Governance

Data and data sets are a mandatory prerequisite for the use of AI systems. The types of data have already been described in section 3.1.

For the different types of data, i. e. training, validation and testing data sets, data governance and data management procedures must be established in accordance with Art. 10 AI Act that are suitable for the purpose of the high-risk AI system. The data and datasets must therefore meet quality criteria that are tailored to the purpose of the high-risk AI system. Depending on the intended use, the data sets must have the necessary special geographical, contextual, behavioral or functional characteristics that are typical for the intended use of the high-risk AI system.

Essentially, the AI Act describes two types of data governance, firstly general data governance and then personal data governance, with a particular focus on special categories of personal data in accordance with Art. 9 GDPR, if this involves combating bias.

General data governance:

- Conceptual decisions with a view to the intended purpose of the AI system
- Data collection method and origin of the data (including the original purpose of the data collection if it is personal data)
- Data preparation processes, such as annotation, labeling, cleansing, updating, enrichment and aggregation
- Making assumptions, particularly with regard to the information to be collected and presented with the data
- Assessment of the availability, quantity and suitability of the required data sets
- Examination with regard to possible bias, especially if this has an impact on health, safety or fundamental rights or can lead to discrimination
- Measures to detect, prevent and mitigate these distortions
- Identification of relevant data gaps or deficiencies and how these can be rectified

Providers may exceptionally process special categories of personal data to detect the correction of distortions or bias, whereby they must also take appropriate protective measures.

Data governance for special categories of personal data:

- Necessity of processing for detection and correction, as these cannot be carried out effectively otherwise
- Existence of technical restrictions that prevent further use, e. g. pseudonymization
- The existence of appropriate security measures, such as strict access controls and documentation, to prevent misuse and to ensure that only authorized persons have access to this type of data
- No transmission to or access by third parties
- Deletion of the data as soon as the distortion has been corrected or the end of the retention period has been reached, whichever comes first
- Maintenance of the procedure directory in accordance with Art. 30 GDPR, including documentation of the reasons why the data processing is necessary for the detection and correction of the bias

A checklist is shown in section 4.1.1.

3.3.2.3.3 Technical Documentation

In accordance with Art. 11 AI Act, the technical documentation of the high-risk AI system must be prepared before it is placed on the market/put into service and kept up to date. It must show compliance with Art. 8 et seq. and be written in a clear and comprehensible form. It must contain at least the information specified in Annex IV AI Act.

SMEs can provide this documentation in a simplified manner. The EU Commission provides a simplified form for this purpose.

In the case of a high-risk AI system in accordance with Annex I Section A AI Act, a single set of documentation must be prepared that contains the requirements of the specific legislation and the AI Act. The joint technical documentation is mandatory, while the maintenance of a joint risk management system in accordance with Art. 9 AI Act is an optional requirement.

3.3.2.3.4 Record-keeping and Logging

A high-risk AI system must be designed in such a way that automatic recording of events is possible throughout the entire life cycle.

Checklist: Specifications for logging functions

- Identification of functions that lead either to a procedure in accordance with Art. 79 AI Act (handling of AI systems that pose a risk) or to a significant change
- Facilitating the monitoring of the AI system after it has been placed on the market (see Art. 72 AI Act)
- Monitoring the operation of the high-risk AI system (see Art. 26 AI Act)

Additional requirements for high-risk AI systems in accordance with Annex III lit a AI Act (**Remote Biometric Identification**)

- Recording the use of the system (date and time, period of use)
- Reference database for data synchronization
- Input data with which the query resulted in a match
- Identity of the natural person involved in the verification of the results (see Art. 14 para. 5 AI Act)

3.3.2.3.5 Transparency and Provision of Information to Deployers

The transparency obligations are discussed in section 3.5.2.

3.3.2.3.6 Human Supervision

High-risk AI systems must be designed and developed in such a way that they can be **effectively** supervised by natural persons **throughout their life cycle**, which may include the use of human-machine interface tools. Human supervision serves to prevent or minimize risks to health, safety or fundamental rights. In particular, attention should be paid to risks that arise even in the case of intended use or foreseeable misuse and that persist despite compliance with Art. 8 et seq. AI Act.

When determining the **supervisory measures**, the risks, the degree of autonomy and the context of use of the high-risk AI system must be taken into account. Art. 14 AI Act provides for the following types of precautions:

- Installation of precautions by the provider, placing on the market or commissioning, if technically feasible

- Determination of the arrangements by the provider so that they can be implemented by the deployer

The AI system must be developed and made available in such a way that human supervision can be carried out **effectively**. Human supervision must be able to do this:

- Understanding the capabilities and limitations of the high-risk AI system and monitoring its operation, including the ability to detect and resolve anomalies, malfunctions and unexpected performance

- Awareness of automation bias (see section 7.1 Discrimination), especially when the system provides information or recommendations on the basis of which natural persons make decisions

- Correct interpretation of the result of the system, taking into account existing interpretation tools and methods

- Decision not to use the system in certain situations or to disregard, override or reverse the result

- Intervention in the system using the stop button

Systems for **remote biometric recognition** in accordance with Annex III no. 1 lit. a AI Act must not be designed in such a way that only the system makes a decision regarding identification, but that a human being is always involved who has the necessary competence, training and authorization to separately check the identification and decide on it.

3.3.2.3.7 Accuracy, Robustness and Cyber Security

The **development and design of** the system in accordance with Art. 15 AI Act is carried out in such a way that an appropriate level of accuracy, robustness and cybersecurity is ensured and can be maintained throughout the entire lifetime of the system.

The accuracy key figures must be specified in the enclosed instructions for use of the system.

With regard to the resilience of the system, the AI Act requires that the system is as resilient as possible to errors, malfunctions or inconsistencies. To this end, the necessary technical and organizational measures must be taken to protect the system. Robustness can be achieved through **technical redundancy**, e. g. through security plans or fault security plans. Systems that "learn" after being placed on the market/commissioned must be developed in such a way that the risk of distorted results that influence future processes ("feedback loops") is kept to a minimum and risk mitigation measures are taken.

The high-risk AI system must be **resistant** to attempts by third parties to change its use, results or performance by exploiting vulnerabilities. The cybersecurity measures taken must be appropriate to the individual case and the risks of the system. Specifically, however, the aim is to prevent

- **Data poisoning:** Manipulation of the training data set

- **Model Poisoning:** Manipulation of pre-trained components used during training

- **Model Evasion/Adversarial Examples:** Use of input data intended to induce the model to make errors

- **Detection and prevention of attacks** on confidential data or model defects

3.3.2.3.8 Obligations of Providers, Deployers and other Parties involved

Table 3.3 Providers

Article	Obligation/Requirement
Art. 6 et seq. AI Act	Fulfill requirements, in particular ■ Consideration of the state of the art ■ Product requirements (see Annex I Section A) ■ Risk management system ■ Data Governance ■ (Technical) documentation ■ Record-keeping and logging
Art. 16 lit. a AI Act	Name/trade name/registered trademark and contact address on high-risk AI system (if not possible, on packaging/documentation)
Art. 17 AI Act	**Quality management system** Written documentation containing at least the following points: ■ Concept for compliance with the AI Act and any other regulations (see Annex I and III AI Act) Conformity assessment procedures, change management ■ Design, design control, design review of the system ■ Development, quality control, quality assurance

Article	Obligation/Requirement

	• Examination, testing and validation procedures
	    • Implementation before, during and after development of the system, documentation of the frequency of execution
	• Applicable technical specifications and standards
	• Data management
	    • Data collection, aquisition, analysis, labeling, storage, filtering, evaluation, aggregation, data retention, etc.
	• Risk management system in accordance with Art. 9 AI Act (see section 3.3.2.3.1)
	• Monitoring system in accordance with Art. 72 AI Act (see section 3.10.7 Monitoring after placing the AI system on the market)
	• Procedure for reporting serious incidents in accordance with Art. 73 AI Act (see section 3.10.8 Sharing information on Serious Incidents)
	• Communication with the relevant authorities
	• Systems and procedures for recording all relevant documentation and information
	• Resource management, security of supply
	• Accountability framework that regulates the responsibilities of management and other staff in relation to quality management (e. g. RACI matrix)
	
	The quality management system may be based on the size of the provider's organization, but it should be noted that the degree of rigor and the level of protection of the system must be taken into account. The quality management system in accordance with the AI Act may be integrated into the quality management system for other sector-specific legislation (see in particular Annex 1 AI Act). It is therefore not necessary to maintain a "double" or second quality management system for compliance with the AI Act; it may be combined or extended.

Art. 18 AI Act	Storage of the **documentation**: • Technical documentation according to Art. 11 AI Act • Documentation of the quality management system in accordance with Art. 17 AI Act • Documentation on approved changes by notified bodies • Decisions and other documents from notified bodies • EU Declaration of Conformity in accordance with Art. 47 AI Act (see section 3.5.2 Conformity Assessment Procedure) They must be stored for at least ten years from the date they are placed on the market/put into service.

Table 3.3 Providers *(continued)*

Article	Obligation/Requirement
Art. 19 AI Act, Art. 12 AI Act	**Records** in accordance with Art. 12 AI Act The minimum storage period is six months, unless other legal provisions applicable to the provider do not provide for a different period.
Art. 43 AI Act	**Conformity assessment procedure** of placing on the market/commissioning
Art. 47 AI Act	Issuing an **EU Declaration of Conformity**
Art. 48 AI Act	Affixing the **CE marking** on system/packaging/documentation
Art. 49 para. 1 AI Act	Fulfillment of **registration obligations**
Art. 20 AI Act, Art. 79 AI Act	Taking **corrective measures** Providing the necessary information If a provider has reason to believe that its system does not (or no longer) comply with the AI Act, it must either restore compliance (e. g. install updates) or be able to withdraw, deactivate or recall the system. They must also inform the distributor or, if applicable, the deployer, authorized representative or importer. If the provider becomes aware that its system poses a risk (see Art. 79 AI Act, see section 3.10.11), it shall carry out an investigation into the causes – if necessary together with the notifying deployer – and inform the competent authorities and, if applicable, the notified body that issued the certificate in accordance with Art. 44 AI Act of the nature of the non-compliance and the measures already taken.

Art. 21 AI Act	**Proof** compliance with the requirements of Art. 6 et seq. AI Act, cooperation with the competent authorities (in the event of inquiries)
	  ▪ Transmission of all information and documentation required to demonstrate compliance with the high-risk AI system:
	    ▫ Easy to understand language
	    ▫ Official language of the Member State concerned
	  ▪ Access to automatically generated logs (on request)

Directives (EU) 2016/2102 and (EU) 2019/882	Ensuring **accessibility requirements** are met

Table 3.4 Authorized Representatives of the Providers of High-risk AI Systems

Article	Mandatory
Art. 22 para. 1, 2, 3 AI Act	Providers with a branch in **a third country/non-EU country** ▪ Written appointment of an authorized representative established in the EU ▪ Commissioning ▫ Enabling the fulfillment of tasks by authorized representatives ▪ Authorization of the authorized representative to serve as a contact person for the competent authority in addition to or instead of the provider ▪ Termination of the contract if the provider has reason to believe that the authorized representative is not fulfilling its duties (notification to the market surveillance authority and/or notified body)
Art. 22 para. 3 AI Act	**Tasks** of the authorized representative ▪ Provision of the assignment ▫ Official language of the Member State ▪ Checking whether the EU Declaration of Conformity and the technical documentation have been drawn up in accordance with Art. 11 ▪ Ensuring the implementation of the conformity assessment procedure
Art. 22 para. 3 AI Act	**Documents** that the authorized representative must have ready ▪ Retention of the provider's contact details (for at least ten years) ▪ Copy of the EU Declaration of Conformity ▪ technical documentation ▪ any certificates issued by the notified body ▪ Transmission of the aforementioned documents to the competent authority (on request) ▪ Access to automated logs in accordance with Art. 12 AI Act (on request) ▪ Cooperation with the competent authority (on request) ▪ Ensuring compliance with the registration obligations pursuant to Art. 49 AI Act ▪ Ensuring the accuracy of the information/listed in Annex VIII Section A AI Act

Table 3.5 Importers

Article	Mandatory
Art. 23 para. 1 AI Act	Ensure that the AI system complies with the AI Regulation by **checking** the following documents: ▪ Carrying out the conformity assessment in accordance with Art. 43 AI Act by the provider ▪ Preparation of technical documentation in accordance with Art. 11 AI Act and Annex IV AI Act by the provider ▪ Presence of the CE marking, the EU Declaration of Conformity and the instructions for use ▪ Appointment of an authorized representative pursuant to Art. 22 para. 1 AI Act
Art. 23 para. 2 AI Act	In the event of **suspected non-compliance** with the AI Regulation, suspected falsified AI system or falsified documentation: ▪ Placing on the market only after conformity has been established ▪ In the case of high-risk AI systems (see Art. 79 AI Act), the importer shall inform ▪ the provider, ▪ the authorized representatives and ▪ the market surveillance authority.
Art. 23 para. 3 AI Act	Disclosure of the following information on the **packaging** or, if applicable, the accompanying documentation ▪ Name ▪ registered trade names ▪ registered trademark ▪ Address where importer can be contacted in connection with the system
Art. 23 para. 4 AI Act	Ensuring the necessary **storage or transportation conditions** (if applicable)
Art. 23 para. 5 AI Act	**Retention of** the following documents for ten years from placing on the market or commissioning: ▪ Copy of the certificate of the notified body ▪ Instructions for use, if applicable ▪ EU conformity assessment

Article	Mandatory
Art. 23 para. 6 and 7 AI Act	**Cooperation** with the competent **authority** (at its request): ▪ Transmission of the documents kept available (Art. 23 para. 5 AI Act) ▪ Information and documentation required to demonstrate compliance of the high-risk AI system in an easily understandable language ▪ Ensuring that the technical documentation can be made available to the authority ▪ Developing and collaborating on measures to reduce or mitigate the risks posed by the system

Table 3.6 Distributors

Article	Mandatory

Art. 24 para. 1 AI Act	**Before provision on the market:**
	▪ Ensure that the system is provided with the necessary CE marking.
	▪ Copy of the EU Declaration of Conformity is attached.
	▪ Instructions for use is enclosed.
	▪ Fulfillment of the provider's obligations:
	  ▫ Disclosure of the following information on the packaging or, if applicable, the enclosed documentation
	    Name
	    Registered trade name
	    registered trademark
	    Contact address
	  ▫ Quality management system (see Art. 17 AI Act)
	▪ Fulfillment of the following obligations of the importer:
	  ▫ Disclosure of the following information on the packaging or, if applicable, the enclosed documentation
	    Name
	    Registered trade name
	    registered trademark
	    Address where importer can be contacted in connection with the system

Table 3.6 Distributors *(continued)*

Article	Mandatory
Art. 24 para. 2 and para. 4 AI Act	In the event of **suspected non-compliance** with the AI Regulation based on the information available to the retailer: ▪ Placing on the market only after conformity has been established ▪ In the case of high-risk AI systems (see Art. 79 AI Act), the importer shall inform ▫ the provider, ▫ the authorized representatives and ▫ the market surveillance authority ▪ Taking the necessary **corrective actions** to achieve compliance ▪ Withdrawal or recall of the system ▪ Ensure that the supplier, importer or anyone else takes the necessary corrective action ▪ In the case of **high-risk AI systems** (see Art. 79 AI Act), the retailer shall inform ▫ the provider, ▫ the importer ▫ competent authority of the Member States in which it has made the system available
Art. 24 para. 3 AI Act	Ensuring the necessary **storage or transportation conditions** (if applicable)
Art. 24 para. 5 and 6 AI Act	**Cooperation** with the competent **authority** (on request): ▪ Transmission of all information and documentation relating to the above obligations ▪ Proof of conformity of the AI system ▪ Developing and collaborating on measures to reduce or mitigate the risks posed by the system

Table 3.7 Responsibilities along the AI Value Chain

Article	Mandatory
Art. 25 para. 1 and para. 2 AI Act	Distributors, importers, deployers or other third parties become providers of a high-risk AI system in the following cases and must therefore fulfill the **provider obligations** of Art. 16 AI Act: ▪ The system placed on the market or put into operation is provided with its own name/trademark (irrespective of any contractual agreements).

Article	Mandatory
	▪ Significant change to the AI system (only if it is still a high-risk AI system pursuant to Art. 6 ff.) ▪ Modification of an originally non-high-risk AI system or AI system for general purposes so that it is classified as a high-risk AI system pursuant to Art. 6 et seq. AI Act The **reclassification** means that the original provider is no longer considered a provider. The initial provider is obliged to cooperate with the new provider and provide it with all the information it needs to establish compliance, unless it can prove that it has clearly determined that its AI system may not be converted into a high-risk AI system and that it is therefore not obliged to hand over the documentation. Intellectual property, confidential business information and trade secrets must be protected.
Art. 25 para. 3 AI Act	For **safety components** of high-risk systems (see Annex 1 Section A AI Act), the product manufacturer is deemed to be the provider of the high-risk AI system and must comply with the provider obligations for: ▪ Placing the system on the market together with the product under the name or trademark of the product manufacturer ▪ Commissioning of the system together with the product under the name or trademark of the product manufacturer after the product has been placed on the market Intellectual property, confidential business information and trade secrets must be protected.
Art. 23 para.4 AI Act	**Agreement** between ▪ provider of a high-risk AI system and ▪ of the third party providing an AI system, tools, services, components or procedures, that are used or integrated in a high-risk AI system. Necessary **content** so that the provider of the high-risk AI system can fulfill its obligations: ▪ Information on ▪ Skills ▪ Technical access ▪ Support ▪ Recognized state of the art No application to tools, services, processes or components that are not made available to the public as a general-purpose AI model under an open source license.

Table 3.8 Obligations of the Deployer of High-risk AI Systems

Article	Mandatory
Art. 26 para. 1, para. 3, para. 6, para. 12 AI Act	**Safeguards:** ■ Appropriate technical and organizational measures to ensure that the system is only used in accordance with the enclosed instructions for use and in accordance with paragraphs 3 and 6 　■ Other obligations of the deployer under EU or national law remain unaffected (see para. 3). 　■ Storage of automatically generated logs for an appropriate period of time (varies depending on the purpose of the system, but at least six months; see. para. 6) Cooperation with the competent authorities regarding the implementation of the AI Regulation
Art. 26 para. 2 AI Act	**Human supervision:** ■ Use of competent persons who have the necessary training and authorization ■ Support for these persons
Art. 26 para. 4 AI Act	Use of representative input data Safeguarding the intended purpose of the AI system
Art. 26 para. 5 AI Act	**Monitoring the operation of** the high-risk AI system: ■ Observe the instructions for use ■ If required, information of the provider in accordance with Art. 72 Act ■ In case of suspicion of high-risk AI (see Art. 79 AI Act), immediate information to the supplier or distributor and the competent market surveillance authority, including suspension of use ■ Informing the supplier, the importer or distributor and the competent market surveillance authorities in the event of serious incidents
Art. 26 para. 7 AI Act	Use of the high-risk AI system in the **workplace**: ■ Information for employee representatives ■ Information for affected employees National labor law must be observed and, if necessary, a company agreement must be concluded.
Art. 26 para. 8 AI Act	Compliance with **registration obligations** pursuant to Art. 49 AI Act Check whether the high-risk system has been registered in the EU database in accordance with Art. 71 AI Act (if not, it must not be used and the provider or retailer must be informed)

Article	Mandatory
Art. 26 para. 9 AI Act	Carrying out a data protection impact assessment in accordance with the GDPR or Data Protection Directive
Art. 26 para. 10 AI Act	Deployers of high-risk AI systems for **subsequent remote biometric identification:** ▪ Request for authorization or use immediately or within 48 hours to the competent judicial or administrative authority, unless it is the first identification of a potential suspect on the basis of objective and verifiable facts directly related to the crime ▪ Limitation to the necessary extent ▪ If the application is rejected, the use and deletion of the personal data already collected will be stopped immediately. ▪ No use of the system in a non-targeted manner and unrelated to a criminal offense, criminal proceedings or an existing or actual and foreseeable risk of a criminal offense or for the search for a specific missing person ▪ Art. 9 GDPR or Art. 10 GDPR or the Data Protection Directive must be observed. ▪ Documentation of the use of the system in the relevant police file ▪ Providing the documentation of the use to the competent market surveillance authority or the competent data protection authority upon request (except for the disclosure of sensitive operational data in connection with law enforcement) ▪ Annual report to market surveillance authorities and competent data protection authority (except for disclosure of sensitive operational data in connection with law enforcement) ▪ Compliance with any stricter national legislation
Art. 26 para. 11 AI Act	**Information to the natural persons concerned** that an AI system has made a decision about them or has assisted an AI system in making a decision

3.4 Fundamental Rights Impact Assessment

Carina Zehetmaier

Fundamental rights, which are fundamental principles on which democratic societies are built, are coming under increasing pressure. Data protection, freedom of expression, equality and the right to privacy are just some of the areas where AI has the potential to have a negative impact. The duality of AI as a tool for progress and as a potential threat to individual freedoms poses complex questions for legislators, developers and society and, to a certain extent, reflects the need for the AI Act: the aim is to strike a balance between technological progress and the protection of fundamental rights.

It is difficult to name a fundamental right that could potentially not be affected and possibly violated by AI. The role of technology in modern surveillance systems, the risks of discrimination through algorithmic decision-making and the data protection challenges posed by the collection and analysis of huge amounts of data are central.

3.4.1 AI Act and Fundamental Rights

To ensure the protection of fundamental rights, the AI Act clarifies the compliance with the Charter of Fundamental Rights of the European Union (the Charter or CFR) that the development, deployment and use of AI systems in the EU are in line with the fundamental rights and freedoms in the Charter.

The relevance of protecting fundamental rights in the development and use of AI can be inferred from **Art. 1 para. 1 AI Act**, which defines the purpose of regulation:

*"... improve the functioning of the internal market and promote the uptake of human-centric and trustworthy artificial intelligence (AI), while ensuring a high level of protection of health, safety, **fundamental rights enshrined in the Charter**, including democracy, the rule of law and environmental protection, against the harmful effects of AI systems in the Union and supporting innovation."*

Affected Fundamental Rights of the Charter

Most, if not all, of the Charter of Fundamental Rights of the European Union could potentially be affected by the application or impact of AI, as AI systems are increasingly integrated into various aspects of social, economic and personal life. The way in which AI systems are designed, developed and deployed directly or indirectly affects a wide range of rights and freedoms. Thus, Recital. 48 AI Act states that *"the extent of the adverse impact caused by the AI system on the fundamental rights protected by the Charter is of particular relevance when classifying an AI system as high risk."* Furthermore, Recital. 48 AI Act also lists the Charter rights affected by AI systems: *"right to human dignity, respect for private and family life, protection of personal data, freedom of expression and information, freedom of assembly and of association, the right to non-discrimination, the right to education, consumer protection, workers' rights, the rights of persons with disabilities, gender equality, intellectual property rights, the right to an effective remedy and to a fair trial, the right of defence and the presumption of innocence, and the right to good administration".* The consideration of the vulnerability of children is emphasized, and the explicit mention of the fundamental right *"to a high level of environmental protection enshrined in the Charter and implemented in Union policies should also be considered when assessing the severity of the harm that an AI system can cause, including in relation to the health and safety of persons"* is noteworthy.

Here are some examples of fundamental rights enshrined in the Charter that may be affected by AI and how this violation could occur:

▪ **Article 1 – Human dignity**

AI systems that make decisions that affect fundamental aspects of human life could compromise human dignity, especially if they are not transparent or do not respect the inherent dignity and autonomy of the individual.

▪ **Article 3 – Right to integrity**

AI applications, e. g. in the medical field, could influence the right to physical and mental integrity, e. g. through decisions on treatment methods.

▪ **Article 8 – Protection of personal data**

AI systems that process large amounts of personal data directly affect the right to data protection in relation to the collection, storage, processing and disclosure of this data.

▪ **Article 21 – Non-discrimination**

AI systems can reinforce social and economic inequalities if they use biased data, which can lead to discriminatory decisions in areas such as hiring, lending or law enforcement.

▪ **Article 23 – Equality between women and men**

AI can unintentionally reinforce gender bias if it is based on unequal training data, which can affect gender equality.

▪ **Article 14 and Article 11 – Right to education and access to information**

AI can revolutionize access to education and information through personalized learning systems or efficient information filtering, but it also poses risks in terms of access to educational institutions.

▪ **Article 13 – Freedom of art and science**

AI raises questions about copyright and creative freedom, especially when it generates works of art or scientific content, leading to debates about the recognition and protection of such works.

■ **Article 47 – Right to an effective remedy and to a fair trial**

The use of AI in the justice system and in decision-making processes can increase efficiency and accuracy, but can also impair transparency and accountability if the basis for the AI's decisions is not comprehensible.

The AI Act Extends the Scope of the Charter to the Private Sector

The AI Act mainly refers to the Charter as the central point of reference for the protection of fundamental rights, which is why this discussion also focuses on the fundamental rights laid down in the Charter.

Fundamental rights are primarily directed at the state and its organs and are conceived as citizens' rights of defense against state interference. They stipulate which actions the state must refrain from or how it must act to protect certain rights. They oblige the state to respect and protect the freedom and rights of the individual.

Although fundamental rights are primarily conceived as defensive rights against state interference, the third-party effect recognizes that the values and principles embodied in fundamental rights can also be relevant in private law relationships. This occurs on the one hand through the enactment of simple laws, e. g. in labor law, and on the other hand through the influence of fundamental rights on the entire legal system.

The Charter sets out the fundamental rights that must be respected in the EU. It is correct that the Charter primarily binds the EU institutions, bodies, offices and agencies. However, it also applies to the Member States, but only where they implement EU law. This includes situations where national authorities or courts apply EU law or where national laws are based on EU law.

The AI Act indirectly extends the scope of the fundamental rights protected by the Charter to the private sector by laying down certain requirements and prohibitions for the development, deployment and use of AI systems that apply to both public and private operators. These legal requirements ensure that private operators must comply with fundamental rights when implementing AI technologies in certain areas, even if they are not originally directly bound by the Charter.

3.4.1.1 Implementation of the Fundamental Rights Impact Assessment

Technology is not an end in itself. Its purpose can only be to benefit us humans and our planet. A human-centered approach is therefore the basis of trust in AI and thus the AI Regulation. The implementation of fundamental rights impact assessments (FRIAs) is a suitable instrument for ensuring that people are placed at the center of technical development, from conception to ongoing operation. The core component of this framework is to identify risks of potential endangerment or violation of fundamental and human rights prior to development and to take appropriate countermeasures.

For a long time, the private sector virtually ignored the implementation of fundamental rights impact assessments. However, the introduction of the fundamental rights impact assessment in the AI Act marks a turning point by making these assessments for defined areas of application an indispensable part of the development and introduction of high-risk AI systems in particular. This legal requirement forces companies to address the profound impact of their technologies on fundamental and human rights and to consider how these risks can be countered.

Art. 27 para. 1 AI Act:

"Prior to deploying a high-risk AI system referred to in Article 6(2), with the exception of high-risk AI systems intended to be used in the area listed in point 2 of Annex III, deployers that are bodies governed by public law, or are private entities providing public services, and deployers of high-risk AI systems referred to in points 5 (b) and (c) of Annex III, shall perform an assessment of the impact on fundamental rights that the use of such system may produce."

Thus, Art. 27 AI Act sets out specific requirements for conducting a fundamental rights impact assessment for the use of high-risk AI systems before they are put into operation. This provision aims to assess the impact of the use of such systems on the fundamental rights set out in the Charter and to ensure that appropriate measures are taken to protect these rights. As explained above, the obligation to conduct a fundamental rights impact assessment applies both to deployers that are public entities or private entities providing public services and to deployers of high-risk AI systems in certain areas listed in Annex III of the Act (e. g. lending, see section 3.3.2.1).

According to Art. 27 AI Act in conjunction with Recital 93 AI Act, the responsibility to carry out a fundamental rights impact assessment lies primarily with the deployers of high-risk AI systems, as they know the specific use case of the AI system:

"Whilst risks related to AI systems can result from the way such systems are designed, risks can as well stem from how such AI systems are used. Deployers of high-risk AI system therefore play a critical role in ensuring that fundamental rights are protected, complementing the obligations of the provider when developing the AI system. Deployers are best placed to understand how the high-risk AI system will be used concretely and can therefore identify potential significant risks that were not foreseen in the development phase, due to a more precise knowledge of the context of use, the persons or groups of persons likely to be affected, including vulnerable groups ..."

It follows from Art. 27 AI Act that only certain deployers of high-risk AI systems must carry out the fundamental rights impact assessment prior to commissioning:

1. Institutions under public law

2. Private institutions that provide public services, e. g. education, healthcare, social services, housing and administration of justice

3. Deployers of AI systems for credit assessment and credit scoring of natural persons, e. g. a bank (Annex III no. 5 lit b)

4. Deployers of AI systems for risk assessment and pricing of health and life insur-
    ance, e. g. insurance undertakings (Annex III no. 5 lit b)

The area of critical infrastructure is explicitly excluded from the obligation to carry
out fundamental rights impact assessments (Annex III no. 2).

Recital 96 AI Act explains why private institutions that provide public services are
also subject to the obligation: *"Services important for individuals that are of public
nature may also be provided by private entities. Private entities providing such public
services are linked to tasks in the public interest such as in the areas of education,
healthcare, social services, housing, administration of justice."*

The fundamental rights impact assessment aims to identify *"specific risks to the rights
of individuals or groups of individuals likely to be affected"* prior to the initial use and
relevant changes to the system and to determine in advance measures to be taken if
the risk actually materializes. The impact assessment should *"identify the deployer's
relevant processes in which the high-risk AI system will be used in line with its intended
purpose, and should include a description of the period of time and frequency in which
the system is intended to be used as well as of specific categories of natural persons and
groups who are likely to be affected in the specific context of use"* (96 Recital AI Act).

Art. 27 para. 1 AI Act also sets out the framework that the deployer must follow for the
fundamental rights impact assessment:

a) **a description of the deployer's processes** in which the high-risk AI system will be
    used in line with its intended purpose;

b) a description of the **period of time** within which, and the **frequency** with which,
    each high-risk AI system is intended to be used;

c) the **categories of natural persons and groups** likely to be affected by its use in
    the specific context;

d) the **specific risks of harm** likely to have an impact on the categories of natural
    persons or groups of persons identified pursuant to point (c) of this paragraph,
    taking into account the information given by the provider pursuant to Article 13;

e) a description of the implementation of **human oversight** measures, according to
    the instructions for use;

f) the measures to be taken in the case of the materialisation of those risks, including
    the arrangements for **internal governance and complaint mechanisms**.

The specific form of this fundamental rights impact assessment may vary depending
on the context of the AI system and the fundamental rights affected. A more precise
formulation of how an AI Act-compliant fundamental rights impact assessment will
look should be announced by the European AI Office no later than three months
before the provisions on high-risk systems come into force, i. e. 21 months after the AI
Act enters into force, on May 2, 2026.

In anticipation of these requirements for deployers, a first attempt will be made here to interpret the process of fundamental rights impact assessment in accordance with Art. 27 para. 1 AI Act:

1. **Analysis of AI system functions (lit a) and deployment (lit b):** A detailed analysis of the functioning of the AI system, including the data used, the decision-making processes and the way in which outputs are generated, is necessary. This helps to understand how the system could specifically influence fundamental rights. Explanation of the period and frequency of use of the system. Recital 96 AI Act requires deployers to "when carrying out this assessment ... take into account information relevant for a proper assessment of the impact, including the information provided by the provider of the high-risk AI system in the instructions for use".

2. **Identification of the fundamental rights and categories of natural persons and groups of persons affected (lit c):** First, it should be determined which fundamental rights of the Charter could potentially be affected by the use of the AI system. To this end, one could go through the rights of the Charter individually and carry out an analysis of which rights could be affected by the possible system. Is compliance with each individual right guaranteed when using the AI application? Which people or groups could be negatively affected by the AI system with regard to each individually identified right? Are there particularly vulnerable groups (e. g. children or people with physical or mental disabilities) that need to be taken into account?

3. **Assessment of risks and impacts (lit d):** Based on the functional analysis, the risks for each identified fundamental right and the possible group of persons affected should be assessed. This includes assessing the likelihood and severity of possible negative impacts on the violation of the fundamental rights of individuals and entire groups. How likely is a violation of one or more fundamental rights and can an interference with the possible fundamental right be justified?

According to Art. 27 AI Act in conjunction with Recital 96 AI Act, the impact assessment should include the "specific risks of harm". According to the author's interpretation, the harm lies in a violation of the rights in the Charter. To illustrate this, a classic example in connection with AI systems is used: Discrimination against individuals or groups of individuals (see section 7.1, Discrimination), such as by Amazon's AI recruitment tool, which favored male candidates [4]. This could constitute a violation of Art. 21 CFR (non-discrimination) and Art. 23 CFR (equality between men and women), unless the interference with the fundamental right is justified by Art. 52 para. 1 CFR (scope of guaranteed rights).

According to Art. 52 para. 1 CFR, *"any limitation on the exercise of the rights and freedoms **recognised by this Charter** must be provided for by law and **respect the essence of those rights and freedoms**. Subject to the principle of **proportionality**, limitations may be made only if they are **necessary** and genuinely meet **objectives of** *general interest recognised by the Union or the need to protect the rights and freedoms of others.".*

Here, it is necessary to examine (1) whether the use of AI may interfere with a fundamental right under the Charter and which persons or groups of persons could have their rights curtailed as a result and (2) whether an interference may also be justified. The higher the probability that a fundamental right will be infringed and that there is no justifiable reason for this under Article 52 para. 1 of the Charter, the higher the risk to be assessed as part of the fundamental rights impact assessment.

In contrast to **relative fundamental rights**, which can be restricted by the reasons set out in Art. 52 para. 1 CFR, so-called **absolute fundamental rights** may not be restricted under any circumstances. An example of an absolute fundamental right that may not be restricted under any circumstances is Art. 1 CFR: *"Human dignity is inviolable. It must be respected and protected."* If an AI system is supposed to recognize and classify people and objects in an image and depicts people of color as "gorillas" [9], the author believes that this is a violation of Article 1 of the Charter, since individual people and an entire group of people are depicted in a condescending, degrading manner and thus the dignity of the human being can be directly affected. There is no legitimate justification for such a violation of Article 1 of the Charter.

In their article "A Framework for Understanding Sources of Harm throughout the Machine Learning Life Cycle", Harini Suresh and John Guttag describe so-called representational harm, which can often form the basis for subsequent discriminatory treatment [12]. According to Recital 96 AI Act, "the assessment should also include the identification of specific risks of harm likely to have an impact on the fundamental rights of those persons or groups". In this context, representational harm must be included in the impact assessment in the same way as distributive harm, where it must be ensured that goods are distributed fairly and that access to certain benefits is available to all.

If necessary, this step can also determine that the risk of a violation of a fundamental right is too great to start development. How is it ensured that potentially affected rights are protected?

Examples of assessments of potential harm caused by AI systems and their impact on the persons or groups of persons affected by the European Fundamental Rights Agency show Figure 3.5.

Annex II: Examples of theoretical assessment of harm and significant impact of AI or automated decisions

Getting the future right: Artificial intelligence and fundamental rights

What happens if the output is wrong or if it works better in comparison with non-AI, human-based decisions?

EXAMPLES OF POTENTIAL HARM

Area	Potential false positive - examples		Potential false negative - examples		If it works better than human decisions on average - examples
	For an individual	At scale/for society	For an individual	At scale/for society	
Social welfare	If a person receives benefits without being entitled to them or receives benefits in excess of what they are entitled to		If a person does not receive any benefits or less than they are entitled to		• Better access to social welfare
	No real negative consequences, unless the wrong decision is found out later and the person needs to pay back money.	Negative consequences for public administration, as this leads to practices not in line with good administration.	Increased poverty and lack of resources for individual to live a dignified life.	Potential shift in societal distribution of resources, which can potentially increase inequalities and social exclusion.	• Improved public administration
Predictive policing	An innocent person is flagged to the police as a suspect		A person engaged in criminal activity is not identified		• More accurate predictive policing can result in higher levels of arrests of suspects/offenders, and a reduced risk of individuals' crime victimisation.
	Potentially humiliating; can be associated with discrimination.	Could increase dissatisfaction with and lack of trust in the police; particularly affecting certain groups.	A person can continue with criminal activity without being sanctioned.	Potential for increased criminality in society, with significant implications for public safety and victimisation.	• Reduced crime rates and higher levels of security.
Medical diagnosis	A diseases is diagnosed wrongly		A disease is not diagnosed		• Higher levels of health
	Wrong (potentially harmful) or unnecessary treatment – negative impact on health and human dignity.	Reduced trust in health system, including negative health implications if people stop going to the doctor. General level of health reduced.	Lack of treatment – negative impact on health, including life expectancy.	Overall increase in health problems in society, and potentially increased mortality rates.	
Targeted advertising	An ad is delivered via a website, but is not relevant to the individual		A potentially relevant ad is not delivered via a website		• Consumers are better informed about offers in different areas, such as products, services and jobs.
	Person receives specific ads and misses information about offers they would potentially be interested in. Potential to receive offending content.	Ads replicate social stereotypes that do not offer equal access to a market. Potential negative economic impact as large parts of the potential customer-base is excluded. Potential manipulation of consumers and citizens. Widespread dissemination of potentially offensive content.	A potential consumer does not receive a relevant ad and misses information about offers they would potentially be interested in.	Less efficient targeted advertising would not contribute to increasing revenues for companies. Potential negative economic impact as large parts of the potential customer-base is excluded.	• Increased economic revenue for companies.

Figure 3.5 Examples of the Assessment of Potential Harm caused by AI Systems and their Impact on the Individuals or Groups of Individuals Affected (source: © FRA – European Union Agency for Fundamental Rights, 2020)

1. **Development of mitigation strategies through human oversight measures (lit e) and internal governance and grievance mechanisms (lit f):** This step involves considering measures to be taken in the case of a materialisation of those risks, including for example governance arrangements in that specific context of use, such as arrangements for human oversight according to the instructions of use or, complaint handling and redress procedures, as they could be instrumental in mitigating risks to fundamental rights in concrete use-cases" (Recital 96 AI Act). This means that strategies must be developed for identified risks in order to prevent the likelihood of their occurrence and, if this is not possible, to minimize them. This can include technical adjustments to the AI system, revision of the database, additional protective measures for data processing and also, for example, measuring fairness, but also refers to procedures for reviewing and challenging AI decisions about end users.

2. **Human oversight measures (lit e)** High-risk AI systems should be designed in such a way that they can be understood and monitored by humans in the best possible way. It must be carefully examined and evaluated how humans can and must

intervene in the systems. Transparency and explainability play just as important a role here as the presentation of the results of AI systems in order to create a basis for human supervision. If a system only says "yes" or "no", a human has de facto no way of checking the system or the result. Here, it is advisable to present decisions made by AI systems in such a way that a person makes the final decision themselves, but has the relevant information at hand to make an independent decision in the first place. In the interests of transparency, a confidence indicator could be used here, for example, to provide the user with information on how reliable the AI system is, e. g. for a classification.

3. **Internal corporate governance and complaint mechanisms (lit f)** In order to ensure continuous compliance with AI legislation, a suitable governance structure (see section 10.2) and code of conduct (see section 10.5) are required. The introduction of AI systems in the company triggers fears among people, including about their own jobs, and therefore often meets with internal resistance. In other words, if the aim here is to accompany a certain process in the company, employees also need training to allay their fears and demonstrate the potential for making work easier and for further development. Only if employees are properly involved in this process will they be able to critically scrutinize the systems and not blindly accept the automated results. It is a question of the right degree of trust in the technology. In this context, deployers also need to consider how best to set up complaints mechanisms that enable stakeholders such as customers, employees or other affected parties to raise concerns or complaints about the functioning of an AI system or its impact. With regard to end users, open communication about the functioning, limitations of the AI system and complaint measures is fundamental in order to minimize the risk of a violation of fundamental rights and to react in a timely manner through complaint channels if this occurs.

As part of the regulatory impact assessment, it is of fundamental importance to involve as many stakeholders as possible in this process – including end users, legal experts and potentially affected groups of people – in order to fully identify potential impacts and risks in the first place. The entire impact assessment should be carefully documented, including the assumptions made, the analyses carried out and the planned mitigation measures.

As part of the fundamental rights impact assessment, it is important to involve as many stakeholders as possible in this process – including end users, legal experts and potentially affected groups of people – in order to fully identify potential impacts and risks in the first place. The entire impact assessment should be carefully documented, including the assumptions made, the analyses carried out and the planned mitigation measures. Recital 96 AI Act states the following: "*Where appropriate, to collect relevant information necessary to perform the impact assessment, deployers of high-risk AI system, in particular when AI systems are used in the public sector, could involve relevant stakeholders, including the representatives of groups of persons likely to be affec-*

ted by the AI system, independent experts, and civil society organisations in conducting
such impact assessments and designing measures to be taken in the case of materiali-
sation of the risks."

According to Art. 27 para. 2 AI Act, the obligation to carry out the fundamental rights
impact assessment set out in Art. 27 para. 1 AI Act applies to the first use of a high-risk
AI system. However, the impact assessment does not have to be started from scratch
every time: *"The deployer may, in similar cases, rely on previously conducted funda-*
mental rights impact assessments or existing impact assessments carried out by provi-
der. If, during the use of the high-risk AI system, the deployer considers that any of the
elements listed in paragraph 1 has changed or is no longer up to date, the deployer shall
take the necessary steps to update the information."

This obligation applies to the first-time introduction of a high-risk AI system, although
in similar cases deployers can rely on impact assessments previously carried out –
primarily by the providers.

A regular review of the impact assessment is recommended to ensure that it remains
relevant and that new risks are taken into account. If circumstances change or the
information is no longer up to date, the deployers must take the necessary steps to
update the information (Recital 96 AI Act). This means that it must be assessed at
regular intervals whether the framework conditions for the use of the AI system have
changed or may have an impact on fundamental rights. This requires monitoring by
designated, responsible persons and systems that document and make visible any
changes and further development of AI systems and their scope of application.

(3) Once the assessment referred to in paragraph 1 of this Article has been performed,
the deployer shall notify the market surveillance authority of its results, submitting
the filled-out template referred to in paragraph 5 of this Article as part of the notifica-
tion. In the case referred to in Article 46(1), deployers may be exempt from that obliga-
tion to notify.

Pursuant to paragraph 3, after carrying out the assessment, deployers are obliged to
notify the results to the market surveillance authority, including the submission of a
standardized questionnaire provided by the AI Office to facilitate compliance with
these obligations (see paragraph 5 below).

Art. 46 para. 1 AI Act defines the exemptions from the conformity assessment procedure in accordance with Art. 43 AI Act and stipulates the following: *"...upon a duly*
justified request, any market surveillance authority may authorise the placing on the
market or the putting into service of specific high-risk AI systems within the territory of
the Member State concerned, for exceptional reasons of public security or the protection
of life and health of persons, environmental protection or the protection of key indust-
rial and infrastructural assets. That authorisation shall be for a limited period while the
necessary conformity assessment procedures are being carried out, taking into account
the exceptional reasons justifying the derogation. The completion of those procedures
shall be undertaken without undue delay." This means that if the criteria of Art. 46

para. 1 AI Act are met, deployers can be exempted from the notification obligation pursuant to Art. 27 para. 3 AI Act. In the author's opinion, there is a risk that this provision could be used by Member States to undermine the protection of fundamental rights and could be used as a justification for any use of AI systems that interferes with fundamental rights (see section 3.5.2).

(4) If any of the obligations laid down in this Article is already met through the data protection impact assessment conducted pursuant to Article 35 of Regulation (EU) 2016/679 or Article 27 of Directive (EU) 2016/680, the fundamental rights impact assessment referred to in paragraph 1 of this Article shall complement that data protection impact assessment.

If a data protection impact assessment has already been carried out in accordance with the GDPR or Directive (EU) 2016/680, it is sufficient for the data protection impact assessment to be supplemented by the fundamental rights impact assessment in accordance with Art. 27 GDPR. It is essential that the data protection impact assessment includes a comprehensive assessment of the impact of the use of the AI system on fundamental rights.

(5) The AI Office shall develop a template for a questionnaire, including through an automated tool, to facilitate deployers in complying with their obligations under this Article in a simplified manner.

As already mentioned above, paragraph 5 of Art. 27 AI Act stipulates that the European AI Office will develop a model questionnaire to facilitate deployers in carrying out the fundamental rights impact assessment.

Pursuant to Art. 77 para. 2 AI Act, each Member State must designate national authorities or public bodies responsible for compliance with Union law on the protection of fundamental rights by November 2, 2024 and make them available in an up-to-date and public list to be communicated to the Commission and the other Member States.

In order to ensure the implementation of fundamental rights at national level, Article 77 para. 1 AI Act provides for the following: *National public authorities or bodies which supervise or enforce the respect of obligations under Union law protecting fundamental rights, including the right to non-discrimination, in relation to the use of high-risk AI systems referred to in Annex III shall have the power to request and access any documentation created or maintained under this Regulation in accessible language and format when access to that documentation is necessary for effectively fulfilling their mandates within the limits of their jurisdiction. The relevant public authority or body shall inform the market surveillance authority of the Member State concerned of any such request.* If this documentation is not sufficient to determine whether there has been a breach of Union law on the protection of fundamental rights, the national authority or public sector body may submit a request for a technical test of the high-risk AI-system to be carried out by the market surveillance authority in cooperation with the requesting authority or body within a reasonable period of time (Art. 77 para. 3 AI

Act). Pursuant to paragraph 4, this documentation shall be treated confidentially in accordance with Art. 78 AI Act.

Recital 157 AI Act states that this Regulation "is without prejudice to the competences, tasks, powers and independence of relevant national public authorities or bodies which supervise the application of Union law protecting fundamental rights, including equality bodies and data protection authorities".

3.4.1.2 Impact Assessment as Part of AI Governance

Conducting fundamental rights impact assessments is a crucial step towards human-centered AI governance (see Chapter 10). These assessments are necessary to ensure that the development and use of AI technologies are in line with the rights enshrined in the Charter. Such an impact assessment serves to raise awareness of the potential impact of specific AI applications on different areas of society and to ensure a structured overview of possible risks and their management. It is about promoting thoughtful planning, ethical design and responsible implementation of AI systems. This includes promoting transparency and accountability as well as ethical decision-making. A fundamental rights impact assessment should be carried out before the AI system is deployed, but should also be regularly monitored during the operation of the AI system and reviewed in the event of any changes.

At the heart of such an assessment is the early detection of potential violations of fundamental rights by AI applications. Each identified risk must be carefully weighed up and evaluated in order to develop suitable risk mitigation measures. This also includes assessing the probability of a violation as well as the severity of a possible violation of fundamental rights. This approach can promote a balanced and responsible use of AI technologies that safeguards and strengthens the rights and freedoms of individuals.

Conducting fundamental rights impact assessments in the development and deployment of AI technologies is a key element in achieving the goal of human-centered AI governance and promotes transparency, accountability and ethical decision-making throughout the AI planning, design and implementation process.

3.4.1.3 Existing Tools for Fundamental Rights Impact Assessments

There is already a long list of tools from various organizations and institutions that illustrate processes for carrying out a fundamental rights impact assessment. These lists are intended to provide a few examples of impact assessments. However, it must be noted here that the tools do not constitute a fundamental rights impact assessment in accordance with the EU GDPR.

Some relevant instruments for carrying out fundamental rights impact assessments:

- *FRAIA* [13] – The Fundamental Rights and Algorithms Impact Assessment is currently used by the Dutch administration to carry out impact assessments.

- *DEDA* [8] – Data Ethics Decision Aid is also used by the Dutch administration.

- *Automated decision-making systems in the public sector* [5] by Algorithm Watch Switzerland

- *Examining the Black Box* [1] des Ada Lovelace Institute und Data Kind UK

- *National Institute of Standards and Technology AI Risk Management Framework (NIST AI RMF)* [3] by the US government

- *Audit Framework for Algorithms* [11] of the Netherlands Court of Audit

- *AI Ethics Impact Group: From Principles to Practice* [2] of the AIEI Group

- *Guidelines on digital administration and ethics* [10] from the Federal Ministry of Arts, Culture, Civil Service and Sport

- *Ethical Impact Assessment: A Tool of the Recommendation on the Ethics of Artificial Intelligence* [7] von der UNESCO zur Evaluierung der ethischen Auswirkungen

- *ALTAI Trusted AI Assessment List* [6] of the independent High Level Expert Group on Artificial Intelligence established by the European Commission

Sources

[1] Ada Lovelace Institute: Examining the Black Box.

[2] AI Ethics Impact Group: Von Prinzipien zur Praxis – VDE. URL *https://www.ai-ethics-impact.org/de*. – accessed: 2024/04/13

[3] AI Risk Management Framework. In: NIST (2021). – Last Modified: 2024-01-05T14:53-05:00

[4] Amazon scraps secret AI recruiting tool that showed bias against women. URL *https://finance.yahoo.com/news/amazon-scraps-secret-ai-recruiting-030000358.html* – accessed: 2024/04/13 – Yahoo Finance

[5] Automatisierte Entscheidungssysteme im öffentlichen Sektor – einige Empfehlungen. URL *https://algorithmwatch.ch/de/adm-offentlichersektor-empfehlungen/* – accessed: 2024/04/13 – Algorithm Watch CH

[6] Best practices. URL *https://ec.europa.eu/futurium/en/ai-alliance-consultation/best-practices* – accessed: 2024/04/13 – FUTURIUM – European Commission

[7] Ethical Impact Assessment: A Tool of the Recommendation on the Ethics of Artificial Intelligence | UNESCO. URL *https://www.unesco.org/en/articles/ethical-impact-assessment-tool-recommendation-ethics-artificial-intelligence* – accessed: 2024/04/13

[8] Franzke, Aline Shakti; Muis, Iris; Schäfer, Mirko Tobias: Data Ethics Decision Aid (DEDA): a dialogical framework for ethical inquiry of AI and data projects in the Netherlands. In: Ethics and Information Technology Volume 23 (2021), no. 3, p. 551–567

[9] Google Fotos bezeichnet Schwarze als Gorillas. In: Der Spiegel (2015)

[10] Leitfaden Digitale Verwaltung und Ethik. Praxisleitfaden für KI in der Verwaltung, Version 1.0

[11] Rekenkamer, Algemene: Understanding algorithms – Report – Netherlands Court of Audit. URL *https://english.rekenkamer.nl/publications/reports/2021/01/26/understanding-algorithms* – accessed: 2024/04/13 – Last Modified: 2021-02-18T11:52

[12] Suresh, Harini; Guttag, John V.: A Framework for Understanding Sources of Harm throughout the Machine Learning Life Cycle. In: Equity and Access in Algorithms, Mechanisms, and Optimization, 2021 – arXiv:1901.10002 [cs, stat], p. 1–9

[13] Zaken, Ministerie van Algemene: Fundamental Rights and Algorithms Impact Assessment (FRAIA) – Report – Government.nl. URL *https://www.government.nl/documents/reports/2021/07/31/impact-assessment-fundamental-rights-and-algorithms* – accessed: 2024/04/13 – Last Modified: 2022-05-04T15:19

3.5 Harmonized Standards, Conformity Assessment, Certificates and Registration

Gabriele Bolek-Flügl

Section 5 of Chapter 3 AI Act, which comprises Articles 40–49 AI Act, defines the framework for assessing conformity of AI systems. This key section clarifies how providers must ensure that their AI systems comply with strict EU standards for safety, transparency and the protection of fundamental rights prior to market launch.

The conformity assessment is intended to strengthen trust in AI technologies and ensure a high level of protection for all natural persons. This should guarantee that AI systems are safe, privacy-friendly and non-discriminatory, thereby promoting their safe use in the European Union for society.

Example

Let's assume that a company develops an AI system to analyze application documents in the recruitment process. This system could be classified as high-risk AI, as it can have a significant impact on the chances of applicants. The company must therefore carry out a conformity assessment before launching it on the market. This includes checking the accuracy of the system, protecting applicants' data and ensuring that the system does not make discriminatory decisions. After a successful assessment, the company issues a declaration of conformity and registers the system in the EU database. This ensures that the system complies with EU regulations and can be used with confidence.

The following table provides an overview of the key elements of Section 5, from harmonized standards and conformity assessment requirements to the registration of AI systems in a dedicated EU database:

Article	Keyword	Explanation
Art. 40 AI Act	Harmonized standards	Manufacturers and suppliers of high-risk AI systems that adhere to harmonized standards can more easily prove that their products meet the requirements of the EU regulation.
Art. 41 AI Act	Common specifications	Describes how the European Commission deals with the standardization of high-risk AI systems.
Art. 42 AI Act	Presumption of conformity	Defines the criteria for when the requirements for data, accuracy, robustness and cybersecurity may be assumed for a high-risk AI system.
Art. 43 AI Act	Conformity assessment	Describes the procedure that providers of high-risk AI systems must carry out to ensure the conformity of their systems with the requirements of the Regulation.
Article 44 AI Act	Certificates	Describes the certificates of conformity and their period of validity.
Article 45 AI Act	Information obligations of notified bodies	Defines the information obligations of the notified body towards other stakeholders.
Article 46 AI Act	Exemption from the conformity assessment procedure	Regulates the circumstances under which the market surveillance authority can approve a high-risk AI system.
Article 47 AI Act	EU Declaration of Conformity	Obliges providers to issue an EU declaration of conformity, which proves that the AI system meets the requirements before it is placed on the market.
Article 48 AI Act	CE marking	Describes the criteria for labeling the AI system.
Article 49 AI Act	Registration	Requires registration of high-risk AI systems (with certain exceptions) by the provider or its authorized representative in the EU database prior to placing on the market or putting into service. Registration by deployers of certain public services prior to their use is also required.

The main requirements for manufacturers, providers and deployers of AI systems are discussed in more detail in the following sections.

3.5.1 Harmonized Standards and CE Marking

Art. 40 AI Act deals with harmonized standards and standardization results for high-risk AI systems. Harmonized standards are technical specifications (European standards or parts thereof) drawn up by the European standardization organizations such as CEN, CENELEC or ETSI at the request of the European Commission. They are intended to facilitate compliance with the basic requirements of certain EU directives or EU regulations. A product, service or process that complies with a harmonized standard is considered to comply with the relevant requirements of the associated EU legislation.

At the time this book was written, no specific standards for the AI Act had been finalized. Therefore, this section can only deal with the basic principles of the procedure.

> Standardization should play a key role in providing providers with technical solutions to ensure compliance with this Regulation in accordance with the state of the art and to promote innovation, competitiveness and growth in the internal market (Recital 121 AI Act).

One example of a harmonized standard is EN ISO 12100, "Safety of machinery". This standard provides guidelines for risk assessment and risk reduction in the design of machinery. It aims to ensure the safety of machine deployers and users.

Compliance with these harmonized standards enables manufacturers to affix the CE marking on their products to indicate that the product complies with the requirements of the relevant EU legislation. This facilitates the free movement of goods within the European Economic Area.

High-risk AI systems that comply with harmonized standards or parts thereof published in the Official Journal of the European Union are deemed to comply with the requirements for high-risk AI systems (Art. 8 et seq. AI Act) or, where applicable, with the requirements via GPAI, provided that these requirements are covered by the standards.

Significance for manufacturers and providers of high-risk AI systems

These requirements mean that manufacturers and providers of high-risk AI systems can more easily demonstrate that their products comply with the requirements of the AI Act by adhering to the harmonized standards. This procedure is intended to ensure safety, transparency and the protection of fundamental rights within the EU, while promoting innovation and growth in the field of artificial intelligence.

For whom is this relevant?

This is particularly relevant for developers and providers of high-risk AI systems who want to offer their products on the European market, as well as for standardization organizations and political decision-makers in the field of digital technologies.

Summary of the Most Important Requirements

1. **Presumption of conformity through compliance with harmonized standards** (Art. 40 para. 1 AI Act)

   If high-risk AI systems comply with the harmonized standards published in accordance with Regulation (EU) 1025/2012, they are presumed to comply with the relevant requirements of the AI Act. This applies as long as the standards cover the specific requirements or obligations.

2. **Standardization mandates from the Commission (Art. 40 para. 2 AI Act)**

   The European Commission will issue standardization mandates to cover all relevant requirements of the AI Act. These mandates also include the consideration of resource efficiency and energy-efficient development of AI models. The Commission will consult the Board and relevant stakeholders.

3. **Consistency and fulfillment of the requirements (Art. 40 para. 2 AI Act)**

   The standardization mandates issued by the Commission are intended to ensure that the standards developed are clear and consistent and that AI systems or AI models placed on the market or put into service in the EU meet the requirements set out in the Regulation. The European standardization organizations are asked to demonstrate their commitment to achieving these objectives.

4. **Promotion of investments and innovation (Art. 40 para. 3 AI Act)**

   Those involved in the standardization process should promote investment and innovation in the field of AI, in particular by increasing legal certainty and strengthening the competitiveness of the Union market. They should also contribute to global cooperation in standardization and ensure that international standards in the field of AI are in line with the values, fundamental rights and interests of the EU.

5. **Powers of the Commission (Art. 41 AI Act)**

   Article 41 allows the EU to respond flexibly to the challenges of standardizing AI systems so that a high standard of safety and ethics can be maintained even without harmonized standards.

CE Marking

The CE marking is a symbol that is affixed to products to show that they comply with the applicable EU regulations. However, the CE marking for high-risk AI systems not only indicates compliance with the specific requirements of the AI Regulation, but also conformity with other applicable EU regulations. The affixing and nature of the CE marking should be designed in such a way that it is easily recognizable and accessible to users, regardless of whether they are physical products or digitally provided services.

Art. 48 AI Act regulates the criteria:

1. **General principles (para. 1)**

   The principles for CE marking are based on the general principles laid down in Article 30 of Regulation (EC) No 765/2008. These regulate, for example, the affixing of the CE marking, including its visibility, legibility and durability.

2. **Digital CE marking for digitally supplied AI systems (para. 2)**

   For high-risk AI systems that are made available digitally, a digital form of CE marking may be used. This must be easily accessible, either directly via the user interface, via a machine-readable code or via other electronic means.

3. **Affixing the CE marking (para. 3)**

   The CE marking must be affixed to high-risk AI systems in a visible, legible and indelible manner. If the nature of the AI system does not allow or justify it (e. g. because of its size or type of use), the marking may instead be affixed to the packaging or accompanying documents.

4. **Identification number of the notified body (para. 4)**

   If the conformity assessment of a high-risk AI system requires a notified body has been used for the conformity assessment of a high-risk AI system, its identification number must be indicated together with the CE marking. The identification number shall be affixed either by the notified body itself or, under its instructions, by the provider or its authorized representative. This number shall also appear on any promotional material indicating that the AI system meets the requirements for CE marking.

5. **Compliance with other EU legislation (para. 5)**

   If a high-risk AI system is also subject to other EU legislation that also provides for CE marking, the CE marking indicates that the AI system also meets these other requirements.

> The CE marking is an administrative mark that indicates the conformity of a product with EU legislation and thus its free marketability within the European Economic Area. For AI systems, especially those classified as high risk, the CE marking means that the system complies with the specific requirements of the EU regulation(s).

3.5.2 Conformity Assessment Procedure

The conformity assessment procedure is primarily relevant for providers of high-risk AI systems to ensure that these systems meet the strict requirements of the AI Regulation before they are offered on the market or put into operation. Other AI systems are subject to less stringent regulations, whereby the exact requirements may vary depending on the area of application and risk profile.

For whom is this relevant?

This article is relevant for providers of high-risk AI systems who need to ensure that their systems comply with the requirements of the AI Act. It helps to identify which procedures need to be carried out to assess the conformity of these systems and provides guidelines for selecting the appropriate procedure, depending on the application of harmonized standards or common specifications and the type of AI system.

Significance for providers of high-risk AI systems

Art. 43 AI Act deals with the conformity assessment procedures for high-risk AI systems. The following procedure must be followed:

1. **Choice of conformity assessment procedure (Art. 43 para. 1 AI Act)**

   Suppliers of certain high-risk AI systems (listed in Annex III/1 AI Act) can choose between two conformity assessment procedures, provided that they have applied either harmonized standards or common specifications:

   a) an internal control in accordance with Annex VI AI Act

   b) Assessment of the quality management system and the technical documentation by a notified body in accordance with Annex VII AI Act

2. **Necessity of a specific conformity assessment procedure (Art. 43 para. 1 AI Act)**

   If no harmonized standards or common specifications are available or the supplier has not (fully) applied them, the conformity assessment procedure must be carried out with the involvement of a notified body.

3. **Selection of a notified body (Art. 43 para. 1 AI Act)**

   Suppliers can appoint a notified body for conformity assessment, unless the system is operated by specific public authorities (e. g. law enforcement, asylum authorities and other EU bodies), in which case the specific market surveillance authority assumes this role (Art. 74 para. 8 AI Act and Art. 74 para. 9 AI Act).

4. **Internal control for other high-risk AI systems (Art. 43 para. 2 AI Act)**

   For other high-risk AI systems listed in Annex III AI Act (no. 2 to 8), the conformity assessment is carried out by internal control without the involvement of a notified body. This includes AI-systems for:

- Critical infrastructure
- Education and vocational training
- Employment, workers management and access to self-employment
- Accessibility and use of basic private and basic public services and benefits
- law enforcement, insofar as their use is permitted under relevant Union or national law
- Migration, asylum and border control, insofar as their use is permitted under relevant Union or national law
- Administration of justice and democratic processes

5. **Compliance with other EU legislation (Art. 43 para. 3 AI Act)**

   AI systems covered by other EU harmonization legislation must follow the relevant conformity assessment procedures and the requirements of the AI Act are included in these assessments.

6. **Reassessment in the event of material changes (Art. 43 para. 4 AI Act)**

   High-risk AI systems that have been substantially modified are again subject to a conformity assessment procedure, regardless of whether the modified system is still to be placed on the market or continued to be used by the current deployer. Changes that were foreseen as part of the continuous learning process after placing on the market are not considered significant changes.

7. **Updating the annexes and procedures (Art. 43 para. 5 AI Act)**

   The European Commission may adopt delegated acts to update Annexes VI and VII and the conformity assessment procedures, in particular with regard to technical progress and the evaluation of the effectiveness of the procedures.

Other AI Systems

For AI systems that are not classified as high-risk, there is no explicit obligation to undergo a conformity assessment procedure. However, these systems must also meet the general requirements of the regulation, particularly with regard to transparency and fundamental rights.

Suppliers of such systems are expected to assess for themselves whether their products comply with the relevant provisions of the AI Regulation, but they are not required to provide formal proof of conformity or to affix a CE marking.

> The difference between the use of an AI system and its provision is important. The obligation to carry out a conformity assessment procedure lies with the providers (those who place the system on the market or put it into operation), not with the deployers who only use the system.

> However, deployers of high-risk AI systems must be aware of the specific require-
> ments and ensure that they use systems that are compliant and bear the CE
> mark.

Example

To illustrate the application of Art. 43 AI Act, let's look at a fictitious example: a high-risk AI system in medical diagnostics, an area that is usually considered high-risk.

Step 1: Determination of the high-risk AI system

- A company, let's call it MedAI, is developing an AI system for the diagnosis of rare diseases based on imaging data. This system falls under the high-risk AI systems listed in Annex I Section A/1 AI Act.

Step 2: Review of harmonized standards and common specifications

- MedAI checks whether there are harmonized standards for your AI system in accordance with Art. 40 AI Act or common specifications in accordance with Art. 41 AI Act that could meet the requirements. You will find a harmonized standard for the safety and performance of medical software.

Step 3: Decision on the conformity assessment procedure

- As MedAI can fully apply the harmonized standard, they follow the relevant conformity assessment procedures from this applicable legal act.

Step 4: Implementation of the internal control

- MedAI performs an internal control that includes the following:
  - Risk assessment and risk reduction in accordance with the harmonized standard
  - Creation of comprehensive technical documentation that shows how the AI system meets the requirements
  - Carrying out internal tests and validation processes to ensure the safety and effectiveness of the system

Step 5: Affixing the CE marking

- Once the internal inspection has been successfully completed, MedAI affixes the CE mark to its product, which means that the AI system complies with EU regulations and can be marketed in the EU.

Step 6: Market launch and monitoring

- MedAI brings the AI system to the market. They are also obliged to carry out continuous monitoring to ensure that the system continues to meet the requirements, especially if there are updates or changes to the system.

By applying the harmonized standard, MedAI was able to simplify the conformity assessment procedure and carry it out on the basis of internal control. This made it possible to obtain the CE marking and market the high-risk AI system within the European Economic Area.

3.5.3 Exemptions from the Conformity Assessment Procedure

Art. 46 AI Act regulates the exemptions from the conformity assessment procedure for certain high-risk AI systems in exceptional circumstances.

For whom and what does the article call for?

Market surveillance authorities may authorize the placing on the market or putting into service of certain high-risk AI systems if (Art. 46 para. 1 AI Act):

- there are exceptional reasons of public safety or the protection of life, health, the environment or important industrial and infrastructure facilities

- this authorization is limited in time to the duration of the necessary conformity assessment procedures.

In urgent cases, law enforcement and civil protection authorities may put a specific high-risk AI system into operation without prior authorization, but must apply for authorization immediately afterwards (Art. 46 para. 2 AI Act).

What steps need to be taken?

Application (Art. 46 para. 3 AI Act)

A duly substantiated application must be submitted to the market surveillance authority if an exemption from the conformity assessment procedure is desired.

- Approval procedure (Art. 46 para. 3 AI Act)

  The market surveillance authority checks whether the AI system meets the requirements and, if necessary, issues a temporary approval.

- Notification and review (Art. 46 para. 4 and 5 AI Act)

  The market surveillance authority shall inform the Commission and other Member States of any approvals granted. Objections can be raised within 15 calendar days.

- Consultation and decision (Art. 46 para. 5 AI Act)

  In the event of objections, consultations are held between the Commission, the Member State concerned and, where applicable, the operator concerned. The Commission then decides whether the authorization is justified. This decision is communicated to all parties concerned.

- Withdrawal of the authorization (Art. 46 para. 6 AI Act)

  If the approval is considered unjustified by the Commission, the market surveillance authority of the Member State that granted the approval must withdraw it.

■ Specific regulations for certain products (Art. 46 para. 7 AI Act)

For high-risk AI systems associated with products covered by specific EU harmoni-zation legislation (listed in Annex I Section A AI Act), only the exemptions from the conformity assessment procedures laid down in that specific legislation apply.

3.5.4 EU Declaration of Conformity

The EU Declaration of Conformity is an essential step for the market launch of high-risk AI systems in the EU. It serves as proof that an AI system meets the strict require-ments of the AI Act and thus ensures public safety, the protection of health and funda-mental rights.

The careful issuing and storage of this declaration not only ensures regulatory com-pliance, but also strengthens confidence in the safety and reliability of AI systems on the market.

Art. 47 AI Act regulates the issuing and storage of the EU declaration of conformity for high-risk AI systems. This declaration is an essential part of the conformity assess-ment procedure and is of great importance for providers of such systems.

For whom is this relevant?

The EU declaration of conformity is essential for providers of high-risk AI systems. With this declaration, they confirm that their AI system complies with the require-ments set out in the AI Act.

This declaration is a key document that forms the basis for the authorization of a high-risk AI system in the European Economic Area.

Criteria and steps

1. Issue of the declaration (Art. 47 para. 1 AI Act)

    ▪ Providers must issue a written, machine-readable, physically or electronically signed EU declaration of conformity for each high-risk AI system.

    ▪ The declaration must be kept for ten years after the system is placed on the market or put into service and made available to the national authorities on request.

2. Content of the declaration (Art. 47 para. 2 AI Act)

    ▪ It must confirm that the AI system meets the specific requirements defined in Section 2 of the AI Act.

    ▪ The declaration shall contain the information set out in Annex V and shall be translated into a language which can be understood by the national authorities of the Member States.

3. Harmonization legislation (Art. 47 para. 3 AI Act)

   If the high-risk AI system is also subject to other EU harmonization legislation that requires a declaration of conformity, a single EU declaration of conformity is issued for all applicable legislation.

4. Responsibility (Art. 47 para. 4 AI Act)

   By issuing the EU declaration of conformity, the provider assumes responsibility for the conformity of the AI system with the specified requirements. The declaration must be updated if necessary to reflect the latest status.

5. Updating (Art. 47 para. 5 AI Act)

   The European Commission has the power to update the content of the EU Declaration of Conformity by means of delegated acts in order to adapt it to technical progress.

> The EU Declaration of Conformity is essential for the introduction of high-risk AI systems in Europe. It confirms compliance with the AI Act and thus ensures the safety and protection of health and fundamental rights. Thorough handling of this declaration ensures regulatory compliance and promotes confidence in the safety and reliability of AI systems on the market

3.5.5 Registration

Art. 49 AI Act deals with the registration obligations for high-risk AI systems in a special EU database. This must be carried out before their market launch or commissioning. This requirement is of key importance as it ensures transparency and traceability for high-risk AI systems in the European single market. The following requirements and steps must be taken by the parties involved:

For whom is this relevant?

Providers (or their authorized representatives) and deployers of high-risk AI systems are the main target group of this article.

Criteria and steps

1. Registration of high-risk AI systems (Art. 49 para. 1 AI Act)

   Providers (or their authorized representatives) must register their high-risk AI system in the EU database before placing it on the market or putting it into operation, with the exception of the systems listed in Annex III/2 AI Act.

2. Registration for systems that are not classified as high-risk (Art. 49 para. 2 AI Act)

   If the provider decides that a system does not meet the high-risk criteria under Art. 6 para. 3 AI Act, it must still register it in the EU database (Art. 71 AI Act).

3. Registration by the deployer (Art. 49 para. 3 AI Act)

    Deployers of high-risk AI systems that are public authorities or institutions must also register in the EU database (Art. 71 AI Act), except for the systems listed in Annex II/2 AI Act.

4. Special registration for certain areas (Art. 49 para. 4 AI Act)

    For certain high-risk AI systems used in sensitive areas such as law enforcement and border control, registration takes place in a non-public part of the EU database. Only the Commission and certain national authorities have access.

5. National registration (Art. 49 para. 5 AI Act)

    High-risk AI systems specifically mentioned in Annex III/2 AI Act must be registered at national level.

Importance of registration

Registration is an essential process to demonstrate the compliance of high-risk AI systems with the requirements of the AI Act. It enables effective market surveillance by the competent authorities and helps to increase confidence in AI systems by ensuring that these systems are safe and legally compliant. The detailed registration also helps to maintain a clear overview of high-risk AI systems in the European market and facilitates cooperation between Member States and the European Commission in terms of monitoring and enforcement.

> The registration requirement helps to ensure a high level of security and the protection of fundamental rights by requiring that an overview of all high-risk AI systems on the European market is possible and that only compliant high-risk AI systems are placed on the market or put into operation in the EU.

3.6 Transparency Obligations in the AI Act

Veronica Cretu

The AI Act imposes transparency obligations to mitigate adverse impacts, maintain public trust, ensure accountability and provide effective legal remedies to create a trusting and accountable environment for the introduction and use of AI.

In the context of the AI Act, **transparency** means that *AI systems are developed and deployed in a way that allows for adequate traceability and explainability, making people aware that they are communicating or interacting with an AI system and properly informing deployers about the capabilities and limitations of that AI system and data subjects about their rights.*

Transparency is particularly important to avoid adverse impacts, maintain public confidence and ensure accountability and effective remedies.

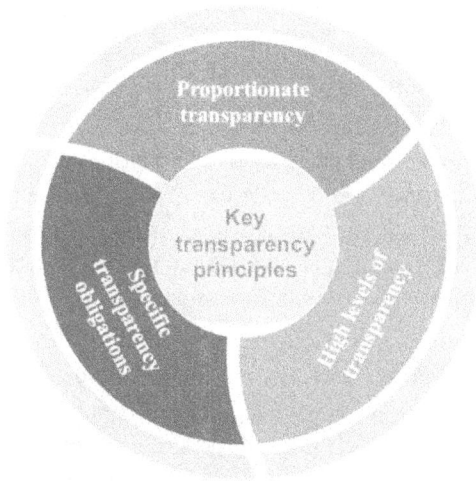

Figure 3.6
Principles of Transparency in the AI Act

While the AI Act does not explicitly explain the theoretical framework or typology of transparency, it sets out differentiated transparency requirements based on the level of risk and specific use cases of AI systems, effectively incorporating the **principles of proportionate, high-level and specific transparency obligations**.

- **The principle of proportionate transparency**

  The principle of **proportionality** is a general principle of EU law. It restricts public authorities in the exercise of their powers by requiring them to strike a balance between the means used and the aim pursued. In the context of fundamental rights, such as the right to the protection of personal data, proportionality is the key to any restriction of these rights [1].

  The AI Regulation requires that the level of transparency should be proportionate to the risk posed by the AI system, which is the essence of **proportionate transparency**: therefore, proportionate transparency measures should be provided for, including the creation and updating of documentation and the provision of information on the general AI model for its use by downstream providers.

- **The principle of high transparency**

  AI models for general purposes published under free and open source licenses should be considered to ensure a **high level of transparency** and openness if their parameters, including weights, model architecture information and model usage information are made publicly available (see Art. 54 para. 5 AI Act).

  For AI systems that pose significant risks or have a significant impact on individual rights and societal values, the AI Act requires a higher degree of openness. This includes detailed documentation, clear explanations of the AI system's capabilities, its limitations and the associated logic, especially for systems that are classified as high-risk. This ensures that stakeholders have access to comprehensive information in order to fully assess, scrutinize and understand the impact of the AI system (see e. g. section 3.3.2.3, Requirements for High-risk AI Systems).

▨ **The principle of special transparency obligations**

AI-systems intended to interact with natural persons or to generate content, whether or not they are classified as high-risk systems, may pose a particular risk of impersonation or deception. In certain circumstances, the use of those systems should therefore be subject to **specific transparency obligations**, without prejudice to the requirements and obligations for high-risk AI-systems, with targeted exceptions to take into account the specific needs of law enforcement.

Art. 50 AI Act introduces specific transparency obligations for certain categories of AI, such as those that interact with humans or generate content that could be misleading or manipulative. This approach is tailored to address specific concerns related to different AI applications and mitigate their potential negative effects.

All of these provisions reflect the EU's commitment to ensuring that AI technologies are used in a way that is safe, ethical and respects fundamental human rights.

Article 6 et seq. AI Act, entitled **Requirements for high-risk AI systems**, transparency requirements are set out in the following articles:

▨ Art. 10 AI Act: **Data and data management**

▨ Art. 13 AI Act: **Transparency and provision of information to deployers**

In addition,Art. 53 AI Act: **Transparency obligations for providers and users of certain AI systems and GPAI** and the information from Annex XI AI Act referred to in Art. 53 para. 1 AI Act: technical documentation for providers of AI models for general purposes to downstream providers who integrate the model into their AI system.

3.6.1 Guidelines for the Implementation of Transparency Obligations for Data and Data Management

Data protection and **Data governance** mean that AI systems are developed and deployed in accordance with applicable privacy and data protection regulations, processing data that meets high standards of quality and integrity.

The following guidance is intended to provide AI system providers with a structured approach to compliance with Art. 10 AI Act, with a focus on data and data governance requirements for high-risk AI systems.

Table 3.9 Overview of Art. 10 AI Act

Provisions of Art. 10 AI Act	Most Important Goals	Actions
Development on the basis of high-quality data sets (para. 1)	Determine whether the AI system can be classified as a high-risk AI system within the meaning of the AI Regulation. Classify data.	Determine whether the AI system is high-risk. Classify the data sets into training, validation and test categories.
Appropriate data management practices (para. 2)	Develop a data management framework that complies with the requirements of Art. 10.	Define clear processes for data collection, including sourcing and the original purpose of data collection. Implement data preparation processes such as annotation, labeling, cleansing and aggregation that are suitable for the intended purpose of the AI system. Evaluate the data sets for their relevance, representativeness and accuracy with regard to the objectives of the AI system. Ensure that the data sets take into account the specific characteristics of the target population or context of use.
Bias-Detection and correction (para. 2 lit f, 2 lit g)	Introduction of mechanisms to detect and mitigate biases in AI systems.	Regular review of data sets and AI results for potential biases that could affect safety or rights or lead to discrimination. Implement suitable measures to detect, avoid and correct distortions.
Relevance and representativeness of the data sets (para. 3)	Ensuring data quality and representativeness	Verify that the data sets are accurate and comprehensive. Confirmation that the data sets reflect the intended use and demographics of the users.
Consideration of special features (para. 4)	Consider the contextual relevance	Include relevant geographical, contextual and behavioral factors in data sets.

Table 3.9 Overview of Art. 10 AI Act *(continued)*

Provisions of Art. 10 AI Act	Most Important Goals	Actions
Processing of special categories of personal data (para. 5)	Processing of special categories of data under strict conditions	Assess the need to process special categories of data to correct bias. Apply advanced security and data protection measures. Ensure a strict access control and data deletion policy. Justify the processing of special categories of data in the documentation.
Applicability to the development of non-training models (para. 6)	Application to testing data sets	For AI systems that are not based on model training, the testing data sets should be aligned with the governance practices described.

General guiding principles for the implementation of Art. 10 AI Act:

- Detailed documentation of all steps and measures not only ensures compliance, but also contributes to transparency and accountability.

- Data governance and bias reduction are ongoing processes. Regularly review and update practices to ensure that they are in line with technological advances and changes in legal requirements.

- The relevant stakeholders should be involved in the development and review of the data governance framework and strategies to avoid bias. This includes data scientists, legal and compliance teams and potentially affected user groups.

- It must be ensured that practices comply not only with the GDPR, but also with other relevant regulations such as the GDPR. Particular attention should be paid to the processing of special categories of personal data.

- Before resorting to special categories of personal data to detect and correct bias, it should be checked whether the same objective can be achieved with synthetic or anonymized data.

3.6.2 Guidelines for the Implementation of the Transparency Provisions Provided for in Art. 13 AI Act

Table 3.10 Overview of Art. 13 AI Act

Provisions of Art. 13 AI Act	Most Important Goals	Actions
Design and development for transparency (para. 1)	Assess and design for transparency, ensuring that the design and development of high-risk AI systems promote transparency.	Evaluate how the system works to ensure that deployers understand and can appropriately use the results of the system. Determine the required level of transparency based on the complexity of the system and the use case.
Instructions for use in digital or other formats (para. 2)	Development of comprehensive and user-friendly instructions for the high-risk AI system.	Create instructions in an accessible format that contains all the necessary information. Ensure that the used language is clear, concise and understandable for all users.
Detailed content of the instructions for use (para. 3)	Provide comprehensive information about the AI system to ensure informed implementation and use.	Provide the contact details of the provider and, if applicable, the authorized representative. Describe the purpose of the AI system, the performance metrics, the limitations and the expected level of accuracy, robustness and cybersecurity. Highlight the circumstances in which the performance of the system may vary and explain the technical means of explaining its performance. Specify the specifications for the input data and all relevant information about the training, validation and testing data sets. Note all known changes to the performance of the system since the first conformity assessment. Explain the measures for human supervision and technical support in interpreting the results of the AI system. Providing information on computer and hardware requirements, expected system life and maintenance logs. If applicable, describe the mechanisms within the AI system for recording, storing and analyzing logs.

Table 3.10 Overview of Art. 13 AI Act *(continued)*

Provisions of Art. 13 AI Act	Most Important Goals	Actions
Ensuring compliance with the regulations and enabling interpretation by the emergency services (throughout para. 3)	Enable effective use and compliance with regulations	Organize training courses for emergency personnel on how to interpret the results of the AI system. Provide support and resources to clarify system usage issues. Regularly update the instructions for use to reflect any changes or updates to the system.

General guiding principles for the implementation of Art. 13 AI Act:

- Ensure that the instructions for use and all information provided are accessible to people with different levels of technical knowledge. Consider the use of multimedia elements or interactive instructions for better understanding.

- Establish a mechanism to regularly update the information provided based on feedback from users, technological advances and regulatory changes.

- Keep detailed records of all steps taken to comply with Art. 13 AI Act, including design decisions, development processes and the creation of instructions for use. This documentation is crucial for demonstrating compliance to the supervisory authorities.

- Create of channels for continuous exchange with users in order to gain insights into the transparency of the AI system, possible improvements and the need for clarification.

- When providing detailed information, ensure that security and data protection are not compromised.

3.6.3 Guidelines on the Implementation of Transparency Obligations for Providers and Suppliers of Certain AI Systems and GPAI Models

Table 3.11 Overview of Art. 52 AI Act

Provisions of Art. 52 AI Act	Most Important Goals	Actions
Transparency for direct interaction (para. 1 and 2)	Inform natural persons	Design AI systems so that it is clearly recognizable when users interact with AI. Implement and document machine-readable labeling systems for AI-generated content that indicate artificial generation or manipulation.

Provisions of Art. 52 AI Act	Most Important Goals	Actions
Disclosure of falsified content (para. 4)	Signal artificial content	Disclose when content is generated by AI, especially in cases of deep fakes, unless it is part of authorized legal activities or editorially reviewed.
Accessibility of information (para. 5)	Ensure clarity and accessibility	Provide clear and understandable information about the AI interaction at the first point of contact. Compliance with accessibility standards to ensure that the information is understandable for all users.
Development of codes of conduct (para. 7)	Development of and compliance with codes of conduct	Participation in or adherence to established codes of conduct for the identification and labeling of AI-generated content. Liaise with industry groups or regulatory bodies involved in the development of these standards.
Technical documentation for GPAI models (Annex XI)	Preparation of comprehensive documentation	Create detailed technical documentation for GPAI models, including descriptions of the model, the development process and the data used. Ensure that the documentation is easily accessible to downstream providers who integrate the model.

General guiding principles for the implementation of Art. 50 AI Act:

- Regularly obtaining feedback from users and deployers in order to improve transparency practices and adapt them where necessary.

- Regularly review updates to the AI Act and related standards and codes of conduct to ensure continuous compliance.

- Collaborate with industry groups, regulators and standards organizations to contribute to or stay informed about best practices for AI transparency.

- Training employees and stakeholders on the importance of transparency in AI deployments and how to effectively implement these requirements.

- Maintaining thorough records of compliance efforts, including design decisions made to inform users about AI interactions, efforts to label AI-generated content, and those for GPAI models technical documentation created for GPAI models.

Sources

[1] Necessity & Proportionality | European Data Protection Supervisor. URL *https://www.edps.europa. eu/data-protection/our-work/subjects/necessity-proportionality_en*. – accessed: 2024/03/31

3.7 General-purpose Artificial Intelligence (GPAI)

Merve Taner

The proposal for a Regulation laying down harmonized rules on artificial intelligence **(AI Act proposal** or **first draft)** was published on April 21, 2021. The increasing presence of generative AI applications such as ChatGPT & Co turned the timetable for the European legislator upside down [6]. The legislator had not considered regulations for the so-called *"general-purpose AI models"* (*GPAIs*) in the first draft.

The need for separate regulation became clear during the legislative process. However, the legislators disagreed for a long time in the negotiations on the necessary level of regulation [10], with the result that general-purpose AI models were only subsequently included in the AI Act.

This section takes a closer look at general-purpose AI models and systems within the meaning of the AI Act.

3.7.1 ChatGPT: the Start of an "AI revolution"? – Implications for the Legislative Process

On November 30, 2022, Open AI released the chatbot ChatGPT and caused a remarkable stir – more than almost any other technology. The company itself had previously classified ChatGPT internally as a *low-threshold research preview* [5]. But the success stories surrounding the use of ChatGPT came thick and fast: ChatGPT passed the American bar exam, the Austrian "Matura" or the German "Abitur" (both being final exams at high school), or invented precedents in Anglo-American case law that lawyers used in ongoing court cases [9].

AI applications have been around for many years. However, the publication of ChatGPT at the end of 2022 helped AI assistance systems gain visibility, made them more accessible to the general public [9] and thus marked a *milestone in the social acceptance of an AI solution* [2].

To a certain extent, *artificial intelligence* in the broadest sense has been commercialized with the help of ChatGPT, so that in my opinion the term "artificial intelligence" is now used almost inflationarily in everyday language. The underlying technology of ChatGPT is a special field of artificial intelligence: Large Language Models (LLM) [9], which represent a special field within generative AI [8].

What does ChatGPT say?

*"**ChatGPT and similar systems** have indeed contributed to the **popularization and commercial use of** of artificial intelligence (AI). This development has brought the term "artificial intelligence" more to the forefront of everyday language. However, it is important to understand that **ChatGPT is an example of applied AI in a specialized field** namely that of natural language understanding and speech generation. The underlying technology, **machine learning (deep learning), is only one aspect of the broad and diverse** of the broad and diverse landscape of AI research and application. The widespread attention and application of such systems [may] **can lead to an inflationary use of the term** of the term, **but should also be seen as an opportunity to raise awareness of the depth and complexity of the field.**"*

Open AI, ChatGPT Plus, Version 4.0 (2023), queried on 10.03.2024 (in German), 1st prompt: "In my opinion, "artificial intelligence" in the broadest sense has been commercialized with the help of ChatGPT, so that the term artificial intelligence is used almost inflationarily in everyday language. However, the underlying technology of ChatGPT is a special field of artificial intelligence. Summarize your point of view succinctly."

ChatGPT: In response to the request to critically examine the previous statement.

"The statement can be viewed critically from several perspectives:

1. ***Definition and understanding of AI:** AI is a broad field that encompasses many different technologies and approaches, from simple algorithms to complex neural networks. The fact that ChatGPT and similar technologies have been popularized **could** actually **contribute to** the **deepen public interest and understanding of AI.** Rather than inflationary use, it could be argued that the increased presence of AI in everyday life **more precise** and **differentiated discussion** about various aspects of AI.*

2. ***Commercialization and accessibility:** [...] of AI technologies like ChatGPT has expanded **expanded access to these advanced tools** and enabled not only companies but also individuals to benefit from AI-powered applications. This could be seen as a **democratization of AI technology** be seen [...]*

3. ***Promoting innovation:** Due to [...] the broad interest in AI technologies [...], research and development in the field of AI is being driven forward. This leads to faster innovation cycles, improved technologies and new use cases that might not have been achieved without popularization and financial support through commercial success.*

4. ***Responsibility and ethics:** A critical view should also include the ethical aspects and responsibility in dealing with AI technologies. The popularization of AI raises questions about data protection, the potential for misuse and the impact on the labor market. [...]*

*In summary, the popularization of AI through technologies such as ChatGPT has **both positive and challenging aspects.** A critical review should take into account the multiple implications of these developments and consider both the opportunities and the risks in order to promote a responsible approach to AI."*

Open AI, ChatGPT Plus, version 4.0 (2023), queried on 10.03.2024 (in German), 2nd prompt: "Critically examine this statement."

3.7.2 Inclusion of GPAI in the AI Act

The proposal for the AI Regulation was published on April 21, 2021, before the hype surrounding generative AI. Considering the rapid technological developments since then, the first version of the AI Regulation was soon considered outdated.

As already mentioned at the beginning, the success of LLMs made separate regulation necessary and there was great disagreement, as the legislator did not want to make innovation more difficult on the one hand, but on the other hand wanted to counter known risks, such as the disclosure of trade secrets or personal data [1].

With the announcement of the political agreement on December 9, 2023 (press release), it was announced for the first time that for general-purpose AI models **(general-purpose AI** or **general-purpose Artificial Intelligence models** or **GPAI** models for short) special regulations will be introduced with the aim of creating transparency along the value chain (*AI Value Chain*). The introduction of the two-stage approach for GPAIs was also announced [7].

In the final spurt, the definition of GPAI models and systems, further obligations, in particular transparency obligations, were actually incorporated into the AI Act.

In section 3.7.4, the specific classification characteristics of GPAIs are presented together with the associated obligations.

For very high-performing models that could pose systemic risks (GPAI models with systemic risk), there are additional binding obligations with regard to risk management, monitoring of serious incidents, model evaluation and attack tests. GPAIs with systemic risk are discussed in section 3.7.4.

Generative AI and Large Language Models

Analytical AI & Generative AI

AI solutions in the field of analytical artificial intelligence are widely tried and tested. Mature AI technologies include data analysis, business intelligence solutions (for the automated creation of visualizations, dashboards, storyboards), anomaly detection, data quality checks, data validation and fraud detection. Classification models, for example for the purpose of recognizing and categorizing numerical data, texts or images, are also included [11].

Analytical AI is contrasted with generative AI. This type of artificial intelligence is used to generate content. Large Language Models (LLMs) for creating texts (e. g. ChatGPT or Google Gemini [formerly Google Bard]), models for generating images (text to image), audio formats or videos are examples of this [11].

Large Language Models (LLMs)

Large language models are one form of AI. Well-known systems include GPT-4 (Generative Pre-Trained Transformer series developed by OpenAI) and the ChatGPT application based on it, PaLM 2 (Google), LLaMA 2 (Meta), Tongyi Qianwen 2.0 (Alibaba) and Luminous (Aleph Alpha).

LLMs can do through statistical calculations what humans can do linguistically through semantics and an understanding of causality. They recognize patterns in language or text data and exploit these with the help of probability calculations. They are increasingly being used in the field of natural language processing (NLP). Here, LLMs deliver extraordinary results, partly due to the gigantic amounts of data with which these models have been trained. This enables the systems to produce content that appears to have been written by humans. [4]

3.7.3 AI Models and AI Systems for General Use

3.7.3.1 Classification Rules for GPAI Models

GPAI models are defined in Art. 3 no. 63 AI Act:

> **☑ GPAI Models pursuant to Art. 3 no. 63 AI Act**
>
> General-purpose AI *Model* means an AI model, including where such an AI model is trained with a large amount of data using self-supervision at scale, that displays significant generality and is capable of competently performing a wide range of distinct tasks regardless of the way the model is placed on the market and that can be integrated into a variety of downstream systems or applications, except AI models that are used for research, development or prototyping activities before they are placed on the market (Art. 3 no. 63 AI Act).

The definition is limited to the essential functional characteristics of a GPAI model:

I. General usability

II. Ability to perform a wide range of different tasks (see Recital 97 AI Act)

Typically, GPAI models are trained using large amounts of data with various methods, e.g:

I. Self-supervised learning

II. Unsupervised learning

III. Reinforcement learning (see Recital 97 AI Act)

They can be brought to market in different ways:

I. in libraries

II. via application programming interfaces (APIs)

III. via direct download

IV. as a physical copy (see Recital 97 AI Act)

The models can be modified or refined into new models. The term GPAI models should be clearly defined and distinguished from the term AI systems in order to create legal certainty (Recital 97 AI Act).

Large generative AI models for the generation of content (text, audio, image, video) are a typical example of GPAI models (Recital 99 AI Act).

> ☑ **Definition: GPAI Systems**
>
> General-purpose AI system, ("General-purpose AI system") *means an AI system which is based on a general-purpose AI model and which has the capability to serve a variety of purposes, both for direct use as well as for integration in other AI systems* (cf.Art. 3 no. 66 AI Act).

AI models are components of AI systems, but are not in themselves an AI system. This requires additional components (e. g. user interface). In any case, the regulations for GPAIs apply regardless of whether they are integrated into AI systems.

The obligations apply to the provideras soon as GPAI models are launched on the market. If the provider of a GPAI model integrates it into its own AI system and makes it available on the market or puts it into operation, the GPAI obligations also apply in addition to the AI system obligations (Recital 97 AI Act).

> → **EXCEPTION: Purely internal process optimization**
>
> If a separate GPAI model is **used for purely internal processes**, the obligations are not applicable. The same applies to AI models that are used exclusively for **research, development and prototyping purposes before they are placed on the market** (Recital 97 AI Act; Art. 3 no. 63 AI Act).

> ! **EXCEPTION: Products and Services for Third Parties**
>
> **Please note:** The exception does not apply if GPAI models are used for purely internal processes but are **essential for the provision of a product or service to third parties** or affect the rights of natural persons (Recital 97 AI Act).

Art. 25 para. 1 lit c AI Act (AI responsibilities along the AI value chain) has been supplemented to the effect that GPAIs are bound to the risk-based approach of the AI Act. Providers of such systems will be obliged to provide downstream providers (*downstream providers*) of high-risk AI systems all information and elements (Art. 25 para. 1 lit c AI Act, Art. 53 para. 1 lit b AI Act, Recital 101 AI Act, Annex XII AI Act).

> ☑ **Downstream Providers**
>
> *Provider of an AI system, including a general-purpose AI system, which integrates an AI model, regardless of whether the AI model is provided by themselves and vertically integrated or provided by another entity based on contractual relations* (Article 3 no. 68 AI Act).

If a GPAI model is integrated into an AI system or is part of an AI system, this system should be considered a GPAI system if it can be used for a variety of purposes due to this integration. A GPAI system can be used directly or integrated into other AI systems (Recital 100 AI Act).

3.7.3.2 Commitments

Commitments for all GPAI models and GPAI models with systemic risk have been included in the compromise agreement for the first time, such as evaluating models, conducting risk assessments, taking risk mitigation measures, ensuring an adequate level of cybersecurity protection and reporting serious incidents to the Office for Artificial Intelligence and the competent national authorities. The most important **obligations for** all providers of *general-purpose AI models* are as follows in the final version of the AI Act:

- **Preparation and updating of the technical documentation listed in** Annex XI (Art. 53 para. 1 lit a AI Act)

- Obligation to make these available to the **European Artificial Intelligence Office (AI Office)** and the competent national authorities **upon request** (Art. 53 para. 1 lit a AI Act)

- Provision of certain information and documentation (capabilities and limitations of the AI model and Annex VII) to **downstream providers** for the purpose of compliance with the AI Act (Art. 53 para. 1 lit b AI Act)

- Compliance with **"EU" copyright law** (Art. 53 para. 1 lit c AI Act)

- **The dissemination of detailed summaries of the content used** (Art. 53 para. 1 lit d AI Act)

The aforementioned obligations do not apply to providers of AI models that are provided under a free and open license. This exception does not apply to general-purpose AI models with systemic risks (see Art. 52 para. 2 AI Act). The EU Commission is to be empowered to amend the annexes by means of delegated acts (changing technological developments) (Recital 101 AI Act, Art. 97 para. 2 AI Act).

The obligations in the AI Act are fundamentally dependent on the role of the obligated party. The majority of the obligations in the AI Regulation apply to the provider.

> **☑ Provider**
>
> Provider is a natural or legal person, public authority, agency or other body that
>
> - **develops** or has developed an **AI system or an AI model for general purposes** and
> - these under their **own name** or **trademark**
>   - **places on the market** or **puts into service**,
>   - regardless of whether this is done in return for payment or free of charge (see Art. 3 no. 3 AI Act).

Distributors, importers, deployers or other third parties are considered to be providers of a high-risk AI-system if they change the intended use of an AI-system that is not classified as high-risk and has already been placed on the market or put into operation, including a *general-purpose* AI-system, in such a way that the AI-system becomes a high-risk AI-system in accordance with Art. 6 AI Act (Art. 25 para. 1 lit c AI Act).

Providers of general-purpose AI models have a particular role and responsibility along the AI value chain: the models they provide can form the basis for a number of downstream systems, often provided by downstream **providers**. This requires a good understanding of the models and their capabilities to enable the integration of such models into their products and to fulfill their obligations (Recital 101 AI Act).

Obligations for Providers of all General-Purpose AI Models

DOCUMENTATION REQUIREMENTS

Technical documentation of the model in accordance with Art. 53 AI Act

Preparation and updating of the technical documentation listed in Annex XI AI Act in accordance with Art. 53 para. 1 lit a AI Act:
- Obligation to prepare the technical documentation of the model, including the training and testing procedure and the results of its evaluation, and
- up to date,
- which contains at least the elements listed in Annex XI,

to make them available **to the AI Office and the competent national authorities on request.**

Information and documentation for downstream providers in accordance with Art. 53 AI Act

Information and documentation for the downstream provider in accordance with Art. 53 para. 1 lit b AI Act:
- Obligation to provide information and documentation for AI system providers who intend to integrate the AI model into their AI system for general purposes,
- to keep it up to date and make it available.

The information and documentation shall enable AI system providers to have a good understanding **of the capabilities and limitations of the AI model** for general purposes and to comply with their obligations under this Regulation and shall include at least the elements listed in Annex VII.

Consideration of the need to protect trade secrets and confidential business information (Recital 107 AI Act; Art. 53 para. 1 lit b AI Act).
This is without prejudice to the need to respect and protect intellectual property rights and confidential business information or trade secrets in accordance with Union and national law.

Obligations for Providers of all General-Purpose AI Models

Detailed summary of the content used for the training in accordance with Art. 53 para. 1 lit d AI Act

Transparency of the training content

In order to increase transparency regarding the data used in the **pre-training and training of** general-purpose **AI models**, including copyrighted text and data, providers of such models must produce and make publicly available a **sufficiently detailed summary** of the **content used** to train the general-purpose model.

The **summary should not be technically detailed** but generally comprehensive to facilitate parties with legitimate interests (including copyright holders) to exercise and enforce their rights under Union law, e. g. by listing the main data collections or sets used to train the model, **such as large private or public databases** or data archives, and by **explaining other data sources used**. The AI Office should provide a template for the summary. (Recital 107 AI Act; Art. 53 para. 1 lit d AI Act).

COPYRIGHT

Policy on compliance with Union copyright law (Recital 104 AI Act)

Obligation to introduce a policy/strategy for compliance with Union law in the area of copyright, to identify legal reservations in accordance with Art. 4 para. 3 of Directive (EU) 2019/790 (Copyright Directive), including through the use of state-of-the-art technologies (Art. 53 para. 1 lit c AI Act).

Detailed summary

Obligation to make publicly available a sufficiently detailed summary of the content used for the training of the GPAI model based on a template provided by the Office of Artificial Intelligence (see above).

Authorization for copyrighted content

- **Any use of copyright-protected content requires the permission of the rights holder concerned, unless relevant copyright exceptions and limitations apply.** Directive (EU) 2019/790 introduced exceptions and limitations that allow, under certain conditions, reproductions and extracts of works or other protected subject matter for the purposes of text and data mining.
- **Rights holders** can reserve their rights to their works or other protected subject matter in order to prevent text and data mining. This does not apply to scientific research purposes. If the right to opt-out has been expressly and appropriately reserved, providers of AI models for general purposes must obtain permission from the rights holders if they wish to carry out text and data mining with such works (Recital 105 AI Act).

3.7.4 GPAI Models with Systemic Risk

For high-performance models with systemic effects ("systemic models") there are additional requirements.

As systemic risks arise from particularly high capabilities, a GPAI model should be considered to pose systemic risks if it has high-impact capabilities or has a significant impact on the internal market due to its scope. This should be assessed on the basis of appropriate technical tools and methodologies. The full range of a model's capabilities could be better understood after it has been released to the market or when users interact with the model (Recital 111 AI Act).

3.7.4.1 Classification Rules for General-Purpose AI Models with Systemic Risk according to Art. 51 AI Act

> ✓ **GPAI Model with Systemic Risk**
>
> A GPAI model is to be classified as a GPAI model with systemic risk if
>
> - it has **High-impact capabilities** (high-impact capabilities) *that are assessed using appropriate technical tools and methods, including indicators and benchmarks (quantitative threshold)* (Art. 51 para. lit 1 a) AI Act).
> - it is on the basis of an ex officio decision by the EU Commission or as a result of a qualified warning by the Scientific Panel that a GPAI model has capabilities or effects that are equivalent to the above point (Art. 51 para. 1 lit a AI Act). The criteria are listed in Annex XIII (Art. 51 para. 1 lit b AI Act).
>   - *"Skills with high impact"* correspond to the capabilities identified in or exceeding the most advanced general-purpose AI models (Art. 3 no. 64 AI Act, Recital 111 AI Act);
>   - "Systemic risk" means a risk that is specific to the **high-impact capabilities** of general-purpose AI models, having a **significant impact** on the Union market **due to their reach**, or due to **actual or reasonably foreseeable negative effects** on public health, safety, public security, fundamental rights, or the society as a whole, that can be **propagated at scale across the value chain** (Art. 3 no. 65 AI Act).

According to the EU Commission, "high impact capabilities" are to be assumed if the cumulative computational effort for its training, measured in floating point operations (FLOPs), is greater than 10^{25} (Art. 51 para. 2 AI Act).

"Floating point operation" or "FLOP" (floating-point operation) describes any arithmetic operation or any assignment with floating-point numbers, which are a subset of the real numbers that are typically represented on computers by the product of an integer with fixed precision and a fixed base with an integer exponent (Art. 3 no 67 AI Act).

SIMPLY PUT:

The **cumulative amount** of **calculations used to train** the GPAI model is one of the relevant approximations for model capabilities. This quantity is made up of the quantity of calculations used for the activities and methods intended to improve the model's capabilities prior to deployment, e. g. pre-training, synthetic *data generation* and *fine-tuning*. The calculation unit are floating point operations "FLOPs" (Recital 111 AI Act).

From the EU's point of view, 10^25 FLOP is a suitable threshold value:

▪ The threshold mentioned includes the currently most advanced GPAI models, namely GPT-4 from OpenAI and probably Gemini from Google DeepMind. Capabilities of models above this threshold are not yet well enough known. They could pose systemic risks and therefore it makes sense to subject their providers to additional obligations. The AI Act can be amended to update the FLOP threshold (by means of a delegated act pursuant to Art. 97 AI Act) [3].

▪ The EU Commission is obliged to adjust the threshold, taking into account technological developments and the capabilities of the most advanced GPAI models in order to keep pace with the state of the art, for example:

  ▪ the improvement of algorithms or

  ▪ increasing hardware efficiency (Art. 51 para. 3 AI Act).

3.7.4.2 Obligations for GPAI Models with Systemic Risk under Article 55

Obligations for Providers of General-Purpose AI Models with Systemic Risk	
GPAI	**Existing obligations under Art. 53 AI Act for GPAI models** In addition to the obligations set out in Art. 53 and Art. 54 AI Act (see section 3.7.3.2), providers of general-purpose AI models with systemic risk must comply with the following obligations (Art. 55 para. 1 AI Act):
Procedure	**Reporting obligations – Procedure according to Art. 52 AI Act** If an AI model for general purposes meets the requirements set out in Art. 51 para. 1 lit a, the provider concerned must notify the Commission **immediately within two weeks** of becoming aware (that these requirements are or will be met). ▪ This notification shall contain the information necessary to demonstrate that the relevant requirements are met. The Commission may decide to classify a model as posing a systemic risk. ▪ The share can provide evidence to the contrary (Art. 52 para. 2 AI Act); if the Commission does not agree, the GPAI model is deemed to pose a systemic risk (Art. 52 para. 3 AI Act).

Obligations for Providers of General-Purpose AI Models with Systemic Risk

Model evaluation
Obligation to carry out a model assessment using standardized protocols and tools that correspond to the state of the art, including the implementation and documentation of attack tests on the model in order to identify and mitigate system risks (Art. 55 para. 1 lit a AI Act).

Possible systemic risks
Obligation to assess and mitigate potential systemic risks at Union level – including their causes – that may arise from the development, placing on the market or use of general-purpose AI models or general-purpose AI models with systemic risk (Art. 55 para. 1 lit b AI Act).

Serious incidents and possible remedial measures
- Duty to record and document relevant information on serious incidents and possible remedial measures, and
- inform the Office for Artificial Intelligence and, where applicable, the competent national authorities without delay (Art. 53 para. 1 lit c AI Act).

Cybersecurity
Obligation to ensure an appropriate level of cybersecurity for the general-purpose AI models with systemic risk and the physical infrastructure of the model (Art. 55 para. 1 lit d AI Act).

Providers of general-purpose AI models with systemic risk can rely on codes of conduct until a harmonized standard is published (Art. 55 para. 2 AI Act). Codes of conduct are regulated in Art. 56 AI Act and Chapter 10 (Art. 95 and 96 AI Act) (see section 3.7.3.2)

3.7.5 GPAI Models and High-risk Systems

General-purpose AI systems are defined as AI systems that are based on a GPAI model and can be used for a variety of purposes. GPAI systems themselves can be classified as high-risk AI systems or act as parts of such systems (Recital 85 AI Act). Providers of such GPAI systems are obliged to make all information and elements available to downstream providers of high-risk AI systems so that they can meet the relevant requirements (including conformity assessment; Recital 86 AI Regulation, Article 25 para. 1 lit c AI Act). Article 25 includes provisions to align them with the risk-based approach of the AI Regulation (cf. Art. 25 para. 1 lit c AI Act).

If a general-purpose AI system that can be used directly by a deployer for at least one purpose is classified as high-risk, market surveillance authorities should cooperate with the AI Office to carry out conformity assessments and inform the Committee and other market surveillance authorities accordingly (Recital 161 AI Act, Art. 75 para. 2 AI Act).

3.7.6 Implementation Period and Penalties

The transposition deadline in the AI Act is in stages. The provisions relating to GPAI models and systems are applicable until August 2, 2025 (Art. 113 lit b AI Act, Recital 179 AI Act). For AI systems already placed on the market or put into operation, a transposition deadline of August 2, 2027 applies in accordance with Article 111 para. 3 AI Act.

Art. 101 AI Act sets out the fines for providers of general-purpose AI models in the event of breaches of obligations or non-compliance with enforcement measures. The EC can impose fines on providers of general-purpose AI models of up to 3% of their total worldwide annual turnover in the previous financial year or EUR 15,000,000 (see Art. 101 para. 1 AI Act). **The maximum amount of the fines has been aligned with that for providers of high-risk AI systems** (see Art. 99 para. 4 AI Act). There is an additional grace period for providers of AI models for general purposes, as no fines can be imposed in the first year after the provisions enter into force (Art. 113 lit b AI Act).

Sources

[1] Anderl, Axel; Ciarnau, Alexandra: Sprach-KI als "systemisches Risiko". In: Der Standard (2023)

[2] Anderl, Axel; Ciarnau, Alexandra: Datenschutzrechtliche Herausforderungen bei Generativer KI. In: Ecolex Volume 2023/12, p. 667

[3] Artificial Intelligence – Q&As. URL *https://ec.europa.eu/commission/presscorner/detail/en/qanda_21_1683* – accessed: 2024/04/20. – European Commission – European Commission

[4] Aschauer, Ricarda: (Juristische) Anwendungsmöglichkeiten von Large Language Models. In: Österreichische Richterzeitung 2024 Volume 2024/1–2

[5] Brühl, Jannis: Künstliche Intelligenz: Was nach einem Jahr Chat-GPT-Hype bleibt. URL *https://www.sueddeutsche.de/wirtschaft/kuenstliche-intelligenz-chat-gpt-ki-open-ai-hype-1.6311444* – accessed: 2024/04/20 – Süddeutsche.de

[6] ChatGPT broke the EU plan to regulate AI. URL *https://www.politico.eu/article/eu-plan-regulate-chatgpt-openai-artificial-intelligence-act/* – accessed: 2024/04/20 – POLITICO

[7] Fülop, Tünde: AI Act: Das Ende europäischer Innovation oder Gefahr für den Datenschutz? – eine Relativierung. In: DaKo Volume 2023/42, p. 82

[8] Gozalo-Brizuela, Roberto; Garrido-Merchan, Eduardo C.: ChatGPT is not all you need. A State of the Art Review of large Generative AI models, arXiv (2023) – arXiv:2301.04655 [cs]

[9] Kopetzky, Theodorich: Technische Hintergründe, Voraussetzungen und Funktionsweisen von KI-Assistenzsystemen. In: Österreichische Richterzeitung 2024 Volume 1–2, p. 6

[10] Mukherjee, Supantha; Chee, Foo Yun; Coulter, Martin; Mukherjee, Supantha; Chee, Foo Yun: Generative AI a stumbling block in EU legislation talks – sources. In: Reuters (2023)

[11] Wegenstein, Karin; Waniczek, Mirko: KI als Game-Changer in der Finanz- und Controlling-Organisation. In: CFO aktuell Volume 2023/6, p. 200

3.8 AI Sandboxes

Natascha Windholz

The AI Act should not slow down or prevent **innovative ideas, developments or technologies** despite the high level of regulation of AI. In order to strengthen and promote innovation, so-called **"regulatory sandboxes"** are created. They are intended to provide a controlled environment in which innovative AI systems can be developed, tested or validated for a limited period of time before they are placed on the market or put into operation. A sandbox can also include real-world testing, which are monitored in the sandbox.

Art. 57 et seq. AI Act regulates the AI sandboxes. According to the definition in Art. 3 no. 55 AI Act, this is a controlled framework created by a competent authority that gives providers or potential providers of AI systems the opportunity to develop, train, validate and test innovative AI systems for a limited period of time under official supervision and, if necessary, under real-world conditions in accordance with a so-called **real-world testing plan**. The provider and the competent authority agree on the sandbox plan. This describes the objectives, conditions, time frame, methods and requirements for the activities to be carried out in the sandbox. A real-world testing plan, on the other hand, is a document that describes the objectives, methodology, geographical, population-related and temporal scope as well as the monitoring, organization and implementation of tests under real-world conditions in accordance with Art. 3 no. 53 AI Act.

3.8.1 Setup and Functionality

Each Member State must have **at least one AI sandbox at national level**, which must be operational 24 months after the AI Act enters into force, i. e. from August 2, 2026 at the latest. However, this sandbox may be operated by one or more other EU Member States. The EU Commission can provide technical support, advice or tools for the introduction or operation of a sandbox. Additional real laboratories may be established at regional or local level or together with authorities from other Member States. Member States must ensure that the authorities are provided with the appropriate resources in good time to operate the real laboratories. Authorities may also operate a sandbox jointly, so it would be conceivable for the competent AI authority to operate a sandbox jointly with the competent data protection authority.

In order to use a sandbox, providers must agree a sandbox plan with the competent authority. The authority may, where appropriate, provide guidance, monitoring and support to identify risks related to fundamental rights, health and safety. It must also provide support with regard to the testing process, risk minimization measures and their effectiveness in connection with the obligations and requirements of the AI Act.

The competent authority must also guide providers and prospective providers of AI systems with regard to the regulatory expectation and how they must fulfill the requirements and obligations of the AI Act. At the request of the providers, the authority must issue **written confirmation** of the activities successfully carried out in the sandbox. In any case, the authority shall issue a report describing the activities carried out, including the results and learning experiences. This documentation may be used by the providers to demonstrate compliance with the AI Act in the conformity assessment procedure or any other market surveillance procedures. Accordingly, the authorities or notified bodies must be positively included in the assessment to a reasonable extent.

Final reports may be inspected by the EU Commission, and if the authority and provider agree, the report may also be published.

The establishment of a sandbox pursues the following **objectives**:

- Improving legal certainty regarding compliance with the AI Act or, where applicable, other EU or Member State legislation

- Support by sharing best practices through cooperation with the authorities

- Promoting innovation and competition and enabling the development of an AI ecosystem

- Contribution to evidence-based learning in the field of regulation

- Enabling and accelerating the access of AI systems to the European market, especially for SMEs and start-ups

If an AI system processes personal data, the competent AI authority must ensure that the data protection authorities are involved in the operation of the sandbox.

The use of a sandbox does not affect the authority's other powers. Significant risks to health, safety and fundamental rights identified during the development or testing of the AI system must be mitigated by means of risk minimization measures. If this is not possible, the authority may suspend operations in the sandbox for a certain period of time or permanently.

Providers or prospective providers remain **liable for damages to third parties** that occur during the experiments in the sandbox. However, if they adhere to the plan and the conditions for their participation and follow the authority's instructions in good faith, no administrative penalties may be imposed. This also applies to other authorities involved in the sandbox.

The national authorities inform the AI Office and its board to set up a sandbox and can request support. A list of planned real-world laboratories is publicly available at the AI Office to promote interaction and cross-border cooperation.

The national authorities also report to the AI Office and its board annually, starting one year after the establishment of the sandbox and thereafter for as long as the sandbox is in operation. The report includes the progress and results of the implementation of the sandbox, including best practices, incidents, lessons learned and recommendations for setting up a sandbox.

The EU Commission is developing an interface with the information on the real-world laboratories to allow stakeholders to interact with the real-world laboratories. They can also raise objections with the authorities to obtain non-binding guidance on the compliance of innovative products, services, business models that incorporate AI technologies.

Concrete **specifications for the functionalities and modes of operation** of the sandbox are regulated in Art. 58 AI Act in order to ensure uniformity within the EU. To this end, the EU Commission issues a **legal act** regulating the establishment, development, implementation, operation and monitoring of real laboratories. The legal act implements the following principles:

- Suitability and selection for participation in a sandbox

- Procedure for the application, participation, monitoring and termination of a sandbox, a r sandbox plan and the final report

- Conditions of participation for applicants

The legal act is intended to ensure that the sandboxes are open to all prospective providers, provided they meet the eligibility and participation requirements. These requirements must be transparent and fair. The authority offering the sandbox must inform applicants of the decision on the application within three months. The real-world laboratories should allow broad and equal access and meet demand. Applicants can also submit applications in partnership with users and other third parties. The modalities and requirements for participation must be kept as flexible as possible. Access to a sandbox is free of charge for SMEs and start-ups, but the authority can demand exceptional costs in a fair and proportionate manner. The legal act is intended to enable prospective providers to use the learning outcomes for the obligations relating to conformity assessment or voluntary application for an industry standard in accordance with Art. 95 AI Act. The real-world laboratories should also be able to be used to involve other relevant operators within the AI ecosystem, such as notified bodies or a standardization institute. SMEs, start-ups, companies, innovators, testing and experimental facilities, research, laboratories, centers for digital innovation, competence centers or researchers should also be given access. Procedures, processes and administrative requirements for the application, selection, participation and termination of participation in a sandbox must be simple, easy to understand and clearly communicated so that SMEs and start-ups with limited legal and administrative resources can also easily understand them. These requirements will be uniform across Europe to prevent fragmentation and to ensure that participation is equally recognized in the EU and has the same legal effects. Participation in a sandbox is limited to a certain period of time that corresponds to the complexity and size of the project, but can be extended by the authority. The sandboxes enable the development of tools and infrastructure for texting, benchmarking, evaluating and explaining the dimensions of AI systems, in particular when it comes to regulatory learning on accuracy, robustness and cybersecurity, measures that can be taken to address risks to fundamental rights, the environment and society as a whole.

Where authorities are considering testing under real-world conditions supervised in a sandbox, they must agree with participants on the conditions of participation and take safeguarding measures to protect fundamental rights, health and safety. They may also cooperate with other authorities to ensure consistency within the EU.

3.8.2 Further Processing of Personal Data

The further processing of personal data in certain AI systems of public interest in sandboxes is possible under the conditions of Art. 59 AI Act.

Personal data that has been lawfully collected for other purposes may be used for the purposes of **developing, training and testing certain AI systems** in sandboxes. However, certain conditions must be met.

The AI system must be developed for the protection of essential public interests by a public authority or other natural or legal person under public or private law in one of the following areas:

- Public safety, public health, including the prevention, control and treatment of diseases and the improvement of the health system

- Ensuring a high level of environmental protection and improving environmental quality, protecting biodiversity, pollution, green change and climate protection

- Energy sustainability

- Security and resilience of transportation systems and mobility, critical infrastructure and networks

- Efficiency and quality of public administration and public services

The processed data must be necessary for the fulfillment of the requirements in Section III, Chapter 2 of the AI Act (requirements for high-risk AI systems). However, processing is only permitted if these requirements cannot be met with anonymized, synthetic or other non-personal data.

Efficient **monitoring measures** must also be taken to mitigate high risks to the rights and freedoms of data subjects (see Art. 4 para. 1 GDPR) that may arise during the sandbox experiment or, if necessary, to terminate the processing at all. All personal data that is to be processed in connection with the sandbox must be stored in a separate, isolated and protected environment under the control of the responsible provider and can only be viewed by authorized persons. Providers may share the originally collected data in compliance with the GDPR, but the data created in the sandbox may not be shared outside the sandbox. This means that processing results from the sandbox that are personal may not be reused. Any processing of personal data in connection with a sandbox must not lead to measures or decisions that adversely affect data subjects or restrict their rights with regard to the processing of personal data. Personal data must be protected by appropriate technical and organizational measures and deleted as soon as participation in the sandbox has ended or the retention period has expired. Log data and protocols generated during processing in the sandbox may be retained for the duration of participation in the sandbox, unless otherwise stipulated by EU or national law. A detailed description of the processes and justification of the training, testing and validation of the AI system must be kept together with the test results as part of the technical documentation in accordance with Annex IV AI Act. A brief summary of the AI project developed in the sandbox, its objectives and expected results must be published on the website of the competent authority. This obligation does not include sensitive operational data related to the activities of law enforcement, border control, immigration or asylum authorities.

These requirements also apply to AI systems in sandboxes for the purposes of the prevention, investigation, detection or prosecution of criminal offenses or the execution of criminal penalties, including the safeguarding against and the prevention of threats to public security. The processing of personal data is also carried out on the basis of a specific legal act of the Member States or the EU.

3.8.3 Tests Outside of AI Sandboxes

Art. 60 AI Act also provides rules for **testing high-risk AI systems under real world conditions** outside of sandboxes. Provider or prospective providers may carry out such tests in accordance with a test plan, subject to certain conditions. However, the prohibitions of Art. 5 AI Act apply. The exact elements of the real world testing plan are issued by the EU Commission in a legal act.

Providers or prospective providers may test high-risk AI systems under real-world conditions at any time before placing them on the market or putting them into operation, either alone or together with others. Testing is without prejudice to any ethical review required under national or EU law.

The performance of real-world testing may only be carried out by providers or prospective providers under certain conditions: The provider or prospective provider has a **testing plan** and submitted it to the market surveillance authority of the Member States in which the test is to be carried out. The market surveillance authority or authorities must **approve** the testing under real-world conditions and the real-world testing plan. If the market surveillance authority has not responded within 30 days, the test is deemed to have been approved. If national law does not provide for explicit approval, the test must at least be authorized. If it is a high-risk AI system pursuant to Annex III, points 1, 6 and 7 in law enforcement, migration, asylum and border control management and a high-risk AI system pursuant to Annex III, point 2 AI Act, the test must be registered in a non-public EU database with an EU-wide unique identification number (see Annex IX AI Act). The provider or prospective provider must have its **registered office** or at least a legal representative in the EU. Data collected and processed for the purpose of real-world testing may only be transferred to **third countries** outside the EU if the relevant applicable safeguards under EU law are complied with (cf. Art. 48 et seq. GDPR). Testing under real-world conditions may not last longer than necessary to achieve the relevant objectives, but in no case longer than **six months**, which in turn may be extended by a maximum of six months. This must be done by prior notification to the competent market supervisory authority and must include an explanation of why the extension is necessary. Persons who belong to **vulnerable groups** due to their age or physical or mental disability must be protected accordingly. If the provider or prospective provider organizes tests under real-life conditions with one or more prospective deployers, the latter must be informed about all aspects of the test that are necessary for their decision to participate. They must also be instructed on the use of the AI system. The provider or prospective provider and the deployers must conclude an **agreement** that defines the roles and responsibilities for the real-world testing. The test subjects must give informed consent in accordance with Art. 61 AI Act. If the test is related to law enforcement and obtaining consent would be contrary to the test, it may be waived if the real-world test has no negative effects on the test subjects and the personal data is deleted after the test. The test must be conducted under the supervision of the provider or prospective provider and the deployer with the help of qualified persons. The predictions, recommendations or decisions of the AI system can be reversed or ignored.

Any **subject of the testing** can withdraw from the testing in real world conditions without giving reasons, revoke their consent and request the deletion of their personal data. The competent market surveillance authority may carry out on-site or remote investigations to monitor the progress of the tests. Any serious incident must be reported to the market surveillance authority. The provider or prospective provider must take immediate action to mitigate or, if this fails, suspend or terminate the test. The provider or prospective provider must establish a process to immediately recall the AI system if such a test is terminated. The market surveillance authority must be informed of the end or suspension of a test and of the final results. The provider or prospective provider is **liable for any damage** caused in the course of participating in the test in a real environment.

3.8.4 Consent for Tests Outside Sandboxes

Art. 61 AI Act describes the rules for informed consent for real-world testing outside of sandboxes. Such consent must be given **voluntarily** and **informed** by the subject of testing before participating. The information must be concise, clear, relevant and understandable. This means that the **nature** and **objectives** of the testing and **possible inconveniences** associated with participation must be clearly stated. The conditions under which the test will take place and the **duration** of participation must be described. The data subject's rights and guarantees with regard to participation must be explained, in particular the right to refuse participation or to withdraw consent to the test at any time without this having negative consequences or requiring justification. The modalities for requesting the withdrawal or disregard of any predictions, recommendations or decisions of the AI system must be set out, as well as the EU-wide unique identification number of the test under real-life conditions and the contact details of the provider or its legal representative from whom further information can be obtained. Consent must be dated and **documented**, and the data subject or their legal representative must receive a copy.

3.8.5 Facilitation for SMEs

Art. 62 AI Act contains facilitations for small providers and deployers, in particular SMEs and start-ups. The EU Member States are obliged to take the following measures: SMEs and start-ups that have an office or branch in the EU are given **priority access to the sandboxes**, provided they meet the requirements and selection criteria. Priority access should not prevent other SMEs and start-ups from gaining access to the sandboxes. Member States shall also organize specific **awareness-raising activities** on the application of the AI Act, tailored to the needs of SMEs and start-ups, but also of deployers and, where appropriate, local governance bodies. In addition, Member States may establish (new) channels of communication with SMEs and start-ups, other innovators and, where necessary, local governance bodies to advise and respond to requests related to the implementation of the AI Act, including the sandboxes. Member States may involve the participation of SMEs and other relevant stakeholders in the development of standardization processes.

The new **AI Office** is also making efforts: On request, it offers standardized templates for the AI Act, it develops and maintains a platform that provides information about the AI Act. The AI Office organizes communication campaigns to raise awareness of the obligations of the AI Act. It evaluates and promotes the bringing together of best practices.

Micro-enterprises as defined in Art. 2 para. 3 of the Annex to Commission Recommendation 2003/361/EC on the definition of micro, small and medium-sized enterprises may meet the requirements of Art. 17 of the Capital Investment Regulation in a simplified manner. The EU Commission is developing its own guidelines for this purpose.

3.9 Authorities

Natascha Windholz

Art. 28 et seq. AI Act distinguish between notifying authorities, conformity assessment bodies and notifying bodies. The Member States may decide that monitoring is carried out by a national accreditation body in accordance with Directive (EC) No 765/2008.

3.9.1 Notifying Authority

Notifying authorities are established in every EU member state. The definition can be found in Art. 3 no. 19 AI Act. This authority is responsible for the establishment of conformity assessment bodies and their monitoring. It may also be an accreditation body in accordance with the Market Surveillance Regulation (Regulation (EC) No. 765/2008). In Austria, these are different authorities, depending on the legal area, federal or state responsibility. This can be, for example, AGES, the Vienna Market Office or the responsible section of a federal ministry. Nationwide coordination is carried out by the Federal Office of Metrology and Surveying. The situation is similar in Germany, where the Market Surveillance Working Committee was set up to ensure uniform enforcement. The complete list of all market surveillance authorities is available from the EU Commission [1].

Member States must set up notifying authorities in such a way that they can work in a structured and organized manner. Conflicts of interest with conformity assessment bodies must be avoided and the objectivity and impartiality of the authority must be guaranteed. Persons working for the authority may not simultaneously work for a conformity assessment body, nor may the authorities take over activities of the conformity assessment bodies. A strict separation is provided for. The authority may explicitly not offer consultancy services and must guarantee confidentiality. The Member States must provide the authority with appropriate resources and the staff must have the relevant expertise.

3.9.2 Conformity Assessment Bodies and Notified Bodies

A conformity assessment body carries out all activities in connection with testing, certification and inspections and acts as an independent third party (see definition in Art. 3 no. 21 AI Act). It is a **notified body** if it has been designated in accordance with the AI Act (or other EU regulations or directives). (cf. Art. 3 no. 22 AI Act).

Conformity assessment bodies must apply for notification in the Member State in which they are established.

The following documents must be enclosed with the **application**:

- Description of conformity assessment activities
- Description of the conformity assessment procedure(s)
- Description of the AI technologies for which the conformity assessment body has competence
- If available, accreditation certificate that the body fulfills the requirements of Art. 31 AI Act
- If available, existing designation as a notified body in accordance with other EU regulations or directives.

If there is no accreditation certificate in accordance with Art. 31 AI Act, the body must prove that it fulfills the requirements of Art. 31 AI Act.

The notified bodies verify the **conformity of high-risk AI systems**, which means that the body must have the necessary resources, appropriate quality management and procedural requirements to perform this task. The organizational structure must be designed in such a way that the body can guarantee trustworthy results in its conformity assessment activities. The body must be independent of the provider, i. e. there must be no overlapping of personnel, economic interests or competitive relationships. No person of the body, neither top-level management nor staff, may be directly involved in the design, development, marketing or use of the high-risk AI or represent a party that was involved in these activities. This applies in particular to consulting services.

The notified body documents the implementation of the procedures and ensures confidentiality. During the procedure, it takes into account the size, sector and structure of the provider as well as the complexity of the AI system to be tested. The aim is to reduce costs and administrative burdens, particularly for small and micro-enterprises (see Art. 34 AI Act).

Compliance with the requirements of Art. 31 AI Act is assumed if the body fulfills the requirements in the relevant EU legal acts.

Liability insurance is mandatory for notified bodies.

The notification procedure is regulated in Art. 30 AI Act. Notifying authorities may only notify bodies that fulfill the requirements of Art. 31 AI Act. The EU Commission must be informed of notifications made by conformity assessment bodies.

A **notification** contains full details of:

- the conformity assessment activities
- the conformity assessment module(s) concerned
- the relevant AI technologies
- the relevant proof of competence (either accreditation in accordance with Art. 29 para. 2 AI Act or proof of compliance with Art. AI Act)

The notified body bears full responsibility for any branch offices used or subcontracts awarded. Activities may only be transferred with the consent of the provider.

The notified body may only commence its activities if neither the EU Commission nor other Member States raise any objections within two weeks in the case of a notification pursuant to Art. 29 para. 2 AI Act, or within two months in the case of evidence pursuant to Art. 30 para. 3 AI Act. If objections are raised, the EU Commission must immediately begin consultations with the Member States concerned. The EU Commission decides whether the objections are justified or not and addresses the decision to the Member State and the notified body.

The EU Commission also assigns the notified bodies an **identification number** that is always the same, even if the body has been notified under several EU legal acts. The list of bodies, including their identification numbers and activities, is published.

The authority must notify the EU Commission immediately of any **changes**. Extensions to the scope of the notification must be carried out in accordance with the procedure set out in Art. 29 and 30 AI Act. If a body wishes to end its assessment activities, the notifying authority and the providers must be informed. If an authority has reasonable grounds to suspect that a body no longer meets the requirements of Art. 31 AI Act or is not fulfilling its obligations, it must investigate immediately. The authority confronts the body with its concerns and gives it the opportunity to comment on them. The notification may subsequently be restricted, suspended or partially or completely revoked. The authority also informs the EU Commission and the notified body informs the AI manufacturers within ten days at the latest. The authority also ensures that procedural documents and files of the body are retained and are available to other authorities or market surveillance bodies on request.

In the event of **restriction, suspension or revocation of the status as a notified body**, the authority is obliged to

- to examine the influence on certifications awarded to the body;
- submit a report to the EU Commission and the other Member States on the changes to the notification within three months;

- to oblige the bodies to suspend or revoke certificates that have been wrongly issued;

- to inform the EU Commission and the Member States about suspended or revoked Member States;

- inform the national competent authorities of the Member States in which providers are based of certificates that have been suspended or revoked. The authorities there will then take the necessary steps to prevent risks to health, safety or fundamental rights.

Under certain conditions, certificates can be maintained in accordance with Art. 36 AI Act: The notifying authority confirms within one month of suspension or restriction that there is no risk to health, safety or fundamental rights and the authority provides a timetable and tasks to lift the suspension or restriction. The second option is that the authority confirms that no certificates are suspended and the notified body still has the possibility to supervise the issued certificates. If this is not the case, the provider has the option of informing the authority within three months of another notified body that will supervise the certificate in the future.

Nevertheless, certificates from a previously notified body remain valid for nine months if the competent authority confirms to the provider that there is no risk to health, safety and fundamental rights in connection with the AI system in question; alternatively, another notified body confirms in writing that it will assume immediate responsibility for these systems and carry out the assessment within twelve months of the revocation. In the first case, the deadline can be extended by a further three months.

The competent authority or the notified body taking over the function of the former notified body shall inform the EU Commission, the Member States and the other notified bodies of the takeover without delay.

In addition, in accordance with Art. 37 AI Act, the EU Commission can investigate all cases in which it has doubts about the competence of a notified body or the continued compliance of the body with the requirements of Art. 31 AI Act. The notifying authority must provide the EU Commission with all relevant information in connection with the notification or the maintenance of the competence of the notified body upon request. The EU Commission ensures the confidentiality of such an investigation. If the EU Commission comes to the conclusion that a notified body no longer meets the requirements, it immediately informs the notifying Member State so that it can take the necessary corrective measures, including, if necessary, suspending or withdrawing the notification. If the Member State does not take the necessary measures, the EU Commission may suspend, restrict or revoke the notification by means of an implementing act in accordance with Art. 98 para. 2 AI Act.

In accordance with Art. 38 Act, the EU Commission ensures coordination and cooperation between notified bodies.

Conformity assessment bodies of third countries with which the EU Commission has concluded an agreement in this regard can assume the tasks of notified bodies under the AI Act, provided that they fulfill the requirements of Art. 31 AI Act or guarantee an equivalent level.

Sources

[1] European Commission. URL *https://single-market-economy.ec.europa.eu/single-market/goods/build ing-blocks/market-surveillance/organisation_en* – accessed: 2024/04/20

3.10 Governance in the AI Act

Natascha Windholz

The AI Act provides for various mechanisms to ensure uniform interpretation and cooperation between the Member States.

3.10.1 AI Office

According to Art. 64 AI Act, the EU Commission is obliged to develop its own expertise and skills in the field of AI. The member states are to provide the **AI Office**. The AI Office was established by Commission Decision of 24.1.2024.

3.10.2 AI Board

A key component of governance is the – also new – **European Artificial Intelligence Board** or "AI Board". In accordance with Art. 65 AI Act, this consists of one representative per Member State. The European Data Protection Supervisor participates as an observer. The AI Office also takes part in the meetings, but has no voting rights. Other national or EU authorities or bodies may be invited if the AI Board discusses topics that are relevant to them.

3.10.2.1 Composition

The members, i. e. the **deputies of the member states,** are appointed for three years, whereby the appointment can be extended to a total term of six years.

Member States must ensure that their deputies have the relevant responsibilities and powers to actively represent the Member State and contribute to the AI Board. The deputy is also the single point of contact with the committee and other stakeholders. The deputy must be authorized to ensure consistency and coordination between the various national authorities with regard to the implementation of the AI Act. They may collect data and information in order to fulfill their duties towards the Committee.

One of the first tasks of the designated members of the committee will be to adopt the **rules of procedure** by a two-thirds majority. In particular, the selection process, the duration of the appointment and the tasks of the chair, the voting modalities and the organization of the activities of the committee and its working groups must be defined. The committee must ensure that it works objectively and impartially.

In any case, **two permanent working groups** will be set up to serve as an exchange platform for the market surveillance authorities and the notifying authorities for their respective topics. Other working groups may be set up by the Board on a permanent basis or for a specific duration to clarify specific issues.

The chair is an elected representative of a member state. The AI Office provides the secretariat for the Board, organizes the meetings and prepares the agenda.

3.10.2.2 Tasks of the AI Board

The tasks of the advisory body are defined in Art. 66 AI Act. The AI Board advises and assists the EU Commission and the Member States in order to ensure the consistent and efficient application of the AI Act. The following tasks are explicitly defined:

The AI Board contributes to the **coordination of the competent national authorities** and, depending on the agreement with the market surveillance authorities concerned, provides support for joint activities of the market surveillance authorities in accordance with Art. 74 para. 11 AI Act.

The Board gathers technical and regulatory expertise and best practices among the Member States. The Board advises on the implementation of the AI Act, in particular with regard to the enforcement of the rules on AI models for general purposes. It contributes to the **harmonization of administrative practice** in the Member States, including the procedures for conformity assessment procedures in accordance with Art. 46 AI Act, the functioning of real laboratories and real-world testing in accordance with Art. 57 et seq. AI Act.

At the request of the EU Commission or on its own initiative, the AI Board may issue **recommendations and written opinions** on any relevant topic concerning the implementation of the AI Act and its consistent and efficient application. These recommendations or opinions should be with regard to the development and application of codes of conduct and practice in accordance with the AI Act or in accordance with the guidelines of the EU Commission. The Board may also issue opinions on the evaluation of the AI Regulation, serious incidents, delegated acts and amendments to Annex I AI Act. Opinions are also possible on technical specifications and existing standards as well as on harmonized standards. The Committee can also comment on trends, such as the competitiveness of the EU, the development of digital skills, AI value chains, etc.

The AI Board also supports the EU Commission in **promoting AI skills**, public awareness and understanding of the benefits, risks, safeguards, rights and obligations associated with the use of AI systems.

The AI Board develops common criteria and assist in establishing a common understanding among market participants and competent authorities of the concepts provided for in the AI Act and contribute to the development of benchmarks. The Board shall cooperate with other EU institutions, bodies, offices and agencies as appropriate and, where necessary, internationally, as well as with relevant expert groups and networks in the EU, in particular in the areas of product safety, cybersecurity, competition, digital and media services, financial services, consumer protection, data protection and the protection of fundamental rights.

The AI Board supports the competent national authorities and the EU Commission in building up the organizational and technical expertise required for the implementation of the AI Regulation, including by helping to identify training needs for Member State staff involved in the implementation of the AI Act. The Board assists the AI Office, which supports the competent national authorities in setting up and developing the sandboxes, and facilitates cooperation and the exchange of information between the sandboxes. The Board advises the EU Commission on international matters related to AI and issues opinions to the EU Commission regarding qualified notifications of AI models for general purposes. Member States also provide opinions to the Board on qualified notifications of AI models for general purposes, but also on national experiences, practices regarding the monitoring and enforcement of AI systems.

3.10.3 Advisory Forum

Art. 67 AI Act also provides for an advisory forum technical. This primarily provides **technical expertise** to the AI Board and the EU Commission. The members are appointed by the EU Commission and they are appointed to the advisory forum for two years, but after a one-time extension for a maximum of four years. **Permanent members** of the advisory forum are the Fundamental Rights Agency FRA, the European Cybersecurity Agency, the European Committee for Standardization CEN, the European Committee for Electrotechnical Standardization CENELEC and the European Telecommunications Standards Institute ETSI. The advisory forum has two chairs, who are also elected for two years, renewable for a further two years. To fulfill its tasks, the advisory forum meets at least twice a year, prepares statements at the request of the AI Board or the EU Commission and draws up an annual report, which is also published.

3.10.4 Scientific Panel

A **scientific panel of independent experts** is also planned in accordance with Art. 68 AI Act. This body is set up by the EU Commission to assist with enforcement tasks. The members are appointed by the EU Commission based on their scientific or technical expertise. They must be independent of providers of AI systems. The scientific panel advises and supports the AI Office with regard to the implementation and enforcement of the AI Act, possible risks, the evaluation of AI models for general purposes, the classification of AI systems, the development of tools and models, the work of market surveillance authorities, the AI Office with regard to its tasks in accordance with Art. 66 AI Act. The scientific panel acts impartially, objectively, confidentially and without instructions.

Member States may use the experts of the scientific panel to assist them with the enforcement tasks of the AI Act. The EU Commission provides timely access to the experts for the Member States and ensures that the combination of supporting activities through the so-called "Union AI testing support" in accordance with Art. 84 AI Act and the experts offers the best possible added value.

3.10.5 National Authorities

The appointment of the national competent authorities is regulated in Art. 70 AI Act.

Each Member State shall establish or designate at least one **notifying authority** and at least one **market surveillance authority** as the national competent authority. These authorities shall exercise their responsibilities independently, impartially, objectively and without bias. The members of these authorities shall refrain from any incompatible activities. Member States shall notify the EU Commission of the appointment, tasks and any changes to the notifying authorities and market surveillance authorities. Information on how authorities can be contacted must be published within twelve months of the AI Act coming into force. Each member state appoints a market surveillance authority as a **"single point of contact"**. The EU Commission in turn publishes a complete list of all these contact details. It also supports the exchange of experience between the authorities.

National authorities must have an appropriate level of cybersecurity measures in place. They are obliged to maintain confidentiality when carrying out their activities.

In carrying out their activities, competent authorities may provide guidance and advice, in particular to SMEs and start-ups. In doing so, they should take into account any guidance provided by the AI Board and the EU Commission. The national authorities implementing the AI Act must, where other EU acts are additionally applicable, consult the authorities responsible for those acts. For example, if an AI system processes personal data, the competent AI authority or the competent data protection authority should be consulted, depending on the circumstances.

3.10.6 EU Database for High-risk AI Systems

Together with the Member States, the EU Commission creates and maintains a database on high-risk AI systems that have been registered in accordance with Art. 49 and 60 AI Act. With regard to the specification of the database, the EU Commission coordinates with the AI Board.

The database contains high-risk AI systems in accordance with Annex VIII AI Act. AI systems in accordance with Section A are registered by the providers or their representatives. AI systems in accordance with Section C are registered by the deployer acting on behalf of the authority, office or institution.

In principle, the database is publicly available and should also be machine-readable. Personal data should only be processed in the database if this is necessary in accordance with the AI Act. Contact details of natural persons who are responsible for the registration of the AI system and who can represent the provider or supplier are named in the database.

3.10.7 Post-market Monitoring

Once the AI system has been placed on the market, providers must ensure that the AI system is monitored in accordance with Art. 72 AI Act and document this accordingly. A **risk-based approach** can be followed. The monitoring measures must correspond to the type of AI technology and the risk of the high-risk AI system.

The purpose of the post-market monitoring system is to actively and systematically collect, document and analyze the relevant data in order to assess the high-risk AI system **throughout its entire life cycle**. The provider must be able to constantly check compliance with the requirements of the AI Act. Checking the interaction with other AI systems can also be part of the monitoring system. This means that the high-risk AI system must at least be in regular contact with the provider in order to provide the relevant data. This must already be taken into account when designing the AI system.

The **post-market monitoring system** must be based on a plan. This plan is part of the technical documentation in accordance with Annex IV AI Act. The EU Commission provides a template for such a plan, including the elements to be included, by means of an implementing act. This model shall be published no later than six months before the AI Act enters into force.

If a monitoring system has already been established for high-risk AI systems in accordance with Annex I, Section A AI Act and in accordance with the legal acts mentioned therein, the elements of the AI Act must also be included.

3.10.8 Sharing Information on Serious Incidents

According to Art. 73 AI Act, providers of high-risk AI systems placed on the market in the EU must report certain incidents. Serious incidents of such AI systems must be reported to the market surveillance authority in whose Member State the incident occurred. In general, the **notification** depends on the severity of the incident. Very serious incidents must therefore be reported as quickly as possible. The notification is made immediately as soon as the provider has established a causal link between the AI system and an incident or has at least identified the obvious possibility. However, no later than 15 days after the provider or provider has become aware of the incident, a report must be made. In the case of a widespread breach or a serious incident in accordance with Art. 3 no. 49 AI Act, however, a report must be made immediately, but no later than two days. If the incident has led to the death of a person, the report must also be made immediately or as soon as the provider or supplier suspects a serious incident, but in any case no later than ten days after becoming aware of the incident. The provider or supplier also has the option of making an initial report and providing the final report at a later date.

After reporting a serious incident, the provider must carry out the necessary investigations. This includes a **risk assessment** of the incident and the corrective measures. The provider shall cooperate with the competent authorities or the notifying body during the investigation. Any change to the AI system that would complicate or prevent the evaluation of the causes of the incident is not permitted without informing the competent authority in advance. "Cover-up actions" of any kind are therefore not permitted.

High-risk AI systems in accordance with Annex III AI Act or high-risk AI systems that contain safety components in accordance with EU Regulation 2017/745 (medical devices) and 2017/746 (in vitro diagnostics) that have been placed on the market or put into service are only required to submit reports in the event of an incident in accordance with Article 3 no. 49 AI Act, i. e. violations of fundamental rights or serious damage to property or the environment.

3.10.9 Law Enforcement

The market surveillance and control of AI systems on the European market are regulated in Art. 74 AI Act. The **Market Surveillance Regulation** 2019/1020 applies to AI systems that fall under this regulation. Economic operators according to the Market Surveillance Regulation are all operators according to Art. 2 para. 1 (suppliers, providers, importers, product manufacturers) AI Act, and AI systems according to the AI Act are also considered products.

The Market Surveillance Regulation grants the competent authorities extensive rights, such as the **requirement of certain evidence** (in particular access to documentation, testing data, safety measures, interfaces, tools for remote access), **unannounced on-site inspections** and the removal of online content. If the providers or suppliers suspect that a product or AI system is dangerous, the market surveillance authority must be informed and corrective measures must be initiated if necessary.

Under certain conditions, market surveillance authorities may also have access to the source code. Access must be necessary in order to check the conformity of the high-risk AI system with the relevant requirements of the AI Act and if the provider's documentation is inadequate with regard to testing and audit procedures.

With regard to AI systems for general purposes, there are additional requirements in Article 75. If the AI system and the AI model are operated by the same provider, the AI Office has the rights to monitor this AI system. In this case, the AI Office has the rights of a market surveillance authority under the Market Surveillance Regulation. If a national authority is of the opinion that an AI system can be used for at least one high-risk purpose and this system does not comply with the requirements of the AI Act, it cooperates with the AI Office.

The monitoring of tests under real-life conditions is carried out by the market surveillance authorities in accordance with Art. 76 AI Act. If the test is carried out under real-world conditions in an AI sandbox, the market surveillance authority checks compliance with the AI Act as part of its supervisory function for the sandbox.

If the market supervisory authority is informed by the prospective provider, the provider or a third party about a serious incident or malfunction, or if it has reason to believe that the requirements for real-world testing is not being met, it may suspend or terminate these tests or instruct the provider to adapt the tests. Reasons must be given for such decisions so that the provider can appeal against them.

Authorities for the protection of fundamental rights have the possibility to request access to any documentation of high-risk AI systems. The authority informs the market surveillance authority of such a step. Member States identify such authorities, publish them and inform the EU Commission and all other Member States. If the documentation is insufficient, the fundamental rights authority can make a reasoned request to the market surveillance authority and require testing of the high-risk AI.

3.10.10 Confidentiality of Procedures

Confidentiality of procedures is repeatedly referred to in the AI Act, but the main requirement is set out in Art. 78 AI Act. The EU Commission, market surveillance authorities, notified bodies and other natural or legal persons entrusted with the application of the AI Act must maintain the **confidentiality of data and information**. This applies to the performance of their tasks and activities, but in particular they must protect the following information and rights:

- Intellectual property confidential business information or trade secrets of natural or legal persons, source code

- the effective implementation of the AI Act, in particular inspections, investigations and audits

- Public and national security interests

- Criminal and administrative proceedings

- Information classified in accordance with EU or national law

When requesting information and data, the authorities are obliged to request only what is absolutely necessary to carry out their tasks or to determine the risk of the AI system. The authorities and bodies are obliged to implement **cybersecurity measures** to guarantee the security and confidentiality of data and information. Data and information must also be deleted as soon as they are no longer required. The AI Act does not specify a specific deletion period; authorities and bodies must refer to other EU or national legal acts.

For matters relating to law enforcement, immigration or asylum authorities, there are additional confidentiality mechanisms if disclosure could jeopardize national and national security interests. The exchange of information between authorities or with the EU Commission requires consultation with the competent national authority or the user. In addition, the technical documentation remains with this authority and the market surveillance authority receives access or a copy of it. In the market surveillance authority, only personnel with a corresponding security clearance may have access.

3.10.11 Procedures at National Level for dealing with AI Systems presenting a Risk

According to Art. 79 AI Act, AI-systems are a product presenting a risk pursuant to Art. 3 no. 19 of the Market Surveillance Regulation if they present a risk to **health, safety or the protection of fundamental rights**. Such products or AI systems affect the aforementioned interests to a greater extent than is considered reasonable and justifiable in relation to their intended purpose or under normal or reasonably foreseeable use of the product or AI system in question.

Has the market surveillance authority reasonable grounds to assume such a risk, it checks the AI system for compliance with the AI Act. If there are **risks to fundamental rights**, the market surveillance authority informs and cooperate with the relevant authority for compliance with the relevant fundamental right. The market surveillance authority also informs the notified body, or if the non-compliance extends be-yond its own territory, it also informs the EU Commission and the other Member States of the results of the examination and any measures to which the supplier/de-ployer/importer has been obliged. The latter ensures that the measures are imple-mented. If he fails to do so, the authority can **ban** the AI system **or restrict its provi-sion** or withdraw the product from the market or recall it. The authority informs the operator of the steps taken. The authority indicates whether the non-compliance con-stitutes a prohibited AI-system, a failure to comply with the requirements for high-risk AI-systems or a failure to comply with the transparency obligations for providers and deployers of certain AI-systems and GPAI-models pursuant to Art. 52 AI Act.

If neither the Member State nor the EU Commission raises objections to this notifica-tion, the measure taken by the competent market surveillance authority is deemed justified. If it is suspected that a prohibited AI system is involved, the period is re-duced to 30 days. Any legal remedies under the Market Surveillance Regulation re-main unaffected (see Art. 18 Market Surveillance Regulation).

3.10.12 Procedures for AI Systems Classified as Non-high-risk AI by the Provider

Art. 80 AI Act provides for procedural rules in the event that the market surveillance authority concludes that the AI system is a high-risk AI system, while the provider has not identified the AI system as high-risk AI and classified it in accordance with Annex III AI Act. The market surveillance authority shall immediately inform the provider of this conclusion and shall require the provider to take the appropriate steps to ensure that the AI-system complies with the requirements for high-risk AI-systems. If the AI-system is not restricted to its own territory, the authority informs the EU Commission. If the provider does not take the necessary **corrective measures**, the same applies as for high-risk AI systems that still pose a risk (see section 3.10.11). If the authority establishes that the provider has deliberately misclassified the AI-system in order to avoid having to comply with the relevant requirements of the AI Regulation, it may impose a **penalty**.

Art. 81 AI Act governs the EU's **safeguard procedure**. If a member state raises objec-tions to the notification of a measure referred to in Art. 81 para. 5 AI Act within three months or if the EU Commission is of the opinion that a measure is incompatible, the EU Commission examines the measure and decides on it within nine months. Justified measures proceed as planned, unjustified measures must be withdrawn by the Mem-ber State.

3.10.13 Compliant AI Systems which present a Risk

It can also happen that an AI system complies with the AI Act but still poses a risk to health or safety or fundamental rights. In this case, in accordance with Art. 82 AI Act, the market surveillance authority requires the provider concerned to provider/deployer/importer to take all appropriate **measures** specified by it to ensure that the AI-system no longer presents that risk when it is placed on the market or put into service, or that the AI-system is withdrawn from the market or recalled. The Member State shall immediately inform the EU Commission and the other Member States thereof. The EU Commission shall immediately enter into **consultation** and examine the national measures taken and decide whether or not they are justified and, if necessary, propose measures itself.

3.10.14 Formal Non-conformity

The following criteria lead to a formal non-conformity in accordance with Art. 83 AI Act and result in a **request** to rectify the non-conformity in question:

- The CE marking was affixed in violation of Art. 49 AI Act.
- The CE marking has not been affixed.
- Registration in the EU database was not carried out.
- If applicable, no authorized representative has been appointed.
- The technical documentation is not available.

If non-compliance persists, the market surveillance authority must take the necessary and proportionate steps to restrict or prohibit the high-risk AI system or recall or withdraw it from the market.

3.10.15 Legal Remedy

In accordance with Art. 85 AI Act, the right to lodge a complaint with the **market surveillance authority** to lodge a complaint. Without prejudice to any other administrative or judicial remedy, any natural or legal person who has reason to believe that there has been a breach of the AI Act may lodge a complaint with the competent market surveillance authority. These complaints will be considered and processed in accordance with the Market Surveillance Regulation.

3.10.15.1 Right to a Explanation of Decision-making

Any data subject who is the subject of a decision made by a deployer on the basis of an output of a **high-risk AI system** may request from the provider a clear and reasonable explanation of the role of the AI system in the decision-making process and the main elements of the decision (see Art. 86 AI Act). The **prerequisites** are that

* this decision has legal effect, or

* it is similarly significantly affected in a way that the decision has an adverse impact on health, safety or fundamental rights.

This right does not apply to AI systems for which there is an exception or restriction under national or EU law. If this right already exists in other legal bases (e. g. Art. 22 GDPR), the right to lodge a complaint pursuant to Art. 86 AI Act does not apply.

3.10.15.2 Legal Remedies for GPAI

Pursuant to Art. 88 AI Act, the **EU Commission** is exclusively authorized to but may delegate this task to the AI Office. The Member States can ask the EU Commission to fulfill its duties.

Downstream providers have the right to lodge a complaint about an alleged breach of the AI Regulation. A **complaint** must be substantiated and contain the following points:

* Contact point of the provider of the GPAI

* Description of the relevant facts, the relevant provisions of the AI Act and the reason why the downstream provider considers the AI model to be in breach of them

* other information that the downstream provider considers relevant and, where applicable, information that it has obtained on its own initiative

The **scientific panel** may issue a qualified warning to the AI Office if it has reason to believe that a GPAI poses a specific, identifiable risk at EU level or that a GPAI meets the requirements for classification as a GPAI with systemic risk. Following such a qualified warning, the EU Commission may, through the AI Office and after informing the AI Board, exercise the following powers to assess the matter.

A **qualified warning** contains at least the following points:

* Contact point of the provider of the GPAI with the system risk

* Description of the relevant facts and the grounds for the suspicion

* any other information that the scientific panel deems relevant and, where applicable, information that it has obtained on its own initiative

The EU Commission may require the provider to document the GPAI and request any additional information in order to assess whether the provider complies with the AI Act. Before submitting the request for information, the AI Office can start a structured dialog with the provider of the GPAI, where internal tests and protective measures are discussed with the provider. In response to a duly substantiated request from the scientific panel, the EU Commission can send a request for information to the provider. The request for information will state the legal basis and purpose, the information required, the deadline for providing the information and a statement that a fine may be imposed if incorrect, incomplete or misleading information is provided.

The AI Office may, after consulting the AI Board, **evaluate the GPAI**. It assesses the provider's compliance with the AI Act on the basis of the information obtained or examines the systemic risks at EU level. The EU Commission can appoint independent experts to carry out the evaluation on its behalf. It can also demand access to interfaces, technical tools and even the source code. It must justify this. The exact test procedure will be defined in separate legal acts.

Where necessary and appropriate, the EU Commission may request the provider to take appropriate **measures** or require the implementation of remedial measures if the assessment carried out has given rise to serious and substantiated concerns regarding a systemic risk at EU level. If necessary, the provider may even be required to restrict the AI model on the market, withdraw it or recall it. Before the measures are imposed, the AI Office again conducts a **structured dialog** with the provider. If measures to mitigate the systemic risk are taken during the structured dialog, the EU Commission can declare these obligations binding and there is then no need for further action.

3.11 Penalties and Sanctions

Natascha Windholz

Art. 99 et seq. AI Act regulate sanctions. Depending on the type of breach of the AI Act, different levels or types of penalties may be imposed.

According to Art. 99 AI Act, Member States are obliged to lay down penalties and take all measures necessary for the proper and **effective enforcement of the AI Act**. These can be finesbut also warnings and other non-financial measures. Sanctions must be **effective, proportionate and dissuasive**. However, they must also take into account the interests of SMEs and start-ups and their economic survival. If penalties are to be imposed on them, the lower of the following calculation bases must be used.

Penalty Amount (whichever is higher)	Nature of the Infringement
Up to ▪ € 30 million or ▪ 7% of total global annual sales in the previous financial year	▪ Art. 5 AI Act (prohibited AI systems)

Penalty Amount (whichever is higher)	Nature of the Infringement
Up to ▪ € 15 million or ▪ 3% of the total worldwide annual turnover of the previous financial year	▪ Obligations of providers pursuant to Art. 16 AI Act ▪ Obligations of authorized representatives pursuant to Art. 22 AI Act ▪ Obligations of importers according to Art. 23 AI Act ▪ Obligations of distributors pursuant to Art. 24 AI Act ▪ Requirements and obligations of notified bodies pursuant to Art. 31, 33 para. 1, 3, 4 and Art. 34 AI Act ▪ Transparency obligations for providers and users pursuant to Art. 50 AI Act
Up to ▪ € 7.5 million and ▪ 1% of the total worldwide annual turnover of the previous financial year	▪ Providing false, incomplete or misleading information to notified bodies and competent national authorities upon their request for information

If a penalty is to be imposed, the authorities are obliged to consider the individual case and must take all circumstances and the specific situation into account. They should take the following points into account:

▪ Nature, gravity and duration of the infringement and its consequences: Taking into account the purpose of the AI system and, where applicable, the number of persons affected and the extent of the harm they have suffered.

▪ Penalties imposed by market surveillance authorities: If market surveillance authorities have already imposed a fine on the operator in the same case.

▪ Penalties imposed: Have other authorities already imposed fines on the same manufacturer or supplier based on the same activity or omission?

▪ Size, annual turnover and market share of the operator who committed the infringement.

▪ Other mitigating or aggravating factors: Advantages gained or losses avoided directly or indirectly as a result of the infringement must be taken into account.

▪ Type of cooperation with the authorities: To what extent has the operator cooperated with the competent authorities to end the violation and mitigate the possible adverse effects.

▪ Responsibility of the operator: Consideration of the technical and organizational measures taken.

- Notification of the breach to the authority: How did the breach come to the attention of the authority and to what extent did the provider report the breach.

- Intent and negligence of the infringement.

- Measures taken by the provider to mitigate the damage suffered by the persons concerned.

Similar to the GDPR, it is up to the Member States to determine the extent to which fines can be imposed on authorities and public bodies established in the Member State concerned. However, the European Data Protection Supervisor can impose fines on EU institutions, bodies, offices and agencies under similar conditions in accordance with Art. 100 AI Act, although these are set at a lower level.

Depending on the structure of the legal system of the member state, these determine whether authorities or courts may impose fines. However, there must be no difference in the effect of the penalties. Appropriate **legal remedies** must be provided for **in national law** against acts of enforcement by market surveillance authorities. In addition, the Member States report all fines imposed and the associated legal disputes or court proceedings to the EU Commission.

There are additional requirements for **penalties relating to GPAI** pursuant to Art. 101 AI Act.

The EU Commission can impose fines on providers of AI models for general purposes. Fines may not exceed **3% of the worldwide annual turnover** of the previous financial year or **€ 15 million**, whichever is higher. Penalties may be imposed no earlier than one year after the entry into force of the AI Act (i. e. after August 2, 2025) so that providers have time to adjust their AI model if necessary, should the EU Commission establish intent or negligence:

- violations of the relevant provisions of the AI Act,

- failure to follow up on a request for documents or information or provision of false, incomplete or misleading documents;

- Failure to provide the EU Commission with access to the AI model with systemic risk in order to carry out an assessment.

- When determining the fine or periodic penalty payment, the EU Commission must take this into account:
  - Nature, gravity and duration of the infringement
  - Principles of proportionality and appropriateness
  - any codes of conduct

Before the EU Commission imposes a fine, it must notify the provider of the AI model with systemic risk of its preliminary findings and give it the **opportunity to comment**. It also communicates the results of the investigation to the AI Board. The ECJ has the power to review the EU Commission's decision. It can revoke, reduce or increase the fine. The exact modalities of the procedure are still to be determined by the EU Commission by means of an implementing act.

3.12 SMEs and Start-ups in the AI Act

Natascha Windholz

The AI Act is intended not only to regulate AI systems and ensure a high level of protection of public interests such as health and safety and the protection of fundamental rights, but also to promote the development, use and dissemination of AI. The AI Act considers SMEs (small and medium-sized enterprises) and start-ups so that they can also pursue innovative approaches. This is already mentioned inArt. 1 para. 2 lit g AI Act, which states that there are *"measures to support innovation, with a particular focus on SMEs, including start-ups"*. This does not mean that SMEs and start-ups are largely spared or that there are clear exceptions to applicability, but the EU had the needs of SMEs and start-ups in mind when drafting the AI Act. The legislator was aware that they often do not have their own legal department and generally have few employees.

For this reason, this section summarizes the numerous exemptions and simplifications for SMEs and start-ups.

According to Recommendation 2003/61 of the EU Commission [1], SMEs are defined as follows:

	Maximum number of employees	Maximum turnover	Maximum balance sheet total
Medium-sized company	250	€ 50 million	€ 43 million
Small company	50	€ 10 million	€ 10 million
Microenterprises	10	€ 2 million	€ 2 million

There is no Europe-wide definition of the term "start-up", but funding applications may specify how long the company may have existed or how large it may be.

3.12.1 Facilitations and Exemptions for SMEs and Start-ups

Facilitating Technical Documentation

In accordance with Art. 11 AI Act, technical documentation must be prepared for high-risk AI systems before they are placed on the market or put into operation. The documentation must also always be up to date, i. e. further developments must always be taken into account (see section 3.3.2.3 High-risk AI Obligations). The minimum content is regulated in Annex IV AI Act.

SMEs and start-ups can provide this content in a simplified manner. The EU Commission provides a simplified form as a template for this purpose. The SME or start-up has the choice of using the simplified form or Annex IV. However, if it opts for simplified documentation, the EU Commission's form must be used. The notified bodies must then accept this for the purposes of conformity assessment.

Simplified Access to AI Sandboxes

AI sandboxes should be available throughout the EU and obstacles for SMEs should be removed.Art. 57 AI Act regulates AI sandboxes with the explicit aim of promoting innovation (see section 3.8 AI Sandboxes). Pursuant to Art. 57 para. 9 lit e AI Act, SMEs and start-ups are given easier and faster access to the real laboratories so that the AI system can be placed on the market or put into operation more quickly. This must be taken into account by the competent authorities when setting up the AI sandbox. Recital 139 AI Act also emphasizes this. Participation in AI sandboxes should focus on issues where there is legal uncertainty among providers and prospective providers. The focus is also on the development, training, testing and validation before the AI system is placed on the market or put into operation.

According to Art. 58 para. 2 lit d AI Act, access to AI laboratories is generally free of charge for SMEs and start-ups; however, the competent authorities may demand exceptional costs, but they must be fair and proportionate. In addition, procedures, processes and administrative requirements for applications, selection, participation and exit from the AI sandbox should be designed in such a way that SMEs and start-ups with limited legal and administrative capacities can also easily fulfill their rights and obligations. Procedures, applications etc. should be easy to understand and clearly communicated (see Art. 58 para. 2 lit g AI Act). The authorities that operate AI laboratories must also refer SMEs and start-ups to institutions that offer guidance on the implementation of the AI Act, provide assistance with standardization documents, etc., where necessary.

Measures for SMEs and Start-ups

Art. 62 AI Act provides for measures for SMEs and start-ups that act as providers and deployers. However, these must first be transposed into national law, which is where the member states and the AI Office in particular come in.

Member States should take the following measures:

- **Priority access to AI sandboxes:** SMEs and start-ups based or with a branch in the EU have priority access, but must still meet the admission requirements and selection criteria despite priority access. However, priority access must not prevent other providers from gaining access.

- **Awareness-raising and training measures:** Member States shall provide awareness-raising and training measures on the application of the AI Act tailored to the needs of SMEs, start-ups, deployers and local authorities. These measures have not yet been implemented in the Member States.

- **Communication channels:** Member States shall use existing or establish new communication channels to provide advice on the implementation of the AI Act and to answer questions regarding participation in AI sandboxes. The aim is to provide support throughout the entire development process, offer guidance and answer questions on the implementation of the AI Act. If there are different channels, they should work together if necessary to create synergies and ensure homogeneity.

- **Participation in the development of standards:** Member States shall encourage the participation of SMEs and other relevant stakeholders in the development of standards.

- **Fees for conformity assessment:** When setting fees in accordance with Art. 43 AI Act, care is taken to ensure that these are set in proportion to the size of the company, the size of its market and its relevant key figures. The EU Commission should regularly assess the certification and compliance costs for SMEs and start-ups and work with the Member States to limit these costs.

The **AI Office** also takes measures specifically for SMEs and start-ups:

- **Examples and templates:** The AI office provides standardized templates.

- **Central information platform:** The AI Office is introducing a central information platform that will provide all stakeholders in the EU with easy-to-use information on the AI Act.

- **Information campaigns:** The campaigns are intended to raise awareness of the obligations resulting from the AI Act.

- **Procurement procedures:** The AI Office evaluates and promotes the consolidation of best practices in procurement procedures involving AI systems.

Microenterprises

Art. 63 AI Act provides for further simplifications for micro-enterprises. These can include certain elements in accordance with Art. 17 AI Act (quality management system see section 3.3.2.3.8 Obligations of Providers, Deployers and other Parties involved) in a simplified manner. To this end, the EU Commission will draw up guidelines that take into account the needs of micro-enterprises on the one hand, but also the level of protection or the need to comply with the requirements relating to high-risk AI. However, this facilitation must not be read as an exemption from the obligations under Art. 9 et seq. AI Act.

Sanctions

According to Art. 99 AI Act, sanctions must be effective, proportionate and dissuasive. At the same time, however, the interests and in particular the economic survival of SMEs and start-ups must also be taken into account. When imposing fines, the lower amount from paragraphs 3, 4 and 5 must therefore be imposed in accordance with Art. 99 para. 6 AI Act (see section 3.10). Pursuant to Recital 168 AI Act, fines are assessed on a case-by-case basis and the relevant circumstances of the situation must be taken into account, in particular the nature, gravity and duration of the infringement and the consequences as well as the size of the provider.

3.12.2 Checklist: Launching a New AI System in Accordance with the AI Act

The following is a rough outline of the questions that an SME or start-up should address when it wants to market or commission a new AI system. The test steps must be documented in any case. The focus is on the necessary steps in accordance with the AI Act.

If an AI system pursuant to Art. 3 no. 1 AI Act exists?

An AI system is *"a machine-based system that is designed to operate with varying levels of autonomy and that may exhibit adaptiveness after deployment, and that, for explicit or implicit objectives, infers, from the input it receives, how to generate outputs such as predictions, content, recommendations, or decisions that can influence physical or virtual environments"* (see in detail section 3.1).

- If **yes**, continue.
- If **no**, end here.

Does the AI system use personal data?

See Art. 4 no. 1 GDPR, according to which personal data is *"any information relating to an identified or identifiable natural person ('data subject'); an identifiable natural person is one who can be identified, directly or indirectly, in particular by reference to an identifier such as a name, an identification number, location data, an online identifier or to one or more factors specific to the physical, physiological, genetic, mental, economic, cultural or social identity of that natural person"*.

It does not matter whether personal data is required for development, testing, training and/or use.

- If **yes**, compliance with the GDPR required, see chapter 4.
- If **no**, e. g. when using anonymized data, no compliance with the GDPR necessary.

Prohibited or High-risk AI Systems

Is a prohibited AI system pursuant to Art. 5 AI Act present?

Prohibited AI systems are, for example, AI systems that deliberately manipulate or deceive and cause people to make a decision that they would not otherwise have made, exploitation of vulnerable groups of people, social scoring, etc. (see section 3.2.1 for details).

- If **yes**, end here, as the AI system may very likely not be put into operation or placed on the market.

- If **no**, continue.

Is a high-risk AI pursuant to Art. 6 Act present?

A high-risk AI system exists either if it is a product or a safety component in accordance with a harmonization regulation in Annex I (list of harmonized legislation) or if it is an AI system in accordance with Annex III AI Act (list of "use cases") (see section 3.3.2.2 for details on classification).

- If **yes**, is there an exception?

  Art. 6 para. 3 AI Act sets out a number of exceptions as to when a high-risk AI system does not exist, e. g. if the AI system only performs a narrowly defined procedural task or if it is intended to recognize patterns without replacing or influencing previously completed human assessments. However, profiling of natural persons always leads to classification as high-risk AI. See section 3.3.1 for the exceptions in detail.

- If there is a high-risk AI and no exception applies, see the following section on compliance and section 3.3.2.3 on obligations and requirements.

- Documentation of the test and the result, regardless of whether a high-risk AI is present or not.

Is a Fundamental Rights Assessment (FRA) necessary?

For certain high-risk AI systems, a fundamental rights impact assessment must be carried out in accordance with Art. 27 AI Act:

- AI-systems listed in Annex III in the case of bodies governed by public law and private bodies providing public services

- AI-systems according to Annex III No. 5 lit. b and c (accessibility and use of basic private and basic public services and benefits), if it is a deployer, regardless of whether it is a body governed by public law and private bodies providing public services

Exceptions:

- Annex III no. 2, critical infrastructure (no fundamental rights impact assessment necessary)

For implementation, see section 3.4, Fundamental Rights Impact Assessment.

According to which role does the company or start-up operate (cf. Art. 3 AI Act)

- Provider is a *"a natural or legal person, public authority, agency or other body that develops an AI system or a general-purpose AI model or that has an AI system or a general-purpose AI model developed and places it on the market or puts the AI system into service under its own name or trademark, whether for payment or free of charge"* in accordance with Art. 3 no. 3 AI Act.

- Deployer According to Art. 3 no. 4 AI Act, a deployer is a *"a natural or legal person, public authority, agency or other body using an AI system under its authority except where the AI system is used in the course of a personal non-professional activity"*.

- Authorized representative pursuant to Art. 3 no. 5 AI Act is *"a natural or legal person located or established in the Union who has received and accepted a written mandate from a provider of an AI system or a general-purpose AI model to, respectively, perform and carry out on its behalf the obligations and procedures established by this Regulation"*.

- Importer according to Art. 3 no. 6 AI Act is *"a natural or legal person located or established in the Union that places on the market an AI system that bears the name or trademark of a natural or legal person established in a third country"*.

- Distributors According to Art. 3 no.7 AI Act is a *"a natural or legal person in the supply chain, other than the provider or the importer, that makes an AI system available on the Union market"*.

- Operator according to Art. 3 no. 8 AI Act is *"a provider, product manufacturer, deployer, authorised representative, importer or distributor"*.

See section 3.1.2 for details of the roles.

Establishing compliance of a high-risk AI system (see Art. 8 et seq. AI Act)

- General obligations of high-risk AI systems pursuant to Art. 8 et seq. AI Act, see section 3.3.2.3 for details

  - Risk management system in accordance with Art. 9 AI Act

  - Data and data governance in accordance with Art. 10 AI AI Act

  - Technical documentation in accordance with Art. 11 AI Act (see exceptions for SMEs and start-ups: Use of the simplified form of the EU Commission)

  - Recording obligations pursuant to Art. 12 AI Act

  - Transparency and provision of information to deployers in accordance with Art. 13 AI Act

  - Human supervision in accordance with Art. 14 AI Act

  - Accuracy, robustness and cybersecurity in accordance with Art. 15 AI Act

■ Compliance depending on the role

■ **Provider, see Art. 16 AI Act**

– Quality management system in accordance with Art. 17 AI Act

– Retention of documentation in accordance with Art. 18 AI Act

– Protocols in accordance with Art. 19 AI Act

– Corrective measures and duty to inform pursuant to Art. 20 AI Act

– Cooperation with the competent authorities pursuant to Art. 21 AI Act

– If applicable, role of the authorized representative of the provider pursuant to Art. 22 AI Act

– If applicable, agreement with third parties from which AI system or parts thereof originate, see Art. 25 para. 4 AI Act

– Compliance with harmonized standards in accordance with Art. 40 AI Act, see section 3.5.1

– If applicable, conformity assessment procedure according to Art. 42 AI Act, see section 3.5.2

– EU Declaration of Conformity in accordance with Art. 47 AI Act, see section 3.5.4

– Registration of the high-risk AI system in accordance with Art. 49 AI Act

– If the AI system interacts with natural persons, compliance with the transparency obligations pursuant to Art. 50 para. 1 AI Act, see section 3.6

– Compliance with transparency obligations in the case of "deep fakes" pursuant to Art. 50 para. 2 AI Act, see section 3.6

– Monitoring of the AI system after placing on the market in accordance with Art. 72 AI Act

■ **Importer, see Art. 23 AI Act**

– If the AI system or parts thereof originate from third parties, see Responsibilities along the AI value chain pursuant to Art. 25 AI Act

■ **Traders, see Art. 24 AI Act**

– If the AI system or parts thereof originate from third parties, see Responsibilities along the AI value chain pursuant to Art. 25 AI Act

■ **Deployer, see Art. 26 AI Act**

– If the AI system or parts thereof originate from third parties, see responsibilities along the AI value chain pursuant to Art. 25 AI Act

– Technical and organizational measures for the operation of the AI system, ensuring AI literacy, etc. (see section 3.2)

– Registration of the high-risk AI system in accordance with Art. 49 AI Act (see section 3.5.5)

– Transparency obligations for emotion recognition systems or systems for biometric categorization pursuant to Art. 50 para. 3 AI Act (see section 3.6)

   – Compliance with transparency obligations for "deep fakes" pursuant to Art. 50 para. 4 AI Act, see section 3.6

   – If applicable, right to explanation pursuant to Art. 86 AI Act when the AI system makes decisions about individuals

AI Systems with General Purpose

Is an AI system with a general purpose or GPAI (General-Purpose Artificial Intelligence) pursuant to Art. 3 no. 63 AI Act present?

GPAI is an *"AI model, including where such an AI model is trained with a large amount of data using self-supervision at scale, that displays significant generality and is capable of competently performing a wide range of distinct tasks regardless of the way the model is placed on the market and that can be integrated into a variety of downstream systems or applications, except AI models that are used for research, development or prototyping activities before they are placed on the market".* Currently, many systems are GPAI, especially generative AI for texts, images, programming code, etc.

- If **yes**, see section 3.7 (GPAI) and section 3.5 (Harmonized Standards, Conformity Assessment, Certificates and Registration)

- If **yes**, sub-question whether there is a GPAI with so-called "systemic risk":

  According to Art. 3 no. 65 AI Act, a systemic risk is *"a risk that is specific to the high-impact capabilities of general-purpose AI models, having a significant impact on the Union market due to their reach, or due to actual or reasonably foreseeable negative effects on public health, safety, public security, fundamental rights, or the society as a whole, that can be propagated at scale across the value chain".*

- If **yes**, see below for the obligations or section 3.7 GPAI.

Establishing compliance of a GPAI model in accordance with Art. 51 AI Act (see section 3.7)

- Notification to the EU Commission pursuant to Art. 52 AI Act

- Obligations of **providers** pursuant to Art. 53 AI Act

  - Technical documentation of the model (see Annex XI AI Act)

  - Information and documentation for downstream providers

  - Cooperation with the EU Commission (see in particular Art. 91 AI Act) or competent authorities

  - Use of harmonized standards in accordance with Art. 56 AI Act or practical guides to demonstrate compliance with Art. 53 para. 1 AI Act

  - Use of delegated acts pursuant to Art. 97 AI Act to demonstrate compliance with Annex XI AI Act

  - Implementing measures provided by the EU Commission in accordance with Art. 93 AI Act

- Obligations of **authorized representatives** of providers of GPAI models pursuant to Art. 54 AI Act
  - (Only applicable if the provider is established in a third country!)
  - Written appointment of an authorized representative
  - Review of the technical documentation
  - Provision of a copy of the technical documentation
  - Provision of all documents required to prove compliance with the obligations under the AI Act
  - Cooperation with AI Office and competent authorities
  - Obligation of the authorized representative to terminate the order if he is of the opinion or has reason to believe that the provider is in breach of his obligations under the AI Act, including the obligation to inform the AI Office

Additional obligations for GPAIs with systemic risk pursuant to Art. 53 AI Act

- Model evaluation
- Assessing and mitigating potential systemic risks
- Information on serious incidents and possible remedial measures, including reporting to the AI office and, if applicable, the competent authorities
- Appropriate cyber security measures
- Use of harmonized standards in accordance with Art. 56 AI Act or practical guides to demonstrate compliance with Art. 55 para. 1 AI Act

Sources

[1] Commission Recommendation of 6 May 2003 concerning the definition of micro, small and medium-sized enterprises (Text with EEA relevance) (notified under document number C(2003) 1422). OJ 124, 2003. Legislative Body: COM; *https://eur-lex.europa.eu/legal-content/EN/TXT/?uri=CELEX:32003H0361 – last accessed: 2025/04/11*

4 Data Protection

Gabriele Bolek-Fügl

In today's world, where humans and machines are increasingly working together and producing large amounts of data, compliance with the General Data Protection Regulation (GDPR) [1] is one of the biggest challenges and opportunities for developers, companies and society. This central EU regulation, which came into force in all member states on May 25, 2018, regulates the processing of personal data that is either fully or partially automated, as well as the non-automated processing of personal data that is stored or is intended to be stored in a file system (Art. 2 para. 1 GDPR).

> ☑ The main objective is to standardize and strengthen the data protection rights of individuals in the digital age without hindering innovation. Another aspect is to facilitate the free movement of data within the European market (Art. 1 GDPR).

The GDPR replaces the previous Data Protection Directive from 1995 and brings significant changes for all companies and public institutions, as the regulation applies to all organizations that process personal data, regardless of size, turnover, company form or industry. This applies to individual tradespeople as well as multinational corporations.

Although the GDPR is an EU regulation, it has a global impact. Any company worldwide that offers services in the EU or processes data of EU citizens must comply with these regulations, regardless of where the organization has its headquarter.

Enforcement of the GDPR is carried out by the local data protection authorities in each EU member state. These have the power to conduct investigations and impose sanctions. The regulation empowers the national data protection authority to impose significant penalties on organizations for violations including fines of up to 20 million euros or 4% of annual global turnover, whichever is higher.

When processing data using artificial intelligence, the GDPR imposes the same high standards that apply to all other types of data processing. These include compliance with the processing principles, the need for a lawful basis for processing, the protection of the rights of data subjects and specific rules for automated decision-making and profiling.

It is therefore advisable to involve data protection experts in the AI project. Have data protection officers been appointed, they should be part of the project team from the beginning.

The central importance of data protection in the context of AI arises from several scenarios:

1. **Training and operation of AI with personal data**

   AI systems often process large amounts of personal data in order to learn, recognize patterns and make decisions. The GDPR regulates how such data may be collected, stored, processed and transferred in order to protect the privacy of individuals.

2. **Transparency and accountability**

   The GDPR requires organizations to be transparent about how and for what purpose personal data is processed. In the case of AI systems, this means that the underlying algorithms and data processing procedures must be disclosed to a certain extent in order to ensure compliance with the law.

3. **Right to explanation**

   The GDPR gives individuals the right to explanations for automated decisions that affect them. This is particularly relevant for AI decisions, which are often based on complex calculations and are difficult for laypersons to understand. Companies must therefore be able to explain how their AI systems work.

4. **Privacy by Design and Privacy by Default**

   The GDPR requires data protection to be integrated into the development of products and services from the outset. For AI, this means that data protection considerations must be taken into account right from the start of system development.

5. **Right to erasure and correction**

   Individuals have the right to request the deletion or correction of their data. AI systems must therefore be designed in such a way that they can meet these requirements. This can be technically challenging, because even through pseudonymization of the data, it is still personal data according to Recital 26 GDPR.

6. **Risk of discrimination**

   AI can consciously or unconsciously reinforce prejudice and discrimination if it is trained on biased data. However, the GDPR aims to promote fairness and equal treatment in the handling of personal data. Correct implementation is of great importance in the development and use of AI systems.

> In summary, the GDPR aims to shape the development and use of technologies in such a way that privacy and fundamental rights are protected. The Regulation creates a legal framework that balances the protection of individuals and the promotion of innovative technologies, including AI.

4.1 General Requirements of the GDPR

The GDPR is therefore based on several key principles that govern the processing of personal data. These principles require organizations to process personal data in a lawful, fair and transparent manner, to use it only for specified purposes and to ensure that the data is kept accurately and only for as long as necessary.

Not all GDPR requirements can be broadly discussed in this book, but the following aspects in particular are relevant when AI is used to process personal data:

1. **Principles for the processing of personal data**

   All processing activities must comply with the principles of the GDPR, such as lawfulness, fairness, transparency, purpose limitation, data minimization, accuracy, storage limitation, integrity and confidentiality as well as accountability (Art. 5 GDPR).

2. **Lawfulness of processing**

   Any processing of personal data must be based on a legitimate legal basis, such as the consent of the data subject, the necessity for the performance of a contract, legal obligations, the protection of vital interests, the performance of a task carried out in the public interest or the pursuit of legitimate interests (Art. 6 GDPR).

3. **Obligation to provide information where personal data is collected**

   If personal data is collected, the data subject must be informed of the name and contact details of the controller. In addition, the purpose of processing, the legal basis and the duration of data storage must be explained (Art. 13–14 GDPR).

4. **Rights of the data subjects**

   Individuals whose data is processed have specific rights under the GDPR, including the right of access, rectification, erasure ("right to be forgotten"), restriction of processing, data portability and objection. When AI processes personal data, these rights must be guaranteed (Art. 15–21 GDPR).

5. **Automated decision making including profiling**

   Data subjects have the right not to be subject to a decision based solely on auto-mated processing which produces legal effects concerning them or similarly sig-nificantly affects them. There are exceptions to this right if, for example, the auto-mated decision is necessary for the conclusion or performance of a contract, is based on legislation or is made with explicit consent (Art. 22 GDPR).

6. **Data protection through data protection-friendly design and default settings**

   When developing and implementing AI systems, data protection principles must be taken into account and integrated from the beginning (Art. 25 GDPR).

7. **Responsibility for processing in compliance with the law**

   A "controller" means any natural or legal person, public authority, agency or other body which, alone or jointly with others, determines the purposes and means of processing of personal data pursuant to Art. 4 para. 7 GDPR. This person is there-fore also responsible for the implementation of all the requirements described above and must prove this in case of doubt.

Developers and users of IT and AI systems are obliged to ensure that their applica-tions and data processing processes comply with the requirements of the GDPR. This can be achieved, for example, by:

- the detailed documentation of all processing steps
- the presentation of the data used and data flows during processing

the entry in the data processing register of the company using the data

- the implementation of data protection impact assessments
- ensuring transparency in automated decision-making processes
- the implementation of adequate technical and organizational measures ("TOM") to protect personal data from unauthorized access, loss, destruction or damage. These include
  - Encryption
  - Anonymization
  - Regular security checks
  - Access controls

Let us now look in more detail at the impact on the use of AI in the company of the seven basic requirements for the use of personal data as outlined above.

4.1.1 The Principles for Processing Personal Data

The principles for the processing of personal data under Art. 5 GDPR form the foundation for the handling of personal data, including processing by artificial intelligence. These principles can therefore be applied in the context of AI processing:

1. **Lawfulness, processing in good faith, transparency**

   Data processing must be founded on a lawful basis, such as the consent of the data subject, the necessity for a contract or legal requirements. In the context of AI, this means that users must be clearly informed about how their data is processed by AI systems, including the purposes and methods of processing.

   Recital 58 GDPR clarifies that all information addressed to the public or the data subject must be concise, easily accessible and easy to understand and that clear and simple language and, where appropriate, additional visualization must be used.

2. **Purpose limitation**

   Data may only be collected for specified, explicit and legitimate purposes and may not be further processed in a manner incompatible with those purposes. If data is to be used for training of AI systems, a check must first be carried out to establish the basis on which the data was collected and stored (for details, see also section 4.1.2). AI systems must also be designed in such a way that they only process data that is relevant and necessary for the specific purpose for which it was collected.

   Further processing for archiving purposes in the public interest, scientific or historical research purposes or statistical purposes (Art. 89 para. 1 GDPR) may be exempt from incompatibility with the original purposes.

3. **Data minimization**

   Only as much data as necessary may be collected and processed. In the development and use of AI, this means that only the minimum amount of data required for the specific processing purpose may be used.

   There is a particular area of tension with AI here. According to Sartor [2], the principle of data minimization should always be considered in the context of proportionality. It allows the inclusion of additional personal data in processing operations if the resulting benefits outweigh the potential risks for the data subjects. The potential benefits of future data processing may also justify the storage of this data, provided that appropriate security measures, such as pseudonymization and other protection mechanisms, are implemented. In addition, the processing of personal data for purely statistical purposes may be subject to looser minimization requirements (see above, 2. Purpose limitation).

4. **Accuracy**

   The data must be accurate and, where necessary, kept up to date. AI systems based on the analysis of personal data must include mechanisms to ensure the accuracy of the data and to either correct or delete incorrect data.

According to Sartor [2], this also applies to personal data used as input for AI systems, especially when personal data is used to make inferences or decisions about data subjects. Inaccurate data can expose data subjects to harm if they are viewed and treated in a way that does not reflect their identity.

In large language models, this is a challenge that cannot be easily solved. OpenAI[1)] states that "factual accuracy in large-scale language models remains an area of active research". To clarify the legal requirements, noyb filed a complaint against OpenAI with the Austrian data protection authority in April 2024. [3] [4] [5] Further details on this process are described in section 4.6.

"Technology must follow the legal requirements, not the other way around"

Maartje de Graaf, data protection lawyer at noyb

5. **Storage limitation**

   Data must not be stored in an identifiable form for longer than necessary for the processing purposes. AI applications must therefore take precautions to anonymize or delete personal data once the purpose of processing has been achieved.

   If the data subjects' information is only considered as input for a training dataset and not used for predictions or decisions regarding individuals, simplified conditions apply. This is supported by Recital 162 GDPR, which states that such data processing is primarily intended for the production of statistical surveys or results. However, these results must not be personal, but must provide aggregated data that is not used to make decisions that affect individuals.

6. **Integrity and confidentiality (Data security)**

   Processing must be carried out in a manner that ensures appropriate security for personal data, including protection against unauthorized or unlawful processing, accidental loss, destruction or damage. For AI systems, this approach must be included in the design of the model to ensure data integrity and privacy protection.

7. **Accountability**

   The controller for data processing must be able to demonstrate compliance with the above principles. For AI, this means that developers and deployers must document how their systems are designed and operated to ensure compliance with the GDPR.

---

[1] OpenAI Inc, San Francisco, is the manufacturer and deployer of the well-known chatbot ChatGPT

In the context of AI processing, these principles require careful planning and implementation of AI systems to ensure that they comply with data protection regulations. This includes, among other things, developing ethical guidelines for AI, conducting data protection impact assessments and establishing procedures to safeguard the rights of data subjects.

When creating internal guidelines Table 4.1 can provide support.

Table 4.1 Content for corporate policies relating to AI and data protection

Principle	Explanation
Lawfulness	▪ Is the processing based on a legal requirement? See also Art. 6 para. 1 GDPR ▪ Proof and documentation of the legal basis. ▪ Otherwise, proof of the required consent of the data subject. Note: Consent is not limited in time, but can be withdrawn at any time. A process for withdrawing consent must therefore be implemented.
Fairness	▪ Informing data subjects about the existence of data processing. where data is collected data, data subjects must be fully and correctly informed about the conditions of this data processing activity.
Transparency	▪ Data subjects must be informed about the current and future processing of their data. ▪ The purpose of processing must be described. The information must be easy to find and written in a language understandable to non-experts.
Purpose limitation	▪ Processing of personal data only for specific, clearly defined and legitimate purposes. ▪ Documentation of the purposes for the processing of personal data. ▪ Definition and documentation of the purpose of AI data processing. ▪ Processing must not be carried out in a way that is incompatible with the defined (and communicated) purposes. For extended data processing, consent may have to be obtained from the data subjects or the data must be anonymized.
Data minimization	▪ Collection and processing must be directly relevant and adequate for the specified purpose. ▪ The amount of personal data processed must be limited to what is absolutely necessary. Be careful when "enriching" or supplementing or linking the data with data from other sources (documentation of lawfulness).

Table 4.1 Content for corporate policies relating to AI and data protection *(continued)*

Principle	Explanation
Accuracy	▪ Personal data must be kept factually correct and, if necessary for processing activity, up to date. ▪ Incorrect personal data must be deleted or corrected immediately with regard to the processing purposes. ▪ Have mechanisms been implemented in the AI system that can identify and correct incorrect data?
Storage limitation	▪ Storage in a form which permits identification of data subjects only for as long as is necessary for the original processing purposes. ▪ Longer storage of the data is only possible for legally defined exceptions. ▪ After the period of use has expired, data must be deleted or anonymized or alternatively consent must be obtained from the data subject. ▪ If consent is withdrawn by the data subject, the data record must be deleted or anonymized (no storage of a possible in the system). The data must always be correct, even with long storage periods, and integrity must be maintained.
Integrity	▪ The integrity of the data must be maintained during processing activity. ▪ Data integrity must be ensured over the entire life cycle of data processing activity (caution with long storage periods). ▪ Implementation of measures that can document and prove integrity (examples include encryption, hash check value, anonymization, etc.) regular security checks, access according to the need-to-know principle, etc.).
Confidentiality	▪ Protection of personal data from unauthorized access, disclosure, modification or transfer. ▪ Implementation of protective measures (TOMs) against unintentional loss, destruction or damage to data.
Accountability	▪ The controller must be able to actively demonstrate compliance with the above principles. ▪ Sufficient documentation, procedures and measures to demonstrate compliance with the principles. ▪ Documentation of the successful implementation of internal controls to demonstrate compliance with the principles. ▪ Regular review of controls by internal auditors/internal audit/data protection officer/compliance officer. ▪ If necessary, regular certification by independent third parties.

4.1.2 Lawfulness of Processing

The lawfulness of processing of personal data is defined in Art. 6 para. 2 GDPR specifies the various conditions under which processing is lawful:

1. **Consent**

   The data subject has given their consent to the processing of their personal data for one or more specific purposes.

   For AI applications, obtaining clear, informed and voluntary consent from data subjects is particularly important, especially if the processing is extensive or involves sensitive data. Consent must be obtained specifically for the processing activities enabled by AI.

2. **Contract fulfillment**

   The processing activity is necessary for the performance of a contract to which the data subject is party or in order to take steps at the request of the data subject prior to entering into a contract.

   When using AI systems to fulfill contracts, such as personalized recommendations in e-commerce, there must be a clear need for processing for the contractually agreed service.

3. **Legal obligation**

   The processing activity is necessary for compliance with a legal obligation to which the controller is subject to..

   If AI systems are used for this purpose, such as fraud detection systems in banking, they must precisely meet the legal requirements and the processing must be necessary to fulfill these obligations.

4. **Vital interests**

   The processing activity is necessary in order to protect the vital interests of the data subject or of another natural person.

   In this case, the use of AI requires particularly careful consideration, especially in situations where the data subject is not in a position to give consent.

5. **Public interest or exercise of official authority**

   The processing activity is necessary for the performance of a task carried out in the public interest or in the exercise of official authority vested in the controller.

   AI applications in the public sector must be clearly justified in the public interest or exercised within the framework of public authority.

6. **Legitimate interest**

   The processing activity is necessary for the purposes of the legitimate interests pursued by the controller or by a third party, except where such interests are overridden by the interests or fundamental rights and freedoms of the data subject which require protection of personal data.

If AI systems are operated on the basis of the legitimate interests of the controller or a third party, careful consideration is required. It must be ensured that the interests, fundamental rights and freedoms of the data subject, which require the protection of personal data, do not prevail. Transparency of processing and the possibility for data subjects to object are particularly important here.

It is important that the controller carefully selects and documents the appropriate legal basis for data processing to ensure compliance with the GDPR. The legal basis chosen must be specific, explicit and legitimate, and the processing must be limited to the achievement of the specified purpose.

Art. 6 para. 4 GDPR sets out the conditions under which the processing of personal data for purposes that go beyond the original purpose of collection is permitted. This paragraph provides a guideline for assessing whether the new data processing is compatible with the original purpose by taking various criteria into account.

> In particular, it is required that various factors must be taken into account when assessing whether further processing for a new purpose is permissible:
>
>   ▫ How closely are the purposes linked? Is the new purpose a logical continuation of the original purpose?
>   ▫ What expectations did the data subjects have regarding possible further processing at the time of data collection?
>   ▫ Is it particularly sensitive data for which stricter protection measures are required?
>   ▫ Could further processing have a negative impact on the persons concerned?
>
> If suitable protective measures such as pseudonymization applied to protect the rights and freedoms of data subjects?

Art. 6 para. 4 GDPR thus enables flexible handling of the further processing of personal data, provided that the compatibility of the new processing purpose is carefully examined and justified. This provision contributes to legal certainty by providing clear criteria for assessing the permissibility of further processing operations while ensuring the protection of data subjects.

4.1.3 Obligation to Provide Information where Personal Data is Collected

The duty to inform when collecting personal data where personal data is collected is set out in Art. 13 and 14 of the GDPR. These obligations aim to ensure transparency in the processing of personal data and to enable data subjects to effectively exercise their rights. The requirements differ slightly depending on whether the data is collected directly from the data subject (Art. 13 GDPR) or not (Art. 14 GDPR).

In the context of artificial intelligence, these information obligations become even more important, as AI systems often carry out complex data processing operations that are not always easy for data subjects to understand. The following areas are essential:

I. **Direct data collection (Art. 13 GDPR)**

    In the case of direct data collection, the controller must must provide the data subject with comprehensive information at the time of data collection:

    i.   Identity and contact details of the controller and, where applicable, of the controller's representative and the data protection officer if available

    ii. Purposes of the data processing and the legal basis for it, if applicable, further explanation of the legitimate interests of the controller

    iii. Recipients or categories of recipients of the personal data

    iv. Information on whether the data is transferred to a third country and which protection mechanism is applied

    v.   Storage duration or criteria for determining this duration

    vi. Information on the rights of the data subject, including the right of access, rectification, erasure, restriction of processing, right to object and right to lodge a complaint with a supervisory authority

    vii. The existence of an automated decision-making process including profiling and meaningful information about the logic involved, as well as the significance and envisaged consequences of such processing for the data subject

II. **Indirect data collection (Art. 14 GDPR)**

    If personal data is not collected directly from the data subject, similar information obligations apply as in Art. 13 GDPR, but with some adjustments. In addition, the controller must, for example, provide information about the source of the data.

> **Specific considerations when using AI**
>
> When using AI, controllers should place particular emphasis on the transparency of data processing. This includes:
>
> - Clear explanations of how AI systems process data and make decisions
> - Information about the training data records used to train the AI, especially if this could have an impact on the data subject
> - Details of measures taken to address inaccuracies, bias and discrimination by AI systems

Compliance with information obligations when processing personal data by AI systems not only contributes to legal compliance, but also strengthens the trust of users and data subjects in the technology.

4.1.4 Rights of the data subjects

The GDPR strengthens the rights of individuals by giving them control over their personal data. These rights are particularly important in the context of processing by artificial intelligence, as AI systems often process large amounts of data and make complex decisions that have a significant impact on individuals. The main rights and their implications when using AI are outlined below:

1. **Right to information (Art. 15 GDPR)**

   Data subjects have the right to know whether their data is being processed and, if this is the case, to obtain access to this data and additional information.

   In the context of AI, this means that individuals can request information about how their data is used in an AI system, including a description of the logic behind automated decisions (Art. 15 para. 1 lit h GDPR).

2. **Right to rectification (Art. 16 GDPR)**

   This right enables individuals to request the rectification of inaccurate personal data concerning them. AI systems that process incomplete data could make incorrect decisions, with negative consequences for the data subject.

3. **Right to deletion ("Right to be forgotten", Art. 17 GDPR)**

   Under certain conditions, individuals can request the deletion of their data. For AI applications that process personal data, mechanisms must be in place to delete data at the request of the data subject, especially if the data is no longer needed for the original purposes or consent has been withdrawn.

4. **Right to restriction of processing (Art. 18 GDPR)**

   Data subjects may request the restriction of processing of their data under certain circumstances, for example if the accuracy of the data is disputed. For AI systems, this may mean that certain data may temporarily not be used for decision-making processes.

5. **Right to data portability (Art. 20 GDPR)**

   Individuals have the right to receive their data in a structured, commonly used and machine-readable format and to transmit those data to another controller. In the AI context, this allows users to transfer their data from one service to another, which is particularly relevant for services that use AI for personalized recommendations.

6. **Right to object (Art. 21 GDPR)**

   Data subjects have the right to object to the processing of their personal data at any time, in particular if this processing is based on the legitimate interests of the controller or for direct marketing purposes. When using AI, this means that individuals can object to the processing of their data by AI systems, particularly in connection with profiling in the case of direct marketing (Art. 21 para. 2 GDPR).

The implementation of these rights in AI systems requires careful planning and technical measures to ensure that the systems can meet the requirements. This can be achieved through transparent data processing practices, the provision of user interfaces for the exercise of rights and the integration of data protection principles into the design process of AI systems.

4.2 Privacy by Design

Art. 25 GDPR is a central element for the promotion of data protection in the development and use phase of products, services and systems. This article is particularly relevant when using artificial intelligence, as it encourages both developers and users of AI systems to integrate data protection measures into their systems from the outset and to establish data protection-friendly settings as standard. The key aspects are:

■ **Privacy by Design**

This principle requires that data protection is already taken into account during the development and design of processing procedures. In the context of AI, this means that data protection considerations must be an integral part of the design process of AI systems, from the selection of the data used to train the AI to the algorithms that make decisions.

■ **Privacy by Default**

This principle requires that only personal data that is absolutely necessary for the specific purpose is processed. For AI systems, this means that they should be configured by default to respect privacy, for example by practising data minimization, restricting the collection and storage of data to what is absolutely necessary and limiting the accessibility of the data.

Art. 25 GDPR underlines the importance of proactive and preventive data protection. When using AI, this means that data protection measures must be carefully planned and implemented - at every stage of the life cycle of an AI system, from data collection and model training through to the practical application of AI. The principles of "privacy by design" and "privacy by default" serve to ensure the protection of privacy and strengthen the trust of users and the public in AI systems.

4.2.1 Implementation

The implementation of the principles of "privacy by design" and "privacy by default" in accordance with the General Data Protection Regulation (GDPR) and the consideration of the AI Act are crucial for the development and operation of AI applications.

1. **Privacy by Design**

   "Privacy by Design" means that data protection is integrated into the design and architecture of AI systems from the start. This includes several aspects:

   - Data protection-friendly technologies: Use of technologies that facilitate data minimization such as data anonymization and pseudonymizationto avoid the identification of individuals.

   - Minimize data collection: Only collect the data that is absolutely necessary. AI models should be trained with the minimum amount of data required to perform the task.

   - Security: Implementation of robust security measures to protect data from unauthorized access and misuse. This includes encryption, secure data transmission and access controls.

   - Transparency and accountability: Ensure that the function and data processing of AI applications are understandable and comprehensible for users.

2. **Privacy by Default**

   "Privacy by Default" means that the most secure data protection settings are activated by default without the user having to make any settings themselves. For AI applications, this implies

   - Data economy by default: By default, only the data that is absolutely necessary for the specific function of the AI is processed.

   - Restricted data access: Standard restrictions on who can access which data and under what circumstances, especially for sensitive information.

   - Automatic deletion: Data that is no longer required must be deleted automatically in order to minimize the risk of data breaches.

3. **AI Act**

   The AI Act, which is specifically aimed at artificial intelligence, supplements the GDPR by introducing specific regulations for AI systems:

   - Risk-based classification: AI systems are classified according to their risk to the rights and freedoms of individuals. High-risk applications are subject to stricter requirements.

   - Transparency obligations: AI providers must ensure that users are informed about how the AI works and the decision-making factors.

   - Monitoring and compliance: Adhering to ethical guidelines and ensuring that AI systems are developed and operated in accordance with legal requirements.

So how can these principles be put into practice? Providers, product manufacturers and other developers should always develop their AI applications in a project with people with diverse knowledge. This includes:

- Early involvement of a data protection expert in the design of the AI

- Carrying out a data protection impact assessment to identify and mitigate potential risks

- When developing AI systems, data protection principles such as data minimization, purpose limitation and transparency must be taken into account from the outset.

- AI systems should be designed in such a way that they limit the collection and processing of personal data to what is necessary to achieve the purpose of processing.

- Continuous documentation of the functionality and monitoring of AI systems in operation to prove compliance. Developers and providers of AI must be able to demonstrate how data protection principles have been integrated into their systems in order to meet the requirements of the GDPR.

Art. 25 GDPR emphasizes the importance of proactive and preventive data protection. When using AI, this requires careful planning and implementation of data protection measures in all phases of the life cycle of an AI system, from data collection to the training of models and the use of AI in practice. Compliance with "privacy by design" and "privacy by default" should ensure that AI systems protect privacy and strengthen the trust of users and the public.

4.2.2 Responsibility for Processing in Compliance with the Law

Art. 4 no. 7 GDPR defines the term "controller". It is defined as the natural or legal person, public authority, agency or other body which, alone or jointly with others, determines the purposes and means of processing of personal data. The controller is therefore the primary decision-making authority as to why (purpose) and how (means) personal data is processed.

In the context of artificial intelligence, the role of the controller is particularly important, as AI systems often carry out complex data processing activities that can have far-reaching implications for the privacy and rights of data subjects. Here are some specific aspects that need to be considered:

1. **Decision-making in the development of AI**

   Providers and deployers of AI systems that use personal data to train AI models or provide AI-supported services are typically considered data controllers, as they decide on the use of these technologies and the use of the data.

2. **Transparency and accountability**

   As controllers, AI providers and deployers must ensure that their processing activities are transparent and comply with the data protection principles of the

GDPR. They must document which data is processed for which purposes, how the processing is carried out and must be able to demonstrate compliance with the GDPR to the supervisory authorities.

3. **Impact assessment and protective measures**

   Data controllers who use AI systems must carry out data protection impact assessments if the type of processing could pose a high risk to the rights and freedoms of data subjects. They must take appropriate technical and organizational measures to mitigate the risks and ensure the protection of personal data.

4. **Compliance with the rights of data subjects**

   The controller must ensure that the rights of data subjects, such as the right of access, rectification, erasure and objection (Art. 15–21 GDPR), are fully guaranteed. When using AI, particular care must be taken to ensure that data subjects can exercise their rights effectively, especially in connection with automated decisions. When designing the AI system, these obligations must therefore become the basis for the implementation requirement.

Conclusion

In the context of AI, Art. 4 no. 7 GDPR emphasizes the central role of the controller in ensuring data protection and compliance with the GDPR. AI providers and deployers must take a proactive approach to integrate data protection principles into their systems, ensure transparency of data processing and protect the rights of data subjects. Identifying and taking responsibility for AI-supported data processing activities is crucial to promote user trust and legal compliance.

4.3 Requirements for Testing Data

The application of the GDPR to testing data for artificial intelligence poses specific requirements, especially if this data contains personal information. Here are some of the most important requirements that can be addressed using the following points:

Lawfulness of data processing

According to the GDPR, the processing of personal data must be carried out on a lawful basis.

For AI testing data, this means that there must be a clear legal basis for the collection and use of this data, such as the express consent of the data subjects, the performance of a contract, legal obligations or legitimate interests (see Art. 6 GDPR). In case of doubt, the data must be anonymized before the test run.

Data minimization and purpose limitation

The GDPR requires that only as much data is processed as is absolutely necessary (data minimization) and that the data is only used for specified, explicit and legitimate purposes.

For AI testing data, this means that only the amount of information required for the specific test objective of the AI may be used. Furthermore, the data may not be used for other purposes.

Transparency and information obligations

Organizations must be transparent and proactive about how and why personal data is used.

In the case of AI tests, this includes the provision of an information document on the intended data processing to the data subjects. Additional data protection information can be created for this specific purpose or the existing information can be supplemented.

Data security

The GDPR requires that appropriate technical and organizational measures are taken to protect personal data.

For AI testing data, this means that security measures such as encryption, access controls and regular security checks must be implemented to protect the data from unauthorized access or loss. Wherever possible, the testing data should also be anonymized or at least pseudonymized to adequately protect it from the developers and testers as well. This reduces the risk that the data can be linked to a specific person.

Rights of the data subjects

Individuals whose data is used for AI testing retain their rights under the GDPR, including the right of access, rectification, erasure and restriction of processing. Organizations must provide mechanisms to ensure these rights. The involvement of the data protection officer in the project team therefore reduces errors in compliant reporting when exercising data subject rights.

Data protection impact assessment (DPIA)

A data protection impact assessment is necessary if a type of processing, in particular using new technologies, is likely to result in a high risk to the rights and freedoms of natural persons due to its nature, scope, circumstances and purposes (Art. 35 GDPR). The controller shall consult the supervisory authority prior to processing if a data protection impact assessment indicates that the processing would result in a high risk, unless the controller takes measures to mitigate the risk (Art. 35 GDPR).

The GDPR therefore requires a DPIA for AI projects that could pose a high risk to the rights and freedoms of natural persons. This should assess and document the specific risks associated with the processing of testing data as well as measures to mitigate these risks.

> For AI projects, it is crucial that data protection considerations are integrated as early as the development phase, including the selection and use of testing data. Document the entire data protection impact assessment process, including the risks identified, the assessments performed and the mitigation measures taken. This serves as proof of compliance with the GDPR.

4.4 Automated Decision Making

Art. 22 GDPR provides an important mechanism to protect individuals from the risks and potential disadvantages of automated decision-making, especially those based on artificial intelligence or other automated processing systems.

This article limits the use of solely automated decision-making by giving data subjects the right not to be subject to decisions that have legal or similarly significant effects on them without human review.

Art. 4 no. 4 GDPR defines the term profiling as any form of automated processing of personal data consisting of the use of personal data to evaluate certain personal aspects relating to a natural person, in particular to analyze or predict aspects concerning that natural person's performance at work, economic situation, health, personal preferences, interests, reliability, behavior, location or movements.

In fact, more and more data is being collected that maps every human activity. Through various AI technologies, individuals can be monitored and influenced based on a wide range of personal characteristics in many cases and contexts. By correlating data about individuals with corresponding classifications and predictions, AI increases the potential for profiling, i. e. deriving information about individuals or groups and making assessments and decisions based on this. [2]

Art. 22 GDPR deals with automated individual decision-making, including profiling. This article is particularly relevant in the context of artificial intelligence, as AI systems are often used for automated decision-making and profiling.

> **Prohibition of automated individual decision-making**
>
> Art. 22 para. 1 GDPR states that individuals have the right not to be subject to a decision based solely on automated processing, including profiling.which produces legal effects or similarly significantly affects them.

Four characteristics are therefore required for the application of the ban:

1. A decision must be made about a natural person, e. g. the assignment of a credit rating.

2. The decision must be based exclusively on automated processing; a human must not have any relevant influence on the outcome of the decision-making process.

3. The technology must include profiling. This requirement is further specified in Recital 71 GDPR.

4. The result must have a legal or at least similarly significant effect.

In principle, IT systems are therefore not permitted to make significant decisions about natural persons. However, there are exceptions to this prohibition, which are set out in Art. 22 para. 2. Such a decision may be made if it:

▪ is necessary for the conclusion or performance of a contract between the data subject and the data controller,

▪ is authorized by EU or Member State law which also lays down suitable measures to safeguard the data subject's rights and freedoms and legitimate interests, or

▪ with explicit consent of the data subject.

The protective measures required in such cases are listed in Art. 22 para. 3 and 4 GDPR. Where decisions are based on automated processing and fall under the exceptions, appropriate measures must be implemented to protect the rights and freedoms as well as the legitimate interests of the data subject. This includes, for example:

▪ the right to human intervention on the part of the controller

▪ the right to present one's own point of view

▪ the right to appeal the decision

What does this look like in concrete terms in interaction with AI systems? The following considerations should be discussed by the project team and measures decided and documented:

1. **Automated decision making**

   Many AI systems are able to make decisions without human intervention, which falls directly under Art. 22 GDPR. This is particularly relevant in areas such as credit scoring, human resources (e. g. automated applicant selection) and health diagnostics.

   The risk to data subjects must therefore be assessed in a data protection impact assessment and appropriate measures must be taken. Examples of these measures include regular reviews of decisions by an expert human, the implementation of an objection option in the AI system or an internal control that randomly selects an issue processed by the AI and forwards it to a human for review.

2. **Profiling**

   AI is often used for profiling, i. e. collecting information about an individual and making predictions or decisions based on that information. Art. 22 GDPR restricts the use of such techniques if they have a significant impact on individuals. Examples of this may include a person's performance at work, economic situation, state of health, personal preferences, interests, reliability, possible behavior in a certain situation or movement patterns.

Profiling is used in many different application scenarios because it enables large amounts of data to be analyzed efficiently and specific findings about individuals or groups to be derived from it. In healthcare, profiling can help to identify patients who are at higher risk of certain diseases, and in finance it helps to assess the credit risk of borrowers.

Although profiling is a powerful technique to identify and exploit patterns and trends in large amounts of data, it also has its limitations, as the results can be influenced by external factors such as economic changes, political events or technological developments that may not be included in the existing data. In addition, one-off or random events that lie outside the patterns and trends identified in the data cannot be predicted.

3. **Consent and transparency**

The use of AI for automated decision-making often requires the clear and explicit consent of the data subjects. In addition, the procedures and criteria on which the decision-making process is based must be transparent. Together with the data protection officer, it must therefore be checked whether the necessary consents have been obtained, whether technical measures have been adequately implemented and whether the rights of the data subjects can be exercised. This also includes easily understandable descriptions of the process used.

4. **Human intervention**

In cases where automated decisions are permitted, there must still be the possibility for human intervention to ensure that the rights of the data subjects are safeguarded. It must be conceptually taken into account that the controller can intervene in the processing and correct the result.

4.5 Guidance and Recommendations on GDPR and AI from Data Protection Authorities

The responsible use of AI in accordance with the GDPR currently raises numerous complex issues. There is a diverse and sometimes considerable potential for conflict that has not yet been fully clarified. Various initiatives by data protection experts are currently aiming to develop practicable solutions to these challenges and achieve legal certainty.

This section serves as a guide for companies and shows several approaches on how AI systems can be implemented and operated in compliance with data protection regulations. Particular emphasis is placed on meeting the requirements of the GDPR and at the same time making the best possible use of the innovation potential of AI technologies.

The guidance and case studies reflect the current status in July 2024. Decisions or other opinions and recommendations made after this date are not part of this overview.

4.5.1 Publications of the European Data Protection Board (Excerpt)

Organisation: European Data Protection Board (EDPB)

Country: EU

Publication: "Statement 3/2024", July 2024 [13]

Content:

In Opinion 3/2024, the EDPB describes its view on the role of national data protection authorities in the context of the AI Act and emphasizes that Union data protection law is fully applicable to the processing of personal data in the context of the lifecycle of AI systems, as explicitly recognized in Art. 2 para. 7 AI Act (see also Recitals 9 and 10).

The EDPB points out that the processing of personal data in the lifecycle of AI systems poses a high risk to fundamental rights, especially as they are often closely intertwined with non-personal data. Therefore, the national competent authorities should work closely with data protection authorities to enforce the AI Act.

Publication: "Report of the work undertaken by the ChatGPT Taskforce", May 2024 [12]

Content:

This task force was established because OpenAI had no establishment in the EU until February 15, 2024 and therefore no single national data protection authority was responsible for the ChatGPT service, which is provided by the US company OpenAI OpCo, LLC.

The EDPB therefore decided in April 2023 to set up a task force to promote cooperation between national authorities and coordinate information on possible enforcement measures in relation to the processing of personal data in connection with ChatGPT.

In this interim report, the members of the ChatGPT task force report on their analysis of the applicability of the GDPR to the ChatGPT service service and come to the following preliminary conclusions:

1. **Lawfulness**

   The processing of personal data must fulfill at least one of the requirements specified in Art. 6 para. 1 GDPR. Lawfulness must be assessed for each of the following
   phases and may differ:

   I. Phases: "Collection of training data", "Pre-processing the data" and "Training". During these phases, there are particular risks to the fundamental rights
   and freedoms of natural persons, as personal data can be collected and processed by means of web scraping (automated collection and extraction of certain information from various publicly accessible sources on the internet). In
   some cases, this may even include special categories of data in accordance
   with Art. 9 para. 1 GDPR, e. g. when people share their medical history on social
   media channels. The assessment of lawfulness is still pending and OpenAI has
   been asked to provide several proofs of GDPR compliance.

   II. Phases: "Prompt input", "Result output" and "Training ChatGPT with
   prompts". OpenAI qualifies the user's input and feedback on the result as "content" and declares that it will use this information to train and improve the
   model, whereby the use of "content" for training purposes can be objected to.
   This must be taken into account when weighing up interests in accordance
   with Art. 6 para. 1 lit f GDPR.

2. **Fairness**

   This GDPR principle requires that personal data must not be processed in a way that
   is unjustifiably detrimental to the data subject, unlawfully discriminatory, unexpected or misleading. Furthermore, there must be no transfer of risk from a company as the controller to data subjects. The task force concludes that, with regard to
   ChatGPT, the responsibility for compliance with the GDPR should not be transferred
   to the data subjects, for example by including a clause in the general terms and
   conditions that the data subjects are responsible for their chat entries. OpenAI has
   held out the prospect of implementing better procedures for checking input.

3. **Transparencyand information obligations**

   The task force notes that in the case of data collection via web scraping, the data
   subjects are not informed and an exception pursuant to Art. 14 para. 5 lit b GDPR
   may apply if OpenAI implements appropriate measures to protect the rights and
   freedoms as well as the legitimate interests of the data subjects, including the provision of this information to the public

   With regard to user input, persons must be made aware that the aforementioned
   "content" (user input) may be used for training purposes.

4. **Principle of data accuracy**

   It should be noted that the current training approach of OpenAI, due to the probabilistic nature of the system, leads to a model that can also produce biased or in-

vented results. In accordance with the principle of transparency pursuant to Art. 5 para. 1 lit a GDPR, the controller must provide adequate information about the probabilistic mechanisms for generating outputs and their limited reliability. This includes an explicit reference to the fact that the generated text may be syntactically correct, but may be distorted or fictitious. While the current measures are considered beneficial to avoid misinterpretation of ChatGPT results, they are not sufficient to comply with the principle of data accuracy.

5. **Rights of data subjects**

   In the European version of the privacy policy, OpenAI provides the option of contacting them by e-mail, whereby some rights of the data subject can also be exercised via the account settings. OpenAI holds out the prospect of implementing further measures for exercising the rights of data subjects.

The report is only an interim result and the task force has sent OpenAI a list of questions to be answered in order to better understand and assess the procedures and measures implemented in ChatGPT.

> The EDPB has published further statements on various topics that may also be of great interest in relation to a specific AI application.

4.5.2 DSK Recommendations

Organization: Conference of Independent Federal and State Data Protection Supervisory Authorities (DSK)

Country: Germany

Publication: DSK guidance on artificial intelligence and data protection, May 2024 [9]

Content:

Many companies and organizations face the challenge of not knowing under which conditions they can use AI applications in compliance with data protection regulations. The so-called Large Language Models (LLM), which are often referred to as chatbots but can also serve as the basis for other applications, represent a cost-effective introduction to AI.

At the beginning of May 2024, the DSK published a guideline that provides an "overview of the data protection criteria that must be observed for the data protection-compliant use of AI applications", with a focus on LLMs and chatbots. It can serve as a guide for organizations when selecting, implementing and using AI applications.

"The guidance is primarily aimed at those responsible who want to use AI applications", but also at developers and technicians who want to design and operate AI systems in compliance with data protection regulations.

The first chapter provides assistance for the design and selection of an AI application, the second chapter addresses implementation, and the third chapter provides information on data protection-compliant use. The following issues are discussed:

1. **Conception and selection of AI applications**

   The data controller under GDPR must explicitly define the areas of application and the purpose of the AI before using the AI application and determine whether personal data is required for this. It must then be checked whether these systems belong to the prohibited systems according to the AI Act, e. g. biometric real-time monitoring of public spaces.

   If no or only partially directly personal data is processed, it must still be assessed whether indirect personal data is processed or occurs in the AI model. This check relates to the entire life cycle of the data and the AI system, starting with the training of the AI. If personal data was used for the AI training, the legal basis for this data processing must be questioned.

   > "Decisions with legal effect may only be taken by humans in accordance with Art. 22 para. 1 GDPR. Exceptions are only permitted in certain cases, such as the consent of the data subject. If an AI application develops proposals that have legal effect for a data subject, the procedure must be designed in such a way that the person making the decision has an actual margin of maneuver and the decision is not primarily based on the AI proposal." [9]

   The DSK also distinguishes between open and closed AI systems, whereby closed AI systems relate to a defined user group and use case and are therefore preferable from a data protection perspective. In the case of open AI systems, which are made available to a large group of participants on the internet, for example, input from individuals can also become responses from other individuals. In this case, it is more difficult to ensure data protection compliance.

   Furthermore, the use of AI applications in relation to the information- and transparency obligations considered by GDPR controller:

   - If the controllers do not develop the AI application themselves, they must receive sufficient information from the provider in order to fulfill the transparency requirements pursuant to Art. 12 et seq. GDPR to be fulfilled. Developers must provide appropriate documentation and, as processors pursuant to Art. 28 para. 3 sentence 2 lit e GDPR, support the controller in implementing the rights of data subjects.

   - The controller must also provide information about the logic involved in automated decision-making in accordance with Art. 22 para. 1 GDPR and its scope and possible effects for the data subject. This requires an explanation of the data processing methods and how the programs work. Visualizations and interactive techniques can be useful to present the complexity of AI in an understandable way.

▪ If input and output data of an AI (e. g. an LLM) is to be used for further training of the AI, the data subjects must be informed. If they do not exclude the use and if personal data may be affected, then a legal basis is required.

▪ If the AI application is controlled by text input and this input is saved for later processing, the data subject must be informed of this. In particular, if other people also have access to this dialog, it must be possible for the data subject to delete the input history.

One focus of the GDPR is the rights of data subjects. The guidance states: "Controllers must ensure that data subjects can exercise their rights to rectification under Art. 16 GDPR and erasure under Art. 17 GDPR. Organizational and technical measures must be designed for both rights so that they can be exercised effectively." Of course, this requirement also applies to the other rights of data subjects.

Specifically for the use of LLMs and chatbots, the DSK states that the right to rectification also exists here. "It must be possible to implement this rectification in an AI application, for example by correcting data or through retraining/fine tuning."

The following procedure is recommended for deleting personal data. "The suppression of unwanted output by means of downstream filters does not generally constitute erasure within the meaning of Art. 17 GDPR. This is because the data that leads to a certain output after a certain input could still be available for the AI model in a personalized form. However, filter technologies can help to avoid certain outputs and thus serve the rights and freedoms of the persons affected by a particular output."

In addition, the DSK recommends the involvement of data protection officers as well as works and staff councils.

2. **Implementation of AI applications**

In terms of data protection, it is important to define who is responsible for the personal data. This is easy to determine if the organization operates the AI application on its own servers and for its own purposes. It is more difficult if an AI application is used as a service. In this case, there may also be joint responsibility.

> "Pursuant to Art. 26 para. 1 sentence 2 GDPR, the bodies involved shall specify in a transparent manner in an agreement which of them shall comply with which obligations under the GDPR, in particular the fulfillment of the rights of data subjects and the information obligations pursuant to Art. 13 and 14 GDPR"

While the clarification of responsibility according to the GDPR is important for the external relationship, it must be clarified internally with the workforce which AI applications can be used and how, and in particular how personal data is handled.

To this end, specific instructions should be drawn up and the workforce sensitized. In addition, the organization should provide employees with a company user ID for external AI systems that does not contain the person's full name.

A risk assessment must be carried out before the processing of personal data begins. If this reveals that there may be a high risk for natural persons, a data protection impact assessment must be carried out (DPIA) pursuant to Art. 35 GDPR is required, which is often the case with AI applications. The data protection authorities also publish regularly updated lists and information on when a DPIA is required and when it is not. Data controllers who are not themselves developers of the AI system require information from the provider for this and should take this into account when selecting an AI application.

The DSK also recommends "data protection-compliant design in the sense of "privacy by design" and "privacy by default", which takes into account the special features of AI systems, as well as the implementation of IT security measures so that no one can access the AI application without authorization.

In order to remain legally compliant in the future, a process should be implemented that regularly assesses the appropriateness of the measures implemented and updates them where necessary.

3. **Use of AI applications**

The last section of the guidance relates to the use of AI applications. The first warning here is against entering personal data into AI systems, especially if the AI models used are not within the EU. Data subjects must be informed about the use of their data and a legal basis is required for the transfer.

The special categories of personal data pursuant to Art. 9 para. 1 GDPR, which include racial and ethnic origin, trade union membership, political opinions, religious or philosophical beliefs, as well as the processing of genetic and biometric data, health data or data on sexual orientation, are particularly worthy of protection. The processing of this data is generally prohibited and only permitted in exceptional cases under the conditions of Art. 9 para. 2 to 4 GDPR.

> "The results of AI applications with personal references must be critically scrutinized. The providers of LLM in particular often make it clear that the texts generated by their application do not claim to be correct and should always be scrutinized. Moreover, AI applications can have different levels of information."

Furthermore, the DSK points out that the results and procedures of AI need to be assessed for any discrimination so that, for example, the German General Equal Treatment Act (AGG) is not violated.

4.5.3 The State Commissioner for Data Protection and Freedom of Information Baden-Württemberg

Organization: State Commissioner for Data Protection and Freedom of Information Baden-Württemberg (LfDI BW)

Country: Germany

Publication: Legal bases for data protection in the use of artificial intelligence, November 2023 (Version1.0) [11]

Content:

In November 2023, the LfDI BW published a comprehensive discussion paper outlining its assessment of the GDPR-compliant handling of AI systems.

With regard to the processing of personal data in AI systems, the LfDI BW points out that the assessment depends on the time of the evaluation. "The natural persons may be identifiable from the outset or only at a later point in time with additional information. In each case, the machine learning methods used must be analyzed as well as the probability that natural persons can be (re-)identified through atypical influence on the systems."

The LfDI BW's assessment relates to the individual phases of processing (from the collection of training data to the output of the AI), the assessment of GDPR responsibility, discusses the legal bases for public and non-public bodies and the processing of special categories of personal data.

Very helpful for use in an AI project are the guiding questions in the document for most wwwwws, which cover the key questions for the content covered. In addition, a short checklist for processing with the five most important questions is included in the appendix, as well as a collection of material that provides points of reference for further, more in-depth analyses.

4.5.4 Hamburg Commissioner for Data Protection on LLMs

Organization: Hamburg Commissioner for Data Protection and Freedom of Information (HmbBfDI)

Country: Germany

Publication: Discussion paper: Large language models and personal data, July 2024 [8]

Content:

In July 2024, the Hamburg Commissioner for Data Protection and Freedom of Information (HmbBfDI) published a discussion paper on the applicability of the GDPR to large language models. (LLMs).

The HmbBfDI states that "the paper is an impetus for debate. It is intended to help companies and authorities to better understand the complexities of data protection law".

The discussion paper [8] summarizes the following three points:

1. The mere storage of an LLM does not constitute processing within the meaning of Art. 4 no. 2 GDPR. This is because no personal data is stored in LLMs. Insofar as personal data is processed in an LLM-supported AI system, the processing operations must comply with the requirements of the GDPR. This applies in particular to the output of such an AI system.

2. Due to the lack of storage of personal data in the LLM, the rights of data subjects under the GDPR cannot relate to the model itself. However, claims for access, erasure or rectification can at least relate to the input and output of an AI system of the responsible provider or deployer.

3. The training of LLMs with personal data must comply with data protection regulations. The rights of data subjects must also be respected. However, training that may violate data protection regulations does not affect the lawfulness of the use of such a model in an AI system.

With these three points, the HmbHfDI is attempting to bring more clarity to the current discussions surrounding the legally compliant use of ChatGPT and Copilot in companies.

First, the AI system "Chatbot" is broken down into its components and described so that the individual modules can subsequently be assessed separately:

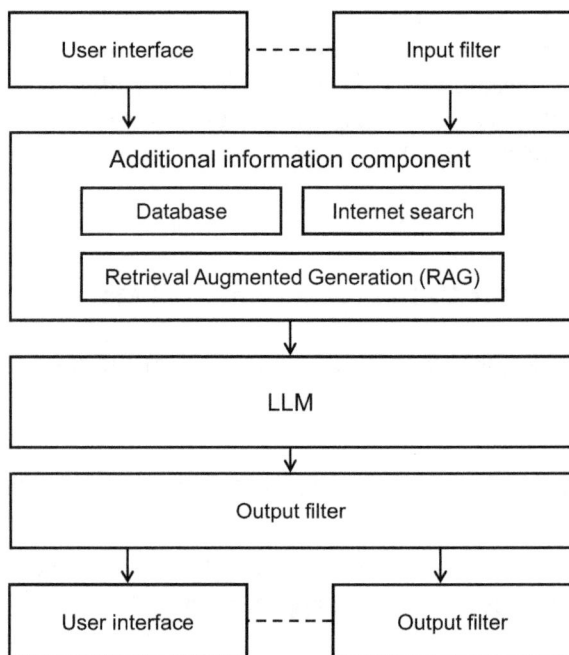

Figure 4.1
Interaction and Information Flow between the Various Components of an AI System that Uses an LLM

The individual components perform the following functions:

User interface: enables the user to interact with the AI system.

Input filter: processes the user input before it is forwarded to the LLM.

Additional information components:

   Database: supplements the user input with additional information.

   Internet search: searches for relevant information on the Internet.

   Retrieval Augmented Generation (RAG): combines and integrates the information found.

LLM (Large Language Model): processes the modified user input and generates corresponding responses.

Output filter: processes the immediate output of the LLM before it is output to the user.

Furthermore, it is explained that a central element of processing of linguistic information in LLMs is tokenization. Here, texts are broken down into small, predefined units, so-called tokens, which are typically smaller than words but larger than individual letters. This makes it possible to work with a limited number of basic elements that can be placed in relation to each other.

For example, the sentence "Data protection is important" is divided into tokens like

   [Dat] [aprot] [ection] [is] [impo] [rtant]

These tokens are then mapped to numerical values and further processed within the model. Texts exist in the model as fragments in the form of these numerical tokens and their so-called embeddings. These make the learned relationships accessible by relating the tokens to each other and organizing them according to probability.

When the model responds to a person's input, it uses the mathematical representation of the learned input. The output of an LLM is first generated as a sequence of tokens, which are then converted into sequences of letters. For example, the LLM can generate the word "project" from the tokens "pro" and "ject" or the word "projectile" from "pro" and "ject" and "il", depending on the context. This shows how flexible and context-dependent tokenization and the text generation based on it works in LLMs.

The HmbBfDI notes that LLMs themselves do not store any personal data within the meaning of Art. 4 no. 1, 2 GDPR in conjunction with Recital 26, as the models only contain mathematical representations of the processed texts.

It is particularly emphasized that the training of LLMs with personal data must comply with data protection regulations, but that training in breach of data protection regulations does not affect the lawfulness of the use of such a model, but only affects the provider of the LLM. For the rights of data subjects, this means that access, erasure or rectification must not relate directly to the model, but to the input and output of the AI systems.

> [!] When using an LLM in the company, the organizational unit using it must therefore ensure that data protection requirements are observed when entering queries and outputting the results from the LLM.

This can take the form of training, a code of conduct (see section 10.5 on codes of conduct) or other guidelines for employees.

4.5.5 FAQ of the Austrian Data Protection Authority

Organization: Austrian Data Protection Authority (dsb)

Country: Austria

Publication: FAQ on the topic of AI and data protection, July 2024 [10]

Content:

At the beginning of July 2024, dsb published an FAQ on its website that addresses the key issues relating to the implementation of AI in the company. These questions are constantly being expanded to include further topics and findings.

In response to the question of whether a deployer who has not developed an AI system must also comply with the GDPR, the answer is as follows: "As soon as a natural or legal person decides on the purposes and means of data processing, they are to be qualified as a controller under data protection law and are obliged to comply with the GDPR. Even if the technical specifications may originate from the provider or deployer, this does not generally change the fact that the entity using the AI system is to be regarded as the controller under data protection law."

In response to the question about the relationship between the GDPR and the AI Act, the following is returned: "Art. 2 para. 7 AI Act states that the GDPR, the work of the data protection authority and the obligations of providers and deployers of AI systems in their role as controllers or processors remain unaffected by the AI Act. The GDPR remains applicable (in parallel) if personal data is processed. The data protection authority is therefore responsible for data protection issues in connection with AI systems."

The answers to the questions often contain links to other authorities and decisions that are suitable for further analysis.

4.6 ChatGPT and the Data Protection Complaint from noyb

A concrete example of the conflicts between the GDPR and the use of generative AI is the case of the complaint [6] [7] by noyb - European Center for Digital Rights, Vienna, against OpenAI OpCo LLC, San Francisco. An employee of the complainant discovered that ChatGPT provided incorrect information about his date of birth. His request for deletion of the incorrect data was answered by the deployer of the generative AI OpenAI to the effect that it is not in a position to completely remove or correct the data relating to the date of birth. He could only prevent the display for users of ChatGPT. According to the complainant, this is a violation of Art. 5 para. 1 lit d GDPR.

In Detail:

According to the complaint, ChatGPT has incorrectly provided the complainant's date of birth, which in its opinion shows that the data used is incorrect. This constitutes a breach of the data accuracy obligation as set out in the GDPR. When the complainant submitted a request for access and erasure, OpenAI only focused on the complainant's account data and did not provide any information about the personal data processed in ChatGPT's Large Language Model.

In its response, OpenAI explained that it was not technically possible to correct the data without affecting other relevant information. However, this contradicts the requirements of the GDPR, which requires immediate correction or deletion of inaccurate personal data. OpenAI further argued that restricting the information provided by ChatGPT would violate the public's freedom of expression and freedom of information, as the complainant is a public figure.

This case illustrates the difficulties that can arise in complying with the GDPR in the context of complex AI systems. OpenAI's inability to completely remove or correct the erroneous data demonstrates the challenges associated with processing personal data in large-scale AI models. At the same time, the AI Act emphasizes the need for AI systems to operate responsibly and transparently, which was not fully ensured in this case. It remains to be seen how the courts will judge this case.

Sources

[1] Regulation (EU) 2016/679 *https://eur-lex.europa.eu/legal-content/DE/TXT/HTML/?uri=CELEX:32016R0679&from=DE*, accessed: 2025/04/13

[2] Sartor, G., in *The impact of the General Data Protection Regulation (GDPR) on artificial intelligence*, (2020) STOA – Scientific Foresight Unit, EU Parlament

[3] noyb, "ChatGPT verbreitet falsche Infos über Personen – und OpenAI kann nichts tun", *https://noyb.eu/de/chatgpt-provides-false-information-about-people-and-openai-cant-correct-it*, accessed: 2024/08/16

[4] Die Presse, "Nicht mal OpenAI kann ChatGPT stoppen": Nach Facebook legt sich Schrems jetzt mit OpenAI an", *https://www.diepresse.com/18420000/nicht-mal-open-ai-kann-chat-gpt-stoppen-nach-facebook-legt-sich-schrems-jetzt-mit-openai-an*, accessed: 2024/08/16

[5] ORF.at, "Beschwerde von Datenschützern zu ChatGPT", *https://orf.at/stories/3355809/*, accessed: 2024/08/16

[6] ChatGPT verbreitet falsche Infos über Personen – und OpenAI kann nichts tun. URL *https://noyb.eu/de/chatgpt-provides-false-information-about-people-and-openai-cant-correct-it* – accessed: 2024/08/08

[7] Complaint noyb vs. Open AI.

[8] Der Hamburgische Beauftragte für Datenschutz und Informationsfreiheit: Diskussionspapier: Large Language Models und personenbezogene Daten.

[9] DSK: Orientierungshilfe der Konferenz der unabhängigen Datenschutzaufsichtsbehörden des Bundes und der Länder vom 6. Mai 2024 – Künstliche Intelligenz und Datenschutz.

[10] FAQ zum Thema KI und Datenschutz. URL *https://www.dsb.gv.at/download-links/FAQ-zum-Thema-KI-und-Datenschutz.html* – accessed: 2024/08/08

[11] Rechtsgrundlagen im Datenschutz beim Einsatz von Künstlicher Intelligenz – Der Landesbeauftragte für den Datenschutz und die Informationsfreiheit Baden-Württemberg. URL *https://www.baden-wuerttemberg.datenschutz.de/rechtsgrundlagen-datenschutz-ki/* – accessed: 2024/08/08

[12] Report of the work undertaken by the ChatGPT Taskforce | European Data Protection Board. URL *https://www.edpb.europa.eu/our-work-tools/our-documents/other/report-work-undertaken-chatgpt-taskforce_en* – accessed: 2024/08/08

[13] Statement 3/2024 on data protection authorities' role in the Artificial Intelligence Act framework. URL *https://www.edpb.europa.eu/our-work-tools/our-documents/topic/artificial-intelligence_en* – accessed: 2024/08/08

5 Intellectual Property

Alexandra Ciarnau

Intellectual property rights ("intellectual property rights"; internationally also "intellectual property rights" or "IP rights")") refers to intangible human creations such as texts, images, software, databases, know-how or inventions. These may be subject to different rights of protection under IP law if the relevant requirements are met in accordance with the respective laws [1]:

- Registered industrial property rights as patents and utility models, trademarks or designs;
- Copyrights or ancillary copyrights;
- Trade secret protection.

The creator or owner of IP rights enjoys protection against unauthorized access or use by third parties [2].

The AI Act does not affect the existing regulation of IP rights, but takes it into account in various contexts as determined fundamental rights (see Recital 1 AI Act, Recital 48 AI Act, Article 17 of the Charter of Fundamental Rights of the European Union). The most important IP correlations include the following:

- The extent of the adverse impact of an AI system on fundamental rights protected by the Charter – including IP rights – is relevant for the classification of high-risk AI under Art. 6 et seq. AI Act and General Purpose AI according to Art. 51 AI Act. In addition, when adopting delegated acts, the Commission must consider the impact on fundamental rights, including IP rights (e. g. when amending the risk classification as high-risk AI according to Annex III pursuant to Art. 7 AI Act).
- The protection of third-party IP rights is also reflected in many obligations of deployers, providers, importers and manufacturers (e. g. risk management, data use and governance, fundamental rights impact assessment for high-risk AI, reporting of serious incidents). This is particularly important when using generative AI. Pro-

viders of General Purpose AI must in particular put a policy in place to protect copyrights and make a sufficiently detailed summary of the content used for training (Art. 53 para. 1 AI Act in conjunction with Recitals 106 et seq. AI Act) available. This should prevent unlawful distribution of copyright protected work. Along the AI value chain, however, the obligations must be fulfilled in such a way that the respective deployers do not jeopardize their IP rights themselves (Recital 88 AI Act).

- The Commission, market surveillance authorities and notified bodies as well as all other natural or legal persons involved in the application of the IPR Regulation are obliged to maintain confidentiality in the course of their activities. They must protect IP rights from unlawful access, use and disclosure (Art. 78 IPR Regulation) [3].

- Access by the notifying body in the context of the conformity assessment of high-risk AI, i. e. access to the training models and trained models of the AI system, including its relevant parameters, is subject to existing EU law on protection of IP and trade secrets (Annex VII AI Act).

- The protection of IP rights is also a checkpoint in the context of AI real laboratories (Art. 57 para. 6 AI Act).

In practice, providers or deployers are faced with the question, if

- AI systems, their components and the accompanying documentation are protected by IP law and

- the use of AI is IP-compliant.

The latter must be evaluated both on the input and output side with regard to third-party rights. In the following, we therefore address these two issues [4].

5.1 Protection of AI and its Components

For assessing the eligibility of protection an initial technical examination is necessary. The definition of AI systems within the meaning of the AI Act is based on the OECD definition of AI. Accordingly, AI systems are machine-based systems consisting of an AI model, input (data) and output, which are designed for a varying degree of autonomous operation, can be adaptable and which derive from the inputs received for explicit or implicit goals how the results can influence the physical or virtual environments (Art. 3 no. 1 AI Act).

a. Build phase, pre-deployment

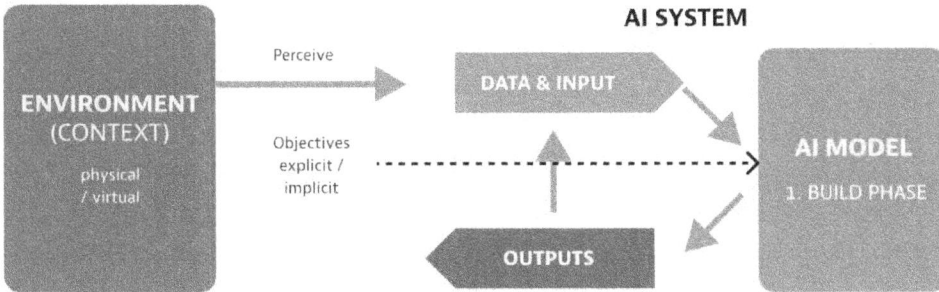

AI SYSTEM

Perceive

ENVIRONMENT
(CONTEXT)

physical
/ virtual

DATA & INPUT

Objectives
explicit /
implicit

AI MODEL

1. BUILD PHASE

OUTPUTS

b. Use phase, post-deployment

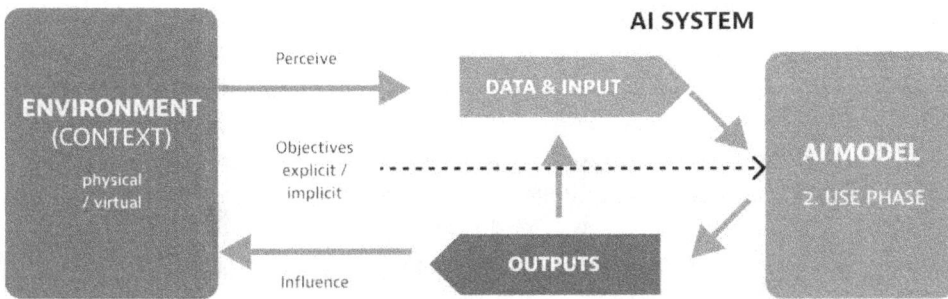

AI SYSTEM

Perceive

ENVIRONMENT
(CONTEXT)

physical
/ virtual

DATA & INPUT

Objectives
explicit /
implicit

AI MODEL

2. USE PHASE

OUTPUTS

Influence

Figure 5.1 Visual Representation of the OECD Definition of AI (source: *https://oecd.ai/ en/wonk/definition*)

Whether AI can be qualified as software is the subject of varying debate [5]. However, the recitals of the AI Act attempt to distinguish AI systems from traditional software (Recital 12 AI Act). Supplementary regulations, such as the amended Product Liability Directive, also apply to AI systems by extending the definition of product including software. In my opinion, this leaves no doubt about the classification of AI as software.

However, the components of AI systems in sum must be distinguished: (i) the AI model, which in many cases represent a collection of possible algorithms, models and methods; (ii) the input data and (iii) the output, which can manifest itself in various forms (e. g. as predictions, content, recommendations or decisions).

Based on this understanding, AI systems and, in some cases, their components may be protected primarily by copyright or ancillary copyright. Patent or utility model law, on the other hand, is often ruled out. This is explained in detail in the following section.

5.1.1 Copyrights and Ancillary Copyrights

5.1.1.1 General Information

Intellectual creations enjoy copyright protection. The work must therefore stand out from day-to-day, commons, ordinarily content and have personal characteristics. Work in the fields of literature, sound art, visual art and cinematography are eligible for protection. Copyright protection arises with the act of creation and does not require separate registration, as is the case with registered IP.

Facts, mere ideas including business ideas, processes, methods, mathematical concepts, style and manner are not protected by copyright [6].

Computer programs can be protected as literature works, if they are the result of an original creation and constitute an individual work [7]. According to Austrian case law [8], computer programs must exhibit a certain degree of complexity, meaning that the solution to the task can be mastered in several ways and the programmer has the freedom to develop individual features [9]. Copyright protection of computer programs covers all forms of expression, such as source code, binary code, object code, byte code, assembler code and compilation and developer materials. Everyday, banal computer programs, on the other hand, whose creation requires neither effort and expense nor any significant intellectual achievement, are not protected by copyright [10].

On this basis, the copyright protection of AI can be assessed as follows.

5.1.1.2 Individually Developed AI Systems

Individually developed AI systems are generally protected by copyright in their entirety due to their complexity and the existing scope for design. After all, they require special expertise in the field and stand out from the ordinary.

5.1.1.3 Individually Developed AI Models

Copyright protection of AI models on the other hand, is controversial. AI models are often based on generally known mathematical methods and calculations. These are generally not protected by copyright [11]. Even in the case of complex models, it is questionable whether there is sufficient room for original creation and thus copyright protection can be assumente for the AI model in the case of a purely technical sequence.

This must be distinguished from the implementation of an algorithm in a program code and the program structure. The combination of many program steps and individually shaped problem solutions can be eligible for protection [14].

Example

The example of machine learning illustrates the difficulty of classifying AI models as proprietary computer programs. On the one hand, the network topology and the weighting defined for training and execution can vary and be complex depending on the machine learning model. The more layers and neurons the network has and the more efficient and reliable the model is designed, the more the component stands out from the ordinary. The high investment costs may also speak in favor of this [12]. However, it is questionable whether this optimization of computing sequences is not merely of a technical nature and does not in fact allow any creative freedom, because the possibilities for designing neural networks are limited [13].

5.1.1.4 Input and Training Data Pool

Not only the AI system as a computer program may be protected, but also its input and training data pool as well as the arrangement of this data. Copyright law provides specific protection for databases. Databases are collections of works, data or other independent elements that are systematically or methodically arranged and individually accessible by electronic means or otherwise. However, copyright protection only applies, if the selection or arrangement of the content constitutes an original creation [15]. This requires a creative achievement, which can arise from the decision to include content in the database or to structure it. Since there is room for maneuver when setting up input and training data pools, I believe that copyright protection is in general possible.

Alternatively, the content arranged in the input and training data pool can enjoy sui generis protection as a simple database. This requires the existence of a database and a substantial investment in terms of type or scope for the procurement, review or presentation of its content. This catch-all provision grants the developer investment protection and protection against a acquisition of their services or essential database parts by third parties.

For the protection of AI-generated results, see section 5.2.2.

5.1.1.5 User Documentation and User Manual

The user documentation and the user manual can achieve the character of a work and enjoy protection as a literary work, if they are original creation [16].

Example

In my opinion, however, it is questionable whether the instructions for use for high-risk AI can constitute an original intellectual creation pursuant to Art. 13 para. 2 AI Act. These must, for example, describe the characteristics, capabilities and performance limitations of the AI system as well as known circumstances of use and possible risks. This has parallels with package leaflets for medicinal products, for which copyright protection has been denied in the past [17].

5.1.1.6 Rights and Claims of the Author

The author enjoys exclusive and moral rights. The exploitation of work is therefore reserved exclusively to the author, as long as no third party has been granted permission to use the work (see section 5.1.1.7).

The author enjoys the exploitation rights listed below. In practice, in the case of AI applications the following are particularly relevant:

- Reproduction right: The author has the exclusive right to reproduce the work in any way, in any number, temporarily or permanently. An exception exists in the context of free use of the work, in particular ephemeral or accompanying reproduction, text and data mining (see section 5.2.1.1) and, in the case of computer programs, additionally in the case of use and decompilation in accordance with the intended purpose.

- Distribution right: Only the author may distribute their work and, for example, place it on the market. However, the distribution right for software is exhausted when it is placed on the market in the EEA with the author's consent [18].

- Right to make available: Furthermore, only the author is entitled to make the work available to the public by wire or wireless means. This exploitation right applies to the provision of AI systems via online interfaces.

- Adaption rights: The work may only be adapted with the consent of the author. Exceptions are adaptions for the intended use and in connection with decompilation. Free use is also excluded. This is the case, if the work merely serves as a source of inspiration for the creation of a new, individual work. The original work may no longer be clearly recognizable in the new work.

In addition, the creator enjoys moral rightssuch as the indispensable right to authorship or the waivable right to author attributions.

The author is entitled to the following rights against an infringement of his or her rights:

- Injunctive relief regardless of fault (in practice the main claim, which can also be enforced by way of a preliminary injunction)

- Claim for removal (e. g. destruction of unlawful copies)

- No-fault claim to appropriate remuneration

- Claim for damages (including a fault-based claim in the amount of twice of the appropriate compensation as liquidated damages)

- Surrender of the profit and accounting claim

- Claim for publication of judgment

5.1.1.7 Granting of Rights

If the author wishes to commercialize his or her work, it requires a licenseof rights. Copyright law distinguishes between permission and the right to use a work:

A permission to use a work grants a third party the non-exclusive right of use. A right to use a work, on the other hand, grants the third party an exclusive right effective against anyone. The third party can even enforce the licensed exploitation rights against the author him/herself. The right to use the work is therefore the stronger right.

In both cases, the scope of the license is freely customizable. It can be limited in terms of time, territory or subject matter.

It must also be taken into account that, according to case law, the granting of rights of use for future, as yet unknown types of exploitation is generally not permitted without prior consent. At the time the contract is concluded, the licensor cannot foresee these. If licenses are also granted for future, currently unknown types of use, the licensor may be entitled to an additional fee. This is a current topic in connection with AI.

A special case applies to computer programs created by an employee in the performance of his or her official duties. Under Austrian law, the "employer's privilege" applies here, which grants the employer an unlimited right to use the work. The intention to this provision is that the employer bears the costs associated with the programming of computer programs and should thus be entitled to the exclusive rights of exploitation. In addition, the employer is entitled to moral rights, in particular the right to author attribution.

> The employer's privilege only applies to employees. Freelancers, for example, are not deemed as employees. In such cases, an explicit license to the work results, including copyright protected work, is required, which is often lacking in practice.[1]

5.1.1.8 Open Source Software

In the course of software development, open source software plays a major role. Open source software enables rapid, resource-saving further development and thus promotes innovation. However, open source software is not in the public domain. It is subject to its own license conditions. They usually provide for the free use of the software including the source code. In return, however, some licenses oblige the licensee to varying degrees. The most relevant obligation concerns the question of the obligation to publish:

---

[1] Anderl/Schelling in Kollar/Balog/Martinetz/Pichler, Das große Handbuch Wirtschaftsrecht, para. 10.196

- **Copyleft license** Under these license conditions, the programming must be distributed under the same license, regardless of any adaptations. Therefore, the same rights and obligations that the licensee receives and is bound by must also be granted or transferred to third parties (including end customers). In addition, the source code must usually be published or at least disclosed to the users of the (processed) software.

- **Non-copyleft License** With these license conditions, there are fewer restrictions on the further distribution of the software. In particular, further development does not have to be distributed under a free license. Therefore, the licensee can also demand fees for commercialization of the software or keep the source code secret.

The biggest challenge is to combine several open source software licenses in one development. They must be compatible with each other and must not contradict each other so that the respective license conditions can be complied with. Before AI systems are built on open source software, a prior open source audit is recommended to evaluate compatibility and the possibility of fulfilling the corresponding obligations [19].

5.1.1.9 Patent and Utility Model Protection

Patents and utility models protect technical inventions. The owners enjoy exclusive rights for a certain period and can exclude anyone else from using the innovation.

In order to obtain patent protection, the invention must

- have a technical effect,

- be new (no prior innovation or publication),

- be inventive (not obvious for a person skilled in this field) and

- be commercially applicable.

In contrast, a utility model ("small patent") only needs to be

- based on an inventive step,

- new (taking into account a grace period of six months for own pre-publications) and

- commercially applicable.

Among other things, mathematical methods and programs for data processing programs are not eligible for protection. These exceptions are relevant for the assessment of patent or utility model protection for AI systems:

Computer programs are excluded from protection, if they consist exclusively of a control instruction for the operation of a computer (e. g. in the form of an algorithm). This form of programming as a mere instruction falls under the legal exception. If, on the other hand, it is a computer-implemented invention whose execution of program in-structions has a further technical effect, software may also be eligible for protection as a patent or utility model [20]. However, the necessary technicality and inventive step must also be present, which are often more difficult to achieve in practice with AI software [21]. Before an innovation is published, it makes sense to check for any patent or utility model protection. This increases the value of the IP assets and there-fore also the value of the company.

5.1.2 Trade Secret Protection

AI systems, their underlying processes, derivations, database structures, functional-ities and the know-how for operation and further development can also be protected as trade secrets. To this end, the information must be

▪ secret,

▪ of commercial value and

▪ subject to appropriate confidentiality measures.

Information is confidential, if it is not generally accessible either as a whole or in its specific composition of its components [22]. The information must therefore not be discoverable without considerable effort.

A commercial value is assumed, if the information has a commercial value or leads to economic disadvantages to the owner in case of disclosure [23].

Example

The accompanying documentation of AI systems is to be qualified as a trade secret apart from copyright protection, if this written know-how is essential for the operation and further development of the AI system, concerns a previously unexplored area and many competitors on the market are interested in selling this AI programming including documentation. In this case, there will be a com-mercial value.

Appropriate confidentiality measures include adequate organizational, technical and contractual measures. The specific measures depend on the circumstances of the case at hand. In principle, document classification according to confidentiality levels, re-stricted access according to the "need-to-know" principle, access logging, content en-cryption, agreement of confidentiality obligations with employees and third parties involved and regular training [24] are possible measures.

5.2　Legal IP Compliance when Using AI

A profound examination of the issue of IP compliance of an AI system is essential. This is also illustrated by the current legal disputes against providers of large-language models. Several publishers and authors are claiming violations of copyrights under the US Digital Millennium Copyright Act, in particular the commercialization of third-party IP and distribution of protected work without consent of the authors [25].

The IP compliance check should therefore focuse on the following aspects:

- Can the use of IP-protected materials on the input side for the creation of an AI corpus or for AI training be lawful?

- Which AI Act requirements must be implemented on the input side of AI design in order to protect the IP rights of third parties, especially when creating texts, images and videos?

- Do the output-side AI-generated results enjoy IP protection, and who may use them and to what extent?

5.2.1　AI Input

5.2.1.1　IP-protected Input Data

The AI input can consist of different types of data. In the course of the AI design, it must be assessed, if IP-protected content should also be scraped, collected from user activities and their prompts, duplicated in the AI corpus and analyzed:

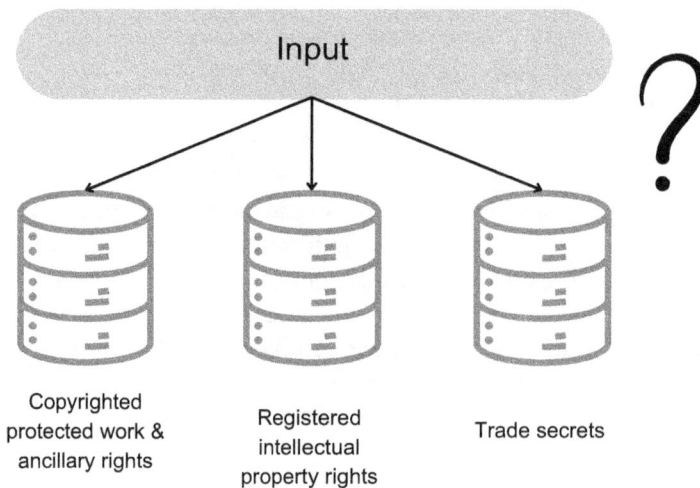

Copyrighted protected work & ancillary rights

Registered intellectual property rights

Trade secrets

Figure 5.2
Exemplary Sources for Input Data

In this case, the following legal limitations must be considered:

- **Copyright protection**

  If copyright protected workare used for the input, they will generally be reproduced within the meaning of copyright law in the course of compiling the AI corpus or training data pool. This requires appropriate justification, which can either be based on legally granted free rights of use or a contractually granted license.

  One possible justification is the free use for text and data mining. Anyone may reproduce a work for a research institution, for a cultural heritage institution or for their own use in order to automatically evaluate digital texts and data in order to obtain information. For the private sector, the free personal use is relevant, which also covers commercial use. The prerequisite is that the user had lawful access (e. g. open source content; contractually granted access rights) to the work and no reservation of use was declared. However, this free use is not unlimited [26]: (i) exploitation by third parties must not lead to more than minimal damage for the author. This protects his economic position. (ii) Furthermore, the free use does not include any modifications beyond those required for automated evaluation and information retrieval. (iii) Finally, a reproduction may only be retained for as long as is necessary to achieve the purposes of data analysis and information retrieval. These principles must be taken into account in the AI design. Depending on the specific design, the use of copyright protected materials may be justifiable based on the text and data mining provision.

  Alternative to text and data mining-use, free use of a work could also be based on the right of a mere "transient" and incidental reproduction. However, the reproduction must (i) be merely temporary, (ii) be an integral and essential part of a technical process, (iii) have the sole purpose of transmission of the work in a network between third parties by an intermediary or a lawful use, (iv) have no independent meaning and (v) must not lead to any modification of the copy [27]. In the case of generative AI, meeting all of these requirements is more challenging in practice because the reproduction is usually non-volatile or accompanying.

  If no free use of a work is applicable, exploitation can only take place based on a corresponding contractual license of rights by the author. The scope of the license and its interpretation are of particular importance in this respect [28].

- **Ancillary copyright**

  In addition, the ancillary copyright of databases must be considered (see section 5.1.1.4). This right can be infringed by scraping. Individual, relatively minor accesses are permitted, but systematic extractions are not. According to case law, the accesses carried out during scraping must be considered in sum and thus added together. This risk should be mitigated in the design.

- **Registered property rights**

  If, for example, trademarks, patent drawings, utility model applications or designs are used as training material, the (il)legal use on the input side also primarily arises from a copyright perspective. These laws only grant the owner certain rights that are aimed at commercial use by third parties, such as the trademark-like use of the protected sign for identical or similar goods and services. However, the effects of the registered property rights can have an impact on the output. If the AI generates similar signs or duplicates them and they are subsequently used by the user for business purposes in a similar context, the specific use may constitute an infringement of the trademark, patent, utility model or design rights of third parties.

- **Trade secret protection**

  The disclosure of trade and business secrets in the AI corpus, which is usually triggered by user prompts, is critical. In the case of a free and open-access AI solution, the confidentiality interest in this information may lapse because an unlimited user group has access and there are no longer any appropriate confidentiality measures in place. In the first few months of the ChatGPT hype, many companies were not even aware of the potential disclosure of user prompts and results via the AI system, which led to a great deal of know-how being lost [29].

  The possible disclosure and consequence of the loss of trade and business secrecy protection must be assessed in the design phase when considering the adoption of user instructions and their generated results in the AI input and, if necessary, counteracted by appropriate technology design and clear user policies.

5.2.1.2 AI Act Requirements for AI Systems

The AI Act provides for the obligation to protect the IP rights of third parties in various provisions, as mentioned above. Of course, this also relates to the input and thus primarily to the development, testing and training of AI systems. The specific requirements for safeguarding IP rights of third parties are not precisely defined in the AI Act. Only the provision in Art. 53 para. 1 lit c AI Act is somewhat more specific, according to which providers of General Purpose AI models are obliged to implement a strategy to comply with copyright and, in particular, to identify and comply with a reservation of use for text and data mining, including through state-of-the-art technologies. In my opinion, the strategy should cover data sources, data flows, examination results of the exploitation acts and statements on permissibility as well as protective measures to prevent copyright infringement. In connection with the traceability of the sources used, the retrieval augmented generation (RAG) method is often discussed [30]. Such technical considerations should also be included in a copyright protection policy.

5.2.2 AI Output

The question of the IP classification of the output plays primarily a role for AI-generated content such as texts, images and videos. From a user perspective, there is a need for a clear assignment of rights in order to define the possibilities of use. These depend on various aspects. The decisive points are described below using the example of a standard AI tool:

- The first step is to question whether the AI-generated content even fulfills the requirements for protection as a copyrighted work, invention or utility model described in section 5.1. If this is the case, the author must be identified.

- The author can either be the creator of the original work from which the AI was "inspired" or from which the performance was adopted, or the user. The AI cannot be an author due to a lack of natural legal personality [31]. However, the user can only claim a work as their own, if it actually derived from their personal human creation [32]. In the AI context, however, the user usually does not know which action leads to which result. Which letters, phrases or image sections are the next logical results of a specific instruction are a black box for the user. As a rule, the derivation of the results is not in the user's hands. However, this should not necessarily lead to a rejection of protection. In practice, attempts are made to determine this based on the height of the prompt: Were the framework conditions set by the user so individual and creative that the AI-generated result can be attributed to him or her?

- In the case of the generated result, a particularly critical question must be asked as to whether the content is adopted unchanged and thus reproduced or edited. In the latter case, a distinction must be made between editing requiring consent and free use. If the AI only makes minor changes and the individual character of the original is retained, this is considered an adaptation requiring consent. This requires a license by the author. If, on the other hand, the original fades in comparison to the edited version and fades noticeably into the background, it is considred as a new creation – i. e. a new work [33]. In this case, the exclusive rights of use belong to the user.

> On the one hand, the issue of unaltered reproduction of third-party content and its processing must be taken into account in the AI design in order to minimize direct copyright infringements. On the other hand, the handling of generated content is a topic of AI literacy and should be a mandatory part of employee training, such as in workshops and accompanying AI guidelines.

- If neither the user has made an intellectual creation, nor is the result based on an original work, there is no copyright-protected work. However, the scope of the permitted use of the generated content can also be regulated independently by the provider via its terms and conditions. Almost all providers of generative AI systems make use of this option. As a rule, they do not grant users exclusive rights because they cannot rule out the possibility of other users receiving exactly the same result or often do not want to grant more rights for reasons of further tool development.

> Before selecting the AI tool, check the terms of use, particularly with regard to commercial use and altering of the results if you are using the results for business purposes.

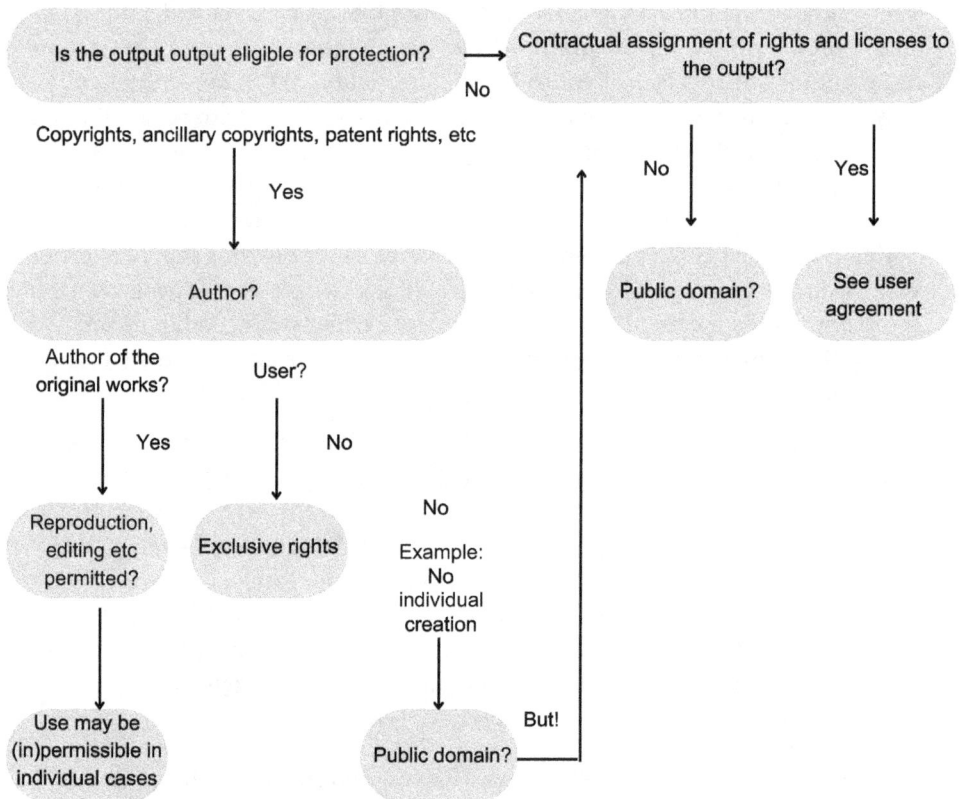

Is the output output eligible for protection? → Contractual assignment of rights and licenses to the output?

No

Copyrights, ancillary copyrights, patent rights, etc

Yes

No   Yes

Author?   Public domain?   See user agreement

Author of the original works?   User?

Yes   No

No

Reproduction, editing etc permitted?   Exclusive rights   Example: No individual creation

Use may be (in)permissible in individual cases   But!

Public domain?

Figure 5.3 Checking the (In)Permissibility of Output Usage

> If it turns out that the user is not the author of the AI result, comprehensive editing makes sense. A redesign of the result may be permissible as free use, as mentioned above. The new creation then originates from the user themselves, so they can also exploit the change exclusively.

In the case of individual AI solutions, these complex assessment can be omitted with appropriate contractual safeguards. In this case, rights to the generated results can already be contractually granted to the customer.

> The provider and user are already liable for any unauthorized use and copyright infringement regardless of fault (see section 5.1.1.6). A lack of knowledge of a copyright infringement therefore does not change the liability risk.

5.3 Checklist

IP compliance concerns both the classification of the respective components and the entirety of the AI system as an IP asset as well as the specific implementation on the input and output side. The following checklist summarizes the key checkpoints once again:

AI design

- Are my AI system or its components protected by IP law?
- Which data sources are used to create the input (AI corpus or AI training data pool)?
- How is the AI input formed from a technical perspective? (Scraping? Reproduction?)
- Are the data sources used legally compliant?
- Does the AI system allow trade secrets to be leaked? Can this be prevented technically or organizationally?
- Is a copyright compliance strategy in place? Are the copyrights of third parties protected within the meaning of the AI Act?

AI development and testing

- Are the parameters defined in the AI design implemented accordingly, and can legally compliant use and mitigation of the risks of infringing third-party rights also be achieved in test environments?

Operation

- Is the license of rights to the AI-generated content contractually defined and clear?
- Have employee training courses been held and AI guidelines issued on the legally compliant use of AI systems?
- Are further adjustments to the AI system, the design or parameterization, configuration and any interface connections necessary due to errors that have occurred?

5.4 Reference Table Legislation

The chapter was based on the Austrian legal framework, but the relevant German standards are referenced below without any claim to correctness.

Context	Austrian Laws	German Laws
Protection of computer programs as linguistic works	§ 40a para. 1 UrhG,A	§§ 69a ff UrhG
Protection of databases	§ 40f UrhG,A	§§ 87a ff UrhG
Protection of simple databases	§§ Sections 76c ff UrhG,A	§ 55a UrhG
Exploitation rights	§§ 14 ff UrhG,A	§§ 7 ff UrhG
Reproduction right	§ 15 UrhG,A	§ 7 UrhG
Transient or accompanying duplication	§ 41a UrhG,A	§ 44a UrhG
Text and data mining	§ 42h UrhG,A	§ 44b UrhG
Intended use	§ 40d UrhG,A	§ 69d UrhG
Decompilation	§ 40e UrhG,A	§ 69e UrhG
Distribution right	§ 16 UrhG,A	§ 17 UrhG
Right to make available	§ 18a UrhG,A	§ 19a UrhG
Infringement of copyrights	§§ 81 ff UrhG,A	§§ 97 ff UrhG
Employer privilege	§ 40b UrhG,A	§ 69b UrhG
Moral rights	§§ 20 and 21 UrhG,A	§§ 12 ff UrhG
Lack of protection for mathematical methods and programs for data processing programs	§ 1 para. 3 PatG,A, GMG	§ 1 PatG, GebrMG
Trade secret	§§ 26 a ff UWG,A	GeschGehG

Sources

[1] In Austria, the Patent Act, Utility Model Act, Trademark Act, Design Act, Copyright Act and the Act against Unfair Competition (*www.ris.bka.gv.at*) are relevant for the assessment of the corresponding IP protection.

[2] Cf. on the scope section 5.1.1.

[3] For details, see also section 3.7.3.2 on obligations when using GPAI.

[4] You can only make use of the exceptions set out in Directive (EU) 2016/943 of the European Parliament and of the Council of June 8, 2016 on the protection of confidential know-how and business information (trade secrets) against their unlawful acquisition, use and disclosure ("Trade Secrets Directive").

[5] Cf. *https://www.itzbund.de/DE/digitalemission/trendstechnologien/kuenstlicheintelligenz/kuenstliche intelligenz.html?nn=303798#bodyText3038001* – accessed: 2024/03/23

[6] Art. 9 Abs. 2 TRIPS; OGH 4 Ob 13/92; OGH 4 Ob 92/12a; OGH 4 Ob 191/19w; OGH 4 Ob 2085/96p; OGH 4 Ob 85/06p; OGH 4 Ob 244/22v; OGH 4 Ob 21/18v; OGH 4 Ob 229/02h; OGH 4 Ob 201/04v.

[7] Cf. Art. 1 para. 20 Software Directive on the concept of a computer program within the meaning of Directive 2009/24/EC of the European Parliament and of the Council of 23.04.2009 on the legal protection of computer programs

[8] OGH 12. 7. 2005, 4 Ob 45/05d; 5. 4. 2005, 4 Ob 35/05h; 16. 1. 2007, 4 Ob 198/06f; Ris-Justiz RS0120097.

[9] Wiebe/Pabst in Handig/Hofmarcher/Kucsko, urheber.recht3 § 40a UrhG point 35.

[10] Anderl/Ciarnau in Blockchain und Immaterialgüterrecht, #Blockchain.

[11] Wiebe/Pabst in Handig/Hofmarcher/Kucsko, urheber.recht3 § 40a UrhG point 83.

[12] Wiebe/Pabst in Handig/Hofmarcher/Kucsko, urheber.recht3 § 40a UrhG point 95 ff.

[13] Wiebe/Pabst in Handig/Hofmarcher/Kucsko, urheber.recht3 § 40a UrhG point 97.

[14] OGH 16. 1. 2007, 4 Ob 198/06 f.

[15] Ciresa in Ciresa, Österreichisches Urheberrecht22 § 40 f. UrhG point 11.

[16] Wiebe/Pabst in Handig/Hofmarcher/Kucsko, urheber.recht3 § 40a UrhG, point 107.

[17] OGH 4 Ob 2202/96v. *https://360.lexisnexis.at/d/u_zivil_OGH_1996_JJT_19960812_OGH0002_0_4dd80ac54d ?origin=lk* – accesed: 2024/03/23

[18] EuGH C-128/11; Anderl, Zur Online-Erschöpfung bei Computerprogrammen, ecolex 2012, 905.

[19] Anderl/Ciarnau in Blockchain und Immaterialgüterrecht, #Blockchain.

[20] Heinzl/Ciarnau in Anderl, IP in der Praxis 67.

[21] The patent offices have already reacted to the advance of patent applications, further refined their approaches and revised guidelines; see European Patent Office on AI patent applications *https://www. itzbund.de/DE/digitalemission/trendstechnologien/kuenstlicheintelligenz/kuenstlicheintelligenz.html?nn= 303798#bodyText3038001* – accessed: 2024/03/23

[22] OGH 4 Ob 188/20f, JusGuide 2021, 19336.

[23] The OHG applies a strict standard when examining the commercial interests of the owner. Thus, there is no commercial value in the case of captured design plans for industrial parts, as the mere (partial) use of these drawings as a template for designs does not yet threaten the owner's competitive position. This would be different if the plans were used for patentable further developments (OGH 4 Ob 188/20f, JusGuide 2021, 19336).

[24] Seling/Woltran in Anderl (Hrsg), Praxishandbuch UWG (2021) 297 f.

[25] Cf. *https://www.nytimes.com/2023/12/27/business/media/new-york-times-open-ai-microsoft-lawsuit. html*; *https://www.derstandard.at/story/3000000209680/immer-mehr-nachrichtenorganisationen-verkla gen-openai-und-microsoft* – accessed: 2024/03/30

[26] Art. 5 Abs. 5 Richtlinie 2001/29/EG; ErlRV 1178 BlgNR 27. GP 25; vgl auch von Welser, Generative KI und Urheberrechtsschranken, GRUR-Prax 2023, 516 (517); Schack, Auslesen von Webseiten zu KI-Trainingszwecken als Urheberrechtsverletzung de lege lata et ferenda, NJW 2024, 113 (114).

[27] EuGH C-302/10 point 53.

[28] More details in Jonas in Thiele/Burgstaller4 § 24c UrhG point 38.

[29] Cf. *https://www.forbes.com/sites/siladityaray/2023/05/02/samsung-bans-chatgpt-and-other-chatbots -for-employees-after-sensitive-code-leak/?sh=365c432c6078* – accessed: 2024/03/30

[30] Cf. *https://www.derstandard.at/story/3000000204643/so-laesst-sich-das-urheberrechtsproblem-der-kuenstlichen-intelligenz-loesen* – accessed: 2024/03/30

[31] Zankl, Künstliche Intelligenz und Immaterialgüterrecht bei Computerkunst, ecolex 2019, 244.

[32] Wiebe/Pabst in Handig/Hofmarcher/Kucsko, urheber.recht3 § 40a UrhG, point 101.

[33] Cf. § 5 öUrhG; Schumacher in Handig/Hofmarcher/Kucsko, urheber.recht3 § 5 UrhG, point 41.

[34] Anderl/Schelling in Kollar/Balog/Martinetz/Pichler, Das große Handbuch Wirtschaftsrecht, point 10.196

6

AI and IT Contract Law

Alexandra Ciarnau, Merve Taner

The digital value chain is undergoing constant change. It is becoming increasingly global, more complex and affects more and more areas of life. In addition to the numerous transformation potentials, AI also brings new complexity. Questions arise around product safety standards, potential discrimination and trustworthiness. In order to ensure the protection of health, safety and fundamental rights, the AI Act takes into account **global interdependencies** and, in accordance with Art. 2 para. 1 of the AI Act includes all **operators along the supply chain**.

- Provider[1] means any person, irrespective of their place of business, who places AI systems on the market or puts them into service in the EU

- Deployer[2] of AI systems that are based in the EU or are located in the EU

- Providers and deployers of AI systems based or residing in a third country if the AI results are used in the EU

- Importer[3] and distributor[4] of AI systems

---

[1] Provider means a natural or legal person, public authority, agency or other body that develops an AI system or a general-purpose AI model or that has an AI system or a general-purpose AI model developed and places it on the market or puts the AI system into service under its own name or trademark, whether for payment or free of charge.

[2] Deployer means a natural or legal person, public authority, agency or other body using an AI system under its authority except where the AI system is used in the course of a personal non-professional activity.

[3] Importer means a natural or legal person located or established in the Union that places on the market an AI system that bears the name or trademark of a natural or legal person established in a third country.

[4] Distributor means a natural or legal person in the supply chain, other than the provider or the importer, that makes an AI system available on the Union market.

- Product manufacturers who place AI systems on the market or put them into operation together with their product under their own name or brand

- Authorized representatives of providers who are not established in the EU

Depending on the respective role and classification of the AI system, these actors have different obligations. In very few cases, however, providers or deployers will develop and maintain AI systems entirely themselves. Instead, they will also rely on the expertise of third parties and procure software/hardware (components) or maintenance and support services. The reasons for this may vary, such as financial savings, increased efficiency, expertise, transfer of responsibilities and expansion of the liability pool, particularly in the case of new technologies.

When procuring IT services, the new **requirements of the AI Act to ensure legal compliance must now also be taken into account in IT contracts**.[5] Customers must assess where it makes sense to additionally oblige a service provider to comply with specific obligations under the AI Act (e. g. additional information, support in fulfilling their own obligations, etc.). Any regulations directly applicable to the customer must then be bound accordingly to the provider.[6] This is intended to ensure that the respective party subject to specific obligations in the value chain can use the AI system in compliance with the AI Act. This is particularly relevant for deployers who use AI for certain use cases under their oversight and regularly rely on service providers. For this reason, the following section briefly outlines the new issues triggered by the AI Act in IT contracts using **the example of the deployer as the customer**. The regulatory points to which particular attention should be paid when drafting the contract depend on the specific service and the type of contract. We provide an overview of (i) Licensing of standard software(ii) customized software development, (iii) software maintenance and (iv) hardware purchase/-maintenance.

Questions about the scope of performance arise for all types of contract. They are dealt with in the respective context, while warranty and liability are addressed generally in section 6.6.

---

[5] IT contracts touch upon different areas of law, such as traditional civil law, company law, intellectual property law and data protection law, as well as industry-specific, regulatory obligations in regulated business fields.

[6] "Overbinding" in this context refers to the obligation of the provider to fulfill certain obligations that apply directly to the client by law or contract.

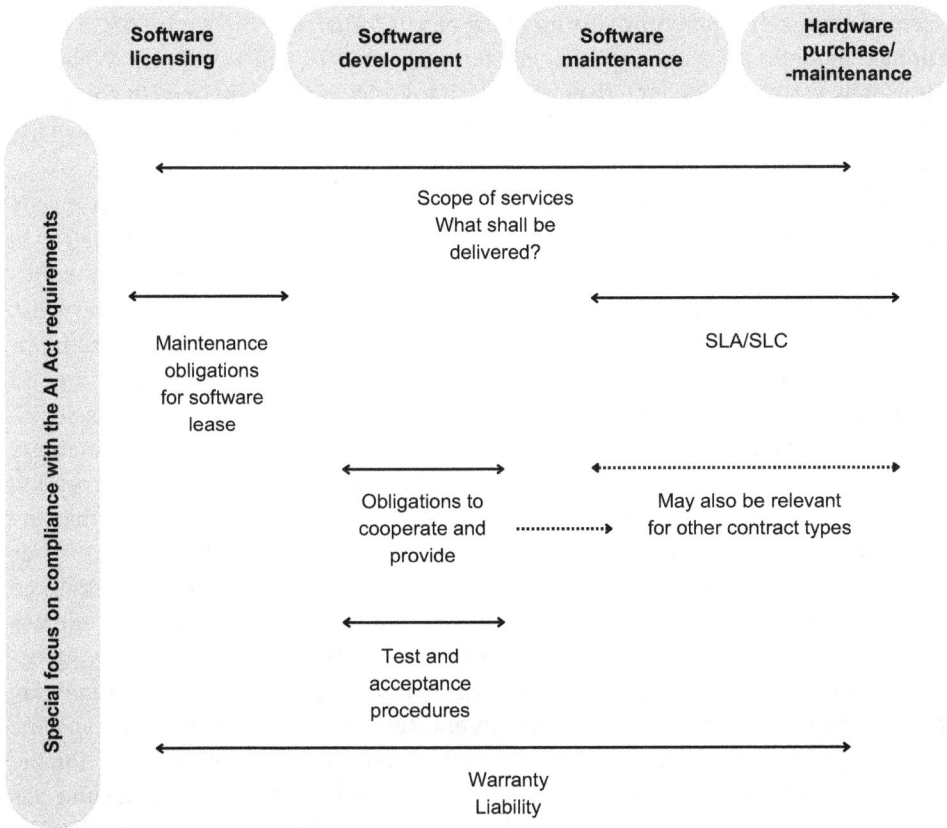

Figure 6.1 Visual Representation of the Focal Points of the Most Relevant IT Contracts

6.1 Licensing of Standard Software

Standard software is currently primarily made available via purchase or lease models.

Buying software is characterized by the following features [4]:

- One-off payment

- License to use for an indefinite period of time

- Provision of software to the agreed extent

- Contract termination through fulfillment (target debt relationship)

In the AI context, questions arise – not only for software licensing, but also for all other types of contracts – in particular regarding the **subject matter of the service** and its **specifications**. The agreement is decisive here, i. e. the stipulated and usually assumed characteristics within the meaning of § 922 Austrian Civil Code (ABGB). Conditional characteristics are explicitly agreed performance characteristics. What one can usually assume to be included, on the other hand, is based on objective expectations, which must be interpreted in each individual case, taking into account the public perception and the nature of the transaction [1].

The service contractually agreed must be provided. The customer intends to specify its service as precisely as possible; the provider, on the other hand, wants to define in scope and out of scope services in order to be able to make a realistic offer. The explicitly specified services may represent the required properties. However, not every task can be described. The scope of services can therefore also be partially open to interpretation. The usually assumed characteristics therefore play a significant role in the interpretation. However, this is open to debate. For example, are a certain stability, compatibility, user-friendliness, response times, expandability or maintainability usually assumed to be included although not explicitly stated? The public perception of AI systems is still evolving. For example, it is currently being discussed that the operational and traffic safety of AI systems within the meaning of the AI Act and thus compliance with the new obligations of the regulation are indeed usually assumed characteristics of a product. After all, the purpose of the AI Act is excactly to address the associated risks and enable safe use. However, there exist also the following opposing arguments: However, the specific risks and implementation obligations depend on the classification of the AI system and therefore also partly on the specific use in the deployer's environment. The latter in particular is often difficult for the service provider to assess in advance. This applies in particular to standard solutions provided that are intended for different applications. This case should therefore be assessed differently from a provider's offer for an AI system that can be used for a specific purpose. In this case, the provider knows the use case and the customer can expect that the necessary safety requirements for commissioning have already been taken into account. However, any disclaimers from the provider must also be considered during the design process.

Example

One provider advertises an AI system for the screening of job applications, automated decisions for recruitment and selection of job applicants. The AI system is obviously intended for the use as high-risk AI in accordance with Annex III Z 4 lit a AI Act. The provider, importer or distributor thus signals that his product can be used on the respective market. In my opinion, this speaks for an objectively expectable compliance with a fundamental, general operational and traffic safety of the software.

Practical Tip

The subject matter and specifications of the AI system must be carefully described in order to avoid legal disputes and frustrated investments. This should be done at the following levels:

- **Quantitative requirements** (e. g. provision of an AI model, an algorithm, an entire AI system, provision of a certain size of neural network, provision of additional functionalities, provision of a test environment, creation of a user manual and documentation, performance of conformity assessment for high-risk AI, etc.).
- **Qualitative requirements** (e. g. technical, organizational and legal requirements, such as AI Act compliance, compliance with the market standard or the provision of state-of-the-art services, availability of AI expertise among the personnel deployed and any subcontractors; training with a balanced data set to avoid bias, CE marking in accordance with Art. 48 AI Act)

Software lease is generally characterized by the following features [4]:

- Recurring remuneration;
- Limited or unlimited use;
- Software license to the agreed extent;
- Maintenance obligation of the provider (e. g. bug fixes, updates) for software as a service;
- Termination of contract (continuing obligation).

Under Austrian law, in addition to the above-mentioned challenges for the specification of services, the scope of the maintenance obligation also plays a role in the software as a service/lease models. Unless otherwise agreed, the provider is responsible for maintaining the software. He therefore guarantees that the AI system not only has the agreed properties at the time of handover, but also owes the ongoing, contractual maintenance over the lease period. However, the maintenance obligations are usually specified in more detail in the contract.

Example

High-risk AI systems must be as resilient as possible to errors, malfunctions or inconsistencies within the system or the environment in which the system is operated in accordance with Art. 15 para. 4 AI Act. In this context, technical and organizational measures must be taken. From the customer's perspective, it is therefore advisable not only to agree compliance with this obligation, but also to provide examples of the expected technical and organizational measures for troubleshooting. These include, for example, the provision of security updates to maintain the contractually compliant status.

6.2 Software Development

The core elements of a **software development contract** include [4]:

- Individual development taking customer needs into account;
- Usually a committment to realize the development;
- Generally, exclusive right to the individual software;
- Termination of contract through fulfillment (usually successful acceptance; target debt relationship).

If an AI system is developed individually, the parties agree to implement software that is specifically tailored to the customer. From the deployer's perspective as the customer, the agreement should therefore be structured as a **contract for work for hire**. This also corresponds to the classification of the Austrian Supreme Court (see OGH 21.1.2015, 1 Ob 229/14d). The service contract is to be distinguished from the contract for work. In the case of the provision of services, only mere effort and no success is owed. Of course, this weakens the position of the customer and is inappropriate in view of the financing of the individual development by customer. In my opinion, different rules apply if the parties consciously enter into a research partnership and in the case of individual development of high-tech AI systems that are far beyond the state of the art and whose achievement of the objective depends on several unclear factors.

Also for software development the issues described under 6.1 also arise with regard to the **service description**.

Another specific aspect is the **obligations to cooperate** of customer is the client's **obligation to cooperate**. Project realization is usually also dependent on support services from customer's side. These must be agreed separately. Common obligations to cooperate are, for example

- Creation and maintenance of certain framework conditions such as hardware, special requirements for the IT infrastructure (connections, computers, capacities, etc.);
- Access and access rights of the provider's employees;
- Provision of human resources for ongoing coordination;
- Acceptance tests.

When procuring AI systems, the following obligations to cooperate may be relevant, for example:

- Information on the intended use in order to be able to classify the software in accordance with the AI Act and implement the necessary requirements for software production

- For high-risk AI:
    - Provision of training, validation and testing data sets in accordance with Art. 10 AI Act;
    - Support in carrying out tests in accordance with Art. 10 AI Act;
    - Information on existing data/AI governance and risk management systems in order to link the obligations under Art. 9 AI Act with the existing framework;
    - Carrying out an initial fundamental rights impact assessment in accordance with Art. 27 AI Act in order to be able to make any necessary changes to the software design in time (see also section 3.4 for the fundamental rights impact assessment).
- For certain AI systems:
    - Provision of proprietary data if the AI system is also to interact with people on the basis of other sources of information.

Finally, the development of AI systems also changes the technical test points and requirements in the **acceptance procedure**. In the provider's test procedure, which is usually carried out before the acceptance procedure, the provider should ensure compliance with the specific **testing requirement**s of the AI Act:

- Compliance with the specific obligations for tests under real-world conditions within the meaning of Art. 2 para. 8 AI Act in conjunction with Art. 3 no. 57 AI Act, such as obtaining the informed consent of users in accordance with Art. 60 AI Act;
- Testing of high-risk AI systems in order to comply with the identified appropriate risk management measures within the meaning of Art. 9 para. 6 AI Act;
- Testing based on pre-defined parameters and probabilistic thresholds within the meaning of Art. 9 para. 8 AI Act that are suitable for the intended purpose of the high-risk AI system;
- Testing with training, validation and testing data sets, taking into account the requirements of Art. 10 para. 2 et seqq. AI Act;
- Carrying out attack tests to determine system risks (e. g. for general purpose AI models with systemic risk in accordance with Art. 55 AI Act).

6.3 Software Maintenance

In a software maintenance contract the parties agree on the **operational readiness** of the standard or customized software provided. The specific scope of maintenance is determined by the agreement. There is a great deal of room for maneuver here, and various services are offered on the market – individually or in combination – such as [4]:

- Troubleshooting (error correction);
- Preventive error correction through bug-fixing (maintenance);
- Provision of updates;
- Provision of upgrades;
- Provision of a support hotline;
- Back-up.

Similar to the considerations in 6.4 the **scope of maintenance** must also be specified in the contract. The service agreement is usually specified via **service level agreements** (SLA) in more detail. SLAs contain objectively measurable targets that must be achieved by the provider. These are often availability and quality commitments. Compliance with the SLA must be monitored and reported. It mus also be aexplicitly, who fulfills these monitoring and reporting obligations. If the SLA is not met, **service level credits** (SLC) can be agreed as a penalty (contractual penalty).

In SLA the following AI-specific regulations in particular must be taken into account:

- If all AI systems are used, staff must have AI literacy in accordance with Art. 4 AI Act (see section 3.1.6 for details). This requirement must be agreed in the quality of the personnel deployed.

- High-risk AI

    - According to Art. 13 para. 3 lit e AI Act, high-risk AI requires all necessary maintenance and care measures, including their frequency, to ensure the proper functioning of this AI system, including with regard to software updates. This must therefore be taken into account when defining availability, response time, errors, troubleshooting and response times, updates and upgrades in the SLA.

    - The necessary maintenance and care measures include, in particular, the obligations set out in Art. 9 et seq. AI Act, such as regular monitoring, risk assessment, review of mitigation and control measures, notification obligations, testing, cleansing, updating, enrichment and aggregation of data, identification of data gaps or deficiencies, detection and correction of distortions in data sets, technical documentation and recording obligations, human oversight, etc.

- AI systems with a general purpose

    - At general purpose AI models, for example, compliance with transparency regulations, ongoing improvement of the model to prevent interference with third-party rights (in particular copyrights) and technical documentation in accordance with Art. 53 AI Act are relevant.

- For general purpose AI models with systemic risk, additional model assessments, tests to identify and eliminate systemic risks, ongoing documentation and fulfillment of reporting obligations in the event of serious incidents must be contractually taken into account in accordance with Art. 55 AI Act.
  - For further details on the specific obligations when using general purpose AI, see section 3.7.
- Certain AI systems
  - The AI Act obligations when operating certain AI systems are primarily limited to compliance with the transparency regulations and ensuring that the rights and freedoms of third parties are protected in accordance with Art. 50 AI Act.

The examples make it clear that maintenance contracts will also have to be re-assessed in future and adapted to AI-specific errors.

6.4 Open Source Software

Merve Taner

Sovereignty over the programming code i. e. the digital infrastructure, is important for a free society. An independent digital infrastructure is needed to be able to shape digitalization itself. Genuine democratic control over the code and the associated hardware is part of digital sovereignty [20] and, according to *Lessig*, goes hand in hand with free and open software (open source) [15]. This section provides an overview of the definition of open source software, use cases, legal problems and the relevance for the EU, including the legal provisions in the AI Act.

6.4.1 Open Source AI – Paving the Way for the Future?

Zuckerberg looks at open source AI as the way forward. His company META is taking the next steps to establish open source AI as an industry standard. To this end, Meta published Llama 3.1 405B (according to Zuckerberg, the first frontier-level open source AI model) and the improved Llama 3.1 70B and 8B models [19]. Other examples include BLOOM (BigScience Large Open-Science Open-Access Multilingual Language Model), developed under the leadership of the AI company Hugging Face, MPT-7B, introduced by MosaicML Foundations, Falcon 2, the latest generation of open-source large-scale language models from the Technology Innovation Institute (TII) in Abu Dhabi, and Vicuna-13B [16]. Over 84% of companies state that open source software is used in important or business-critical areas [21].

Advantages of Open Source from a Developer's Perspective

- **Training, fine-tuning your own models:** Companies have a wide variety of requirements. Ideally, these requirements can be met with models of different sizes that are trained or fine-tuned with a specific data set. Open source models such as Llama can be trained with your own data and reduced to the required size.
- **No dependence on closed providers ("vendors"):** With market-leading vendors of closed AI models, there is a certain degree of risk of dependency. Open source can enable a broad ecosystem of companies with compatible toolchains. Companies can become dependent if they
    - rely on **models**:
        - that they **cannot carry out** and **control themselves**;
        - which the provider can **change at any time**,
        - whose **terms of use** the provider can change or
        - where provision is even **stopped completely**.
    - are tied to **a single cloud** that has exclusive rights to a model [19].
        An example of this is Microsoft Azure Open AI, where, in contrast to OpenAI without Azure context, access security to data is ensured by a stored authorization model (RBAC) [11]. However, modifiable (and therefore controllable) content filters and/or modifiable misuse monitoring for the Azure OpenAI service are only available for managed customers and partners who work with Microsoft account teams and are subject to additional requirements. Only customers who meet these requirements can apply for this [13].
- **Protection of (personal and non-personal) data:** One of the most striking opportunities associated with digitalization and the development of new technologies is big data and big data analytics. This is a generic term for various developments in connection with data, divided into the following v-categories:
    - *v*olume (scope, data volume),
    - *v*elocity (speed at which the data volumes are generated and transferred),
    - *v*ariety (range of data types and sources) and
    - *v*eracity (authenticity of data).

Related to this are *data processing capacities* (also known as big data analytics) – including the methods and tools used-which have taken on a significant dimension and represent a large part of a company's value in many industries [3, 10].[7] This makes it all the more important to protect the company's data.

---

[7] Wimmer, Auswirkungen der Digitalisierung auf das Wirtschaftsprivatrecht – Ausgewählte Fragen zum Gesellschafts-, Kartell- und Lauterkeitsrecht, JBl 2021, 288 (291); see also Rupprecht, Die 9. Novelle des Gesetzes gegen Wettbewerbsbeschränkungen (GWB), 48 f. The opinion emphasizes that the digital economy is increasingly data-driven and that this is reflected in the fact that the German legislator expressly anchored "access to competition-relevant data" in Section 18 para. 3a no. 4 ARC as part of the 9th amendment to the ARC in 2017. Wimmer in FN 32: The German legislator thus standardized access to competition-relevant data as a criterion relevant to market power.

Open source models make it possible to run the models anywhere and to (further) develop them transparently. Companies often work with confidential data that they want to keep secure [19]. The trust of customers and the security of confidential data (personal and non-personal data such as trade secrets) are a company's greatest asset.

- **(Cost) technical efficiency:** Developers can often run open source models on their own infrastructure more cheaply [21], if not for free. The range is between 0.2 and 7.5 USD per 1 M token [8, 17]. For example, Llama 3.1 405B can be run on one's own infrastructure at around 50% of the cost of using closed models such as GPT-4o.
- **Sustainable Ecosystem:** Open source models are used to build the company's own infrastructure and embed AI systems in it. The creation of a long-term architecture would be sustainable and open source would therefore be an integral part of this solution (on sustainability, see also).

6.4.2 Definition of Open Source and Legal Basis

Open Source Software (OSS)-solutions offer an alternative to paid software [1]. The use of OSS is becoming increasingly established in the software industry. With the digitalization of everyday life, the use of OSS is also increasing [21]. The first definition of OSS goes back to the Free Software Foundation at the end of the 1990s. It defined OSS as the freedom of users to run, copy, distribute, study, modify and improve the software [4]. The definition of the Open Source Initiative [24] states that OSS is not just access to the source code and lists further sub-items.

The distribution conditions must meet certain criteria:

1. **Free distribution:** The license may not restrict the sale or distribution of the software.

2. **Source code:** The program must contain the source code and allow its distribution in source and compiled form.

3. **Unrestricted editing rights/derived works:** The license must allow modifications and derived works and permit their distribution under the same conditions as the original software.

4. **Integrity of the author'ssource code:** The license may only restrict the source code in modified form if the distribution of patch files is permitted.

5. **No personal or group discrimination**

6. **No discrimination** of fields of activity

7. **Distribution of the license:** The rights associated with the program must apply to everyone to whom the program is distributed.

8. **No product-specific license:** The rights must not depend on the program being part of a specific software distribution.

9. **No restriction of** other software

10. **Technology neutrality** of the license: No provision of the license may be based on a specific technology or interface type.

> ✅ **Definition of Open Source**
>
> Software licensed under an OS license license has the following characteristics:
>
> 1. **Public access** to the source code: With commercial software, the source code is not accessible. In contrast, with freely accessible source code, users and programmers collaborate on the OSS and develop it further [4]. The source code is available free of charge. However, OSS can also be used commercially [21]. Due to the distinctions in the license conditions, the software is not always suitable for commercial use [14]. The program must contain the source code and allow its distribution in source and compiled form.
> 2. **Modifiability** of the software by anyone;
> 3. **Free of charge;**
> 4. **Provision for download** on the Internet directly from the website of the author, editor or manufacturer. However, OSS can also be obtained from dealers, so-called distributors [18]. Depending on the respective license, further obligations may be imposed on the user or licensee [4].

The licensee of an OS license is granted the work use permit (§ 24 para. 1 öUrhG (Austrian IP Act), § 31 dtUrhG (German IP Act)), a right to edit (§ 5 öUrhG (Austrian IP Act), § 3 dtUrhG (German IP Act)), reproduction right (§ 15 öUrhG (Austrian IP Act), § 16 dtUrhG (German IP Act)) and distribution right (§ 16 öUrhG (Austrian IP Act), § 17 dtUrhG (German IP Act)), whereby the licensee must comply with the obligations set out in the license.

6.4.3 Legal Problem Areas in Connection with Open Source According to Existing Legal Bases

OSS can entail the following legal difficulties:

1. Every person who co-develops an OSS develops it on the basis of the open source license. This can result in a **large number of co-authors** (several programmers). It is not possible to agree the rights of use for individual cases [4, 18].

2. There are **different types of OSS license agreements** under which OSS products are distributed [1]. Permissive licenses, weak copyleft licenses and strong copyleft licenses [7, 22]. In any case, attention should be paid to the type of license, as these

entail different rights and obligations, which can lead to breaches of contract in the event of non-compliance.

Table 6.1 Overview of OSS License Agreement Types

PERMISSIVE LICENSES	COPYLEFT WEAK LICENSES	COPYLEFT STRONG LICENSES
These licenses grant users extensive freedom to use, modify and distribute the software with minimal restrictions and require only minimal obligations: for example, the inclusion of the original copyright notice and license terms in all copies or substantial portions of the software and documentation [5].	Weak copyleft licenses strike a balance between permissive and strong licenses. They allow the code to be freely used, modified and distributed, but with certain conditions so that derivative works under the same license remain open source. The conditions are less strict than strict copyleft licenses and allow proprietary use under certain circumstances [1].	Strong copyleft licenses ensure that all works derived from the software **are also distributed under the same license conditions**. Changes to the software and any software that contains them must be distributed under the same license. Strong copyleft licenses are intended for projects that want to guarantee the freedom of the software and prevent *proprietary forks**.
The following licenses fall under the category **Permissive Licenses**: *MIT license*used by Facebook; *BSD license*, which is used by Google [5]; *Universal Permissive License* [21]	The following licenses fall under the category **Weak Copyleft Licenses**: *Mozilla Public Licence* (MPL); *Common Development and Distribution License* (CDDL) [1]; *Apache License 2.0*, which is used by AWS; *Microsoft Public License* [21]	The following licenses fall under the category **Strong Copyleft Licenses**: The *GNU General Public License* (GPL), under which the Linux operating system or the OpenOffice.org software are distributed, was considered the most widely used OSS license and contains a **strong copyleft**. This category also includes: *Affero General Public License* (AGPL) und *The Linux Kernel*, licensed under GPL [5] *Eclipse Publice License* (EPL-1.0) *European Union Public License* *German Free Software License* *Open Software License* [21]

Table 6.1 Overview of OSS License Agreement Types *(continued)*

PERMISSIVE LICENSES	COPYLEFT WEAK LICENSES	COPYLEFT STRONG LICENSES
MIT license: The licensee only has to retain existing copyright notices (= license text). This license is also suitable for closed source software where the source code is not disclosed [4]. **BSD license:** Copyright notices, license and liability clause must be retained (2-clause). Rights holders or (co-)authors may not be named for advertising purposes (3-clause) [4].	**Apache license:** Modified passages must be marked as such, and license conditions and copyright notices must be retained or included [1]. Depending on how "aggressively" the copyleft effect is formulated, a distinction is made between the three categories illustrated here [4].	**GPL license:** It contains a strong copyleft in versions 2.0 and 3.0; this is somewhat weaker in the LGPL ("Lesser"). Licensees are usually obliged to make the source code available to the public. Explicitly no license fees may be charged [2].

*　Proprietary forks = a process in which developers take a copy of the source code of a software package and begin independent development on it to create a distinct and separate piece of software, available at *https://en.wikipedia.org/wiki/Fork_(software_development)* (last accessed: 2024/07/29).

Not all licenses fall into these categories. For example, the *LLAMA 2 Community License Agreement* is a *"non-exclusive, worldwide, non-transferable and royalty-free limited license […]."* However, it also has some restrictions[8] while the LLAMA3 *Community License Agreement* has even more specific provisions.[9]

1.　If a strong "copyleft" clause has been agreed, the **link to proprietary software** may constitute a further development to which the open source license extends [4]. If the OSS is further developed and published, the (new) source code must be made available to the general public. The concept of the public domain can already be realized in the provision within a company or an authority [2].

2.　The **technical implementation and the compatibility of the licenses** (cf.) **must** be checked when using OSS in commercial software, as otherwise the licence may be violated or "adhere" to the software based on it ("viral" [4] or "immunizing effect" [21]):

---

[8]　Github, LLama 2 License, available at *https://github.com/Meta-Llama/llama/blob/main/LICENSE* (accessed: 2024/07/28). For example, the license rights require that copies of the LLama license be distributed to third parties (1.b).

[9]　Github, Llama 3 License, available at *https://github.com/meta-llama/llama3/blob/main/LICENSE* (last accessed on 28.07.2024): "Provide a copy of this Agreement with any such LLAMA Materials." […] "Prominently display 'Built with Meta LLAMA 3' on a related website, user interface, blog post, about page, or product documentation." […] "Include 'LLAMA 3' at the beginning of any AI model name that is created, trained, fine-tuned, or otherwise improved using the LLAMA Materials and is distributed or made available."

- In one of the world's first decisions on the effectiveness of open source licenses, the Munich Regional Court dealt with the then best-known and most common license GNU GPL at the time. Contrary to the opinions that the license model originating from American law was not transferable to European and German legal relationships, the court found that it was fundamentally valid under German law [23].[10] In the meantime, this view has been confirmed several times by courts and, for example, the possibility of a claim for damages in the event of an infringement of OS licenses has been established [21].

- *Wiebe* noted in this regard that no gross disadvantage to the user could be assumed under Austrian law either. The admissibility of such a condition results from §§ 696, 704 öABGB (Austrian Civil Code).

- Any software that is derived from or based on GPL-protected programs must be made available to third parties free of royalties in source code in the event of publication or distribution as a whole under the terms of the GPL. The GPL thus differs fundamentally from Austrian - and German - copyright law. However, if parts of programs consisting of GPL code and non-GPL code can be regarded as independent programs, these non-GPL parts may be distributed commercially independently. The relevant demarcation issues are very complex and difficult; appropriate technical and legal checks are recommended in each individual case [21].

3. Violations of open source licenses can amount to **copyright infringement** can amount to copyright infringement. The possible legal consequences are: Claims for injunctive relief, claims for removal, claims for reasonable compensation, damages; criminal prosecution; publication of judgment. Users of software can be prosecuted even if they had no knowledge of the unlawful use of the software. When purchasing, commissioning or investing in software, it should therefore be checked whether the software complies with any OS licenses ("open source due diligence", OSS), or the supplier should be obliged to create an OS-compliant state. If a software company or individual software products are acquired, it makes sense to include corresponding clauses regarding OSS in the contract [21].

4. The characteristic legal obligations that often accompany OSS are:

- Delivery of the license text, publication of the source code, author's note; a disclaimer, prohibition of OSS restrictions [21], obligation to transfer the OSS license to the end user [4].

---

[10] Wiebe, Open Source Software-Lizenz-Wirksamkeit, Medien und Recht 2004, 269 (272); Munich 21 O 6123/2004 (19.05.2004). In this case, it was decided that the clauses of the open source software license GNU GPL that were the subject of the lawsuit did not contain any unreasonable disadvantages for a contracting party and were to be regarded as effective. The envisaged reversion of rights in the event of a breach of the license conditions constitutes a resolutory condition of the granting of rights in rem, so that no circumvention of Section 31 (1) dUrhG (permissible restriction of the right of use) arises.

6.4.4 Open Source Software Strategy of the European Commission

On October 21, 2020, the European Commission adopted its new open source software strategy for the period from 2020 to 2023. Under the guiding principle "Think Open", the strategy aims to harness the transformative and innovative power of open source software and strengthen the collaborative use and reuse of software solutions and expertise across Europe. The Commission is committed to intensifying the use of open source software not only in the IT sector, but also in other strategically important areas: by setting up open source innovation labs, reducing the administrative burden of publishing open source software and promoting skills and talent in the field of open source software [12]. Open source is recognized as a catalyst for change. The main points of the strategy are:

- emphasizing the importance of open source software for Europe's digital autonomy and measures to promote the use and reuse of open source software
- Promoting open source as a means of achieving digital autonomy and control over technologies
- Implementation of the digital strategy [6]

6.4.5 Exceptions for Open Source in the AI Act

The AI Regulation does not apply to AI systems that are *licensed under free and open source licenses* ("OSS"), unless they are classified as high-risk AI systems or placed on the market or put into service as an AI-system falling under Article 5 or 50 (Art. 2 para. 12 AI Act, Recital 89 AI Act, see also). Free and open source AI components include software and data, including models and general purpose AI models, tools, services or procedures of an AI system (Recital 103 AI Act).

> In practice, the misunderstanding can arise that open source software has been completely excluded from the scope of the AI Act, or the counter-exceptions, in particular those of Art. 50 AI Act, are overlooked. The exception should therefore be treated with caution for the following reasons:
>
> 1. It is not inconceivable that OSS could be used for the development of a specific AI system (Art. 50 AI Act). Here, not only the applicability of the AI Act would have to be examined, but also the legal framework conditions outside the regulatory requirements of the AI Act would have to be clarified (see section 6.3.3).
> 2. Even if the party providing the OSS (provider) is not itself subject to the regulations, as it is an OSS that neither engages in prohibited practices (Art. 5 AI Act) nor uses it in a high-risk AI system or specific AI system, the party using the OSS to develop and operate an independent AI system is not covered by the exception.

Open Source and General Purpose AI Models

The AI Act provides for an exception for providers of general purpose AI models (see section 3.7) that are provided under a free and open source license *that allows access, use, modification and distribution of the model and whose parameters, including weights, model architecture information and model usage information, are made publicly available.*

The obligations under Art. 50. 1 lit. a and b AI Act do not apply in this case. The opposite exception applies to general purpose AI models with systemic risks (Art. 50 para. 2 AI Act; Recital 104 AI Act).

For third parties that make tools, services, processes or components (other than general purpose AI models) publicly available under a free and open source license, Art. 50 para. 4 AI Act does not apply. As a result, they do not record the information, capabilities, technical access and other support in accordance with the generally recognized state of the art in a written agreement, which is necessary for the provider of the high-risk AI system to fully comply with the obligations laid down in this Regulation (see Art. 25 para. 4 AI Act on "Responsibilities along the AI value chain").

Outlook

Finally, it should be noted that the European Commission is responsible for drawing up guidelines in accordance with Art. 96 AI Act, which are intended to address the prohibited practices (Art. 5 AI Act), high-risk AI systems (Art. 6 AI Act) and certain AI systems (Art. 50 AI Act) and the associated obligations in more detail.

It therefore remains to be seen when and to what extent Art. 96 AI Act will be implemented in order to be able to conclusively assess the delimitation pursuant to Art. 2 para. 12 AI Act. At the same time, there is the problem that the deadline of Art. 113 AI Act applies to the implementation of Art. 96 AI Act and therefore the implementation should take place by February 2, 2026 [9].

In order to avoid short implementation periods after publication of the guidelines, companies should already consider the extent to which open source software is part of their corporate and AI strategy and subject any development projects to a legal review.

Sources

[1] Andréewitch, Markus: Open Source und proprietäre Software: Das Verknüpfungsproblem. In: MR2005, issue 5, 240–243

[2] Andréewitch, Markus: Risiken bei firmen- und behördeninterner Bearbeitung von Open Source Software. In: MR 2005 issue 1, 36–39

[3] Auswirkungen der Digitalisierung auf das Wirtschaftsprivatrecht – Ausgewählte Fragen zum Gesellschafts-, Kartell- und Lauterkeitsrecht | Lexis 360. URL *https://360.lexisnexis.at/d/artikel/aus wirkungen_der_digitalisierung_auf_das_wirtschaf/z_jbl_2021_5_jbl_2021_05_0288_3a608b4100* – accessed: 2024/08/03

[4] Bisset, Katharina: Open Source Softwarelizenzen. URL *https://360.lexisnexis.at/d/lexisbriefings/open_ source_softwarelizenzen/h_80004_3864683696566738385_df06868344* – accessed: 2024/08/03

[5] Choosing the Right Open Source License in 2024: A Comprehensive Guide – Threatrix. URL *https:// threatrix.io/blog/open-source-compliance/choosing-the-right-open-source-license-in-2024-a-compre hensive-guide/* – accessed: 2024/08/03

[6] Europäische Kommission: Mitteilung an die Kommission, Open-Source-Software-Strategie 2020– 2023 Offen Denken.

[7] Freizügige Open-Source-Lizenz. Wikipedia.

[8] Götz, Charlotte: KI Kosten – Welche Lösungen gibt es für Ihr Budget? URL *https://konfuzio.com/de/ ki-kosten/* – accessed: 2024/08/03 – Konfuzio

[9] kaizenner: The AI Act: responsibilities of the European Commission (AI Office). URL *https://www. kaizenner.eu/post/ai-act-responsibilities-commission* – accessed: 2024/08/03 – Digitizing Europe

[10] Kersting, Christian; Podszun, Rupprecht; Grave, Carsten: Die 9. GWB-Novelle: Kartellschadens- ersatz – Digitale Ökonomie – Fusionskontrolle – Bußgeldrecht – Verbraucherschutz. München: C. H. Beck, 2017 – ISBN 978-3-406-71080-3

[11] KI und Recht: ChatGPT versus Microsoft Azure OpenAI und Copilot. URL *https://www.cio.de/a/ chatgpt-versus-microsoft-azure-openai-und-copilot,3734533* – accessed: 2024/08/03

[12] Kommission verabschiedet neue Strategie für Open-Source-Software – Europäische Kommis- sion. URL *https://germany.representation.ec.europa.eu/news/kommission-verabschiedet-neue-strategie- fur-open-source-software-2020-10-21_de* – accessed: 2024/08/03

[13] krlaird: Limited access to Azure OpenAI Service – Azure AI services. URL *https://learn.microsoft. com/en-us/legal/cognitive-services/openai/limited-access* – accessed: 2024/08/03

[14] Lanzinger, Michael; Bisset, Katharina: Softwarevertrag | Lexis 360. URL *https://360.lexisnexis.at/d/ lexisbriefings/softwarevertrag/h_80001_4172893168535162674_8cc3e5d8e8* – accessed: 2024/08/03

[15] Lessig, Lawrence; Lessig, Lawrence: Code. Version 2.0. New York: Basic Books, 2006 – ISBN 978-0- 465-03914-2

[16] McFarland, Alex: Die 5 besten Open Source LLMs (August 2024). URL *https://www.unite.ai/de/beste- Open-Source-Filme/* – accessed: 2024/08/03 – Unite.AI

[17] Model & API Provider Analysis | Artificial Analysis. URL *https://artificialanalysis.ai* – accessed: 2024/08/03

[18] ÖJZ 2004/39: Open Source Software Rechtliche Rahmenbedingungen nach österr. Recht (Andreas Wiebe *) / Felix Prändl *)): RDB Rechtsdatenbank. URL *https://rdb.manz.at/document/rdb.tso.LI04091 40023* – accessed: 2024/08/03

[19] Open Source AI Is the Path Forward. URL *https://about.fb.com/news/2024/07/open-source-ai-is-the- path-forward/* – accessed: 2024/08/03 – Meta

[20] Rosengrün, Sebastian: Künstliche Intelligenz zur Einführung, Zur Einführung. Hamburg: Junius, 2021 – ISBN 978-3-96060-323-8

[21] Tretzmüller: Handbuch Softwarerecht

[22] Verschiedene Lizenzen und Kommentare – GNU-Projekt – Free Software Foundation. URL *https:// www.gnu.org/licenses/license-list* – accessed: 2024/08/03

[23] Wiebe, Andreas: Open Source Software-Lizenz-Wirksamkeit Volume Medien und Recht 2004, 269 (272)

[24] *https://opensource.org/osd* accessed: 2024/08/03

6.5 Hardware Purchase and Maintenance

Alexandra Ciarnau

The hardware purchase is particularly relevant in certain areas, such as in industry with **robotics and sensor components**. Procurement is usually structured as a classic purchase agreement. The buyer owes the purchase price, whereas the supplier owes the transfer of unencumbered ownership, including any other necessary rights to any software supplied.

Hardware procurements with AI components focus on the following topics:

The requirements under the AI Act also apply to hardware procurements. Finally, the AI definition also covers software embedded in hardware (see section 6.4 for further details). This means that predominantly high-risk AI systems are also subject to obligations in terms of **accuracy, technical robustness and cybersecurity** throughout the entire life cycle of the product (Art. 15 AI Act), the requirement for **CE marking**, **conformity assessment and compliance with standards** (e. g. ISO, DIN, Ö-Norms and other standards). The provider must be obliged to fulfill these (AI Act) requirements as part of the **specification of the subject matter of the service**.

With regard to maintenance, the considerations set out in section 6.3 apply mutatis mutandis. In addition, customers should also contractually regulate the provision of **spare parts** and the performance of **repair obligations** to not jeopardize the ongoing operation of an AI system.

6.6 General Information on Liability

For IT contract draftings the following liability provisions are relevant:

- Warranty;
- Compensation for damages;
- Penalty and indemnification irrespective of fault.

Warranty

The **service provider is liable for tany defects of** the services provided. A defect is deemed, if the services deviate from the agreed specifications at the time of handover. This includes the stipulated and usually assumed characteristics (see section 6.1 on stipulated and usually assumed characteristics). If these properties are missing, the customer is entitled to warranty claims (improvement, replacement, price reduction and withdrawal from the contract).

The statutory warranty period is **two years from handover of the product**, but is regularly restricted in the B2B sector. In the first six months from handover, it is legally presumed that the defect already existed at the time of handover. The presumption rule is also often excluded.

In addition, the obligation to give notice of defects is agreed in B2B relationships. The buyer must inspect the service within a reasonable period of time and give notice of any defects, otherwise claims will be forfeited. However, the obligation to give notice of defects is usually excluded and an acceptance procedure is agreed.

> **Practical Tip**
>
> Warranty claims generally play a subordinate role in IT software contracts. This is due to different circumstances:
>
> - On the one hand, it is difficult to prove that a defect existed at the time of handover (taking into account that no software is 100% error-free). Finally, the aforementioned presumption rule is generally excluded.
> - On the other hand, the acceptance procedure for software development contracts is of particular importance. Testing and acceptance procedures are intended to identify and correct errors that prevent acceptance. In addition, the warranty is pushed further into the background, if software maintenance is seamlessly linked to the transfer and bug fixes are planned as part of this run period.
>
> The situation is different when buying hardware, especially standard goods. The warranty is essential here.

Compensation for Damages

In addition, the service provider is liable for damages caused due to **fault** (contractual or tort liability) or **strict liability** (e. g. Product Liability Act in Germany and Austria, Austrian Railway and Motor Vehicle Liability Act). This is one of the most important regulatory issues in the procurement and use of AI. According to the current Austrian legal provisions, the service provider is liable

- in case of fault according to §§ 1203 ff. ABGB (Austrian Civil Code) taking into account expert liability pursuant to § 1299 ABGB (Austrian Civil Code)[11] for negligently and intentionally caused positive damages (including loss of profit)[12],

---

[12] The determination of fault depends on compliance with the duty of care according to the usual abilities of an average person. Experts are subject to a stricter standard and must have the skills that are objectively expected in their profession.

[13] In the context of contractual liability, the customer enjoys certain advantages, such as the reversal of the burden of proof or the attribution of vicarious agents. In the case of tort liability, there is no reversal of the burden of proof and no vicarious liability.

▪ as a (quasi-)manufacturer or importer for property damage and personal injury under the PHG (Austrian Product Liability Act), depending on fault, if this is caused by a defective product.[13] are caused.

In future, the liability regulations will be adapted to current developments with the **Directive on AI Liability** [2] and the **amendment of the Product Liability Directive** [3]. For the first time, they will create a harmonized legal framework for damage caused by AI. The focus is on consumer protection and enabling the de facto enforcement of claims for damages. As plaintiffs, injured parties bear the full burden of proof. Of course, in practice they face difficulties in providing evidence when they have to claim and prove that they have suffered damage due to the use of AI. It is therefore a question of the causal link. Easier proof and extensive information rights should now change this and ensure effective compensation. In addition, the product definition in product liability law will also be extended to software in future and the product defect will be described in a new way.

In B2B contract practice, however, **exclusions and limitations of liability** are common. Liability in Austria can be limited

▪ according to the type of damage (e. g. for atypical damage, certain types of damage),

▪ the amount (e. g. amount cap as a percentage, in euros or based on the order value) or

▪ fault (e. g. exclusion for slight negligence).

However, liability **cannot** be excluded for

▪ intent,

▪ blatant gross negligence,[14]

▪ Damage to life, limb and health and

▪ Claims under the Product Liability Act.[15]

---

[14] A product within the meaning of the PHG (Austrian Product Liability Act) is a movable tangible good. AI systems as pure software do not fall under the product definition. An exception exists if the software is connected to hardware. See alsoRabl, Produkthaftungsgesetz (2016) on Section 4 PHG, Rz 54; Posch/Terlitza inDeixler-Hübner/Kolba (eds.), Handbuch Verbraucherrecht (2015). Das Recht der Produkthaftung, 373 f.; Posch/Terlitza inSchwimann/Kodek (eds.), ABGB Praxiskommentar⁴ (2016) on Section 4 PHG, para. 10.

[15] The exclusion for simple gross negligence is permissible up to the limit of immorality. This is a case-by-case decision. See also OGH 7 Ob 666/84; 6 Ob 836/83.

[16] The limits of the exclusions of liability relate to the B2B sector. For B2C relationships, more favorable regulations apply for consumers.

Practical Tip

The potential risks associated with the use of AI systems should be adequately covered by the contractual indemnification provisions from a customer perspective. These include at least liability for data damage and loss, fines under the AI Act or parallel applicable penalties under the GDPR or other provisions and infringements of third-party rights when using AI.

Penalty and Indemnification and Hold Harmless Agreements

As the parties often encounter difficulties in providing evidence when enforcing claims for damages (see also the above explanations in the AI environment), no-fault penalties (contractual penalties) are popular to be included in IT contracts[16] as liquidated damages[17] and indemnification agreements (indemnity agreements).

Common use cases are

- Penalty for
    - delay;
    - failed acceptance;
    - data breaches and breaches of confidentiality obligations;
    - breach of material contractual obligations, such as compliance with statutory provisions;
    - violation of SLA (see SLC in section 6.4).
- Damage and claim indemnification:
    - Infringement of third-party rights by the software, in particular IP rights;
    - Violation of agreed certifications, norms and standards,
    - Violations of restrictions on use.

In IT contracts for AI systems, the specific risks in the penalty and indemnification clauses can also be taken into account, for example as follows:

- Penalty for breach of contractual and statutory obligations to comply with the AI Act requirements (analogous to data protection violations or other breaches of the law);
- Indemnification and hold harmless in the event of infringement of third-party rights by the AI model and/or AI system;

---

[17] Unless otherwise agreed, penalties under Austrian law are independent of fault; see OGH 2 Ob 9/14h.

[18] Damages in excess of the penalty can be claimed independently of this if the requirements for damages are met.

- Indemnification and hold harmless in case of infringement of the creation and implementation of general purpose AI's copyright compliance strategy;

- Indemnification and hold harmless in the event of violation of fundamental rights and freedoms through the development, testing and commissioning of AI systems, including reasonable legal advice and defense costs.

The new AI regulation with the AI Act will also have a significant impact on the responsibilities and liability regulations in IT contracts.

6.7 Reference Table Legislation

The chapter was written based on the Austrian legal framework, but the relevant German standards are referenced below without any claim to correctness.

Context	Austrian Law	German Law
Attribution of public advertising statements	§ 922 Abs. 2 ABGB,A (Austrian Civil Code)	§ 434 BGB (German Civil Code)
Scope of the maintenance obligation	§ 1096 ABGB,A (Austrian Civil Code)	§ 535 BGB, § 538 BGB (German Civil Code)
Freedom from defects of the services provided	§§ 922 ff. ABGB,A (Austrian Civil Code)	§ 434 ff. BGB (German Civil Code)
Obligation to give notice of defects	§ 377 UGB (Austrian Corporate Code)	§ 377 HGB (German Corporate Code)
Fault	§§ 1203 ff. ABGB,A (Austrian Civil Code)	§ 823 BGB (German Civil Code)
Attribution of assistants	§ 1313a ABGB,A. (Austrian Civil Code)	§ 278 BGB (German Civil Code)
Auxiliary liability	§ 1315 ABGB,A. (Austrian Civil Code)	§ 831 BGB (German Civil Code)
Expert liability	§ 1299 ABGB,A (Austrian Civil Code)	§ 839a BGB (German Civil Code)
Definition of a product	§ 4 PHG,A (Austrian Product Liability Act)	§ 2 PHG (German Product Lability Act)

Sources

[1] Bydlinski, Peter; Perner, Stefan; Spitzer, Martin; Bydlinski, Michael; Danzl, Karl-Heinz; Dehn, Wilma: Kommentar zum ABGB: Allgemeines bürgerliches Gesetzbuch, EheG, KSchG, VGG, IPR-G, Rom I-, Rom II- und Rom III–VO. 7th edition. Wien: Verlag Österreich, 2023 – ISBN 978-3-7046-9081-4

[2] Proposal for a DIRECTIVE OF THE EUROPEAN PARLIAMENT AND OF THE COUNCIL adapting the rules on non-contractual civil liability to artificial intelligence (Directive on AI liability), 2022

[3] Proposal for a DIRECTIVE OF THE EUROPEAN PARLIAMENT AND OF THE COUNCIL on liability of defective products, 2022

[4] Anderl/Buchmann in Kollar/Balog/Martinetz/Pichler, Das große Handbuch Wirtschaftsrecht, Wien: Manz, 2024 ISBN 978-3-214-25440-7

7 Private Sector

Kristina Altrichter, Gabriele Bolek-Fügl, Karin Bruckmüller,
Alexandra Ciarnau, Julia Eisner, Isabella Hinterleitner,
Manuela Machner, Renate Rechinger, Carina Zehetmaier,
Klaudia Zotzmann-Koch

7.1 AI – from Prejudice to Discrimination

Carina Zehetmaier

AI is often described as a tool that can be used with a neutral and objective perspective for a wide variety of purposes, both to benefit and to harm. This approach implies that AI is neither good nor bad in itself, but that its effects depend on the user's intentions. By assuming that the systems are objective and neutral, prejudices that can lead to discrimination are concealed, and this can lead to a reproduction and reinforcement of existing prejudices:

- Reproduction of social prejudices: AI systems learn from data that is generated and selected by humans. If this data is biased or reflects social inequalities, AI can reproduce these biases in its decisions and recommendations. *This can be seen in facial recognition technology, for example, where some systems perform differently for people of different skin colors due to the predominant use of light skin color image data during training.* [14]

- Reinforcement of existing inequalities: The unconscious embedding of bias in AI systems can reinforce existing social and economic inequalities. *For example, AI-powered recruiting tools based on historical data may tend to favor candidates who fit the typical profile of successful male employees in the past, potentially putting women at a disadvantage.* [5]

The key terms in this context are:

- **Machine learning** is a branch of artificial intelligence that uses algorithms to give computers the ability to learn from data and make decisions or predictions without being explicitly programmed. It is based on the idea that systems can recognize patterns and structures in large amounts of data in order to independently develop solutions.

- **Objectivity** refers to the ability to make judgments or decisions free from personal bias and subjective influences, based on fact-based criteria.

- **Neutrality** means impartiality and the absence of preferential treatment or bias towards all sides of an issue or conflict.

- **Bias** is considered in this chapter from a legal, socio-political perspective and refers to a bias or partiality in the decision-making of a person, an institution or, an AI system, which can lead to unfair treatment or discrimination based on characteristics such as origin, gender, age or religion. In the context of AI systems, the term bias refers to systematic distortions in the data or algorithms that lead to prejudices in the AI's decisions or predictions. These distortions can originate from the training data, the design decisions of the algorithms or the implicit assumptions of the developers and often result in unfair or discriminatory treatment of certain groups or individuals. Note: The term "bias" described here is to be distinguished from the technical term "bias" in statistics, which refers to a systematic distortion that leads to a deviation of the estimated value from its actual value and will not be explained further here.

- **Automation Bias** refers to the tendency of people to question decisions and judgments that are made or suggested by automated systems or technologies and to favor them excessively, even if better or equivalent human decisions are available.

- **Discrimination** is any form of unjustified disadvantage or unequal treatment of individuals or groups on the basis of various perceptible or non-perceptible characteristics. Perceptible characteristics include, for example, age, ethnicity or disability.

- **Equal rights (Equality)** means the formal and legal equality of persons and groups.

- **Equality (Equity)** means that everyone has the same opportunities, regardless of where they come from, their gender or age. This also requires targeted measures to promote and support people from unequal backgrounds in such a way that true equality is made possible.

One goal of trustworthy AI is for AI systems to be "fair". Fairness is a complex concept, usually defined as the quality (someone is fair) or state (something is fair) of being treated fairly. But what is considered fair and what is not can mean different things to different people in different contexts. Accordingly, there is not one metric to measure fairness in machine learning, but *at least 21 ways to define fairness according to Arvind Narayanan.* [18]

A Confusion Matrix is a tool used to measure the performance of an AI system. This matrix makes it possible to calculate several important performance metrics and thus evaluate the accuracy of a classification model, such as Accuracy, Precision, Recall or

Sensitivity and the F1 score, which is the harmonic mean of Precision and Recall. It also helps to understand how a model performs across different classes.

In the context of machine learning, the term black box refers to a model or system whose internal functioning is not 100% explainable and comprehensible. This is particularly problematic when it comes to the traceability of decisions, the identification of bias or ensuring fairness. Black box models are often found in complex machine learning systems such as deep neural networks, where the number and type of processing layers make it difficult to understand exactly how the input data led to a particular result.

Proxies are substitute variables that are not directly related to a sensitive characteristic, but can still be used to indirectly infer this characteristic. For example, zip codes could serve as proxies for ethnicity or socio-economic status. AI systems could use these proxies to recognize patterns that lead to discriminatory decisions, even if the sensitive characteristics themselves are not present in the data.

Profiling according to Art. 4 para. 4 GDPR means any form of automated processing of personal data consisting of the use of personal data to evaluate certain personal aspects relating to a natural person, in particular to analyze or predict aspects concerning that natural person's performance at work, economic situation, health, personal preferences, interests, reliability, behavior, location or movements (see Chapter 4).

Technology is a multiplier, meaning that it can impact the lives of millions, both positively and negatively. In the context of AI systems that are already being used to make life-changing decisions, these systems can inadvertently become amplifiers of prejudice and discrimination. While some applications are intentionally deployed to harm people and society, such as autonomous weapon systems or deep fake images designed to influence public opinion, and others are recklessly developed applications, such as software designed to detect sexual orientation[6], most AI systems are developed and deployed with the best of intentions. Nevertheless, there is a risk that they can introduce unintentional biases to discriminate against individuals, but moreover, entire groups of people at once. These unconscious biases, also known as unconscious bias are internal beliefs or stereotypes that influence our understanding, actions and decisions in ways we are usually unaware of. A large part of the human thought process takes place in the subconscious. This shapes our perceptions and actions without us realizing it and can be transferred to technological developments. This is part of the problem, when AI systems are developed by a less diverse group such as the stereotypical young white men from Silicon Valley, these systems can be unintentionally biased and neglect or discriminate against entire populations, which has happened many times in the past, such as with health apps or lending algorithms. While developers strive to act neutrally, their cognitive blindspots can still be incorporated into the technologies and potentially cause harm.

Examples of bias in AI systems:

- Amazon's AI recruitment tool that favored male candidates [2]

- Facial recognition algorithms with lower accuracy for dark-skinned people [14]

- Automatic translation tools that reinforce gender stereotypes [7]

- Health apps that better recognize skin diseases in light skin [8]

- Lending processes that disadvantage minorities [10]

- Autonomous vehicles that are less able to recognize people of color [9]

- AI-based application tools that put women at a disadvantage [15]

- Search algorithms that promote racist stereotypes [19]

- AI monitoring systems that monitor minorities more frequently [1]

- Algorithms in healthcare that disadvantage African-American patients [3]

Interdisciplinary and diverse development teams thus play a crucial role in the early detection and sensitization of biases in AI development. For example, a team consisting of different cultures and genders might be better suited to recognize gender or cultural biases in a language assistant. However, this alone is not enough. Biases need to be identified, understood and eliminated throughout – ideally from the start, while constant monitoring and adjustments are necessary throughout the AI lifecycle. Diverse teams and careful testing are essential, as is an understanding of the social dynamics that can influence AI. The challenge is to **recognize, understand and ultimately eliminate biases**.

- Biases in AI systems can primarily be identified through targeted testing and validation, as well as by measuring the performance of AI systems using metrics such as the Confusion Matrix. Precise measurements can reveal whether a system systematically favors or disadvantages certain groups. This makes it possible to identify injustices and take measures to improve fairness. The fundamental rights impact assessment can help to identify and mitigate risks of discrimination before they occur.

- To understand where the biases in AI systems come from, a critical examination of the role of AI in our society is essential. To ensure that technological progress benefits all members of society, rather than reinforcing prejudice and discrimination, it is necessary to view AI as a complex socio-technological system and raise broad awareness of the complexity and pressing issues that lie at the intersection of AI, ethics and social justice. A critical analysis of the role of AI in society can reveal how societal biases feed into technologies.

- Artificial intelligence cannot solve our deep-rooted social problems, but it can help us to recognize them when entire groups are systematically disadvantaged or discriminated on a large scale. Eliminating bias in AI systems is a challenging task that has no simple, universal solution. It is questionable whether it will ever be possible to completely eliminate all biases in AI systems, as these must always be considered in the context of the respective culture and the social and political circumstances of their time. Nevertheless, if we want to use AI systems to make decisions in sensitive areas that could potentially lead to discrimination, we must ensure that biases in AI systems are eliminated as far as possible and create technical and legal mechanisms to ensure fairness in the use of AI.

Example

A person applies for a job that seems to be a perfect fit, but is rejected. The reason for the rejection: the AI system used by the company has decided that the applicant is unsuitable for the position. When AI systems are used in areas where discrimination may occur, it is important to question what data and criteria the AI system is basing its decision on in order to assess whether the decision is fair. The sole justification of a rejection by referring to an AI decision must be considered insufficient here. There is also a risk that the AI will reflect systemic biases contained in the training data. It is therefore essential that decisions made by AI systems in the recruitment process are comprehensible and contestable for applicants.

This highlights another problem with AI-supported decisions based on machine learning, deep learning and neural networks, a field of AI that has made great progress thanks to big data and increased computing power. These complex systems are often opaque, which leads to the term "black box" and outlines the problem of traceability. The lack of explainability makes it difficult to understand how AI systems arrive at their conclusions and results, and is therefore closely linked to issues of fairness and accountability. The argument is often formulated that not everyone knows how a car works, and yet people would still drive it. In the author's opinion, this argument is not valid in this context because, on the one hand, those who build the vehicles know how they work and cars do not make decisions about us, unless we are talking about self-driving cars, where the problem of decision-making arises anew.

Figuratively speaking, the black box problem describes the fact that we cannot simply enter the algorithm in order to identify and eliminate the source of decision-making and prejudices in AI systems. Instead, biases and potential for discrimination must be identified using adequate test and measurement methods. Discrimination comes to light during operations at the latest, for example when it becomes apparent that women are systematically not invited to job interviews. If it is discovered during testing or deployment that an AI system is biased, the question of correcting the algorithm arises. The obvious solution would be to anonymize the training data so that it is no longer possible to identify the gender of an applicant. However, this shows that simply anonymizing data is not always sufficient for training AI systems, because AI systems independently recognize patterns and establish correlations that can lead to discriminatory results – even without explicit information about gender. For example, an AI can indirectly infer sensitive attributes such as gender or ethnicity via seemingly neutral variables (periods of care, empty periods in a CV, words that tend to be used by women), so-called proxies. Another prominent example is the seemingly neutral place of residence or the zip code as proxy variables, which can often be used by an AI system as a "proxy" for socio-economic circumstances or ethnic groups, and play a role above all in the granting of credit, as well as in predictive policing.

Although automated systems promise efficiency and objectivity, their use harbors the risk that people will follow AI recommendations uncritically, even if they could be incorrect (cf. automation bias). [13]

Finally, it must be recognized that any classification we make is in the political, social and cultural context of the era, region or country in which we find ourselves. This manifests itself in the use of surveillance technologies: While in some countries cameras are used to monitor compliance with dress codes such as the correct wearing of the veil, other countries where this is prohibited might use similar technologies to ensure that no veil is worn. Or the consideration of developing systems to recognize people's sex, gender or sexual orientation could have far-reaching consequences, including the death penalty. Such examples make it clear that the orientation of AI systems is deeply rooted in the prevailing norms and values and that AI technologies cannot be viewed in isolation from the social and legal frameworks in which they are developed and used.

7.1.1 Right to Equality and Non-discrimination

The right not to be discriminated against has its origins in the idea that all people are equal before the law and must therefore be treated equally. However, the principle of non-discrimination goes further: it recognizes that people are different in their individuality and that equality before the law does not necessarily mean treating all people identically. To achieve true equality, we must go beyond simple equal treatment and recognize the different conditions and challenges that people face. [11]

In accordance with Article 1 of the Universal Declaration of Human Rights all human beings are born free and equal in dignity and rights. Article 2 states that everyone is "entitled to the rights and freedoms set forth in this Declaration without distinction of any kind, such as race, color, sex, language, religion, political or other opinion, national or social origin, property, birth or other status".

In Europe, we find the non-discrimination clause primarily in Article 14 of the European Convention on Human Rights (ECHR) which prohibits any discrimination based on sex, race, color, language, religion, political or other opinion, national or social origin, association with a national minority, property, birth or other status.

The EU Charter of Fundamental Rights contains an entire chapter – Chapter III, Articles 20–26 of the Charter – on principles of equality. Discrimination based on sex, race, color, ethnic or social origin, genetic characteristics, language, religion or belief, political or other opinion, membership of a national minority, property, disability, age or sexual orientation is declared unlawful. Furthermore, the Charter also includes the recognition of cultural, religious and linguistic diversity, equality between men and women, the protection of the rights of children and the elderly, as well as measures for integration and the rights of persons with disabilities.

The right to equality and non-discrimination enjoys extensive protection beyond the EU Treaties, based on Article 19 of the EU Treaty, which provides for the possibility of taking appropriate measures to combat discrimination based on sex, racial or ethnic origin, religion or belief, disability, age or sexual orientation. These directives oblige Member States to implement legislation and policies to combat discrimination. [11]

In implementing the EU legal framework, national laws have been enacted and specialized bodies have been created in all EU Member States to help victims of discrimination, enforce their complaints, conduct independent reports and surveys and formulate recommendations to combat discrimination. Some of these bodies are also empowered to make decisions in cases of discrimination and thus act as a quasi-judicial body.

Article 3 of the Basic Law of the Federal Republic of Germany stipulates in paragraph 1: *"All people are equal before the law."* Paragraph 3 stipulates that no one may be *"disadvantaged or favored because of their gender, origin, race, language, homeland and origin, faith, religious or political views"*. No one may be disadvantaged because of their disability. Furthermore, according to paragraph 2, men and women have equal rights. In this sense, the state promotes *"the effective implementation of equal rights for women and men and works towards the elimination of existing disadvantages"*.

In Austrian constitutional law, this principle is enshrined in Article 7 B-VG (Austrian Federal Constitutional Law) in the principle of equality and declares that all federal citizens are equal before the law and that *"privileges of birth, sex, status, class and creed"* are excluded. The Basic Law confirms this in Article 2: *"All citizens are equal before the law."* Art. 14 ECHR (European Convention on Human Rights) goes beyond citizens and describes the prohibition of discrimination as follows: *"The enjoyment of the rights and freedoms set forth in this Convention shall be secured without discrimination based on any ground such as sex, race, color, language, religion, political or other opinion, national or social origin, association with a national minority, property, birth or other status."* The principle of equality entails a ban on unobjective differentiation, which means that the same is to be treated equally and unequal is to be treated unequally.

In order to invoke the above-mentioned Art. 14 ECHR, there must be an interference with a right protected by the ECHR. According to the ECHR, a difference in treatment is lawful if it is justified by a legitimate aim and subject to proportionality between the means used and the aim pursued. [12] The 12th Additional Protocol to Art. 14 ECHR, which contains a comprehensive prohibition of discrimination, has not yet been ratified by either Germany or Austria.

The principle of equality is a fundamental right and is therefore primarily directed against the state and has no general validity in legal relationships between private individuals or between private individuals and companies. It is the task of the state to enact laws to extend the scope of protection of fundamental rights to legal relationships between natural and legal persons and to impose equal treatment or a ban on discrimination for certain relationships. The principle of equal treatment thus prohibits in employment law prohibits employers from discriminating against individual employees without objective reason. § 1 para. 5 Austrian Data Protection Law expressly binds private operators in that private legal entities can assert the fundamental right to data protection in civil proceedings [12]

This means unequal treatment must

- objectively justified by a legitimate aim and

- the funds must be appropriate and necessary.

Exceptions to the principle of non-discrimination must be justified by a legitimate aim and may be appropriate means of achieving that aim. This can be, for example, a genuine and determining occupational requirement or a positive action measure implemented to achieve greater equality of opportunity. A job campaign is launched for people with disabilities that is not open to unemployed people without disabilities because unemployment among people with disabilities is particularly high. [11]

United Nations treaties on protection against discrimination:

- the International Convention on the Elimination of All Forms of Racial Discrimination (CERD)

- the Convention on the Elimination of All Forms of Discrimination against Women (CEDAW)

- the UN Convention on the Rights of Persons with Disabilities (CRPD)

All of these treaties contain prohibitions of discrimination, but show different lists of protected grounds. [11]

7.1.2 How Prejudices Find their Way into AI

This section describes how biases find their way into AI systems. To this end, the standard work *A Framework for Understanding Sources of Harm throughout the Machine Learning Life Cycle* by Harini Suresh and John V. Guttag [17] is particularly valuable in explaining how biases can find their way into AI systems and forms the ideal basis for this section, which is largely based on this scientific work.

Artificial intelligence, in the form of machine learning, is increasingly being used in decision-relevant areas that have a direct impact on human life. This works by training models based on existing data sets in order to make predictions or decisions for new, unknown data. In the course of data collection, modeling and application, a wide variety of problems can arise that have harmful consequences. The potential of AI systems to discriminate has already been explained above. Another example from the USA is the COMPAS software, which is used to assess the risk of defendants in order to predict the likelihood of a defendant reoffending or not. According to *ProPublica* [10], this software falsely classifies African-American defendants as having a higher risk of reoffending.

When discrimination by AI systems occurs, the first reaction is usually to assume that the data is biased or prejudiced. While many biases may indeed be embedded in the process of data generation, it is crucial to understand that not all problems should be attributed solely to the data. The process of machine learning involves a variety of decisions and practices from the selection of the mathematical model to the user interfaces used in implementation. Each step in this process carries the risk of leading to undesirable results.

Harini Suresh and John V. Guttag provide the following examples:

- A medical researcher wants to develop a model to improve the detection of heart attacks. She trains the model with medical records of a specific group of patients in a hospital, including information about whether and when these people have had a heart attack. She finds that the model tends to correctly identify heart attacks in women less often, suggesting that it may not have been able to adequately learn the symptoms in women due to a lack of relevant data. By integrating additional data representing women with heart attack experiences into the dataset and retraining the model, she can improve accuracy for female patients.

- At the same time, a colleague who is responsible for hiring new lab technicians is trying to develop an algorithm to predict the suitability of female and male applicants based on their CVs and manually assigned ratings. He found that the model was significantly less likely to identify women as suitable candidates than men. Despite attempts to expand the data set by adding more female examples, the discriminatory behavior of the AI system persisted.

The reason for the different effects lay in the different causes: In the first example, a lack of data on women meant that adding more data was helpful, while in the second example, the discriminatory predictions were due to the use of human ratings as quality indicators and simply expanding the dataset did not remedy the situation.

These examples illustrate that distortions or prejudices occur at different points in the life cycle of machine learning and can therefore lead to discrimination and other negative consequences. In addition to the potential for discrimination by AI systems, it is also common for AI systems to misrepresent certain groups, such as language models that reinforce and propagate stereotypes.

Most AI systems are based on machine learning. To understand how biases are incorporated into the system, which can lead to unfair results, the individual steps of machine learning are considered:

- **Data collection:** The process begins with defining a target group and collecting the data required for the model. When developing a credit scoring system, the selection of the target group should reflect pre-existing socio-economic inequalities, e. g. if the data collection excludes people in lower income brackets or certain geographical areas, this can lead to a historical bias.

- **Data processing and preparation:** In this phase, data is cleaned, normalized and converted into a format that can be processed by algorithms. This can lead to measurement biases, such as when the way variables are measured or categorized systematically disadvantages certain groups. For example, if "credit history" is used as a proxy for "creditworthiness", systemic differences in access to credit between different social groups may not be taken into account (historically, fewer people from immigrant backgrounds have applied for credit than Americans).

- **Model development:** In this step, algorithms are trained to recognize patterns in the data and make predictions. Learning biases can occur if the selection of features, the training data or the type of learning algorithm systematically favors certain patterns over others. An example of this is a face recognition system that performs worse on women and people of color due to a predominantly white male training dataset.

- **Model evaluation:** Here the performance of the model is assessed on the basis of testing data. Evaluation bias occurs when the testing data is not representative of the diversity of real-world use cases. An algorithm tested on an insufficiently diverse data set may achieve high accuracy scores, but still be unfair in the real world because the testing data set was collected predominantly on data from a demographically biased group, such as mainly SME applicants.

- **Model insert:** Even if a model has passed all tests, discrimination may occur in actual use. This may be the case if the deployment environment or user interactions with the model do not exactly match the conditions under which the model was developed and tested. An example of this could be a recruitment algorithm that is used in an environment in which certain qualifications or experience are systematically undervalued.

To minimize the potential for discrimination, it is important to look critically at the entire lifecycle of machine learning and proactively implement strategies to identify and mitigate bias. This includes incorporating expert knowledge, selecting representative data sets, applying trustworthy AI practices and continuously reviewing and adapting models based on real-world feedback.

This is followed by a description of which biases (biases) can flow into the AI system [17]:

A Framework for Understanding Sources of Harm throughout the Machine Learning Life Cycle

EAAMO '21, October 5–9, 2021, –, NY, USA

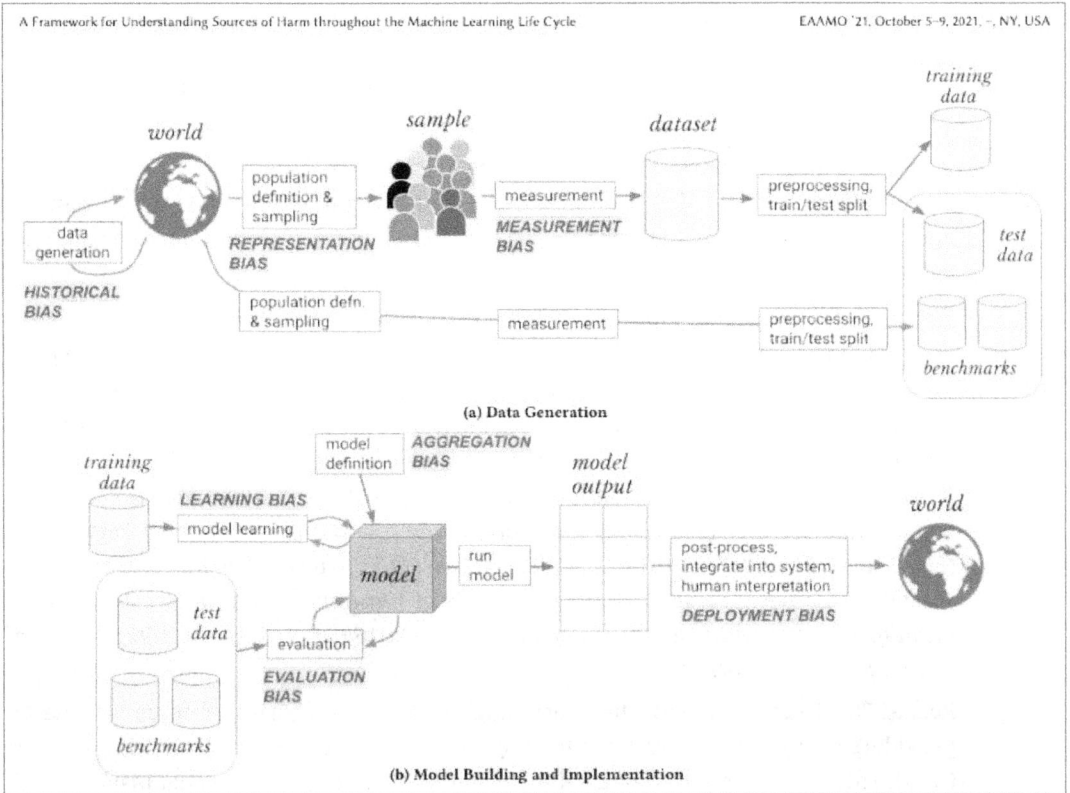

(a) Data Generation

(b) Model Building and Implementation

Figure 7.1 Incorporation of Bias into AI Systems

7.1.2.1 How the AI Act Addresses Discrimination

Through algorithms can become discriminatory if they lead to an unjustified disadvantage for individuals. This applies in particular to cases in which people are disadvantaged on the basis of characteristics worthy of protection such as age, gender, ethnicity, religion, sexual orientation or disability. Protection against discrimination by AI systems is one of the main objectives of the AI Act, which aims to ensure a high level of protection for the fundamental rights and safety of citizens while creating an environment that promotes innovation and the development of AI systems.

The AI Act addresses the issue of discrimination mainly by establishing rules and requirements for high-risk AI systems to ensure that these systems respect fundamental rights, including non-discrimination:

- **Requirements for high-risk AI systems:** The AI Act defines certain requirements for AI systems that are classified as high-risk in order to ensure their compliance with fundamental rights. These requirements include the accuracy, robustness and security of the systems, the verification and validation of data quality, and the transparency of the AI systems (see section 3.3.2).

- **Prohibited AI practices:** The AI Act prohibits specific practices that could constitute a serious violation of fundamental rights, such as manipulative practices that could alter the behavior of individuals in a way that impairs their freedom of choice, or systems that classify sensitive characteristics such as gender, race or sexual orientation based on biometric data (see section 3.3.1).

These rules are designed to minimize the risk of discrimination by AI systems and to ensure that the development and use of AI is in line with the fundamental rights and values of the EU.

Recital 70 EU AI Act is explicitly dedicated to the topic of discrimination:

"In order to protect the right of others from the discrimination that might result from the bias in AI systems, the providers should, exceptionally, to the extent that it is strictly necessary for the purpose of ensuring bias detection and correction in relation to the high-risk AI systems, subject to appropriate safeguards for the fundamental rights and freedoms of natural persons and following the application of all applicable conditions laid down under this Regulation in addition to the conditions laid down in Regulations (EU) 2016/679 and (EU) 2018/1725 and Directive (EU) 2016/680, be able to process also special categories of personal data, as a matter of substantial public interest within the meaning of Article 9(2), no. (g) of Regulation (EU) 2016/679 and Article 10(2), no. (g) of Regulation (EU) 2018/1725."

Recital 70 AI Act deals with the processing of special categories of personal data by providers of high-risk AI systems for the purpose of detecting and correcting biases (Bias). This is intended to safeguard the right of others to protection against discrimination that could result from such biases. The processing of such data is permitted by way of exception and to the extent strictly necessary to ensure the detection and correction of bias. Appropriate safeguards must be put in place to protect the fundamental rights and freedoms of natural persons and all conditions laid down in the Regulation must be complied with, in addition to the provisions of GDPR (EU) 2016/679, Regulation (EU) 2018/1725 and Directive (EU) 2016/680. This processing is classified as a matter of substantial public interest pursuant to Art. 9 para. 2 lit g GDPR and Art. 10 para. 2 lit g of Regulation (EU) 2018/1725, which constitutes a legal basis for data processing (see section 3.3).

In this context, Art. 22 GDPR is also relevant, which protects data subjects against fully automated decision-making processes without human involvement if an automated individual decision has legal consequences for the data subjects (such as the conclusion or termination of a contract) or significantly affects the data subjects in any other way. Data subjects have the right to request a human review of such decisions, to present their own point of view and to challenge the decision (see Chapter 4).

Art. 86 AI Act supplements and specifies the **right to an explanation of the decision-making process in individual cases for persons** in the context of high-risk AI systems by giving data subjects the right to receive an explanation of the role of the AI system in the decision-making process and the most important elements of the decision taken. This applies to decisions based on data processed by high-risk AI systems according to Annex III AI Act, with the exception of critical infrastructure (Annex III no. 2), and which have legal effects or similarly significantly affect the data subject. The following AI systems according to Annex III have a particular potential to discriminate against individuals or groups of individuals:

- Biometrics, as current facial recognition systems deliver varying results for different skin colors and have a high error rate for dark-skinned women [4].

- Education and vocational training (no. 3), e. g. AI systems that decide on access or admission to educational institutions or are intended to be used for the assessment of learning outcomes.

- Employment, Personnel management and access to self-employment (number 4), e. g. AI systems that automate the selection process by placing targeted job advertisements and filtering and evaluating applicants.

- Accessibility and use of basic private and basic public services and benefits (no. 5), e. g. AI systems that assess whether natural persons are entitled to basic public assistance and support services, including health services, and whether such benefits and services should be granted, restricted, withdrawn or reclaimed.

- AI systems that carry out a credit check and credit score assessment of natural persons or calculate a risk assessment and pricing for health and life insurance.

- etc.

Both Art. 22 GDPR and Art. 86 AI Act ensure transparency and fairness of automated decision-making processes and grant data subjects rights to defend themselves against such decisions. While Art. 22 GDPR establishes a general right not to be subject to decisions based solely on automated processing, Art. 86 AI Act provides a specific right to explanation for decisions made by certain AI systems in order to further improve the understanding and verifiability of these decisions.

Accordingly, the European Court of Justice (ECJ) has also ruled that an "automated decision" within the meaning of the GDPR also exists if a probability value is calculated automatically and a decision by a person depends significantly on this probability value (ECJ 7.12.2023, C-634/21 – Schufa). Specifically, this legal dispute concerned a bank's refusal to grant a loan to the plaintiff based on a calculation of creditworthiness of the plaintiff (credit score) by the German credit reference agency Schufa. According to the ECJ's decision, an automated decision also exists if the final decision is taken by a person, provided that the person's decision depends "significantly" on an automated calculation carried out beforehand. In other words, any automated preparation of a downstream human decision is to be considered an automated decision within the meaning of Art. 22 GDPR. This decision by the ECJ significantly expanded the scope of application of the GDPR on automated decisions (see ECJ 7.12.2023, C-634/21).

This in turn means that when developing and using certain AI systems that process personal data, both the requirements of the AI Act and those of the GDPR must be met by the providers and deployers of such systems.

7.1.2.2 Can We Fix Bias in AI?

Eliminating bias in AI systems is a multifaceted challenge for which there are no simple solutions exist. Prejudices can flow into AI systems via data, algorithms and human decision-making processes and subsequently lead to discrimination against individuals or entire groups. Accordingly, it is important to combat biases in AI systems and their effects using various strategies, most of which are described above:

- **Diverse teams:** The inclusion of diverse perspectives in the development process can help to incorporate as many points of view, different experiences, cultural backgrounds and specialist knowledge as possible into development and to identify blind spots at an early stage. This reduces systematic biases and unintentional prejudices in algorithms and improves the creation of AI systems that are fairer and more representative of the diversity of users.

- **Fundamental rights impact assessments:** The aim of a fundamental rights impact assessment is to analyze and evaluate the potential impact of a planned AI system on fundamental rights before it is developed. This is intended to minimize risks to fundamental rights and proactively take measures to ensure the protection of fundamental rights and to understand, actively address and reduce the impact on various groups and people (see section 3.4).

- Development or use according to **trustworthy AI Ethic Guidelines** (see section 9.1 or section 9.4)

- **Test and validation data sets:** Good test and validation datasets are essential for AI development to ensure accuracy, fairness and robustness. They enable developers to evaluate the performance of AI under different conditions. Careful selection and diversification of these datasets helps to identify and minimize biases and prejudices.

- **Fairness measurement:** Since AI systems have a high potential for discrimination, it is essential to measure the fairness of critical systems. In practice, various metrics and approaches, such as the Confusion Matrix, are used to evaluate fairness and biases in AI systems. Each of these metrics focuses on different aspects of fairness and helps to identify and address biases in their models. According to "21 fairness definitions and their politics" by Arvind Narayanan [18], there are at least 21 mathematical ways to measure fairness.

- **Lifecycle monitoring:** Continuous monitoring and adaptation of AI systems are crucial to counteract discrimination in the long term and ensure fairness.

- **Creation of Code of Conducts:** (see section 10.5)

AI can help to make human prejudices visible, but it cannot solve them. Technology reflects the data and decisions made by humans. Therefore, effective solutions to overcome biases and inequalities are only possible through an integrated approach that combines technological, ethical and social perspectives.

Sources

[1] Alba, Davey: Facial Recognition Moves Into a New Front: Schools. In: The New York Times (2020)

[2] Amazon scraps secret AI recruiting tool that showed bias against women. URL *https://finance. yahoo.com/news/amazon-scraps-secret-ai-recruiting-030000358.html*. – accessed: 2024/04/13 – Yahoo Finance

[3] Beuth, Patrick ; Breithut, Jörg: USA: Algorithmus benachteiligt afroamerikanische Patienten. In: Der Spiegel (2019)

[4] Buolamwini, Joy ; Gebru, Timnit: Gender Shades: Intersectional Accuracy Disparities in Commercial Gender Classification. In: Proceedings of the 1st Conference on Fairness, Accountability and Transparency: PMLR, 2018, p. 77–91

[5] Dastin, Jeffrey: Insight – Amazon scraps secret AI recruiting tool that showed bias against women. In: Reuters (2018)

[6] david.kotrba: KI erkennt sexuelle Orientierung von Menschen anhand Fotos. URL *https://future zone.at/science/ki-erkennt-sexuelle-orientierung-von-menschen-anhand-fotos/285.083.652*. – accessed: 2024/04/20

[7] Ghosh, Sourojit; Caliskan, Aylin: ChatGPT Perpetuates Gender Bias in Machine Translation and Ignores Non-Gendered Pronouns: Findings across Bengali and Five other Low-Resource Languages, arXiv (2023). – arXiv:2305.10510 [cs]

[8] Groh, Matthew ; Badri, Omar ; Daneshjou, Roxana ; Koochek, Arash ; Harris, Caleb ; Soenksen, Luis R. ; Doraiswamy, P. Murali; Picard, Rosalind: Deep learning-aided decision support for diagnosis of skin disease across skin tones. In: Nature Medicine Volume 30, Nature Publishing Group (2024), no. 2, p. 573–583

[9] Hawkinson, Katie: The pedestrian detection systems in self-driving cars are less likely to detect children and people of color, study suggests. URL *https://www.businessinsider.com/self-driving-cars-less-likely-detect-kids-people-of-color-2023-8*. – accessed: 2024/04/20 – Business Insider

[10] Mattu, Julia Angwin, Jeff Larson,Lauren Kirchner,Surya: Machine Bias. URL *https://www.propublica. org/article/machine-bias-risk-assessments-in-criminal-sentencing*. – accessed: 2024/04/20 – ProPublica

[11] Nowak, M. (Hrsg.): All human rights for all: Vienna manual on human rights, All human rights for all. Wien Graz : NWV, 2012 – ISBN 978-3-7083-0853-1

[12] Öhlinger, Theo ; Eberhard, Harald: Verfassungsrecht. 13th, revised edition.. Wien: Facultas, 2022 – ISBN 978-3-7089-2094-8

[13] Orwat, Carsten: Diskriminierungsrisiken durch Verwendung von Algorithmen.

[14] Project Overview ‹ Gender Shades. URL *https://www.media.mit.edu/projects/gender-shades/ overview/*. – accessed: 2024/04/20 – MIT Media Lab

[15] Reuters: Amazon ditched AI recruiting tool that favored men for technical jobs. In: The Guardian (2018)

[16] Studie "Digitalisierung Finanzmarkt". URL *https://www.fma.gv.at/publikationen/studie-digitalisierung-finanzmarkt/*. – accessed: 2024/04/20 – FMA Österreich

[17] Suresh, Harini; Guttag, John V.: A Framework for Understanding Sources of Harm throughout the Machine Learning Life Cycle. In: Equity and Access in Algorithms, Mechanisms, and Optimization, 2021. – arXiv:1901.10002 [cs, stat], p. 1–9

[18] TL;DS – 21 fairness definition and their politics by Arvind Narayanan. URL *https://shubhamjain0594. github.io/post/tlds-arvind-fairness-definitions/*. – accessed: 2024/04/20

[19] Yekkehkhany, Ali; Nagi, Rakesh: Blind GB-PANDAS: A Blind Throughput-Optimal Load Balancing Algorithm for Affinity Scheduling, arXiv (2020). – arXiv:1901.04047 [cs]

7.2 AI in the Financial Sector

Alexandra Ciarnau

The European Commission emphasizes *"The future of our financial system is digital."*, in its strategy for digital finance in the EU [1]. In addition to cloud solutions and block-chain, big data and AI are of particular importance. After all, a huge amount of data is the basis of all analytics. AI can be used to optimize derivations from data input. This enables new products and innovations. From automated trading algorithms and fraud detection to personalized financial advice, lending, risk and complaint manage-ment – the use cases are endless and have already been used in the highly regulated sector for years [2]. However, the potential is far from exhausted and rapid progress and benefits still await us. However, the technology also poses specific **challenges** in this sector. In the highly regulated financial sector, for example, questions arise re-garding (i) regulatory admissibility and risk management and (ii) the legally compli-ant implementation of AI.

The first question is insofar exciting as the decisions made with various AI systems and models are only comprehensible to a limited extent. It must therefore first **be examined whether AI may be used at all from a regulatory perspective. Gover-nance** plays a key role here (see section 10.2). The supervisory authorities currently expect any lack of traceability, hidden discrimination, misuse or copyright infringe-ments to be avoided through careful governance [3].

Legally compliant implementation is complex because **various sector-specific legal acts** (national laws, regulations and directives) including formal and informal recom-mendations and orders of the competent (supervisory) authorities and courts must be observed in the IT sector (e. g. CRR Regulation, CRD Directive, Market Infrastructure Regulation, Markets and Financial Instruments Directive, Market Abuse Regulation, Network and Information Security Directive, Regulation on the Operational Stability of Digital Systems in the Financial Sector, EBA Guidelines on ICT and Security Risks EBA/GL/2019/04, etc.). If AI is used within the meaning of the AI Act (see section 3.1), the requirements of all sector-specific regulations must also be implemented. A deep understanding of the different regulations and their interactions with each other is therefore required, in order to implement AI efficiently.[1]

---

[1] Cf. *https://data.consilium.europa.eu/doc/document/ST-9930-2024-INIT/en/pdf* Council, Conclusions on Financial Literacy

The aspects of the AI Act relevance to the financial sector are discussed below:

- Exceptions to the scope of application

- Prohibited AI practices

- High-risk AI systems

- General Purpose AI models

- Certain AI systems

- Authority competences

7.2.1 Exceptions to the Scope of Application

Art. 2 AI Act regulates the scope of application and explicit exemptions (see section 3.1). The following exceptions are particularly relevant for the financial sector:

- **Research, testing and development activities outside of real-world conditions**

  According to Art. 2 para. 8 AI Act, the regulation does not apply to product-oriented research, testing and development activities on AI systems or AI models before they are placed on the market or put into service, **unless** the **tests are carried out under real-world conditions**.

  "Tests under real-world conditions" means temporary tests of an AI system for its intended purpose, which are carried out under real-world conditions outside a laboratory or other simulated environment in order to collect reliable, robust data and to assess and verify the conformity of the AI system. For the testing of high-risk AI systems under real-life conditions, there are special regulations in Art. 60 et seq. AI Act (e. g. test plan, approval by the market surveillance authority, maximum duration of six months, informed consent, safeguards, etc.).

  The distinction between tests under real and non-real-world conditions is not trivial. In most cases, the purpose of development and validation in a test environment is ultimately to obtain reliable, resilient results for productive use. Therefore, there is often a great interest in simulating real-world conditions as closely as possible. However, the conditions and therefore also the results of a test and development environment often differ from the conditions in the production environment. A successful pilot in a protected environment can lead to different or worse performance in the production system [4]. Against this background, I believe that only the simulated environment can be the decisive criterion for tests under real or non-real-world conditions.

> **Example**
>
> A bank is developing an AI system to detect fraudulent transactions. For this purpose, it uses a simulated, closed test infrastructure and synthetic (fictitious) data. In my opinion, there are many arguments in favor of a non-real test environment, so that the exception applies and this use is not yet subject to the AI Act.
>
> The case is different if a credit institution tests the AI system in a closed productive environment with real data. In this case, the obligations under Art. 60 et seq. AI Act must be complied with.

- **Free, open source license**

  According to Art. 2 para. 12 AI Act, AI systems provided under a free and open source license are not covered by the Act. This does not apply to prohibited AI systems, certain AI systems including general purpose AI systems[2] The exception does not apply to systematic risks, emotion recognition systems or biometric categorization systems referred to in Article 50.

  Software, data and models that are provided as open source, allow them to be shared openly and that users can access, use, modify and redistribute free of charge are not regulated under the AI Regulation. This takes account of the idea of promoting growth and innovation. However, the exemption provision should be treated with caution. According to Recital 102 et seq. AI Act, this should not include AI components that are provided for a price or otherwise monetized.

> **Example**
>
> A software service provider offers an AI system for market segmentation and optimization of sales activities for the regulated financial sector. Its software is based on proprietary software and integrated open source machine learning components. Due to the provision of the free, open-source AI components for a fee, the AI system or parts thereof do not fall under the exemption of Art. 2 para. 12 AI Act.

7.2.2 Prohibited AI Systems

Every AI system within the scope of the AI Act must be checked against the list of prohibitions in Art. 5 AI Act (see section 3.1 for details). Several prohibitions may apply in the financial sector and therefore the following practices in particular should be critically assessed:

---

[2] Exemptions to the transparency requirements apply to providers of general purpose AI models that are released under a free and open source license and whose parameters, including weights, model architecture information and model usage information, are made publicly available. However, this exception to the transparency requirements does not apply to systematic risks.

▪ Subliminal influence, manipulative or deceptive techniques

Art. 5 para. 1 lit a AI Act prohibits AI systems that use techniques of subliminal influence outside a person's awareness or intentionally manipulative/deceptive techniques,

- to significantly change the behavior of people (groups),
- by significantly impairing their ability to make an informed decision,
- causing them to make a decision that they would not otherwise have made, and
- which causes or is reasonably likely to cause substantial harm to such person(s).

The ban thus supplements the provisions of the UCP Directive, the GDPR and the sector-specific requirements in the financial sector.

Example

Targeted emotional influencing of consumers in order to force them to make a certain decision can constitute manipulative techniques. These for example include dark patterns.

As EIOPA points out, this is the case, for example, if consumers are made to believe that they are agreeing to a certain financial risk without appropriate insurance. If AI is used for this purpose, this practice may be prohibited under Art. 5 AI Act.

Example of toying with customers' emotions & usage of a testimonial

Select Yes or No to continue booking:

○ Yes, I want Hotel Booking Insurance for my trip   **71€** per person

○ No, I am willing to risk my 2585€ trip. — — — → Emotions: usage of the notion of risk and fear of losing the travel costs

"Things happened outside of my control which caused the trip to be cancelled. The travel insurance was valuable in reducing the loses when I had to cancel my trip." - Mr Rodman — — → Testimonial

Source: *https://www.eiopa.europa.eu/tools-and-data/behavioural-insights-insuranceand-pensions-supervision/dark-patterns-insurance-practices-exploit-consumer-biases_en?prefLang=de* (accessed: 2024/05/19)

Manipulative user interface designs can also affect people (groups) below the conscious perception threshold. For example, different presentation and design of decision-relevant buttons on trading apps are already inadmissible due to regulatory requirements if equivalent button options are worse or barely perceptible and thus dishonestly nudge the user towards a certain action [5]. If AI systems are used for this purpose, this also constitutes a violation of the AI Regulation. Further indications of manipulative techniques can be, for example, coercive actions or fake offers, the conveyance of urgency, pre-selected options or inaccurate rankings [6].

- **Exploitation of vulnerability or need for protection of persons (groups) due to certain characteristics with significant potential for harm**

  Art. 5 para. 1 lit b AI Act prohibits AI systems that create vulnerability or vulnerability of a person (group).

  - due to their age, a disability, a particular social or economic situation
  - with the aim or effect of influencing their behavior,
  - which will (probably) cause it considerable damage.

  The prohibition supplements manipulative and deceptive techniques to the extent that it does not require any special methodology and already penalizes the influencing of the decision-making power of persons worthy of protection.

- **Social evaluation and classification of people**

  The AI Act also prohibits AI systems to evaluate or classify individuals over a period of time based on their social behavior or known, inferred or predicted personal characteristics or personality traitsif the social assessment leads to

  - leads to a disadvantage or discrimination in social contexts that are unrelated to the original data collection;
  - is unjustified or disproportionate with regard to their social conduct or its scope.

  The ban therefore covers social scoring but is not limited to the public sector.

  > **Example**
  >
  > If a financial institution uses AI to assess the creditworthiness of an applicant on the basis of their social behavior (e. g. incorrect parking, extroverted, loud manner, etc.), a prohibition may be justified.

- **Emotion recognition in the workplace**

  According to Art. 5 para. 1 lit f AI Act, the use of AI systems for emotion recognition is, among other things of persons in the workplace is not permitted. An exception only exists if the AI system is introduced for medical or safety reasons (e. g. detection of fatigue of a pilot and the associated safety risk for all passengers).

  > **Example**
  >
  > With the consent of the call participants, a financial institution records the calls made via the service hotline, transcribes them due to legal documentation obligations and also analyzes them for training purposes. If, in the course of this, hotline employees are recorded and their emotions are derived with the help of AI (e. g. happy, sad, tired, annoyed, demotivated, etc.), this constitutes unauthorized use in accordance with Art. 5 AI Act.

On the other hand, the classic evaluation of employee satisfaction questionnaires does not constitute impermissible emotion recognition. In these cases, the automation is usually only aimed at the overall evaluation, but not at the evaluation of the individual questionnaires under profiling. In addition, employee surveys are usually anonymous.

- **Biometric categorization**

  Finally, in the financial sector, attention must be paid to the ban on the use of AI systems for biometric categorization. Article 5 para. 1 lit g AI Act prohibits the identification or inference of the race, political opinions, trade union membership, religious or philosophical beliefs, sex life or sexual orientation of natural persons on the basis of categorization using biometric data. Narrow exceptions exist only in the area of law enforcement.

  Example

  If the enclosed passports (which contain biometric data) are used in the course of opening an account for the purpose of deriving racial or ideological beliefs, this is an impermissible use of AI in accordance with Art. 5 AI Act.

7.2.3 High-risk AI Systems

In the area of finance and insurance, the catalog of high-risk AI systems is also essential. What qualifies as high-risk AI is defined inArt. 6 et seq. AI Act, Annex I and III AI Act (details on high-risk AI in section 3.3.2). In addition to the prominent examples of credit scoring and credit assessment a number of high-risk applications from the catalog in Annex III AI Act are possible in this sector.[3]

7.2.3.1 Classification

- **Biometrics**

  According to Art. 6 para. 2 AI Act in conjunction with no. 1 Annex III AI Act, the following biometric applications are considered high-risk:

  - Biometric remote identification systems, except systems for verifying the authenticity of a person;

---

[3] The areas listed in Annex I in which AI is used as a security product or component tend to be of little relevance to the financial sector.

  ▨ AI systems that are intended to be used for biometric categorization according
     to sensitive or protected attributes or characteristics based on inferences about
     those attributes or characteristics;[4]

  ▨ AI systems that are intended to be used for emotion recognition.[5]

Examples

The use of biometric authentication solutions with facial recognition when opening bank accounts online or for the login check to the personal bank account are
not high-risk AI systems according to no. 1 Annex III AI Act. Biometric identification through facial recognition is ultimately necessary to verify that the person is
who they say they are. This also applies to AI-supported vein scanners that only
allow authorized persons access to the server rooms. According to Recital 54 AI
Act, such applications whose sole purpose is to confirm the identity of a person
in order to gain access to a service, unlock a device or gain secure access to
premises should be excluded from the high-risk area.

▨ **Critical infrastructure**

According to Article 6 para. 2 AI Act in conjunction with no. 2 of Annex III AI Act,
AI systems for the management and operation of critical digital infrastructures
are considered high-risk AI. "Critical digital infrastructures" are the areas listed in
no. 8 of the Annex to the Critical Infrastructure Resilience Directive:

  ▨ Deployers of Internet nodes

  ▨ DNS service providers (except deployers of root name servers)

  ▨ TLD name register

  ▨ Provider of cloud computing services

  ▨ Provider of data center services

  ▨ Deployers of content delivery networks

  ▨ Trust service provider

  ▨ Providers of public electronic communications networks

  ▨ Providers of electronic communications networks, insofar as their services are
     publicly accessible

AI systems detect safety componentsthat are used to protect the physical integrity
of critical infrastructure or the health and safety of people and property. Failures
and malfunctions of such components can ultimately lead directly to risks (Recital
50 AI Act).

---

[4] In this context, the prohibition in Article 5(1)(g) must be observed.

[5] In this context, the prohibition under Article 5(1)(f) must be taken into account.

> **Example**
>
> A banking group has a subsidiary that provides internal IT services throughout the group. It operates a data center for all operating companies. The data center uses AI systems for access control security. The system therefore fulfills a security function and the failure or malfunction of the AI system also endangers the health and safety of people or property. Access could also be possible for third parties. These AI systems are to be classified as high-risk in accordance with no. 2 of Annex III (see Recital 55 AI Act).

▪ Employment and personnel management

In addition, AI systems in employment and personnel management are classified as high-risk AI in accordance with no. 4 Annex III AI Act if they

- are to be used for the recruitment or selection of natural persons, in particular to place targeted job advertisements, to screen or filter applications and to evaluate applicants;
- used for decisions affecting the terms of employment, promotions and terminations, for assigning tasks based on individual behavior or personal characteristics or traits, or for monitoring and evaluating performance.

These applications can have a significant impact on individuals, their privacy, their employee rights and their fundamental rights to data protection and are therefore subject to stricter regulation. These restrictions are also relevant and must be observed in the financial sector – just as in all other sectors.

> **Example**
>
> Due to sector-specific requirements, a careful risk management system and documentation are required in many areas. In the course of this, employee data may also be processed (e. g. via log files to ensure secure IT systems). If this data about specific employees from various sources is also used to make decisions about the employment relationship, this is generally a high-risk AI application.

▪ Access to and use of basic private and public services and benefits

The most important regulations for the financial sector are no. 5 lit b and lit c Annex III AI Act:

▪ Credit scoring and credit rating

Accordingly, AI systems that are to be used to **assess the creditworthiness and credit rating** of natural persons are to be classified as high-risk AI. They are capable of denying individuals access to financial resources or other essential services, such as housing, electricity and telecommunications services (see Recital 58 AI Regulation). In addition, there is a high risk that such AI systems could lead to discrimination of individuals or groups and perpetuate historical distortions. For this reason, the EU legislator has opted for stricter regulation of this application.

However, there is an expressis verbis exception for the use of such systems to **detect financial fraud**. These should not constitute high-risk AI. In addition, the Recitals also do not want to qualify AI systems that are intended for supervisory purposes to calculate the capital requirements of credit institutions and insurance companies as high-risk AI (see Recital 58). In my opinion, the latter is not possible ex lege because the catalog only mentions financial fraud, but not the calculation of capital requirements required for supervisory purposes. This only appears possible by **refuting the high-risk status pursuant to Art. 6 para. 3 AI Act** (see Section 3.3.2) if no profiling is carried out.

> **Example**
>
> The creditworthiness assessment of a credit institution in the course of checking the granting of a loan will generally fall under no. 5 lit. b Annex III AI Act. In practice, the credit assessment is not only carried out to detect financial fraud, but also to assess the solvency of a customer.
>
> Whether an AI-supported credit assessment of a ltd. falls under the high-risk application is questionable. In my opinion, according to the wording, the risk classification is only limited to the assessment of "natural persons", but not of legal entities. Therefore, in my opinion, such AI use should not be classified as high-risk.

Risk assessment and pricing of life insurance policies

No. 5 lit c Annex III AI Act may also have a scope of application in the financial sector. This provision covers AI systems that are used for **risk assessment and pricing** in relation to natural persons in the case of **life and health insurance**. They entail a high risk because AI-supported assessment and pricing can have a significant impact on people's livelihoods, which can lead to financial exclusion and discrimination.

> **Example**
>
> An AI system calculates the conditions of a life insurance policy on the basis of individual characteristics, in particular life expectancy based on gender, lifestyle, state of health, income, existing insurance policies, etc. Irrespective of its data protection concerns, this application must in any case be classified as a high-risk application in accordance with no. 5 lit c Annex III.

7.2.3.2 Refutation of the High-risk Property

The high-risk characteristic according to Annex III AI Act can be refuted in accordance with Art. 6 para. 3 AI Act if the AI system does not profile natural persons. For this purpose, there must be no significant risk of harm to the health, safety or fundamental rights of natural persons because, among other things, the AI system does not influence the outcome of the decision-making significantly. To this end, one of the conditions specified in Art. 6 para. 3 AI Act must be met.[6]

Example

An AI system is designed to process incoming applications to the respective job advertisements without reviewing or evaluating their content. This form of categorization represents a **narrowly defined procedural task** in accordance with Article 6 para. 3 lit a (see Recital 53 AI Act). It can increase the risk of discrimination or distortion and enables an exclusively human decision on recruitment. If a mere categorization and no profiling takes place, the high-risk characteristic can be refuted.

An AI-supported risk assessment of life insurance policies is only used after a previously completed review of conditions and application processing **to identify decision-making patterns or deviations from previous decisions**. This means that the AI system no longer harbors the presumed risk of financial disadvantage or exclusion and can be refuted in accordance with Art. 6 para. 2 lit c AI Act.

A credit institution obtains the following for the individual credit rating of a loan applicant for various purposes from credit reference agencies and the scoring carried out by credit reference agencies. It analyzes this data with the support of AI using a wide range of other criteria (e. g. own experience from the existing customer relationship, accuracy or inconsistency of information provided, household income, own funds, etc.) in order to get a better picture. In this case, the credit agency's scoring is merely one of many **preparatory measures** and is not exclusively or primarily relevant to the decision. This process fulfills the condition of Article 6 para. 3 lit d. However, if **profiling** is carried out in the course of using AI is carried out in the course of the use of AI, the refutation as a high-risk AI system is excluded (see Art. 6 para. 2 last paragraph AI Act)

Risk classification must be clearly documented to demonstrate compliance with the AI Act.

7.2.3.3 Interactions between Financial Regulations and the AI Act

If an AI system is classified as high-risk, the requirements listed in Art. 8 et seq. AI Act must be fulfilled by every operator in the value chain must be implemented (see section 3.3.2.1). The AI Act provides for simplifications for financial institutions insofar as the implementation of some obligations is deemed to be fulfilled or can be simplified if sector-specific legislation provides for similar requirements. When financial

---

[6] After consulting the AI Panel, the EU Commission will provide guidelines in which this practical implementation is explained in detail and supplemented by a comprehensive list of examples.

institutions may refer to the **existing regulations and implementations** is explicitly regulated in the AI Act, in particular in the following sections:

■ The requirements for the **quality management system** in accordance with Art. 17 AI Act apply to providersthat are financial institutions and are subject to internal corporate governance in accordance with financial services legislation are deemed to have fulfilled the requirements if they comply with the regulatory require-ments. This does not include the obligation pursuant to Art. 17 para. 1 lit g AI Act (risk management system), lit h (establishment, implementation and maintenance of a system for monitoring the AI system after it has been placed on the market) and lit i (notification of a serious incident) are excluded.

■ Providers that are financial institutions and in accordance with financial services legislation, maintain the **technical documentation** in accordance with Art. 18 AI Act as part of the documentation in accordance with the special regulations in the financial sector.

■ Financial institutions as providers or deployers may use the **logs automatically generated** by their high-risk AI systems in accordance with Art. 19 AI Act and Art. 26 para. 6 AI Act as part of the documentation within the meaning of the spe-cial provisions in the financial services sector.

■ Financial institutions as deployers can fulfill their **monitoring obligations** set out in Art. 26 para. 5 subpara. 1 AI Act by complying with the provisions on rules, pro-cedures or mechanisms of internal corporate governance in accordance with the relevant regulatory provisions.

In addition, Art. 27 para. 1 AI Act stipulates that a fundamental rights impact assess-ment is also required when using high-risk AI, in particular for (i) credit scoring and creditworthiness assessment and (ii) risk assessment and pricing of (health and) life insurance policies. This is particularly relevant for the financial sector. For details on fundamental rights impact assessments, see section 3.4.

7.2.4 General Purpose AI Systems/Models

General Purpose AI systems or models that are integrated into AI systems also may be used in the financial sector.

Example

General Purpose AI models can be used for text or voice-based chatbots, process optimization, automation or complaint management, for example.

In the area of General Purpose AI, particular attention must be paid to the separte classification: simple General Purpose AI or with systematic risk. For details on the classification of General Purpose AI systems and models and the associated obligations, see section 3.7.

7.2.5 Certain AI Systems

If a regulated company only uses AI systems for **direct interaction** with natural persons (without General Purpose AI models), these are deemed as certain AI systems. The persons interacting with the system must be informed about the human-machine interaction, if not not already obvious to an appropriately informed and reasonable person considering the circumstances of the individual case. For chatbots in the financial sector, in my opinion, it cannot necessarily be assumed that a machine-supported system is clearly recognizable because personal contact is regularly assumed here due to the sensitivity of the inquiries. For details on the associated transparency obligations and restrictions, see section 3.6.

7.2.6 Authority Competencies

The AI Act provides for one or more authorities formarket surveillance. This can be bundled with the notifying body. Which insitution(s) shall be designated as the market surveillance authority is not yet clear (as of 19.5.2024) in Germany and Austria. The AI Act leaves this open to the member states. For the financial sector, however, Art. 74 para. 6 AI Act stipulates that the authority designated under national financial regulations is responsible for market surveillance of compliance with the provisions for high-risk AI systems by supervised financial institutions, provided that the AI systems are directly related to the provision of these financial services. In Austria, this is the Financial Market Authority (FMA) and in Germany the Federal Financial Supervisory Authority (BaFin). However, a deviating responsibility of the authorities is possible according to Art. 74 para. 7 AI Act, provided that coordination between the relevant authorities is ensured. See also section 3.9 for the structure of the authorities and their tasks and powers.

Irrespective of market surveillance under the AI Act, the existing competencies under other regulations remain in place. A breach of the AI Act can therefore also constitute a breach of other laws or regulations and open up parallel proceedings. This must be taken into account with regard to the potential risk when using AI systems from a governance and compliance perspective in regulated areas.

Sources

[1] Communication to the European Parliament, the Council, the European Economic and Social Committee and the Committee of the Regions on a Digital Finance Strategy for the EU, 2020

[2] Jahresbericht der BaFin 2023. URL *https://www.bafin.de/SharedDocs/Downloads/DE/Jahresbericht/dl_jb_2023.html*. – accessed: 2024/05/22 – BaFin

[3] Risiken im Fokus 2024. URL *https://www.bafin.de/DE/Aufsicht/Fokusrisiken/Fokusrisiken_2024/RIF_Trend_1_Digitalisierung/RIF_Trend_1_Digitalisierung_Artikel.html*. – accessed: 2024/05/22 – BaFin

[4] Beyond the prototype – Erfolgsfaktoren und Herausforderungen einer erfolgreichen Implementierung KI-basierter Services in der Produktion. URL *https://blog.iao.fraunhofer.de/beyond-the-prototype-erfolgsfaktoren-und-herausforderungen-einer-erfolgreichen-implementierung-ki-basierter-services-in-der-produktion/*. – accessed: 2024/05/22 – Fraunhofer IAO – BLOG

[5] BaFin erklärt Dark Patterns in Trading Apps für unzulässig. URL *https://www.bafin.de/SharedDocs/Veroeffentlichungen/DE/Meldung/2022/meldung_2022_11_21_Dark_Patterns_in_TradingApps_Verbraucher.html*. – accessed: 2024/05/22 – BaFin

[6] Guidelines 3/2022 on Dark patterns in social media platform interfaces: How to recognise and avoid them | European Data Protection Board. URL *https://www.edpb.europa.eu/our-work-tools/documents/public-consultations/2022/guidelines-32022-dark-patterns-social-media_en.%20-%20abgerufen%20am%202024-05-22*. – accessed: 2024/05/22 – BaFin

7.3 AI in the Insurance Industry

Renate Rechinger

The insurance industry in Austria plays a central role in protecting against risks and ensuring the financial stability of the population. It is a complex system that is characterized by state regulations and offers a wide range of insurance products.

The Austrian insurance industry is governed by a complex network of laws and regulations designed to ensure that insurance contracts are transparent, fair and understandable for consumers. The central legal bases are:

- Austrian Insurance Contract Act (VVG): The VVG is the central law for all insurance contracts in Austria. It regulates the rights and obligations of policyholders and insurers, the conclusion of contracts, the obligation to pay benefits and the termination options.

- Austrian Civil Code (ABGB): The ABGB contains general provisions on contracts and serves as a supplementary legal basis to the VVG.

- Austrian Financial Market Supervision Act (FMAG): The FMAG regulates the supervision of the financial markets, including the insurance sector. The Financial Market Authority (FMA) monitors insurers' compliance with the statutory provisions.

One of the latest developments in insurance is the integration of artificial intelligence (AI) into the insurance industry, which will revolutionize the way risks are assessed, products are designed and customers are served. The vast amounts of data generated by insurers provide fertile ground for the use of AI algorithms that can recognize patterns, make predictions and automate processes.

AI can be used in the following areas:

- Risk assessment and prioritization:
  - **More precise risk assessment:** AI models can use extensive data to analyze historical events and forecast future risks more accurately.
  - **Personalized tariffs:** By analyzing individual customer profiles, tailor-made insurance products can be offered.
  - **Fraud detection:** Anomaly detection and pattern analysis help to identify fraudulent activities at an early stage.
- Customer service:
  - **Chatbots and virtual assistants:** AI-supported chatbots take over routine customer service tasks and are available around the clock.
  - **Personalized advice:** AI algorithms can better understand customer needs and make individual recommendations.
  - **Faster claims processing:** Automation of claims notifications and processing speeds up the process considerably, for example omni:us [3].
- Process optimization:
  - **Automation:** Recurring tasks such as data processing and document checking can be automated, reducing costs and increasing efficiency.
  - **Predictive analytics:** AI makes it possible to predict future events and thus take proactive measures.

Artificial intelligence will permanently change the insurance industry. Insurers who invest in AI technologies at an early stage can gain a competitive advantage and serve their customers even better.

The following specific application examples result from the topics listed:

- **Claims settlement:** AI-based image analysis for fast and precise assessment of damage to vehicles or buildings.
- **Credit scoring:** AI models for assessing the creditworthiness of potential customers.
- **Product development:** Development of new insurance products based on AI-supported market research data.
- **Customer loyalty:** Personalized marketing campaigns and offers to increase customer satisfaction, for example with deepassist [1].

The challenge for these areas of application is that the quality of the data is crucial for the accuracy of the AI models. Furthermore, it will be essential that the results of the AI models are comprehensible and explainable.

Despite these challenges, the use of AI in the insurance industry offers numerous advantages:

- **Increased efficiency:** automation of processes and reduction of manual activities.

- **Cost reduction:** optimization of resources and avoidance of errors.

- **Improved customer satisfaction:** personalized offers and faster service.

- **New business models:** development of innovative products and services.

Depending on which AI system is used, it will be necessary to classify it in the existing AI Act.

7.3.1 Dynamic Underwriting and Risk Assessment in Health Insurance

Example

The applicant is guided through an interactive digital dialog. The same number of questions are asked as required and an immediate underwriting-decision is made. Big data and data analytics make it possible to optimize the questioning process and assess risk on the basis of several hundred million insurance years, far more than a risk assessor has available. The applicant's pre-existing conditions are recorded using a special tool for context-sensitive diagnostic recording. The risk assessment is then carried out on the basis of the recorded health data using an evidence-based risk assessment system [2].

Relevant roles

Provider is the company that developed and sells the AI system, and deployer is the company that uses the AI system in its business.

Classification as high-risk AI

Such AI system are classified as a high-risk AI because it is listed in Annex III no. 5 lit c AI Act, if the AI system that is intended to be used for risk assessment and pricing in relation to natural persons in the case of life and health insurance. It is categorized as a high-risk AI system in accordance with Art. 6 para. 2 AI Act. The obligations can be found in detail in section 3.3.2.4.

Classification as a high-risk AI system means that the following requirements in particular must be met:

- A risk management system must be set up, applied, documented and maintained in accordance with Art. 9 AI Act.

- According to Art. 10 AI Act, if techniques are used in which AI models are trained with data, developed with training, validation and testing data sets, these must meet the quality criteria specified in paragraphs 2 to 5 if such data sets are used.

- According to Art. 11 AI Act, technical documentation of a high-risk AI system must be prepared before this system is placed on the market or put into operation and must be kept up to date.

- The technology of high-risk AI systems must enable the automatic recording of events (hereinafter referred to as "logging") in accordance with Art. 12 AI Act during the life cycle of the system.

- In accordance with Art. 13 AI Act, a high-risk AI system shall be designed and developed in such a way that its operation is sufficiently transparent to enable deployers to interpret and use the outputs of a system appropriately.

- The high-risk AI system shall be designed and developed in such a way that it can be effectively supervised by natural persons in accordance with Art. 14 AI Act for the duration of its use, including with appropriate human-machine interface tools.

- In accordance with Art. 15 AI Act, the high-risk AI system shall be designed and developed to achieve an adequate level of accuracy, robustness and cybersecurity and to function consistently in this respect throughout its life cycle.

In addition, **providers** of high-risk AI systems in particular must comply with the following requirements in accordance with Art. 16 AI Act, namely:

a) ensure that their high-risk AI systems meet the requirements set out in para. 2;

b) indicate on the high-risk AI system or, if this is not possible, on its packaging or in the accompanying documentation, their name, registered trade name or registered trade mark and contact address;

c) have a quality management system that complies with Art. 17 AI Act;

d) retain the documentation referred to in Art. 18 AI Act;

e) retain the logs automatically generated by their high-risk AI systems in accordance with Art. 19 AI Act if these are subject to their control;

f) ensure that the high-risk AI system is subject to the relevant conformity assessment procedure in accordance with Art. 43 AI Act before it is placed on the market or put into operation;

g) issue an EU Declaration of Conformity in accordance with Art. 47 AI Act;

h) affix the CE marking to the high-risk AI system or, if this is not possible, on its packaging or in the accompanying documentation to indicate conformity with this Regulation in accordance with Art. 48 AI Act;

i) comply with the registration obligations set out in Art. 49 para. 1 AI Act;

j) take the necessary corrective measures and provide the information required under Art. 20 AI Act;

k) demonstrate, upon reasoned request from a national competent authority, that the high-risk AI system complies with the requirements set out in para. 2;

l) ensure that the high-risk AI system meets the accessibility requirements in accordance with Directives (EU) 2016/2102 and (EU) 2019/882.

Decisions about people

According to Art. 86 AI Act, persons affected by a decision taken by the deployer on the basis of the output of a high-risk AI system listed in Annex III AI Act, with the exception of the systems listed in no. 2 of that Annex, and which has legal effects or similarly significantly affects them in a way that they consider to be detrimental to their health, safety or fundamental rights, have the right to receive a clear and meaningful explanation from the deployer on the role of the AI system in the decision-making process and on the main elements of the decision taken. (see section 3.10.15.1)

In the case in question, no direct decision is made about health (e. g. determination of a specific treatment method), but a decision is made about the possible conclusion of a health insurance policy or its conditions. A broad interpretation of the ECJ could lead to the application of Art. 86 AI Act.

In any case, Art. 22 GDPR applies because an automated decision is made on a case-by-case basis. Therefore, the requirements and measures contained in Art. 22 para. 2 GDPR must be complied with (see also Chapter 4, Data protection).

Sources

[1] Automate processsing of customer service requests. URL *https://deepsearch.net/* – accessed: 2024/08/28 – deepsearch

[2] RISK-CONSULTING. URL *https://risk-consulting.de/* – accessed: 2024/08/28 – RISK-CONSULTING

[3] Claims automation with AI for insurance companies – omni:us. URL *https://omnius.com/de/* – accessed: 2024/08/28

7.4 AI and Whistleblowing

Gabriele Bolek-Fügl

The EU Whistleblower Directive 2019/1937 (Whistleblower Directive for short) has applied in all member states since December 2023 (end of the transition period) for organizations with more than 50 employees and the public administration. It is intended to improve the conditions for whistleblowers across the EU and offer them more security (Art. 1 Whistleblower Directive). The law prescribes secure reporting channels both within organizations and to external bodies in order to guarantee the anonymity and security of whistleblowers when submitting a report. It also stipulates sanctions to prevent retaliation against whistleblowers.

This chapter deals with the effects of the provisions of the AI Act on compliance with the respective whistleblower protection lawas each Member State had to transpose this EU Directive into local law. This law now plays a central role in organizations because it offers protection to people who report violations of certain legal provisions. The scope of application is broader in some countries than in others. The EU Directive itself only specifies a minimum scope of ten categories (see table).

An internal reporting channel in accordance with the EU directive fundamentally promotes a culture of openness and a sense of responsibility in organizations, which is essential for compliance and effective monitoring of regulations. In the modern economy, compliance is more than just adhering to legal requirements. It has become an integral part of corporate governance and risk management.

The European Union's AI Act will now be a further material scope of the Whistleblower Directive to ensure that the development, implementation and operation of artificial intelligence is carried out responsibly and in accordance with applicable laws and ethical standards in companies.

> **Art. 87 AI Act – Reporting of Breaches and Protection of Whistleblowers**
> The Whistleblower Directive applies to the reporting of breaches of this Regulation and the protection of persons who report such breaches.

Local whistleblower protection laws in each EU Member State take an important step towards strengthening transparency and integrity in business and the public sector by encouraging and protecting whistleblowers.

The following table provides a rough overview of the (minimum) requirements of the Whistleblower Directive:

Category/Article	Content of Directive (EU) 2019/1937
Objective of the Directive (Art. 1 Whistleblower Directive)	The EU Whistleblower Directive aims to protect people who report breaches of EU law. It is intended to ensure that whistleblowers can report without fear of retaliation.
Material scope (Art. 2 Whistleblower Directive)	The Directive applies to internal and external reports and public disclosures relating to breaches affecting the EU's financial interests or other areas such as: ▪ Public procurement ▪ Financial services ▪ Financial products and financial markets, prevention of money laundering and terrorist financing ▪ Product safety and conformity ▪ Road safety ▪ Environmental protection ▪ Radiation protection ▪ Food and feed safety, animal health and animal welfare ▪ Public health ▪ Data protection ▪ Member States can extend the material scope!

Category/Article	Content of Directive (EU) 2019/1937
Protective measures (Art. 6 and 19 Whistleblower Directive)	Whistleblowers who act lawfully are protected from dismissal, demotion and other forms of retaliation. Other prohibited actions include: ▪ Relocation of tasks or change of place of work ▪ Salary reduction ▪ Change in working hours ▪ Refusal to participate in further training measures ▪ Negative performance appraisal or issue of a poor reference ▪ Disciplinary measure, coercion, intimidation ▪ Bullying or exclusion ▪ Discrimination ▪ This protection also extends to related persons and supporting third parties.
Establishment of an internal reporting channel (Art. 7–9 Whistleblower Directive)	Legal entities under private law with more than 50 employees or with an annual turnover of more than 10 million euros must set up internal reporting channels. These channels must protect the confidentiality of the whistleblower and allow them to remain anonymous. In addition, legal entities in the public sector with > 50 employees: ▪ State administrative offices ▪ Regional administrations and departments ▪ Other legal entities under public law ▪ Municipalities with > 10,000 inhabitants or > 50 employees
Reporting procedure (Art. 9 Whistleblower Directive)	It should be possible to submit the report in written or oral form or in both forms. In addition, a physical meeting must be possible within a reasonable timeframe at the request of the whistleblower.
Duty to respond (Art. 9 Whistleblower Directive)	Organizations must respond to reports within specified deadlines. An acknowledgement of receipt must be sent within seven days and a description of the follow-up measures within three months.
External reports and public disclosures (Art. 10–15 Whistleblower Directive)	If internal reporting channels do not exist or do not work, or if it is unlikely that internal reports will provide a remedy (for example, if there is a direct threat to the public interest or a risk of retaliation), the whistleblower can turn to external authorities. If there is no response, the whistleblower can make the information public.

Whistleblowers are only protected (Art. 6 Whistleblower Directive) if they had reasonable grounds to believe that the reported information about breaches was true at the time of the report and that this information falls within the scope of the Directive.

According to Art. 23 Whistleblower Directive, Member States must impose effective, proportionate and dissuasive sanctions on natural or legal persons who:

- Obstruct or attempt to obstruct reports

- Taking reprisals against whistleblowers

- initiate malicious legal proceedings against whistleblowers

- violate the obligation to maintain the confidentiality of the identity of whistleblowers

What Needs to be Done?

If a company has already implemented an internal reporting channel, it must now be checked whether the extended scope of application of the AI Act is already included in the categories and descriptions of the whistleblowing system or must be supplemented:

1. Addition to the categories of the internal reporting channel

2. Supplementing the descriptions of the internal reporting channel (e. g. help texts, description of facts, examples of potential violations, etc.)

3. Appointment of a person responsible for processing potential notifications under the AI Act

4. Expansion of defined workflows/processes in the company

5. Expansion of the internal whistleblowing policy

6. Expansion of the training and training materials

7. Expansion of internal compliance descriptions (e. g. texts and examples on the intranet, onboarding documents, texts in employment contracts or works agreements, etc.)

8. Expansion of reporting to include the AI Act category

It should be noted that the material scope of application may differ from one Member State to another. In addition, the use of AI can also fall within the scope of the Whistleblowing Directive via detours, for example if personal data is processed by AI.

7.4.1 Whistleblower for the AI Category

A whistleblower who reports wrongdoing or unethical behavior in connection with the use of AI in an organization is protected by EU Directive 2019/1937. The report can concern the development and implementation of AI systems as well as their use and impact.

With the increasing use of AI in companies and the capabilities of AI systems, the risk that such technologies do not meet all legal requirements or are misused also increases. This in turn increases the need for whistleblowers to draw attention to potentially harmful or illegal behavior.

> **Example of a Whistleblower Report in the Context of the AI Act**
>
> Andra works in the HR department of a medium-sized company that is introducing a new AI-based system for evaluating job applications. This system is designed to increase the efficiency of the recruitment process and help identify the best talent. During her work with the system, Andra notices that while the system identifies many qualified candidates, it misses a significant number of applicants with unconventional resumes or career paths who could potentially bring valuable skills and perspectives to the organization.
>
> Andra realizes that overlooking these candidates could weaken the company's innovative strength and diversity in the long term. Concerned about the potential problem, Andra first turns to the project team responsible for implementing the AI system. She suggests adapting the model so that it can also better evaluate unconventional career paths. However, the project team is reluctant to take Andra's suggestions on board, fearing that additional adjustments could overrun the project budget and delay the schedule.
>
> After her concerns were not taken on board by the project team, Andra decides to report the issue via the internal whistleblowing channel. In her report, she emphasizes not only the short-term financial and time-related concerns, but also the long-term benefits of more comprehensive talent tracking for the company.
>
> The management takes Andra's advice seriously and recognizes the strategic importance of her suggestions. It commissions a team of data scientists and HR specialists to revise the AI system accordingly. The adjustment leads to an improved assessment system that can recognize and include a greater variety of talent, thereby improving the quality and diversity of new hires.
>
> The company benefits enormously from Andra's proactive approach: the quality and diversity of new hires improve and the company is perceived as a progressive and attractive employer. Andra's initiative shows how whistleblowing not only serves to uncover grievances, but also to drive constructive change within the company and ensure its long-term success.

There are several reasons why whistleblowing could become more important in the field of AI:

- Increased number of regulatory requirements for AI systems. Not only in Europe, but also in the USA and Asia, there are more and more laws and regulations that companies have to comply with.

- With the increasing use of AI, regulatory control over its use is also increasing. Regulatory authorities such as the Securities and Exchange Commission (SEC) and the US Department of Justice (DOJ)[7] have already established programs to monitor and enforce regulations related to AI. The AI Act will also establish national supervisory authorities in the EU.

- In Europe, national data protection authorities are also paying increasing attention to the GDPR-compliant use of data when training AI and in productive use.

- With the implementation of AI technology, values that are derived from data generated in past processes are also digitized. This increases the requirements for ethical decisions that need to be made during an AI project. However, not everyone involved in the project realizes that they can only influence the future results of AI by selecting the right data. Negligence in this context can therefore cause a project to fail and could trigger an internal report.

When employees know they can safely point out challenges in an AI project without fear of retribution, they feel encouraged to speak openly about problems and opportunities for improvement. This can lead to better internal communication and a more proactive approach to compliance issues, saving the company from paying fines.

A tip-off can also provide valuable insight into vulnerabilities and risks in existing AI systems that might otherwise go undetected. This information is crucial for changing processes before they can cause harm or improving the overall efficiency and security of AI applications.

> **Example of a Whistleblower Report for a High-risk AI**
>
> I would like to draw your attention to a serious ethical issue that has arisen in the use of our AI system for medical diagnostics. The Diagnosis AI v2.3 system is currently being used in several hospitals to assist in the diagnosis of diseases. Although the system officially meets the requirements of the AI Act, I have found that it systematically discriminates against certain patient groups.
>
> Diagnostic AI v2.3 shows significantly lower accuracy in diagnosing diseases in patients of a certain ethnicity. This leads to incorrect diagnoses or delayed treatment, which can have serious health consequences for these patients.
>
> The AI system does not provide sufficient transparency about the decision-making processes, and doctors and medical staff do not receive clear information about how certain diagnoses are made. This makes it difficult to recognize errors and to question or correct the results.
>
> Please investigate this problem and rectify it.

---

[7] *https://www.debevoisedatablog.com/2024/04/24/preparing-for-ai-whistleblowers/* of July 27, 2024

By creating an environment that supports whistleblowing, companies can not only better comply with legal and ethical standards, but also strengthen their own competitiveness and innovative power.

7.4.2 Areas of Application of AI in the Implementation of the Whistleblowing Directive

One particular AI use case is an AI-supported whistleblowing platform which offers companies an innovative solution to deal with grievances more efficiently and respond more quickly to reports. By combining various automated actions and techniques, companies can strengthen their compliance and ethics programs and promote a transparent and trustworthy corporate culture.

Task Definition

Implementation of a whistleblowing platform in which some essential tasks are taken over by an AI to minimize manual, time-consuming actions. This internal reporting system should be able to fulfill all legal requirements and help whistleblowers feel safe and address issues internally first before informing external bodies.

7.4.2.1 Challenges in the Whistleblowing Process

Traditional whistleblowing platforms are often faced with a large number of reports that need to be reviewed manually. This can lead to delays and inconsistent assessment. There is also a risk that the confidentiality of whistleblowers is not sufficiently protected, especially if managers are accused or the names of employees appear in the reports. In addition, reports are often received at a time when employees are not online (off-peak hours) and are therefore unable to respond quickly to communication with the whistleblower.

An AI-supported system should therefore help with the following challenges:

- Assess the relevance and accuracy of incoming reports according to legal requirements before the whistleblower officially submits the report and inform the whistleblower that the legal protection only applies to a limited number of criteria.

- Evaluate the quality of the reports in terms of the scope and detail of the content and provide information on what information is still required in order to start the analysis efficiently.

- Propose appropriate actions and follow-up questions based on previously analyzed cases.

- Identify whether names of whistleblowing officers are included in the reports and do not grant them access to these reports to ensure independent processing.

- Identify whether executives from the top circle are accused and assign these reports only to a specific officer.

Challenges in the AI Project

An AI whistleblowing project poses a number of specific challenges, particularly with regard to training the AI models and collecting sufficient and representative data for case processing. Some of the main challenges are:

- **Sufficient number of messages:** A large amount of data is required to train AI models, often several thousand. In the context of whistleblowing, it can be difficult to collect a sufficient number and variety of cases to train a robust model. Many companies may only have a few documented cases, and these are often confidential, further limiting access to this data.

- **Data quality:** The quality of the data available for training is crucial to the success of the project. Missing, incomplete or inconsistent data can have a negative impact on model performance. However, the reports processed in the past are often not documented in a standardized way.

- **Mapping different cases:** An AI model must be able to recognize and process a variety of whistleblowing scenarios. This includes different types of misconduct (e. g. financial irregularities, ethical violations, environmental offenses). If the training is based on a limited number of cases, the model may struggle to respond appropriately to new or rare cases.

- **Bias and fairness:** There is a risk that the training data may contain biases or other systematic distortions that influence the model's predictions. If certain types of misbehavior or certain groups of people are over- or under-represented in the data, this could lead to unbalanced performance.

- **Data protection requirements and confidentiality of reports:** As whistleblowing reports often contain personal or very sensitive information, it is a challenge to use this data for the training of an AI model without violating GDPR or other data protection regulations, for example because a former whistleblower does not want to give their consent for the training of the AI. Anonymization techniques can help, but they need to be applied carefully to ensure that the data is still useful for training.

- **Model complexity:** The complexity of the AI model for the whistleblowing application can be a challenge, as these models must be able to recognize not only simple patterns but also complex relationships and anomalies that could indicate misconduct.

- **Competence of the project team:** An AI project is carried out differently to rule-based software projects because the focus is very much on domain knowledge and the appropriateness of the data. This must be reflected in the project team, and those involved must have a minimum level of knowledge of AI techniques, data management, ethics and legal requirements.

The selection and quantity of data in particular will pose a challenge when implementing the project.

Advantages of an AI Whistleblowing Application

However, processing tips with AI support has a number of advantages that should be considered and weighed up more carefully:

- **Increased efficiency:** Automated evaluation and prioritization of notifications reduce manual effort and speed up the response process.

- **Improved quality in the processing of reports:** Consistent and objective assessment of reports through AI-supported analyses (AI in the Loop).

- **Protection of people:** The anonymity and confidentiality of the persons named in the submitted reports can be increased.

- **Better decision-making:** Well-founded recommendations for action and prioritization support the compliance team in the effective processing of reports.

- **Conflict avoidance:** Preventing clerks from accessing messages in which they themselves are mentioned and targeted assignment of sensitive messages.

Even in companies that only receive a few reports per year, the use of a pre-trained AI whistleblower solution would be would be advantageous, as people need to be continuously trained in the correct handling of reported information so that all legal requirements are reliably met during the analysis. An AI system could guide people here so that no errors occur.

Assessment of the Risks for the Target Group

The following people are among those affected by the whistleblowing system and must be considered in the AI project with regard to the specific risks:

- **Whistleblowers:** With the introduction of the AI system, it must be ensured that the names and any information referring to the person are treated confidentially.

- **Persons named in tip-offs:** With the introduction of the AI system, it must be ensured that the names, the reference of information pointing to the person and their status in the tip-off (e. g. witness or potential perpetrator) are treated confidentially and are also not used for further AI training.

- **Compliance team:** The performance of the persons responsible for processing must not be used to measure or assess performance.

7.4.2.2 Procedure of the Whistleblowing Use Case

The following processes and functions could be supported by an AI-supported whistleblowing platform in cooperation with the compliance team:

1. A person submits a report that indicates a possible offense in a particular department.
   - If the report was submitted by name, the AI can recognize the name and anonymize it for internal analysis.

2. The AI analyzes the notification and assesses whether it is relevant according to the legal requirements and whether the contents of the notification are sufficient to start the analyses efficiently.
   - If the report does not meet any of the legal criteria, the whistleblower will be informed, as legal protection is not guaranteed in this case. He or she could then withdraw the report.
   - If essential content is not included in the report, the AI automatically asks the person providing the information for further information.
   - Key information is identified in the notification and provided for storage in case management. This could include, for example, the following: Names of potential offenders, name of a department, locations, dates, totals, etc.

3. The system notifies the right person in the compliance team to process the report.
   - This ensures that employees whose names are mentioned in the report do not have access to it.
   - The AI could only assign reports concerning top-level managers to a specific administrator.
   - Different reporting categories could be assigned to different people in the compliance team.

4. The AI system generates recommendations for the internal investigation so that the compliance team can take immediate action.
   - Based on investigations already carried out in the past, AI proposes audit procedures that are expedient for clarification.

5. AI could support communication between compliance staff and the whistleblower by evaluating the content of reports and automatically generating any follow-up questions.

An AI system could therefore support people in processing various tasks, especially when it comes to correctly assigning, structuring and grouping information, as well as responding quickly to a report while a whistleblower is online.

Use of Digital Techniques in the Whistleblowing Use Case

The following AI techniques could be used in this AI project:

Ref	Function	Non-AI Functions	AI Functionality	AI Techniques	IT Security Features	Groups of People Affected
1	Admission portal and anonymization	Secure web portal for the (anonymous) submission of a report	Anonymization of personal data for identity protection	Named Entity Recognition (NER), masking of names using placeholders	Encryption, data anonymization	Indicator
2	Content analysis	Review and extraction of relevant information	Analysis and extraction of relevant information from the text of the messages	Natural Language Processing (NLP), Named Entity Recognition (NER)		Compliance-Team
2	Relevance and accuracy assessment	Manual assessment of relevance and legal accuracy	Automated assessment of relevance and accuracy in accordance with legal requirements	Machine learning, rule-based systems	Good selection of training data	Compliance-Team
2	Evaluation of the message quality	Manual analysis of the level of detail and consistency of the messages	Evaluation of the quality of the reports in terms of the scope and detail of the content	Natural Language Processing (NLP), pattern recognition		Compliance-Team
3	Conflict and confidentiality detection	Manual check for conflicts and confidentiality	Recognition of names of defined persons in messages and prevention of their access, assignment of sensitive messages	Named Entity Recognition (NER), rule-based systems	Access control mechanisms, confidentiality check	Compliance-Team

Ref	Function	Non-AI Functions	AI Functionality	AI Techniques	IT Security Features	Groups of People Affected
4	Recommendations for action and follow-up	Manual generation of recommendations for action and other questions	Automatic generation of recommendations for action and specific questions for follow-up	Decision trees, rule-based systems		Compliance-Team
5	Communication and notification system	Real-time monitoring and notification of the relevant decision-makers	Automatic notification and real-time monitoring and analysis of message content	Natural Language Processing (NLP), Automated Notification System	Encryption	Compliance team, whistle-blowers

This concept is intended as a proposal and only represents a basis for an AI project. However, the functions can also be implemented using other technologies.

Further Development and Implementation

The following phases must continue to be implemented in the AI project after the AI has been developed:

- **Pilot phase:** Introduction of the AI system in selected areas of the company to validate and fine-tune the functionalities. The criteria must be defined in advance.

- **Scaling:** After a successful pilot phase (according to defined criteria), expansion to the entire company.

- **Continuous improvement:** Regular monitoring of AI (review of results and assessment of accuracy by domain users) and adaptation of AI models and systems based on feedback and new findings.

This use case illustrates how AI can be integrated into whistleblowing platforms to improve the quality and efficiency of processing of reports and thus strengthen the integrity and ethics of a company. It is also clear that joint processing by AI and humans brings the greatest benefits and minimizes the risks.

7.5 Use of AI in Future and Existing Employment Relationships

Renate Rechinger

Austrian labor law regulates the relationship between employers and employees. It covers a wide range of topics, from the establishment of an employment relationship to its termination.

The most important legal sources of labor law in Austria are:

- **Laws:** The most important law in Austrian labor law is the **Employees Act (Ange-stelltengesetz** – AngG). In addition, there are a number of other laws that are relevant to labor law, e. g. the **Austrian Civil Code (Allgemeines Bürgerliches Gesetzbruch** – ABGB), the Industrial Code (Gewerbeordnung – **GewO**), etc.

- **Collective agreements:** Collective agreements are contracts between employee representatives (labor union) and employer representatives that apply to certain industries or professions. They usually stipulate wages, working hours and other working conditions.

- **Works agreements:** Company agreements are contracts between the employer and the works council of a company. They regulate company-specific matters, e. g. working hours, vacation and rest periods.

- **Individual employment contracts:** Individual employment contracts are contracts between the employer and the individual employee. They regulate the employee's individual working conditions, e. g. salary, working hours and duties.

The most important topics of labor law are:

- **Employment contract:** The employment contract regulates the basic conditions of the employment relationship, e. g. the type of work, pay, working hours and vacation.

- **Working time:** Working time is the time during which the employee is obliged to work. The statutory maximum working time in Austria is forty hours per week.

- **Wage:** The wage is the remuneration for the employee's work. It is usually agreed in euros per hour or per month.

- **Vacation:** The employee is entitled to paid vacation. The statutory minimum vacation in Austria is 25 days per year.

- **Termination:** The employment relationship can be terminated by either party. The notice periods are regulated by law.

- **Employee protection:** Employee protection comprises a range of regulations designed to protect the health and safety of employees in the workplace.

In Austria, employers must comply with certain legal provisions when looking for new employees to ensure that the process is fair and non-discriminatory.

General principles:

- **Equal treatment:** All applicants, regardless of gender, race, religion, age, disability, sexual orientation or ethnicity, have the right to equal treatment.

- **Prohibition of discrimination:** Direct and indirect discrimination in the job advertisement, in the application process and during the employment relationship is prohibited.

- **Transparency:** The job advertisement should clearly describe the requirements for the applicant and the working conditions offered.

- **Data protection:** Applicants' personal data must be protected in accordance with data protection regulations.

Special requirements:

- **Obligation to report:** Employers with more than twenty employees must report vacancies to the Public Employment Service Austria (AMS).

- **Disability-friendly applications:** Applications from people with disabilities must be given equal consideration. Employers are obliged to take appropriate measures to facilitate the application process for people with disabilities.

- **Foreigners employment law:** When hiring foreign employees, the provisions of employment and residence law must be observed.

Application platforms use AI to automatically screen CVs for the advertised position. **CV parsing** (to parse = analyze) is already a common field of application for artificial intelligence. The technology analyzes application documents and extracts relevant information such as qualifications and professional experience. This data is then made available in a standardized format such as a database for further processing and analysis or processing.

ATS systems (Applicant Tracking Systems) help companies to manage application processes, publish job vacancies and manage potential candidates. CV parsing and ATS systems often work together. Examples of such ATS systems are Oracle Taleo [5] or Greenhouse [1].

Employers can also use AI or certain platforms to test and assess the required skills of applicants. Codility [2] and HackerRank [3] are used by large companies in particular to check technical skills.

AI can be used to varying degrees. This ranges from the complete creation of a job advertisement to AI-supported video analysis.

7.5.1 Writing Job Ads with AI

Example

Direct use of common LLM tools (e. g. Google Gemini, ChatGPT) to obtain results from the AI via prompts (input). In principle, all text tasks can be completed with an AI.

Identify job title alternatives:

The right job title is a key success factor for job advertisements. Tools such as Google Trends can be used to check how often the different variants are searched for. This allows you to make a data-based decision in favor of the job title that is most frequently used by candidates. There are two options for identifying suitable or alternative job titles: Either you already have a job title and would like to receive alternative suggestions from the AI based on this. Or you have an outline of the qualifications you are looking for and the planned tasks and first search for those titles that could basically fit the position.

Example of a prompt to use ChatGPT or Google Gemini to search for suitable alternatives:

"Please support me in identifying alternative job titles for the search for [POSITION]. The alternatives should, on the one hand, show different designation possibilities and, on the other hand, be designed to have a high search volume of job seekers. The title should be close to the source term without reading too much into the role. It is a company in [INDUSTRY; optional], which could be included in the title, but is not a must."

Create and optimize company description:

An essential part of every job advertisement is the company's self-description. This should show what makes the company stand out as an employer. An AI can help with the wording, but also with the optimization of the texts.

Define job-related requirements and tasks:

Here you specify exactly what you are looking for and what tasks future employees should take on in the company.

Example of a prompt to get useful results using ChatGPT or Google Gemini:

"Create a list of tasks and requirements for a job advertisement for the search for [position]. Use non-discriminatory, German and formal language. The position is to be used in particular in [specialization] – i. e. [specific tasks, if nameable]. [Another important area of responsibility] is an essential area of responsibility."

Channel mix for the publication of the job advertisement:

Once the job ad has been created, it's time to get it to the right candidates via the right channels. To do this, you can use generative AI tools to search for suitable channels for publication. For example, Google Gemini could be used as a research tool.

Example of a prompt:

"I need a mix of suitable channels to publish my job advertisement for the search for [position] in [location]. Create a list of suitable job portals, industry media and social media channels that I could use to advertise my job."

Relevant roles

The deployer of ChatGPT within the meaning of the AI Act is the company OpenAI, which is dedicated to AI research.

Classification as high-risk AI

No, there is no high-risk AI.

Points of contact with prohibited AI

No, there are no points of contact with prohibited AI.

Transparency obligations

Transparency rules apply in principle in accordance with Art. 50 AI Act. If, for example, an image, video or audio content is created or modified by an AI, this fact must be disclosed. This also applies if an AI creates or modifies a text that is disseminated for the purpose of public information.

7.5.2 AI Support for Applicant Selection by Means of Video Analysis [4]

Example

Applicants applying for a job are asked to record a one-minute video in addition to their traditional CV. In this video, applicants answer the question: "Why are you looking forward to working for XY?" These videos are recorded and subsequently evaluated by the AI tool.

Artificial intelligence creates a personality profile. The Big 5 model (McCrae & John, 1992) describes a person's personality on the basis of five dimensions: openness, conscientiousness, extraversion, agreeableness and neuroticism. The model classifies candidates according to these five different personality dimensions, which are universally and interculturally recognized. Together with the personality profile, a communication profile of the applicant is also provided. By combining the profiles, the company receives an objective profile of all applicants, which can significantly speed up the entire pre-selection process.

Relevant roles

In this use case, all roles can be relevant, depending on the constellation.

Classification as high-risk AI

Yes, because Annex III no. 4 lit a AI Act defines an AI system that is intended to be used for the recruitment or selection of natural persons, in particular to place targeted job advertisements, to screen or filter applications and to evaluate applicants, as a high-risk AI system pursuant to Art. 6 para. 2 AI Act. The obligations can be found in detail in section 3.3.2.4.

Classification as a high-risk AI system means that the following requirements in particular must be met:

- A risk management system must be set up, applied, documented and maintained in accordance with Art. 9 AI Act.

- According to Art. 10 AI Act, if techniques are used in which AI models are trained with data (training, validation and testing data sets), these must meet the quality criteria specified in paragraphs 2 to 5.

- According to Art. 11 AI Act, technical documentation of a high-risk AI system must be prepared before this system is placed on the market or put into operation and must be kept up to date.

- The technology of high-risk AI systems must enable the automatic recording of events (hereinafter referred to as "logging") in accordance with Art. 12 AI Act during the life cycle of the system.

- In accordance with Art. 13 AI Act a high-risk AI system shall be designed and developed in such a way that its operation is sufficiently transparent to enable deployers to interpret and use the outputs of a system appropriately.

- The high-risk AI system shall be designed and developed in such a way that it can be effectively supervised by natural persons in accordance with Art. 14 AI Act for the duration of its use, including with appropriate human-machine interface tools.

- In accordance with Art. 15 AI Act, the high-risk AI system shall be designed and developed to achieve an adequate level of accuracy, robustness and cybersecurity and to function consistently in this respect throughout its life cycle.

Decision about natural persons

According to Art. 86 AI Act, persons affected by a decision taken by the deployer on the basis of the output of a high-risk AI system listed in Annex III, with the exception of the systems listed in no. 2 of that Annex, and which has legal effects or similarly significantly affects them in a way that they consider to be detrimental to their health, safety or fundamental rights, have the right to receive a clear and meaningful explanation from the deployer on the role of the AI system in the decision-making process and on the main elements of the decision taken, see section 3.10.15.1)

The AI in the use case in question can interfere with fundamental rights, in particular if it does act in a discriminatory manner. The right to the protection of personal data, freedom to choose an occupation and the right to work or protection against discrimination could be impaired (see section 7.1, Discrimination, for details).

However, Art. 22 GDPR applies because an automated decision is made on a case-by-case basis. Therefore, the requirements and measures contained in Article 22 para. 2 GDPR must be complied with.

Obligations of the providers

In addition, **providers** of high-risk AI systems in particular must comply with the following requirements in accordance with Art. 16 AI Act, namely

a) ensure that their high-risk AI systems meet the requirements set out in Section 2;

b) indicate on the high-risk AI system or, if this is not possible, on its packaging or in the accompanying documentation, their name, registered trade name or registered trade mark and contact address;

c) have a quality management system that complies with Art. 17 AI Act;

d) retain the documentation referred to in Art. 18 AI Act;

e) retain the logs automatically generated by their high-risk AI systems in accordance with Art. 19 AI Act if these are subject to their control;

f) ensure that the high-risk AI system is subject to the relevant conformity assessment procedure in accordance with Art. 43 AI Act before it is placed on the market or put into operation;

g) issue an EU Declaration of Conformity in accordance with Art. 47 AI Act;

h) affix the CE marking to the high-risk AI system or, if this is not possible, on its packaging or in the accompanying documentation to indicate conformity with this Regulation in accordance with Art. 48 AI Act;

i) comply with the registration obligations set out in Art. 49 para. 1 AI Act;

j) take the necessary corrective measures and provide the information required under Art. 20 AI Act;

k) demonstrate, upon reasoned request from a national competent authority, that the high-risk AI system complies with the requirements set out in Section 2 AI Act;

l) ensure that the high-risk AI system meets the accessibility requirements in accordance with Directives (EU) 2016/2102 and (EU) 2019/882.

Sources

[1] Bewerbermanagementsystem & Einstellungssoftware. URL *https://www.greenhouse.com/de/* – accessed: 2024/08/28 – Greenhouse

[2] Codility. URL *https://www.codility.com/* – accessed: 2024/08/28 – Codility

[3] HackerRank – Online Coding Tests and Technical Interviews. URL *https://www.hackerrank.com/* – accessed: 2024/08/28 – HackerRank

[4] Identify and Drive Winning Behaviors | Retorio. URL *https://www.retorio.com* – accessed: 2024/08/28

[5] Taleo | Oracle Österreich. URL *https://www.oracle.com/at/human-capital-management/taleo/* – accessed: 2024/08/28

7.6 AI in Education

Julia Eisner

Artificial intelligence (AI) in education is an interdisciplinary interface between computer science, pedagogy, psychology, social sciences and educational science. Ongoing research and development in this area shows how education systems around the world are evolving and adapting to the needs of an increasingly digitalized society [1, 2]. The aim is to optimize and personalize teaching and learning processes through the use of intelligent systems to improve educational outcomes. These technologies aim to fundamentally transform the education sector by enabling automation, customization and efficiency gains. In addition to implementation, educational institutions take on a facilitator role. The role includes the teaching and transfer of AI skills so that learners and teachers acquire the necessary digital skills and competences to be able to actively participate in the economy, society and democratic processes in the future (Recital 56 AI Act).

AI systems are used in a variety of applications. Areas of application include automated assessment of exams, adaptive learning platforms that offer personalized curricula and learning paths, and predictive analytics to predict learning behavior and dropout risks [1, 2]. Initial international studies show that immersive learning environments [1, 2] use technologies such as virtual reality (VR), augmented reality (AR) and mixed reality (MR) to immerse learners in realistic, interactive and three-dimensional worlds. Furthermore, AI-supported monitoring systems are used to detect cheating attempts during exams. In addition, ChatGPT, a text-based AI chatbot, opens up various possibilities for teachers and students. The creation of own GPTs enables the development of scenarios, for example for counseling sessions. It also offers the option of receiving answers to exam literature depending on the learning level. AI systems for a general purpose such as ChatGPT are treated separately in the AI Act and are subject to special requirements (see section 3.7 GPAI). This includes, among other things, the transparency obligation of the systems (Art. 50 AI Act). The wide range of technologies and possible applications allow teachers to respond to the individual needs of learners and adapt lessons accordingly.

Educational institutions at all levels, from elementary school to tertiary educational institutions, as well as adult and vocational institutions, are increasingly integrating AI technologies to address the individual learning needs of learners, streamline administrative processes and increase the quality of teaching in terms of innovation and digitalization. The use of AI enables teachers and lecturers to make informed decisions based on data-driven analysis, making the learning environment more interactive and effective. However, the implementation of AI in education is not without its challenges and risks. The ethical use of these technologies is of paramount importance to prevent discrimination and data breaches. In addition to the internal policies and guidelines of the educational institution, the AI Act provides an essential framework to ensure the safe and ethical use of AI in education. In particular, the classification of certain AI systems as high-risk or prohibited requires an examination of the AI Act. Nevertheless, even AI systems with "limited risk" (Art. 50 AI Act) entail certain risks that can be minimized by means of transparency obligations [3]. For AI systems with "minimal risk", no further obligations apply for deployers, apart from ensuring the AI literacy of users. The risk-based approach thus sets essential framework conditions to ensure that the regulations are effective and binding (Recital 26 AI Act) so that the use of AI in education is both innovative and safe.

The following aspects are discussed below:

- Roles in the AI Act
- AI literacy
- AI systems with "limited" risk in education
- High-risk AI systems in education
- Prohibited AI systems in education

7.6.1 Roles in the AI Act

The AI Act aims to promote the safe and ethical use of artificial intelligence. The introduction of clearly defined roles is fundamental to assigning responsibilities and ensuring compliance. This should prevent misuse and ensure that AI technologies are used both effectively and (ethically) responsibly.

Provider (Art. 3 no. 3 AI Act): Companies and developers that develop or provide AI systems for the education sector must ensure that the systems comply with regulatory requirements and also disclose whether they are, for example, high-risk AI.

Deployer (Art. 3 no. 4 AI Act): Educational institutions such as schools, colleges and universities, but also natural persons who implement or use AI systems, i. e. are responsible for the integration and operation of AI. Deployers transfer the necessary competence, authorization and training to natural persons. They also provide them with the necessary support and human supervision. Educational institutions are therefore not only responsible for integrating AI into the curriculum, but must also ensure that the systems used meet regulatory requirements. They must also provide resources, training and infrastructure to ensure responsible use and develop the necessary skills among teachers (see also Annex IV AI Act).

Users are, for example, teachers who use AI systems in day-to-day education and are regarded as mediators between technologies and students, but also use AI to support their teaching. However, users in educational institutions can also be IT departments. Users must have the necessary AI literacy skills (Annex IV AI Act) and must, for example, be aware of a high-risk classification and comply with the AI Act.

Market Surveillance Authority (Art. 3 no. 26 AI Act): is the national authority that carries out the activities and takes the measures provided for in the AI Act;

Regulatory authorities: Institutions that monitor compliance with the AI Act, ensuring compliance with legal requirements and sanctioning violations.

See also section 3.1.2 for details of the roles.

7.6.2　AI Literacy (Art. 4 AI Act)

The use of AI systems in education or training is crucial to promote high-quality digital and vocational education and training (Recital 56 AI Act). It enables learners and teachers to acquire and pass on the necessary digital skills, media literacy and critical thinking. Providers, deployers and data subjects (Recital 20 AI Act) must be equipped with the necessary skills and competences to make informed decisions about AI systems. **Fundamental rights, health and safety** must also be safeguarded in order to enable democratic control. The promotion of AI literacy is therefore an important prerequisite for ensuring that citizens can continue to actively participate in the economy, society and democratic processes in the future (Recital 20 AI Act). The definition of AI literacy according to the AI Act (Art. 3 no. 56 AI Act) is as follows:

"AI literacy means skills, knowledge and understanding that allow providers, deployers and affected persons, taking into account their respective rights and obligations in the context of this Regulation, to make an informed deployment of AI systems, as well as to gain awareness about the opportunities and risks of AI and possible harm it can cause."

In addition to the provider, deployers of AI systems are also obliged to demonstrate a sufficient level of AI literacy (Art. 4 AI Act in conjunction with Art. 3 no. 56 AI Act). The scope of the deployer's obligations differs depending on the risk classification of the AI system, i. e. high-risk AI systems have the most obligations and AI systems with minimal risk have the fewest [3]. However, all risk levels have the necessary AI literacy skills (Art. 4 AI Act) in common as an obligation. This illustrates the relevance of AI literacy. In addition to practical application, it is also necessary to deal with and understand data processing, including **privacy issues, ethical understanding, understanding of bias and discrimination in systems** and in application. Careful design and use form the basis for the use of AI in education in order to avoid negative effects (see also section 3.2 AI literacy). Regular training and further education is required to expand teachers' knowledge of AI and improve their didactic skills. It is advisable to integrate practical applications of AI-based learning tools and platforms into lessons. This promotes the use of technology and prepares learners for future challenges. The development of appropriate curricula, training and practical applications is an important measure to promote comprehensive AI skills that meet the requirements of modern digital education.

7.6.3 AI Systems with "Limited" Risk (Art. 50 AI Act) in Education

For AI systems with limited risk in accordance with Art. 50 AI Act (see section 3.6), the **transparency obligation** towards downstream actors (Art. 50 para. 3 of the AI Act, Art. 50 para. 4 AI Act) must also be taken into account in addition to AI competence (Art. 4 AI Act). According to Art. 50 AI Act, the transparency obligation can minimize a limited risk. Information about the use of AI systems must be provided clearly and unambiguously at the latest at the time of first use or first contact. The current accessibility requirements must be taken into account (see Art. 50 para. 5 AI Act). The following are examples of AI systems with "limited" risk in the education sector.

Example I: Chatbots

Chatbots can be used for administrative tasks such as answering general inquiries or making appointments. These systems increase efficiency and reduce the administrative burden in educational institutions. However, users must be informed that they are communicating with a chatbot and not with a natural person, but with an AI (transparency obligation pursuant to Art. 50 AI Act). In addition to this transparency obligation, Union and national rights remain in place that regulate, for example, the use and processing of personal data in accordance with the GDPR.

Example II: Image and video creation

If visual learning content was created or supported by an AI, the transparency obligation pursuant to Art. 50 AI Act also applies here. Learners must be informed that the content was created or manipulated by an AI.

Exceptions to the transparency obligation arise if there is an editor who assumes responsibility for the content and form of AI-generated and manipulated texts. The review and approval process ensures that the content is correct and of high quality, which removes the specific transparency obligation.

Example III: Adaptive learning environment

An adaptive mathematics learning system uses AI to analyse students' learning progress in order to offer them personalized learning paths. The system adjusts the difficulty of the tasks based on individual performance and learning behavior to ensure optimal learning success. However, the AI system does not assess performance. When using or registering for the first time, learners must be informed that the system uses AI to adapt learning content.

Adaptive learning systems carry the risk of also being used for assessment. As a result, there is a possibility that the AI system will be classified as a high-risk AI system. For example, if (1) the system makes automated decisions as to whether a learner may progress to the next course or class. (2) The system automatically awards certifications and assessments that can influence the learner's further educational and career path. Possible high-risk AI systems in education are outlined below.

7.6.4 High-risk AI Systems in Education

AI systems used in education and training can also control access to educational institutions and programs, assess learning outcomes, evaluate educational attainment and enable the monitoring of learners during exams, among other things. These systems have the potential to significantly influence the course of a person's educational and professional life. They are therefore also classified as high-risk AI systems (Recital 56 AI Act). High-risk AI systems in education can have a very invasive effect if not designed and used properly. They can violate the right to education and training and the right to non-discrimination. These systems carry the risk of perpetuating historical patterns of discrimination, in particular against women, certain age groups, people with disabilities or people with a certain ethnic origin or sexual orientation (Recital 56 AI Act). High-risk AI systems are defined in the AI Act as a separate category with specific obligations for deployers. In contrast to AI systems with "limited" risk, a transparency obligation is not sufficient for high-risk AI systems. In this case, the AI Act provides for comprehensive obligations during use (see section 3.3.2.3).

Annex III no. 3 AI Act, Art. 6 para. 2 subpara. 3 AI Act classifies high-risk AI systems in education and training. This definition is illustrated below using practical examples to provide a better understanding of the classification and its implications.

a) *AI systems that are intended to be used to determine access or admission or to allocate natural persons to institutions at all levels of education and training (Annex III/3, AI Act, Art. 6 para. 2 subpara. 3).*

Example I for a) Automated approval systems

An AI system evaluates applications for university places based on school grades, standardized test results and extracurricular activities. This system determines the access or admission of individuals to educational institutions and thus directly influences their educational and career prospects.

Example II for a) Automated scholarship awarding

An AI system evaluates applications for scholarships based on school grades, standardized test scores and extracurricular activities. This system determines the access or admission of individuals to educational institutions and thus directly influences their educational and career prospects.

Both AI systems (example I & II) would be classified as high-risk AI systems in accordance with Annex III/, Section a) AI Act. According to the classification, no automated, AI-based decisions may be made with regard to access or admission of natural persons to educational institutions.

b) *AI systems that are intended to be used for the assessment of learning outcomes, including where these outcomes are used to guide the learning process of natural persons in institutions or programs at all levels of education and training (Annex III/3 AI Regulation, Art. 6 para. 2 subpara. 3 AI Act).*

Example I for b) Automated assessment of examinations and/or submissions

An AI system evaluates written exams and essays, analyzes the answers and assigns grades that learners use for assessment. The system is used to assess learning outcomes and thus directly influences the learning process and academic performance of students. According to Annex III/3, b) AI Act, it would therefore be classified as a high-risk AI system.

Example II for b) Immersive learning environment

An AI-supported VR system for training. In order to create a realistic situation for students (e. g. medicine), an AI-supported VR system is used in training. The AI evaluates the students' performance in real time, provides feedback and adjusts the difficulty of the tasks to the progress of the learners. This system is used to assess learning outcomes and directly influences the learning process and performance assessment.

These AI systems can therefore influence the (professional) career of this person and would be classified as a high-risk AI system in accordance with Annex III/3 AI Act, Art. 6 para. 2 lit. b AI Act.

c) *AI systems that are intended to be used for the purpose of assessing the appropriate level of education that a person will receive or to which they will have access in or within institutions of all levels of education and training (Annex III/3 AI Act, Art. 6 para. 2 subpara. 3 AI Act);*

Example I for c) Identification of support needs

An AI system analyses the learning progress and behavior of learners in order to identify individual support needs and suggest programs. The system thus assesses the appropriate level of education and influences the support measures that a person receives. According to Annex III AI Act, Art. 6 para. 2 lit. c AI Act, the system would be classified as a high-risk system.

d) *AI systems that are intended to be used for the monitoring and detection of prohibited behavior of students during examinations in or within institutions of all levels of education and training (Annex III AI Act, Art. 6 para. 2 no. 3 AI Act);*

Example I for d) AI-supported plagiarism scanner

An AI system analyzes submitted work for plagiarismby checking text similarities and matches with existing sources. The system is used to monitor and detect prohibited behavior (plagiarism) in examinations and assignments and thus influences the grading. According to Annex III AI Act, Art. 6 para. 2 lit. d AI Act, this is classified as a high-risk AI system.

Example II to d) Monitoring and detection of prohibited conduct during examinations

An AI system is used during an online exam, in which all students have the camera switched on, to detect prohibited behavior such as talking, cheating, etc.. The system thus monitors and detects potential fraudulent behavior during the exams and thus influences the grading. According to Annex III AI Act, Art. 6 para. 2 lit. d AI Act, this is classified as a high-risk AI system.

Use cases can also combine different sections, such as a predictive analysis for drop-out risk. An AI system analyzes behavioral and performance data to identify learners at risk of dropping out of school/university/teaching and offers interventions. A high-risk AI system according to Annex III AI Act, no. 3. b) and c) AI Act assesses learning outcomes and educational attainment and can initiate measures that influence the educational pathway of individuals.

In summary, the use of AI in education, particularly in the assessment of learning outcomes, presents significant challenges as well as opportunities. While AI systems can provide valuable real-time feedback and dynamically adapt learning content, the final assessment of performance should always remain in the hands of human in-structors. Trainers and teachers should be able to view the recommendations gener-ated by the AI and adjust them as they see fit. AI-based evaluations must not have a direct impact on official performance evaluations in order to maintain the fairness and transparency of the educational process. It is crucial that AI does not become the sole authority for assessments and evaluations that influence students' professional or academic careers. To avoid being categorized as a high-risk AI system, it is essential to clearly define the role of AI and ensure human oversight. This is the only way to ensure that the benefits of AI are exploited without jeopardizing the rights and op-portunities of students.

However, if there is a high-risk AI and no exception applies (Art. 6 para. 3 AI Act), the following obligations for deployers of high-risk AI systems come into force:

Table 7.1 Obligations of Deployers of High-risk AI Systems [3], see in detail section 3.3.2.3

Obligations of deployers under the AI Regulation	High-risk AI System
AI literacy	Art. 4 AI Act
Transparency towards downstream players	Art. 26 para. 1 AI Act
Use of the AI system according to the instructions for use	Art. 26 para. 1, 3, 4 AI Act
Human supervision	Art. 26 para. 2 AI Act
Monitoring the AI system	Art. 26 para. 5 AI Act
Reporting of serious incidents	Art. 26 para. 5 AI Act, Art. 73 AI Act
Storage of generated logs	Art. 26 para. 6 AI Act
Where relevant, data protection impact assessment	Art. 26 para. 9 AI Act

Obligations of deployers under the AI Regulation	High-risk AI System
Cooperation with competent national authorities	Art. 26 para. 12 AI Act
Right to an explanation of the decision-making process in individual cases	Art. 86 para. 1 AI Act
Duty to inform the employee representative body if the employer uses high-risk AI systems in the workplace	Art. 26 para. 7 AI Act
Obligation to register if EU institutions, EU bodies and other EU bodies	Art. 26 para. 8 AI Act, Art. 49 AI Act
Authorization required from a judicial or administrative authority if used for subsequent remote biometric identification	Art. 26 para. 10 AI Act
Preparation of a fundamental rights impact assessment if, among other things, public or private institutions provide public services.	Art. 27 AI Act

7.6.5 Prohibited AI Systems in Education

While high-risk AI systems can be deployed through appropriate measures, there are certain AI systemswhose use in education is completely prohibited (see section 3.3.1). The next chapter will provide examples of such prohibited AI systems and explain why they are classified as prohibited in order to ensure the integrity and safety of the education system.

Example I: Emotion recognition

An AI system analyzes learners' emotions in real time during lessons. The lecturer wants to use the results to assess the learners' participation. The use of AI to infer the emotions of natural persons in educational institutions is prohibited, except for medical or safety reasons (Art. 5 para. 1 lit f AI Act).

Even if the assessment were to be omitted, this would still be a prohibited practice. So even if the teacher wants to use the results to adapt and adjust their teaching style, for example, it remains a prohibited practice, as the following example is intended to underline once again.

Example II: Emotion recognition

An AI system monitors learners during exams for signs of stress or anxiety in order to provide timely support. Deriving the emotions of natural persons (during examinations) is a prohibited practice under Art. 5 para. 1 lit f AI Act, unless there are medical or safety reasons.

If there is a prohibited AI system in accordance with Art. 5 AI Act, the test must be completed and the AI system may not be put into operation or placed on the market.

Sources

[1] Zhai, X., Chu, X., Chai, C. S., Jong, M. S. Y., Istenic, A., Spector, M. et al. (2021). A Review of Artificial Intelligence (AI) in Education from 2010 to 2020. Complexity, 2021(1), 8812542.

[2] Zhang, K., & Aslan, A. B. (2021). AI technologies for education: Recent research & future directions. Computers and Education: Artificial Intelligence, 2, 100025.

[3] *https://www.rtr.at/rtr/service/ki-servicestelle/ai-act/Betreiberverpflichtungen.de.html*; accessed: 2024/07/23

7.7 AI in Healthcare

Karin Bruckmüller/Kristina Altrichter

Artificially intelligent (assistance) systems in healthcare are increasingly being used. There has even been a real **boom in AI systems and AI research** and development, especially in recent years in the medical field, and the potential for revolution is evident [15] [6].

Finding AI systems in **hospitals** In addition to their use in administration, AI systems are also used directly in connection with the treatment of patients, in particular for diagnostics, individualization of treatments [12], in surgical assistance robots [8] [4], for the analysis of large amounts of data in intensive care medicine [13] and for triage [12]. Patients themselves also use AI-supported devices or apps to (self-)monitor certain values in chronic diseases [1] [13].

AIs in the field of **diagnostics** currently provide the most support in the hospital sector [1], for example in radiology, where images are evaluated by AI systems within a very short time [10], or/and in other departments, where analyses and interpretations of health data such as blood samples of various diseases, such as Alzheimer's, leukemia and colon cancer[10] [1] are detected. This enables earlier diagnosis and therefore usually creates less complicated and less invasive treatment options [1] [10].

In skin cancer detection in particular, AI has already been shown [9] to achieve roughly the same diagnostic accuracy as experienced doctors, and the algorithm is sometimes even significantly superior to inexperienced (assistant) doctors [16] [9] [10] [7]. Certain AI systems not only achieve (at least) equivalent results to experienced practitioners, but also reach the diagnostic goal much faster [10] [5].

It is therefore understandable that the question of a possible right to AI integration in the context of diagnostics is being raised in the legal debate [3]. This is why hospitals are already integrating more and more AI systems and will continue to do so in the future.

A skin diagnostics AI is therefore assumed as a use case, whereby the measures for the AI Act also apply in principle to other diagnostic systems and the above-mentioned systems in hospitals.

7.7.1 Example: AI Diagnosis of Skin Diseases

An AI-supported system for the diagnosis of skin diseases is being implemented in a hospital that uses medical **image data** (in particular images of skin changes) and patient data (e. g. laboratory results, previous illnesses) [2]. It is a medical device that uses machine learning to recognize patterns that indicate certain skin diseases. The results are used by dermatologists to support diagnosis and decision-making, particularly in the case of skin cancer [2] (Recital 12 AI Act, Art. 3 para. 1 AI Act). Early detection is therefore more likely, which optimizes treatment outcomes and individual patient care.

The procedure is mainly as follows.

1. **Data recording:** Patients are examined and their medical image data and relevant health information are recorded.

2. **Data analysis:** The AI system analyzes the collected data in real time. It compares the information with an extensive database of disease patterns and progressions.

3. **Suggested diagnosis:** Based on the analysis, the AI system provides doctors with recommendations for possible diagnoses and points out abnormal findings.

4. **Medical review:** The doctors review the AI system's suggestions, take their clinical experience into account and carry out further tests if necessary.

5. **Treatment plan:** Once the diagnosis has been confirmed by the doctor, an individual treatment plan is drawn up for the patient.

Applicability of the AI Act

Since the system uses machine learning it falls under the AI Act (Art. 2 para. 1 AI Act, Art. 3 no. 1 AI Act).

Deployers within the meaning of the AE Act – hospitals and doctors

The **hospital** is to be regarded as a deployer within the meaning of the AI Act (Art. 3 no. 4 AI Act), as it is a legal entity that uses an AI system under its own responsibility. This also applies to the **doctors** using the AI system as natural persons who do not use the AI system as part of their personal but professional activities.

Deployers have various obligations under the AI Act, depending on the risk category classification of the AI system used.

7.7.1.1 High-risk AI Classification within the Meaning of the AI Act

Even though the EU is using the AI Act to promote systems – including those related to health – in the internal market through innovation, marketing and confidence-building, it is also aware of the particular risks associated with this, especially in this area [10].[8] However, intelligent diagnostic (assistance) systems are not prohibited per se, but are permitted in principle. However, particular attention must be paid to ensuring a high level of protection of health and safety (Art. 1 AI Act). AI diagnostic systems are therefore regularly classified as high-risk AI, not only because they are used in an area of critical infrastructure – healthcare [11].

In any case, the skin cancer diagnostic AI is to be categorized as such a high-risk AI system, as it is a **medical device** within the meaning of the Medical Devices Regulation (EU) 2017/745 (MDR for short) [11], to which explicit reference is made in the Annex to the AI Act (Recital 50 AI Act; Art. 6 para. 1 lit a AI Act; Annex I no. 11 AI Act).

An AI algorithm to support skin cancer diagnostics is a medical device within the meaning of the MDR, as it is software which, according to the manufacturer, is intended for human use and is intended alone or in combination to fulfill the medical purpose, in particular diagnosis, but also for the prediction, prognosis and treatment of diseases (Art. 2 Z 1 MDR) and is subject to a **conformity assessment** within the meaning of the Medical Devices Regulation and has thus been certified (Art. 6 para. 1 lit. b Medical Devices Regulation, Art. 52 para. 6 Medical Devices Regulation). It is not the deployer, i. e. not the hospital, but the **provider** who must ensure that the product complies with the applicable requirements of the MDR (Art. 8 para. 2 AI Act).

7.7.1.2 Requirements and Obligations of the Hospital Deployer According to the AI Act

The AI Act attaches a number of requirements and obligations to the category of high-risk AIs for the deployer and thus also for the hospital and its management staff and committees.

Obtaining and understanding information on transparency

To this end, the management or management board of the hospital must – the provider should – if the system provider has not already done so or has not done so completely – ensure that all available information on transparency is obtained.

This information, such as the degree of accuracy of the diagnosis, known and foreseeable circumstances affecting the accuracy of the diagnostic proposal, foreseeable misapplications that could lead to a risk to health or fundamental rights in particular, as well as the data disclosed for this purpose that was used in the development process and, for example, maintenance and care work (Art. 13 AI Act), must not only be read

---

[8] European Commission: White Paper on Artificial Intelligence – a European approach to excellence and trust. In: COM(2020) 65 final, p. 1; reference is made here, for example, to opaque decision-making processes or discrimination.

but also understood by the employees of the relevant departments, primarily the compliance department, in order to be implemented correctly.

Where there is uncertainty or ambiguity, ask the provider accordingly or take part in the training courses offered by the provider so as not to run the risk of (civil and/or criminal) liability if damage to health occurs in connection with the AI due to failure to act in accordance with one's duties.

Set measures according to instructions for use

According to the enclosed instructions for use and the information from the provider mentioned above, suitable technical and organizational measures must be taken to use the system in the relevant dermatology ward and outpatient clinic (Art. 26 AI Act).

Data management

As additional data, namely patient data, is entered, this is subject to the deployer's control. These must correspond to the purpose of the high-risk AI system and be sufficiently representative (Art. 26 para. 4 AI Act). In addition, the provisions of the **GDPR** must be complied with.

Monitor system and report errors

The hospital must monitor the operation of the AI diagnostics system using the instructions for use with the help of IT, the doctors using the system and, if necessary, the nursing staff (Art. 26 para. 5 AI Act).

The log fileswhich are automatically generated by the AI system must be kept for at least six months according to the AI Act, unless national law provides otherwise (Art. 26 para. 6 AI Act). In the event of a risk to health, safety or fundamental rights (Art. 26 para. 5 AI Act and Art. 79 subpara. 1 AI Act) or a serious incident, such as a (possibly unforeseeable) misdiagnosis (see also Art. 73 AI Act), these must also be sent to the provider or distributor (possibly the importer) and, if the other two cannot be contacted, to the competent market surveillance authority without delay.

In the event of such risks or serious system errors, the system must be suspended immediately (for the time being).

Risk management

In order to avoid risks in the best possible way, a risk management system in the hospital or hospital group (Art. 9 AI Act) must be set up by the compliance department – which should be staffed by doctors, lawyers, technicians and, ideally, ethicists. This means that the AI must be continuously and regularly reviewed and, if necessary, updated in order to eliminate foreseeable risks that could affect the health, safety or fundamental rights of patients. This is because the deployers in particular can still identify risks during appropriate use that were not (yet) foreseeable in the development phase (Recital 93 AI Act).

Risk management – whereby, according to the AI Act, the technical knowledge, experience and level of education that can be expected of the deployer must be taken into account accordingly (Art. 9 para. 5 AI Act) – includes in particular the identification, analysis and assessment of not only known but also **reasonably foreseeable risks** or**misuse**that could affect health, safety or fundamental rights when used for their intended purpose (Art. 9 para. 2 AI Act). It must be taken into account if the system is likely to have adverse effects on persons under 18 years of age, i. e. young patients, or, where appropriate, vulnerable groups, whereby patients are generally to be classified as vulnerable, especially if they are disabled (Art. 9 para. 9 AI Act).

The measures must eliminate or reduce the risks as far as possible; the residual risk must be assessed as acceptable. Appropriate **mitigation and control measures** must be defined to manage risks that cannot be ruled out (Art. 9 para. 5 AI Act).

Based on this assessment, measures must be taken to manage the risks and designed in such a way that the residual risk and the overall residual risk are deemed acceptable.

To be able to do this, not only must the information be understood and implemented, but providers must also be **trained** to ultimately apply appropriate risk mitigation and control measures.

Human supervision

In addition, human supervision of the system, by natural persons who have the necessary competence, training and authorization, by the deployer of the (Art. 14 AI Act in conjunction with Art. 26 AI Act).

The **check** must be carried out by an appropriate doctor who has the special knowledge and experience to monitor the AI, interpret the AI's suggested diagnosis and check the state of the art in dermatology. It must also be possible to recognize malfunctions or misdiagnoses. In the use case, this is a doctor, in this case a dermatologist in particular.

The deployer must provide to doctors the necessary support (Art. 26 para. 2 AI Act) to ensure that employees are fully informed about the use of AI can be provided, for example, through training on the system, its procedures, training data, accuracy and susceptibility to errors and the like. In addition, doctors must be made aware of and informed about possible bias in order to raise awareness of the need to avoid automatic or excessive trust in the diagnosis and, where applicable, the treatment proposal produced by the AI system (**"automation bias"**).

As it is predominantly doctors who have to implement the control measures in this area, they must also be appropriately trained and informed, as it is ultimately the doctors who make the diagnosis based on and supported by the AI output. In doing so, they must recognize and take into account misapplications or reasons for deviating decisions (e. g. due to a specific pre-existing condition of the patient that was not included in the training data) and make further treatment decisions – taking into account the autonomy of the patient and medical ethics. It is therefore advisable for the hospital to provide an appropriate information and consent form or for the doctor to explain that the initial diagnosis will be made with the help of AI, but that the final decision will be made by the medical staff.

Sanctions

The Member States are still responsible for issuing provisions for "sanctions and other enforcement measures, which may include warnings and non-monetary measures" (Art. 99 AI Act) in the event of breaches of the AI Act, including for deployers who do not diligently comply with their obligations under Art. 26 AI Act (see above).

Sources

[1] Ahmidi, Narges: Künstliche Intelligenz im Gesundheitswesen (2023).

[2] Barata, Catarina; Rotemberg, Veronica; Codella, Noel C. F.; Tschandl, Philipp; Rinner, Christoph; Akay, Bengu Nisa; Apalla, Zoe; Argenziano, Giuseppe; u. a.: A reinforcement learning model for AI-based decision support in skin cancer. In: *Nature Medicine* Volume 29, Nature Publishing Group (2023), no. 8, p. 1941–1946.

[3] Botta, Jonas: (K)ein Recht auf Behandlung mit KI? – Zugang zu intelligenten Medizinprodukten. In: ZfPC 2024, p. 42 mwN. In: *ZfPC* Volume 2024, p. 42

[4] Eichelberger, Jan: Arzthaftung beim Einsatz von KI und Robotik. In: *Zeitschrift für Product Compliance (ZfPC)* Volume 2 (2023), no. 5, p. 209–214.

[5] Jorzig, Alexandra; Kemter, Luis: Der Einsatz Künstlicher Intelligenz in der Medizin im Spannungsfeld zwischen Medizinprodukte- und KI-Recht. In: ZfPC 2023, p. 172. In: *ZfPC* Volume 2023, p. 172.

[6] *Künstliche Intelligenz in der Medizin – Fraunhofer IKS*. URL *https://www.iks.fraunhofer.de/de/themen/kuenstliche-intelligenz/kuenstliche-intelligenz-medizin.html* – accessed: 2024/08/16 – Fraunhofer-Institut für Kognitive Systeme IKS

[7] *"Künstliche Intelligenz" schlägt Hautärzte bei Krebsdiagnose*. URL *https://www.aerztezeitung.de/Medizin/Kuenstliche-Intelligenz-schlaegt-Hautaerzte-bei-Krebsdiagnose-256254.html* – accessed: 2024/08/16 – AerzteZeitung.de

[8] Lobe, Analyse / Adrian: *Technischer Fortschritt im Gesundheitswesen – Chance oder Risiko?* URL *https://www.derstandard.at/story/3000000217797/technischer-fortschritt-im-gesundheitswesen-chance-oder-risiko* – accessed: 2024/08/16 – DER STANDARD

[9] Menzies, Scott W; Sinz, Christoph; Menzies, Michelle; Lo, Serigne N; Yolland, William; Lingohr, Johann; Razmara, Majid; Tschandl, Philipp; u. a.: Comparison of humans versus mobile phone-powered artificial intelligence for the diagnosis and management of pigmented skin cancer in secondary care: a multicentre, prospective, diagnostic, clinical trial. In: *The Lancet Digital Health* Volume 5 (2023), no. 10, p. e679–e691.

[10] Parlament, ARGE ITA-AIT: KI im Gesundheitswesen.

[11] *Regulation – 2017/745 – EN – Medical Device Regulation – EUR-Lex*. URL *https://eur-lex.europa.eu/eli/reg/2017/745/oj* – abgerufen am 16.08.2024 – Doc ID: 32017R0745Doc Sector: 3Doc Title: Regulation (EU) 2017/745 of the European Parliament and of the Council of 5 April 2017 on medical devices, amending Directive 2001/83/EC, Regulation (EC) No 178/2002 and Regulation (EC) No 1223/2009 and repealing Council Directives 90/385/EEC and 93/42/EEC (Text with EEA relevance.) Doc Type: RUsr_lan: en.

[12] Schneeberger, David: *Dako 2024/3: Intelligente Medizinprodukte: Rechtsfragen am Schnittpunkt von DSGVO, MPVO und AI Act*. URL *https://rdb.manz.at/document/rdb.tso.LIdako20240103* – accessed: 2024/08/16

[13] Wegenstein, Karin; Waniczek, Mirko: KI als Game-Changer in der Finanz- und Controlling-Organisation. In: *CFO aktuell* Volume 2023/6, p. 200.

[14] WEISSBUCH Zur Künstlichen Intelligenz – ein europäisches Konzept für Exzellenz und Vertrauen, 2020.

[15] *Wie KI die Medizin revolutioniert*. URL *https://www.helmholtz.de/newsroom/artikel/wie-ki-die-medizin-revolutioniert/* – accessed: 2024/08/16 – Helmholtz-Gemeinschaft Deutscher Forschungszentren

[16] Wien, Medizinische Universität: Hautkrebs-Diagnosen mittels KI sind ähnlich zuverlässig wie jene von Ärzt:innen | MedUni Wien. URL *https://www.meduniwien.ac.at/web/ueber-uns/news/2023/news-im-oktober-2023/hautkrebs-diagnosen-mittels-ki-sind-aehnlich-zuverlaessig-wie-jene-von-aerztinnen/* – accessed: 2024/08/16 – Medizinischen Universität Wien

7.8 AI in Advertising

Klaudia Zotzmann-Koch

Advertising is a creative field of work and also one in which trends have always been adapted at an early stage. It is therefore not surprising that so-called "artificial intelligence" also plays a role here – particularly in the form of generative models. In addition, there is the algorithmic evaluation of user behavior for advertising purposes, which has been common practice for more than 15 years and has been considered legally and ethically problematic for just as long. The mass of information collected over the years through this type of analysis represents a huge data basis for processing by AI systems. This is because two areas meet here for which AI systems are particularly suitable: Mass data processing (keyword: **Big Data**) and pattern recognition. However, just because algorithmic processing can work well in these areas does not mean that it is permitted everywhere. It is worth taking a look at other laws such as the Austrian Competition Act (UWG), copyright laws and the General Data Protection Regulation (GDPR).

7.8.1 Legal Requirements for AI in Advertising

7.8.1.1 Prohibited AI Systems

The algorithmic evaluation of user behavior for advertising purposes can be divided into two areas:

1. the targeting for finding target groups, i. e. locating and targeting groups or individuals, usually based on information collected and evaluated about the individuals, their circumstances and their behavior;

2. the influencing of groups or individuals by displaying personalized information and/or advertising messages, usually based on targeting or micro-targeting.

> The **manipulation of people** into behavior that they have not consciously chosen themselves is prohibited under Art. 5 para. 1 lit. a AI Act. According to Recital 29 AI Act, manipulative techniques are prohibited if they have a material effect of "materially distorting human behaviour, whereby significant harms, in particular having sufficiently important adverse impacts on physical, psychological health or financial interests". In particular, and regardless of whether the effects are explicitly detrimental, subliminal influence that is not recognizable to humans is prohibited, as these stimuli are outside the range of perception.

The following practices are prohibited under Art. 5 AI Act: "the placing on the market, the putting into service or the use of an AI system that deploys subliminal techniques beyond a person's consciousness or purposefully manipulative or deceptive techniques, with the objective, or the effect of materially distorting the behaviour of a person or a group of persons by appreciably impairing their ability to make an informed decision, thereby causing them to take a decision that they would not have otherwise taken in a manner that causes or is reasonably likely to cause that person, another person or group of persons significant harm." (Art. 5 para. 1 lit. a AI Act)

The exploitation of vulnerable groups is also prohibited under the AI Act. Art. 5 A 1 lit. b AI Act prohibits AI systems that exploit "any of the vulnerabilities of a natural person or a specific group of persons due to their age, disability or a specific social or economic situation, with the objective, or the effect, of materially distorting the behaviour of that person or a person belonging to that group in a manner that causes or is reasonably likely to cause that person or another person significant harm". Recital 29 AI Act adds that these persons are more susceptible to exploitation, for example persons living in extreme poverty and ethnic or religious minorities.

Recital 29 AI Act also clarifies that the provider or deployer of an AI system must not have the intention to cause significant harm. Explicit reference is made here to unfair commercial practices and Directive 2005/29/EC (EU Directive on Unfair Commercial Practices [7], see below). However, common and legitimate commercial practices in the area of advertising should not be prohibited. However, Recital 29 AI Act does not define what is "common". An argument that certain methods or systems are ingrained and used by everyone is nevertheless likely to fall short with regard to prohibited practices.

On targeting and political advertising, see also Regulation (EU) 2024/900 of the European Parliament and of the Council on the transparency and targeting of political advertising [8], Annex III no 8 lit. b AI Act and section 8.3, AI in Elections and Democratic Processes.

7.8.1.2 Overlaps with Other Laws

Recital 29 AI Act refers to the EU Directive on Unfair Commercial Practices. Therein, the law on fair trading between companies and consumers was harmonized as far as possible at European level. As this is an EU directive, it had to be incorporated into national law. In Austria and Germany, this was done through the respective national law on competition (e. g. the Austrian UWG).

Competition law is intended to ensure fair competition. It provides legal remedies against practices that would give companies an unfair advantage over competitors. "Unfair business practices" are defined as misleading or aggressive business practices.

Aggressive business practices are those that are likely to restrict a person's freedom of choice or behavior by

- harassment,

- coercion or

- undue influence

and cause him to take a business decision that he would not have taken otherwise (see Art. 8 Unfair Commercial Practices Directive).

Misleading commercial practices in accordance with Art. 7 Unfair Commercial Practices Directive exist when false statements are made or people are misled in any other way about a product or service. This also includes the concealment of important information.

Annex 1 Unfair Commercial Practices Directive contains a **blacklist of commercial practices** which are considered unfair under all circumstances. In connection with AI systems, this could be, for example, the unauthorized affixing of a CE marking, but also advertising disguised as information. Claims that an AI system can cure diseases, malfunctions or deformities, persistent and unwanted contact with people or direct appeals to children are also included.

Not only fair competition law plays an important role in connection with advertising, but also the GDPR; in particular Art. 22 GDPR, which regulates **automated decisions** in individual cases and **profiling**. If personal data is processed, a person has the right to a decision that was not made exclusively by AI, especially if this decision either has a legal effect on them or significantly affects them in a similar way (see Chapter 4, Data protection, for details).

In a nutshell: Just because something is "permitted" under the AI Act does not mean that it is not prohibited under other laws.

7.8.1.3 Data Trading

Another area that became the focus of authorities in 2024 is data trading. This was triggered by the research of an investigative team from netzpolitik.org and Bayrischer Rundfunk, which discovered the names, home and work addresses, hobbies and other occupations of people, including others in the civil service, from a "sample" of a data trader with 3.6 billion data points [6]. German authorities were alarmed, and in the USA the Pentagon became involved in the matter [4]. It is to be expected that there will be further regulations in the area of data collection, but especially in data trading, in addition to the laws already in force. In Austria, for example, data trading is already regulated in the Trade Regulation Act (Gewerbeordnung). Furthermore, **purpose limitation** applies throughout Europe according to Art. 6 para. 1 lit. b GDPR, which states that data may only be collected for specified, explicit and legitimate purposes. Further processing of the data for purposes that are incompatible with the original purposes is only permitted to a limited extent (Art. 6 para. 4 GDPR).

In principle, any data processing, including data trading, must have a **legal basis** for data processing. This may mean that the data subjects must give their voluntary and informed **consent** as an unequivocal expression of will (Art. 4 para. 11 GDPR and Art. 7 GDPR).

As it does not seem very promising to prohibit the use of such data sets by European companies alone, as the data can still be collected and used by companies in third countries, it is quite conceivable that personalized advertising could be banned altogether. In October 2023, the European Data Protection Board (EDPB) proposed to ban Meta from processing personal data for advertising purposes without the explicit, voluntary and informed consent of the data subjects [5]. This led to Meta introducing a "pay or okay" in spring 2023, where you can either consent to personalized advertising or take out a subscription to be able to use Facebook, Instagram and co. without advertising. In July 2024, the model was already on the EU consumer protection authorities' checklist due to possible lack of transparency and misleading information [2].

7.8.1.4 Personalization

The targeted addressing and display of personalized content, which has been practiced for years, means that timelines and web experiences look different for all individuals. However, as this is not only used by companies to encourage people to buy certain goods or services, but also by other stakeholders such as news portals, NGOs or even political parties, people have different perceptions of factual situations. The algorithmically controlled display of personalized content **creates a bubble**. This in turn means that there is no longer a socially uniform basis for discussion, which could ultimately endanger democracy. In addition to this initial situation, AI systems are now being used to further optimize personalization. It is therefore hardly surprising that there are strict rules for this area.

It is worth taking a close look at the standards here: Is what we are doing good just because it is effective? Manipulating and targeting vulnerable groups "at just the right moment" is not ethically good practice and is also prohibited under the AI Act.

For more information on prohibited AI, in particular in the case of election advertising, see the box above on prohibited AI practices under Art 5 para. 1 lit a AI Act and Art 5 para. 1 lit b AI Act and Annex III AI Act.

7.8.2 Energy Consumption and Sustainability

In addition to all other aspects, the AI Act also explicitly addresses the protection of the environment from the harmful effects of AI systems. Generative AI models in particular consume ever-increasing amounts of resources and already emit vast quantities of CO_2. On the other hand, socially responsible action according to ESG criteria, i. e. environment, social and governance (see section 10.6 on sustainability).

But sustainability does not only involve a life cycle assessment component. The "S" in **ESG** should also not be forgotten, as the AI Act repeatedly points out. Socially responsible action also means setting up a diverse team whose members cover as many perspectives and subject areas as possible. Today, this not only includes equal representation of people of all genders, but also a resilient division of labor that includes creative people. Employing creatives not only has the advantage that they – just like technicians – often have their own perspectives on problems and their solutions, but they also bring real human depth to communication with the target group through their work on texts, graphics, photos, videos, etc. While AI generators are fascinating due to their rapid results with minimal effort, as a study on **Design Aesthetics** [3] shows, the mediocrity of the content generated is now causing a certain weariness among the population. According to a study [1], the mention of "AI" in product names or product descriptions leads to a **decrease in emotional trust** and thus to a reduction in purchase intentions. The results were the same for different product and service categories, so there is a corresponding trend. Using human intelligence to shape communication is more sustainable on many levels, not least in terms of medium and long-term business success.

7.8.3 Best Practice: Generative AI in Creation

If there is no prohibited use of AI within the meaning of the AI Act, the GDPR, the Austrian Competition Act (UWG) or copyright law and it is ethically and sustainably justifiable to use generative AI models in advertising, a number of best practice rules have been established among creatives that provide good ethical and legal advice.

1. When using generative models, you should not use the names of living or dead artists or other people in the prompts. Even if it is unlikely that you can create an exact **plagiarism** with a generative model it is possible to uncover the database by reverse-engineering the AI model. Under certain circumstances, this can lead to **data breaches** and **copyright infringements**. By not mentioning names in the prompts, you ensure that copyright holders have no reason to take action against the material created.

2. In addition, we don't want to copy colleagues whose style we like, but rather develop our own works with a genuine **Unique Selling Proposition** (USP), uniqueness and recognition value. Even if generated material is not subject to copyright, it is fair to the artists and their work.

3. The use of generative models is interesting and exciting for some people. It can be a help for creative people, but it doesn't have to be. There are creative people who have their own ideas and want to implement them. In terms of unique selling points (USP) alone, it is a good idea to let **human intelligence** and creativity implement the corporate texts, images and musical elements. Under no circumstances should those responsible for creation be forced to use AI tools. Conversely, AI tools are now so frequently integrated into commercially available software solutions by manufacturers that a strict ban no longer makes sense.

4. AI-generated content should always be **labeled** as such, even if the AI Act only requires the identification of AI in cases such as chatbots in customer support or deepfakes (see Art. 50 AI Act). A basic declaration ensures that people know what they are dealing with and can assess the content accordingly.

5. In addition, depending on the tool used, it may be contractually required under the **license** that the tool used to generate the content is named. If this mandatory naming is omitted, this leads to a breach of contract, which can be expensive under certain circumstances.

Sources

[1] Cicek, Mesut; Gursoy, Dogan; Lu, Lu: Adverse impacts of revealing the presence of "Artificial Intelligence (AI)" technology in product and service descriptions on purchase intentions: the mediating role of emotional trust and the moderating role of perceived risk. In: *Journal of Hospitality Marketing & Management* Volume 34, Routledge Issue 1 (2025), p. 1–23.

[2] *EU-Verbraucherschützer prüfen Meta-Bezahlmodell*. URL *https://www.derstandard.at/story/300000022 9435/eu-verbrauchersch252tzer-pr252fen-meta-bezahlmodell* – accessed: 2024/08/17 – DER STANDARD

[3] Hekkert, Paul: Design aesthetics: Principles of pleasure in design. In: *Psychology Science* Volume 48 (2006).

[4] ingo; Sebastian: *Databroker Files: US-Senator schaltet Pentagon ein; Bundesministerium fordert EU-Gesetze*. URL *https://netzpolitik.org/2024/databroker-files-us-senator-schaltet-pentagon-ein-bundesminis terium-fordert-eu-gesetze/* – accessed: 2024/08/17 – netzpolitik.org

[5] Pitz, Leonhard: *Soziale Netzwerke: Europäischer Datenschutzausschuss verbietet Meta personalisierte Werbung*. URL *https://netzpolitik.org/2023/soziale-netzwerke-europaeischer-datenschutzausschuss-verbie tet-meta-personalisierte-werbung/* – accessed: 2024/08/17 – netzpolitik.org

[6] Sebastian; ingo: *Databroker Files: Die große Datenhändler-Recherche im Überblick*. URL *https:// netzpolitik.org/2024/databroker-files-die-grosse-datenhaendler-recherche-im-ueberblick/* – accessed: 2024/08/17 – netzpolitik.org

[7] *Unlautere Geschäftspraktiken | EUR-Lex*. URL *https://eur-lex.europa.eu/DE/legal-content/summary/ unfair-commercial-practices.html* – accessed: 2024/08/17 – Doc ID: I32011Doc Sector: otherDoc Title: Unfair commercial practicesDoc Type: otherUsr_lan: en

[8] Verordnung (EU) 2024/900 des Europäischen Parlaments und des Rates vom 13. März 2024 über die Transparenz und das Targeting politischer Werbung (Text with EEA relevance), 2024 – Legislative Body: EP, CONSIL.

7.9 Tourism

Manuela Machner

The tourism industry encompasses a variety of services and activities aimed at providing travelers with an enjoyable and memorable experience. This industry plays an essential role in the global economy by creating jobs, promoting cultural exchange and contributing to regional development. The tourism industry can be divided into several **segments**:

1. **Accommodation:** Hotels, hostels, vacation rentals, resorts, bed and breakfasts and campgrounds. These facilities offer travelers a variety of options for accommodations and comfort.

2. **Transportation:** airlines, railroads, bus companies, car rental services, cruise ships and other forms of public and private transportation that move travelers to and within their destination.

3. **Catering:** Restaurants, cafés, bars and other dining establishments that offer travelers culinary experiences that often reflect the local cuisine and culture.

4. **Leisure activities:** Amusement parks, beaches, sporting events, outdoor activities such as hiking, diving, skiing and other leisure facilities that offer visitors entertainment and adventure.

5. **Cultural experiences:** Museums, historical sites, art galleries, theaters, festivals and other cultural events that showcase a destination's heritage and traditions.

6. **Cultural experiences and events:** Museums, historical sites, art galleries, theaters, festivals and other cultural events that showcase a destination's heritage and traditions.

7. **Travel agencies and tour deployers:** Travel agencies provide advice and booking services for travelers, while tour deployers put together complete travel packages that include transportation, accommodation, meals and activities. Both play an important role in the planning and organization of trips by offering tailor-made services and often acting as intermediaries between customers and service providers.

8. **Tourism information and services:** Information centers, online platforms and mobile apps that provide travelers with information about attractions, activities, local events and services. These resources help with travel planning and execution by providing up-to-date and useful information.

9. **Business travel and MICE (Meetings, Incentives, Conferences, Exhibitions):** Companies that offer services for business travel and the organization of meetings, incentives, conferences and exhibitions. This segment includes event planning, accommodation and transportation bookings as well as special services for business customers.

10. **Health and well-being tourism:** Facilities and services that focus on health and well-being, including spas, wellness centers, medical tourism offerings and other health-related services. These facilities offer programs to improve the physical and mental health of travelers.

7.9.1 Use case: Operational efficiency

In the tourism industry, operational efficiency and smooth processes play a crucial role in maximizing service quality and minimizing operating costs. AI technologies contribute significantly to the optimization of various operational processes by automating tasks, managing resources efficiently and enabling data-driven decisions. By using AI, companies in the tourism sector can increase their efficiency by freeing up staff while ensuring a high quality of service.

1. **Automated booking systems (segments: all)**
   - **Description:** AI-powered systems manage bookings in real time by automatically updating availability, processing booking requests and sending confirmations.
   - **Examples – AI use cases**
     - Real-time reservation systems that synchronize requests across different platforms (websites, apps, travel agencies)
     - Management of bookings in real time
     - Automatic update of availability
     - Processing of booking requests
     - Sending booking confirmations
   - **Roles relevant (Art. 3 AI Act)**
     - Provider (Art. 3 no. 3 AI Act): Companies that develop the booking systems
     - Deployer (Art. 3 no. 4 AI Act): Hotels, tour deployers, travel agencies
   - **Advantages:** Reduction of double bookings, improvement of customer satisfaction through quick confirmation, optimized room occupancy
   - **Risk levels:**
     - **High-risk KI according to Art. 6 AI Act:** No, neither listed in Annex I or III
     - **Are there any points of contact with prohibited AI?** No, no prohibited applications identified
     - **Transparency obligations acc. Art. 50 AI Act** For direct interaction with natural persons

2. **Dynamic pricing (Segments: 1, 2, 3, 4, 5, 6)**
   - **Description:** Systems adjust prices for rooms, flights etc. based on current demand, season, events in the area and competitor prices in real time.
   - **Examples – AI use cases**
     - Yield management systems that increase prices when demand is high or offer special discounts when booking rates are low
     - Adjustment of room rates based on demand and season

- Dynamic pricing for flights depending on competitor prices and events
- Automatic discount promotions for low booking rates

- **Roles relevant (Art. 3 AI Act)**
  - Providers (Art. 3 no. 3 AI Act): Companies that develop the dynamic pricing systems
  - Deployers (Art. 3 no. 4 AI Act): Hotels, airlines, tour deployers
- **Advantages:** Maximization of revenue, higher utilization, competitive pricing
- **Risk levels:**
  - **High-risk AI according to** Art. 6 AI Act: No, not listed in Annex I or III
  - **Are there points of contact with prohibited AI?** Yes, e. g. if the system uses manipulative techniques or exploits vulnerable groups
  - **Transparency obligations pursuant to** Art. 50 AI Act: For direct interaction with natural persons

3. **Predictive Maintenance (segments: 1, 2, 3, 4, 8, 9)**
   - **Description:** AI systems monitor the condition of facilities, vehicles, etc. and predict maintenance work before problems occur.
   - **Examples – AI use cases**
     - Sensors and AI algorithms that detect anomalies in machines and provide maintenance recommendations to prevent breakdowns
     - Sensors and AI algorithms that detect anomalies in vehicles and provide maintenance recommendations. Predicting and planning maintenance work
     - Sensors and AI algorithms that detect anomalies in fitness equipment and medical devices and provide maintenance recommendations
   - **Roles relevant (Art. 3 AI Act)**
     - Providers (Art. 3 no. 3 AI Act): Companies that develop the predictive maintenance systems
     - Deployers (Art. 3 no. 4 AI Act): Hotels, transport companies, health centers, leisure facilities
   - **Advantages:** Reduction of downtimes, cost savings through preventive maintenance, longer service life of the systems
   - **Risk levels:**
     - **High-risk AI according to Art. 6 AI Act:** No, not listed in Annex I or III
     - **Are there any points of contact with prohibited AI?** No, no prohibited applications identified

4. **Capacity management and visitor control (segments: 4, 5, 7)**
   - **Description:** AI-supported systems analyze visitor data in real time to optimize capacity and manage visitor flows.
   - **Examples – AI use cases**
     - Systems that predict visitor numbers and take appropriate measures to prevent overcrowding
     - Systems that predict staffing and material requirements based on participant numbers and event schedules
   - **Roles relevant (Art. 3 AI Act)**
     - providers (Art. 3 no. 3 AI Act): Companies that develop the capacity management systems
     - Deployers (Art. 3 no. 4 AI Act): Venues, amusement parks, museums
   - **Advantages:** Avoidance of congestion, increased safety and comfort for visitors, efficient use of resources
   - **Risk levels:**
     - **High-risk AI acc. Art. 6 AI Act:** No, not listed in Annex I or III
     - **Are there any points of contact with prohibited AI?** No, no prohibited applications identified
     - **Transparency obligations acc. Art. 50 AI Act** For direct interaction with natural persons

5. **Automated ticketing systems (segments: 4, 5)**
   - **Description:** AI systems manage the sale and distribution of tickets, including seat allocation and ticket validity checks.
   - **Examples:**
     - Online ticketing platforms that process orders in real time and issue digital tickets
     - Automatic allocation of seats
     - Checking the validity of the ticket
   - **Roles relevant (Art. 3 AI Act)**
     - Providers (Art. 3 no. 3 AI Act): Companies that develop the ticketing systems
     - Deployers (Art. 3 no. 4 AI Act): Venues, amusement parks, museums
   - **Advantages:** Increased efficiency, reduction of queues, simplified ticket management
   - **Risk levels:**
     - **High-risk AI acc. Art. 6 AI Act:** No, not listed in Annex I or III
     - **Are there any points of contact with prohibited AI?** No, no prohibited applications identified

- **Transparency obligations acc. Art. 50 AI Act** For direct interaction with natural persons

6. **Automated access control (segments: 4, 5)**

- **Description:** AI systems for automated verification of tickets and access authorizations, including facial recognition and biometric data

- **Examples – AI use cases**
  - Real-time verification of tickets and access authorizations
  - Use of facial recognition and biometric data for access control
  - Combination of facial recognition and QR code scans to speed up entry

- **Roles relevant (Art. 3 AI Act)**
  - Providers (Art. 3 no. 3 AI Act): Companies that develop the conditional access systems
  - Deployers (Art. 3 no. 4 AI Act): Venues, amusement parks, museums

- **Advantages:** Faster processing at the entrance, increased security, reduction of queues

- **Risk levels:**
  - **High-risk AI pursuant to Art. 6 AI Act:** When using biometric recognition methods, Annex I No. 1 AI Act may be applicable.
  - **Are there points of contact with prohibited AI?** Possibly, if real-time remote biometric identification is involved
  - **Transparency obligations acc. Art. 50 AI Act** For direct interaction with natural persons

7. **Route optimization and traffic management (Segment: 2)**

- **Description:** AI-supported systems analyze traffic conditions in real time to determine the best routes for vehicles and avoid traffic jams.

- **Examples – AI use cases**
  - Real-time analysis of traffic conditions
  - Suggest alternative routes to avoid traffic jams
  - Consideration of traffic data, accidents and roadworks when planning routes

- **Roles relevant (Art. 3 AI Act)**
  - Providers (Art. 3 no. 3 AI Act): Companies that develop the route optimization systems.
  - Deployer (Art. 3 no. 4 AI Act): Transport company.

- **Advantages:** Reduction in travel time, lower fuel consumption, increased punctuality

- Risk levels:
    - **High-risk AI acc. Art. 6 AI Act:** No, not listed in Annex I or III
    - **Are there any points of contact with prohibited AI?** No, no prohibited applications identified

8. **Fleet Management (Segment: 2)**
    - **Description:** AI systems monitor and manage vehicle fleets to predict maintenance needs and optimize vehicle use
    - **Examples – AI use cases**
        - Real-time monitoring of vehicle data
        - Prediction of maintenance requirements
        - Optimization of vehicle deployment
        - Systems that analyze vehicle data in real time and make recommendations for maintenance or spare parts
    - **Roles relevant (Art. 3 AI Act)**
        - Providers (Art. 3 no. 3 AI Act): Companies that develop the fleet management systems
        - Deployer (Art. 3 no. 4 AI Act): Transport company
        - Operator (Art. 3 no. 8 AI Act): Fleet manager, maintenance personnel
    - **Advantages:** Reduction of downtimes, longer service life of vehicles, cost efficiency
    - **Risk levels:**
        - **High-risk AI acc. Art. 6 AI Act:** No, as the main effects are of an operational nature and no direct decisions are made about people
        - **Are there any points of contact with prohibited AI?** No, no prohibited applications identified

9. **Automated ordering systems (Segment: 3)**
    - **Description:** AI-supported systems that process orders in real time, forward them to the kitchen and monitor stock levels
    - **Examples – AI use cases**
        - Real-time processing of orders
        - Automatic forwarding of orders to the kitchen
        - Monitoring and management of inventories
        - Digital menus and self-service kiosks that send orders directly to the kitchen
    - **Roles relevant (Art. 3 AI Act)**
        - Providers (Art. 3 no. 3 AI Act): Companies that develop the ordering systems
        - Deployer (Art. 3 no. 4 AI Act): Restaurants

- **Advantages:** Reduction of waiting times, accurate order processing, improved inventory control
- **Risk levels:**
  - **High-risk AI acc. Art. 6 AI Act:** No, not listed in Annex I or III
  - **Are there any points of contact with prohibited AI?** No, no prohibited applications identified
  - **Transparency obligations pursuant to Art. 50 AI Regulation:** For direct interaction with natural persons

10. **Smart Room/House Management (segments: 1, 4, 9)**

- **Description:** Automated control of lighting, heating/cooling and other room functions based on occupancy and guest preferences
- **Examples – AI use cases**
  - Automatic adjustment of the room temperature
  - Lighting control based on presence and time of day
  - Adaptation of other room functions to the preferences of guests
- **Roles relevant (Art. 3 AI Act)**
  - Providers (Art. 3 no. 3 AI Act): Companies that develop the smart room systems
  - Deployers (Art. 3 no. 4 AI Act): Hotels, well-being centers
- **Benefits:** Energy savings, improved guest experience through customized environments
- **Risk levels:**
  - **High-risk AI acc. Art. 6 AI Act:** No, not listed in Annex I or III
  - **Are there any points of contact with prohibited AI?** No, no prohibited applications identified
  - **Transparency obligations pursuant to Art. 50 AI Regulation:** For direct interaction with natural persons

11. **Automated scheduling (Segment: 9)**

- **Description:** AI-powered systems that manage and optimize appointments for treatments and services in real time
- **Examples – AI use cases**
  - Systems that automatically find available times for wellness treatments and accept bookings
  - Managing appointments in real time
  - Optimization of resource utilization through automatic appointment allocation
  - Avoidance of double bookings and missed appointments

- **Roles relevant (Art. 3 AI Act)**
  - Providers (Art. 3 no. 3 AI Act): Companies that develop the scheduling systems
  - Deployers (Art. 3 no. 4 AI Act): Well-being centers, wellness facilities
- **Advantages:** Avoidance of double bookings and missed appointments, optimized use of resources
- **Risk levels:**
  - **High-risk AI according to Art. 6 AI Act:** No, not listed in Annex I or III
  - **Are there any points of contact with prohibited AI?** No, no prohibited applications identified
  - **Transparency obligations pursuant to Art. 50 AI Act:** For direct interaction with natural persons

7.9.2 Use Case: Guest Experience

An outstanding guest experience is at the heart of the tourism industry. With the help of AI technologies, individual guest needs and preferences can be better understood and fulfilled. AI-powered systems offer personalized recommendations, enable smooth and fast service processes and create immersive experiences. These technologies help to take the guest experience to a new level by providing customized offers and immediate assistance. The use of AI not only increases guest satisfaction, but also their loyalty and likelihood to return.

1. **Personalized recommendations (Segments: all)**
   - **Description:** AI-based systems provide personalized recommendations for local attractions, restaurants and activities based on guest data.
   - **Examples – use cases of AI**
     - Apps or interactive screens in the lobby that make personalized excursion suggestions based on previous bookings and preferences
     - Digital menus that make personalized suggestions based on previous orders and preferences
     - Apps or interactive screens that offer personalized tips or tailored event tips
     - Personalized event apps, with timetables, parking options, driving tips
     - Digital platforms that make tailored travel suggestions based on traveler data
   - **Roles relevant (Art. 3 AI Act)**
     - Providers (Art. 3 no. 3 AI Act): Companies that develop the recommendation systems
     - Deployers (Art. 3 no. 4 AI Act): Hotels, tour deployers, event planners

- **Advantages:** Improved guest experience through customized recommendations, increased satisfaction and return rate
- **Risk levels:**
  - **High-risk AI according to Art. 6 AI Act:** No, not listed in Annex I or III
  - **Are there points of contact with prohibited AI?** Possibly, if manipulative techniques are used
  - **Transparency obligations acc. Art. 50 AI Act:** For direct interaction with natural persons
  - **Important other areas of law:** Art. 22 GDPR, § 160 ff. öTKG (Austrian Telecommunications Act), § 25 para. 1 dtTDDDG (German Telecommunications Act), see section 7.8 on advertising

2. **Virtual assistants/chatbots (segments: all)**
   - **Description:** Chatbots and voice assistants offer round-the-clock answers to questions and services.
   - **Examples – AI use cases**
     - Voice assistants in the rooms that make restaurant reservations, order room service or provide information about the hotel and the surrounding area
     - Chatbots on restaurant websites or in apps that answer questions about the menu, opening hours and reservations
     - Chatbots on the phone that are available to answer questions
     - Chatbots that can make bookings, answer questions, etc.
   - **Advantages:** Service available around the clock, relief for staff, fast problem solving
   - **Risk levels:**
     - **High-risk AI acc. Art. 6 AI Act**: No, not listed in Annex I or III
     - **Are there any points of contact with prohibited AI?** No, no prohibited applications identified
     - **Transparency obligations pursuant to Art. 50 AI Act:** For direct interaction with natural persons

3. **Automated check-in and check-out/boarding processes (segments: 1, 2)**
   - **Description:** Face recognition and mobile apps speed up and simplify the check-in and check-out process.
   - **Examples – AI use cases**
     - Self-Check-in-Kioske
     - Automatic baggage drop-off
     - Boarding gates with facial recognition

- Mobile apps that allow guests to access their room directly without having to wait at reception or check-in
- **Roles relevant (Art. 3 AI Act)**
  - Providers (Art. 3 no. 3 AI Act): Companies that develop the check-in/check-out systems
  - Deployers (Art. 3 No. 4 AI Act): Hotels, airlines
- **Advantages:** Time savings, improved customer experience, reduction of queues
- **Risk levels:**
  - **High-risk AI acc. Art. 6 AI Act**: see Annex I no. 13 AI Act (Regulation on Aviation Safety), Annex III no. 1 AI Act (biometric facial recognition), Annex III no. 2 AI Act (critical infrastructure)
  - **Are there any points of contact with prohibited AI?** No, no prohibited applications identified.
  - **Transparency obligations acc. Art. 50 AI Act:** For direct interaction with natural persons

4. **Interactive and immersive experiences (segments: 4, 5)**
   - **Description:** Use of AI and augmented reality (AR) or virtual reality (VR) to create interactive and immersive experiences
   - **Examples – AI use cases**
     - AR apps that bring historical sites to life or VR experiences that allow visitors to relive past events
     - Events & Events that merge real experiences with mixed reality (MR)
     - Creating interactive and immersive experiences through AR and VR
     - Use of MR to merge real and virtual experiences
     - Bringing historical sites and past events to life through AR and VR
   - **Roles relevant (Art. 3 AI Act)**
     - Providers (Art. 3 no. 3 AI Act): Companies that develop AR, VR and MR technologies
     - Deployers (Art. 3 no. 4 AI Act): Museums, event venues
   - **Advantages:** Greater attractiveness of cultural sites and events, deeper emotional connection with visitors, innovative forms of presentation
   - **Risk levels:**
     - **High-risk AI acc. Art. 6 AI Act:** No, not listed in Annex I or III
     - **Are there any points of contact with prohibited AI?** No, no prohibited applications identified
     - **Transparency obligations pursuant to Art. 50 AI Act:** For direct interaction with natural persons

5. **Real-time feedback and analysis (segments: all)**

- **Description:** AI-powered systems to collect and analyze visitor feedback in real time to continuously improve the event experience
- **Examples – AI use cases:**
  - Mobile apps and social media monitoring that collect and analyze visitor feedback to enable immediate adjustments
  - Collection of visitor feedback in real time
  - Analysis of the feedback collected to improve the experience
  - Immediate adjustments based on feedback
- **Roles relevant (Art. 3 AI Act)**
  - Providers (Art. 3 no. 3 AI Act): Companies that develop feedback and analysis systems
  - Deployers (Art. 3 no. 4 AI Act): Venues, museums, amusement parks, hotels
- **Advantages:** Improved adaptability, higher visitor satisfaction, continuous improvement
- **Risk levels:**
  - **High-risk AI acc. Art. 6 Act:** No, not listed in Annex I or III
  - **Are there any points of contact with prohibited AI?** No, no prohibited applications identified
  - **Transparency obligations pursuant to Art. 50 AI Act:** For direct interaction with natural persons

6. **Real-time translations (segments: all)**

- **Description:** AI-supported systems for real-time translation of conversations and texts to break down language barriers
- **Examples – AI use cases:**
  - Mobile apps and kiosks that offer instant translations in multiple languages
  - Collection of visitor feedback in real time
  - Analysis of the feedback collected to improve the experience
  - Immediate adjustments based on feedback
  - Real-time translation of conversations
  - Translation of texts into several languages
- **Advantages:** Reduction of language barriers, improved communication with international guests
- **Risk levels:**
  - **High-risk AI acc. Art. 6 AI Act:** No, not listed in Annex I or III
  - **Are there any points of contact with prohibited AI?** No, no prohibited applications identified

    – **Transparency obligations acc. Art. 50 AI Act:** For direct interaction with natural persons

7. **Personalized wellness programs (Segments: 9)**

    ⊕ **Description:** AI-based systems that create individual wellness and health programs based on guest data

    ⊕ **Examples – AI use cases:**

        – Systems that suggest personalized nutrition plans and training programs based on health data and preferences

        – Customization of wellness and health programs based on guests' preferences and health data

    ⊕ **Roles relevant (Art. 3 AI Act)**

        – Providers (Art. 3 no. 3 AI Act): Companies that develop wellness and health programs

        – Deployers (Art. 3 no. 4 AI Act): Well-being centers, wellness facilities

    ⊕ **Benefits:** Improved health and satisfaction of guests through customized programs

    ⊕ **Risk levels:**

        – **High-risk AI acc. Art. 6 AI Act:** No, not listed in Annex I or III

        – **Are there any points of contact with prohibited AI?** No, no prohibited applications identified

        – **Transparency obligations pursuant to Art. 50 AI Act:** For direct interaction with natural persons

        – **Other important legal provisions:** Art. 9 GDPR

7.9.3 Use Case: Smart Companies

Smart companies in tourism rely on advanced AI technologies to promote sustainability and operational efficiency. AI-based systems monitor and control energy consumption, optimize supply chains and ensure the safety of guests and staff. Through the intelligent management of resources and predictive maintenance of equipment, businesses can reduce costs while helping to protect the environment. These innovative approaches help companies to operate more sustainably and efficiently without compromising the quality of guest service.

1. **Energy efficiency (segments: 1, 2, 3, 4)**

    ⊕ **Description:** AI systems monitor and optimize energy consumption in real time to reduce costs and promote sustainability. Buildings, vehicles (emission reduction)

- **Examples – AI use cases:**
  - Systems that control lighting and air conditioning in public areas and guest rooms based on occupancy data
  - Systems that monitor fuel consumption and give drivers tips on how to drive more efficiently
  - Systems that monitor the energy consumption of kitchen appliances and provide recommendations for optimization
- **Roles relevant (Art. 3 AI Act)**
  - Providers (Art. 3 no. 3 AI Act): Companies that develop energy efficiency systems
  - Deployers (Art. 3 no. 4 AI Act): Hotels, transportation companies, restaurants
- **Advantages:** Reduction of energy costs, sustainable operation, environmental friendliness
- **Risk levels:**
  - **High-risk AI acc. Art. 6 AI Act:** No, not listed in Annex I or III
  - **Are there any points of contact with prohibited AI?** No, no prohibited applications identified

2. **Safety management (segments: 1, 2, 4, 5, 6)**
   - **Description:** Use of AI to monitor security cameras, identify anomalies and support security personnel
   - **Examples – AI use cases:**
     - Intelligent monitoring systems that detect suspicious behavior and alert security personnel in real time
     - Systems for monitoring driver conditions (e. g. drowsiness detection), real-time analysis of vehicle data to prevent accidents
     - Systems for monitoring attractions and visitor areas that detect anomalies and alert security staff
     - Venue monitoring systems that detect anomalies and alert security personnel
     - Support for security personnel through real-time alarms
   - **Roles relevant (Art. 3 AI Act)**
     - Providers (Art. 3 no. 3 AI Act): Companies that develop the monitoring systems
     - Deployers (Art. 3 no. 4 AI Act): Hotels, event venues, transportation companies
   - **Advantages:** Increased security for guests and staff, faster response times to security incidents

- **Risk levels:**
  - **High-risk AI pursuant to Art. 6 AI Act:** Annex I no. 1 AI Act (Biometrics)
  - **Are there points of contact with prohibited AI?** Yes, if biometric systems are used for law enforcement purposes, this is only permitted to a limited extent.
  - **Transparency obligations acc. Art. 50 AI Act:** For direct interaction with natural persons

3. **Supply Chain Management (segments: 1, 2, 3, 4, 5)**
   - **Description:** Optimizing the supply chain through AI-powered forecasting and inventory management to ensure there is always sufficient stock on hand
   - **Examples – AI use cases:**
     - Systems that automatically trigger orders based on consumption and delivery time patterns to avoid bottlenecks
     - Forecasting consumption and stock requirements
     - Automatic triggering of orders based on consumption and delivery time patterns
     - Optimization of warehouse management and supply chain
   - **Roles relevant (Art. 3 AI Act)**
     - providers (Art. 3 no. 3 AI Act): Companies that develop supply chain management systems
     - Deployers (Art. 3 no. 4 AI Act): Hotels, restaurants, event venues, transportation companies
   - **Advantages:** Cost efficiency, avoidance of bottlenecks, better planning and warehouse management
   - **Risk levels:**
     - **High-risk AI acc. Art. 6 AI Act:** No, not listed in Annex I or III
     - **Are there any points of contact with prohibited AI?** No, no prohibited applications identified

4. **Maintenance management (segments: 1, 2, 3, 4, 5, 6)**
   - **Description:** AI systems to monitor and predict maintenance needs of attractions and facilities to minimize downtime
   - **Examples – AI use cases:**
     - Sensors and AI algorithms that monitor the condition of rides and facilities and provide maintenance recommendations
     - Prediction of maintenance requirements based on sensor data and algorithms
     - Optimization of maintenance planning to minimize downtimes

- **Roles relevant (Art. 3 AI Act)**
  - Providers (Art. 3 no. 3 AI Act): Companies that develop maintenance management systems
  - Deployers (Art. 3 no. 4 AI Act): Amusement parks, event venues, transportation companies, hotels, restaurants
  - Operator (Art. 3 no. 8 AI Act): Maintenance personnel, facility managers, IT service providers
- **Advantages:** Avoidance of breakdowns, extended service life of the systems, increased safety
- **Risk levels:**
  - **High-risk AI acc. Art. 6 AI Act:** No, not listed in Annex I or III
  - **Are there any points of contact with prohibited AI?** No, no prohibited applications identified

Risk levels:

5. **Quality control and hygiene monitoring (segments: 3, 9)**
   - **Description:** AI-supported systems that monitor the quality and hygiene of food and kitchens
   - **Examples – AI use cases:**
     - Sensors and AI algorithms that detect anomalies in food quality or monitor compliance with hygiene standards
   - **Advantages:** Ensuring high quality and hygiene standards, avoiding food waste, protecting the health of guests
   - **Risk levels:**
     - **High-risk AI according to Art. 6 AI Act:** No, not listed in Annex I or III
     - **Are there any points of contact with prohibited AI?** No, no prohibited applications identified

6. **Transportation and traffic management (segments: 2, 4, 5)**
   - **Description:** AI-powered systems to optimize traffic flow around event venues, including parking and public transport management
   - **Examples – AI use cases:**
     - Systems that analyze traffic flows and create dynamic traffic routing plans to minimize congestion
     - Creation of dynamic traffic routing plans to avoid traffic jams
     - Optimization of parking space management and public transport
   - **Roles relevant (Art. 3 AI Act)**
     - Providers (Art. 3 no. 3 AI Act): Companies that develop traffic management systems
     - Deployers (Art. 3 No. 4 AI Act): Event venues, amusement parks

- **Advantages:** Reduction of traffic problems, improved accessibility of the venue, higher participant satisfaction
- **Risk levels:**
  - **High-risk AI acc. Art. 6 AI Act** No, not listed in Annex I or III
  - **Are there any points of contact with prohibited AI?** No, no prohibited applications identified
  - **Transparency obligations pursuant to Art. 50 AI Act:** For direct interaction with natural persons

7.10 AI in Autonomous Driving

Isabella Hinterleitner

The term *autonomous* means independence and self-reliance and is often used in connection with autonomous vehicles. It implies that vehicles can steer, accelerate and brake independently in traffic. The path to vehicle autonomy is described by the SAE J3016 standard [1], which is based on the associated standard. The standard defines levels 0 to 5, which describe self-driving vehicles, starting with no automation (level 0), driver assistance (level 1), partial automation (level 2), conditional automation (level 3) through to high automation (level 4) and full automation (level 5).

In addition to the term autonomous, the term *automated* can also be found in the literature. An autonomous, independent system is also an automated system. According to IEC60050351 [2], the meaning of automated is defined as "the equipping of a device so that it operates completely or partially without human intervention". This is also reflected in the automation levels for automated driving. The higher the level of automation, the less the human has to act as a safe fallback level. In this context, the term *automated driving* means the execution of process steps without human control.

Figure 7.2 describes these levels of autonomous driving, whereby level 1 means driver assistance such as cruise control, level 2 is considered partial automation, in which the vehicle can steer and accelerate. Level 3 involves conditional automation, in which the vehicle can steer and accelerate as well as take over the perception of its surroundings, but humans still have to intervene, e. g. in automated shuttles. At level 4 (highly automated), the vehicle performs all driving tasks under certain conditions, whereby human intervention is possible under certain conditions. At level 5 (fully automated), the vehicle performs all known, learned driving tasks.

Level 2 autonomous vehicles (partial automation) have one or more partial functions that support the driver, e. g. automatic cruise control or automatic lane changes. Level 4 (highly automated) autonomous vehicles, on the other hand, are able to drive autonomously without the driver being involved in operational decisions. There are currently no vehicles in Europe that are allowed to drive highly automated (level 4) or fully autonomous (level 5) without an operator according to the national road traffic regulations (StVO, Austrian Road Traffic Code).

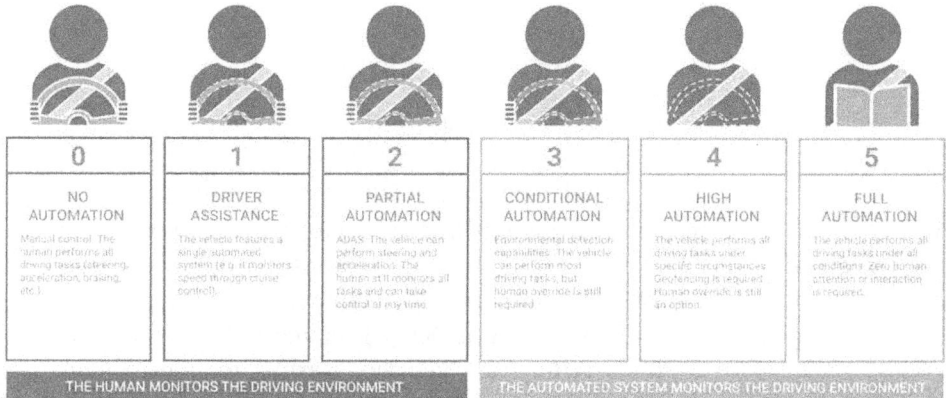

Figure 7.2 Automation stages (Source: *https://www.synopsys.com/blogs/chip-design/ autonomous-driving-levels.html*)

In addition to the SAE standard, there is another classification due to a lack of technical depth. This is the Operational Design Domain (ODD), which defines specific operating conditions under which the automated driving system should work properly and safely. The ODD therefore specifies road types, speed ranges, environmental conditions (including weather, day/night time), applicable traffic laws and regulations, and other constraints (SAE, 2018) [3]. Each Level 1–4 automation use case is only usable in its specific ODD. It is possible that the ODD of a use case is very limited, e. g. a segregated road or a single fixed route on public roads with low speed.

7.10.1 Austrian & International Legislation

In Austria, the **AutomatFahrV** [4] (Austrian Regulation for Autormated Driving) was issued in 2016. With the entry into force of the second amendment in April 2022, the development of the legal framework for testing automated systems was further advanced. The second version of the regulation created further use cases for the automated testing of vehicles.

The regulation consists of eight cases, five of which are intended for testing: the automated vehicle for transporting goods, for transporting passengers, the automated minibus, the automated work machine and the army vehicle. There are also three further use cases for real-life operation, such as the automated parking assistant.

In addition to the test cases, new requirements were introduced for route analysis and risk assessment when registering a mobility solution.

One point of criticism of the design of the AutomatFahrV is the case-based approach, which is specific but not designed for the general public. Due to the rapid technical progress in the field, further amendments to the original ordinance were necessary. It can therefore be assumed that a law for autonomous driving will be defined from a general perspective in the future, similar to what has been the case in Germany since 2021 with the law for autonomous driving. [5]

In addition, new requirements have been introduced for route analysis and risk assessment with regard to the introduction of a vehicle. This risk assessment includes a thorough analysis of the route in the public area in individual route sections of 100–200 m and currently means a great deal of effort for deployers and approvers. In the future, the introduction of a route analysis and assessment tool will be of great importance when manufacturers enter the Austrian market.

The General Safety Regulation exists at international level (EU Regulation 2019/2144) – this EU regulation stipulates mandatory assistance systems for all new first registrations, such as intelligent cruise control, reversing assistants, drowsiness warning systems and emergency brake lights for passenger cars.

Implementing Regulation EU 2022/1426 is also relevant at European level. The regulation, which came into force in September 2022, applies with regard to uniform procedures and technical specifications for the type approval of the automated driving system of fully automated vehicles. The term fully automated vehicles refers to vehicles that are to be used in a defined operating range (the aforementioned ODD), whereby there is no longer a driver in the vehicle. The regulation currently covers small series of a maximum of 250 units of vehicles per year in a Member State. The implementing regulation was introduced to assess the safety of the systems before approval can be granted in the EU. In Austria, there is currently (as of 2024) no company that has made use of this approval, as the current regulation (AutomatFahrV) for automated passenger transport only allows testing.

Last but not least, there is UNECE-R 157, which came into force in January 2021 and which, with regard to Automated Lane Keeping Systems) regulates the situation for level 3 systems. ALK systems take over automatic lane keeping on the highway or on highway-like roads up to a speed of 60 km/h. In Germany, the first type approval for an ALK system has already been granted to Mercedes Benz.

The General Data Protection Regulation (GDPR) is also relevant from an international, European perspective. Autonomous vehicles consist of a large number of control units and associated sensors that read out data and pass it on to the manufacturer. Mercedes, for example, records GPS position data, mileage, fuel consumption, tank filling, tire pressure and the levels of operating fluids in the vehicle.

In this context, the 2015 activity report on data protection already stated that insufficient precautions are being taken to ensure that no personal movement profiles can be created in the car-to-car sector on the basis of the exchanged driving data. According to the GDPR, movement profiles are also personal data (see chapter 4).

The vehicle's perception of its surroundings ensures that objects and people are recognized by cameras and that the vehicle reacts to them by braking. Artificial intelligence (AI) methods are used in the development of these person recognition algorithms. The algorithm "You look only once" (YOLO) ensures that people are recognized in real time, whereby the process consists of a "trained" neural network. YOLO belongs to the group of grid-based deep learning -This means that the image is broken down into a raster and the feature is searched for in the raster image. The identity or personal characteristics of the person are irrelevant to the process; a recognized object is simply marked with a rectangle.

7.10.2 Development of Autonomous Driving Functions

In the development of autonomous driving, the ISO 26262 [5] standard defines functional safety. It is defined here as the "absence of unreasonable risks due to hazards that can occur as a result of erroneous behavior of systems". Whereby misbehavior is the "failure or unintended behavior of an element in relation to its design intent during development".

The V-model is a step-by-step process model that is used for the integration and development of software in autonomous driving. As a rule, not one function is developed, but multiple requirements for object recognition are defined in the requirements analysis, which are then implemented in the system architecture (step 2) and in the software architecture (step 3). The actual software code can be found in the software architecture and in the design. The right-hand part of the diagram defines the testing of the functions – depending on the stage on the left-hand side, the corresponding test is carried out on the right-hand side.

ISO 26262 also includes a risk assessment of autonomous driving functions. This is carried out using a failure mode and effects analysis (FMEA), event tree analysis (ETA) or fault tree analysis (FTA) is supported. In the development of AI-based functions for autonomous driving, development in accordance with ISO 26262 is a standard method for getting from the software requirements to the system test and thereby ensuring transparency transparency.

The approach according to ISO 26262 for achieving an acceptable risk is shown in Figure 7.3 with reference to a similar discussion of the Safety Integrity Level (SIL) of IEC 61508. A high provisional risk (ASIL D) implies a large required risk reduction during development, resulting in stringent requirements for the development of a product. A low provisional risk (e. g. ASIL A), on the other hand, implies a low level of risk reduction required, resulting in less stringent requirements for the development of an item. The acceptable risk is not explicitly defined in ISO 26262, but is determined by the ASIL-specific requirements via the specification of the safety objectives for product development.

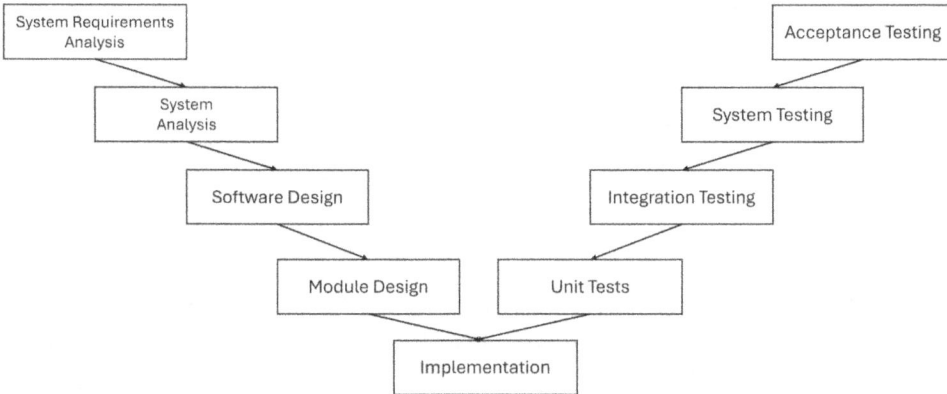

Figure 7.3 V-Model of Software Development

7.10.3 The AI Act and Autonomous Driving

Based on the software development model presented, it can be seen that a lot of sub-functions are involved in the development of software for autonomous driving, which makes classification in the case of the AI Act non-trivial.

In the context of autonomous driving, a shortening of the development – validation/testing – and homologation in compliance with all legal and qualitative framework conditions will be necessary. In particular, it can be observed that AI will increasingly be used in the validation of software. This is the only way to make the amount of software code manageable.

In the future, the AI Act will start at the development stage and stipulate that object recognition systems used in (semi-)autonomous vehicles must undergo strict testing and validation procedures to ensure their safety and reliability, as they are classified as high-risk applications. The reason for this is that if an object recognition function fails, the person is not recognized and can therefore be hit and injured.

The aforementioned procedures from the V-model will have to be incorporated into the development of AI-based validation systems in order to enable efficient control of systems. Nevertheless, it will still be necessary to include people in real operation in the overall context of validation and testing.

Together with AVL LIST, TÜV Süd has developed a procedure for testing autonomous vehicles in the future. For efficient validation and homologation, i. e. the approval of vehicles and vehicle components, a combination of virtual and real tests on the test bench and at the proving ground is absolutely essential in order to be able to map the complexity and variety of situations. There are currently no applicable international legal regulations for automated driving functions, but there are ongoing activities, for example at the United Nations.

With regard to the AI Act, reference should also be made to Annex I, which does not claim to be exhaustive. The applicability of a legal act listed in Annex I leads to the assumption that it is a high-risk AI system. To this end, the AI system used has to be a safety component of a product in accordance with one of the aforementioned legal acts, or the product itself is the AI system or the AI system must undergo a conformity assessment of a listed legal act as a product (see section 3.4).

In addition to the AI Act, Annex I contains the following provisions in connection with autonomous vehicles:

- Regulation (EU) No 168/2013 of the European Parliament and of the Council of January 15, 2013 on the approval and market surveillance of two- or three-wheel vehicles and quadricycles

- Regulation (EU) 2018/858 of the European Parliament and of the Council of 30 May 2018 on the approval and market surveillance of motor vehicles and their trailers, and of systems, components and separate technical units intended for such vehicles

- Regulation (EU) 2019/2144 of the European Parliament and of the Council of 27 November 2019 on type-approval requirements for motor vehicles and their trailers, and for systems, components and separate technical units intended for such vehicles, with regard to their general safety and the protection of occupants and vulnerable road users

Sources

[1] On-road automated driving (ORAD) committee. Taxonomy and definitions for terms related to driving automation systems for on-road motor vehicles. SAE International, 2021

[2] Austrian Standards International. IEC60050351 International Electrotechnical Vocabulary (IEV) – Part 351: Automatic control. Wien: Austrian Standards International, 2016

[3] Czarnecki, Krzysztof. Operational design domain for automated driving systems. Taxonomy of Basic Terms ", Waterloo Intelligent Systems Engineering (WISE) Lab, University of Waterloo, Canada, 2018

[4] *https://www.austriatech.at/assets/Uploads/Fokusseiten/Kontaktstelle-Automatisierte-Mobilitaet/Dokumente/294145da59/AutomatFahrV-Fassung-vom-12.04.2022.pdf*, accessed: 2024/03/19

[5] *https://bmdv.bund.de/SharedDocs/DE/Anlage/Gesetze/Gesetze-19/gesetz-aenderung-strassenverkehrsgesetz-pflichtversicherungsgesetz-autonomes-fahren.pdf?_blob=publicationFile* accessed: 2024/03/19

[6] ISO 26262-2:2018–12 Straßenfahrzeuge – Funktionale Sicherheit – Teil 2: Management der Funktionalen Sicherheit

[7] *https://www.tuvsud.com/de-at/-/media/de/auto-service/pdf/atzextra-autom-fahren_tv-sd.pdf* accessed: 2024/03/19

8 Public Sector

Kristina Altrichter, Karin Bruckmüller, Veronica Cretu,
Theresa Tisch, Natascha Windholz

8.1 "Public Decision Making" and AI

Theresa Tisch

When considering the use of AI systems in the area of decision-making in the public sector, it is important to bear in mind that **fully automated administrative procedures** for example in the context of issuing tax assessments in the tax administration, are already established in Austria and correspond to the standard procedure. The systems used here are usually based on clear coding principles that are designed in the form of if-then commands and therefore always process data in the same way. In this context, one speaks of so-called rule-based systems, which are not to be classified as AI (see § 96 öBAO (Austrian Federal Fiscal Code)) [3] [1].

In contrast, an AI system, which is utilized by users as a **decision-making aid** or fully automated decision-making tool, that analyzes the patterns and rules underlying the data in order to apply them, for example, to various application documents as part of the subsumption process of factual characteristics of a claim basis [3]. The more complex the self-learned mechanism becomes, the more difficult it is for the responsible persons to understand individual steps in the decision-making process. Such decision-making tools not only open up the scope of application of the AI Act, but are also classified as high-risk according to its methodology, depending on the purpose of awarding the claim for the service to be checked, and are subject to stricter usage regulations. In addition to the provisions arising from the AI Act, it should always be borne in mind that the same relevant national procedural provisions apply to automated decision-making tools as to traditional administrative procedures, regardless of whether they are AI systems. This includes, in particular, the applicant's right to be heard, the right to a statement of reasons for the decision and the **right to effective legal protection** [2].

8.1.1 Use Cases in Annex III AI Act

Annex III AI Act contains a list of possible applications of AI systems for which a certain level of risk has already been identified or is foreseeable. The existing use cases relate in particular to areas in which the use of AI is considered to be particularly "sensitive" due to the corresponding field of activity and the functioning of the respective system. In these cases, the increased requirements for high data quality, documentation and traceability, transparency, human oversight, precision and robustness provided for in the AI Act are intended to mitigate risks of interference with fundamental rights or security risks associated with these AIs that are not covered by other existing legislation (see Recitals 72 and 73 AI Act).

Classification rules for **high-risk AI systems** can be found in Art. 6 AI Act, whereby Art. 6 para. 2 and 3 AI Act are particularly relevant for the cases of application of the AI Act listed in Annex III AI Act. As an essential prerequisite for the cases listed in Annex III AI Act to be classified as high-risk systems, Art. 6 para. 3 AI Act states that they do not pose a significant risk of harm to the health, safety or fundamental rights of natural persons and do not significantly influence the outcome of decision-making, among other things.

In addition, a system within the scope of Annex III is not considered high-risk pursuant to Art. 6 para. 3 AI Act if

- the AI system is intended to perform a narrowly defined procedural task (lit a),

- the AI system is intended to improve a result that was previously achieved by human activity (lit b),

- the AI system is intended to recognize decision patterns or deviations from previous decision patterns and is not intended to replace or influence the previously completed human assessment without appropriate human review (lit c),

- the AI system is intended to perform a preparatory task for an assessment relevant for the purposes of the use cases listed in Annex III (lit d).

8.1.2 Example: Allocation of Social Benefits

One use case for high-risk Annex III systems is AI systems that are intended to be used "by public authorities or on behalf of public authorities to assess whether natural persons are entitled to basic public assistance and services, including health services, and whether such benefits and services are to be granted, restricted, withdrawn or reclaimed" (see Annex III no. 8 lit a AI Act). This already implies that these are cases in which an authority acts as a deployer within the meaning of Art. 3 no. 4 AI Act.

One possible scenario for the granting of social benefits to natural persons by the competent authorities is the payment of social welfare benefits to people at acute risk of poverty. According to the respective national legal basis (cf. for example in Germany § 27 SGB XII. (German Social Code) or § 5 SH-GG (German Social Aid Basic Law)), anyone who is unable or not sufficiently able to cover their necessary living expenses from their own resources and means is entitled to benefits. The competent national authority must check the extent to which the person's own financial resources are available, in particular their own income and existing assets or outstanding claims against third parties, etc., as well as the living situation of the person entitled to benefits.[1] The verification of the documents received and the reconciliation with other authorities such as asylum authorities, employment service, etc. can be carried out using automated systems. The **subsumption process** for individual facts to be checked can potentially be taken over by AI systems. In addition, there is a subsidiary entitlement to social assistance (needs-oriented minimum social benefits in Austria) if the applicant does not receive benefits from other sources such as unemployment benefit.

Assuming that the verification of eligibility for social benefits, such as needs-oriented minimum social benefits, can be carried out by automated systems, this would be a case in which an authority has to verify the eligibility of a person for a basic public social benefit, the existence of corresponding requirements such as main residence, income limit, coverage of housing needs, etc. If such applications are now used by administrative staff as deployers within the meaning of Art. 3 no. 4 AI Act to make decisions in the context of administrative procedures that grant or deny *entitlements to basic public assistance and services* (Annex III no. 5 lit. a AI Act) or distribute existing resources, this affects the scope of application of high-risk AI systems and is then regulated more stringently. The system used must then meet the requirements set out in Sections 2 and 3 AI Act. In accordance with Art. 26 AI Act, the administration as the deployer of the system is obliged to take appropriate technical and organizational measures to ensure that such systems can be used in accordance with the instructions for use attached to the systems (see Art. 13 para. 2 AI Act). The deployers must assign human supervision to natural persons who have the necessary competence, training and authorization and provide the necessary support (Art. 13 AI Act; Art. 14 para. 2 AI Act).

If a natural person has approached the public body as an applicant and is significantly disadvantaged by the legally effective **decision-making process** in the award of a public service or service provision or if there are other adverse effects on the health, safety or fundamental rights of the applicant, Art. 86 AI Act provides a transparency obligation. The applicant shall be entitled to receive clear and meaningful explanations from the public body on the role of the AI system in the decision-making process and on the most important elements of the decision taken.

---

[1] A detailed list of the criteria for eligibility can be found in the relevant national regulations §§ 27–40 SGB XII in Germany and in Austria at state level, e. g. the Vienna Minimum Welfare Act (WMG).

The transparency should be designed in such a way that the deployers are able to understand how the AI system works, how its functionality is to be evaluated and how its strengths and limitations are to be identified (Recital 72 AI Act). Provider of such systems within the meaning of Art. 3 para. 3 AI Act must take appropriate measures to enable transparent decision-making by the public body as deployer when placing on the market and putting into operation.

The question of whether support services and services provided by a public authority or other public body are considered high-risk within the meaning of the AI Act will be "significance". There may be the potential for a demarcation problem in individual cases when it comes to the question of whether an AI system is to be assessed as high-risk.

Irrespective of the GDPR, applicants are always protected by Art. 22 GDPR when using fully automated decision-making tools if these are used to evaluate personal aspects of the individual ("**profiling**"), the decision has a legal effect on the person and/or significantly affects them in a similar way [5] (see also Chapter 4, Data protection).

8.1.3   Example: Allocation of Kindergarten Spots

An AI system is already in use in the Warsaw administration for the allocation of kindergarten spots, which is based on the data provided by parents to calculate a certain number of points and allocate the respective child, who is "applying" for a kindergarten spot, to a facility using an algorithm [6] [4].

The system thus assumes the allocation function of a (potential) resource issue. In terms of how AI works, this is a combination of expert- and rule-based systems, which are combined with systems for the purpose of algorithmic decision-making, i. e. two different AI developments with the purpose of facilitating and largely automating decision-making processes. As a result, this system is not only used in the private sector, but also in the public sector and thus extends to decision-making processes in which the administration acts as the deployer of AI.

One such use case of the use of an AI system by a public institution is covered by Annex III no. 3 lit. a AI Act and refers to AI systems that are intended to be used to determine the access or admission or allocation of natural persons to institutions at all levels of education and training and are therefore considered high-risk.

As already mentioned in 8.1.2 the obligations set out in the AI Act for providers, deployers etc. apply to high-risk systems (see in particular Art. 6, 13, 26 AI Act).

Sources

[1] Denk, Michael: *ZTR 2019, 189: Der maschinell erstellte Bescheid (Teil I) (Michael Denk): RDB Rechts-datenbank*. URL *https://rdb.manz.at/document/rdb.tso.LIztr20190403* – accessed: 2024/08/15

[2] Eisenberger, Iris; Merli, Franz: *Automatisierung, Algorithmen und künstliche Intelligenz in der öffent-lichen Verwaltung. Eine Positionsbestimmung | JRP issue 1, May 2023, Volume 31.* URL *https://www.verlag oesterreich.at/automatisierung-algorithmen-und-kuenstliche-intelligenz-in-der-oeffentlichen-verwaltung.-eine-positionsbestimmung/99.105005-jrp202301002501* – accessed: 2024/08/15 – Verlag Österreich

[3] Fernbach, Sarah Anna: *ZfV 2024/11 – Bescheiderlassung durch Künstliche Intelligenz aus rechtsstaatlicher Sicht – LexisNexis Zeitschriften*. URL *https://lesen.lexisnexis.at/_/bescheiderlassung-durch-kuenstliche-intelligenz-aus-rechtsstaatl/artikel/zfv/2024/2/ZfV_2024_02_011.html* – accessed: 2024/08/15

[4] Henning, Arian; Langenbach, Pascal: Bridging the Human-Automation Fairness Gap: How Providing Reasons Enhances the Perceived Fairness of Public Decision-Making. In: *SSRN Electronic Journal* (2024).

[5] Haidinger in Knyrim Rainer (Hrsg.): *Der DatKomm – Praxiskommentar zum Datenschutzrecht*, 2022, Art 22 DSGVO Rz 1 – ISBN 978-3-214-17316-6

[6] Misuraca, Gianluca; Van, NOORDT Colin: *AI Watch – Artificial Intelligence in public services*. URL *https://publications.jrc.ec.europa.eu/repository/handle/JRC120399* – accessed: 2024/08/15 – JRC Publications Repository

8.2 AI in Criminal Prosecution

Kristina Altrichter/Karin Bruckmüller

The recently adopted AI Act of the European Union also provides rules for the use of AI systems in the area of criminal law. The background to the measures explained in more detail below was, among other things, the increasing [1] use of AI in criminal prosecution throughout Europe, which is associated with possible (fundamental) rights interference [1]. These AI systems can be used for risk assessments of individuals and crime predictions and influence further criminal prosecution [1] [2].

Specifically, it concerns the use of so-called biometric real-time remote identification systems namely AI-supported systems which, according to Article 3 AI Act, can be used to identify natural persons without their active involvement and, as a rule, remotely (see Article 3 para. 41 AI Act). This is done by comparing biometric, i. e. personal data – which relate to certain characteristics of a person, e. g. facial images and are obtained from "live material" or "near-live material" (e. g. video recordings, see Recital 17 AI Act) – with the biometric data of persons stored in a reference database (see Art. 3 no. 41 AI Act). The function of a biometric remote identification system in real time allows "the collection of biometric data, matching and identification to take place without significant (time) delay" (see Art. 3 no. 42 AI Act). This makes it possible to carry out proactive police work to find people who are potentially dangerous, suspects or victims.

Despite the crime prevention and protection for victims associated with these systems, they can also lead to violations of fundamental rights of the persons to whom such systems are applied [2]. This concerns, for example, human dignity, the right to non-discrimination and, in the area of criminal law, the presumption of innocence and thus the right to a fair trial [1].

In addition, the use of such systems can also be detrimental to the privacy of a large part of the population and lead to a feeling of constant surveillance. It can thus indirectly discourage the exercise of freedom of assembly and other fundamental rights (see Recital 32 AI Act). There is also the risk that technical inaccuracies in AI systems may lead to incorrect results and thus cause discrimination, particularly with regard to age, ethnic origin, race, gender or disability (see Recital 32 AI Act).

The fundamental objective of ensuring that AI in the context of law enforcement is also in line with the values of the European Union is therefore to be taken into account by the Regulation that has now been adopted (see Recitals 1, 3, 33 AI Act). Accordingly, the legislative process for the AI Regulation was consensual, at least with regard to a fundamental ban on predictive policing in relation to individuals. In contrast, the exceptions to the ban, i. e. when such systems may nevertheless be used, were a major point of contention that led to lengthy and intensive negotiations. By balancing the various interests, it was not until December 2023 that a compromise was finally reached and the final regulations for the criminal authorities in the European Union [3] [4].

8.2.1 Use of Biometric Real-time Remote Identification Systems

Fundamentally Prohibited Practice

Article 5 AI Act regulates the prohibited practices in connection with AI and also mentions the real-time biometric remote identification systems of natural persons in publicly accessible areas by l criminal prosecution authorities. It includes systems of immediate identification, but also those with "limited short delays" in order to prevent circumvention (Art. 3 no. 42 AI Act). This explicitly establishes a ban on such AI systems. Although these systems are prohibited, their use is nevertheless permitted under certain conditions, provided it is necessary in exceptional cases.

Permitted Use under Strict Conditions

Biometric real-time remote identification systems are permitted underArt. 5 para. 1 lit h AI Act for the protection of potential crime victims and missing persons on the one hand and for the (criminal) prosecution of persons on the other.

These AI systems may be used if it is necessary to search for specific victims of kidnapping, human trafficking or sexual exploitation and missing persons (in general) is inevitable (see Art. 5 para. 1 lit h sublit i AI Act).

In addition, the use of biometric real-time remote identification systems is also permitted for the prevention of a specific, significant and immediate threat to the life or physical integrity of natural persons or for the prevention of an existing or foreseeable threat of a terrorist attack (see Art. 5 para. 1 lit. h sublit. ii AI Act).

Permissibility is also given for tracing or identifying persons who are believed to have committed a serious crime and who are therefore being prosecuted for certain explicitly named serious crimes (see Art. 5 para. 1 lit. h sublit. iii AI Act). Specifically, these include the offenses of terrorism,human trafficking, sexual exploitation of children and child pornography, illicit trafficking in drugs and psychotropic substances, illicit trafficking in arms, ammunition or explosives, murder, serious bodily harm,trafficking in human organs or human tissue, trafficking in nuclear or radioactive substances, kidnapping, deprivation of liberty or hostage-taking (see Annex II AI Act). This refers to the purpose of conducting criminal investigations,criminal proceedings or the execution of a criminal penalty for such criminal offenses, provided that a Member State imposes a custodial sentence or a detention order for a minimum period of at least four years (see Art. 5 para. 1 lit. h sublit. iii AI Act). This point also changed before the final resolution of the AI Act. The penalty for an offense that justifies the use of the system for law enforcement purposes has been increased from three to four years since the Commission's original draft [5].

How Use is Permitted in Exceptional Cases

- **Exclusively for confirmation of identity**

  If one of the aforementioned exceptions for the use of biometric real-time remote identification systems is given, these are subject to further requirements arising from the AI Act in order to actually be allowed to use such an AI application. For example, the use by criminal prosecution authorities are only permitted to confirm the identity of the specific person concerned in the cases specified above (see Art. 5 para. 2 AI Act).

  In addition, the use of such AI systems must always be carried out by weighing up the effects in the specific case; on the one hand, with regard to the severity, probability and extent of the potential harm if the system is not used and, on the other hand, with regard to the severity, probability and extent of the consequences for the rights and freedoms of the affected person if the system is used (see Art. 5 para. 2 AI Act).

  In addition, the use of real-time biometric remote identification systems in publicly accessible spaces, must be based on the legal boundaries at national level and must therefore be limited to the necessary minimum in terms of time, geographical and personal scope of application of the persons concerned and taking into account available evidence (see Art. 5 para. 2 and 3 AI Act; Recital 34 AI Act).

- **Based on an authorization and registration**

  An authorization must be obtained before the system is used. This is issued by the competent national judicial- or independent administrative authority – at the request of the criminal prosecution authorities (see Art. 5 para. 3 AI Act, Recital 35 AI Act) – if an impact assessment has been carried out with regard to fundamental rights and the system to be used is also included in the EU database. Only in justi-fied urgent cases can a system be used without registration, as long as this is done immediately afterwards (Art. 5 para. 2 AI Act).

The basis for the decision to authorize the use of the system by the authorities in the course of prosecution is the objective evidence or clear indications presented to the authority that the use of the system is necessary and proportionate for the identification and achievement of one of the above-mentioned purposes and is limited to what is strictly necessary (see Art. 5 para. 3 AI Act).

The decision on whether or not to grant authorization for a specific case is in any case binding for the requesting law enforcement authority. In urgent and justified cases, however, provisional use without authorization is also possible in this con-text if the application for authorization is submitted no later than 24 hours after use of the system has begun (see Art. 5 para. 3 AI Act). The decision may not be made solely on the basis of the result of the real-time biometric remote identifi-cation system, which results in a negative legal consequence for a person. If an application is ultimately rejected, any use of biometric real-time remote identifica-tion systems that has already begun in the course of criminal prosecution must also be discontinued immediately and all previous data and results must be de-leted without delay.

Under supervision through reporting obligations

The AI Act now also provides for a type of monitoring mechanism that makes the use of the systems rather restrictive [5]. The key point here is that any use of a real-time biometric remote identification system in publicly accessible areas for law enforcement purposes must also be reported to the competent national mar-ket surveillance authority and national data protection authority (see Art. 5 para. 4 AI Act). The national authorities responsible for supervision must also report annually to the Commission on the cases of use (see Art. 5 para. 6 AI Act).

Based on the data provided by the Member States, the Commission will publish an-nual reports on the use of real-time biometric remote identification systems in pub-licly accessible spaces for law enforcement purposes in the EU, although no sensi-tive operational data on the specific cases is included (see Art. 5 para. 7 AI Act).

8.2.2 Implementation Obligations of the Member States

In retrospect and taking into account the conflicting substantial interests in this pro-vision – on the one hand, to prevent serious interference with fundamental rights and freedoms by means of a comprehensive ban, and on the other hand to nevertheless allow exceptions for the use of real-time biometric remote identification systems in public interest (see Recital 33 AI Act) – it is now up to the Member States to implement the provisions in their national law. They must specify the use of such systems in publicly accessible areas for law enforcement purposes with regard to the application, granting, exercise and supervision and also notify these provisions to the Commission within 30 days of their adoption (see Art. 5 para. 5 AI Act).

Sources

[1] AI, data analysis and algorithms | Campaign. URL *https://www.fairtrials.org/campaigns/ai-algorithms-data/* – accessed: 2024/03/31 – Fair Trials

[2] Automating Injustice. URL *https://www.fairtrials.org/articles/publications/automating-injustice/* – accessed: 2024/03/31 – Fair Trials

[3] Artificial intelligence act: Council and Parliament strike a deal on the first rules for AI in the world. URL *https://www.consilium.europa.eu/de/press/press-releases/2023/12/09/artificial-intelligence-act-council-and-parliament-strike-a-deal-on-the-first-worldwide-rules-for-ai/* – accessed: 2024/03/31

[4] Commission welcomes political agreement on Artificial Intelligence Act. URL *https://ec.europa.eu/commission/presscorner/detail/de/ip_23_6473* – accessed: 2024/03/31 – European Commission

[5] Proposal for a Regulation of the European Parliament and of the Council laying down harmonized rules on Artificial Intelligence (Artificial Intelligence Act) and amending certain union legislative acts, 2021

8.3 AI in Elections and Democratic Processes

Veronica Cretu

"The year 2024 is unique (so far) in human history as more people will vote in elections than ever before. Known challenges to the integrity of elections this year include political attacks on the independence of electoral bodies, a polarized political environment, disinformation, and even public health crises and natural disasters." [20]

According to the Anchor Change Election Cycle Tracker [11] and additional data from Statista [18], elections will be held in more than 60 countries around the world in 2024, with around 2 billion people, or about a quarter of the world's population, going to the polls. This year is being called a "super election year" or possibly the biggest election year ever, with elections in populous countries such as the United States, Mexico, India and Indonesia being of great importance. In addition, the citizens of the 27 countries of the European Union will elect a new European Parliament in a supranational election.

IDEA International provides a comprehensive map with relevant details on the 2024 elections [21].

8.3.1 Emerging Discussions about the Impact of AI on Democracy and Electoral Processes

IDEA International's report on perceptions of democracy [20] shows that the continuous evolution of technology has consistently impacted elections, from the introduction of radio and television to the rise of the internet and social media. However, recent advances in generative artificial intelligence (AI) may have a profound, yet not fully understood, impact on elections and the perceived integrity of electoral processes. In addition, there is evidence that disinformation campaigns, potentially amplified by AI, affect voters' ability to properly evaluate the legitimacy of elections. The IDEA report recognizes the growing influence of technology and AI on democracy and advises a cautious approach to the use of these tools. The report looks at how advances in generative AI are impacting perceptions of the credibility of elections.

- There is a concern that AI-driven disinformation campaigns could undermine voters' ability to properly assess the credibility of elections. This highlights the dual role of AI as a potential tool to promote democratic engagement and as a threat that could affect public understanding and trust in electoral processes.

- While the impact of AI has not been covered in detail in all sections of the report, the overarching impact of the technology on democracy is clear. The report suggests that as technology becomes increasingly integrated into daily life and democratic processes will play a crucial role in shaping public perceptions of democracy. This integration requires careful regulation and oversight to ensure that it supports, rather than undermines, democratic values.

- The findings suggest that while AI and other technologies offer opportunities to improve democratic processes – such as more accessible and efficient elections – they also pose significant challenges. These include ensuring the security of electoral processes, protecting against the misuse of personal data and combating the spread of misinformation.

- The results of the survey conducted by IDEA underscore the need to establish standards for the use of AI in democratic processes. This includes developing frameworks that can effectively balance the benefits of AI in improving participation and transparency while addressing the risks related to privacy, security and the potential for AI to be used in manipulative ways.

According to Freedom House [22], many discussions about AI are rooted in long-standing questions about internet governance [25], such as how regulations can protect people from harmful state and non-state operators while promoting a vibrant and innovative private sector. What legal obligations should companies have when their products are misused? Lessons learned from discussions over the past decade about government oversight, the importance of active participation by civil society, and the pitfalls of excessive self-regulation provide guidance for navigating this new area. Given the role of AI in digital oppression, it is critical to create a carefully crafted legal framework to protect human rights in the digital age.

The same report paints a grim picture of declining internet freedom worldwide for the 13th consecutive year, highlighting the rise of digital repression in countries such as Iran, Myanmar and the Philippines. Even countries like Costa Rica, once lauded for their internet freedom, are now facing challenges from policies that make use of online harassment. The emergence of generative AI poses new risks and can fuel disinformation campaigns. The use of this technology to manipulate online discussions has doubled in the last ten years and now affects at least 47 governments. The role of AI in censorship is increasing, with advanced authoritarian states using chatbot technologies to tighten their control, and at least 21 countries using machine learning to silence unwanted posts.

Despite the oppressive potential of AI, lessons from the history of internet governance provide a roadmap for protecting internet freedom. The democratic world must develop human rights-based standards for AI that take into account the threats posed by state and non-state operators. This approach requires collaboration between democratic policy makers and civil society experts to ensure a free and open internet. The current state of AI use underscores the importance of proactive and informed policy to preserve the integrity of human rights online. While the advances in technology are worrying, they also offer opportunities – if managed properly – to strengthen the protections needed for internet freedom.

The Ipsos report [12] from October 2023 provides valuable insights into the global perception of the impact of AI on information integrity, particularly in the context of elections, based on an analysis conducted in 29 countries around the world. The report concludes that there is a strong awareness across countries that AI technologies are making it increasingly easy to create realistic fake news reports and images. This underlines the growing concern that AI could exacerbate the problems of misinformation and disinformation that are already a major problem in the digital age. However, confidence in distinguishing between real and fake news varies greatly from region to region. While some populations are relatively confident in their ability to distinguish truth from falsehood, others are much less so. These differences could influence how different societies respond to and regulate AI technologies in their electoral processes. These and other reports highlight the critical intersection between AI technology and democratic integrity and underscore the urgent need for proactive measures to mitigate risk and strengthen the resilience of electoral systems worldwide.

There is great concern that generative AI could significantly disrupt the electoral process, according to Chatham House [15]. This technology can clone voices, create fake videos and generate persuasive narratives that could undermine the authenticity of campaign messages. Unfortunately, the use of AI for disinformation has escalated, with AI being used to create doubt, smear opponents, or influence public debate. Here are two examples, but there are hundreds of such examples around the world in the context of elections:

- A political ad published by the Republican National Committee *depicts* a dystopian scenario in the event that President Joe Biden is re-elected: Explosions in Taipei as China invades, waves of migrants cause panic in the US, and martial law is declared in San Francisco [24].

- In a video generated by an artificial intelligence [23], Hillary Clinton appears to offer her support to a Republican: "I have great admiration for Ron DeSantis. He's exactly the kind of leader our country needs."

8.3.2 How Should AI be Defined in the Context of Elections?

In the area of electoral processes, the definition of AI includes understanding its application in the lifecycle of elections, from voter registration and education to the actual casting and counting of votes and the analysis of election results.

In the European context, the reference to the AI Regulation is key: *"'AI system' means a machine-based system that is designed to operate with varying levels of autonomy and that may exhibit adaptiveness after deployment, and that, for explicit or implicit objectives, infers, from the input it receives, how to generate outputs such as predictions, content, recommendations, or decisions that can influence physical or virtual environments."* (See section 3.1, Introduction to the AI Act [10])

The 2024 definition by the OECD [19] is another good reference: *"An AI system is a machine-based system that, for explicit or implicit objectives, infers, from the input it receives, how to generate outputs such as predictions, content, recommendations, or decisions that can influence physical or virtual environments. Different AI systems vary in their levels of autonomy and adaptiveness after deployment."*

Based on the existing definitions of an AI system, in the broader context of elections, AI systems are becoming dynamic tools that are able to learn and evolve. For example, they can analyze voter and constituent data to improve the targeting of campaign messages, monitor social media trends to detect misinformation, or optimize the allocation of election resources. Operating with a degree of autonomy, these systems can learn from new data and adapt their functions after deployment to improve performance in achieving predefined goals, whether to increase voter turnout, ensure the security and integrity of the electoral process, or provide fair access to electoral information.

8.3.3 Exploiting Opportunities and Minimizing Risks through the Use of AI

The integration of AI into the electoral context is a relatively new field. In the absence of a comprehensive framework, one can incrementally build on the general guidelines and principles that address the use of technology in democratic processes and address the specific challenges of AI by building on the practice of internet governance, data governance and other areas. The current lack of a robust, dedicated framework for AI in elections underscores the need for urgent, dedicated action by global leaders, technologists and civil society.

The following proposes a framework for a multi-layered, multi-stakeholder approach to the use of AI elections.

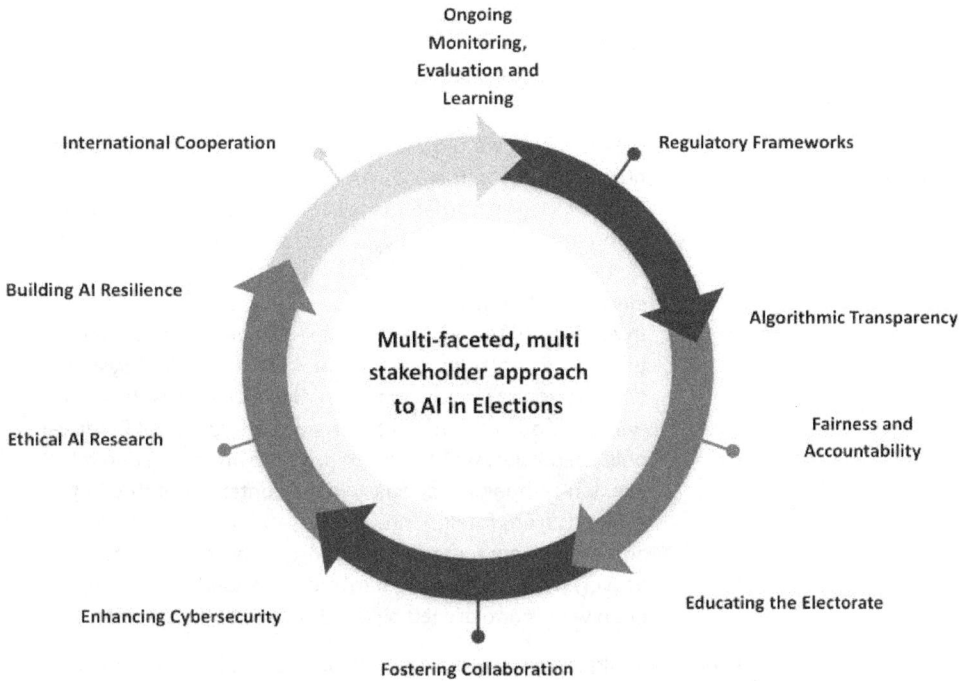

Figure 8.1 Multi-faceted, Multi-stakeholder Approach to the Use of AI in Elections

Central to this approach is the need to create a robust and resilient framework that continuously adapts and is characterized by continuous monitoring, evaluation and learning. This dynamic process feeds into and is informed by the development and enforcement of rigorous legal frameworks that govern the ethical use of AI in elections. Transparency of AI algorithms is necessary. Educating the electorate is crucial to the effectiveness of AI in elections. By fostering dialogue and partnership between governments, private sector companies, civil society and international organizations, a more holistic and proactive stance on the challenges and opportunities of AI in elections can emerge. The improvement of cybersecurity is an ongoing priority as cyber threats evolve alongside advances in AI. Protecting election data and the integrity of elections from these threats is an ongoing task that requires vigilant mechanisms. Ethical AI research must guide the development of AI in a way that upholds democratic values and test these systems rigorously against the highest ethical standards. At the international level, collaboration is paramount, not only in sharing best practices and lessons learned, but also in aligning global standards that transcend national borders, as digital election influencing knows no borders. Building AI resilience means anticipating future challenges and threats, even the unknown ones. By going through this continuous loop of innovation and reflection, democratic societies can strive to maintain integrity and trust in their electoral processes in the age of AI.

Table 8.1 Trust-building Measures for the Use of AI in Elections

Component	Examples
Development of regulatory frameworks	Governments should enact comprehensive laws and regulations that govern the use of AI in elections. This includes defining clear parameters for the ethical use of AI, setting standards for transparency and accountability, and ensuring that AI tools are not used to manipulate voter behavior or election outcomes. In addition to the provisions of the AI Act (classification of the use of AI in elections, see section 3.3.2 High-risk AI Systems), an important example related to AI in elections is the adoption of a Code of Conduct [7] on April 9, 2024 by all European political parties, which aims to promote an ethical and fair election campaign, especially in the context of protecting elections from foreign interference and disinformation. This agreement represents a joint effort by these parties to proactively avoid reinforcing narratives that undermine European values and are led by entities outside the EU [13].
Algorithmic transparency	AI algorithms used in election processes should be transparent so that it is possible to check and understand how they work, make decisions and influence users. This transparency is crucial for trust and for checking these systems for bias or manipulation. An important example of an institution that can provide guidance and support to stakeholders working on AI in elections in Europe is the European Center for Algorithmic Transparency (ECAT) [2] – a European Commission body that plays a central role in ensuring the transparency of algorithms. By providing technical support to enforce the Digital Services Act (DSA), researching the societal impact of algorithmic systems and evaluating platform algorithms, ECAT helps to ensure that the digital landscape upholds democratic integrity. Through collaboration and community building, it promotes methods for fair and responsible AI applications that are critical to maintaining the transparency and neutrality of

Component	Examples
	algorithmic decision-making in electoral processes. ECAT's efforts are an essential part of protecting elections from the risks associated with AI-driven content editing and disinformation. The UK government is a good example, as it was among the first to introduce an algorithmic transparency standard for government departments and public sector bodies in November 2021, in partnership with the Centre for Data Ethics and Innovation. In February 2024, the government announced that the use of ATRS (The Algorithmic Transparency Recording Standard) will be mandatory for all central government departments, with the intention of extending this to the entire public sector over time [6].
Fairness and responsibility	There must be mechanisms to hold the developers and users of AI systems accountable for their work. This means not only setting standards for fairness and accuracy, but also enforceable consequences for the misuse of AI. Providers of AI tools should adhere to high quality, privacy and security standards for their products [5]. They should disclose the external training data used to develop their AI models, as this data may contain biases that could influence the election result. They should be able to demonstrate their AI tools using state and local voter data to provide a realistic picture of the tool's performance. After acquisition, state election authorities should retain control and ownership of all data processed by the AI system.
Educating the electorate	Raising awareness and educating voters about the role of AI in elections can enable them to critically evaluate the information they receive. Voter education campaigns can include information on how to counter AI-generated disinformation and the importance of fact-checking. "Planned and strategic voter education campaigns can mitigate the impact of misinformation and disinformation generated by AI tools" [1]. Here is an example of a voter education initiative at US called "BEHIND THE HEADLINES." This campaign, which runs through Election Day 2024, targets women, dark-skinned and Hispanic voters to raise awareness about the impact of AI in elections and the risks of misinformation. It includes multilingual resources, including social media content, webinars and explainer videos, such as one showing how deepfakes are created using AI-generated voiceovers. The main goals of the campaign are to highlight the personalization of AI-driven

Table 8.1 Trust-building Measures for the Use of AI in Elections *(continued)*

Component	Examples
	messaging, expose the prevalence of misleading deep fake content, and emphasize the impact of AI-generated misinformation on individual voting behavior [3].
Promoting cooperation	Creating a collaborative ecosystem that includes government agencies, technology companies, civil society and academia can facilitate the sharing of best practices and the development of sound strategies to address the challenges posed by AI in elections. The Tech Accord to Combat Deceptive Use of AI in 2024 Elections [4] is a collective initiative by leading technology companies to combat the spread of harmful AI-generated content that misleads voters. Companies such as Adobe, Google, Microsoft, Meta and others have committed to developing technologies that can detect AI-generated audio, video and image content aimed at manipulating the appearance and messages of political figures or misinforming voters about electoral processes. The agreement contains eight specific commitments, including the development of open source tools, the ongoing assessment of the risks posed by such technologies and efforts to curb the spread of misleading content on their platforms. In addition, the agreement emphasizes transparency, public engagement and education campaigns to improve media literacy and strengthen society's resilience to these threats. The agreement builds on the existing efforts of individual companies and aims to protect the digital space from the dangers of misleading AI in election periods. Another compelling example is the value of country-led election coalitions, which are proving to be an effective mechanism for combating misinformation. By bringing together news outlets, fact-checking organizations and local groups within a country, these coalitions work together to address the specific needs of voters and provide targeted support and information in the run-up to elections [17].
Improving cyber security	Strengthening cyber security of election systems against AI-powered threats must be a priority. This means protecting infrastructure against hacking and securing data against unauthorized AI analysis that could affect the integrity of elections. One example of a tool is the Cybersecurity Toolkit with free tools, services and resources provided by CISA (Cybersecurity and Infrastructure Security Agency of the United States of America [9]).

Component	Examples
Promotion of ethical AI research	Supporting research into the ethical implications of AI in elections can provide deeper insights into the potential consequences of its use and guide the development of technologies that strengthen democratic principles. An example of a study on the impact of new technologies on free and fair elections ("Elections Study") can be found in the sources. Although the literature review is from 2021, it provides an overview and analysis of the relevant literature identified and reviewed in the context of a study on the impact of new technologies on free and fair elections. The following research questions were used in the search: How might the use of new technologies such as artificial intelligence and blockchain/distributed ledger technology (DLT) and new online techniques such as microtargeting and algorithmic filtering, which rely on voter data to create and disseminate online disinformation and target different categories of voters, could have an impact on the outcome of elections and public trust in them? What are the potential risks and opportunities of these technologies when used in the electoral context? How can the risks be minimized and the opportunities of the technologies maximized to strengthen the rule of free and fair elections as the backbone of democracy? [16]
Building AI resilience	As AI technologies evolve, so should the strategies to combat their misuse. This means investing in AI that can detect and defend against disinformation and creating rapid response mechanisms to counter AI threats in real time. At the same time, election officials, IT staff and other stakeholders are better able to identify, address and neutralize cyber threats through comprehensive cybersecurity training. Education and training not only prepares people to deal with immediate threats, but also provides the foundation for continued resilience to evolving AI challenges and ensures that election systems remain robust and trustworthy [14].

Table 8.1 Trust-building Measures for the Use of AI in Elections *(continued)*

Component	Examples
International cooperation	International cooperation is crucial in the context of elections, as the influence of AI transcends national borders, making joint efforts to mitigate its risks essential. While elections are primarily national affairs, they are influenced by global digital ecosystems in which AI technologies play an important role. In addressing AI-related challenges in elections, countries can benefit from a unified approach to intelligence sharing that includes sharing information on emerging AI threats and effective countermeasures. In addition, the standardization of regulations is crucial. By aligning laws and policies on AI use, countries can create a coherent framework that ensures consistency and fairness in electoral processes worldwide. The AI Act is a groundbreaking example of comprehensive legislation regulating AI applications and a precedent for other regions. Its focus on high-risk AI systems, including those used in elections, demonstrates a proactive approach to dealing with the impact of AI on democracy. Similarly, the Council of Europe's draft Framework Convention on Artificial Intelligence, Human Rights, Democracy and the Rule of Law [8] provides a comprehensive structure for member states and potentially non-member states to ensure that AI technologies are developed and used in a way that respects democratic values and human rights. This framework and the accompanying explanatory report outline principles and guidelines that can facilitate harmonized regulations among countries and foster a collaborative environment for addressing the global challenges of AI. Such international frameworks not only increase the effectiveness of individual countries' efforts, but also ensure that the further development of AI technologies takes place in a global context that respects and upholds democratic integrity. This collective approach can lead to a more robust defense against AI-driven interference in elections, promoting a healthier democratic process at the international level.
Ongoing monitoring, evaluation and learning	As AI technologies and their applications in elections evolve, so must the strategies to address them. Regular evaluation and revision of policies, regulations and educational materials is essential to stay ahead of new threats. AI tools must be continuously evaluated throughout their development, from conception to integration and operation in electoral processes, and the procurement of all other products/services that rely on AI must be closely scrutinized [5].

8.3.4 AI and Election Integrity: a Hypothetical Analysis of the Cambridge Analytica Scandal in the Context of the AI Act

Description of the case: The Cambridge Analytica controversy has dominated the landscape of data privacy, political campaigning and social media in a new way. It has prompted governments and companies to take protective measures, balancing data protection with the need for transparency and research.

The Cambridge Analytica scandal [26], uncovered in 2018, revealed how the data analytics company collected millions of Facebook profiles of US voters without authorization. This data was used to create a powerful software program to predict and influence voting behavior, which impacted both Donald Trump's election team and the Brexit campaign. Whistleblower Christopher Wylie revealed that Cambridge Analytica, under the direction of Steve Bannon and funded by Robert Mercer, used Facebook to profile voters and target individuals with personalized political advertising. The data was collected via an app developed by academic Aleksandr Kogan, which not only collected user data but also data from their Facebook friends, thus amassing a huge pool of data.

The Guardian and the New York Times revealed that Facebook knew about the data misuse in late 2015, but failed to warn users and took only limited steps to protect data. The scandal led to widespread outrage and prompted legislative action around the world, including the EU's Digital Services Act [28] and the Digital Markets Act [27]. Facebook has taken steps to protect user data, but the revelations have raised significant concerns about the platform's role in political targeting and data privacy. The scandal also led to various investigations and hearings by government agencies in the US, the UK and other countries.

Applicability of the AI Act

The practices of Cambridge Analytica, in particular the use of psychological profiling and targeted political advertising could be classified as prohibited AI practices under Art. 5 para. 1 lit a and possibly Art. 5 para. 1 lit b AI Act. Their techniques included manipulative approaches that distorted the behavior of voters and impaired the ability of individuals to make informed decisions, thereby likely causing significant harm.

The AI Act classifies AI systems into four risk categories: prohibited, high risk, limited risk (transparency obligations) and minimal risk. Given the nature of Cambridge Analytica's activities – using data analytics and AI for targeted political advertising and influencing voter behavior – the AI systems fall into the "high risk" category according to Annex III AI Act, which explicitly mentions the use of AI in elections:

> No. 8 lit b) AI systems intended to be used for influencing the outcome of an election or referendum or the voting behaviour of natural persons in the exercise of their vote in elections or referenda. This does not include AI systems to the output of which natural

persons are not directly exposed, such as tools used to organise, optimise or structure political campaigns from an administrative or logistical point of view.

If Cambridge Analytica's methods involved manipulation that significantly undermined voter autonomy or exploited vulnerable groups, some of their practices could fall into this prohibited category, such as:

Art. 5 para. 1 lit a AI Act – manipulative or deceptive techniques: the placing on the market, putting into service or use of an AI-system that employs subliminal techniques beyond a person's awareness or intentionally manipulative or deceptive techniques intended to or having the effect of significantly influencing the behavior of a person or a group of persons, materially interferes with the person's ability to make an informed decision, causing the person to make a decision that he or she would not otherwise have made, in a way that causes or is likely to cause significant harm to that person, another person or a group of persons.

> **Cambridge Analytica** used data collected by Facebook to create targeted political advertisements designed to influence voting behavior by exploiting psychological vulnerabilities. This would likely fall under the prohibited practices as their techniques were aimed at manipulating voter behavior without their informed consent, which could significantly impair an individual's ability to make independent decisions.

Art. 5 para. 1 lit b AI Act – Exploitation of vulnerable groups of persons: the placing on the market, putting into service or use of an AI system that exploits a vulnerability of a person or a specific group of persons due to their age, disability or particular social or economic situation, with the aim or effect of significantly influencing the behavior of that person or a person belonging to that group in a way that causes or is reasonably likely to cause significant harm to that person or another person.

> **Cambridge Analytica** targeted individuals based on psychological profiling in order to influence their voting behavior. If it can be proven that the company targeted vulnerable groups based on their social or economic situation, this practice would also fall under this prohibited category.

Art. 5 para. 1 lit c AI Act – Social scoring the placing on the market, putting into service or use of AI systems to evaluate or classify natural persons or groups of natural persons over a period of time on the basis of their social behavior or known, inferred or predicted personal or personality characteristics, where the social evaluation results in one or both of the following: (i) adverse or unfavorable treatment of certain natural persons or entire groups of them in social contexts unrelated to the contexts in which the data were originally generated or collected; (ii) adverse or unfavorable treatment of certain natural persons or groups of them that is unjustified or disproportionate to their social behavior or the seriousness thereof.

> **Cambridge Analytica** created detailed psychological profiles and used them for political microtargeting. Their profiling-practices could be considered a form of

social scoring if they result in disproportionate treatment or targeted political messages, although this is more nuanced and depends on the specifics of their data use.

The above analysis shows the potential breaches of the AI Act by Cambridge Analytica's practices. The scandal underscores the importance of robust AI governance to protect the integrity of elections and the need for continued vigilance and regulation in the use of AI in political processes. For Cambridge Analytica to comply with the provisions of the AI Act, the company would need to comply with the following:

- Establish a risk management system to identify and mitigate the risks associated with their AI systems.

- Ensure high quality data sets, maintain data sets and implement sound data management practices to avoid bias and inaccuracies.

- Maintaining comprehensive technical documentation detailing the design, development and operational processes of your AI systems.

- Clearly informing users when they interact with AI systems or consume AI-generated content.

- Implementation of measures to ensure adequate human oversight of the operation of the AI system, including contingency plans in the event of AI failure.

- Ensure that AI systems are robust, accurate and secure and include mechanisms to prevent and mitigate risks.

- Compliance with GDPR and other relevant data protection laws to protect personal data and ensure privacy rights.

- Continuous monitoring of AI systems after implementation to ensure compliance and resolve any emerging risks or issues.

Furthermore, ethical considerations play a crucial role in the use of AI in political processes. The scandal shines a spotlight on the broader implications of AI misuse on democracy, including the erosion of public trust and the potential manipulation of voter behavior. Ensuring ethical AI practices and maintaining transparency in AI applications are essential to upholding democratic values and protecting the integrity of electoral systems. By adhering to these principles, organizations can contribute to a fair and transparent electoral process and thus strengthen public confidence in the democratic system.

Sources

[1] 8 best practices for state election officials on AI. URL *https://www.brookings.edu/articles/8-best-practices-for-state-election-officials-on-ai/* – accessed: 2024/05/04 – Brookings

[2] About – European Commission. URL *https://algorithmic-transparency.ec.europa.eu/about_en* – accessed: 2024/05/04

[3] AI & Elections. URL *https://aiandyou.org/elections/* – accessed: 2024/05/04 – AIandYou

[4] AI Elections Accord – Munich Security Conference. URL *https://securityconference.org/en/ aielectionsaccord/* – accessed: 2024/05/04

[5] AI in Elections: The Battle for Truth and Democracy. URL *https://www.ie.edu/insights/articles/ai-in-elections-the-battle-for-truth-and-democracy/* – accessed: 2024/05/04 – IE Insights

[6] Algorithmic Transparency Recording Standard Hub. URL *https://www.gov.uk/government/collections/ algorithmic-transparency-recording-standard-hub* – accessed: 2024/05/04 – GOV.UK

[7] Code of Conduct for the 2024 European Parliament Elections. URL *https://www.idea.int/european-code-of-conduct-2024* – accessed: 2024/05/04

[8] Committee on Artificial Intelligence (CAI) – Artificial Intelligence – *www.coe.int*. URL *https://www.coe. int/en/web/artificial-intelligence/cai* – accessed: 2024/05/04 – Artificial Intelligence

[9] Cybersecurity Toolkit and Resources to Protect Elections | CISA. URL *https://www.cisa.gov/cyber security-toolkit-and-resources-protect-elections* – accessed: 2024/05/04

[10] Die Gesetzestexte | EU-Gesetz zur künstlichen Intelligenz. URL *https://artificialintelligenceact.eu/ de/das-gesetz/* – accessed: 2024/05/04

[11] Election Cycle Calendar. URL *https://www.anchorchange.com/election-cycle-calendar* – accessed: 2024/05/04 – Anchor Change – Civic Tech Strategies

[12] Global views on A. I. and disinformation. In: New Zealand (2018)

[13] Griera, Max: EU parties and Commission sign campaign rulebook against foreign interference, disinformation. URL *https://www.euractiv.com/section/elections/news/eu-parties-and-commission-sign-campaign-rulebook-against-foreign-interference-disinformation/* – accessed: 2024/05/04. – *www.euractiv. com*

[14] Here's what to know about elections, cybersecurity and AI. URL *https://www.weforum.org/ agenda/2023/11/elections-cybersecurity-ai-deep-fakes-social-engineering/* – accessed: 2024/05/04. – World Economic Forum

[15] How AI could sway voters in 2024's big elections | Chatham House – International Affairs Think Tank. URL *https://www.chathamhouse.org/publications/the-world-today/2023-10/how-ai-could-sway-voters-2024s-big-elections* – accessed: 2024/05/04

[16] *https://commission.europa.eu/system/files/2022-12/Annex%20I_LiteratureReview_20210319_clean_dsj_ v3.0_a.pdf* – accessed: 2024/05/04

[17] *https://static1.squarespace.com/static/605bcb01669c157444b9a21e/t/661577d77925c1179611a0ca/171 2682969565/AnchorChange_ElectionCoalitionsPlaybook.pdf* – accessed: 2024/05/04

[18] Infographic: 2024: The Super Election Year. URL *https://www.statista.com/chart/31604/countries-where-a-national-election-is-was-held-in-2024* – accessed: 2024/05/04 – Statista Daily Data

[19] OECD: Explanatory memorandum on the updated OECD definition of an AI system. Paris: OECD, 2024

[20] Perceptions of Democracy: A Survey about How People Assess Democracy around the World: International Institute for Democracy and Electoral Assistance, 2024 – ISBN 978-91-7671-757-8

[21] The 2024 Global Elections Super-Cycle | International IDEA. URL *https://www.idea.int/initiatives/ the-2024-global-elections-supercycle* – accessed: 2024/05/04

[22] The Repressive Power of Artificial Intelligence. URL *https://freedomhouse.org/report/freedom-net/2023/repressive-power-artificial-intelligence* – accessed: 2024/05/04 – Freedom House

[23] Video of Hillary Clinton endorsing Ron DeSantis is AI-generated. In: Reuters (2023)

[24] Vincent, James: Republicans respond to Biden reelection announcement with AI-generated attack ad. URL *https://www.theverge.com/2023/4/25/23697328/biden-reelection-rnc-ai-generated-attack-ad-deep fake* – accessed: 2024/05/04 – The Verge

[25] What are 5 Digital Policy Trends for 2022 – Diplo. URL *https://www.diplomacy.edu/resource/an-introduction-to-internet-governance/* – accessed: 2024/05/04

[26] Cadwalladr, Carole; Graham-Harrison, Emma: Revealed: 50 million Facebook profiles harvested for Cambridge Analytica in major data breach. In: The Guardian (2018) *https://www.theguardian.com/ news/2018/mar/17/cambridge-analytica-facebook-influence-us-election*

[27] The Digital Markets Act. URL *https://digital-markets-act.ec.europa.eu/index_en* – accessed: 2024/07/13

[28] The Digital Services Act. URL *https://commission.europa.eu/strategy-and-policy/priorities-2019-2024/europe-fit-digital-age/digital-services-act_en* – accessed: 2025/03/25

8.4 AI in the NIS Sector

Natascha Windholz

8.4.1 Introduction NIS and NIS 2

The NIS Directive dates back to 2016 and was implemented in Austria in the öNISG (Austrian Federal Act to Ensure a **High Level of Security** of Network and Information Systems – Network and Information System Security Act for short). The NIS Directive and the NISG are intended to ensure and harmonize a higher level of security for network and information systems throughout the EU. The companies concerned must take appropriate and proportionate technical, operational and organizational measures for cybersecurity risk management and pursue an "all-hazards approach" (see Art. 21 NIS2 Directive).

The network and information system are

- electronic communication networks pursuant to § 3 Z 11 öTKG (Austrian Telecommunications Act)

- spatially distributed, digital processing devices for the technical support of the collection, processing, storage, maintenance, use, transmission, processing or disposition of digital information

- digital data processed in such an electronic communications network or in such devices

The addressees of the current öNISG are **providers of essential services** in the energy, air, road and rail transport, financial market infrastructure, healthcare, drinking water supply and digital infrastructure sectors. Certain **public administration institutions** are also covered, and these services are specifically regulated because they play a key role in economic and social activities and are of crucial importance to them. Security incidents in these areas can impair the performance of economic activities, cause financial losses and undermine the trust of users.

The NIS Directive requires a high level of security in the sectors concerned, but also cooperation between the Member States, the establishment of national authorities and computer emergency teams and the reporting of significant incidents to them.

Network and information security means not only being able to ward off security incidents, but also to prevent them, detect and eliminate faults that have already occurred and restore normal operations. Threats must be identified, assessed and tracked. Faults must be dealt with and the ability to act and function must be restored.

The competent authority is the Austrian SCIRT, which is set up at the Federal Ministry of the Interior.

8.4.1.1 NIS2

However, the NIS Directive has been replaced by the NIS2 Directive. However, the NIS2 Directive has not been transposed into national law neither in Germany nor in Austria. The directive must be implemented by October 18, 2024 at the latest, otherwise there is a risk of infringement proceedings against the EU.

The NIS2 Directive, like NIS, should strengthen the affected sectors in terms of preparing for and responding to security incidents. The scope of application is extended to better protect essential social and economic activities. Risk management measures are just as much a part of the obligations as certain reporting obligations.

Sectors affected:

Sectors with High Criticality	Other Critical Sectors
▪ Energy	▪ Postal and courier services
▪ Traffic	▪ Waste management
▪ Banking (priority applicability of the DORA Regulation 2022/2554)	▪ Chemistry
▪ Financial market infrastructures (priority applicability of the DORA Regulation 2022/2554)	▪ Food
	▪ Processing/manufacturing industry
	▪ Provider of digital services
▪ Healthcare	▪ Research (optional)
▪ Drinking water	
▪ Waste water	
▪ Digital infrastructure	
▪ Management of ICT services B2B	
▪ Public administration	
▪ Space	

A distinction is also made according to **company size**, whereby the number of employees, annual turnover and annual balance sheet total must be taken into account. Small companies (fewer than 50 employees, maximum annual turnover of € 10 million or maximum annual balance sheet total of € 10 million) are not covered by NIS2, although there are exceptions.

The **size categories** are:

Full-time Equivalents/Annual Sales/Annual Balance Sheet Total	Company Class
▪ More than 50 full-time equivalents *and* ▪ equal to or more than € 10 million in annual sales *or* ▪ equal to/more than € 10 million annual balance sheet total	Small company
▪ More than 250 full-time equivalents *and* ▪ equal to/more than € 50 million annual turnover *or* ▪ equal to/more than € 43 million annual balance sheet total	Medium-sized company
▪ Equal to/more than 250 full-time equivalents *or* ▪ more than € 50 million in annual sales *and* ▪ more than € 43 million annual balance sheet total	Large company

The Directive refers to the Commission Recommendation on the definition [1] of SMEs, which also contains further specifications regarding the calculation of the size of the company, in particular for affiliated companies, i. e. **groups** or **groups of companies**.

Small businesses are generally not covered by NIS2, but there are exceptions, particularly if they are a trust service provider or act as a service provider or supplier to affected companies.

A distinction is also made between **essential and important companies**, which determines whether security checks are carried out ex ante or ex post in the event of reasonable suspicion. Significant facilities are large companies, e. g. from the energy, transport, health and drinking water sectors. Important companies are medium-sized companies from these sectors and large and medium-sized companies from the postal, waste, chemicals, food, digital services, etc. sectors. There are exceptions for digital infrastructure, e. g. communication services, cloud services, data center services, etc. The complete lists can be found in the annexes to NIS2.

The NIS2 Directive imposes various obligations on companies, including **risk management measures** supply chain security and reporting obligations. The directive provides for high penalties for non-compliance.

The management bodies of the facility concerned are responsible. They must ensure and supervise compliance. They are liable if the company suffers culpably caused damage due to non-compliance.

8.4.2 Importance of NIS2 for the Supply Chain

NIS2 not only requires compliance of companytoo which NIS2 is directly applicable, but also requires the supply chain to be secured. "IT" is becoming increasingly global, multi-layered, networked and ultimately more complex. Hardly any company still has "the one" IT service provider that does everything for them; instead, a large number of systems are used, which in turn come from a large number of service providers and suppliers. These systems then no longer run "on premise", i. e. on the company's own servers, but often in the cloud.

NIS2 therefore requires rigorous **third party risk management** i. e. risk management for precisely these service providers and suppliers. Not only the individual supplier is taken into account, but also the relationships between the individual facilities and their service providers and suppliers. Risk management must take into account the vulnerabilities of suppliers and service providers as well as the overall quality of the products and their IT security, the security of their development processes and what protective measures have been taken.

The service providers and suppliers of NIS2 companies can demonstrate compliance with these requirements in various ways, e. g. through certifications, audits or individual verification.

The Austrian NIS authority recommends the following standards and best practices [3]:

- ÖISHB: Cooperation with external parties, evaluation of certifications, supplier relationships

- ISO/IEC 27001: Information security in supplier relationships

- IEC 62443 2-1: Security of the supply chain

- CIS CSC v8.0: Management of service providers

- KSÖ Cyber Risk Rating: Requirement for A or B rating

NIS2 has already been taken into account in the ENISA guideline "Good Practices for Supply Chain Cybersecurity" [2]. The guide can therefore serve as an implementation aid.

8.4.3 Use of AI in NIS Companies

The use of AI by NIS and NIS2 companies is regulated in two ways. **Annexes I and III** specify certain directives or regulations and the use of AI systems in the critical infrastructure.

The use of AI systems as a **safety component** is essential. According to Art. 3 no. 14 AI Act, a safety component of a product or system is a component of a product or system that fulfills a safety function for it or whose failure or malfunction endangers the health or safety of persons or property.

The AI Act itself justifies the classification of the use of AI systems in critical infrastructure by stating that a malfunction or failure can **endanger the lives and health** of many people and lead to considerable **disruption to social and economic life**. Safety components are systems that are used to protect the physical integrity of the critical infrastructure or the health and safety of people or property, but are not essential to the functioning of the system. Failure or malfunction of such components can lead to risks to physical integrity and therefore to risks to the health and safety of people or property. Components that are used solely for cyber security purposes do not qualify as security components. Examples of safety components in critical infrastructure are systems for monitoring water pressure or fire alarms in cloud computing centers.

8.4.3.1 Annex I AI Act

AI systems that are used as a **safety component of a device**, or if the AI system itself is the device and listed in Annex I, are considered high-risk AI-systems. The same applies to devices whose safety component is an AI system, whereby the AI system or device must undergo a conformity assessment before it is placed on the market or put into service.

Depending on the sector, the following EU legal acts in particular may be relevant for NIS2 companies:

- Machinery Directive 2006/42/EC: Applicable to machinery, safety components, chains, ropes, belts, etc.

- Regulation on protective equipment (EU) 2016/425: equipment that can be worn or held by people as protection against one or more risks to their health or safety

- Medical Devices Regulation (EU) 2017/745: Medical devices intended for human use and their accessories, including associated clinical investigations; e. g. devices, instruments, software or implants for the purpose of diagnosis, prognosis, palliation or investigation

- Regulation for medical devices for in-vitro diagnostics (EU) 2017/746: reagents, kits, instruments, devices, software for in-vitro testing

- Civil Aviation Regulation (EC) 300/2008 and Regulation 2018/1139: flights of civil aircraft; aviation security is the combination of measures and human and material resources designed to protect civil aviation from acts of unlawful interference that jeopardize the security of civil aviation.

- Directive on the interoperability of the rail system (EU) 2016/797: Provisions on interoperability constituents, interfaces and procedures and for the overall coherence of the EU rail system to ensure the safe and continuous movement of trains

If the NIS2 company therefore uses AI-based components that fall under one of the legal acts in Annex I, it must ensure compliance with the requirements for high-risk AI (see section 3.3.2). If it uses a supplier for this purpose, it must also ensure compliance with the NIS2 requirements regarding supply chain security.

8.4.3.2 Annex III AI Act

All AI systems listed in Annex III are considered high-risk AI systems. The exception would be if the AI-system does not pose a significant risk to the health, safety or fundamental rights of natural persons, including a non-material influence on the outcome of a decision. This **exception** applies if one or more of the following criteria are met:

- The AI system only carries out a narrowly defined process step;
- the AI system is used to improve the results of an activity previously carried out by humans;
- the AI system should detect decision-making patterns or deviations from them and not replace assessments previously carried out by humans without proper human review; or
- the AI system performs preparatory tasks for an assessment that are relevant for one of the use cases from Annex III.

However, an AI system is always assessed as a high-risk system if it includes **profiling** of natural persons.

A provider who is of the opinion that it is not high-risk AI must document this assessment accordingly before the AI system is placed on the market or put into operation. Such a provider is subject to the obligation to register in accordance with Art. 49 para. 2 AI Regulation and must be able to present this upon request by the authority. The EU Commission will issue delegated acts on Annex III or adapt them to Annex III as a whole.

The main overlap between NIS2 and the AI Act concerns no. 2 of Annex III, which defines high-risk AI systems in critical infrastructure as AI systems that are to be used as **security components for the management and operation of critical digital infrastructure, road transport and the supply of water, gas, heat and electricity**.

The definition in Annex III no. 2 is therefore not consistent with all sectors in NIS2, whereby Article 3 no. 62 AI Act refers to Article 2 para. 4 CER Directive 2022/2557 (Regulation on the resilience of critical facilities) with regard to the definition of critical infrastructure. According to the CER Directive, essential critical infrastructure services are all services that are critical to the maintenance of important societal functions, important economic activities, public health and safety or the preservation of the environment. The member states must define and determine these. Neither Germany nor Austria have yet passed legislation to implement the CER Directive. It is therefore not yet possible to make a final statement on the interaction between the CER Regulation and NIS2.

Therefore, according to the wording, only the following are considered **critical infrastructure** in accordance with Annex III AI Act:

- Digital infrastructure, e. g. providers of internet nodes, providers of cloud services, providers of data center services, providers of public electronic communications networks, providers of publicly accessible electronic communications services

- Road traffic, in particular road traffic authorities, operation of intelligent traffic systems

- Water supply, in particular drinking water suppliers (the wording does not cover wastewater disposal)

- Gas, e. g. natural gas suppliers, providers of plants for refining and processing natural gas

- Heat, e. g. district heating provider

- Electricity, e. g. electricity companies, distribution network providers, charging station providers

If an operator of critical infrastructure from the sectors listed here uses an AI system as a safety component, it must meet the requirements for high-risk AI systems.

Checklist for the use of AI in NIS2 companies:

Is there a high-risk AI system in accordance with Annex III? Does the AI system serve as a safety component in accordance with one of the legal acts from Annex I?	Art. 6 et seq. describes the classification and obligations for deployers and providers of high-risk AI systems; see section 3.3.2.3
Is it another AI system for which there is a transparency obligation pursuant to the AI Act?	Article 52 AI Act contains transparency obligations for providers and deployers of certain AI systems and AI models for general purposes; see section 3.6
Is it an AI model for general purposes?	Article 52 et seq. AI Act contains the rules for the classification of GPAI with systemic risk and the obligations for providers; see section 3.7.

Sources

[1] Commission Recommendation of 6 May 2003 concerning the definition of micro, small and medium-sized enterprises (Text with EEA relevance) (notified under document number C(2003) 1422) – Legislative Body: COM

[2] Good Practices for Supply Chain Cybersecurity. URL *https://www.enisa.europa.eu/publications/good-practices-for-supply-chain-cybersecurity* – accessed: 2024/03/16 – ENISA

[3] Bundesministerium des Innern, Bundeskanzleramt: Sicherheitsmaßnahmen für Betreiber wesentlicher Dienste

9 Ethics

Gabriele Bolek-Fügl, Valerie Hafez, Sabine Singer

The following chapter deals with the ethical implications of the use of AI. Useful tools are provided, such as guidelines for trustworthy AI or for ethical innovation. The focus is broadened beyond the AI Regulation and global guidelines are considered, as well as the bodies, committees and panels that deal with artificial intelligence.

9.1 Ethical Guidelines for Trustworthy AI

Valerie Hafez

This chapter presents the ethical guidelines for trustworthy AI [11], which were published in April 2019 by the European Commission's High-Level Expert Group on Artificial Intelligence.[1] The evaluation list for trustworthy AI, which accompanies the guidelines, is also referred to. Although these guidelines explicitly exclude legal discussions, they are given greater significance by the AI Act, as it refers to them. Finally, approaches are briefly presented that are similar to these ethics guidelines or develop them further and may therefore be valuable for certain areas of application.

9.1.1 What is it About?

First of all, an important point: the ethical guidelines regard AI systems as socio-technical systems. This means that the ethics guidelines do not only refer to technical components such as the model, the weights or the code, but also to topics such as data

---

[1] In the German version of the guidelines, the group is referred to as the High-Level Expert Group although female experts were also represented. To ensure consistency, the High-Level Expert Group is also referred to here, but reference is made to authors.

work, the organization around AI systems or governance processes[2] such as in connection with human oversight. The ethics guidelines thus also represent an attempt to move away from a mere list of requirements (such as the accessibility requirements of the WRC (Workplace Relations Commission)) towards the development of context-sensitive evaluation competence according to ethical principles.

The ethical guidelines of the High-Level Expert Group on AI are intended for all stakeholders who design, develop, introduce, implement, use or are affected by AI systems. They are intended to enable the most holistic and practical implementation of ethical principles in connection with AI systems. The authors of the guidelines consider ethics to be a component of trustworthy AI systems (p. 6):

> *(15) A trustworthy AI is characterized by three components that should be fulfilled during the entire life cycle of the system:*

1. It should be lawful and therefore comply with applicable law and all statutory provisions;

2. it should be ethical and thus guarantee compliance with ethical principles and values; and

3. it should be robust, both technically and socially, as AI systems may cause unintended harm even if they are based on good intentions.

These components must all be fulfilled for an AI system to be considered trustworthy. For the guidelines, ethics and robustness are two intertwined principles that must be implemented together, because: Only if an AI system both serves an ethical purpose, is in line with ethical norms and can also keep these ethical promises technically and socially should it be considered trustworthy.

The ethics guidelines attempt to shed more light on the second and third aspects of trustworthy AI, as the first aspect – a legal framework – was excluded by the experts themselves, but later led to the development of the AI Act. This includes the definition of four ethical principles, which can be derived from the Charter of Fundamental Rights of the European Union. In this context, the group of experts particularly emphasized respect for human dignity, the freedom of the individual, respect for democracy, justice and the rule of law, equality, non-discrimination and solidarity, as well as civil rights. These values serve as a guide to what should be done with AI systems (as opposed to what can be done with AI systems).

---

[2] These terms are discussed in more detail in section 10.2 in connection with governance.

9.1.2 Ethical Principles of the Guidelines

The ethical principles formulate principles that should be incorporated as formative values in the development and use of AI systems (see Table 9.1). In practice, there may be tensions between these principles, which must be considered and resolved by the participating organizations. These organizations are also responsible for taking appropriate and risk-appropriate measures to protect against negative effects.

Table 9.1 Principles for the Development and Use of AI Systems

Ethical principle	Description
Respect for human autonomy	AI systems should implement measures that promote, strengthen and complement people's cognitive, social and cultural skills. (Guideline 50, p. 14–15)
Loss prevention	AI systems should have no or as few negative effects as possible on people or the environment (material or immaterial) and show special consideration for persons (groups) worthy of protection. (Guideline 51, p. 15)
Fairness	AI systems should ensure that advantages and disadvantages are distributed equally and fairly, proportionately and with consideration for the freedom of choice of those affected, which also includes the possibility of objection. (Guideline 52, p. 15)
Explainability	The processes, capabilities and purpose of AI systems must be transparent and communicated so that those directly and indirectly affected can challenge decisions in case of doubt. (Guideline 53, p. 16)

Building on these four principles, the guidelines propose seven core requirements to facilitate the implementation of the ethical principles in practice.

9.1.3 Core Requirements

With these core requirements, the expert group is addressing developers of an AI system, as well as users and stakeholders. In any case, the requirements should be monitored, evaluated and taken into account throughout the entire life cycle of the AI system. All seven core requirements are equally important, although some requirements are more important than others in certain use cases. For example, if AI systems are used in industrial contexts, diversity or data protection will play a lesser role than in applications where people are directly affected.

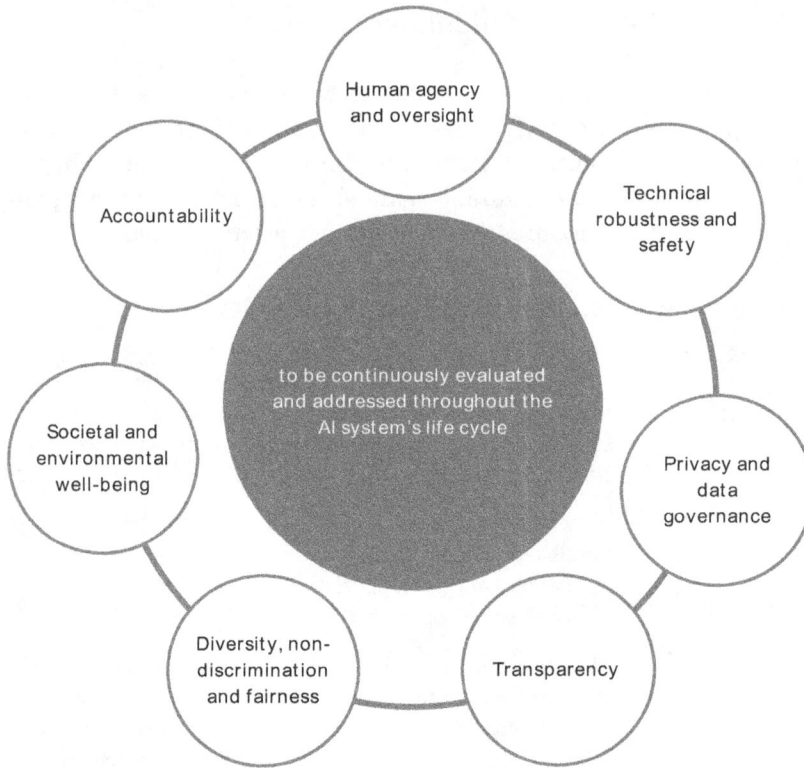

Figure 9.1 Core Requirements for Trustworthy AI Systems According to the Ethics Guidelines (p. 16)

The seven requirements for trustworthy AI are described in detail in Table 9.2.

Table 9.2 Requirements for Trustworthy AI

Core Requirements *Reference to Principles*	Description
Primacy of human action and supervision *Respect for human autonomy*	▪ Evaluate fundamental rights in advance (Guideline 63) ▪ Enable informed decisions and assessments by users and stakeholders (Guideline 64) ▪ Enable human supervision operationally by human-in-the-loop, human-in-command or human-in-control [8] as well as externally by supervisory authorities (Guideline 65)

Core Requirements *Reference to Principles*	Description
Technical robustness and security *Damage prevention*	▪ Ensure resistance to and protection against attacks and security breaches at both software (e. g. data poisoning, model leakage) and hardware level (Guideline 67) ▪ Develop safety precautions and containment plans, ensure proper functioning and identify, assess and counteract risks through measures (Guideline 68) ▪ Ensure the precision of results through an appropriate development and evaluation process and information on the degree of precision provided to users (Guideline 69) ▪ Ensure reliability (perfect functioning despite a wide range of inputs and application situations) and reproducibility (same behavior under the same conditions) (Guideline 70)
Protection of privacy and data quality *Damage prevention*	▪ Protect personal data and private information at all stages of the life cycle and not use it unlawfully or in a discriminatory manner (Guideline 72) ▪ Data sets must be of high quality even before AI systems are trained to avoid deficiencies, biases, errors and inaccuracies, and the input of harmful data that would compromise the integrity of the system must be ensured; data sets and processes to ensure the quality and integrity of data should be tested and documented at all stages of the life cycle (Guideline 73) ▪ Establish appropriate protocols to ensure that only appropriately qualified personnel can access personal data under the necessary circumstances (Guideline 74)
Transparency *Explainability*	▪ Make data records, processes and results of the AI system traceable through documentation (Guideline 76) ▪ Communicate results that affect people's lives to those affected in a timely and needs-based manner (Guideline 77) ▪ Inform people about the interaction with an AI system and its capabilities and limitations in line with their needs and offer them the opportunity to interact with a human being in the event of potential impacts on fundamental rights (Guideline 78)

Table 9.2 Requirements for Trustworthy AI *(continued)*

Core Requirements *Reference to Principles*	Description
Diversity, non-discrimination and fairness *Fairness*	▪ Avoid distortions both in the function of the AI system and by exploiting the distortions of users and stakeholders (e. g. unfair competition) and counteract existing distortions during development and through appropriate supervisory processes and diversity of staff ▪ Make AI systems usable and accessible for all people, regardless of their personal characteristics or abilities, with the help of universal design or design for all (Guideline 81) ▪ Involve stakeholders and employees in development and during the use phase (Guideline 82)
Social and environmental well-being *Fairness and damage prevention*	▪ Evaluate and minimize environmental impacts during all phases of the life cycle and throughout the supply chain (Guideline 84) ▪ Consider the effects on social relationships and bonds and maintain social agency (Guideline 85) ▪ Assess impacts on democracy, society and institutions and avoid negative impacts (Guideline 86)
Accountability *Fairness*	▪ Ensure verifiability through the assessment of internal and external auditors, the latter especially for applications with an impact on fundamental rights and for safety-critical applications (Guideline 88) ▪ Identify, assess, minimize and report negative impacts, enable incident reporting and conduct life cycle impact assessments (Guideline 89) ▪ Identify interests and values and make compromises taking into account ethical principles and fundamental rights or – if compromises are not possible – develop, introduce or use AI systems differently; justify all compromises, document them, continuously review their appropriateness and obtain changes if necessary (Guideline 90) ▪ Make provisions for adequate legal protection, paying particular attention to vulnerable persons and groups (Guideline 91)

9.1.4 Methods for Implementing the Core Requirements

The ethical requirements can be implemented using technical or non-technical methods that are used throughout the entire life cycle.

The technical processes include methods that are already known from other areas of software development as well as methods that are the subject of intensive research.

Table 9.3 Technical Methods for the Implementation of Ethical Requirements for AI

Technical Procedures	Examples
Creating architectures for trustworthy AI	▪ Definition of desirable (White List) and undesirable (Black List) behavior or conditions as well as appropriate restrictions (Guideline 95) ▪ Sense-Plan-Act cycles that ensure that the AI system recognizes all environmental elements necessary to meet the requirements (sense), executes only plans that meet the requirements (plan), and executes only actions that realize those requirements (act) (Guideline 96)
Integrating ethics and the rule of law into design (Ethics by Design)	Integrate approaches such as privacy-by-design, security-by-design and similar principles during development (Guideline 98)
Realizing explanatory methods	Approaches such as explainable AI (xAI) (Guideline 99)
Test and check	▪ Non-deterministic and context-specific properties of AI systems during testing for stability, robustness and functionality under defined conditions in order to validate the results of the system and the underlying process (Guideline 100) ▪ Throughout the entire lifecycle and as early as possible, AI systems should be tested holistically, including all components and in all environments, with diversity of testing teams and external testing options such as Red Teams or bug bounties create broader reliability (Guideline 101)
Quality of service parameters develop	Develop quality of service indicators that can be used to evaluate outcomes and training of the AI system, including traditional software metrics such as functionality, performance, usability, reliability, security and maintenance (Guideline 102)

The non-technical methods that can be used to comply with the requirements include a range of measures that can be used by organizations independently or require the cooperation of broader social institutions.

Organizations can ensure that both external and internal codes of conduct are developed and implemented, as well as drive the implementation of accountability as the basis for internal and external frameworks for the governance and control of AI systems (including appropriate oversight processes, compliance checks and sharing of best practices). This also includes ensuring diversity and inclusion in the teams that develop, implement, deploy, test, maintain, deploy and monitor AI systems and the involvement of a broad and diverse range of stakeholders in these processes.

While other measures can support individual organizations, they require broader institutional involvement. These include regulation (including legislation), standardization (including official standards, sector-specific norms or quality labels), education and development of AI skills as well as the involvement of stakeholders and the promotion of social dialogue.

9.1.5 Tools for Implementation

To accompany the ethics guidelines, the High-Level Expert Group has developed a rating list for trustworthy AI (Assessment List for Trustworthy AI or ALTAI). Following a pilot phase in 2019, the first final version of the assessment list was published as a PDF and as a web-based tool in June 2020 [8]. This assessment list contains questions on the individual core requirements, which are intended to serve as inspiration for stakeholders involved in different phases of the life cycle of AI systems.

As emphasized by the members of the High-Level Expert Group on AI, ethics should be designed to be as practical as possible. For this reason, it is not surprising that many ethics guidelines have since been developed for specific contexts. These include, for example, the Digital Administration and Ethics: Practical Guidelines for AI in Administration (Version 1.0) [5], which were developed by experts from the Austrian Institute of Technology (AIT) for the Federal Ministry of Arts, Culture, Civil Service and Sport (BMKÖS). For the ethical development and use of AI systems in research and science, a guideline was developed as part of Horizon 2020 funding to support applicants in dealing with ethical criteria and demonstrating compliance (Ethics by Design and Ethics of Use Approaches for Artificial Intelligence) [6]. The ETAPAS consortium's toolkit (Ethical Technology Adoption in Public Administration Services) [7], which can be used to support the use of disruptive technologies (including AI), is also intended for public administration.

To support the implementation of ethical principles, the AI Ethics Impact Group, led by the Association for Electrical, Electronic & Information Technologies (VDE) and the Bertelsmann Stiftung, has developed a framework for their assessment (From principles to practice: How can we make AI ethics measurable?) [4]. This presents a method for assessing ethical aspects and also a risk matrix for classifying applications. In 2021, Fraunhofer IAIS developed a guideline for the design of trustworthy artificial intelligence (AI testing catalog) [23], which contains the dimensions of fairness, autonomy and control, transparency, reliability, security and data protection as well as a cross-dimensional assessment.

Beyond Europe, there are also efforts to develop ethical guidelines. The UNESCO Recommendation on the Ethics of Artificial Intelligence [26], which was adopted in 2021, identifies the following core values: respect for, protection and promotion of human rights, fundamental freedoms and human dignity; environmental and ecosystem thriving; diversity and inclusivity; and living in peaceful, just and interconnected societies. Based on this, principles were formulated which should be observed by AI systems: Proportionality and harmlessness; Protection and safety; Fairness and non-discrimination; Sustainability; Right to privacy and data protection; Human oversight and control; Transparency and explainability; Responsibility and accountability; Awareness and training; and Multi-stakeholder and adaptive governance and collaboration. Although not identical to the European Ethics Guidelines, similar topics are covered. This points to the global importance of dealing with ethical issues, which, however, can only find answers on a situational and local basis. Many other ethical guidelines can be found, for example, in the AI Ethics Guidelines Global Inventory from AlgorithmWatch.[3]

Sources

[1] Adensamer, Angelika; Gsenger, Rita; Klausner, Lukas Daniel: "Computer says no": Algorithmic decision support and organisational responsibility. In: Journal of Responsible Technology Volume 7–8 (2021), Article 100014

[2] Advancing accountability in AI: Governing and managing risks throughout the lifecycle for trustworthy AI, OECD Digital Economy Papers (OECD Digital Economy Papers no. 349). Volume 349, 2023

[3] Arnold, Zachary; Toner, Helen: AI Accidents: An Emerging Threat. What Could Happen and What to Do (CSET Policy Brief): Center for Security and Emerging Technology – Georgetown University, 2021

[4] Bertelsmann Stiftung; VDE: From Principles to Practice: An interdisciplinary framework to operationalise AI ethics [object Object] (2020)

[5] Biegelbauer, Peter; Lackinger, Caroline; Schlarb, Sven; Subak, Edgar; Weinlinger, Pia: Leitfaden Digitale Verwaltung und Ethik: Praxisleitfaden für KI in der Verwaltung, Version 1.0. Wien: Bundesministerium für Kunst, Kultur, öffentlichen Dienst und Sport (BMKÖS) Sektion III – Öffentlicher Dienst und Verwaltungsinnovation, 2023

[6] Dainow, Brandt; Brey, Philip; Kuyumdzhieva, A. (Hrsg.): Ethics By Design and Ethics of Use Approaches for Artificial Intelligence. Brussels: European Commission, 2021

[7] ETAPAS Consortium: ETAPAS toolkit. URL *https://joinup.ec.europa.eu/collection/govtechconnect/solution/etapas?f%5B0%5D=solution_content_bundle%3Adocument* – accessed: 2024/03/17

[8] European Commission. Directorate General for Communications Networks, Content and Technology.: The Assessment List for Trustworthy Artificial Intelligence (ALTAI) for self assessment. LU: Publications Office, 2020

---

³ *https://inventory.algorithmwatch.org/*

[9] Gebru, Timnit; Morgenstern, Jamie; Vecchione, Briana; Vaughan, Jennifer Wortman; Wallach, Hanna; Daumé III, Hal; Crawford, Kate: Datasheets for Datasets, arXiv (2021) – arXiv:1803.09010 [cs]

[10] Green, Ben: The Flaws of Policies Requiring Human Oversight of Government Algorithms. In: SSRN Electronic Journal (2021)

[11] High-Level Expert Group on Artificial Intelligence: Ethics Guidelines for Trustworthy AI. Brussels: European Commission, 2019

[12] Kaminski, Margot E; Malgieri, Gianclaudio: Algorithmic impact assessments under the GDPR: producing multi-layered explanations. In: International Data Privacy Law Volume 11 (2021), no. 2, pp. 125–144

[13] Laux, Johann: Institutionalised Distrust and Human Oversight of Artificial Intelligence: Toward a Democratic Design of AI Governance under the European Union AI Act. In: SSRN Electronic Journal (2023)

[14] Mäntymäki, Matti; Minkkinen, Matti; Birkstedt, Teemu; Viljanen, Mika: Defining organizational AI governance. In: AI and Ethics Volume 2 (2022), no. 4, pp. 603–609

[15] Minkkinen, Matti; Mäntymäki, Matti: Discerning Between the "Easy" and "Hard" Problems of AI Governance. In: IEEE Transactions on Technology and Society Volume 4 (2023), no. 2, p. 188–194

[16] Mishra, Saurabh; Aria, Amin; Renda, Andrea: Ensuring AI's trustworthiness: reliability engineering meets data-driven risk management. URL *https://oecd.ai/en/wonk/reliability-engineering-data-driven-risk-management* – accessed: 2024/03/17

[17] Mitchell, Margaret; Wu, Simone; Zaldivar, Andrew; Barnes, Parker; Vasserman, Lucy; Hutchinson, Ben; Spitzer, Elena; Raji, Inioluwa Deborah; u. a.: Model Cards for Model Reporting. In: Proceedings of the Conference on Fairness, Accountability, and Transparency, 2019 – arXiv:1810.03993 [cs], pp. 220–229

[18] Morgan, Deborah; Hashem, Youmna; Straub, Vincent J.; Bright, Jonathan: "Team-in-the-loop" organisational oversight of high-stakes AI, arXiv (2023) – arXiv:2303.14007 [cs]

[19] Nicholson Consulting; Ministry of Social Development: Governance Guide: Model Development Lifecycle (no. A13094818), 2021

[20] OECD: OECD Due Diligence Guidance for Responsible Business Conduct, 2018

[21] Park, Tina M.: Making AI Inclusive: 4 Guiding Principles for Ethical Engagement (White Paper): Partnership on AI, 2022

[22] Perrow, Charles: Normal Accidents: Living with High Risk Technologies. Princeton: Princeton University Press, 2011 – ISBN 978-1-4008-2849-4

[23] Poretschkin, Maximilian; Schmitz, Anna; Akila, Mara; Adilova, Mara; Becker, Daniel; Cremers, Armin B.; Hecker, Dirk; Houben, Sebastian; u. a.: Leitfaden zur Gestaltung vertrauenswürdiger Künstlicher Intelligenz: Fraunhofer-Institut für Intelligente Analyse- und Informationssysteme IAIS, 2021

[24] Society Inside; European Center for Not-for-Profit Law: Framework for meaningful engagement: ECNL

[25] Stocktaking for the development of an AI incident definition, OECD Artificial Intelligence Papers (OECD Artificial Intelligence Papers no. 4). Volume 4, 2023

[26] UNESCO: Recommendation on the Ethics of Artificial Intelligence. Paris: UNESCO, 2021

[27] UNESCO: Ethical impact assessment. A tool of the Recommendation on the Ethics of Artificial Intelligence: UNESCO, 2023

9.2 Relevant AI Guidelines & Policies

Gabriele Bolek-Fügl

There are a large number of ethical guidelines for artificial intelligence around the world. These include not only national frameworks for individual countries, but also specially developed guidelines from interest groups, non-governmental organizations (NGOs) and private companies, all of which aim to ensure the safe use and development of AI technologies.

The challenge is therefore not a lack of theoretical descriptions or guidelines on AI ethics, but rather the practical implementation in day-to-day work and in projects.

This section is dedicated to presenting some of the most important and widely recognized AI ethics guidelines. Particular attention has been paid to those guidelines that have both global relevance and have been issued by organizations that are leaders in AI research and application. Some also provide information, resources and tools to implement AI with confidence.

9.2.1 OECD Council Recommendation on Artificial Intelligence

Designation

OECD/LEGAL/0449 Recommendation of the Council on Artificial Intelligence

(References in this subsection refer to this recommendation).

Publisher

Organization: OECD Digital Economy Committee (Organization for Economic Co-operation and Development)

Authority and influence: The OECD has no direct legislative power over its members (38 countries). Instead, its authority and influence are based on its ability to collect and analyze data, make independent policy recommendations and provide a framework for dialogue and cooperation between countries. The OECD publishes a variety of reports that provide insights into best practices and recommendations. However, implementation is always voluntary.

Target group

Addressees: Members (38 countries) and non-members as well as AI stakeholders who play an active role in the life cycle of an AI system, including organizations and individuals who use or operate AI (Chapters I and II of the Recommendation).

Area of application: The recommendations are cross-sectoral.

> **Why is this Guideline Important for our AI?**
> On its online platforms, the OECD provides relevant information on the use of AI in its member countries and for non-members and shares best practices.

Contents

Ethical principles The first section sets out five principles that are relevant to all stakeholders in the use of AI. In line with these, the second section contains five recommendations for members and non-members who have signed up to the draft recommendation to implement them in their national and international policies.

1. Principles for the responsible use of trustworthy AI:

    I. inclusive growth, sustainable development and well-being

        AI should benefit people and the planet by promoting inclusive growth, sustainable development, nature conservation and quality of life (Section 1.1).

    II. People-centered values and fairness

        Throughout the lifecycle of an AI system, the fundamental principles of the rule of law, human rights and democratic values should be respected and appropriate safeguards, commensurate with technological progress, should be implemented to ensure freedom, justice and human autonomy. This may include the possibility of human intervention where necessary. The goal is a fair and just society (Section 1.2).

    III. Transparency and explainability

        AI systems should ensure transparency and disclosure so that people can understand and challenge AI-based outcomes, as well as give people negatively assessed by an AI system the opportunity to challenge that decision (Section 1.3).

    IV. Robustness, safety and protection

        AI systems must function robustly and safely over their entire life cycle. Potential risks should be continuously assessed and monitored by AI stakeholders (Section 1.4).

    V. Accountability

        AI operators should be responsible for the proper functioning of AI systems and for compliance with the aforementioned principles, based on their roles, the context and in line with the state of the art (Section 1.5).

2. Recommendations for national guidelines and international cooperation for trustworthy AI:

    I. Investments in AI research and development

        Facilitate public and private investment in research and development of AI systems and open datasets to foster innovation in trustworthy AI (Section 2.1)

    II. Promotion of a digital ecosystem for AI

        Such an ecosystem includes, in particular, digital technologies and infrastructure and, where appropriate, mechanisms for sharing AI knowledge and data (Section 2.2).

III. Shaping a conducive political environment for AI

Governments should foster a policy environment that supports an agile transition from the research and development phase to the deployment and operational phase for trustworthy AI systems (Section 2.3).

IV. Building human capacity and preparing for the transformation of the labor market

Governments should work closely with stakeholders to prepare for the transformation of the world of work and society. They should enable people to use AI systems effectively in all application areas and distribute the benefits of AI widely and fairly (Section 2.4).

V. International cooperation for trustworthy AI

Governments should work together to promote the exchange of AI knowledge and international, cross-sectoral and open multi-stakeholder initiatives (Section 2.5).

Definition of AI: An AI system is a machine-based system that derives how to generate outputs such as predictions, content, recommendations or decisions for explicit or implicit goals from the inputs it receives, which can influence physical or virtual environments. Different AI systems differ in their degree of autonomy and adaptability after deployment (Chapter I).

Areas of application: No restriction to specific AI applications or technologies

Instructions for action: Recommendations are aimed at countries and stakeholders (organizations and individuals) that are directly or indirectly involved in or affected by AI systems (Chapter I).

Validity and topicality

Publication date: current version dated August 11, 2023 (adaptation of the original version dated May 22, 2019)

Published under: Legal instruments of the OECD *https://legalinstruments.oecd.org/en/instruments/OECD-LEGAL-0449*

Implementation and monitoring

Implementation mechanisms: Member States agree to a recommendation document on a voluntary basis and with the intention to consider or implement the principles or measures contained therein at national level, at their own pace and according to their own procedures.

Monitoring and evaluation: The OECD will support the implementation of the Principles by providing data and guidance on metrics, policies and practices in the field of AI and will be a center for dialogue and exchange of best practices for AI policies. Results can be found at *https://oecd.ai/* or *https://goingdigital.oecd.org/* respectively.

Legal and regulatory integration

Legal status: Member countries agree to a recommendation document on a voluntary basis. The OECD's strength lies in its ability to influence the policy-making of its member countries through research, analysis and the exchange of best practices.

Integration into existing laws: The recommendations reflect common goals and agreed standards among members and can be considered or implemented in national laws or measures.

Global applicability: The recommendations have an international impact.

9.2.2 The Executive Order on the Safe, Secure, and Trustworthy Development and Use of Artificial Intelligence

Designation

Executive Order 14110 on the Safe, Secure, and Trustworthy Development and Use of Artificial Intelligence

(References in this subsection refer to the Executive Order.)

Publisher

Organization: Executive Office of the President of the United States of America

Authority and Influence: An Executive Order directly reflects the President's authority over the executive branch and is binding on all administration officials in the interpretation of laws.

Target group

Addressees: The Executive Order applies primarily to the federal authorities with spillover effects on private companies in numerous sectors.

Scope of application: An executive order does not replace a law, but is based on the discretionary powers granted by US federal law. However, it contains specific mandates for various agencies, e. g. "to train the federal workforce on AI issues, the head of each agency shall establish or increase the availability and use of AI training and familiarization programs for employees, managers, and executives (Sec 10.2 (g))".

Why is this Guideline Important for our AI?

The Executive Order provides specific information on the (future) use of AI in the USA.

Contents

Ethical principles According to Sec 2, the development and use of AI should be driven and managed according to eight guiding principles and priorities:

1. AI must be safe and secure. Achieving this goal requires robust, reliable, repeatable and standardized assessments of AI systems as well as policies, institutions and other mechanisms as appropriate (Sec 2 (a)).

2. Promote responsible innovation, competition and collaboration, including investment in AI-related education, training, development, research and capacity. At the same time, clarify intellectual property (IP) issues to protect inventors and creators. In addition, promote a fair, open and competitive ecosystem and marketplace for AI and related technologies (Sec 2 (b)).

3. Supporting American workers. This requires adapting job training and education to facilitate access to the opportunities created by AI for a diverse workforce. In the workplace itself, AI should not be used in a way that undermines rights, degrades job quality, creates inappropriate monitoring of employees, reduces competition in the marketplace, introduces new health and safety risks or causes harmful disruption in the workplace (Sec 2 (c)).

4. Promoting justice and civil rights to limit the irresponsible use of AI systems that reproduce existing inequalities and new types of harmful discrimination and exacerbates online and physical harm (Sec 2 (d)).

5. Protect consumers, patients, passengers and students by improving existing consumer protection laws and putting in place appropriate safeguards against fraud, unintentional bias, discrimination, privacy violations and other harms caused by AI (Sec 2 (e)).

6. Improve privacy protection to make the collection, use and storage of data lawful and secure and minimize risks to data protection and confidentiality (Sec 2 (f)).

7. Promote the use of AI by the federal government. All federal employees should receive appropriate training to understand the benefits, risks and limitations of AI for their job functions and to modernize the federal government's IT infrastructure, remove bureaucratic barriers and ensure that safe and rights-respecting AI is deployed and used (Sec 2 (g)).

8. Strengthen U. S. leadership abroad, including pioneering the systems and security measures necessary for responsible use of this technology (Sec 2 (h)).

Definition of AI The term "artificial intelligence" refers to a machine-based system that is capable of making predictions, recommendations or decisions that affect real-world or virtual environments for a given set of human-defined goals. Artificial intelligence systems use machine and human input to (A) perceive real-world and virtual environments, (B) abstract these perceptions into models through analysis in an automated manner, and (C) formulate information or action options through model inference (Sec 3 (b) and 15 USC 9401(3) [1]).

Areas of application: No restriction to specific AI applications or technologies.

Instructions for action: The executive order contains specific instructions for action, including a timetable and the authority responsible for implementation.

Validity and topicality

Publication date: Executive Order signed on October 30, 2023, published on November 1, 2023

Published: Federal Register under *https://www.federalregister.gov/documents/2023/11/01/2023-24283/safe-secure-and-trustworthy-development-and-use-of-artificial-intelligence*

Implementation and monitoring

Implementation mechanisms: An executive order applies directly to all civil servants.

Monitoring and Evaluation: The White House AI Council is established within the Executive Office of the President. It coordinates the activities of federal government agencies to ensure effective development, communication, and industry involvement in AI activities (Sec 12).

Legal and regulatory integration

Legal status: supplements existing US laws (discretionary powers) and mandates various agencies to hire and develop IT talent and integrate (generative) AI systems into daily work processes.

Integration into existing laws: Specifications for the discretionary scope of laws, but in accordance with applicable law and subject to the availability of funds (Sec 13).

Global Applicability: Executive Orders are primarily applicable nationally in the U.S., however Sec 11 mandates "strengthening U.S. leadership abroad" with several activities to be implemented such as:

- Expand cooperation with international allies and partners in relevant bilateral, multilateral and multi-stakeholder forums
- create a strong international framework for managing the risks and reaping the benefits of AI
- drive responsible global technical standards for AI development and use outside military and intelligence sectors, such as:
  - AI nomenclature and terminology
  - Best practices in terms of data collection, processing, protection, privacy, confidentiality, handling and analysis
  - Trustworthiness, verification and security of AI systems
  - AI risk management (based on the principles of the NIST AI 100-1 Risk Management Framework)

9.2.3 Compliance Tools for Many Occasions

There are many good reasons why supervision and risk management should be practiced with regard to AI systems. These good reasons include the AI Act, which will only actually affect very few applications, but mainly oversight and risk management simply facilitate good project management. Thinking about transparency and accountability from the beginning of an AI project is much easier than having to build them in after the fact.

The previous chapters have already explained how other areas of law borders on the AI Act. This section is dedicated to common tools that are used to support governance processes both in connection with the AI Act and with adjacent areas. The aim is not to provide an exhaustive list, as this list will expand rapidly in the coming months, but to provide initial points of contact and an overview of different ways.

Before we approach these tools, a few caveats are in order. There is currently no quality management for the creation or use of these tools, and, among other things, there is wide variation in the extent and quality of documentation and contextualization or testing of these tools. The Plan-Do-Check-Act cycle can be helpful in evaluating governance tools, which originates from ISO 9001:2015. The first step is to formulate the purpose for which the tool is being used and the objectives that the governance tool is intended to fulfill. The achievement of these objectives is then systematically tested and, based on the results of these tests, the purpose and objectives as well as the test process are evaluated. This process should then be incorporated into the documentation of the AI system and made available to deployers.

In any case, it is important to use the right tool for the right phase and, for example, to check fairness in connection with the development of an AI system, but also during ongoing operations. This also prevents risks associated with data drift.[4] or Model Drift[5] can arise. Technical tools should also be treated with caution, as evaluation methods, e. g. for explainability based on SHAP[6] or LIME[7] are found to be insufficient

---

[7] Data drift refers to a phenomenon in which the data set originally used to train an AI system is no longer relevant to events in the real world. This can happen, for example, if an AI system was trained to provide recommendations for drinks in summer and a data set was used for training for a period in which a soft drink with passion fruit was popular. Next year, however, a soft drink with mint is in vogue, which means that the data set used for training no longer reflects current preferences and the recommendations derived from it lose their validity.

[8] Model drift or concept drift refers to a phenomenon in which the framework conditions of the task that an AI system based on machine learning is supposed to perform change over time (or even suddenly). This can happen, for example, if a system was developed to predict long waiting times based on the number of visitors. If more rooms or more services are suddenly offered and these are not taken into account by the system, high waiting times will continue to be predicted for a high number of visitors, even though the actual waiting times remain stable or become shorter.

[9] SHAP (SHapley Additive exPlanations) refers to a game-theoretical approach for explaining the results of AI systems based on machine learning.

[10] LIME (Local Interpretable Model-agnostic Explanations) can provide explanations about the environment of results for models based on supervised machine learning.

or unreliable by academic experts. All governance processes and tools should be well documented so that, in the event of changes, it is possible to trace up to which point in time which methods were used.

Regular monitoring makes it easier to mitigate risks. On the one hand, this includes monitoring the performance(s) of the AI system in terms of ongoing quality assurance, but also the use of the AI system and its expenditure: Is there improper use of the AI system? Which governance measures work in practice and which do not? A core pillar of good governance remains the pursuit of understanding how well the tools that are used actually work.

Comprehensive Approaches

The first comprehensive approach to meeting the requirements of the AI Act comes from a Finnish consortium of academics and companies. The governance checklist of the AI Governance and Auditing project[8] covers essential requirements for documents and processes. Another tool is, for example, the Responsible AI Framework of the Responsible AI Lab[9] which can be used to identify initial risk points on the basis of a self-assessment.

Basic rights

Human rights and fundamental rights impact assessments are increasingly being requested by organizations, not least due to the new Corporate Sustainability Due Diligence Directive[10] which will contain requirements for the review of supply chains that could presumably also apply to companies in the AI sector. AI systems developed or deployed by organizations are no different in this context than other products, ingredients or relationships if they are part of the company's value chain.

A number of useful guidelines already exist to facilitate impact assessments for fundamental rights. These include, for example, the UNESCO Guide for the Implementation of Ethical Principles in the Context of AI Systems [27]. The Danish Human Rights Institute has developed one of the most comprehensive guides for conducting AI impact assessments, while also providing a step-by-step guide through the process.[11] Impact assessments for fundamental rights are usually also a core element of ethical guidelines, which are discussed in section 9.1.

---

[11] *https://ai-governance.eu/ or https://ai-governance.eu/ai-governance-framework/task-list/*

[12] *https://facets.netlify.app/*

[13] *https://commission.europa.eu/business-economy-euro/doing-business-eu/corporate-sustainability-due-diligence_en*

[14] *https://www.humanrights.dk/tools/human-rights-impact-assessment-guidance-toolbox*

Data Protection

There are already a number of helpful tools in connection with data protection. We recommend, for example, the how-to sheets[12] from the French data protection authority CNIL. These guides help organizations to identify the legal basis and purpose of data processing and to clarify the legal status of providers of AI systems. The CNIL also provides guidance on data protection impact assessments, which are required for all AI systems that process personal data.

There is also an attempt to use the data protection impact assessment to carry out algorithmic impact assessments. The aim is to create multi-layered explanations that, on the one hand, provide an explanation of the system as a whole and, on the other, make it possible to derive the algorithmic decision in each specific case. Margot Kaminski and Gianclaudio Malgieri propose specific elements for this [12]. It should be noted that the AI Act also requires multi-layered explanations, as Art. 86 AI Act insists that data subjects receive explanations on the role of the high-risk AI system in decision-making and on the most important elements for the results of high-risk AI systems from Annex III AI Act (with the exception of AI systems in critical infrastructures).

Environment and sustainability

As in the context of fundamental rights, the upcoming Corporate Sustainability Due Diligence Directive requires an increased focus on sustainability and supply chains, which will also be relevant for AI systems.[13] There are already a number of tools that can be useful for determining and monitoring environmental aspects, such as the Machine Learning CO_2 Impact Calculator[14], the CO_2 Sustainability Calculator[15] or the Carbon Intensity Specification software.[16] However, these tools currently focus on the carbon footprint of AI systems and at best translate other impacts (such as resource consumption) into carbon equivalents. Further tools will be needed to better understand water consumption, raw material consumption, waste and similar environmental impacts. In addition, many of these tools are designed for developers and are therefore not suitable for organizations elsewhere in the value chain, making reporting more difficult for deployers.

---

[15] *https://www.cnil.fr/en/ai-ensuring-gdpr-compliance* and *https://www.cnil.fr/en/self-assessment-guide-artificial-intelligence-ai-systems*

[16] *https://commission.europa.eu/business-economy-euro/doing-business-eu/corporate-sustainability-due-diligence_en*

[17] *https://mlco2.github.io/impact/*

[18] *https://carboncalculator.ldco.ai/home*

[19] *https://github.com/Green-Software-Foundation/sci/blob/main/Software_Carbon_Intensity/Software_Carbon_Intensity_Specification.md*

Model Cards and Data Sheets

Model cards and data sheets are among the best-known tools for creating transparency regarding the capabilities, structure and inputs of AI systems. Model maps were first proposed by Margaret Mitchell and other researchers in an academic article published in 2018 [17]. When creating model maps, the Hugging Face template can provide inspiration[17] which also includes instructions on how to create them.

Datasheets for datasets are also based on an academic article published by Timnit Gebru and other researchers in 2018 [9]. In contrast to model maps, datasheets only refer to the datasets and are therefore well suited for fulfilling dataset documentation requirements.

Risk Management

The first standardized approach to AI-related risks can be found in ISO/IEC 23894:2023[18] where recommendations for dealing with AI-specific risks and possible risk management processes have been developed. The ISO 31000 series on risk management and ISO/IEC 31010:2019 in particular can also be adapted for the use of AI systems. The AI Risk Management Framework of the US National Institute of Standards and Technology is also widely used.[19]

Involving Stakeholders

As already mentioned several times, in some cases it can be useful to involve external stakeholders in the development and oversight of AI systems. To facilitate these processes, the European Center for Not-for-Profit Law, together with Society Inside, has developed a framework for participatory processes [24]. This framework builds on three elements – a common purpose, a trusted process and visible change as a result of engagement – and includes methodologies for successful engagement.

9.2.4 Artificial Intelligence Risk Management Framework

Designation

Artificial Intelligence Risk Management Framework (AI RMF 1.0 or NIST AI 100-1) (References in this subsection refer to this framework).

---

[20] *https://huggingface.co/docs/hub/model-cards*

[21] *https://www.iso.org/standard/77304.html*

[22] *https://oecd.ai/en/catalogue/tools/artificial-intelligence-risk-management-framework-(ai-rmf-1.0)* and *https://oecd.ai/en/catalogue/tools/nist-ai-rmf-playbook*

Publisher

Organisation: National Institute of Standards and Technology (NIST)

Authority and Influence: NIST is an agency of the U. S. Department of Commerce and plays a central role nationally and internationally in the development of standards, measurements and technologies aimed at promoting business competitiveness, improving innovation and enhancing the quality of life.

Target group

Addressees: The framework is aimed at organizations and individuals who design, develop and operate AI systems (Executive Summary NIST AI 100-1). The description is aimed equally at managers, AI experts, AI users and other interested parties.

Area of application: Support for the implementation and operation of risk management for AI applications (see also section 10.2).

> **Why is this Guideline Important for our AI?**
> NIST AI 100-1 provides guidance for implementing AI-related risk management in organizations during the development and operation of AI systems.

Contents

Ethical principles: According to Chapter 3, several criteria must be met for a trustworthy AI system. The characteristics of trustworthy AI systems include

1. Valid and Reliable

   The validity and reliability of AI systems is often ensured through continuous testing and monitoring to confirm their correct functioning. Measuring validity, accuracy, robustness and reliability contributes to trustworthiness. AI risk management should prioritize minimizing potential negative impacts and may include human intervention in cases where the AI system cannot detect or correct errors (Section 3.1).

2. Safe

   The integration of safety measures throughout a system's lifecycle, starting at the earliest stages of planning and design, is critical to avoid potential failures or dangerous conditions. Effective AI safety strategies often include comprehensive simulations, in-application testing, continuous real-time monitoring, and the ability to safely shut down, adapt or enable human intervention in the event of deviations from their intended functionality (Section 3.2).

3. Secure and Resilient

   AI systems that can maintain confidentiality, integrity and availability through protective mechanisms that prevent unauthorized access and use can be described as secure (Section 3.3).

4. Accountable and Transparent

   Transparency refers to how accessible information about an AI system and its out-comes is to the people interacting with that system, even if they are not aware of the AI system's existence. Accountability means that AI developers and deployers must proactively adapt their transparency and accountability measures, espe-cially in high-risk contexts, to mitigate risk (Section 3.4).

5. Explainable and Interpretable

   Transparency, explainability and interpretability support each other. Transpar-ency can answer the question of "what happens in the system". Explainability an-swers "how" a decision was made in the system. Interpretability answers "why" a decision was made by the system and what meaning or context it has for the user (Section 3.5).

6. Privacy-enhanced

   Privacy values such as anonymity, confidentiality and control should generally guide decisions for the design, development and deployment of AI systems. Pri-vacy-related risks can influence security, bias and transparency and come with trade-offs to the other characteristics (Section 3.6).

7. Fair – with Harmful Bias Managed

   Fairness in AI encompasses a concern for equality and justice, addressing issues such as harmful bias and discrimination. Methods for fairness can be complex, as the perception of fairness varies from culture to culture and can also change de-pending on the AI application. A proactive approach is required (Section 3.7).

Definition of AI NIST AI 100-1 refers to an AI system as an engineered or machine-based system that can produce outcomes such as predictions, recommendations, or decisions that affect real-world or virtual environments for a specific set of goals. AI systems are designed to operate with varying degrees of autonomy (adapted from: OECD Recommendation on AI:2019; ISO/IEC 22989:2022).

Areas of application: No restriction to specific AI applications or technologies

Instructions for action: NIST AI 100-1 describes the procedure for identifying, avoid-ing or minimizing risks in relation to AI systems.

Validity and topicality

Publication date: January 2023

Published under: National Institute of Standards and Technology at *https://nvlpubs. nist.gov/nistpubs/ai/nist.ai.100-1.pdf*

Implementation and monitoring

Implementation mechanisms: Specifications by the NIST

Monitoring and evaluation: The description characterizes the framework as a "living document" that is continuously evaluated by NIST and adapted to changing require-ments and findings.

Legal and regulatory integration

Legal status: Organizations can implement the AI Risk Management Framework on a voluntary basis.

Integration into existing laws: NIST AI 100-1 is referenced in some requirements (e. g. laws, executive orders, invitation to bid or funding).

Global applicability: NIST AI 100-1 is primarily applicable nationally in the USA, but is also referenced internationally.

9.2.5 Further Formative Ethical Guidelines

It is not so easy to identify the "first" global AI ethics guideline, because the development of ethical AI guidelines has been an ongoing process, taking place simultaneously in different organizations and countries. Nevertheless, there are some early or influential documents that are considered pioneers in the AI ethics debate and are the basis for the development of subsequent guidelines.

The Montréal Declaration for a Responsible Development of Artificial Intelligence

On November 3, 2017, the Université de Montréal led the process to co-create the Montréal Declaration dedicated to the responsible development of artificial intelligence. Dozens of events aimed at an in-depth discussion of the societal challenges posed by AI. In addition, around 15 deliberative workshops were held, in which over 500 citizens, experts and stakeholders from various sectors of society took part. The following year, the results of this comprehensive citizen consultation were published under the name "Montreal Declaration for the Responsible Development of Artificial Intelligence" [2].

The declaration not only contains an explanation of ten principles on the ethical use of AI, but also recommendations on how to deal with the digital transformation. The principles include the demands for democratic participation, solidarity, well-being, protection of privacy, equality, diversity and inclusion.

The website also offers toolkits and best practices for different areas of AI use, describing tips and activities for concrete implementation in organizations, including those for the healthcare industry, municipalities and the financial sector.

The discussions are still ongoing and new information will be published successively on the website.

Ethically Aligned Design

One of the first comprehensive documents to deal with the ethical aspects of AI development is the "Ethically Aligned Design" guideline [3] of the IEEE Global Initiative on Ethics of Autonomous and Intelligent Systems, which was published in 2016. A second, adapted version is available.

This guide represents the Institute of Electrical and Electronics Engineers' (IEEE) vision that human well-being must be prioritized in autonomous and intelligent systems and combines scientific analysis with pragmatic, application-oriented recommendations. It serves as a key reference for technology, education and policy professionals and addresses the design of standards, certification regulations and legislation in this area.

The IEEE guideline covers a wide range of topics, including transparency, accountability and data protection, as well as respecting human rights and enhancing human well-being.

The Ethically Aligned Design guideline has also been the starting point for the creation of a number of standards (IEEE P7000™ series and beyond) and associated certification programs, among others:

- IEEE P7001™ – Transparency of Autonomous Systems
- IEEE P7002™ – Data Privacy Process
- IEEE P7003™ – Algorithmic Bias Considerations

Recommendation on the Ethics of Artificial Intelligence

When UNESCO member states adopted the "Recommendations on the Ethics of Artificial Intelligence" [4] in November 2021, it was an act of collective consent that shows that countries around the world recognize the importance of ethical considerations in dealing with AI. The UNESCO emphasized that these recommendations were unanimously adopted by all 193 member states. Countries such as the USA, China and Russia, major players in the field of AI technology, also agreed.

Before the UNESCO recommendations were adopted by consensus, this was preceded by a long process involving many hours of negotiation. Especially about human rights were the subject of particularly controversial negotiations, according to the minutes of the 41st UNESCO General Conference.

The UNESCO recommendations on the ethical use of AI systems cover eleven key policy areas, ranging from the impact on labor, health and education to previously neglected aspects such as the interests of the Global South, gender bias, discrimination and sustainability issues. This holistic approach provides a basis for countries worldwide to shape the diverse potential of AI development in an ethically responsible manner.

It is planned to evaluate the initial UNESCO recommendations at regular intervals and adapt them if necessary.

Sources

[1] Legal Information Institute, Cornell Law School, Definitions Artificial Intelligence, *https://www.law.cornell.edu/uscode/text/15/9401#3* – accessed: 2024/03/18

[2] Université de Montréal, *https://montrealdeclaration-responsibleai.com/* – accessed: 2024/03/10

[3] IEEE, *https://standards.ieee.org/industry-connections/ec/ead-v1/* – accessed: 2024/03/10

[4] General Conference of the United Nations Educational, Scientific and Cultural Organization (UNESCO), *Recommendation on the Ethics of Artificial Intelligence,* (2022), UNESCO, Paris

9.3 EU and Global Bodies, Boards and Committees

Gabriele Bolek-Fügl

The regulation and standardization of artificial intelligence is a global concern that is attracting the attention of many important bodies, working groups and authorities. The following organizations deal with the ethical, legal and technical aspects of AI development and application across countries.

Board	Tasks	Authority	Legal Status	Global Impact	Concrete Statement
High-Level Expert Group on AI (EU)	Recommendations on AI ethics, investment and research	European Commission	Advisory	High	AI ethics guidelines (see section 9.1)
European Artificial Intelligence Board	Monitoring AI regulation in EU member states	European Union	Regulating	High	AI Act
International Telecommunication Union (ITU)	Standards for AI in telecommunications	United Nations	Standardizing	High	AI standardization framework
UNESCO	Global standards for the ethics of AI	United Nations	Advisory	High	AI ethics recommendations
National Institute of Standards and Technology (NIST)	Standards and guidelines for AI technologies	USA	Standardizing	Medium	Trustworthy AI guidelines
White House Office of Science and Technology Policy (OSTP)	Coordination of AI research and policy	USA	Coordinating	High	US AI Initiatives

Board	Tasks	Authority	Legal Status	Global Impact	Concrete Statement
OECD	Principles for dealing with AI	International Organization	Advisory	High	AI principles
Global Partnership on Artificial Intelligence (GPAI)	Promotion of responsible AI development	Internationale Initiative	Promoting	High	Responsible AI development
Institute of Electrical and Electronics Engineers (IEEE)	Ethical standards and guidelines for AI technology	International professional organization	Standardizing	High	IEEE P7000 series
Partnership on AI	Promotion of best practices in AI development	Multi-Stakeholder-Organisation	Promoting	High	Best Practices in AI
World Economic Forum (WEF)	Working groups on AI and governance	International Organization	Promoting	High	AI und Governance

For the European Union, the High-Level Expert Group on Artificial Intelligence, set up by the European Commission, plays a central role in the formulation of ethical guidelines and recommendations for the development and application of AI. This group of proven experts from various fields – from academia to business and civil society – has made a decisive contribution to shaping the EU strategy for artificial intelligence. Its aim is to ensure that AI development and use within the EU is based on ethical principles in order to create trustworthy AI that serves the well-being of all citizens.

The IEEE Global Initiative on Ethics of Autonomous and Intelligent Systems is an ambitious effort to establish global standards for the ethical design and use of autonomous and intelligent systems. This initiative brings together experts in engineering, ethics, philosophy and policy to develop comprehensive guidelines to ensure that technologies such as AI and robotics contribute to the benefit of humanity. Through its work, in particular through the publication of the document "Ethically Aligned Design", the initiative has addressed fundamental ethical issues ranging from privacy and transparency to accountability and social justice. Its guidelines serve as the foundation for various certification programs as proof that an organization adheres to ethical guidelines.

The European Artificial Intelligence Board is a key component of the AI Act. This new body will play a central role in monitoring and ensuring the consistent application of

AI regulations in all Member States. By creating such a board, the EU aims to ensure a high level of protection for citizens and consumers, while providing an innovation-friendly framework that positions Europe at the forefront of responsible AI development and use.

9.4 From Digital Humanism to a Value-based AI System

Sabine Singer

The rapid development of generative AI presents us with one of the greatest challenges of our time and at the same time offers unprecedented opportunities. Applications like ChatGPT, Dall-E and Sora impressively demonstrate the disruptive potential of this new generation of AI systems. It is foreseeable that generative AI will fundamentally change almost all industries and business areas in the coming years. This will also be accompanied by social upheaval.

The first generation of algorithmically controlled digital applications have made this very clear. Social media, the most prominent digital service, provides a vivid example of the negative ethical impact AI-driven services can have. From the manipulation of decisions, the influencing of democratic processes and interference in elections and opinion-forming, to the spread of deepfakes and overbearing technological paternalism – digital services that are misused and controlled unilaterally curtail the autonomy and credibility of media, companies and public bodies.

The challenges and risks on the path to digital excellence are manifold and can hardly be predicted using traditional IT design methods. These risks are now being exponentially amplified with the brilliant emergence of generative AI systems on the world stage. This new technology carries the risk of scaling biases in unprecedented ways. AI-generated content is already almost indistinguishable from authentic content. Realistic images, videos and texts present unprecedented opportunities to manipulate facts and perceptions – generated by simple voice commands, without technical knowledge or complex IT systems. Numerous lawsuits for violation of data protection rights and unlawful use of intellectual property for the training of large language models are the first consequences.

To avoid data misuse corporate GPTs and to make consciously transparent decisions about the design of AI applications, it is essential to apply new strategy methods that recognize unwanted ethical risks at an early stage and implement them in the system design in good time.

It is crucial for companies and decision-makers to face up to these challenges, and not just in light of the AI Act. The aim must be to develop systems that identify the impairment of ethical values in good time and thus actively promote conscious control of the development of AI-supported applications.

Digital Humanism

Digital humanism is a manifesto and committment that places people and their environment at the center of technology. In contrast to transhumanists, who strive for a fusion of humans and technology, digital humanism emphasizes that technology respects and supports human values. This philosophy forms an initial basis for the development of ethically responsible AI systems.

The AI Act

The AI Act will be the first law that places human values firmly in the foreground and provides legal protection in the development and use of AI systems. It aims to create a binding legal framework that ensures that AI systems protect the fundamental rights, freedoms and democratic rights of people and society. In doing so, it translates the principles of digital humanism into applicable law.

9.4.1　Value-based Engineering

Method for value-based AI system design

From the idea of digital humanism, a methodology was developed at WU Vienna (University of Economics), led by Prof. Dr. Sarah Spiekermann, which makes it possible to translate values into concrete requirements for IT and AI systems. Value-based engineering (VbE) is THE strategic thinking method of the 21st century. VbE follows a structured approach that takes human values into account in the IT design process. Using a set of philosophical questions, ethical considerations can be systematically integrated into the development of AI systems. Based on this ethical value analysis, expectations of the functions of the AI system are evaluated and it is anticipated how and which human values could be negatively influenced by its use. Value-based engineering thus forms the bridge between ethical guidelines, legal requirements, corporate objectives and pragmatic, concrete system requirements. The methodology enables risks to be identified at an early stage, addressed and mitigated in good time.

Independent Trailblazer for a Successful Audit

Value-based engineering and other standards such as ISO 42001 for AI management systems complement each other perfectly: the value-based engineering method is used to systematically develop a value-based AI system design that not only meets the requirements of ISO 42001 for AI management systems, but also targets the currently planned criteria and legal regulations of the AI Act. Organizations are thus prepared for planned or mandatory audits and create comprehensible transparency for all relevant stakeholders.

> **Excursus: ISO 42001 – a Guide for the Considered Use of AI Management Systems**
>
> ISO 42001 is a guideline for the introduction, use and development of AI management systems. It sets requirements for the establishment, implementation, maintenance and continual improvement of an AI management system within an organization. The standard aims to support organizations in fulfilling their role in relation to AI systems in a responsible manner.

In summary, the idea of digital humanism, the legal requirement of the AI Act, value-based engineering as a strategic thought process and ISO 42001 as a guideline form a strong foundation for the responsible development and use of AI. They complement each other and show a clear way in which we can make sensible use of the opportunities offered by AI without jeopardizing values and rights. Value-based engineering is the method of choice for putting these principles into practice and designing AI systems that put people at the center. It is now up to all of us – companies, politicians, scientists and society – to consistently pursue this approach and work together to develop human-centered, trustworthy AI.

Value-based Engineering – an Overview of the Process

Flowchart of the value-based engineering process according to ISO 24748:IEEE7000, which describes the steps from context analysis to system development.

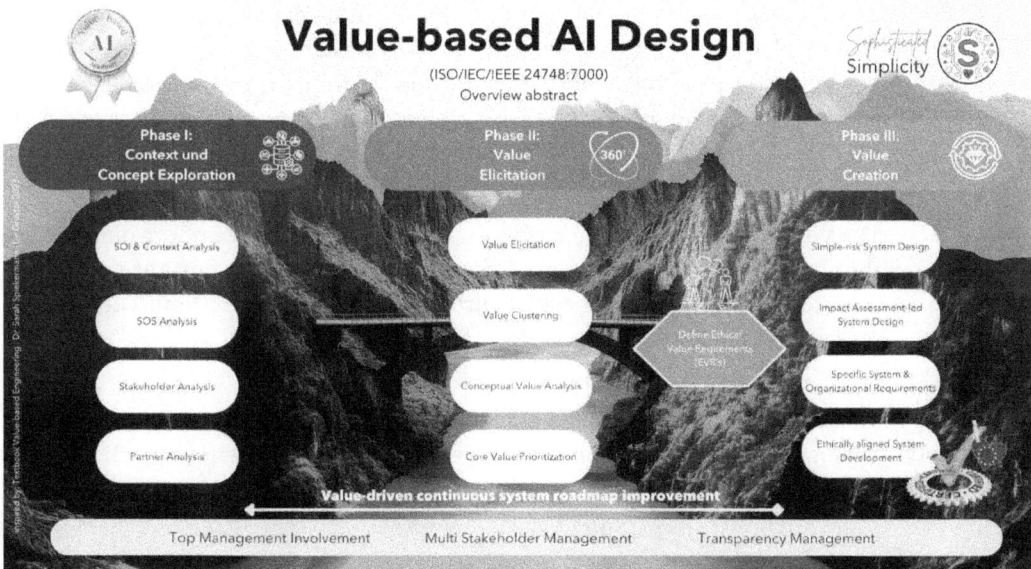

Figure 9.2 Value-based Engineering Process According to ISO 24748:IEEE7000 (Source: Textbook Value-based Engineering, Dr. Sarah Spiekermann, WU Vienna; Verlag DeGruyter 2023; own illustration by Sophisticated Simplicity)

Phases of Value-based Engineering

1. **Concept and context exploration**

    The concept and context exploration process is designed to develop a deep under-
    standing of the operational concept and the context in which the system will be
    deployed. This step is crucial to evaluate the entire economic ecosystem and con-
    sider all relevant stakeholders.

    The determination includes a detailed description of the planned use of the sys-
    tem, its connection to surrounding systems, the identification and analysis of
    stakeholders, their value expectations and the potential impact of the system on
    these values. The result is a defined concept in the context of use and the stake-
    holders affected.

2. **Identifying and prioritizing ethical values**

    The next step is to identify the ethical values of all relevant decision-makers and
    stakeholders, anticipate potential impairments and prioritize core values. This
    process uses centuries-old ethical theories such as utilitarianism, virtue ethics and
    duty ethics to identify the values relevant to the system and its stakeholders.

    As a result, a comprehensive analysis is developed that takes into account value
    expectations according to ethical guidelines and core values. that guides and en-
    sures a comprehensible, value-based system design:

    ▪ Utilitarian analysis

      This analysis evaluates the usefulness of functions and possible negative impli-
      cations according to the principle of highest value expectation from different
      stakeholder perspectives. It aims to evaluate the consequences of scaled use of
      the AI system and to develop functions that generate the greatest benefit and
      enjoyment of using the product or service for as many stakeholders as possi-
      ble.

    ▪ Virtue ethics analysis

      The virtue ethics analysis focuses on the possible influence of ongoing use on
      the character traits and virtues of users. It addresses the importance of virtues
      such as responsibility, honesty, courage, self-determination and compassion
      for a long-term positive perception of the AI system.

    ▪ Obligatory ethical analysis

      The ethical analysis is based on the idea that certain actions are dictated by the
      personal maxims of the company's decision-makers, universally valid obliga-
      tions and principles. It refers to universal moral principles as formulated by
      Immanuel Kant in his "categorical imperative".

3. **Definition of ethical value requirements (EVRs)**

    Based on the prioritized values, ethical value requirements (EVRs) are defined for
    the AI system. These EVRs are expectations to the system that aim to anchor and

promote the identified ethical values in the AI system in the form of functionalities.

4. **Risk-based design**

As part of the risk-based design, potential risks and negative impacts that could affect the ethical value requirements (EVRs) are analyzed. In this step, explicit system requirements are formulated and technical and organizational risk mitigation measures are developed. This involves identifying and analyzing risks associated with EVRs and implementing functional control mechanisms for risk avoidance that are integrated into the system design.

5. **Transparency management**

Transparency management aims to develop a communication strategy that proactively and clearly explains decisions for the implementation of ethically based functions in the system. This process is fundamentally important to ensure that decisions made are comprehensible to all relevant stakeholders and ensure long-term acceptance.

9.4.2 Advantages and Strategic Importance of Value-based Engineering

At a time when digital technologies are having a profound impact on our behavior and our interactions in society, the need for ethical considerations when using AI systems is essential. The challenges posed by the business models of large digital companies – from collecting and selling personal data to manipulating people's behavior and influencing democratic processes – make it clear that a rethink is needed. Value-based engineering (VbE) offers an approach that not only anticipates the ethical risks, but also creates a solid foundation for investment decisions, encourages proactive stakeholder engagement and secures long-term support from top management and investors. The meaningful use of this method offers companies the following benefits:

■ **Anticipated risk analysis**

VbE enables a comprehensive risk analysis that goes far beyond technical aspects. It takes into account the ethical implications of AI systems, such as bias, the indistinguishability of machine-generated content and potential manipulation of user behavior. This proactive approach enables risks to be identified at an early stage and countermeasures to be taken before they become real-world problems that can be expensive to fix.

■ **Basis for investment decisions**

By taking ethical values into account at an early stage, VbE provides a solid basis for investment decisions. Companies can ensure that their products and services are not only economically viable, but also ethically justifiable, which not only strengthens their own market position in the long term, but also provides a sound basis for investment decisions.

- **Proactive involvement of stakeholders**

  Corporate decision-makers play a crucial role in the implementation of VbE. Their support and commitment are essential in order to sustainably integrate ethical considerations into the corporate culture and strategy and to create the necessary cultural framework for a value-based design of AI services.

- **Continuous involvement of top management**

  Corporate decision-makers play a crucial role in the implementation of VbE. Their support and commitment are essential to sustainably integrate ethical considerations into the corporate culture and strategy and to provide the necessary resources for a value-based design of AI services.

- **Comprehensive transparency management**

  VbE emphasizes the importance of transparency in all phases of system design. A transparent approach promotes stakeholder trust and enables a consensual basis for communication about the jointly developed ethical requirements of the system.

- **Anticipation of economies of scale**

  By taking economies of scale into account, companies can use VbE to ensure that their systems deliver on the expected value proposition even in the face of broad growth. This is particularly important in a world where AI systems and services can scale rapidly and exponentially.

- **Forward-looking and future-proof design**

  VbE aims to develop systems that not only meet current but also future ethical requirements. This approach helps to ensure that products and services remain relevant and responsible in the long term.

- **Iterative optimization process**

  The iterative process of continuous application of the VbE methodology enables an agile and targeted approach that ensures continuous improvements and understanding of the adjustments to the system design on the basis of a generally agreed value compass.

- **Traceability of ethical system design**

  VbE creates traceability in the development of value-based systems. This makes it easier to review and evaluate the strategic direction and promotes the integrity of management, developers and partner networks.

- **MValP instead of MVP**

  In contrast to methods that develop purely functional prototypes (so-called "Minimal Viable Products, MVPs"), VbE aims to develop "Maximal Valuable Products" (MValPs) that are both functional and ethically valuable in the long term.

- **Catalog of measures for comprehensive success monitoring**

  The developed value register not only records technical system requirements that address risks in good time, but also provides a basis for measures to monitor success. This makes it possible to measure the success of a product or service not only on the basis of financial indicators, but also on the basis of ethical criteria.

- **Sustainable and comprehensive stakeholder management**

  Through sustainable stakeholder management, VbE ensures that all relevant groups are included in the decision-making process for the development process and that their requirements and values are taken into account. This ensures a lasting commitment on the part of those involved and lays the foundation for trusting business relationships.

- **Long-term market acceptance and compliance**

  VbE helps to ensure long-term market acceptance and compliance with new legislation such as the AI Act by supporting companies in ensuring transparency and traceability of ethical considerations in product design and documenting them accordingly.

9.4.3 Conclusion

Value-based engineering is a key strategy for ethical IT innovation that is ideally suited for the evaluation and prudent development and use of AI systems. The application of value-based engineering is a crucial step for companies to act proactively and responsibly in an increasingly AI-driven world and thus strengthen their long-term economic market position. This integrated approach promotes value-based development of AI systems that take ethical, social and legal standards into account. VbE is a key methodology for the digital excellence of companies that rely on the trustworthy and sustainable use of artificial intelligence with their AI systems.

10 Governance in the Company

Gabriele Bolek-Fügl, Karin Bruckmüller, Veronica Cretu, Valerie Hafez, Klaudia Zotzmann-Koch

10.1 Practical Example: Assessment of a Use Case in Accordance with the AI Act

Gabriele Bolek-Fügl/Karin Bruckmüller

This chapter deals with a practical example (use case) that highlights the implementation and operation of an AI-supported system for early fire detection and automatic alerting in a company building. This use case serves to make the theoretical aspects of the AI Act tangible using a real-life scenario and to show how companies can overcome the challenges of integrating such AI systems.

In our processing, we refer to information that was available on the AI Act until July 2024. Other laws were not included in the assessment.

This specific use case is intended to show an exemplary approach without covering all legal requirements, as the relevant laws are heavily dependent on the location of the company, its industry, the products manufactured and the guidelines and processes already in place. In reality, this should therefore be supplemented with the support of a lawyer.

10.1.1 Description of the Use Case: AI-supported Fire Detection and Alarm System

The use case is about the introduction of an AI-supported fire detection system that uses cameras, smoke and heat sensors to detect potential fire development on the premises of an electricity supply company in real time. The AI continuously analyzes all the data generated by the sensors installed throughout the site and buildings. This enables the AI to detect signs of fire at an early stage and verify them in order to minimize false alarms. The AI system works around the clock and can also detect fire development at night.

In an emergency, the AI automatically activates the fire alarm system, dials the emergency number for the fire department and simultaneously sends relevant information to safety officers and notifications to all employees to initiate a rapid evacuation.

By applying this technology, the fictitious company aims to use AI to protect lives and minimize property damage by detecting fires early and taking the necessary measures immediately before the fire becomes a threat to the company itself, the workforce or the neighborhood.

The fictitious company plans to purchase the video cameras, the smoke and heat sensors and the AI-supported evaluation programs for monitoring from a specialist manufacturer. The installation, commissioning and regular maintenance will also be carried out by the component provider.

10.1.2 How do You Start?

The successful implementation of the AI-supported fire detection system requires a structured approach. Even if the company does not develop the AI-supported system itself, a comprehensive project is required for implementation and operation. A project team must be defined for this.

Who Should Be on the Team?

Putting together an interdisciplinary team with different expertise within the company is essential for the successful implementation of this AI-supported system. The project team should include the following expertise and can be made up of internal or external people:

- AI development skills:

  People with specialized knowledge in programming and artificial intelligence who can implement the purchased AI system from a technical point of view and monitor it during operation in order to identify problems at an early stage and ensure safe operation.

- Lawyers:

  Legal experts who ensure compliance with relevant laws and advise the company on liability and compliance issues.

- Data protection officer:

  Data protection experts to ensure that the processing of personal data, e. g. the processing of images from the video cameras, complies with the requirements of the GDPR and that the privacy of employees is maintained.

- Ethics officer:

  Responsible for the ethical aspects of AI usage to ensure that the system is implemented and operated in accordance with the company's ethical policies and principles.

- Employee representatives:

  Communication of the workforce's concerns and, if necessary, change requests to the project team. Integration into the test phase in order to be able to assess the impact on the workforce.

- Safety engineers:

  Specialists in fire protection and safety technology who specify, test and monitor the technical requirements of the system during operation.

- Project managers:

  Management of the project within the company, including monitoring the schedule and budget, coordination of tasks and communication between the various stakeholders within and outside the company.

According to Art. 4 AI Act, all persons involved in the operation of the AI system must have appropriate training and experience in the context of the AI system. It is certainly an advantage if training is provided for all team members at the start of the project.

Challenges

A number of challenges should be considered when implementing such an AI system. The following are particularly relevant in the context of the AI Act:

- Ethical concerns:

  The extensive use of cameras and sensors for surveillance on company premises can cause unease among the workforce. Various measures must therefore be taken to ensure that the system is used ethically and that the privacy of the workforce is respected during data analysis. The principles of AI ethics such as autonomy, harm reduction, fairness and transparency must be observed and integrated into the system design.

- Technical complexity:

  The development and implementation of such a system requires advanced technologies and expertise. The AI must be able to distinguish precisely between real dangers and harmless events in order to avoid false alarms.

  The more often a false alarm is triggered, the more likely it is that staff will assume that the next alarm is a mistake and may not reliably follow the evacuation measures.

- Legal framework:

  Compliance with the AI Act and the GDPR is essential. The company must ensure that the system complies with the legal requirements, particularly with regard to the processing of personal data and the transparency of the decisions made by the AI. More details in the next paragraphs.

- Risk management:

  As AI makes decisions in critical situations that even affect lives and property, robust risk assessment and risk mitigation measures must be implemented. In addition, regular monitoring and adaptation of the system is necessary to ensure its reliability.

Role of the Company

To this end, it must first be determined what role the company plays in the value chain within the meaning of the AI Act.

The company plans to purchase the video system and the sensors as well as the evaluation program and the AI analysis software that evaluates the data and makes the emergency call to the fire department and alerts the relevant departments of the company.

Therefore, the company, as a legal entity, uses an AI system under its own responsibility and is therefore to be classified as an "deployer" within the meaning of the AI Act (Art. 3 no. 4 AI Act). This also applies to employees who, as natural persons, do not use the AI system as part of their personal but professional activities.

With regard to the GDPR, the company is the controller in relation to the personal data, as it can determine the use, such as the storage of videos for a longer period of time.

Classification of the Risk Category of the AI System

The first step is to determine the risk category of the AI system used in order to be able to present the company management with the specific obligations in accordance with the AI Act.

AI for fire detection and alerting in critical infrastructure is generally classified as a high-risk system. This is because it is designed to evaluate emergency calls and trigger operations, for example by the fire department. In addition, the system processes personal data when it is used, particularly that of the workforce, and makes decisions largely autonomously. This may pose risks to the health and fundamental rights of the monitored persons, in particular through the permanent monitoring of the workforce and other persons present on the company premises (Art. 6 et seq. in conjunction with Annex III point 2).

For the use of high-risk AIs, the AI Act imposes a number of requirements and obligations on the deployer (Art. 26 AI Act).

Key Points of the Requirements for Companies with High-risk AI

In order to operate a high-risk AI system for early fire detection in compliance with the law, the company must take the following measures in accordance with Article 26 AI Act:

Set technical and organizational measures for implementation and realization

The company must ensure that the AI system is implemented and used in accordance with the manufacturer's or provider's instructions for use. Suitable technical and organizational measures for using the system in the company must be defined in accordance with the instructions for use and other information provided by the provider.

The following technical measures could be implemented:

- Regular calibration and maintenance of video cameras to prevent faulty detections caused by blurred or misaligned cameras
- All recorded and transmitted video data should be protected by strong encryption methods to prevent unauthorized access to sensitive information.
- Several cameras or additional smoke and heat sensors could be installed at critical points to increase detection accuracy and compensate for failures of individual components.
- Regular retraining of AI systems on new data sets to continuously improve their fire detection capabilities
- The AI system should keep detailed logs of all identifications, detections, decisions and alarm triggers.
- Organizational measures could include the following:
- Definition of clear responsibilities within the company for the monitoring, maintenance and further development of the AI system and for communication with the authorities
- Regular training for the employees
- Regular training for security staff to inform them about the operation of the system, how to handle alarms and emergency protocols
- Development and regular review of emergency and evacuation plans based on the AI system's alarm signals
- Regular tests of the feasibility and appropriateness of the plans
- Establishment of guidelines and processes to ensure compliance with all relevant laws and regulations
- Regular communication to the workforce about the use of the AI system and the processing of personal data as well as the associated data protection measures

- Conducting and regularly updating a data protection impact assessment (in accordance with Art. 35 GDPR) to ensure that the processing of personal data by the system does not pose disproportionate risks to data subjects

The local fire department must also be informed about the functioning of the system and possible measures must be coordinated.

Use human supervision

Qualified and trained persons must be appointed who are responsible for monitoring the AI system. These persons receive the necessary support from the company to carry out their tasks effectively.

Even if the AI sends the emergency call to the fire department autonomously, human supervision of the system by natural persons who have the necessary competence, training and authorization must be ensured by the deployer on an ongoing basis (Art. 14 in conjunction with Art. 26 AI Act). The supervision must be appropriate to the degree of autonomy and the context of use of the AI system and must be demonstrably carried out by persons who have the special knowledge and experience and are capable of doing so:

- Understand the limitations of the AI system

- Detect and resolve anomalies, malfunctions and unexpected performance

- to be aware of the automation bias, i. e. that the results of AI systems are not neutral and correct

- interpret the results of an AI system correctly, using existing interpretation tools if necessary

- to decide not to use the AI system in a specific situation or to disregard, override or reverse the result

- interrupt the AI system operation with an appropriate procedure, allowing the system to come to a standstill in a safe state

Monitor system and report errors

The company must monitor the operation of the AI system by the IT department, among others, but also by the other safety officer(s).

If serious risks to health, safety or fundamental rights (Art. 79 AI Act) arise or a serious incident occurs (see also Art. 73 AI Act), for example due to a (possibly unforeseeable) misjudgement of the AI, the incident description must be sent immediately to the supplier or distributor (such as the importer) and, if the other two cannot be contacted, to the competent market surveillance authority. The system must be suspended (for the time being) if such risks or serious system errors occur.

Logging

The company must retain the logs generated by the AI system for an appropriate period of time, but for at least six months. These logs must be handled in accordance with the applicable data protection regulations and stored securely against deletion or access by unauthorized persons.

The AI system documents all information recorded by the sensors and cameras as well as its detections, findings, decisions and alarm triggers. These logs should be available for audits and troubleshooting. They could also form the basis for follow-up training.

Data management

As far as possible, the company must ensure that the input data used for the AI system is fit for purpose and sufficiently representative. This requirement aims to ensure the reliability and accuracy of the AI system while minimizing the risks that could arise from incorrect or inappropriate data.

Even if a company uses a pre-trained AI system in our fictitious example, the AI must be trained at the deployment site after all sensors and software have been installed. Data from different scenarios in the operational area should be trained in order to ensure broad representativeness. For example, data from different times of day, weather conditions and different areas of the building could be collected and used.

The training is checked with validation data and tested with a test phase and testing data sets before commissioning.

It is advisable to create traceable documentation for all data used and to version the data. If the training, validation and testing data records are to be archived for a longer period of time, they must be made unrecognizable or deleted before the personal data is stored.

Suitable measures for the input data must then be implemented in the company:

- Ensuring data quality by regularly checking incoming data to ensure that it is complete, up-to-date and correct.

- Set up a control system that automatically checks whether all cameras and sensors are working properly and whether their data is being transmitted without errors

- Filtering of irrelevant data to ensure that only relevant data is used for fire detection

- Verification of data sources in order to only evaluate data from your own defined sensors

- Regular maintenance and calibration of sensors and other devices used to ensure accurate data is always provided

- Implementation of a real-time monitoring system that immediately detects and reports malfunctions or anomalies

- The data collection should take into account specific risk factors of the respective environment, e. g. particularly fire-prone areas or proximity to machines that generate heat.

- Strict access controls should be implemented so that only authorized persons can access the data. This minimizes the risk of data misuse or industrial espionage, for example if the video cameras record production processes.

- Use of encryption technologies for the transmission and storage of data

- Conduct regular audits of data collection and processing processes to ensure that data remains representative and fit for purpose

Risk management

Every company must avoid and minimize the risks that may arise from the use of AI as far as possible. It is therefore necessary to set up a risk management system in accordance with Art. 9 AI Act, which is overseen in particular by the compliance department. This department should include not only lawyers, but also technicians and ideally ethicists. The system must continuously and regularly monitor foreseeable risks that affect the health, safety and fundamental rights of all employees – from board members to employees – as well as visitors to the company. If necessary, the AI must be updated to eliminate these risks. In addition, further risks may arise during operation that were not foreseeable during the development phase of the AI (Recital 93 AI Act).

According to the AI Act, risk management includes in particular the identification, analysis and assessment of known and reasonably foreseeable risks or misuse that could affect health, safety or fundamental rights when used for their intended purpose, taking into account the technical knowledge, experience and level of training that can be expected of the deployer (Art. 9 AI Act).

The risks must be eliminated or at least reduced as far as possible by means of measures to be defined. The residual risk must be deemed acceptable. Appropriate mitigation and control measures must be defined and provided to manage risks that cannot be ruled out.

The following technical risks could be identified in the use case:

- False alarms (false positives): The system could mistakenly interpret harmless situations as a potential fire and trigger an alarm. This can lead to unnecessary evacuations, business interruptions and false calls to emergency services.

- Failure to detect fires (false negatives): A serious risk is that the AI system fails to detect a fire or reacts too late. This could lead to significant property damage, injuries or even fatalities

- System failures: The failure of cameras, sensors or AI could lead to fires not being detected or being detected too late. Redundant systems and regular maintenance can prevent this.

- Data processing errors: Incorrect decisions due to incorrect or incomplete data. This can significantly impair the reliability of the early fire detection system.

Data protection and security risks include

▪ Invasion of privacy: The system's cameras and sensors continuously monitor the company environment and also record personal data of employees and visitors.

▪ Data misuse: There is a risk that the collected data may be misused for other purposes or accessed by unauthorized persons.

▪ Cyberattacks: The system could become a target of cyberattacks where hackers attempt to take control of the cameras, sensors or AI to cause damage or steal confidential information.

Ethical risks include:

▪ Monitoring of employees: The constant use of cameras for fire monitoring can be interpreted as unauthorized surveillance of the workforce, which can affect the working atmosphere and raise legal issues.

▪ Unjustified discrimination: If the AI contains unconscious bias, certain groups of people or behaviors could be disproportionately classified as suspected cases, which could lead to discrimination.

Corporate risks include

▪ Insufficient human supervision: Despite automation through AI, human supervision is necessary as proof that the system is functioning correctly. Insufficient supervision could lead to problems not being detected and rectified in time.

▪ Lack of training and contingency plans: Without adequate training for those affected and clear contingency plans, delays or misconduct could occur in an emergency, reducing the effectiveness of the system.

▪ Regulatory non-compliance: If the AI system does not meet the legal requirements, the company could risk fines or liability claims.

▪ Dependence on technology: Over-reliance on the AI system could lead to other fire safety measures being neglected, which could have serious consequences in the event of a system failure

▪ Adaptation to new sources of danger: The AI system must be continuously adapted to new sources of danger and environmental conditions, otherwise the system could become vulnerable to newly emerging risks. For example, it could be discovered that certain sensors in the immediate vicinity of machines are not functioning reliably.

By identifying and continuously managing these risks, the company can ensure that the AI-powered early fire detection system operates safely and effectively while meeting legal and ethical requirements.

Informing the workforce

Before commissioning the AI system, the company must inform the data subjects and their representatives that they will be partially monitored by the system. According to the GDPR, the purpose must be defined.

Obtaining, understanding and implementing information and instructions for use

In order to enable risk management, the company must ensure in advance that the provider has passed on all available information on transparency and instructions for use to the company.

In particular, the following information must be included:

- the degree of accuracy in fire detection

- known and foreseeable circumstances affecting the accuracy of the generation of the data triggering the emergency call

- foreseeable misuse, which in particular could lead to a false alarm or a non-alarm, which could lead to damage to health, even death of persons or damage to products, machines and the like

- the data used for this purpose, which was used for training during the development process, as well as new data about the workforce (Art. 13 AI Act)

These instructions for use must not only be read but also understood by the employees of the relevant departments, primarily the security engineers, IT department and compliance department, in order to be implemented correctly. This means that in the event of uncertainty or ambiguity, the provider must be contacted or the training offered by the provider must be attended.

Entry in the data processing register and preparation of the data protection impact assessment

Before commissioning, the AI system must be entered in the data processing register and the data protection declaration must be completed. The company must also carry out a data protection impact assessment in accordance with the GDPR, as personal data is processed.

10.1.3 Conclusion

The successful implementation of the AI-supported early fire detection system requires a structured approach:

- Needs analysis:

  First of all, a detailed needs analysis should be carried out to determine the company's specific requirements. This includes identifying the areas to be monitored, selecting suitable sensors and cameras and defining the desired response times.

▪ Legal and ethical analysis:

The legal and ethical framework conditions must be clearly defined before techni-cal implementation. This includes checking compliance with the AI Act, the GDPR and relevant occupational health and safety laws as well as taking ethical guide-lines into account.

▪ Technical implementation:

The technical implementation is based on the needs analysis and takes into ac-count the legal requirements. This involves installing the cameras and sensors, developing and training the AI and integrating it into the alarm system and the emergency call chain.

▪ Test and validation:

After implementation, the system must be comprehensively tested to ensure its functionality and reliability. Both technical tests and ethical tests should be car-ried out to ensure that all requirements are met.

▪ Training and communication:

Employees must be informed about the new system and trained accordingly. In addition, clear communication channels and emergency protocols should be de-fined to ensure a smooth evacuation in the event of an emergency.

▪ Continuous monitoring and adjustment:

Continuous monitoring is required after the system has been commissioned. The system should be checked regularly and adjusted as necessary to minimize new risks and optimize performance.

10.2 Risk Management, Human Supervision and Useful Tools

Valerie Hafez

Governance from an organizational perspective is a broad field and essential for com-pliance with the AI Regulation, but remains under-defined in the AI Act. This makes the practice of governance within an organization particularly important, and at the same time raises several questions. The following definition of AI governance is used for this chapter is used:

AI governance is a system of rules, practices, processes, and technological tools that are employed to ensure an organization's use of AI technologies aligns with the organization's strategies, objectives, and values; fulflls [sic] legal requirements; and meets principles of ethical AI followed by the organization. [14]

Governance often forms part of the risk management processes and consists of the collection, ongoing monitoring, documentation, coordination and communication of risks together with the embedding of governance processes in the organization. [2] This limits us to the "simple" problem of AI governance, namely how organizations can use AI systems responsibly (see [15]). However, AI governance is always embedded in the broader context of corporate due diligence, IT governance and data governance. An isolated approach is therefore neither possible nor sensible: it is much more a question of embedding the governance of AI systems in existing governance structures. [14] To ensure that this is successful, two dimensions of governance in particular are discussed below, namely human oversight in general and risk management in particular.

The need for governance gives rise to important questions relating to transparency, explainability and security, which have already been dealt with in previous chapters. Issues relating to quality management are not addressed, as there are currently no generally recognized indicators or processes for this. The aim of this chapter is, on the one hand, to break down complex issues relating to legal requirements and, on the other hand, to point out practical tools, such as codes of conduct, that organizations can use to strengthen their AI governance.

10.2.1 Embedding Governance in the Life Cycle of an AI System

In the context of AI systems, governance means dealing with the nature and embedding of AI systems, their effects and possible measures to prevent negative developments throughout the entire life cycle of an AI system (see Figure 10.2). Governance therefore begins when the decision is made to develop an AI system – and only ends when an AI system is decommissioned.

In connection with AI systems, the question of when arises particularly often, as AI systems can be designed in such a way that they change their parameters over time. The environment in which AI systems are used can also change. For this reason, ongoing monitoring of development is essential.

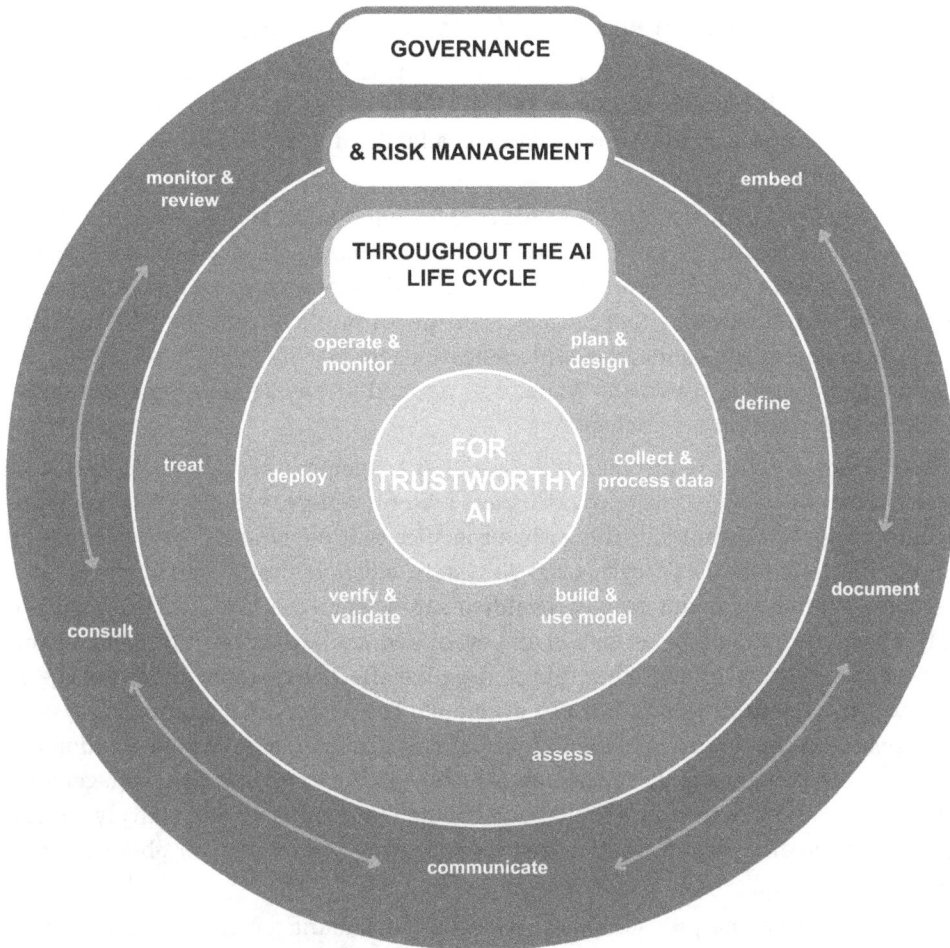

Figure 10.1 Life Cycle of an AI System [2]

10.2.2 Recognizing and Addressing Risks

The AI Act is a risk-based regulation with two special features: Firstly, the most important risk assessment is carried out in the legal text itself by assigning areas of application to certain risks. It is therefore not the product itself, but the area of application
that justifies extended obligations. Secondly, the AI Act does not contain any instructions for risk assessment. Standardization will certainly follow in this area, but there
are already some tools and initiatives that can support risk assessment and risk management.

10.2.2.1 Approaches to Risks, Incidents, Accidents and Affected Parties

First of all, it is important to clarify some basic terms. There are different definitions of riskdamage, incidents, accidents and also affected parties. This section breaks down the definitions in the AI Act – where available – and enriches them with established research.

Risks are defined in Art. 3 para. 2 AI Act as the combination of the probability of occurrence of harm and the severity of that harm. The definition of risks in the AI Regulation is therefore process-oriented or methodological in nature and does not specify any criteria for risk areas that must be considered in a risk assessment. This definition is only made in connection with obligations for certain systems, which are defined for high-risk AI systems in Annex I AI Act and Annex III AI Act and certain AI systems with transparency obligations.

Art. 9 AI Act contains requirements for a risk management process for high-risk AI systems that developers must provide (users are only obliged to follow this risk management system). Essentially, this article specifies that ongoing risk management is required throughout the lifecycle of an AI system, which identifies and analyzes foreseeable risks to fundamental rights, health or safety when the AI system is used properly. These risks should be estimated and evaluated, both in terms of proper use and foreseeable misuse. Among other things, negative effects on people under the age of 18 or other vulnerable groups must be evaluated. The post-market monitoring system in Article 72 AI Act is also an essential part of risk management. The information obtained in this context should subsequently be taken into account in risk management. This in turn must be based on a plan and should systematically and actively collect, document and analyze information that is either provided by users or obtained from other sources.

Based on this risk analysis, suitable and targeted risk management measures should be developed to counteract the identified risks. Any remaining risk must be considered acceptable and suitable mitigation and control measures must be taken. But beware: only those risks should be addressed that can be mitigated or eliminated through the development or design of the high-risk AI system or through the provision of technical documentation. Measures must be taken on the basis of tests that can also take place under real-world conditions (Article 60 AI Act). In any case, these tests must be based on probabilistic threshold values and previously established metrics. Providers that are subject to sector-specific risk management requirements can implement the requirements in Article 9 AI Act as part of their existing risk management system or in combination with it.

Apart from the obligations related to high-risk AI-systems, there is also the possibility that market surveillance authorities may inspect AI-systems and require corrective action if a risk has been identified (Art. 79 AI Act). It is therefore advisable to implement risk management regardless of the classification of a system as a high-risk AI system.

The AI Act defines serious incidents as incidents or failures of AI systems that directly or indirectly result in death or serious harm to the health of a person, a serious and irreversible disruption to the management and operation of critical infrastructure, a breach of legal obligations relating to fundamental rights or serious damage to property or the environment (Art. 3 para. 44 AI Act). Accidents are not defined, but the preparatory work of the OECD [25] suggests that a definition will be developed in the foreseeable future that can be incorporated into risk management. Accidents in connection with AI systems could, for example, result from failures in robustness (unexpected inputs lead to malfunctions), specification (the purpose of the AI system deviates from the intentions of the developers or deployers) or governance (inadequate monitoring or control during operation). [3]

The AI Act does recognize the concept of data subject(s)but it does not specify what types of affected persons there may be. This makes it more difficult to assess affectedness in the risk assessment, as it can be helpful to consider different degrees of affectedness when considering risks. The distinction between first party victims and fourth party victims helps with orientation, e. g. where stakeholder involvement is possible or which measures need to be taken for different forms of affectedness: Consent to the process, transparency about the AI system and training are possible and sensible for first-degree affected parties, while they must be designed differently for second-degree affected parties in the best case and third-degree affected parties already do not enjoy any protection as a result. In this context, it is also important to know your own role in the value chain, as offering AI systems to other organizations may result in contractual obligations towards them. [2]

Table 10.1 Typology of Affectedness [22]

Affected...	Refers to
... first degree	Those directly involved in the process, e. g. developers, deployers and supervisors of an AI system
... second degree	Indirect participants, e. g. users of a service in which an AI system is integrated
... third degree	People affected by the AI system without direct involvement, e. g. people living in an area where biometric surveillance by AI systems is being introduced
... fourth degree	Future generations who are affected by the AI system without direct involvement, e. g. if the classification of parents is used to send their children to certain schools

10.2.2.2 Measuring Risks

In the AI Act, risks are defined as the combination of the probability of occurrence of harm and the severity of that harm (Art. 3 para. 2 AI Act). In order to operationalize risk management and the development of measures, a common understanding of risks and thresholds must be developed within an organization (or even within a sector). This also includes determining when which levels (or degrees of severity) are reached and which measures are to be taken. It should also be made clear whether the AI system is developed by the organization itself or is obtained or even operated from external sources, as this results in different options for action and responsibilities.

Similar to HACCP, the risk management system for food and gastronomy, risks associated with AI systems should be based on a detailed analysis of the operational area of application and an environmental analysis. A threat model could be used for this, for example[1] or a threat analysis could be carried out. The Governance Guide: Model Development Lifecycle [19], in which a risk assessment (based on the probability and impact of a risk occurring) is carried out using a matrix, is also helpful. Section 9.2 also discusses the AI Risk Management Framework of the US National Institute of Standards and Technology (NIST). Many risks that have already been identified in connection with corporate due diligence [20] can be re-evaluated when an AI system is introduced: Does the AI system mitigate a risk, e. g. negative impact on the environment? Will other risks, e. g. to employees, be increased? Such considerations can be included directly in corporate due diligence reporting.

Based on this risk assessment, very different scenarios can arise to which an organization may wish to respond. OpenAI, for example, has come to the conclusion that the alignment of its AI systems is one of the most significant risks and has therefore introduced a number of preventive measures.[2] OpenAI thus clearly prioritizes fourth-degree stakeholders in the risk assessment, but at the same time cites little empirical and context-specific evidence for these risks. This approach will be inappropriate for the majority of organizations: instead, it is usually more appropriate to develop risks and thresholds for different risk categories in dialogue with affected parties.

An important element in measuring risks is the measurement of errors or faults. Concepts from the field of reliability engineering such as Mean Time to Failure, Mean Time Between Failures or Reliability Function can be used [16]. Such measured values help to develop a common understanding of how the performance of an AI system can be observed and compared.

---

[1] https://owasp.org/www-community/Threat_Modeling

[2] https://openai.com/safety/preparedness

10.2.2.3 Responsibility in the Event of Incidents and Accidents

For high-risk AI systems, the AI Act stipulates that providers must provide a framework for managerial responsibilities and other personnel in the context of quality management; in addition, reporting processes in connection with serious incidents must be clarified (Art. 17 AI Act). If the high-risk AI system is or could no longer be compliant with the AI Act, providers, distributors and deployers must take immediate corrective action – especially if a risk within the meaning of Art. 79 para. 1 AI Act has been identified (Art. 20 AI Act). In the latter case, the causes must be clarified immediately and the market surveillance authority informed.

Responsibility can only be assumed once responsibilities have been clarified. This is particularly relevant with regard to liability issues, which in the worst case can be fought out in court; but long before that, clear responsibilities can help to avoid or mitigate risks. The Governance Guide: Model Development Lifecycle [19] recommends that risks at each level of development should be taken by a responsible person. This ensures that at least one person can take responsibility for remaining risks based on their detailed knowledge of the AI system, the area of application and the risk measures taken. VERA follows a similar approach, which is[3] an online tool that can assist in the formulation of responsibilities in connection with AI [1].

If an incident or accident does occur, qualified experts should be called in as quickly as possible to gain an overview of the situation. To do this, it must first be possible to answer questions on the following aspects:

1. Extent of the event: What happened? What did it affect? Which systems or processes contributed to the event? What is the impact of shutting down or suspending the AI system?

2. Persons affected by the event: What degree of affected persons must we assume? How can these affected persons be reached (information, measures ...)? What are the consequences of the event for those affected?

3. Legal situation: What reporting obligations exist (insurance, authorities, etc.)? What measures can be taken?

Ideally, the experts should be made up of a heterogeneous group in which those who work with the system on a daily basis are represented as well as those who are affected by the incident or accident.

10.2.2.4 Perceiving and controlling the unknown

Some risks can be discovered in advance and addressed with suitable measures, but a conclusive breakdown of all risks in advance will never be possible [2]. In order to nevertheless have the broadest possible field of perception for risks, red teaming or

---

[3] *https://wien.arbeiterkammer.at/interessenvertretung/arbeitdigital/DataPolitics/Algorithmen_in_der_Entscheidungsfindung.html*

the exchange with challengers, for example, are useful. Red teaming means subjecting an AI system to the most systematic and thorough troubleshooting possible, which is preferably carried out by external parties and includes the AI system as well as organizational processes and measures. Challengers on the other hand, are stakeholders who are likely to have a negative attitude towards the project. They can be involved early on in a project as critics in order to increase the robustness of the use case by developing appropriate countermeasures. In both cases, involving as many different perspectives as possible helps to identify and assess risks and stabilizes knowledge processes.

When dealing with the unknown, people often prefer caution (according to the precautionary principle). This does not necessarily mean that resistance to change means a rejection of technologies – objections are often raised for serious reasons and can be well addressed with well thought-out measures. Responsible innovation has played an important role in research for over a decade and is gradually becoming more important in the corporate context through legislation such as the Corporate Due Diligence Directive and the Corporate Sustainability Reporting Directive. The various approaches that have been developed in this area can help organizations to deal responsibly with unknown risks and different approaches to minimizing risks.

10.2.3 Human Supervision

When organizations use high-risk AI systems, they must ensure that human oversight is carried out by people with the necessary skills, training and authority and that they have access to the necessary support – both when the oversight processes have been defined by providers and when they design them themselves (Art. 26 AI Act).

AI-based processes often fall back on humans to avert or rectify errors. There are different models for this, such as human-in-the-loop, human-on-the-loop or human-in-command [11].

1. Human-in-the-Loop stands for a model in which human intervention is possible at every stage of the AI system.

2. Human-on-the-Loop refers to a model in which human intervention is provided for during the design phase and during the operating phase.

3. Human-in-Command on the other hand, represents a model in which humans retain control over the activity of the AI system and decide whether, when and how an AI system should be used in individual situations. This includes the decision not to use the AI system as well as the decision to provide for human intervention during operation or to challenge and reverse decisions made by the AI system.

Art. 14 AI Act sets out the framework for human oversight of high-risk AI systems and clarifies that these systems must be designed and developed in a way that enables effective human oversight during the use phase. Human oversight is intended to prevent or minimize risks to health, safety or fundamental rights during proper operation or foreseeable misuse. These supervision options must be adapted to the risks, the degree of autonomy and the context of the AI system. To this end, measures should be taken that are identified by providers and, if possible, built into the AI system before it is made available on the market or put into operation, and/or measures that are identified by providers and implemented by users before it is made available on the market or put into operation. For AI systems for biometric monitoring, it should additionally be ensured that users do not take any further steps before the results of the AI system are confirmed by two different people who are able to do so due to their suitability, training and function. Supervisory measures should enable people to do this:

1. know the capabilities and limitations of high-risk AI systems and monitor the operation of these systems, including to detect anomalies, errors and unexpected outcomes

2. remain vigilant against the risk of automation bias (especially if the system provides information or recommendations)

3. correctly interpret the results of the high-risk AI system using the interpretation tools and methods provided

4. make a decision not to use a high-risk AI system or to disregard, change or reverse the result

5. intervene in the operation of the AI system with high risk or interrupt it with a "stop button" that leads to the safe shutdown of the AI system

In principle, we can assume that human-in-command is practiced in the organization-in-command variant – after all, organizations make decisions about whether AI systems should be used and what they should (not) be used for. Although there are variations in practice, the law is very clear that organizations are liable for the use of AI systems in connection with activities within that organization. Workers and employees, on the other hand, cannot always decide whether they want to use AI systems and what they want to use them for. When using AI systems, it is therefore important to establish and document the level at which decisions on this use are made and what options for action result from this for different positions in the organizations.

It is also important to distinguish between high-risk applications and AI systems in low or medium-risk applications [13]. In the case of high-risk applications, oversight options must be provided at the development stage and implemented by deployers; further measures are welcome but not mandatory.

The focus of the measures mentioned here is that they can be taken independently of manufacturer specifications. The aim is to open up different purposes of human supervision and to enable a careful examination of different supervision models. Just as

AI systems cannot be taken as a technology in their own right, but always in the context of their development and use, there are no stand-alone supervision models that can be used for every case. This makes it all the more important to develop a good understanding of the logic and dynamics of different supervisory models.

10.2.3.1 Break Down Supervision

But what is actually meant when we talk about supervision? As a rule, it refers to human supervision, which ultimately goes hand in hand with responsibility in the event of damage. This can be anchored individually, organizationally or socially. While the AI Act represents a societal oversight measure by legally establishing expectations, organizations must take their own oversight measures to comply with this legal framework.

When developing supervisory measures, it can be helpful to clarify the counterfactual and corrective influence of a supervisory measure. If direct counterfactual influence on the outputs of an AI system, then these outputs only become effective when they are implemented by humans. This is often the case in the medical field: the doctor receives an assessment from the AI system as to whether a finding indicates breast cancer and then decides whether and, if so, what further steps she would like to take based on this assessment. In highly automated areas such as telecommunications, on the other hand, AI systems are often used that only apply indirect counterfactual supervision, e.g. when mobile phone cells forward traffic at high or low utilization. Corrective supervision, on the other hand, exists when the decision of an AI system can be changed afterwards.

Table 10.2 Typology of Supervision [13]

	Type of Counter-factual Influence	Type of Process	Time of Intervention	Required by Law
First degree supervision	Directly counterfactual – result depends on human decision	Partially automated	At any time, also corrective	no?
Second degree supervision	Indirectly counterfactual – result depends on threshold values	Fully automated	Before the introduction of the AI system or corrective after the decision	yes

It is also clear here that in practice, supervision can come from different places. Corrective supervision can, for example, be anchored in the organization itself, currently often in combination with similar responsibilities such as data protection or IT issues. External supervision may be exercised by certification or conformity assessment bodies which, although independent of the organization, have an economic relationship with it. Regulatory supervision, on the other hand, relates almost exclusively to the legal framework from which it arises. Counterfactual supervision must be anchored much deeper in the process or "closer" to the AI system in order to be effective.

10.2.3.2 Develop and Maintain Supervisory Skills

Our training and education contribute significantly to strengthening our ability to assess the results of an AI system. This includes AI competencewhich is an in-depth knowledge of how AI systems work, as well as data literacy, or a good understanding of how data can be collected, structured, processed and interpreted. Training in the field of data science can be helpful in acquiring and developing data and AI skills. Incidentally, the AI Act requires all operators in the value chain of an AI system to ensure that the persons involved in the operation and use of the system have appropriate knowledge (Art. 4 AI Act) – this obligation applies to all AI systems and is not limited to systems with high or medium risk, as is the case with most of the other requirements.

However, when supervising AI systems, it is equally important to have expertise in the area of application. So-called domain experts can build on experience to evaluate the performance of AI systems in specific contexts. This means they play a key role in preventing accidents and can often better assess the effects of certain errors and intervene in a targeted manner in the event of problems. Data scientists also need this domain-specific knowledge in order to deal with AI systems in a mature and responsible manner.

In connection with AI systems, as in other highly automated areas, the problem arises of how people whose work has been taken over by systems remain capable of intervening in an emergency [18]. Practice makes perfect, not only literally but also practically: the more experience people can gain in operation, the faster and safer they can intervene in an emergency. Therefore, if the use of an AI system means that key skills in certain areas can no longer be developed, organizations must make provisions for this in their career planning and internal training processes. One possibility is, for example, the introduction of simulation processes or regular renewal of qualifications, for example through seminars or examinations.

10.2.3.3 Making Supervision Context-sensitive

Human oversight of AI systems can only be effective if the system is designed in such a way that supervisors have sufficient information to make informed decisions and the design of the system minimizes bias or bias towards certain decisions [18]. This means that AI systems must be embedded in existing decision-making contexts and supervision options must be tailored to the skills and knowledge of supervisors. In many areas, e. g. in the medical context, it is also necessary to create decision-making capabilities for a group of supervisors from different disciplines, because diagnoses or treatment plans are developed by a multidisciplinary team. These teams need supervision options that meet different requirements, knowledge and prerequisites in order to allow them to be embedded in existing clinical practice.

These requirements demonstrate the importance of a detailed examination of existing supervisory regulations in a specific area of application [18]. Existing regulations also influence the expectations of the AI system itself: Medical professionals, for example, expect AI systems for clinical applications to pass the same tests – including randomized controlled trials, systematic tests and peer reviews – as other medical devices, remedies or diagnostic tools in order to use them as competent tools.

At the same time, however, this example also illustrates that AI systems can never be introduced just like that, but must be accompanied by organizational measures [18]. This may mean hiring one or more data scientists and ensuring that suitable processes are developed for collaboration between employees with different functions and qualifications. However, it may also mean creating alternative development paths so that parts of existing professions that are performed by AI systems do not lead to an erosion of the profession or to insurmountable obstacles to career progression, for example by making it impossible to develop certain skills.

10.2.3.4 Involving External Parties in Supervision

Many supervisory processes will be anchored in organizations themselves. However, it can make sense to involve external parties in oversight. A famous example is the Facebook Oversight Board, which investigates a small number of controversial cases each year and creates precedents for dealing with similar cases. External oversight can also be obtained, for example, through sectoral supervisory authorities or certifications for certain standards.

Standards play an important role in governance processes as they codify expectations of the process and create model processes. On the one hand, this allows all organizations (and their legal departments) to know that legal requirements are being met to a sufficient degree. At the same time, new employees can be trained more easily if they are familiar with a certain standard that is used in the organization.

ISO/IEC 42001:2023 [4] is the first standard to define a management system for AI systems. It does not refer to quality management with regard to the results of an AI system, but specifies how organizations can develop and use AI systems responsibly and what organizational measures could be taken to achieve this. All criteria in this standard are currently classified as recommendations, not requirements for certification, which is why a further standard specifically for high-risk systems in accordance with the AI Act is to be expected. However, ISO/IEC 42001 provides helpful guidance for organizations wishing to set up governance processes in all other areas of application.

---

[4] See in detail at *https://www.iso.org/standard/81230.html*

Several certification offers are currently being developed for quality management. For example, TÜV Austria offers Trusted AI[5] a certification that proves the quality, safety and suitability of AI applications. The certification process covers functional criteria (e. g. data and model), security (including risk assessment), ethical requirements (including fundamental rights and accessibility) and data protection. The external audit is carried out by TÜV Austria, which ensures objectivity in the examination of the requirements.

In many cases, however, it makes sense to involve external parties – especially stakeholders – before developing an AI system in order to oversee the design of a project. This type of second-degree oversight has an impact on the thresholds used by an AI system to classify and categorize, and can be crucial to the social robustness of an AI application, particularly in sensitive areas such as administration, human resources management, education, medicine or justice. Approaches such as inclusive design[6] The aim of inclusive design is to create the broadest possible inclusion [21]. Similarly, if people are affected on an ongoing basis – regardless of whether they are employees or outsiders, for example – it can make sense to set up complaint mechanisms and feedback loops and thus involve them in the ongoing co-design of the AI system and monitoring of risks.

10.2.3.5 Human Supervision: Pros and Cons

There are good reasons why humans are not suitable for practicing supervision over AI systems [10]. Automation bias, for example, is very difficult. The unconscious tendency is to trust automated decisions more than our own experience. Complacency, or the tendency not to question well-functioning systems later on, also leads to ineffective human supervision. At the same time, however, there is also algorithm aversion, the rejection of algorithmic decisions, even if they are correct or conclusive. Finally, algorithmic recommendations can influence the approach to certain questions: This refers to the tendency to attribute more weight to those factors that are evaluated algorithmically and to no longer consider other types of information.

Trust is therefore a double-edged sword. We can have too much trust in technology and also too little – and at the moment when we make decisions, it is difficult to tell which side the coin has come down on. But the same applies to the developers of technologies and to those who control the technology from a distance. This is a very important point, because we often automatically assume that those who are involved in the operation have too much or too little trust in the technology rather than those

---

[5] See in detail at *https://www.tuv.at/trusted-ai-by-tuev-austria/*

[6] Inclusive design is an approach that strives to meet as many user needs as possible with a product. This includes accessibility, whereby barriers are not only seen as problematic for people with disabilities; rather, inclusive design assumes that everyone experiences barriers in certain situations and that these barriers should be kept as low as possible.

who have planned the technology or its use. Unfortunately, this is not true, because distance alone does not protect us against mistakes.

In fact, there are important reasons why human supervision remains essential in automated contexts. In highly critical areas such as nuclear power plants or aerospace, as well as less life-threatening areas such as warehouses, a pattern runs throughout: A lot can go wrong, even though the design should prevent accidents. Especially when processes are characterized by highly complex interactivity, unforeseen interactions between content, components or individual parts as well as with the environment can occur. Sometimes the very components that should prevent accidents are responsible for disasters. If these processes are also closely coupled, the possibilities for intervention are reduced, as interactions spread quickly in closely coupled processes, and this speed makes it difficult to act in time in emergency situations.

People are amazingly good at averting bad consequences. To do this, however, people must also be in a position to intervene. However, in processes that are increasingly complex and interactive (where many components interact and error analysis is therefore difficult at the moment) and closely coupled, there are conflicting requirements for the development of supervisory skills: Tightly coupled processes require centralization, while complex-interactive processes are better structured in a decentralized manner [22]. If the introduction of an AI system leads to tighter coupling and increased complex interactivity, caution is therefore required with regard to the organization of supervision and decision-making authority. Particularly in critical areas, supervisory processes should be co-developed from the outset together with the introduction of an AI system, taking particular account of the respective supervisory requirements.

10.2.4 Conclusion

The AI Act places high demands on governance, which organizations must meet in various areas. One of these requirements – sufficient training of personnel – applies to all organizations, regardless of the risk level of the application. Most of the governance requirements are legally required for high-risk AI systems, but remain useful for low or medium-risk applications, as they promote the realization of ethical and humanistic principles and other laws also require a level of control and accountability (such as the GDPR).

Governance is not about controlling the technology – because control is always context-specific and sufficient control to cover every case can never be achieved. Rather, it is about guiding the impact of a technology. How do AI systems affect the world and how do we deal with them? A good governance strategy can answer these questions for each specific use case. In this sense, AI systems are not much different from cars, for which we have product safety requirements as well as traffic regulations and also requirements for the qualifications of users; or biotechnology, for which we have introduced ethical standards as well as professional qualification processes. This means that governance must be developed in a context-sensitive manner and with the broad involvement of the people involved – and this is where the interdisciplinary challenge of AI systems arises.

For this reason, the communication of governance measures is also crucial. Governance creates trust in an organization's ability to deal with a technology. This trust-building aspect works best when governance measures are comprehensible to outsiders and have been reviewed by experts [2]. This also enables organizations to meet their obligations to supervisory boards, for example, as a precautionary measure.

Sources

[1] Adensamer, Angelika; Gsenger, Rita; Klausner, Lukas Daniel: "Computer says no": Algorithmic decision support and organisational responsibility. In: Journal of Responsible Technology Volume 7–8 (2021), Article 100014

[2] Advancing accountability in AI: Governing and managing risks throughout the lifecycle for trustworthy AI, OECD Digital Economy Papers (OECD Digital Economy Papers no. 349). Volume 349, 2023

[3] Arnold, Zachary; Toner, Helen: AI Accidents: An Emerging Threat. What Could Happen and What to Do (CSET Policy Brief): Center for Security and Emerging Technology – Georgetown University, 2021

[4] Bertelsmann Stiftung; VDE: From Principles to Practice: An interdisciplinary framework to operationalise AI ethics, [object Object] (2020)

[5] Biegelbauer, Peter; Lackinger, Caroline; Schlarb, Sven; Subak, Edgar; Weinlinger, Pia: Leitfaden Digitale Verwaltung und Ethik: Praxisleitfaden für KI in der Verwaltung, Version 1.0. Wien: Bundesministerium für Kunst, Kultur, öffentlichen Dienst und Sport (BMKÖS) Sektion III – Öffentlicher Dienst und Verwaltungsinnovation, 2023

[6] Dainow, Brandt; Brey, Philip; Kuyumdzhieva, A. (Hrsg.): Ethics By Design and Ethics of Use Approaches for Artificial Intelligence. Brussels: European Commission, 2021

[7] ETAPAS Consortium: ETAPAS toolkit. URL *https://joinup.ec.europa.eu/collection/govtechconnect/solution/etapas?f%5B0%5D=solution_content_bundle%3Adocument* – accessed: 2024/03/17

[8] European Commission. Directorate General for Communications Networks, Content and Technology.: The Assessment List for Trustworthy Artificial Intelligence (ALTAI) for self assessment. LU: Publications Office, 2020

[9] Gebru, Timnit; Morgenstern, Jamie; Vecchione, Briana; Vaughan, Jennifer Wortman; Wallach, Hanna; Daumé III, Hal; Crawford, Kate: Datasheets for Datasets, arXiv (2021) – arXiv:1803.09010 [cs]

[10] Green, Ben: The Flaws of Policies Requiring Human Oversight of Government Algorithms. In: SSRN Electronic Journal (2021)

[11] High-Level Expert Group on Artificial Intelligence: Ethics Guidelines for Trustworthy AI. Brussels: European Commission, 2019

[12] Kaminski, Margot E; Malgieri, Gianclaudio: Algorithmic impact assessments under the GDPR: producing multi-layered explanations. In: International Data Privacy Law Volume 11 (2021), no. 2, pp. 125–144

[13] Laux, Johann: Institutionalised Distrust and Human Oversight of Artificial Intelligence: Toward a Democratic Design of AI Governance under the European Union AI Act. In: SSRN Electronic Journal (2023)

[14] Mäntymäki, Matti; Minkkinen, Matti; Birkstedt, Teemu; Viljanen, Mika: Defining organizational AI governance. In: AI and Ethics Volume 2 (2022), no. 4, pp. 603–609

[15] Minkkinen, Matti; Mäntymäki, Matti: Discerning Between the "Easy" and "Hard" Problems of AI Governance. In: IEEE Transactions on Technology and Society Volume 4 (2023), no. 2, pp. 188–194

[16] Mishra, Saurabh; Aria, Amin; Renda, Andrea: Ensuring AI's trustworthiness: reliability engineering meets data-driven risk management. URL *https://oecd.ai/en/wonk/reliability-engineering-data-driven-risk-management* – accessed: 2024/03/17

[17] Mitchell, Margaret; Wu, Simone; Zaldivar, Andrew; Barnes, Parker; Vasserman, Lucy; Hutchinson, Ben; Spitzer, Elena; Raji, Inioluwa Deborah; u. a.: Model Cards for Model Reporting. In: Proceedings of the Conference on Fairness, Accountability, and Transparency, 2019 – arXiv:1810.03993 [cs], pp. 220–229

[18] Morgan, Deborah; Hashem, Youmna; Straub, Vincent J.; Bright, Jonathan: "Team-in-the-loop" organisational oversight of high-stakes AI, arXiv (2023) – arXiv:2303.14007 [cs]

[19] Nicholson Consulting; Ministry of Social Development: Governance Guide: Model Development Lifecycle (no. A13094818), 2021

[20] OECD: OECD Due Diligence Guidance for Responsible Business Conduct, 2018

[21] Park, Tina M.: Making AI Inclusive: 4 Guiding Principles for Ethical Engagement (White Paper): Partnership on AI, 2022

[22] Perrow, Charles: Normal Accidents: Living with High Risk Technologies. Princeton: Princeton University Press, 2011 – ISBN 978-1-4008-2849-4

[23] Poretschkin, Maximilian; Schmitz, Anna; Akila, Mara; Adilova, Mara; Becker, Daniel; Cremers, Armin B.; Hecker, Dirk; Houben, Sebastian; u. a.: Leitfaden zur Gestaltung vertrauenswürdiger Künstlicher Intelligenz: Fraunhofer-Institut für Intelligente Analyse- und Informationssysteme IAIS, 2021

[24] Society Inside; European Center for Not-for-Profit Law: Framework for meaningful engagement: ECNL

[25] Stocktaking for the development of an AI incident definition, OECD Artificial Intelligence Papers (OECD Artificial Intelligence Papers no. 4). Volume 4, 2023

[26] UNESCO: Recommendation on the Ethics of Artificial Intelligence. Paris: UNESCO, 2021

[27] UNESCO: Ethical impact assessment. A tool of the Recommendation on the Ethics of Artificial Intelligence: UNESCO, 2023

10.3 Data and Knowledge Management

Veronica Cretu

In the last two decades, there has probably not been a single expert in the field of data governance who has not heard the catchy phrase "data is the new oil". It was introduced by Clive Humby, a British mathematician, in 2006 [12]. This term has since been taken up by numerous managers and industry experts. However, it only sparked a broad discourse after an article in The Economist [11] in 2017 entitled "The world's most valuable resource is no longer oil, but data." Since then, this buzzword has become a symbol of the fourth industrial revolution.

In some ways, this analogy illustrates the immense value of data in today's digital economy and ever-changing governance landscape. Comparable to the central role of oil in recent history, this digital resource gives companies the power to shape outcomes and realities, mirroring the influence once wielded by the masters of oil reserves.

At the heart of modern business strategy and operational efficiency today is the question of how organizations can ensure proper data management, security and use. The question is, how should data be managed to drive innovation, ensure compliance and promote growth?

Today, it is becoming clear that unlike oil, which fueled the engines of the past, data is powering the algorithms of the future. It is not just a commodity, but a dynamic catalyst that, if properly managed and governed, can lead to advances and solutions that are tailored to emerging needs and implemented quickly. This shift in perspective is critical for businesses that want to thrive and for governments that want to design policies that protect, serve and empower their citizens. This evolving asset requires a governance model that is as adaptable and forward-thinking as the technology that governs it.

Data governance evolved over time away from being primarily an IT function, while with the advent of digital transformation and the big data era, companies began to realize the potential they could derive from their diverse data assets, leading to Data Governance 2.0. This phase focused on collaboration, breaking down silos and spreading accountability [10].

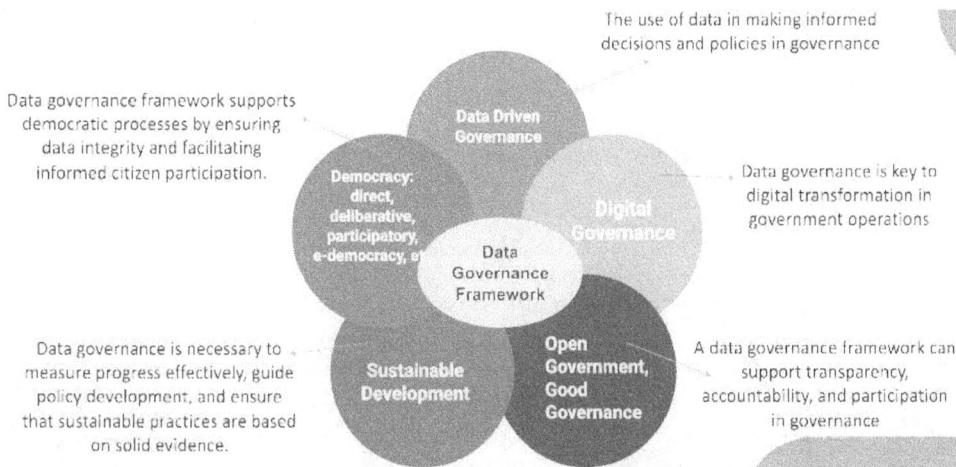

The use of data in making informed decisions and policies in governance

Data governance framework supports democratic processes by ensuring data integrity and facilitating informed citizen participation.

Data Driven Governance

Data governance is key to digital transformation in government operations

Democracy: direct, deliberative, participatory, e-democracy, et

Digital Governance

Data Governance Framework

Data governance is necessary to measure progress effectively, guide policy development, and ensure that sustainable practices are based on solid evidence.

Sustainable Development

Open Government, Good Governance

A data governance framework can support transparency, accountability, and participation in governance

Figure 10.2 Framework Conditions for Data Governance

A solid data governance framework is crucial for supporting democratic processes and other new governance frameworks. It ensures the integrity of data, which in turn facilitates informed participation of the people affected. By maintaining accurate and reliable data, such frameworks contribute to the direct, scrutinizing and participatory dimensions of democracy, including in the field of e-democracy. Data governance plays a crucial role in promoting data-driven and data-driven governance. This is achieved through the use of data to make informed decisions and policies, which is increasingly recognized as a fundamental aspect of competent governance. Such data-driven decision-making processes improve the effectiveness and relevance of government actions.

Furthermore, a framework for data governance is crucial for sustainable development and the realization of the SDGs (Sustainable Development Goals). It enables the effective measurement of progress, guides the development of sound policies and ensures that sustainable practices are supported by robust evidence. This evidence-based approach is key to achieving long-term development goals. Data governance is seen as one of the key pillars for the digital transformation of government operations. It underpins the modernization and efficiency of public services and ensures that digital strategies are based on reliable data.

A data governance framework supports the principles of open government and good governance, and national and local governments that are part of the Open Government Partnership (OGP, see) have systematically made national or local commitments to data for better governance. They underpin transparency, accountability and citizen participation, all of which are central to building trust between the public and government. By making data accessible and government processes more transparent, citizens are empowered and democratic processes are enhanced.

Therefore, data management is not only a technical necessity, but a fundamental element for the promotion of democratic values, sustainable development, digital innovation and transparent administration.

Excursus: The Emerging Need for Consolidated Data Governance in the Public Sector

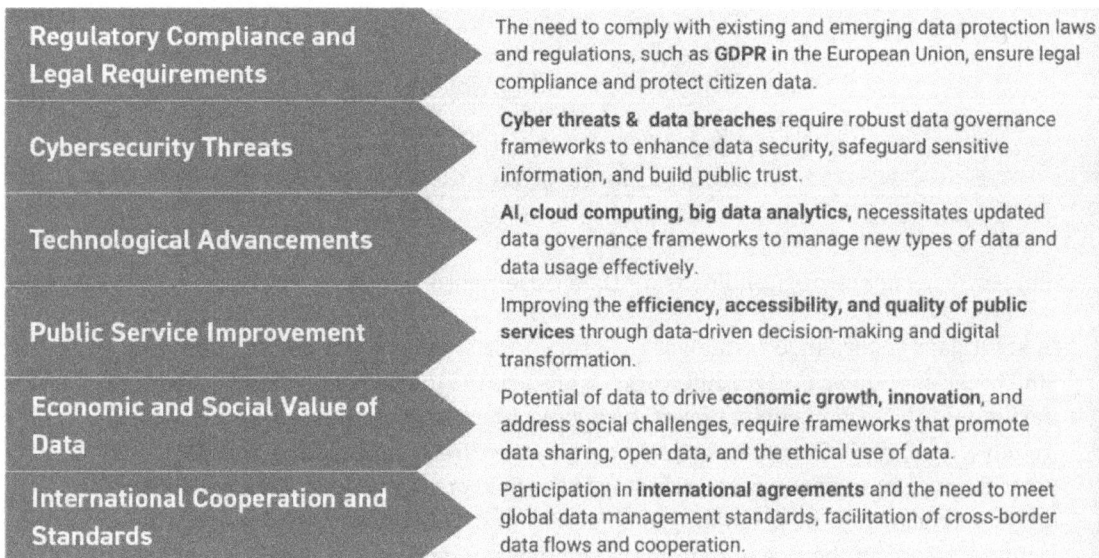

Regulatory Compliance and Legal Requirements	The need to comply with existing and emerging data protection laws and regulations, such as **GDPR** in the European Union, ensure legal compliance and protect citizen data.
Cybersecurity Threats	**Cyber threats & data breaches** require robust data governance frameworks to enhance data security, safeguard sensitive information, and build public trust.
Technological Advancements	**AI, cloud computing, big data analytics,** necessitates updated data governance frameworks to manage new types of data and data usage effectively.
Public Service Improvement	Improving the **efficiency, accessibility, and quality of public services** through data-driven decision-making and digital transformation.
Economic and Social Value of Data	Potential of data to drive **economic growth, innovation,** and address social challenges, require frameworks that promote data sharing, open data, and the ethical use of data.
International Cooperation and Standards	Participation in **international agreements** and the need to meet global data management standards, facilitation of cross-border data flows and cooperation.

Figure 10.3 Data Governance in the Public Sector

Data governance in the public sector is increasingly becoming a necessity due to various new requirements:

- **Compliance with regulations and legal requirements:** With data protection laws and regulations such as the General Data Protection Regulation (GDPR) in the European Union, there is an urgent need to ensure legal compliance and protect citizens' data. Data governance frameworks help public sector organizations comply with these legal requirements and protect personal data.

- **Cybersecurity threats:** The increasing number of cyber threats and data breaches requires robust data governance frameworks that improve data security, protect sensitive information and promote public trust. These frameworks help prevent unauthorized access to sensitive data.

- **Technological advances:** Advances in AI, cloud computing and big data analytics require the introduction of robust data governance frameworks. These frameworks are critical to managing new types of data and ensuring that they are used securely and effectively, especially as technologies evolve.

- **Improving public services:** Data management improves the efficiency, accessibility and quality of public services. By enabling data-driven decision-making and digital transformation, public services can be delivered more efficiently and better respond to the needs of citizens.

- **Economic and social value of data:** Data has the potential to drive economic growth and innovation and address social challenges. Frameworks that promote data sharing, open data and ethical data use are crucial to harnessing this potential for the common good.

- **International cooperation and standards:** Data governance is essential for international cooperation and compliance with global data management standards. In an interconnected world, facilitating cross-border data flows and collaboration depends on common governance standards and practices.

Definition of Data Governance

There is currently no standard definition of data governance that could summarize a single specialist area.

- Data Governance (OECD) [3]: Data governance refers to various arrangements, including technical, policy, regulatory or institutional provisions that affect data and its cycle (creation, collection, storage, use, protection, access, sharing and deletion) across policy domains and organizational and national boundaries.

- Data governance (Davies, 2022) [5]: Data governance concerns the rules, processes and behaviors related to the collection, management, analysis, use, sharing and disposal of data – personal and/or non-personal data. Good data governance should both promote benefits and minimize harm at every stage of the relevant data cycles.

Several other approaches to defining data governance can be found at Informing the Global Data Future: Benchmarking Data Governance Frameworks [9]

Emerging Trends in the Introduction of Data Governance Frameworks

The landscape of data governance frameworks today is characterized by its diversity and adaptability. A one-size-fits-all approach is not practical, as evidenced by the different implementation practices observed in recent years. Data governance has been introduced at various levels, from government-wide initiatives to localized municipal strategies to sector-specific regulations and within individual institutions.

- **Whole-of-government level:** A centralized approach to data governance is crucial. This includes the introduction of consistent data governance frameworks and policies across government. By establishing consistent data standards and practices and implementing government-wide platforms for data analytics and management, a concerted effort is being made to improve decision-making and service delivery across all areas and functions of government. The Singapore government, for example, is using government-wide application analytics to improve government services through data [13].

- **Local/municipal level:** Data governance will be tailored to the specific context and needs of municipalities. This includes a focus on the development of smart cities and smart villages through the integration of data governance practices that support local service initiatives and aim to make service delivery more efficient, responsive and tailored to the specific characteristics of the local population. The City of Vienna's Data Excellence Strategy, for example, envisages taking all necessary measures to ensure the timely provision of reliable, high-quality data to make the city a "data excellent" data capital [2].

- **Sector-specific level:** Certain sectors that require specialized knowledge or need to comply with specific regulations – such as healthcare [7], financial services and education – often use specific data governance models. These models are designed to address the specific privacy, security and ethical considerations of each sector and ensure that sector-specific regulations and requirements are met with precision and care.

- **Organizational level:** Within individual organizations or companies, data governance has an internal focus. Policies are developed to maximize the value of data by treating it as a key business asset. This approach often includes detailed rules for handling data within the organization to improve internal processes and use data to support business goals and strategies. Some organizations are investing in improving data literacy so that their employees can understand, interpret and use data effectively and responsibly, as Airbnb has done with its internal education initiative [1].

Together, these levels of data governance ensure that data is managed effectively and ethically from the highest levels of government down to communities and individual sectors, recognizing the multi-faceted nature of data as a resource for public good, economic growth and social development.

Connection between Data and Knowledge Governance

The existence of a robust data governance framework facilitates the efficient and secure transition of data, as described in the DIKW pyramid [8]. It ensures that data is accurate, accessible and reliable and forms the basis for the creation of information. By establishing policies, standards and procedures, data governance ensures that data is properly captured, stored and managed, enabling effective transformation of raw data into meaningful information.

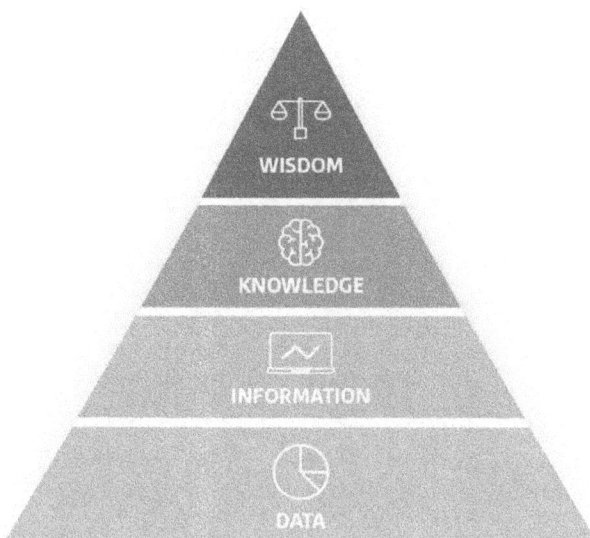

Figure 10.4
DIKW Pyramid

Based on a solid data foundation (based on the data governance framework), the information is then systematically analyzed to extract patterns and generate knowledge. This phase is crucial as data governance ensures that the information is consistent, well documented and maintained so that the organization can gain accurate insights and understand the implications of the information.

Data governance supports the translation of this process into knowledge by ensuring that knowledge is aligned with ethical and legal considerations, regulatory compliance and business objectives. It provides a structured approach to decision making by placing the insights gained from knowledge in the broader context of the organization's strategy and values. With a comprehensive data governance strategy, organizations and government agencies can not only collect data, but also use it to make smart, forward-looking decisions that are ethical and aligned with their long-term goals.

10.3.1 Pillars of the Data Governance Framework

There is no one size fits all when it comes to developing a data governance framework that works, yet there are certain pillars and components that should be considered to ensure a balanced approach, as the data governance framework works optimally when there is a balance between its core pillars – each component is critical and must be given due consideration to create a harmonious and effective system. The proposed framework is built on fundamental pillars – governance and institutions, values, trust, foundations and capabilities – each containing important sub-components that enable a comprehensive understanding of data governance. This framework has been developed based on the recommendations of the WDR21 report [14], the methodology of the Global Data Barometer [6], OECD recommendations [4] and others. It can or must be adapted and tailored to specific needs or requirements.

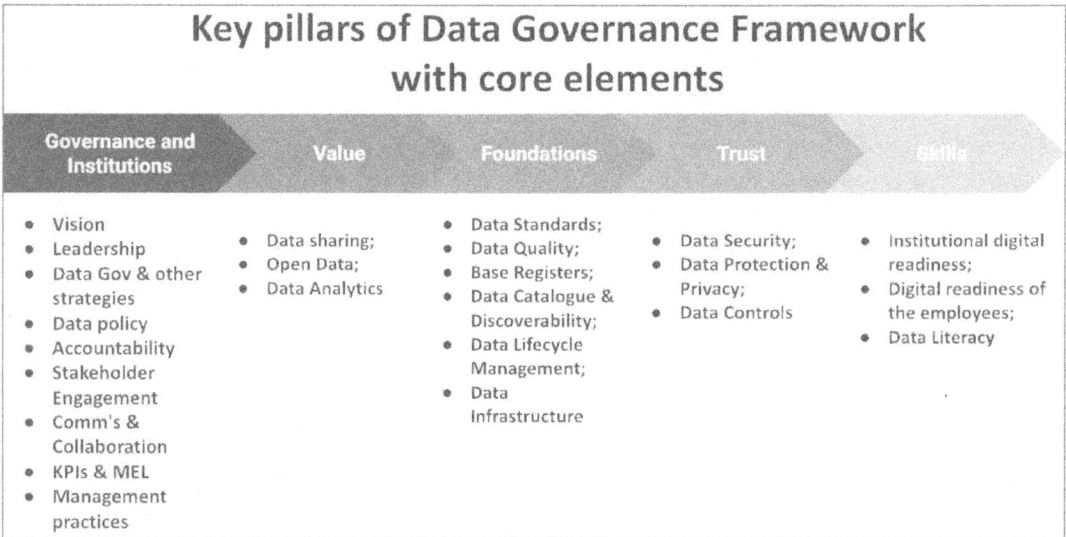

Key pillars of Data Governance Framework with core elements

Governance and Institutions	Value	Foundations	Trust	Skills
• Vision • Leadership • Data Gov & other strategies • Data policy • Accountability • Stakeholder Engagement • Comm's & Collaboration • KPIs & MEL • Management practices	• Data sharing; • Open Data; • Data Analytics	• Data Standards; • Data Quality; • Base Registers; • Data Catalogue & Discoverability; • Data Lifecycle Management; • Data Infrastructure	• Data Security; • Data Protection & Privacy; • Data Controls	• Institutional digital readiness; • Digital readiness of the employees; • Data Literacy

Figure 10.5 Pillars of a Data Governance Framework

The **governance and institutions pillar** is the cornerstone of a data governance framework. It prescribes clear rules, policies and procedures to ensure that data is managed, shared and protected in an open and transparent manner. Governance structures underpin and promote the establishment of these requirements and facilitate their proper implementation and ongoing monitoring. However, these must be accompanied by the flexibility to adapt to evolving data landscapes and technological advances to ensure that governance does not hinder innovation.

Examples of possible strategic measures to develop this pillar are as follows:

- **Establishing a data governance working group:** The main tasks of the data governance working group are to make strategic decisions in connection with data governance and to ensure the implementation of data governance strategies and practices.

- **Defining a data governance framework:** This involves setting a clear vision and a well-defined set of longer-term goals, identifying key stakeholders, defining roles and responsibilities and establishing governance structures and processes to achieve these goals.

- **Appointing a Chief Data Governance Officer (CDGO):** The CDGO and his/her team are responsible for setting priorities, organizing funding and establishing policies, procedures and standards related to data governance initiatives. The CDGO plays a key role in promoting a culture of data-driven decision making.

- **Establishing clear lines of communication and collaboration:** Communication must be prioritized as a critical function and adequate financial and human resources must be allocated to support its implementation. Regularly assess and evaluate the effectiveness of communication efforts using metrics such as reach, engagement and impact. In this way, public institutions and companies can continuously improve their communication strategies on data governance issues.

- **Developing and implementing of an internal data governance scorecard:** The scorecard could be an internal online reporting tool that enables both the visualization and understanding of how the responsible areas or departments are progressing in achieving the goals of their data governance agenda. The results are expressed by numbers (numerical values of the indicators), which are used to calculate the overall assessment of progress on the selected indicators.

The **pillar of value** ensures the comprehensive use and equitable sharing of the benefits of data. It is dedicated to using data as a strategic resource, facilitating informed decision-making and strengthening risk management and regulatory compliance. This pillar focuses on harnessing the potential of data while reducing the risks and costs associated with its governance. Extracting value from data drives the goals of the framework, but this pursuit must be balanced with ethical considerations. Maximizing data utility goes hand in hand with respecting individual rights and promoting collective benefit.

Examples of possible strategic measures to develop this pillar include

- Definition of data governance guidelines: This includes clear guidelines and frameworks that define data governance principles, data standards and protocols for data sharing. This ensures that data is collected, managed and shared in a standardized and transparent manner.

- By jointly creating a culture of data sharing both within authorities and with external partners, the exchange of data and knowledge is facilitated.

- Improving data analytics capabilities and investing in the development of data analytics capabilities, such as machine learning and artificial intelligence, to gain insights from data and make decisions.

- Encourage and support the release of open data that citizens, businesses and researchers can access and use to promote transparency and accountability.

The **pillar of fundamentals** serves as a foundation for sound data governance practices and includes essential elements such as basic registries, data catalogs, infrastructure, lifecycle management, quality and standards. A solid foundation promotes a unified approach to data management, improves consistency, accessibility and organization, and prevents fragmentation and inefficiency. This pillar forms the foundation for data practices. A balanced approach here means investing in a solid data infrastructure and sound data governance, while being flexible enough to accommodate new data types and sources.

Examples of possible strategic measures to develop this pillar include

- Strengthening the data infrastructure, which includes hardware, software and networks to support data collection, storage, processing and analysis.

- Improve data standards and definitions to ensure consistency and interoperability of data between different departments, agencies and systems in the public sector, especially for new systems.

- Improve data quality, including policies, procedures and controls to measure, monitor and improve data quality across all organizations.

- Improve data lifecycle management to ensure that data is appropriately managed and secured at every stage of its lifecycle.

- Creation of data catalogs containing a comprehensive list of the data available in the public institutions.

- Establish basic registers to ensure that data is consistent, accurate and accessible to all stakeholders. Establish procedures and rules for the use of base registers by public bodies, with clear roles for data owners and data managers.

The **pillar of trust** is the ethical backbone of data governance, ensuring the privacy and security of data and its ethical use. This pillar is central to building and maintaining trust between individuals, institutions and society by promoting responsible, ethical and transparent data management practices. Trust must be dynamically maintained, not just built. This requires constant engagement with stakeholders to understand their concerns and evolving expectations.

Examples of possible strategic measures to develop this pillar include

- Improve data security policies and procedures to ensure the confidentiality, integrity and availability of data. This can include data encryption, access controls and threat monitoring.

- Ensuring compliance with data protection regulations: Ensuring compliance with relevant data protection regulations based on existing regulations such as the GDPR.

- Strengthening cyber security measures by investing in firewalls, intrusion detection and prevention systems and regular security audits to protect against cyber-attacks and data breaches.

- Conduct data protection training and awareness programs for employees to ensure that they understand the importance of data protection and privacy and to promote a culture of data protection.

- Establish effective data controls, such as data access controls, data retention policies and data disposal procedures, to ensure that data is used only for its intended purpose and is properly retained and disposed of.

In the **skills pillar**, digital skills are proving to be crucial for sound data management. As the volume of data in public institutions increases, it is essential that employees have the digital skills required to manage and use data. This includes not only technical knowledge and data handling skills, but also soft skills such as effective communication and collaboration, ensuring that data is used ethically, securely and in line with relevant standards. It empowers employees to maintain the integrity and accessibility of data, reinforcing best practice in data governance. Qualifications enable employees to handle data appropriately. Balancing this pillar means providing training in the latest digital tools while creating an environment that fosters soft skills such as critical thinking and collaboration.

Examples of possible strategic measures to develop this pillar include

- Development of training programs to improve employees' digital skills, including training on digital tools and platforms and digital security.

- Provision of training programs to improve employees' data skills, including data analysis, interpretation and visualization.

- Develop a comprehensive plan to improve the digital readiness of institutions, including the development of digital policies, procedures and governance frameworks.

- Build partnerships with other private/public sector organizations, academic institutions and other stakeholders to share best practices, knowledge and resources. Establish communities of practice (CoP) to facilitate ongoing mutual support and professional development in the area of data governance.

In summary, a balanced approach to data governance ensures that no one pillar overrides another, fostering an environment where data is not only secure and compliant, but also actionable and a driver of innovation and public trust.

Sources

[1] 5 Data Governance Examples: Case Studies, Takeaways & More. URL *https://atlan.com/data-governance-examples/* – accessed: 2024/04/20

[2] Data Excellence of the City of Vienna.

[3] Data governance – OECD. URL *https://www.oecd.org/digital/data-governance/#:~:text=Data%20governance%20refers%20to%20diverse,and%20organisational%20and%20national%20borders* – accessed: 2024/04/20

[4] Data Governance in the Public Sector.

[5] Davies, Tim: Data governance and the Datasphere Literature Review (2022). Tim Davies

[6] Global Data Barometer. URL *https://globaldatabarometer.org/* – accessed: 2024/04/20 – Global Data Barometer

[7] IT, Brian Eastwood Twitter Brian Eastwood is a freelance writer with more than 15 years of experience covering healthcare; Delivery, Healthcare; IT, enterprise; Technology, Consumer; leadership, I. T.; Education, Higher: What Is the Role of Data Governance in Healthcare? URL *https://healthtechmagazine.net/article/2023/04/data-governance-in-healthcare-perfcon* – accessed: 2024/04/20 – Technology Solutions That Drive Healthcare

[8] Jain, Manas: The Pyramid of Data, Information, and Knowledge: A Guide for Better Decision Making. URL *https://medium.com/@manas.jain/the-pyramid-of-data-information-and-knowledge-a-guide-for-better-decision-making-d74f271bdd0d* – accessed: 2024/04/20 – Medium

[9] Marcucci, Sara; Alarcón, Natalia González; Verhulst, Stefaan G.; Wüllhorst, Elena: Informing the Global Data Future: Benchmarking Data Governance Frameworks. In: Data & Policy Volume 5 (2023), S. e30

[10] The Effects of Data Governance in Theory and Practice. URL *https://www.compact.nl/articles/the-effects-of-data-governance-in-theory-and-practice/* – accessed: 2024/04/20 – Compact

[11] The world's most valuable resource is no longer oil, but data. In: The Economist

[12] Watson, Poppy: Why data is the new oil. URL *https://futurescot.com/why-data-is-the-new-oil/* – accessed: 2024/04/20 – FutureScot

[13] Whole-of-Government Application Analytics (WOGAA) – Improve Government Services with Data. URL *https://www.developer.tech.gov.sg/products/categories/analytics/wogaa/overview.html* – accessed: 2024/04/20 – Singapore Government Developer Portal

[14] World Development Report 2022: FINANCE for an Equitable Recovery. URL *https://www.worldbank.org/en/publication/wdr2021* – accessed: 2024/04/20

10.4 Audit of Artificial Intelligence

Gabriele Bolek-Fügl

AI systems are capable of analyzing large amounts of data, predicting market trends and even automating customer interactions. These technologies can give companies a significant competitive advantage, but with success comes **new responsibilities**.

A good example of this is the case Moffatt v. Air Canada (2024 BCCRT 149[1]). The Canadian court British Columbia Civil Resolution Tribunal dealt with **liability of a com-**

pany for misinformation provided by its AI chatbot. This decision from February 14, 2024 shows what companies need to consider when integrating AI into customer-facing workflows.

The case involved plaintiff Jake Moffatt, who inquired about bereavement fares on Air Canada's website with the airline's AI chatbot. The chatbot incorrectly told him that he could apply for a retroactive bereavement fare within ninety days of purchasing his ticket. The chatbot also linked to the website where the information was available, but the customer, trusting the chatbot's statement, did not open it and bought a flight. If he had accessed the website, he would have realized that the chatbot's statement was incorrect. He later applied for a partial refund. However, Air Canada rejected his request on the grounds that company policy did not allow retroactive claims for bereavement fares, which contradicted the AI chatbot's response.

The Canadian court has now ruled in favor of the plaintiff. It ruled that Air Canada was liable for the chatbot's statements, which are equivalent to descriptions on the company's website and are binding. The ruling highlights the legal and ethical obligations of companies that use AI technologies.

Although this case relates to Canadian jurisdiction, central questions arise if AI is to be integrated into a company's business processes:

- How can company management be sure that these AI systems are not only effective, but also ethical and legally compliant?

- How can it be guaranteed that the decisions made by the AI are correct, fair, transparent and comprehensible?

- And how is it ensured that customer trust in the company is not damaged by faulty or biased algorithms? is jeopardized?

One possible answer lies in the audit of AI systems. A systematic and thorough audit process is the first step in ensuring that AI models are properly implemented and continuously monitored. Such an audit includes both the technical review and the assessment of data quality, checking model interpretability, analyzing ethical implications, compliance with legal regulations and the appropriateness of the processes surrounding the operation of the AI.

10.4.1 Fundamentals of the Audit

An audit is a systematic, independent and reproducible investigation with the aim of determining whether certain activities, processes, products or systems comply with specified requirements, standards or regulations. Audits are an integral part of corporate reality and are carried out in many areas, such as financial reporting, quality assurance, environmental management and IT security.

The main features of an audit include

1. **Audit objective:** The defined audit objective describes the exact purpose or background of the audit. It determines which aspects, processes, systems or organizational units are to be audited and which questions the audit should answer. The audit objective thus determines the direction and scope of the audit and ensures that the audit is focused on the relevant areas.

1. **Systematic:** An audit follows a structured and methodical approach. There is a clear audit plan and a defined procedure for gathering, collecting and analyzing the necessary information.

2. **Independence:** An audit must be conducted by an independent person or entity that is not directly involved in the activities being audited so that the results, findings and recommendations are objective and unbiased.

3. **Traceability:** All steps of the audit as well as the results and conclusions must be documented. This serves both the traceability and transparency of the audit process. Finally, an audit report is created that contains the procedure, assessment methodology and all results of the audit.

4. **Verification of conformity.** The main objective of an audit is to check whether the processes, products or systems to be examined comply with the specifications from company guidelines, selected standards and legal requirements or, if applicable, follow best practice. Deviations from the specifications are treated as findings and documented in the audit report.

5. **Evaluation and recommendation:** Based on the audit results, recommendations are often made to rectify any deviations or make improvements.

6. **Regularity:** Audits can be carried out once or regularly, depending on the organization's requirements and objectives. Regular audits are often part of a continuous improvement process.

Audits of AI systems can only be carried out if the company has defined specifications for this. Individual aspects, such as conformity with certain legal requirements, can also be checked during the implementation project if necessary.

10.4.2 Audit Team

It is the responsibility of the management to initiate the audit process and ensure that it is carried out thoroughly and regularly. This can be carried out by an in-house audit unit or by an external team of experts.

The commissioning of external auditors has several advantages:

- Independence from the management and the implementing project team

- Independent perspective on the AI systems
- Experience from other audit projects
- Up-to-date knowledge on regulation
- Knowledge of various audit methods and best practices
- Comprehensive reporting on the identified risks

Setting up an internal team to check and ensure the compliance of AI systems also brings advantages:

- Good knowledge of internal processes, specific technical details and the underlying data structures
- Possibility of continuous monitoring and improvement with changing focal points instead of selective testing
- Protection of sensitive company data, trade secrets and intellectual property
- An internal team lives and understands the corporate culture and values of the company and integrates this into its audit.

In terms of the cost of setting up an internal team, the investment should be weighed against the long-term savings from regular audits and independence from external providers. External auditors may require higher short-term expenses, but offer specialized expertise, experience and objectivity.

10.4.3 Difference Between Risk Management and Audit

AI risk management and the AI audit both aim to keep the company safe and legally compliant. They help to identify and control risks at an early stage and ensure compliance with regulations. The main difference between them lies in their objectives, methods and when they are carried out.

Table 10.3 Differences between AI Risk Management and AI Audit

Criterion	AI Risk Management	AI Audit
Goal	Identification, assessment and mitigation of risks	Checking and evaluating compliance with guidelines, standards and regulations
Focus	Proactive and continuous monitoring of risks	Retrospective evaluation of compliance with specifications and economic efficiency
Methods	Continuous risk analysis, scenario planning, implementation of control measures	Systematic examination and evaluation of compliance with defined guidelines, controls and processes

Table 10.3 Differences between AI Risk Management and AI Audit *(continued)*

Criterion	AI Risk Management	AI Audit
Time of implementation	Continuously, throughout the entire life cycle of the AI system	Time-related and according to a defined audit plan
Application	At every stage of AI development and implementation	After the development of the AI or at fixed intervals

Risk management aims to identify risks before they become a problem for the organization and to find and implement suitable risk mitigation measures. The technical and organizational measures derived for the risks become part of the internal control system of the company and regularly reviewed by the audit unit.

The AI audit is the retrospective assessment of whether the AI system was developed and is operated in accordance with regulatory requirements, company guidelines and ethical standards. The audit can also evaluate the effectiveness of the risk management method.

Audits are always geared towards a defined period of time and a defined objective. Past actions are reviewed and evaluated based on the relevant requirements in this context.

10.4.4 Helpful Audit Checklists

There are checklists and standards specifically aimed at assessing the appropriateness, accuracy, safety and ethical defensibility of AI systems. Each of these standards focuses on a slightly different topic area, and each organization must determine its own focus. Here are some of the most important checklists and standards you can use. Checklists that have already been presented in other chapters, for example in risk management or data protection, are no longer listed here:

Ethics Guidelines for Trustworthy AI (EU) [2]

Publisher: European Commission

Country: EU

Release date: 2019

The following document can be used to review the ethics guideline presented in detail in section 10.1:

Assessment List for Trustworthy Artificial Intelligence (ALTAI) for self-assessment

Release date: 2020

Purpose: To ensure that AI systems are developed and used in a trustworthy manner and in accordance with European values.

Content: Audit questions on the seven key requirements from the EU ethics guidelines, including transparency, security, fairness and data protection. The ALTAI checklist contains very detailed and practical tips for implementing trustworthy AI. If you follow this checklist, you cannot forget any areas.

Use: Basically suitable for any organization that wants to develop or operate trustworthy AI systems.

AI4People Ethical Framework [4]

Publisher: AI4People Initiative

Country: EU (international influence)

Release date: 2018

Purpose: To ensure that AI systems are designed in accordance with ethical principles that promote the well-being of society. Further different research results on the use of AI can be found at.

Content: Framework that focuses on principles such as beneficence, non-harm, autonomy and justice

Use: Suitable for all organizations that implement ethical AI development. Provides a comprehensive ethical foundation that goes far beyond technical requirements.

Ethical AI Checklists [8] [3] [6] [5]

Publisher: Various technology companies such as Microsoft and Google publish their own checklists, which can also be used by other companies

Land: International

Release date: Since 2019

Purpose: To support companies in implementing ethical guidelines for the development and use of AI

Content: Practical checklists and reporting on your own dealings with AI systems, covering various aspects such as fairness, transparency and data protection

Use: Easily applicable and often specifically tailored to the needs of developers and companies. Individual issues may focus on the specific interests of the issuing organization and may not comprehensively cover all ethical aspects. For example, in May 2022, Google explains in detail the progress made in recognizing people with different skin tones "Improving skin tone evaluation in machine learning".

IDW PS 861 [7]

Published by: Institute of Public Auditors in Germany (IDW)

Country: Germany

Release date: 2023

Purpose: Guidance on auditing algorithms and AI systems as part of the audit of companies' financial statements

Content: Guidelines for assessing the compliance and appropriateness of AI systems, in particular with regard to their use in financial processes

Use: Provides a clear standard for auditors to assess the compliance and adequacy of AI systems. Specifically tailored to the audit focus, which may limit its application in other areas.

IIA's Updated AI Auditing Framework [9]

Published by: The Institute of Internal Auditors (IIA)

Country: International (headquarters in the USA)

Release date: 2023

Purpose: The framework is designed to provide internal auditors with the necessary tools and guidelines to comprehensively audit AI systems. It focuses on ensuring that AI applications in organizations are robust, secure, ethical and compliant.

Content: The framework provides a structured approach to auditing AI systems, including the assessment of governance, risk management, model validation, ethical implications and compliance with regulatory requirements. It contains specific checklists, guidelines and best practices to support auditors in identifying and mitigating risks in AI systems.

Further checklists for testing AI systems will be developed and published in the coming months and years. In particular, to map conformity with the AI Act. It is important to ensure that the checklist used has always been developed by trustworthy organizations and is appropriate for your own audit objective.

10.4.5 Example of a Simple AI Audit Checklist

The following AI audit checklist can be used as a basis for your own AI audit planning and contains questions that are independent of a specific AI system. For your own audit planning, we recommend adding further audit procedures from the above checklists.

1. **Review of the governance structure for AI systems**
   - Are there documented, clear responsibilities and decision-making processes?
   - Are the decisions and measures taken documented in a comprehensible manner?
   - Are there guidelines for the implementation and monitoring of AI projects?
   - Has a definition of ethical and legal standards been drawn up?
   - Are there guidelines for the assessment of AI algorithms?
   - Are changes to legal requirements monitored and, if necessary, integrated into the processes?

- Is there an internal control system for the AI use cases?
- Is an external opinion (outside the team) regularly sought?

2. **Review of ethics and compliance requirements**

- Are there minimum requirements and a procedure for ethical considerations?
- Who is responsible for implementation?
- Is the assessment carried out by a diverse team?
- How are the results documented?
- Have guidelines been created with reference to the ethical use of the AI tool?
- Is there an AI Code of Conduct/Code of Conduct for the proper use of AI?
- What definition of fairness is used for the AI systems and how is it measured/evidenced?
- How are transparency, discrimination and data protection dealt with in AI systems?
- How and by whom is the proper operation of the AI application monitored?
- Is the specialist department/domain user appropriately involved in AI projects and operations?

3. **Examination for the selection of AI applications (use cases)**

- Is the decision-making process for selecting the use case comprehensible and plausible?
- Are sufficiently trained people part of the selection process, the project and the operation?
- Have all stakeholders for the use case been identified?
- Was a state-of-the-art AI tool selected or AI model developed?
- Have all necessary legal requirements been identified?
- Have the correct assessments been made with regard to role and risk in accordance with the AI Act?

4. **Test for the selection of AI components**

- Is certification/registration necessary for the AI tool?
- Were specifications for trustworthy AI systems adhered to during development?
- Are the requirements for explainable AI being met?
- Were the affected parties/stakeholders of the AI use case surveyed?
- Has appropriate risk management been implemented for the AI application?
- Have the best case/worst case scenarios and KPIs for the use case been identified?

5. **Technology review & infrastructure**
   - On what basis was the decision made to develop the AI yourself or to buy it?
   - Does the company have sufficient trained personnel or experience to carry out the project and operation?
   - Has an appropriate infrastructure been designed for the project phases and operation of the AI tool?
   - Was the use of cloud functionality assessed for the training phase?
   - Does the planned AI system environment fit into the existing infrastructure?
   - Was performance data taken into account in the design phase?

6. **Data strategy audit**
   - How was the data required for the AI tool selected?
   - Is the required data available in the company or does it have to be procured?
   - Is there "consent" or a legitimate purpose for the personal data?
   - If personal data is processed, has the AI application been correctly entered in the data processing register?
   - Are there requirements for the quality of the data and is it defined how this is measured and monitored?
   - Who is responsible for the various data and data types? Has a responsible person already been appointed?
   - Are there implemented security measures, monitoring tools and control measures for the data?

7. **Talent and competence development test**
   - Have the required competencies and skills been identified, defined and documented?
   - Is the project team/team sufficiently diverse for the operation?
   - Is a transfer of knowledge from external to internal persons ensured?
   - Does the team have the necessary experience?
   - Do the people involved know the company's goals and AI strategy?
   - Are the competencies regularly assessed and supplemented if necessary?
   - How is continuous further training ensured, especially for ethical aspects?

8. **Testing the operation of the AI application**
   - Is continuous measurement and assessment of risks ensured?
   - Is the initial assessment regularly questioned?
   - Are the results of the AI tool monitored in a traceable manner?
   - Are the people monitoring the system adequately trained and familiarized with its operation?

- Are the target values of the results known?
- Does the company have sufficient knowledge to eliminate inappropriate results?
- Are the users/administrators/clerks and supervisors informed about the ethical implications/risks for stakeholders?
- How are new findings incorporated into the AI use case?
- Was the use case explained to those affected in clear language?
- Can those affected ask questions, object to a result or lodge a complaint?
- Are the relevant interest groups regularly informed?
- Is feedback actively obtained from those affected?
- How is the feedback processed and are ethical concerns also addressed?

Not all of these areas always have to be audited in the respective AI audit. Each audit should focus on specific areas and examine the individual issues in depth.

Sources

[1] Air Canada's Chatbot case: More questions than answers – Law360 Canada. URL *https://www.law360.ca/ca/articles/1815402/air-canada-s-chatbot-case-more-questions-than-answers* – accessed: 2024/08/16

[2] Assessment List for Trustworthy Artificial Intelligence (ALTAI) for self-assessment | Shaping Europe's digital future. URL *https://digital-strategy.ec.europa.eu/en/library/assessment-list-trustworthy-artificial-intelligence-altai-self-assessment* – accessed: 2024/08/16

[3] Empowering responsible AI practices | Microsoft AI. URL *https://www.microsoft.com/en-us/ai/responsible-ai* – accessed: 2024/08/16

[4] Floridi, Luciano: AI4People Ethical Framework (2018) URL *https://ai4people.org/PDF/AI4People_Ethical_Framework_For_A_Good_AI_Society.pdf* – accessed: 2024/08/16

[5] Google: KI-Grundsätze – Ziele für die Entwicklung nutzbringender künstlicher Intelligenz. URL *https://ai.google/static/documents/DE-AI-Principles.pdf* – accessed: 2024/08/16

[6] Google AI Principles. URL *https://ai.google/responsibility/principles/* – accessed: 2024/08/16 Google AI.

[7] IDW PS: Prüfung von KI-Systemen (IDW PS 861 (03.2023). URL *https://shop.idw-verlag.de/IDW-PS-Pruefung-von-KI-Systemen-IDW-PS-861-03.2023/20685* – accessed: 2024/08/16 –IDW Verlag.

[8] Microsoft: Responsible AI Transparency Report (2024). URL *https://query.prod.cms.rt.microsoft.com/cms/api/am/binary/RW1l5BO* – accessed: 2024/08/16

[9] The IIA's Updated AI Auditing Framework. URL *https://www.theiia.org/en/content/tools/professional/2023/the-iias-updated-ai-auditing-framework/* – accessed: 2024/08/16

10.5 Code of Conduct

Gabriele Bolek-Fügl

A code of conduct (CoC), is a document that defines the ethical principles and guidelines for the conduct and decisions of people, systems or organizations. The aim is to strengthen ethical integrity and professional behavior in business conduct and to prevent risks and misconduct.

The idea of a code of conduct is very old and can be traced back through history in various forms. In many cultures, there were moral and ethical guidelines that governed the behavior of individuals within a community. In the business context, companies and professional associations began to develop formal codes of conduct in the 20th century to set ethical standards that met the growing expectations of society, customers and the workforce. The first formal code of conduct for business was drawn up by the International Chamber of Commerce (ICC) in 1937 with the aim of regulating business competition and preventing it from harming the environment and society [1].

Codes of conduct were created in a variety of contexts and for different purposes long before artificial intelligence played a role in the business world. Some of the traditional areas of application are:

- communicate the values of an organization

- promote fair play, respect and integrity in sport, both on and off the pitch

- ensure integrity in the academic environment and create a safe, respectful environment for all members of the educational community

- ensure ethical fundraising practices, transparency and the effective use of resources in NGOs

Regardless of the respective application context, a code of conduct aims to create a culture of integrity and ethical conduct in an organization or community. It serves as an instrument for clearly defining expectations, strengthening stakeholder trust and providing guidance for decision-making.

> In cases where ethical dilemmas or uncertainties arise, the Code of Conduct proves to be an indispensable resource that enables people to make informed decisions.

In the DIN ISO 19600 Compliance Management System standard, a code is generally defined as a description of practices that have been developed internally or by an external industry organization (see section 3.20 DIN ISO 19600 CMS). A code of conduct, on the other hand, is a document that specifies the central duties and values of an organization on the basis of a voluntary commitment.

In principle, there are no formal requirements for the creation of a code of conduct. It is an agreement by an author, usually an organization or interest group, which is aimed at one or more stakeholders and which the publisher has voluntarily undertaken to comply with [2]. However, it is useful if the document is consistent with the corporate identity, e. g. in relation to other company guidelines, strategy documents or company brochures.

As artificial intelligence continues to make inroads into business processes and decision-making, the scope of codes of conduct is expanding to address the specific challenges and ethical considerations of implementing AI technologies.

> The aim of a code of conduct for the use of AI in the organization is to promote a sense of responsibility, transparency and ethical conduct among the workforce and to communicate the intended behavior to stakeholders and target groups.

The following consideration deals with the specific aspects that should result from the use of artificial intelligence or other complex technologies, such as robotics, etc., through a code of conduct. A distinction is made between external and internal effects for the target groups in order to gain a comprehensive understanding of the different perspectives and requirements:

Table 10.4 Aspects for a Code of Conduct

Aspect	Internal Effects	External Effects
Building trust & correlation	Signals to employees the importance of the potential risks and ethical implications of AI. Strengthens confidence in the technology, reduces fears and promotes acceptance. Promotes an inclusive work environment in which employees feel valued and are actively involved in ethical considerations and decisions.	Customers, partners and the public gain trust in the company's use of technology. This is important with regard to the protection of personal data and the fairness of processes. Strengthens customer loyalty through transparent communication and ethical behavior, which increases customer confidence in products and services.

Table 10.4 Aspects for a Code of Conduct *(continued)*

Aspect	Internal Effects	External Effects
Risk management, legal compliance & global standards	Supports the identification, minimization and management of AI-related risks such as data breaches and unfair decision-making. Ensures that the workforce complies with defined laws and regulations for the use of AI and adheres to international standards to prevent errors and reputational damage. Supports the harmonization of standards of conduct across borders, facilitates international cooperation and collaboration.	Transparency about how legal and ethical requirements are handled enables (potential) business partners to better assess the company, e. g. which management systems are used [3]. Promotes global partnerships and trust between companies, industries and countries by adhering to internationally recognized (ethical) standards.
Promoting innovation	Creates an environment that promotes innovation by providing clear guidelines for the ethically responsible use of AI. Steers research and development in an ethical direction.	A company that is perceived as an innovation leader improves its image among customers, partners and within the industry. This will position it as an attractive business partner and strengthen its negotiating position.
Recruiting and developing talents,	A clear code of conduct can attract talented individuals who value ethical standards and corporate culture and help to retain this talent in the long term.	
Competitive advantage	Promoting a culture of continuous learning and adapting to new (ethical) challenges arising from technological developments.	Creates an advantage over competitors by demonstrating transparency, ethical behavior and social responsibility, which is appreciated by customers and partners [4].
Sustainability & Crisis management	Motivates more sustainable business practices and use of technology, supports environmental and social responsibility. Improves the organization's ability to respond effectively to ethical dilemmas and crises by establishing clear policies and processes in advance.	Improves corporate image and fosters positive relationships with environmental groups and the general public. Can increase public confidence in times of crisis by demonstrating that the company proactively incorporates ethical considerations into its responses.

The content of an effective AI code of conduct requires the approval of top management, as only senior management is in a position to determine the scope and appropriate use of AI systems within the company.

> In an era where AI tools are often available at low cost or even for free, it is imperative that it is not left to the workforce, but management to make the decisions on how and which AI applications may be used.

There are several companies that also publish their AI code of conduct. The following organizations are good examples and sources of ideas:

- KI Guidelines of Deutsche Telekom AG, Bonn [5]
- AI Compass of the City of Vienna, Austria [6]
- AI strategy of the city of Linz, Austria [7]
- AI guidelines of the APA – Austria Press Agency, Vienna [8]
- Guideline of the Ministry of Schools and Education of the State of North Rhine-Westphalia, Düsseldorf [9]

It is not absolutely necessary to create your own AI code of conduct. An existing code of conduct can simply be expanded to include issues relating to digital technologies. One example of this is The European Code of Conduct for Research Integrity [10].

The 2023 update of the European Code of Conduct for Research Integrity has been revised to ensure its continued relevance and applicability across all disciplines, including new research fields and methods. The European Commission recognizes this Code as an authoritative reference for research integrity, especially for projects supported by EU funds. In addition, the European Code of Conduct is increasingly becoming a model for organizations and researchers across Europe and beyond [11].

10.5.1 Example of a Code of Conduct for the Use of Artificial Intelligence in the Organization

Individual aspects can be selected from the following formulations that could be taken into account in a code of conduct when using artificial intelligence in an organization. Of course, the descriptions must be adapted and expanded to suit the company, the specific AI use cases and the scope of use.

Preamble or foreword

This Code of Conduct (Code of Conduct/AI Guidelines) sets out the approach and commitments that our organization pursues in the development, implementation and use of artificial intelligence (AI). Our aim is to ensure that our AI systems are used responsibly, transparently and for the benefit of [name of stakeholder].

We express not only the ethical standards that we set for our own work with AI, but also the expectations that we have of our partners and all those involved in the field of AI technologies. We will refrain from business practices that run counter to the principles of this Code. At the same time, we welcome it when our [mention stakeholders] are guided by similar ethical standards and values.

This Code of Conduct is the ethical framework for the use of AI in our business environment and strengthens our efforts to use technology for the benefit of society and in line with our values.

Every person in our organization has a responsibility to live this Code of Conduct when dealing with AI and related business activities. Managers and [dedicated contact persons] are available for ethical questions relating to AI in the event of uncertainties or questions about the application of the guideline in specific situations.

If you are confronted with a situation that potentially violates our Code or poses a risk to the integrity of our AI initiatives, we encourage you to report it through our whistleblower system. This ensures that transparency, safety and ethical responsibility are always at the forefront of all our AI activities and that the trust of our [customers, clients, employees and society] is strengthened and maintained.

[Management/declared contact persons]

Scope of application

The Code of Conduct is addressed to all employees of the [organization and affiliates], regardless of their position or department, as well as to our [list of stakeholders, such as partners, suppliers] and any third parties who use or interact with AI technologies on behalf of the [organization].

The guidelines apply to all activities and processes in which AI systems are developed, implemented or used. This includes, but is not limited to, research and development, the use of AI in our products and services, the analysis of data by AI systems and any interactions with AI-supported interfaces that are used as part of our business activities.

Violations of this Code will be taken seriously and may result in actions that vary depending on the severity of the violation.

1. Responsibility and accountability

The responsibility for any use of AI systems in our organization and the use of AI-generated results lies with a human being. All AI systems are developed and put into operation with clearly defined objectives and taking into account their potential impact on individuals and society.

Throughout the operation of an AI system, decisions made by AI systems are clearly identified and accountability for monitoring the accuracy of AI results is assigned to a department/position. A mechanism for review and adjustment of AI systems must be established to minimize unintended harm or bias.

In order to make appropriate decisions in increasingly demanding scenarios in the professional environment, the following key questions can provide guidance:

1. Do my actions comply with the legal requirements and the guidelines of the [organization]?

2. Do I have all the necessary and sufficient information and knowledge to make a decision in accordance with the [organization's] requirements?

3. Is my decision in line with the values and ethical guidelines of the [organization]?

4. Can I openly explain and defend my decision and my approach to colleagues, managers, other stakeholders, authorities and the public?

5. Would I feel comfortable if my actions inside or outside the organization were open to public discussion, for example in the media?

In the event of uncertainty or doubt, it is important to proactively seek support from managers, the relevant topic managers or via other designated channels.

2. Transparency and explainability

We stand for trustworthiness and therefore we will inform users and data subjects about the use of AI systems in the processing of their [request, specific service, product or service] and provide access to information about how they work.

The description of how AI systems work and how they make decisions should be clear and comprehensible for the respective target group. It should be clearly communicated when decisions are made by AI systems and how or with what criteria they were made. This applies in particular to the processing of information in critical or sensitive areas (health, lending, job applications, etc.).

The decisions made by AI must lie reliably within our predefined expectation corridor and must be evaluated regularly.

3. Fairness and non-discrimination

Our AI systems shall be designed and monitored to ensure fair processing of our [insert stakeholder name]'s data and avoid discrimination based on age, gender, race, religion, disability or other characteristics that may be relevant to the outcome.

There will be regular reviews of the results of the AI systems during operation to ensure that the AI systems do not exhibit unconscious bias or discriminatory patterns. Where technically unavoidable, other organizational measures will be put in place to minimize undue impact on [name of stakeholder].

4. Data protection and data security

We are committed to data protection. As a matter of principle, no personal data is processed in our organization without a corresponding legal basis. The protection of personal data and the guarantee of data security are of the highest priority in the development and use of AI systems.

Appropriate measures are taken to ensure the confidentiality, integrity and availability of data. The processing of personal data and the protection mechanisms are explained in our privacy policy [alternatively, the description can also be found here]. For specific questions and new data processing operations, the Data Protection Officer must be consulted [contact details].

When using data, attention must always be paid to the quality and accuracy of the required information. If outdated or inconsistent data is used for a calculation or AI training, the results will most likely be disappointing. It is important to implement measures that ensure consistently appropriate data quality.

5. Training and further education of our employees

To ensure the importance of and compliance with our AI Code of Conduct, we offer our employees a comprehensive program of training. This program is designed to provide all employees – from management level to specialist teams – with the necessary knowledge and skills to understand and responsibly manage the ethical, legal, social and technical implications of AI use.

The training initiatives include:

- Induction events for new employees to familiarize them with the principles and guidelines of this AI Code of Conduct from the outset

- Regular courses and events that address current topics in AI, ethics, privacy and security to deepen awareness of potential risks and the importance of responsible decision-making

- Specific training modules for teams directly involved in the development and implementation of AI systems to ensure that technical decisions are always in line with our Code and organizational values

- Ongoing training programs that enable everyone involved to continuously develop their skills and keep abreast of the latest technological developments and ethical discussions

We recognize that the artificial intelligence landscape is rapidly evolving and are therefore committed to regularly evaluating and adapting our training and development programs. This ensures that our employees not only have the skills and knowledge to use AI responsibly, but also that they are empowered to use these technologies for the benefit of [name stakeholder] and society as a whole.

Active participation in these educational initiatives is mandatory for the [organization] workforce to support our shared goal of promoting the ethical and responsible use of AI.

6. Collaboration and stakeholder engagement

Our organization encourages collaboration with other organizations, regulators and the public to promote best practices for the use of AI and to share our findings. We strive to understand and address the perspectives and concerns of our [insert stakeholder name] regarding AI systems.

Our department [contact person and contact details] will support you with all questions.

10.5.2 Further Considerations on the AI Code of Conduct

An AI code of conduct is a living document that needs to be reviewed and updated at short intervals to keep pace with technological developments and societal expectations. New AI tools are currently coming onto the market on a weekly basis, and the major manufacturers update their AI systems at least every six months. The interpretation of ethical requirements and the assessment of risks are also adapting to this rhythm of change. This requires the definition of a short assessment period to evaluate whether the guidelines still adequately support business practices or need to be adapted.

For this reason, it is advisable to provide specific and detailed instructions for the workforce in a format that can be easily updated by those responsible and is also easily accessible to the target group. For example, current information and developments in the following areas could be published on the intranet:

- Responsibility of the user for the correct results when using generative AI in the work processes

- Listing of the (generative) AI tools explicitly released by the organization, including version designation and reference to the license, if applicable

- Explanations on the correct use of the released (generative) AI tools and reference to the risks, e. g. "hallucinating" or "inappropriate prompting", and how these can be avoided or minimized

- Note on legally compliant handling (data protection, copyright, rights of use) with sensitive or personal data and business secrets

- Presentation of the labeling obligation when using AI-generated results, e. g. for images, videos or texts

- Audit obligation and critical scrutiny of information received from third parties or data seen on the Internet
    - Refers to texts, voice messages/phone calls, images and videos
    - Indications of how this information can be checked for false messages (AI-generated deepfakes), for example

These topics are of course not exhaustive, must be appropriate to the company in question and do not take into account future developments in AI technology. Therefore, the range of AI tools must be regularly evaluated, including an assessment of how this could affect the daily work of the workforce.

Sources

[1] Mamic, Ivanka, in *Implementing Codes of Coduct*, (2004) International Labour Organization, Genf, p. 36

[2] Mamic, Ivanka, in *Implementing Codes of Coduct*, (2004) International Labour Organization, Genf, p. 13

[3] Gyamfi, Sandra, in *Verhaltenskodizes im UWG, Corporate Social Responsibility Standards und Rahmenwerke für die nichtfinanzielle Erklärung nach HGB* (2022) LIT Verlag Münster, p. 29

[4] Gyamfi, Sandra, in *Verhaltenskodizes im UWG, Corporate Social Responsibility Standards und Rahmenwerke für die nichtfinanzielle Erklärung nach HGB* (2022) LIT Verlag Münster, p. 37

[5] Deutsche Telekom AG, *https://www.telekom.com/de/konzern/digitale-verantwortung/details/ki-leit linien-der-telekom-523904* accessed: 2024/04/13

[6] Stadt Wien, *https://www.telekom.com/de/konzern/digitale-verantwortung/details/ki-leitlinien-der-telekom-523904* accessed: 2024/04/13

[7] Stadt Linz, *https://www.linz.at/digitaleslinz/ki-strategie.php* accessed: 2024/02/12

[8] APA – Austria Presse Agentur, *https://www.linz.at/digitaleslinz/ki-strategie.php* accessed: 2024/02/12

[9] Ministerium für Schule und Bildung des Landes Nordrhein-Westfalen, *https://www.schulministerium. nrw/system/files/media/document/file/handlungsleitfaden_ki_msb_nrw_230223.pdf* accessed: 2024/03/18

[10] ALLEA All European Academies, *The European Code of Conduct for Research Integrity*, (2023) ALLEA, Berlin

[11] ALLEA Secretariat (Berlin-Brandenburg Academy of Sciences and Humanities), *https://allea.org/ portfolio-item/european-code-of-conduct-2023/* accessed: 2024/04/13

10.6 AI and Sustainability

Klaudia Zotzmann-Koch

The protection of the environment from harmful effects of AI systems is laid down in the definition of objectives in the AI Act. Art. 1 para. 1 AI Act refers to the principle of the protection of fundamental rights set out in the **Charter of Fundamental Rights**:

"The purpose of this Regulation is to improve the functioning of the internal market and promote the uptake of human-centric and trustworthy artificial intelligence (AI), while ensuring a high level of protection of health, safety, fundamental rights enshrined in the Charter, including democracy, the rule of law and environmental protection, against the harmful effects of AI systems in the Union and supporting innovation." (Art. 1 para. 1 AI Act)

Accordingly, according to Art. 3 no. 49 AI Act, serious **damage to property or the environment** constitutes a serious incident that must lead to corresponding consequences (for the reporting obligation, see Art. 73 AI Act). In addition, **environmental crime** is listed alongside terrorism, human trafficking, murder and illegal arms trafficking (and several others) in the "List of criminal offenses pursuant to Art. 5 para. 1 first subparagraph lit. h sublit iii" (Annex II AI Act).

The fact that environmental protection and sustainability are given such central importance in the AI Act is intended to promote the development and operation of ethical and trustworthy AI solutions so that environmentally friendly standards, interoperability and standardization of systems spread from Europe to the rest of the world. The AI Act calls for standardization in line with the state of the art, which manufacturers must also demonstrate (see Recital 121 AI Act). The standards should be developed "with the involvement of all relevant stakeholders, in particular SMEs, consumer organizations and environmental and social stakeholders" (Recital 121 AI AI Act).

The development of and compliance with uniform standards for the development and operation of environmentally friendly AI solutions will strengthen Europe as a business location as a source of ethical and environmentally friendly AI solutions in the medium to long term.

10.6.1 ESG – Environmental, Social and Corporate Governance

Defined rules in the areas of environmental, social and corporate governance are just as forward-looking as uniform standards for AI solutions. ESG-criteria and framework conditions have become an integral part of all corporate, public authority and government strategies. In the AI Act, ESG criteria are implicitly included when talking about **equity, ethical solutions, inclusion or environmental sustainability**. The aim is always to ensure that the requirements of all interest groups are taken into account.

> "Social and environmental well-being means that AI systems are developed and used in a sustainable and environmentally friendly way and for the benefit of all people, while monitoring and assessing the long-term impact on individuals, society and democracy. The application of these principles should, where possible, inform the design and use of AI models. In any case, they should serve as a basis for the development of codes of conduct under this Regulation. All stakeholders, including industry, academia, civil society and standardization bodies, are encouraged to take the ethical principles into account when developing voluntary best practices and standards, as appropriate." (Recital 27 AI Act)

In the medium and long term, compliance with ESG criteria leads to a strengthening of the economic position of the respective company as well as Europe as a business location. Anyone familiar with the stock market will have noticed the positive economic development of companies that adhere to ESG criteria and of sustainable funds and ETFs in recent years.

10.6.2 Diversity, Inclusion, Justice

In addition to regulations, the AI Regulation also relies on the voluntary factor in the form of codes of conduct, including with regard to ethical guidelines and environmental sustainability (Recital 165 AI Act). In this context, reference is also made to inclusive and diverse development teams and accessibility. These contribute to the development and operation of inclusive, ethical AI systems that last for many years and can form the basis for further developments. A non-inclusive system with a bias in the training data, for example, will foreseeably only be in use for a short time and cause more costs in the medium term than if attention had been paid to inclusion and diverse training data from the outset and those affected had been involved in the decision-making process, cf. the following example.

Example of Correlations that Go Beyond the Training Data

A transport company uses an AI system that carries out a **capacity utilization analysis** of the means of transport used in rural areas. It was trained using utilization information from the past 15 years. However, the data collected during this time only shows the status quo, for example that a bus route to city A was underutilized. Over the years, the rail line in the direction of city B was at medium capacity, the rail line in the direction of city A was also at medium capacity and the highway ramp in the direction of city B was consistently well utilized. However, the information does not say anything about the reason for this. In our example, a large company in city A closed shortly before the start of the measurement, and people from the region looked for work in other nearby towns such as city B. There is no bus line to the train station, and the highway entrance is closer to the village than the train station and has very limited parking capacity.

If the AI system were now to calculate that it would be more efficient to cancel the bus line to town A and expand the highway to town B, this would be logical based on the available data, but neither sustainable in terms of the ecological transport transition we are striving for, nor would it meet the needs of people who live in rural areas and work in one of the towns or towns in between. A barrier-free conversion of the station, more frequent rail services, the reopening of an abandoned stop in a small town halfway to town B and a bus route to the station could lead to significantly greater satisfaction. People in the region can complain about the highway expansion and the inaccessible train station with too few parking spaces. In that case, both the AI system and the resulting investment costs would have been a bad investment. Added to this would be the legal costs and the costs for new planning and construction costs at the station.

Designing and developing systems inclusively and ethically from the beginning and **training themwith diverse (rather than simply more) training data** is therefore both more cost-effective and more sustainable and therefore in line with the green transition. It also makes sense not to rely solely on the forecasts and predictions of an AI (as these are always based on data from the past), but to ask citizens directly what would help them.

10.6.3 Benefits for the Environment

The AI Act assumes that the development of AI should also have a benefit for the environment. For example, there is talk of *"environmental monitoring, the conservation and restoration of biodiversity and ecosystems and climate change mitigation and adaptation"* (Recital 4 AI Act).

However, AI systems can only benefit the environment if the water and energy consumption of AI systems themselves is significantly reduced and also ensured by renewable energies. At the time of publication of the AI Act, however, the trend is going in the opposite direction: new nuclear power plants are being considered for the operation of AI solutions [1]. This does not allow for the sustainable operation of AI systems in the long term, as the disposal of the resulting radioactive material is a problem that is likely to become increasingly difficult to solve in the face of more severe storms and flooding.

Overall, the AI Act is designed with a view to medium to long-term developments. Environmental protection and sustainability are key requirements in the regulation, which are discussed from various perspectives in the recitals. Phrases such as "sustainable and responsible data processing" or "ecological well-being" clearly show where the journey should – and must – take us if we want to preserve, or rather reclaim, our own living space. In view of the enormous **computing power** that is inevitably associated with AI systems and thus the amounts of energy, CO_2 emitted and, above all, water used to cool the data centers, it is only logical to focus on the sustainability of product development.

Above all, it is necessary to develop specialized AI models instead of using Large Language Models (LLM) for all use cases. OpenAI has few figures on energy consumption of their ChatGPT models. Open source manufacturers such as Hugging Face are more forthcoming with regard to their Bloom model [3]. While a simple Google search query consumes 0.3 watt hours, a text query to Bloom consumes ten times as much, i. e. three watt hours [5]. This adds up massively; Google, for example, has nine billion search queries per day (the figure still refers to search queries to the database-based Google search before the introduction of AI-supported Google search).

The training of OpenAI's ChatGPT consumed 1280 megawatt hours. Based on Bloom's figures, however, this results in operating costs of 500 megawatt hours per day. These figures are expected to rise further, as the generation of image and video material by generative models consumes ten to 15 watt hours per request [4], i. e. three to five times more than text requests to LLMs.

In view of these accumulating megawatt hours, it is hardly surprising that the AI Act explicitly calls for **energy-efficient programming** (Art. 95 ff. AI Act).

The area of sustainability is therefore particularly suitable for attracting research funding to enable innovations for the environmentally friendly and sustainable operation of AI systems.

Member States are required to support and promote AI solutions *"socially and environmentally beneficial outcomes"* (Recital 142 AI Act). This explicitly includes *"AI-based solutions to increase accessibility for persons with disabilities, tackle socio-economic inequalities, or meet environmental targets.* "Funding is to be provided for projects that are *"based on the principle of interdisciplinary cooperation between AI developers, experts on inequality and non-discrimination, accessibility, consumer, environmental, and digital rights, as well as academics"* (Recital 142 AI Act). These are all areas that help to create trust on the part of people towards companies, authorities and NGOs.

10.6.4 High-risk AI Systems

For high-risk AI systems, providers are required to operate a **monitoring** system ("post-market surveillance system") to keep a constant eye on the respective system. This should also include an analysis of the interaction with other AI systems as well as other devices and software. An efficient and timely response must be ensured, especially for systems that learn during operation.

There is also an **obligation to report** certain serious incidents. Providers should set up a system to report incidents to the authorities quickly and efficiently. This also explicitly refers to incidents or malfunctions that **cause serious damage to property or the environment** (Recital 155 AI Act).

Upon a duly **justified request and for exceptional reasons** of public security, the protection of life and health of persons, the protection **of the environment** or the protection of important industrial and infrastructure facilities, supervisory authorities should be allowed to authorize the commissioning of certain high-risk AI systems. The recitals and the final legislative text now contain different information in this regard. While it sounds clearer in Recital 130 AI Act, namely that the supervisory authorities"may authorize the placing on the market or putting into service of AI-systems that are not subject to **a conformity assessment** c, conformity assessment is clearly required in Art. 46 para.1 AI Act. Here, the possibility of approval is followed by the addition: *"That authorisation shall be for a limited period while the necessary conformity assessment procedures are being carried out, taking into account the exceptional reasons justifying the derogation. The completion of those procedures shall be undertaken without undue delay."* (Art. 46 para. 1 AI Act). (see section 3.5)

If **personal data** lawfully **collected for other purposes** is available for further use in the AI sandbox to develop, train or test an AI system, this is possible, but subject to strict conditions. However, *"improvement of the quality of the environment, protection of biodiversity, protection against pollution, green transition measures and climate change mitigation and adaptation measures"* is also one of the areas for which this derogation can be applied (Art. 59 AI Act). This means that for the development of AI, e. g. to protect against pollution, it is possible to use personal data lawfully collected for other purposes in the AI sandbox.

10.6.5 Supply Chains

With regard to sustainability, it is worth looking beyond the scope of the AI Act to the Supply Chain Act of the EU (also known as the **Corporate Sustainability Due Diligence Directive**, CSDDD or CS3D [2]). This is about improving both social and ecological standards along global supply chains. Companies, NGOs and authorities are required to identify, end, mitigate and, where possible, completely prevent **potential negative impacts on human rights and the environment**; not only within their own company, but also in subsidiaries and with business partners. These due diligence obligations also apply to the supply chains of AI solutions. It is therefore part of the business process to pay attention to and address human rights violations and environmental impacts in subcontractors and suppliers.

10.6.6 Conclusion

The AI Act and the EU Supply Chain Act attach great importance to environmental protection. Companies and organizations are also required to develop sustainable solutions in the area of AI. With regard to the economic development of companies that pursue ESG criteria, this requirement is not just a mere requirement, but also economically forward-looking, as the value of listed companies with ESG or SRI (Socially Responsible Investing) standards develops more positively over time than that of companies that do not represent these values. However, ethical and inclusive framework conditions are also important for authorities and NGOs in order to establish a basis of trust for people in the long term. Ultimately, it is up to European companies, NGOs and authorities to develop and establish AI systems that focus on environmental sustainability, energy efficiency and minimizing the harmful effects on the environment and social well-being in order to establish global standards and have a lasting impact on technological development.

Sources

[1] *AI is exhausting the power grid. Tech firms are seeking a miracle solution.* URL *https://www.msn.com/en-us/money/technology/ai-is-exhausting-the-power-grid-tech-firms-are-seeking-a-miracle-solution/ar-BB1oDl5z* – accessed: 2024/07/20

[2] Directive (EU) 2024/1760 of the European Parliament and of the Council of 13 June 2024 on corporate sustainability due diligence and amending Directive (EU) 2019/1937 and Regulation (EU) 2023/2859. Text with EEA relevance. 2024

[3] LUCCIONI, ALEXANDRA SASHA; JERNITE, YACINE; STRUBELL, EMMA: Power Hungry Processing: Watts Driving the Cost of AI Deployment? In: *The 2024 ACM Conference on Fairness, Accountability, and Transparency*, 2024 – arXiv:2311.16863 [cs], p. 85–99

[4] *Making an image with generative AI uses as much energy as charging your phone.* URL *https://www.technologyreview.com/2023/12/01/1084189/making-an-image-with-generative-ai-uses-as-much-energy-as-charging-your-phone/* – accessed: 2024/07/20 – MIT Technology Review

[5] DE VRIES, ALEX: The growing energy footprint of artificial intelligence. In: *Joule* Volume 7 (2023), no. 10, p. 2191–2194

Natascha Windholz, MSc, studied law in Vienna and information security management in Krems. After many years as a data protection officer, she now works as a senior information security officer for a NIS company. She is an active member of Women in AI Austria, regularly gives lectures and publishes on the topics of data protection, information security and AI. She also teaches at the University for Continuing Education Krems and at the IMC Krems University of Applied Sciences.

https://www.linkedin.com/in/natascha-windholz-96464a18b/

Kristina Altrichter, LL.M, studied law and works as a university assistant (prae doc) to Prof. Karin Bruckmüller at the Sigmund Freud Private University Her independent and joint research activities focus in particular on the areas of medical criminal law and the rights of victims and defendants. In addition to her studies, she completed training as a mediator in accordance with the Austrian Civil Mediation Act (ZivMediatG) and is an associate member of the Austrian Mediation Association.

Gabriele Bolek-Fügl is the founder and CEO of Compliance 2b GmbH and PaiperOne GmbH, which deal with the compliant mapping of laws in companies. She is a lecturer at St. Pölten University of Applied Sciences and Krems University of Applied Sciences and holds a degree in business mathematics with over 22 years of professional experience at international auditing firms in IT compliance auditing and risk management. Her publications include a book on the legal aspects of the Whistleblower Protection Act.

Her expertise lies in the development and implementation of compliance and risk management systems. As Vice President of Women in AI Austria, she actively promotes the visibility of women in artificial intelligence. Together with Carina Zehetmaier, she developed the AI Design Sprint Legal & Ethics method for ethical and legally compliant AI use and also developed a trustworthy AI algorithm that she operates for clients. As a sought-after expert and speaker, she gives talks at international conferences on IT compliance, risk management and AI.

Contact: *gabriele.bolek-fuegl@compliance2b.com* (aus dt. Ausgabe entnommen)

Dr. Karin Bruckmüller studied law and is a criminal law expert at the Sigmund Freud Private University in Vienna and at the Johannes Kepler University in Linz. Her research and teaching focus on medical and care law in connection with ethical issues. She is a regular speaker at important nursing congresses and conferences, such as the 2019 Nursing Congress in Vienna.

Mag. Alexandra Ciarnau is a lawyer at DORDA Rechtsanwälte GmbH in the areas of IT/IP and data protection, Co-Head of the Digital Industries Group and Head of Metaverse. The multiple award-winning lawyer supports companies in the implementation of innovative business models, particularly in the field of AI. She also lectures at various universities and is the author of numerous articles and works.

www.linkedin.com/in/alexandra-ciarnau

Copyright: Natascha Unkart and Isabelle Köhler

Veronica Cretu is an expert on governance and data4development, a representative of the Open Government Partnership, a member of the Committee on Artificial Intelligence and the Access Info Group at the Council of Europe and co-founder of the Moldova4EU Diaspora Task Force.

With over 20 years of experience, Veronica is a driving force in the areas of open government, data governance, AI, internet governance, civil society development and gender equality. Her work in these areas has had an impact on the EU, the Eastern Partnership, Central Asia, South Asia, the Western Balkans, Africa and Latin America, among others.

She has also played a key role in promoting Moldova's open government initiatives and has actively participated in global committees such as the Open Government Partnership Steering Committee.

Julia Eisner, BA MA, studied sociology at the University of Vienna and is currently working on her doctorate with a focus on generative AI in corporate communication. She is a lecturer at the University of Applied Sciences Wiener Neustadt and is active in national and international research projects. Her expertise lies in a socio-technical perspective on AI, with a special focus on ethical and socially responsible aspects. She also gives lectures and workshops in various industries on the topic of AI literacy and is involved in the Women in AI association.

https://at.linkedin.com/in/juliaeisner

Julia Fuith has a degree in law and Slavic studies and specializes in European law. After numerous stays abroad in London and Brussels, she has been working for three years in the department of the Federal Chancellery (previously the Federal Ministry of Finance), which is responsible, among other things, for negotiating EU legislation in the digital sector. Her focus there has always been on AI and the AI Act, which she helped negotiate as part of the Austrian negotiating team.

Julia Fuith's scientific contributions do not (necessarily) reflect the opinion of the Federal Chancellery.

https://at.linkedin.com/in/juliafuith

Valerie Hafez uses her expertise in anthropology and technology research to promote practice-oriented approaches to technology. As Policy Lead of Women in AI Austria, she has driven statements on the AI Act and other legislative proposals, developing innovative approaches such as the poster series and briefing on the AI Act. With over five years of experience in telecoms regulation, she now works on the strategic development of AI at the Federal Chancellery.

The scientific contributions by Valerie Hafez do not (necessarily) reflect the opinion of the Federal Chancellery.

Copyright:
Benita Donschachner

Dr. DI. Mag. rer. soc. oec. Isabella Hinterleitner M.Sc. is a scientist specialized in machine learning and has expertise in the fields of reinforcement learning, recommender systems, neural networks and knowledge graphs in application.

In 2020, she founded TechMeetsLegal GmbH, an alternative legal service provider that offers legal services for interdisciplinary projects and develops functional prototypes for national and international R&D initiatives. TechMeetsLegal focuses on innovations in the field of mobility of the future (connected vehicles, automated vehicles, teleoperation, etc.) and supports compliance with legal frameworks.

Manuela Machner, tourism expert specializing in AI. She supports tourism companies, destinations and providers on their way to using AI optimally. Her focus is on the practical application of AI in people's day-to-day work. She has written a humorous book "Künstliche Intelligenz – Interview mit ChatGPT" for beginners, in which she asks the AI model about the possibilities of artificial intelligence in an interview. Together with a digital psychologist, she also publishes a weekly podcast on AI topics in which the two of them chat about AI in a very down-to-earth way. She founded the company KiNET.ai and uses her social media channels and platforms to bring the topic of artificial intelligence closer to people in a simple way.

Contact: *www.kinet.ai*

Mag. Renate Rechinger studied law and completed the accounting course for lawyers in Graz. After working for many years as a lawyer in the field of IT law, she is now employed as an IT lawyer in an IT company and specializes in AI issues in the field of employment law and the insurance sector. She is also an external data protection officer for companies operating throughout Europe. She gives lectures and is a lecturer in adult education in the field of law & ethics.

Sabine Singer is a pioneer of the ISO/IEC/IEEE 24748:7000 standard and has further developed the methodology for developing AI strategies and data projects. As an experienced digital strategist and authorized training partner of Austrian Standards, she offers Certified VbE Ambassador and Certified AI Manager training courses. She supports companies in building AI awareness and literacy as well as in developing individual, ethically sound AI strategies that are compliant with the EU AI Act.

Copyright: Karin Winter

Merve Taner works in the legal department of Erste Bank der oesterreichischen Sparkassen AG in the "Products and Processes" team. There she is responsible in particular for the legal assessment of AI products in the operational business as well as AI processes, for example for internal process optimization. At the same time, she provides legal advice to Erste Digital GmbH and Erste Group Bank AG on AI law issues such as the establishment of AI governance. As part of an AI training project, she is responsible for the further training of Erste Group lawyers in this area of law and gives lectures on the subject.

During her training as a lawyer, she worked for various renowned law firms, including bpv Hügel Rechtsanwälte GmbH in the areas of M&A, corporate law and commercial law as well as HASCH & Partner Anwaltsgesellschaft mbH in the areas of real estate law, civil law and civil procedure law and most recently as an independent lawyer in commercial law.

She is currently doing her doctorate at the University of Vienna on the use of AI applications in the banking sector.

www.linkedin.com/in/merve-taner

Theresa Tisch works as a university assistant (prae doc) for Prof. (SFU) Dr. Konrad Lachmayer at the Sigmund Freud University. As part of her work, she is involved in several research projects commissioned by the BMK as part of the "Digital Transformation in Mobility 2022" program. She completed her studies at the University of Vienna and is currently writing her dissertation at the Institute for Environmental Law at the JKU Linz.

Carina Zehetmaier is a keynote speaker, AI entrepreneur, lawyer and expert on human rights and democratization. After representing the European Union and Austria at the United Nations in Geneva, she founded her first AI company in 2019. Today she is Managing Director of Paiper. One, a platform that supports companies in AI strategy development and compliance and accompanies them in AI change processes. She is also CEO of AILands GmbH, where she organizes AI Business Leader Bootcamps in Austria and Tenerife and helps companies develop trustworthy AI. As President of the "Women in AI Austria" association, an interdisciplinary network of female AI experts, she is committed to the development and use of artificial intelligence for the benefit of society and in the interests of human rights. She has also been a member of the Advisory Board of the Austrian Federal Government since the beginning of the year.

Klaudia Zotzmann-Koch, M. A. studied Philosophy and English in Hanover and has been involved with web technologies and the social impact of the internet since the 1990s. She put aside a doctorate in philosophy at the University of Vienna for a full-time job as a project manager in web development and recently studied Creative Nonfictional Writing in Cambridge for another year. She approaches the topic of AI from both a creative and an IT security perspective. She works as a freelance author, data protection expert and speaker on IT security awareness, AI and media literacy.

https://www.zotzmann-koch.com/

Index